D017 75506

Berlin

"All you've got to do is decide to go
and the hardest part is over.

So go!"

TONY WHEELER, COFOUNDER – LONELY PLANET

THIS EDITION WRITTEN AND RESEARCHED BY
Andrea Schulte-Peevers

Contents

Plan Your Trip 4

Explore Berlin 70

Understand Berlin 233

Survival Guide 283

Berlin Maps 311

(left) Beach bar on the Spree River

(above) Norman Foster–designed dome at the Reichstag (p76)

(right) Canal-side cafes, Treptow

Welcome to Berlin

Berlin is a mix of glamour and grit that will fascinate lovers of history, art, architecture, restaurants and nightlife.

Time Travel

Berlin is like a virtual 3D textbook where you find history staring you in the face at every turn. Strolling around, you pass by legendary sights that reflect key eras in city history. Schloss Charlottenburg, the Brandenburg Gate and Unter den Linden take you back to the period of Prussian glory. The dark ages of the Third Reich reverberate through the Scheunenviertel, the old Jewish quarter. Checkpoint Charlie and the East Side Gallery reflect the tense times of the Cold War. Potsdamer Platz and the new government quarter stand representative of a forward-looking, post-reunification Berlin.

Art & Culture

With 600 galleries, 175 museums, three opera houses, five major symphony orchestras and scores of theatres and cabarets, Berlin's extraordinary cultural landscape is the envy of many a small country. It's a pillar of the fashion, art, design and music worlds, not just keeping up with but setting new trends. An influx of creatives has turned it into a cauldron of cultural cool comparable to New York in the '80s. It's Berlin's legendary spirit of tolerance and experimentation infused with a dose of gritty subculture that gives this exciting city its edge.

Nightlife

Forget about New York – Berlin is the city that truly never sleeps. Sometimes it seems as though Berliners are the lotus eaters of Germany, people who love nothing better than a good time. The city's vast party spectrum caters for every taste, budget and age group. From tiny basement clubs to industrial techno temples, chestnut-canopied beer gardens to fancy cocktail caverns, saucy cabarets to ear-pleasing symphonies – Berlin delivers hot-stepping odysseys, and not just after dark and on weekends but pretty much 24/7. Pack your stamina!

People & Quality of Life

Berlin may be 10 times the size of Paris but its key areas are pleasingly compact and human-scale with plenty of green and open spaces. Public transportation is brilliant, you can walk without fear at night, few clubs have velvet ropes, and your restaurant bill would probably only buy you an appetiser in most other European capitals. It's a multicultural metropolis infused with the unpretentious charm of an international village. Berliners are a laid-back bunch who follow the credo 'live and let live' and put greater emphasis on enjoying life than accumulating material wealth.

Why I Love Berlin

By Andrea Schulte-Peevers, Author

To me, Berlin is truly one of the world's great capitals and nothing short of addictive. I fell in love with the city the first time I visited, mere months before the Wall's 1989 collapse. Since then, it's been exciting to see Berlin shed its Cold War–era brooding and blossom into a vibrant, sassy yet wonderfully relaxed capital city. I simply love the energy of the place, its ability to reinvent itself time and again. The nightlife, the people, the museums, the landmarks – the mix is an intoxicating cocktail that I'll never get tired of drinking.

For more about our authors, see p336.

Wilfried Fitzenreiter's sculptures, *Three Girls and a Boy*, outside Berliner Dom (Berlin Cathedral; p106)

Berlin's
Top 10

DEM DEUTSCHEN VOLKE

Reichstag *(p76)*

1 This famous Berlin landmark has been set on fire, bombed, left to crumble, and wrapped in fabric before emerging as the home of the German parliament (the Bundestag) and focal point of the re-united country's government quarter. The plenary hall can only be seen on guided tours but, with advance booking, you're free to catch the lift to the dazzling glass cupola designed by Lord Norman Foster. Enjoy not only the mesmerising views but learn about the building and surrounding landmarks on a free audiotour.

⊙ *Historic Mitte*

Brandenburg Gate *(p78)*

2 Prussian emperors, Napoleon and Hitler have marched through this neoclassical royal city gate that was once trapped east of the Berlin Wall. Since 1989 it has gone from a symbol of division and oppression to the symbol of a united Germany. The powerful landmark, which overlooks the stately Pariser Platz square with its embassies and banks, is at its most atmospheric – and photogenic – at night when light bathes its stately columns and proud Goddess of Victory sculpture in a mesmerising golden glow.

⊙ *Historic Mitte*

MAREMAGNUM / GETTY IMAGES ©

Museumsinsel *(p95)*

3 Berlin's 'Louvre on the Spree', this imposing ensemble of five treasure houses is the undisputed highlight of the city's museum landscape. Declared a Unesco World Heritage Site, it represents 6000 years of art and cultural history, from the Stone Age to the 19th century. Feast your eyes on majestic antiquities at the Pergamonmuseum and Altes Museum, report for an audience with Egyptian queen Nefertiti at the Neues Museum, take in 19th-century art at the Alte Nationalgalerie and marvel at medieval sculptures at the Bodemuseum.
PERGAMON ALTAR, PERGAMON-MUSEUM (P96)

👁 *Museumsinsel & Alexanderplatz*

Nightlife *(p50)*

4 Berlin's your oyster when the moon's high in the sky. Cosy pubs, riverside beach bars, beer gardens, underground dives, DJ bars, snazzy hotel lounges, designer cocktail temples – with such variety, finding a party location to match your mood is not exactly a tall order. If you're not into hobnobbing with hipsters at hot-stepping bars or clubs, you could always relive the Roaring Twenties in a high-kicking cabaret, indulge your ears with symphonic strains in iconic concert halls or point your highbrow compass towards the opera.
RESTAURANTS AND BARS ALONG SIMON-DACH-STRASSE

🍷 *Drinking & Nightlife*

Schloss Charlottenburg *(p192)*

5 We can pretty much guarantee that your camera will have a love affair with Berlin's largest and loveliest remaining royal palace. A late-baroque jewel inspired by Versailles, it backs up against an idyllic park, complete with carp pond, rhododendron-lined paths, two smaller palaces and a mausoleum. The palace itself is clad in a subtle yellow typical of the royal Hohenzollern family and wonderfully adorned with slender columns and geometrically arranged windows. An ornate copper-domed tower overlooks the forecourt and the imposing equestrian statue of the Great Elector Friedrich Wilhelm.

👁 *City West & Charlottenburg*

Potsdamer Platz (p113)

6 No other area around town better reflects the 'New Berlin' than this quarter forged from the death-strip that separated East and West Berlin for 28 years. The world's biggest construction site through much of the 1990s, Potsdamer Platz 2.0 is a postmodern take on the historic area that until WWII was Berlin's equivalent of Times Square. A cluster of plazas, offices, museums, cinemas, theatres, hotels and flats, it shows off the talents of seminal architects of our times, including Helmut Jahn and Renzo Piano.
SONY CENTER'S CANOPY, POTSDAMER PLATZ

⊙ *Potsdamer Platz & Tiergarten*

Street Art & Alternative Living (p34)

7 Berlin has world-class art, cultural events galore and increasingly sophisticated dining – but so do most other capital cities. What makes this metropolis different is the legendary climate of openness and tolerance that fosters experimentation, a DIY ethos and a thriving subculture. Hip and funky Kreuzberg, Friedrichshain and the northern reaches of Neukölln are hotbeds of diversity and creativity where tomorrow's trends take shape. No surprise, then, that some of the city's finest street art is brightening facades and house entrances around here. STREET ART AT KUNSTHAUS TACHELES (P132)

☆ *Art Galleries & Street Art*

8

Holocaust Memorial
(p79)

8 Listen to the sound of your footsteps and feel the presence of uncounted souls as you make your way through the massive warped labyrinth that is Germany's central memorial to the Jewish victims of the Nazi-orchestrated genocide. New York architect Peter Eisenman poignantly captures this unspeakable horror with a maze of 2711 tomblike concrete plinths of varying heights that rise from an unsettlingly wavy ground. The memorial's abstract design contrasts with the graphic and emotional exhibits in the subterranean information centre.

⊙ *Historic Mitte*

Kulturforum *(p119)*

9 Conceived in the 1950s, the Kulturforum was West Berlin's answer to Museumsinsel and is an equally enthralling cluster of museums and concert halls, albeit in modern buildings. The most stunning are the New National Gallery in a glass temple stunner by Ludwig Mies van der Rohe and Hans Scharoun's honey-coloured freeform Berliner Philharmonie. The depth and breadth of the art collections here is mind-blowing. Rembrandt to Picasso, fragile Dürer prints to a flute played by a Prussian king, famous medieval masters to German 1920s expressionists – it's all here in one neat package. BERLINER PHILHARMONIE (P120)

⊙ *Potsdamer Platz & Tiergarten*

Berlin Wall *(p40)*

10 Few events in history have the power to move the entire world. The Kennedy assassination. The moon landing. The events of 9/11. And, of course, the fall of the Berlin Wall in 1989. If you were alive and old enough back then, you will probably remember the crowds of euphoric revellers cheering and dancing at the Brandenburg Gate. Although little is left of the physical barrier, its legacy lives on in the imagination and in such places as Checkpoint Charlie, the Gedenkstätte Berliner Mauer and the East Side Gallery with its colourful murals. EAST SIDE GALLERY (P168), BERLIN WALL

⊙ *Berlin Wall*

What's New

Berlin Brandenburg Airport
With several well-publicised delays, we're not betting the farm but remain hopeful that planes will start flying into Berlin's shiny new international airport in autumn 2013, the projected opening date at press time. (p235)

Northern Neukölln ('Kreuzkölln')
Once a headline-making 'bad-rap ghetto', northern Neukölln has catapulted to uber-hipness thanks to a deluge of cash-poor but idea-rich newcomers from around the world. Great for offbeat DIY exploring. (p146)

Tempelhofer Park
The decommissioned Tempelhof Airport has taken on new life as a humongous public park where you can jog or cycle along the tarmac and explore an ever-changing landscape of improvised playgrounds – art installations to minigolf, dog parks to urban gardening. (p150)

Trends in Eating
Berlin chefs have rediscovered German country cooking and reinterpreted it in innovative and sophisticated ways. Long-ignored 'lowly' vegetables like turnips and parsnips are paired with organic meats and other ingredients from sustainable farms in the surrounding region of Brandenburg. (p44)

Berlin Wall Panorama
The bleakness of daily life along the Berlin Wall is artistically captured in this 15m high and 60m long panorama in its own custom-built steel rotunda. The scene, set on a random autumn day in the 1980s, is a reflection of artist Yadegar Asisi's personal memories of the divided Berlin. (p85)

Tränenpalast
This former pavilion between East and West Berlin was the site of many tearful goodbyes and now houses an exhibit that documents the experience at the checkpoint and the emotional ramifications of life in a divided city. (p82)

Humboldt-Box
The biggest building project on the horizon is the reconstruction of the Prussian royal city palace, which will house museums, a library and spaces for public events. The Humboldt-Box provides a preview and a viewing platform of the construction site, which is set to go live in 2014. (p106)

Gedenkstätte Berliner Mauer
This newly expanded central memorial site of German division uses indoor and outdoor exhibits to portray what the Berlin Wall looked like and how it impacted on the daily lives of Berlin citizens on both sides of it. (p130)

Museumsinsel Masterplan
By 2025, all five museums will have been restored and modernised. There will also be the James-Simon-Galerie as the central entrance and the Archaeological Promenade connecting the buildings underground. (p95)

For more recommendations and reviews, see **lonelyplanet.com/ germany/berlin**

Need to Know

Currency
Euro (€). 100 cents = €1.

Language
German

Visas
Generally not required for tourist stays up to 90 days (or at all for EU nationals); some nationalities need a Schengen visa.

Money
ATMs widespread. Cash is king; credit cards are not widely used.

Mobile Phones
Mobile phones operate on GSM900/1800. If you have a European or Australian phone, save money by slipping in a German SIM card.

Time
Central European Time (GMT/UTC plus one hour).

Tourist Information
Visit Berlin has offices at the Hauptbahnhof, the Brandenburg Gate and on Kurfürstendamm, and a **call centre** (📞2500 2333) for information/bookings.

Your Daily Budget

Budget under €60
➡ Dorm beds, shared rental apartment €10–20

➡ Self-catering, quick meals, cafes

➡ Take advantage of happy hours and free or low-cost museums or entertainment

Midrange €60–150
➡ Private apartment or double room €80–120

➡ Two-course dinner with wine €30

➡ Concert or club admission €10

Top end over €150
➡ Fancy loft apartment or double in top-end hotel €150–200

➡ Gourmet two-course dinner with wine €70

➡ Cab rides €20

➡ Orchestra seats at the opera €120

Advance Planning

Two to three months Book tickets for the Berliner Philharmonie, the Staatsoper, Sammlung Boros and top-flight events.

Up to one month Make online reservations for the Reichstag dome, the Neues Museum and the Pergamonmuseum.

Up to one week Reserve a table at trendy and Michelin-starred restaurants, especially for dinner on Friday and Saturday.

Useful Websites

➡ **Lonely Planet** (www.lonelyplanet.com/berlin) Destination information, hotel bookings, traveller forum and more.

➡ **Visit Berlin** (www.visitberlin.de) Official tourist authority info.

➡ **Museumsportal** (www.museumsportal-berlin.de) Gateway to the city's museums.

➡ **Resident Advisor** (www.residentadvisor.net) Guide to parties and clubbing.

➡ **Exberliner** (www.exberliner.com) Online version of monthly English-language magazine.

WHEN TO GO

July and August are busiest but often rainy. May, June, September and October offer colder, though often more stable, weather. Winters are cold and quiet.

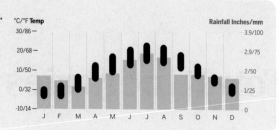

Arriving in Berlin

Berlin Brandenburg Airport
Scheduled to open in autumn 2013; check www.berlin-airport.de for the latest. Airport-Express trains planned for city centre every 15 minutes; €3.10; taxi €40.

Tegel Airport TXL express bus to Alexanderplatz (40 minutes) and bus X9 for the western city centre (eg, Kurfürstendamm, 20 minutes) €2.40; taxi €20–25.

Schönefeld Airport Airport-Express trains (RB14 or RE7) to central Berlin twice hourly (30 minutes) and S9 train for Friedrichshain or Prenzlauer Berg €3.10; taxi €40.

Hauptbahnhof Central train station in the city centre and served by S-Bahn, U-Bahn, bus and taxi.

For much more on
arrival see p284

Getting Around

➡ **U-Bahn** Most efficient way to travel; operates 4am to 12.30am and all night Friday, Saturday and public holidays. From Sunday to Thursday, half-hourly night buses take over in the interim.

➡ **S-Bahn** Not as frequent as U-Bahn trains but fewer stops and thus useful for longer distances. Same operating hours as the U-Bahn.

➡ **Bus** Slow but useful for sightseeing on the cheap. Run frequently 4.30am to 12.30am; half-hourly night buses in the interim; MetroBuses (M1, M19) operate 24/7.

➡ **Tram** Only operate in the eastern districts; MetroTrams (M1, M2) run 24/7.

➡ **Cycling** Designated bike lanes and rental stations abound; bikes are fine in designated U-Bahn and S-Bahn carriages.

➡ **Taxi** Can be hailed and are fairly inexpensive; avoid during day-time rush hour.

➡ For information and trip planning, see www.bvg.de.

For much more on
getting around
see p286

Sleeping

There's over 130,000 hotel rooms but the most desirable properties book up quickly, especially in summer and around major holidays, festivals and trade shows; prices soar and reservations are essential during these periods. Otherwise, rates are mercifully low by Western capital standards. Options range from luxurious ports of call to ho-hum international chains, trendy designer boutique hotels to Old Berlin-style B&Bs, happening hostels to handy self-catering apartments.

Useful Websites

➡ **Visit Berlin** (www.visitberlin.de) Official tourist office books rooms at partner hotels.

➡ **Hostelworld** (www.hostelworld.de) Hostel and budget hotel bookings.

➡ **HRS** (www.hrs.com) Good for last-minute bargains.

➡ **Booking.com** (www.booking.com) General site, often has bargains.

➡ **Lonely Planet** (www.lonelyplanet.com/hotels) Reviews of Lonely Planet's top choices.

For much more on
sleeping see p218

Top Itineraries

Day One

Historic Mitte (p74)

One day in Berlin? Follow this whirlwind itinerary to earn bragging rights for having seen all the key sights. Book ahead for an early lift ride up to the dome of the **Reichstag**, then snap a picture of the **Brandenburg Gate** before exploring the maze of the **Holocaust Memorial** and admiring the contemporary architecture of **Potsdamer Platz**. Before lunch, reflect on Nazi history at the **Topographie des Terrors** and Cold War madness at **Checkpoint Charlie**.

> **Lunch** Renew your energies at Augustiner am Gendarmenmarkt (p87).

Historic Mitte (p74)

After lunch, soak up the glory of **Gendarmenmarkt**, drop by **Fassbender & Rausch** for a chocolate treat and get a dose of retail therapy at the **Friedrichstadtpassagen**. Follow Unter den Linden east to **Museumsinsel** and spend at least an hour marvelling at the antiquities in the **Pergamonmuseum**. Beer-o'-clock! Head over to **Strandbar Mitte**.

> **Dinner** There are plenty of dinner spots in the Scheunenviertel (p127).

Scheunenviertel (p127)

After dinner, stroll over to the all-ages **Clärchen's Ballhaus** for a spin on the dance floor, then process the day's impressions over drinks at the trendy **King Size Bar**.

Day Two

Scheunenviertel (p127)

Spend a couple of hours coming to grips with what life in Berlin was like when the Wall still stood by exploring the **Gedenkstätte Berliner Mauer**. Relax over coffee at **Barcomi's Deli**, then nose around designer boutiques or check out the latest exhibit at **C/O Berlin** and the galleries at the **Jüdische Mädchenschule**.

> **Lunch** At Mogg & Melzer (p138) or Pauly Saal (p138).

Museumsinsel & Alexanderplatz (p93)

Start the afternoon's sightseeing by peeking into daily life behind the Iron Curtain at the **DDR Museum**, then let the sights drift by on a one-hour **river cruise** around Museumsinsel. Afterwards, budget an hour for your audience with Queen Nefertiti at the stunningly reconstructed **Neues Museum** and, if time and energy permit, perhaps pop into the nearby **Humboldt-Box** to learn about the reconstruction of the Prussian royal city palace.

> **Dinner** Make reservations at the riverside Spindler & Klatt (p157).

Kreuzberg (p146)

After dinner, you might catch a concert at **Magnet Club** or **Lido**, find your favourite libation station along Schlesische Strasse or head straight to hip and idyllic **Club der Visionäre** for a waterfront nightcap.

Day Three

City West & Charlottenburg (p190)

 Day three starts at **Schloss Charlottenburg**, where the Neuer Flügel (New Wing) and the palace garden are essential stops. Take the U2 to Zoologischer Garten and meditate upon the futility of war at the **Kaiser-Wilhelm-Gedächtniskirche**, then – assuming it's not Sunday – satisfy your shopping cravings along **Kurfürstendamm** and its side streets. Finish up at **KaDeWe's** mind-boggling food hall.

> **Lunch** Enjoy a casual lunch in the KaDeWe (p202) food hall.

Kreuzberg (p146)

 Spend an hour or two at the amazing Daniel Libeskind–designed **Jewish Museum**, then go local on a stroll down Bergmannstrasse, building in a cafe stop for a pick-me-up. Follow your nostrils to the **Marheineke Markthalle**, perhaps picking up some gourmet treats. Then either amble east along the Landwehrkanal or take the U-Bahn to Schönleinstrasse.

> **Dinner** Enjoy upmarket Turkish fare at Defne (p154).

Kreuzberg (p146)

You're already in party central, so hit the bars around Kottbusser Tor and along Oranienstrasse or check out who's playing at **Festsaal Kreuzberg** or **SO36**. For all-night dancing, try **Watergate**.

Day Four

Potsdam (p111)

 There's plenty more to do in Berlin proper, but we recommend you spend the better part of the day exploring the parks and royal palaces in Potsdam, a mere half-hour S-Bahn ride away. Arrive early to beat the crowds to **Schloss Sanssouci**, a rococo jewel of a palace. Once that's done, explore the surrounding park and its many smaller palaces at leisure. The **Chinesisches Haus** is a must-see.

> **Lunch** Have lunch at the charming Drachenhaus (p209) in the park.

Potsdam (p111)

Continue your park explorations or head to Potsdam's old town for a spin around the **Holländisches Viertel** (Dutch Quarter) and a look at the **Nikolaikirche**, designed by Karl Friedrich Schinkel. If you're starving, stay for dinner here, otherwise head back into town, to Prenzlauer Berg.

> **Dinner** Try Oderquelle (p182) or another eatery on Oderberger Strasse.

Prenzlauer Berg (p178)

Wrap up a long day over a mug of beer at **Prater**, Berlin's oldest beer garden. Still got stamina? Turn your evening into a bar-hop, perhaps stopping at buzzy **August Fengler** or classy **Becketts Kopf**.

If You Like...

Museums

Pergamonmuseum A veritable treasure trove of monumental architecture from ancient civilisations, including the namesake altar. (p96)

Jüdisches Museum Comprehensive exhibit goes beyond the Holocaust in tracing the rich history of Jews in Germany. (p148)

Museum für Naturkunde Meet giant dinos in Berlin's own 'Jurassic Park', then learn about the universe, evolution and even the anatomy of a housefly. (p133)

Neues Museum Pay your respects to Queen Nefertiti, star of the Egyptian collection, then explore other priceless artefacts from ancient Troy and elsewhere. (p98)

Neue Nationalgalerie A roll-call of 20th century art world hotshots on parade in an edgy glass-and-steel temple. (p119)

Gemäldegalerie This Aladdin's cave of Old Masters has heads turning in this expansive Kulturforum space. (p116)

Clubbing

Berghain/Panorama Bar Big, bad Berghain is still Berlin's quintessential dancing den of iniquity. (p175)

Watergate Two floors, a stunning riverside setting, electro DJ royalty and plenty of eye candy. (p159)

://about blank Wild, trashy, unpredictable and with a great garden for daytime chilling. (p174)

KIERAN SCOTT / GETTY IMAGES ©

A cyclist rides through the Tiergarten (p120)

Cookies Grown-up club that's sleek and sexy amid art deco glamour and top DJs. (p90)

Clärchens Ballhaus Salsa, tango, ballroom, disco and swing's the thing in this grand retro ballroom. (p140)

Felix Well-heeled weekend warriors press the flesh at this tricked-out party zone at the ritzy Hotel Adlon. (p90)

1920s & Cabaret

Chamäleon Varieté Intimate former ballroom delivers an alchemy of acrobatics, artistry and sex appeal. (p142)

Bar Jeder Vernunft Gorgeous mirrored tent makes you feel as if you're on the set of *Cabaret*. (p202)

Friedrichstadtpalast Europe's largest revue theatre has long-legged beauties putting on sparkly Old Vegas–style shows. (p143)

1. Absinth Depot Berlin Make a date with the 'green fairy' at this eccentric libation station. (p144)

Hotel Askanischer Hof Channel 1920s glamour by bedding down in chintz-laden rooms filled with frills and antiques. (p229)

Views

Fernsehturm Check off the landmarks from the needle-like TV Tower, Germany's tallest building. (p103)

Reichstag Dome Book ahead for the lift ride to the Norman Foster–designed glass dome of the historic German parliament building. (p76)

Panoramapunkt Catch Europe's fastest lift at Potsdamer Platz for an eyeful of the eastern city. (p114)

Berlin Hi-Flyer Soar above Berlin in this tethered hot-air balloon near Checkpoint Charlie. (p83)

Berliner Dom Climb into Berlin's largest church dome for gobsmacking views of the historic city centre. (p106)

Siegessäule Clamber up this gilded goddess-topped column for superlative views of the Tiergarten park. (p121)

Quirky Experiences

Peristal Singum Take a journey to your soul while climbing, crawling and slithering around this surreal underground labyrinth/art installation. (p176)

Monsterkabinett Descend into a dark and bizarre underworld inhabited by a small army of endearingly spooky mechanical monsters. (p135)

Madame Claude Reality is literally flipped on its head in this kooky bar and concert space where the furniture hangs on the ceiling. (p159)

Badeschiff Cool off in summer, heat up in winter in this river-barge-turned-swimming pool. (p154)

Art Collections

Sammlung Boros World-class contemporaries in a rambling WWII bunker. (p134)

Sammlung Scharf-Gerstenberg A journey to the surreal fantasy worlds of Goya, Dalí and other mind-benders. (p194)

Museum Berggruen Priceless Picassos plus works by Klee and Giacometti in a newly expanded building. (p194)

For more top Berlin spots, see the following:
→ Eating (p44)
→ Drinking & Nightlife (p50)
→ Entertainment (p62)
→ Shopping (p67)

PLAN YOUR TRIP IF YOU LIKE...

Brücke Museum Groundbreaking canvases by Germany's first modern-artist group (1905–13). (p213)

Emil Nolde Museum Brightly pigmented landscapes and nature scenes by leading German expressionist in a former bank building. (p84)

Parks & Gardens

Tiergarten Take pleasure in getting lost amid the lawns, trees and paths of one of the world's largest city parks. (p120)

Schlossgarten Charlottenburg Stake out a picnic spot near the carp and ponder royal splendours. (p192)

Park Sanssouci Find your favourite corner away from the crowds for a little time 'without cares'. (p205)

Volkspark Friedrichshain Rambling 'people's park' offers plenty of diversions and covers two 'mountains' made from WWII debris. (p169)

Royal Encounters

Schloss Charlottenburg Inspired by Versailles this pretty Prussian power display delivers a glimpse into the lsumptuous ifestyles of the rich and royal. (p192)

Schloss Sanssouci In nearby Potsdam, this most famous palace in Park Sanssouci drips in opulence and overlooks vine-draped terraces and a big fountain. (p205)

Berliner Dom The royal court church has impressive dimensions, a palatial design and elaborately carved sarcophagi for the remains of kings and queens. (p106)

Humboldt-Box Get a preview of how the soon-to-be-reconstructed royal Stadtschloss (city palace) will fit within the historic centre. (p106)

Cold War History

East Side Gallery The longest stretch of Berlin Wall turned art canvas by over 100 international artists. (p168)

Gedenkstätte Berliner Mauer Large indoor–outdoor exhibit is Germany's central memorial to the victims of the Berlin Wall. (p130)

Stasimuseum Learn about the machinations of East Germany's secret police in its historic headquarters. (p171)

Stasi Prison Take a tour for a behind-the-scenes look at East Berlin's most notorious prison. (p171)

Checkpoint Charlie Though a tourist trap, this famous crossing is an essential Cold War hotspot. (p85)

WWII Sites

Topographie des Terrors Exhibit peels away the layers of brutality of the Nazi regime on the site of the SS and Gestapo command centres. (p86)

Gedenkstätte Deutscher Widerstand Tells the stories

of the brave men and women of the German Nazi resistance, including Stauffenberg's failed 'Operation Valkyrie'. (p121)

Haus der Wannsee-Konferenz Get shivers while standing in the very room where Nazi leaders discussed the 'Final Solution' (Jewish extermination). (p214)

Sachsenhausen A visit to one of Nazi Germany's first concentration camps, in Oranienburg just north of Berlin, will leave no one untouched. (p210)

Deutsch-Russisches Museum Berlin-Karlshorst The signing of the Wehrmacht's unconditional surrender, ending WWII, took place here. (p217)

Music

Berliner Philharmonie Berlin's most iconic classical concert venue and home of the world-famous Berliner Philharmoniker. (p126)

Konzerthaus This Schinkel-built jewel graces Gendarmenmarkt and is another fabulous concert venue. (p91)

Sonntagskonzerte Enjoy intimate concerts amid the faded glamour of a century-old mirror-clad hall. (p63)

Astra Kulturhaus Mid-size concert hall with Commie-era decor draws big names from rock, pop and electro. (p176)

Magnet Club Good chance to see tomorrow's headliners today, plus dance parties till dawn. (p161)

Authentic Berlin Food

Schusterjunge Cosy corner pub kicks German comfort food into high gear. (p185)

Zur Letzten Instanz Industrial-weight specialities served with a side of misty-eyed nostalgia since 1621. (p107)

Max und Moritz Meat lovers will be in pig heaven at this century-old gastropub. (p156)

Henne Roast chicken is the thing in this charmer from 1907 – take it or leave it. (p156)

Naughty Berlin

KitKatClub Dive in and be as nice or nasty as you want – but do follow the dress code. (p162)

Insomnia Worship at the altar of hedonism at this sassy, sexy dance club with performances and playrooms. (p162)

Schwarzer Reiter Classy purveyor of anything boys and girls with imagination might need for a fun encounter. (p145)

Lab.oratory The place for gays to live out their most frisky, completely uncensored, fantasies. (p176)

Modern Architecture

Jüdisches Museum Daniel Libeskind's astonishing zigzag-shaped architectural metaphor for Jewish history. (p148)

Neues Museum David Chipperfield's reconstructed New Museum ingeniously blends old and new into something bold and beautiful. (p98)

Sony Center Helmut Jahn's svelte glass-and-steel complex is the most striking piece of architecture on Potsdamer Platz. (p113)

IM Pei Bau Relentlessly geometrical, glass-spiral-fronted museum annexe by the 'Mandarin of Modernism'. (p80)

(Top) A stallholder at Flohmarkt am Mauerpark (Sunday flea market; p180)
(Bottom) The Badeschiff, a former river barge that's now a swimming pool (p154)

Markets

Flohmarkt am Mauerpark Gets deluged with visitors in summer but still offers a primo urban archaeology experience. (p180)

Antikmarkt am Ostbahnhof Ferret for old-timey treasure in this sprawling Sunday antiques market. (p177)

Türkenmarkt Berlin meets the Bosphorus at this colourful canalside market. (p164)

Kollwitzplatzmarkt Discerning gourmets can source the finest morsels for that ultimate picnic. (p189)

Flohmarkt am Boxhagener Platz Treasure-hunting grounds with plenty of entertainment, cafes and people-watching as a bonus. (p177)

Tours

Berlin on Bike Repertory includes a superb Berlin Wall bike tour and intriguing 'nightseeing' excursions. (p288)

Trabi Safari Turn the clock back while driving yourself around the city in an original East German Trabant car. (p289)

Berliner Unterwelten Get a look at Berlin from below as you explore a dark and dank WWII bunker. (p182)

Fritz Music Tours Find out what Bowie, U2, Depeche Mode and other seminal musicians were up to in Berlin. (p289)

Walking Tours Get Berlin in a nutshell on a general walk – or opt for a themed one for a more in-depth experience. (p288)

Month by Month

January

New Year's Eve may be wrapped up, but nighttime hot spots show no signs of slowing down, especially during Fashion Week. Cold weather invites extended museum visits and foraging at the International Grüne Woche ('Green Week') food fair.

🔒 Berlin Fashion Week

Twice a year (again in July), international fashion folk book up all the trendy hotels (and restaurants) while here to present or assess next season's threads. See www.fashion-week-berlin .com for public events.

✕ Internationale Grüne Woche

Find out about the latest food trends and gorge on global morsels at this nine-day fair (www.gruenewoche .de) for food, agriculture and gardening.

☉ Lange Nacht der Museen

Culture meets entertainment during the Long Night of the Museums (www .lange-nacht-der-museen. de), when dozens of museums welcome visitors until at least midnight.

February

Days are still dark but Berlin perks up when glamour comes to town during the famous film festival. A full theatre, opera, concert and party schedule also tempts people out of the house.

✴ Berlinale

Berlin's international film festival (www.berlinale.de) draws stars, starlets, directors, critics and the world's A-to-Z-list celebrities for two weeks of screenings and glamour parties around town. The lucky ones go home with a Golden or Silver Bear.

March

Could there be spring in the air? This is still a good time to see the sights without the crowds, but hotel rooms fill to capacity during the big tourism fair.

✴ Internationale Tourismus Börse

Take a virtual trip around the globe at the world's largest international travel expo (www.itb-berlin.de); it's trade-only during the week but open to the public at the weekend.

☆ MaerzMusik

'Music' or 'soundscapes'? You decide after a day at this contemporary music festival (www.berliner festspiele.de) that explores and celebrates a boundary-pushing palette of sounds – from orchestral symphonies to experimental recitals.

April

Life starts moving outdoors as cafe tables appear on pavements and you start seeing budding trees on walks in the park. Hotels get busy over the Easter holidays.

★ Achtung Berlin

Flicks about Berlin and at least partially produced in the city compete for the New Berlin Film Award at this festival (www.achtung berlin.de). Screenings are often attended by writers, directors, producers and actors.

☆ Festtage

Daniel Barenboim, music director of Berlin's internationally renowned Staatsoper opera house, brings the world's finest conductors, soloists and orchestras to Berlin for this 10-day highbrow hoedown of gala concerts and operas (www.staatsoper-berlin.org).

◉ Gallery Weekend

Join collectors, critics and other fellow art-aficionados in keeping tabs on the Berlin art scene on a free hop around 40 of the city's best galleries (www.gallery -weekend-berlin.de) held over a three-day weekend.

May

Spring is in, making this a fabulous month to visit Berlin. Time for beer gardens, picnics and walks among blossoming trees. White asparagus appears in markets and on menus. Don't forget your sunglasses!

★ Karneval der Kulturen

Berlin's answer to London's Notting Hill Carnival (www.karneval-berlin .de) celebrates the city's multicultural tapestry with parties, exotic nosh and a fun parade of flamboyantly dressed dancers, DJs, art-

ists and musicians shimmying through the streets of Kreuzberg.

June

Festival season kicks into high gear around the summer solstice with plenty of alfresco events, thanks to a rising temperature gauge.

★ Berlin Biennale

This biennial curated forum for contemporary art explores international trends and invites newcomers to showcase their work around town for about eight weeks (www.berlin biennale.de). Next in 2014.

★ Fête de la Musique

Summer starts with good vibrations thanks to hundreds of free concerts during this global music festival (www.lafetedela musique.com) that first came online in Paris in 1982. Held each year on 21 June.

★ Christopher Street Day

No matter what your sexual persuasion, come out and paint the town pink at this huge pride parade featuring floats filled with naked torsos writhing to loud techno music. For a less commercial version, head to the Transgenialer CSD in Kreuzberg.

July

Hot summer days send Berliners scurrying to the lakes in town or the surrounding countryside. Gourmets rejoice in the

bounty of fresh local produce in the markets. Expect long lines at main attractions.

☆ Classic Open Air Gendarmenmarkt

Five days, five alfresco concerts – from opera to pop – delight an adoring crowd hunkered on bleachers before the regal backdrop of the Konzerthaus (www .classicopenair.de).

August

More outdoor fun than anyone can handle with concerts in parks, daytime clubbing, languid boat rides, beach-bar partying, lake swimming and a huge beer festival.

★ Berliner Bierfestival

Who needs Oktoberfest when you can have the 'world's longest beer garden' (www.bierfestival -berlin.de)? Pick your poison from over 300 breweries from nearly 100 countries along 2km of Karl-Marx-Allee as the bands play on.

★ Tanz im August

Step out gracefully to this international dance festival (www.tanzimaugust.de) that attracts loose-limbed talent and highly experimental choreography from around the globe.

☆ FuckParade

Relax! It's not what you think but simply your average techno street parade founded as an anti-event to the now defunct Love Parade (www.fuckparade.org). Wear black.

⚜ Berliner Gauklerfest

Comedians, magicians, puppeteers, musicians, clowns, fire eaters, jugglers and other street performers (*Gaukler*) take over a square in historic Mitte for 10 merry days from late August (www.gauklerfest.de).

⊙ Lange Nacht der Museen

The summer edition of the January event (www.lange -nacht-der-museen.de).

September

Kids are back in school but there's still plenty of partying to be done and often fine weather to enjoy it. As days get shorter, the new theatre, concert and opera season begins.

☆ Berlin Music Week

Catch tomorrow's headliners during this four-day celebration of global music (www.berlin-music-week .de) in Berlin's best clubs in Friedrichshain and Kreuzberg. One ticket buys access to all venues and the New Music Award closing party.

⚜ Berlin Art Week

Inaugurated in 2012, this contemporary art fair (www.berlinartweek.de) brings together galleries and artists with the hotshots of the international scene.

🏃 Berlin Marathon

Sweat it out with the other 50,000 runners or just cheer 'em on during Germany's biggest street race (www .berlin-marathon.com), which has seen eight world records set since 1977.

(Top) A Christmas market in Gendarmenmarkt (p84)

(Bottom) A costumed participant at Christoper Street Day

✯ Musikfest Berlin

Famous orchestras, choirs, conductors and soloists come together for 20 days of concerts (www.berliner festspiele.de) at the Philharmonie and other venues.

October

It's getting nippy again and trees start shedding their summer coats, but Berlin keeps a bright disposition and not only during the Festival of Lights.

✯ Festival of Lights

For two weeks, Berlin is all about 'lightseeing' during this shimmering festival (www.festival-of-lights.de) when historic landmarks such as the TV Tower, the Berliner Dom and the Brandenburg Gate sparkle with illuminations, projections and fireworks.

✯ Porn Film Festival

Vintage porn, Japanese porn, indie porn, sci-fi porn - the 'Berlinale' of sex (www.pornfilmfestival berlin.de) brings alternative skin flicks out of the smut corner and onto the big screen.

November

A great time to visit if you don't like crowds but are keen on snapping up hotel bargains. Weatherwise it's not the prettiest of months.

✯ BerMuDa

A celebration of electronic dance music, BerMuDa (Berlin Music Days) brings the world's best DJs to Berlin's top clubs for sweaty dance-a-thons culminating in a huge festival at Tempelhof airport (www .bermuda-berlin.de).

✯ JazzFest Berlin

This top-rated jazz festival (www.jazzfest-berlin.de) has doo-wopped in Berlin since 1964 and presents fresh and big-time talent in dozens of performances all over town.

December

Days are short and cold but the mood is festive, thanks to dressed-up shop windows, illuminated streets and facades, and Christmas markets redolent with the aroma of roast almonds and mulled wine.

🔒 Christmas Markets

Pick up shimmering ornaments or indulge in mulled wine at dozens of yuletide markets held throughout the city.

✯ Silvester

Ring in the new year hugging strangers, cooing at fireworks, guzzling bubbly straight from the bottle and generally misbehaving. The biggest party is at the Brandenburg Gate.

With Kids

Travelling to Berlin with kids can be child's play, especially if you keep a light schedule and involve them in day-to-day planning. There's plenty to do from zoos to kid-oriented museums and magic and puppet shows. Parks and imaginative playgrounds abound as do public pools.

A child views a giant spider at the Museum für Naturkunde (p133)

Museums

Not just for rainy days...

Museum für Naturkunde (Museum of Natural History)

Meet giant dinosaurs, travel through space back to the beginning of time and find out why zebras are striped in this wonderful museum (p133).

Deutsches Technikmuseum (German Museum of Technology)

It's vast, so concentrate time and energy on two or three sections that interest your tech-loving kids the most. Little ones love clambering around the trains and locomotives and marvelling at the windmills. The one-hour kid-geared audioguide tour (also in English) is an excellent introduction to the museum (p150).

Madame Tussauds

Kids of any age are all smiles when posing with the waxen likeness of their favourite pop star or celluloid celebrity (p82).

Legoland Discovery Centre

The milk-tooth set should delight in this Lego wonderland with rides, entertainment and interactive stations (p114).

Computerspielemuseum (Computer Games Museum)

Teens can get their kicks in this universe of computer games – Pac-Man to World of Warcraft (p171).

Mauermuseum (Wall Museum)

Older children with some history background and a decent attention span will likely be engrossed by the documentation of ingenious escape attempts from East Germany (p85).

Loxx Miniatur Welten

Berlin in miniature built around a huge model railway (p104).

Labyrinth Kindermuseum

Slip into a fantasy world while learning about tolerance, working together and just having fun. See www.labyrinth -kindermuseum.de.

Parks, Pools & Playgrounds

Tiergarten Park

Let the kids run wild in this huge park (p120) where they can play hide and seek among the rhododendrons, rent a boat to putt around the lake or have pizza in an outdoor cafe-beer garden.

Kollwitzplatz

This square (p181) sports three playgrounds for different age groups, including one with giant wooden toys. All get busy in the afternoon and on weekends. Cafes are just a hop, skip and jump away.

Kinderbad Monbijou

Keep cool on hot days splashing about this family-friendly public pool. See www.berlinerbaederbetriebe.de.

Volkspark Friedrichshain

Play cowboys and Indians in the 'Indian Village', gather your pirate mateys on the boat in the 'harbour' or find your favourite fairy-tale characters at the enchanting Märchenbrunnen at this park (p169).

Animals

Berlin Zoo & Aquarium

If the 18,000 finned, feathered and furry friends fail to enchant the little ones, the enormous adventure playground most likely will (p196).

NEED TO KNOW
....

➡ Get an English-speaking babysitter at **Babysitter Express** (www.babysitter-express.de) or **Welcome Kids** (www.welcome-kids.de).

➡ On public transport, children under six travel for free and those between six and 14 pay the reduced fare (*Ermässigungstarif*).

➡ Many museums, monuments and attractions are free to anyone under age 18, but the cut-off might also be age 12 or 14.

Tierpark Berlin

Expect plenty of ooa and aah moments when kids watch baby elephants at play or see lions and tigers being fed at this vast animal park.

SeaLife Berlin

Little ones get to press their noses against dozens of fish-filled tanks, solve puzzles and touch starfish and sea anemones – ever so gently, of course (p103).

Domäne Dahlem

Kids can interact with their favourite barnyard animals, help collect eggs or clean out the stalls, harvest potatoes and just generally watch daily farm life unfold at this fun working farm (www.domaene-dahlem.de).

Eating with Kids

It's fine to eat out as a family any time of day, especially in cafes, bistros and pizzerias. Many offer a limited *Kindermenü* (children's menu) or *Kinderteller* (children's dishes) to meet small appetite requirements. If they don't, most will be happy to serve half-size portions or prepare a simple meal. Popular dishes include *schnitzel*, *Pommes mit Ketchup and/or Mayonnaise* (fries with ketchup and/or mayo), *Nudeln mit Tomatensosse* (noodles with tomato sauce) and *Fischstäbchen* (fish sticks).

Large malls have food courts where kids can browse and pick what they like. Same goes for self-service cafeterias in larger department stores. Farmers markets also have food stalls. Bakeries selling scrumptious cakes or sandwiches are plentiful. The most popular snacks-on-the-run are bratwurst in a bun and doner kebab (sliced meat tucked into a pita pocket with salad and sauce). And of course, if nothing else will do, there's no shortage of the usual international fast food burger chains. Note that you have to pay extra for ketchup.

Baby food, infant formulas, soy and cow's milk, disposable nappies (diapers) and the like are widely available in supermarkets and chemists (drugstores).

Like a Local

Local life in Berlin is not as settled upon as in other cities but defined, to some extent, by the enormous influx of neo-Berliners from abroad and other parts of Germany. As such, it's comparatively easy to mingle with locals and to partake in their customs.

Cheese for sale at Winterfeldtmarkt, Schöneberg (p122)

MICHAEL TAYLOR / GETTY IMAGES ©

Dining Like a Local

Berliners love to dine out and, taking advantage of the many reasonably priced cafes and restaurants, do so quite frequently. This can mean scarfing down a quick doner at the local kebab joint or indulging in a four-course meal in a foodie hotspot. Eating out is rarely just about getting fed but is also a social experience. Meeting friends or family over a meal is considered a great way to catch up, to engage in heated discussions or to exchange the latest gossip.

Going out for breakfast has been a beloved pastime for years, although the trend seems to have peaked. With the exception of business people, few Berliners go out for lunch. The traditional German afternoon coffee and cake ritual, too, is not practised as widely in Berlin, and is pretty much the realm of older generations. The main going-out meal is dinner, with restaurant tables usually filled at 7.30pm or 8pm. Since it's customary to stretch meals to two hours and then to linger over a last glass of wine, restaurants only count on one seating per table per night. No one will arrive and present you with the bill as soon as you've swallowed your last bite.

For more information on eating out in Berlin, see p44.

Partying Like a Local

Most Berliners will start the night around 9pm or 10pm in a pub or bar, although it's also common to first meet at someone's home for a few cheap drinks in a ritual called 'Vorglühen' (literally 'pre-glowing'). Once out on the town, people either stay for a few drinks at the same place or pop into several before moving on to a club around 1am or 2am at the earliest.

In most bars, it's common practice to place orders with a server rather than pick up your own drinks at the bar. Only do this if you see a sign saying 'Selbstbedienung' (self-service). In pubs, the number of drinks is often recorded on round cardboard coasters sporting a brewery logo and paid for when you're ready to leave, rather than with each round. It is not customary to buy entire rounds for everyone at the table.

Once in the club, how long one stays depends on individual stamina and alcohol and drug consumption. Hardy types stagger out into the sunshine around midday, although the most hardcore may last even longer. Don't feel bad if you want to go home at 5am. Partying in Berlin takes some practice....

For more on what to expect from Berlin nightlife, see p50.

NEED TO KNOW

For many Berliners, the preferred way of getting around town is by bicycle, so why not join them and rent your own two-wheeler (p286). Alternatively, and especially in bad weather, take advantage of Berlin's excellent public transportation system (p286). For sightseeing on the cheap, hop aboard bus 100 or 200 (p286).

PLAN YOUR TRIP LIKE A LOCAL

Shopping Like a Local

Berliners pretty much fulfil all their shopping needs in their local *Kiez* (neighbourhood). There will usually be three or four supermarkets within walking distance, but grocery shopping is not done in one fell swoop but, rather, in several smaller trips spread over the course of the week. The local farmers market is the preferred source for fresh produce and speciality products like handmade noodles, artisanal cheese or Middle Eastern cheese spreads. Days start with fresh *Brötchen* (rolls) bought from the bakery around the corner. Nonfood needs are also met locally where possible, be it stationery, gifts, flowers, books, hardware, wine and so on.

Clothing will come from a mix of places that may include the high-street chains, upmarket boutiques, vintage stores and flea markets. When Berliners venture out of their neighbourhoods, it's usually to buy big-ticket items like furniture or vehicles or speciality items not available locally. Malls are comparatively rare in Berlin and frequented as much for recreational purposes as for large-scale shopping.

For more information on Shopping in Berlin, see p67.

Living Like a Local

The typical Berlin dwelling is a spacious rented 1½-bedroom flat on at least the 1st floor of a large early-20th-century apartment building (no one wants to live at street level), probably facing onto a *Hinterhof* (back courtyard) full of bicycles and coloured recycling bins. The apartment itself has very high ceilings, large windows and, as often as not, stripped wooden plank floors. The kitchen will almost invariably be the smallest room in the house and used mainly for stacking crates of beer and mineral water. A few flats still have the traditional tiled heating stoves in place, though no one actually uses them.

Berlin flats are usually nicely turned-out, whatever the style favoured by the occupant, and a lot of attention is paid to design, though comfort is also considered. At least one item of furniture will come from a certain Swedish furniture chain. Depending on income, the rest may come from the Stilwerk design centre, Polish craftsmen, a flea market or eBay – or any combination thereof.

Rent is calculated according to space, starting at around €400 a month for 50 sq metres (without utilities, depending on the district). Any conversation about costs with a Berlin tenant will inevitably lead to them asking you how many square metres your place at home is – do some sums before you leave!

Relaxing Like a Local

Although they are passionate about their city, Berliners also love to get out of town, especially in summer. If they're not jetting off to Mallorca or Madagascar, they will at least try to make it out to a local lake on a sunny day. There are dozens right within town, including the vast Müggelsee in Köpenick and the Wannsee in Zehlendorf, and hundreds more a quick car or train ride away in the surrounding countryside of Brandenburg. Everyone's got their favourite body of water and, having staked out the perfect spot, tends to return there time and again.

SILVIA OTTE / GETTY IMAGES ©

Jüdisches Museum (p148), Kreuzberg

With equally easy access to some fabulous parks, Berliners love heading for the greenery to work on their tan, relax in the shade, play frisbee or catch up on their reading. Some parks have sections where barbecuing is permitted, and this is a popular thing to do together with friends.

Sightseeing Like a Local

Most locals – especially those who are recent arrivals – are very appreciative of Berlin's cultural offerings and keep tabs on the latest museum or gallery openings, theatre productions or construction projects. It's quite common to discuss the merits of the latest blockbuster show or exhibit at dinner tables.

Although they love being a tourist in their own city, Berliners stay away from the big-ticket sights in summer when the world comes to town. More likely they will bide their time until the cold and dark winter months or visit on late-opening nights for smaller crowds. The biannual *Lange Nacht der Museen* (Long Night of the Museums), when dozens of museums stay open until midnight, brings out culture vultures by the tens of thousands.

Local Obsessions

Soccer

Many Berliners live and die by the fortunes of the local soccer team, Hertha BSC, which has seen its shares of ups and downs in recent years and is currently relegated to the 2. *Fussball-Bundesliga* (Second Soccer League), much to the dismay of locals. Still, true fans don't quit the team when it's down and, during the season, will inevitably don their blue-and-white fan gear to make the trek out to the Olympic Stadium for home games.

Berlin's other major team, 1. FC Union, also in the second league, has an especially passionate following in the eastern parts of the city.

The Weather

Many locals are hobby meteorologists who never pass up an opportunity to express their opinion on tomorrow's weather or on whether it's been a good summer so far, whether the last winter was mild or brutal, what to expect from the next one, and so on... So if you run out of things to say to a local, get the conversation going again by mentioning the weather. Other popular topics are rising rents, the perceived ineptitude of the local government or the much delayed opening of the Berlin Brandenburg Airport.

For Free

It's no secret that you can get more bang for your euro in Berlin than in any other Western capital. Better still, there are plenty of ways to stretch your budget even further by cashing in on some tip-top freebies, including such sights as the Reichstag dome and Checkpoint Charlie.

Gateway at Checkpoint Charlie (p85)

DAVID CLAPP / GETTY IMAGES ©

Free History Exhibits

Given that Germany has played a dispro-portionate role in 20th-century history, it's only natural that there are plenty of memorial sites and exhibits shedding light on various (mostly grim) milestones. Best of all, none cost even a penny.

World War II

Study up on the SS (Schutzstaffel), Gestapo and other organisations of the Nazi power apparatus at the Topographie des Terrors (Topography of Terror), then see the desk where WWII ended with the signing of Ger-many's unconditional surrender at Museum Karlshorst. You can stand in the very room where the 'Final Solution' was planned at the Haus der Wannsee-Konferenz (House of the Wannsee Conference), get shivers while walking around the Sachsenhausen Con-centration Camp, then pay your respects to Jewish Nazi victims at the Holocaust Memorial. German resistance against the Nazis is the focus of the Gedenkstätte Deutscher Widerstand (German Resistance Memorial Centre).

Cold War

The East Side Gallery may be the long-est surviving section of the Berlin Wall, but also swing by the Gedenkstätte Ber-liner Mauer (Berlin Wall Memorial Site) to get the full picture of what the Wall looked like and the Tränenpalast (Palace of Tears) to learn about the personal hardships of living in a divided city. At Checkpoint Charlie, an outdoor exhibit chronicles milestones in Cold War his-tory, while the nearby Stasi Ausstellung (Stasi Exhibit) peels away the layers on East Germany's sinister secret service. For those years from the point of view of the Allies, swing by the AlliiertenMuseum (Allied Museum).

Free Museums & Galleries
State Museums

Admission to the permanent exhibits at Berlin's state museums (such as the Pergamonmuseum, Neues Museum, Gemäldegalerie and Hamburger Bahnhof) is free for anyone under 18. Admission at the Friedrichswerdersche Kirche is always free for all.

Niche Museums

Although the blockbuster state museums do charge admission to adults over 18, a few niche museums don't. Learn about the history of German democracy at the Deutscher Dom (German Cathedral), life during the Biedermeier at the Knoblauchhaus and Berlin's equivalent of Oskar Schindler at the Museum Blindenwerkstatt Otto Weidt (Museum Workshop for the Blind Otto Weidt). Free art can be enjoyed at the Museum der Verbotenen Kunst (Museum of Forbidden Art), the Daimler Contemporary and the Automobil Forum Unter den Linden. Military and airplane buffs will want to make the trip out to the Luftwaffenmuseum (German Airforce Museum).

Free Guided Tours

Many museums and galleries now include free multilingual audioguides in the admission price; some also offer free guided tours, although these are usually in German.

New Berlin Tours

This company pioneered the concept of the 'free tour', although the guides actually work for tips. The 3½-hour general walking tours leave at 9am, 11am, 1pm and 4pm from Starbucks at the Brandenburg Gate and hit all the major landmarks, including Checkpoint Charlie and the Reichstag.

NEED TO KNOW

➡ **Websites** Search for free stuff by date at www.berlin-eintritt-free.org.

➡ **Discount Cards** The Berlin Museum Pass is a steal for culture lovers. The Berlin Welcome Card and CityTourCard may also be a good investment (p290).

➡ **Wi-fi** Many cafes let their customers get online for free.

Brewers Berlin Tours

Also a 3½-hour tour on a pay-what-you-can basis, the Berlin Express has local experts give you Berlin in a nutshell by taking you to all the major sites in the capital. It leaves daily at 1pm from the ice-cream shop at Friedrichstrasse 96.

Free Music

Free gigs and music events take place all the time, in pubs, bars, parks and churches. See the listings magazines for what's on during your stay.

Summer Concerts

In summer, many of Berlin's parks and gardens ring out with the free sound of jazz, pop, samba, classical and all sorts of other music. Case in point: the lovely Teehaus im Englischen Garten, which presents two concerts (at 4pm and 7pm) every Saturday and Sunday from July to September. Or the enchanting Körnerpark in Neukölln, where crowds gather for the 6pm concerts on Sundays from early June until late August.

Karaoke

The Mauerpark is a zoo-and-a-half on hot summer Sundays, thanks largely to the massively entertaining outdoor Bearpit Karaoke, which has thousands of spectators cramming onto the stone bleachers to cheer and applaud crooners of various talent levels.

Classical

At 1pm on Tuesdays from September to mid-June, the foyer of the Berliner Philharmonie fills with music lovers for free lunchtime chamber music concerts. Students of the prestigious Hochschule für Musik Hanns Eisler also show off their skills at several free recitals weekly.

Rock & Jazz

For one-off free concerts, check the listings magazines. Jazz fans can bop for free at A-Trane on Mondays and at the late-night jam session after 12.30am on Saturday. On Wednesdays, b-flat and Quasimodo have their own free jam sessions.

MARK DAFFEY /GETTY IMAGES ©

Relaxing in the Tiergarten (p120)

Walking in Berlin

The best way to explore Berlin is on foot, and there are certainly some fun city streets. In Mitte, saunter down historic Unter den Linden, flashy Friedrichstrasse, hip Torstrasse or get great views of the government quarter on the car-free Spree promenade. Kreuzberg flaunts indie flair along bohemian Bergmannstrasse and Oranienstrasse. In Schöneberg, walking down from Nollendorfplatz to Haupt-strasse gives you an eyeful of the neigh-bourhood. In Friedrichshain, monumental Karl-Marx-Allee epitomises East Berlin, while the contemporary architecture of Potsdamer Platz reflects corporate post-reunification aesthetics.

For more ideas, check out the neigh-bourhood walks featured in each of the neighbourhood chapters.

PLAN YOUR TRIP FOR FREE

A work by street artist Alias of a person holding their head in their hands

👁 Art Galleries & Street Art

Art aficionados will find their compass on perpetual spin in Berlin. Home to 440 galleries, scores of world-class collections and some 10,000 international artists, it has assumed a pole position on the global artistic circuit. Adolescent energy, restlessness and experimental spirit combined and infused with an undercurrent of grit are what give this 'eternally unfinished' city its street cred.

Alte Nationalgalerie (Old National Gallery; p102)

City of Artists

Since the fall of the Wall, Berlin's abundant space and relatively low cost of living have made it a haven for international emerging artists. Most labour in obscurity but there have also been some notable breakthroughs, including Danish-Icelandic Olafur Eliasson. Other major contemporary artists living and working in Berlin include Thomas Demand, Jonathan Meese, Via Lewandowsky, Isa Genzken, Tino Seghal, Esra Ersen, John Bock and the artist duo Ingar Dragset and Michael Elmgreen.

Nationalgalerie Berlin

The National Gallery of Berlin is a top-ranked collection of mostly European art from the 19th to the 21st century, administered by the **Staatliche Museen Berlin** (Berlin State Museums; www.smb.museum) and presented in six locations scattered around the central city:

Alte Nationalgalerie (p102) Neoclassical, romantic, impressionist and early modernist art, including Caspar David Friedrich, Adolf Menzel and Monet; on Museumsinsel.

Friedrichswerdersche Kirche (p83) German 19th-century sculpture by Christian Daniel Rauch, Johann Gottfried Schadow and Karl Friedrich Schinkel; off Unter den Linden.

Neue Nationalgalerie (p119) Early 20th-century art, especially German expressionists like Grosz and Kirchner, as well as Max Beckmann; part of the Kulturforum.

NEED TO KNOW

Tickets

➡ Buy tickets at the gallery or museum. Blockbuster visiting shows often sell out, so it's best to prepurchase tickets online.

➡ Most private collections require advance registration; reserve weeks ahead for the Sammlung Boros.

➡ Commercial galleries do not charge admission. All hold *vernissage* (opening) and *finissage* (closing) parties.

➡ The Berlin Museum Pass buys admission to about 70 museums and galleries for a three-day period. Available at participating museums and the tourist offices.

Opening Hours

➡ The big museums and galleries are typically open from 10am to 6pm, with extended viewing one day a week, usually Thursday. Many are closed on Mondays.

➡ Commercial galleries tend to be open from noon to 6pm and by appointment.

Tours

GoArt (www.goart-berlin.de) runs customised tours that demystify Berlin's art scene by opening doors to private collections, artist studios and galleries or by taking you to exciting street-art locations.

Websites

➡ **Museumsportal** (www.museums portal.de) Gateway to the city's museums and galleries.

➡ Google 'Berliner Kunstfaltplan' for a comprehensive overview of the latest commercial gallery shows.

Museum Berggruen (p194) Classical modernist, mostly Picasso and Klee; near Schloss Charlottenburg.

Sammlung Scharf-Gerstenberg (p194) Surrealist art by Dali, Magritte, Jean Dubuffet, Max Ernst and more; near Schloss Charlottenburg.

Hamburger Bahnhof (p129) International contemporary art, Warhol to Rauschenberg to Beuys; east of the Hauptbahnhof.

(Top) Street art in Kreuzberg by Italian artist Blu

(Bottom) Graffiti artists in the Mauerpark (p180)

Specialist Galleries

Aside from from the heavy hitters, Berlin teems with smaller museums specialising in a particular artist or genre. You can admire the colourful canvasses of artists group Die Brücke (The Bridge) in a lovely museum (p213) surrounded by forest. See the paintings of Max Liebermann while standing in the very studio in the Liebermann-Villa am Wannsee (p215) where he painted them. Take a survey of a century of Berlin-made art in the Berlinische Galerie (p150). Two museums train the spotlight on women: the Käthe-Kollwitz-Museum (p196), which is dedicated to one of the finest and most outspoken German early-20th-century artists, and the Das Verborgene Museum (p198), which champions lesser-known German female artists from the same period. There are also corporate collections like the Daimler Contemporary and private ones like the Sammlung Boros.

Private Collections

Several private collectors are sharing their precious collections with the public. The most headline-grabbing of these is the Sammlung Boros (p134), an edgy display of contemporary art spectacularly set in up a converted WWII bunker. Others are the Sammlung Hoffmann (p134), in a private apartment in a classic Scheunenviertel courtyard ensemble; the Sammlung Haubrok (p171) on socialist-flavoured Karl-Marx-Allee; and the Me Collectors Room (p134) in a modern building on Auguststrasse.

Public Art

Installations, sculptures, paintings, for free. Public art is big in Berlin, which happens to be home to the world's longest outdoor mural, the 1.3km-long East Side Gallery (p168). But no matter in which neighbourhood you walk, you're going to encounter public art on a grand scale. The Potsdamer Platz area offers especially rich pickings. See our Neighbourhood Walk on p124.

Commercial Art Galleries

The **Galleries Association of Berlin** (www. berliner-galerien.de) counts some 440 galleries within the city, but there are at least 200 noncommercial showrooms and off-spaces that regularly show new exhibitions. Top galleries include **Barbara Wien** (www. barbarawien.de) for works on paper; **Camera**

Work (www.camerawork.de) and **Kicken Berlin** (www.kicken-gallery.com) for photography; **Contemporary Fine Arts** (www.cfa-berlin.de), **Neugerriemschneider** (www.neugerriemsch neider.com) and **Eigen+Art** (www.eigen-art.com) for contemporary art world stars; **Kunstagenten** (www.kunstagenten.de) for tomorrow's stars; and **Thomas Schulte** (www.galerie thomasschulte.de) for conceptual art.

Street Art

Stencils, paste-ups, throw-ups, burners, bombings, pieces, murals, installations and 3D graffiti are the magic words in street art, describing styles and techniques that have little to do with vandalism and tagging. With no shortage of vacant buildings, weedy lots and artists of all stripes, sometimes it seems as though all of Berlin has become a canvas.

Some of the hottest names in international street art have left their mark on local walls, including Banksy, Os Gemeos, Romero, Swoon, Flix, Pure Evil, Miss Van and Blu. But there's plenty of home-grown talent as well. The portrait of a youthful Jack Nicholson behind bird wire is an iconic work by Bonk, while Bimer's signature subject is an angry-looking Berlin bear. Kripoe is known for his yellow hands and El Bocho for the cat-hating Little Lucy.

WHERE IS IT?

There's street art pretty much everywhere, but the area around U-Bahn station Schlesisches Tor in Kreuzberg has some house-wall-sized classics, for instance by Blu and Os Gemeos.

The Boxhagener Platz area in Friedrichshain is another hub sporting nice works by Boxi, Alias and El Bocho. Alias handily signs his work; look for his 'Asian Girl' cut-out near the corner of Gabriel-Max-Strasse and Grünberger Strasse.

There's also some good work in Mitte, especially in the fashionable Scheunenviertel, where you'll find several examples by the prolific XoooX, known for his black-and-white stencils of models (eg Gipsstrasse near Joachimstrasse; Weinmeisterstrasse near the U-Bahn station).

Prenzlauer Berg has the Mauerpark, where budding artists may legally polish their skills along a section of the Berlin Wall.

Here are some of our street-art favourites (see maps for locations):

Astronaut (Map p324) Kreuzberg; stencilling by Victor Ash.

Rounded Heads (Map p324) Kreuzberg; pictogram by Nomad.

Yellow Man (Map p324) Kreuzberg; painting by Os Gemeos.

Brothers Upside Down & Chains (Map p324) Kreuzberg; two side-by-side paintings by Blu and JR.

Leviathan (Map p324) Kreuzberg; by Blu.

Fish (Map p328) Friedrichshain; by Ema.

Sad Girl with Rabbit Ears (Map p328) Friedrichshain; by Boxi.

Lads (Map p324) Kreuzberg; painting by The London Police.

HOW TO SEE IT

A quick way to see plenty of urban art is by riding the S-Bahn lines S41 or S42, especially between Alexanderplatz and Treptow. The above-ground U1 line through Kreuzberg is another good one and ideal for seeing the famous, wall-sized Astronaut by Irish artist Victor Ash (on the north side of the tracks, between Kottbusser Tor and Görlitzer Bahnhof stations).

The gallery **ATM** (0176 3416 4222; www.atmberlin.de; Eylauerstrasse 13; by appointment only; Platz der Luftbrücke) also keeps its finger on the pulse of the scene, although unfortunately it's open by appointment only. Alternative Berlin Tours (p288) runs a 2½-hour street-art walking tour for €15 where you even get to meet local artists and pick up tips and techniques in a mini-workshop. **Hidden Path** (www.thehiddenpath.de) also does customised tours for small groups.

To read up on the subject, pick up *Urban Illustration Berlin: Street Art City Guide* by Benjamin Wolbergs.

Art Galleries & Street Art by Neighbourhood

➡ **Historic Mitte** (p74) Emil Nolde Museum; galleries around Checkpoint Charlie.

➡ **Museumsinsel & Alexanderplatz** (p93) Alte Nationalgalerie; Contemporary Fine Arts.

Tetes et Queue sculpture by Alexander Calder at the Neue Nationalgalerie (New National Gallery; p119)

➡ **Potsdamer Platz & Tiergarten** (p111) Neue Nationalgalerie, Gemäldegalerie, Bauhaus Archiv, Martin-Gropius-Bau.

➡ **Scheunenviertel** (p127) Top-notch galleries around Auguststrasse; street art; Sammlung Boros; Hamburger Bahnhof.

➡ **Kreuzberg & Northern Neukölln** (p146) Best for street art; Berlinische Galerie.

➡ **Friedrichshain** East Side Gallery and more good street art.

➡ **City West & Charlottenburg** High-end galleries, eg on Fasanenstrasse, Mommsenstrasse and Kurfürstendamm; art museums near Schloss Charlottenburg.

Lonely Planet's Top Choices

Gemäldegalerie (p116) Sweeping collection of European old masters, Rembrandt to Renoir.

Hamburger Bahnhof (p129) All aboard the contemporary-art express at this former train station.

Sammlung Boros (p134) Cutting-edge works in a WWII bunker.

Brücke Museum (p213) Forest-framed gem focused on modern-art pioneers.

Martin-Gropius-Bau (p119) First-rate travelling exhibits in a gorgeous Renaissance-style building.

Best Big Art Museums

Gemäldegalerie (p116)

Hamburger Bahnhof (p129)

Neue Nationalgalerie (p119)

Alte Nationalgalerie (p102)

Best Small Art Museums

Neuer Pavillon (p193)

Brücke Museum (p213)

Berlinische Galerie (p150)

Best Single Artist Galleries

Käthe-Kollwitz-Museum (p196)

Emil Nolde Museum (p84)

Dalí - Die Ausstellung (p119)

Liebermann-Villa am Wannsee (p215)

Best Artistic Genre Galleries

Museum Berggruen (p194; classical modernism)

Sammlung Scharf-Gerstenberg (p194 surrealism)

Alte Nationalgalerie (p102 romanticism)

Bauhaus Archiv (p122; Bauhaus)

Best Private Collections

Sammlung Boros (p134)

Sammlung Hoffmann (p134)

Sammlung Haubrok (p171)

Me Collectors Room (p134)

Best Contemporary-Art Galleries

Hamburger Bahnhof (p129)

Sammlung Boros (p134)

KW Institute for Contemporary Art (p133)

Daimler Contemporary (p115)

Best Museum & Gallery Cafes

Martin-Gropius-Bau (p119)

Hamburger Bahnhof (p129)

Bauhaus Archiv (p122)

Bodemuseum (p100)

Liebermann-Villa am Wannsee (p215)

Best Museum Architecture

Bauhaus Archiv (p122)

Martin-Gropius-Bau (p119)

Hamburger Bahnhof (p129)

Neue Nationalgalerie (p119)

Best Public Art

Jonathan Borofsky's *Molecule Man* (p172)

East Side Gallery (p168)

Keith Haring's *Boxers* (Map p316)

Robert Rauschenberg's *Riding Bikes* (Map p316)

Karl Biedermann's *Der Verlassene Raum* (Map p316)

Ben Wagin's *Parlament der Bäume* (p81)

Best Exhibition Halls

Martin-Gropius-Bau (p119)

Haus der Kulturen der Welt (p81)

Automobil Forum Unter den Linden (p82)

Akademie der Künste (p78)

Best Street Art

Leviathan (Map p324)

Brothers Upside Down (Map p324)

Astronaut (Map p324)

Sad Girl with Rabbit Ears (Map p328)

Berlin Wall murals, East Side Gallery (p168)

The Berlin Wall

It's more than a tad ironic that Berlin's most popular tourist attraction is one that no longer exists. For 28 years the Berlin Wall, the most potent symbol of the Cold War, divided not only a city but the world.

Memorial, Gedenkstätte Berliner Mauer (p130)

NEED TO KNOW

Mauerweg

If you're feeling ambitious, rent a bike and follow all or part of the 160km-long **Berliner Mauerweg** (Berlin Wall Trail; www.berlin.de/mauer), a signposted walking and cycling path that follows the former border fortifications with 40 multilingual information stations posted along the way.

The Beginning

Shortly after midnight on 13 August 1961, East German soldiers and police began rolling out miles of barbed wire that would soon be replaced with prefab concrete slabs. The Wall was a desperate measure launched by the German Democratic Republic (GDR, East Germany) government to stop the sustained brain and brawn drain the country had experienced since its 1949 founding. Some 3.6 million people had already headed to western Germany, putting the GDR on the brink of economic and political collapse.

The Physical Border

Euphemistically called the 'Anti-Fascist Protection Barrier', the Berlin Wall was continually reinforced and refined. In the end, it was a complex border-security system consisting of not one, but two, walls hemming in a 'death strip' riddled with trenches, floodlights, patrol roads, attack dogs, electrified alarm fences and watchtowers staffed by guards with shoot-to-kill orders. From the West, artists tried to humanise the grey concrete scar by covering it in colourful street art. The West Berlin government erected viewing platforms, which people could climb up on and peek across into East Berlin.

Escapes

Nearly 100,000 GDR citizens tried to escape, many using spectacular contraptions like homemade balloons or U-boats. There are no exact numbers, but it is believed that hundreds died in the process of escaping by drowning, suffering fatal accidents or killing themselves when caught. More than 100 were shot and killed by border guards – the first only a few days after 13 August 1961. Guards who prevented an escape were rewarded with commendations, promotions and bonuses.

The End

The Wall's demise came as unexpectedly as its creation. Once again the GDR was losing its people in droves, this time via Hungary, which had opened its borders with Austria. Major demonstrations in East Berlin culminated in a gathering of half a million people on Alexanderplatz on 4 November 1989, vociferously demanding political reform. Something had to give.

It did, on 9 November when government spokesperson Günter Schabowski announced during a press conference on live TV that all travel restrictions to the West would be lifted. When asked by a reporter, when this would become effective, he said: 'As far as I know, immediately.' It later turned out that the ruling was not supposed to take effect until the following day, only no one had informed Schabowski. The news spread through East Berlin like wildfire, with hundreds of thousands heading towards the Wall. Border guards had no choice but to stand back.

Amid scenes of wild partying and mile-long parades of GDR-made Trabant cars, the two Berlins came together again.

Today

The dismantling of the hated barrier began almost immediately, leaving only about 2km of the Berlin Wall standing. By now the two city halves have visually merged so perfectly that it takes a keen eye to tell East from West. Fortunately, there's help in the form of a **double row of cobblestones** that guides you along 5.7km of the Wall's course. Walking along the East Side Gallery (p168), at 1.3km the longest remaining

(Top) Open-air gallery (p85),
Checkpoint Charlie

(Left) Cyclist rests near the Berlin Wall,
Potsdamer Platz

Berlin Wall Sights

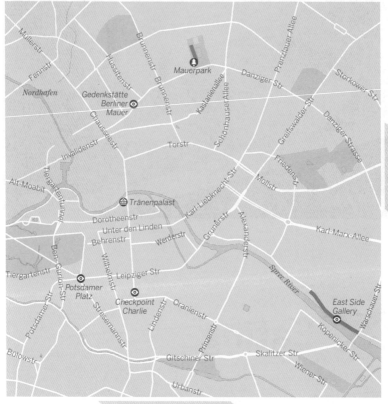

stretch turned outdoor gallery in 1990, is an essential Berlin experience, but there are a few other ways to engage with this element of the city's past.

Museums & Exhibits

For comprehensive background, visit the in-door-outdoor Wall memorial Gedenkstätte Berliner Mauer (p130), which will help you visualise how all the elements of the wall and the death strip fit together. Another exhibit in a former border-crossing pavilion known as Tränenpalast (p82) documents the wall's social impact on the daily lives of Germans on both sides of the border. Right at Checkpoint Charlie, the Mauermuseum (Wall Museum; p85) highlights some of the more spectacular escapes to the West, while

the new 360-degree Berlin Wall Panorama (p85) transports you back to a grey autumn day in 1980s Berlin.

Tours

Fat Tire Bike Tours (p288) and Berlin on Bike (p288) offer guided bike trips along the course of the Wall. Also, see the Nauer-weg (Berlin Wall Trail; p41).

A high-tech way to walk the Wall is with the **Mauerguide** (☏8871 3624; www.mauerguide. com; adult/concession per 4hr €8/5, per 24hr €10/7), a hand-held GPS-guided minicomput-er that provides intelligent commentary and historic audio and video. Hire stations are at Checkpoint Charlie, in the U-Bahn station Brandenburger Tor and at the Documenta-tion Centre of the Berlin Wall Memorial.

Lunch, Prater (p185)

Eating

If you crave traditional German comfort food, you'll certainly find plenty of places to indulge in pork knuckles, smoked pork chops and calf's liver in Berlin. These days, though, 'typical' local fare is lighter, healthier, creative and more likely to come from organic eateries, a UN worth of ethnic restaurants and gourmet kitchens, including 13 flaunting Michelin stars.

Berlin Cuisine

If you want to try classic Berlin food, you better not be squeamish, a vegetarian, a health nut or a waist-watcher. Traditional dishes are hearty, rib-sticking and only give a passing nod to the vegetable kingdom. Pork is a staple, prepared in umpteen ways, including *Kasseler Rippchen* (smoked pork chops) and *Eisbein* (boiled pork hock), which is typically paired with sauerkraut and boiled potatoes. Other regulars are roast chicken, schnitzel and *Sauerbraten* (beef marinated in vinegar and spices). Minced meat tends to come in the form of a *Boulette,* a cross between a meatball and a hamburger, which is eaten with a little mustard and perhaps a dry roll. If local fish is on the menu, it'll most likely be *Zander* (pike-perch) or *Forelle* (trout).

Modern Berlin Cuisine

A growing league of local chefs has jumped on the locavore bandwagon, letting the trifecta of 'seasonal-regional-organic' ingredients steer their menus. Many now travel to Brandenburg, the rural region surrounding Berlin, to source free-range meats, wild-caught fish, farm-fresh fruit and vegetables, handmade cheeses and other delectables, preferably sustainably grown. Menus increasingly champion traditional (and long underrated) ingredients such as root vegetables (like parsnip, turnips and parsley root), old-fashioned grains like barley and buckwheat, and game and other meats like *Blutwurst* (blood sausage), *Zickleinleber* (baby goat liver) or *Ochsenbäckchen* (ox cheeks).

Seasonal Specialities

What's white, hard and about 20cm long? Hey, not what you think, though dirty thoughts shall be forgiven in view of the unmistakably phallic shape of chlorophyll-deprived *weisser Spargel* (white asparagus). Between late April and late June Berliners go nuts for the erotic stalks, which are best enjoyed steamed alongside ham, hollandaise sauce or butter, and boiled potatoes. They also show up as asparagus soup, in quiches and salads and even as ice cream. Locavores will be pleased to hear one of Germany's most celebrated *Spargel* hails from the sandy soils of Beelitz, just outside of town.

Spargelzeit (asparagus season) is a highlight of the culinary calendar that actually kicks off a bit earlier with *Bärlauch* (wild garlic), which starts showing up in salads and as pesto in early spring. Fresh fruit, especially all sorts of berries (strawberries, blueberries, raspberries, gooseberries and red currants) and cherries, brightens up the market stalls in summer. In late summer and early autumn, handpicked mushrooms such as *Steinpilze* (porcini) and earthy *Pfifferlinge* (chanterelles) show up on menus everywhere. A typical winter meal is cooked *Grünkohl* (kale) with smoked sausage, which is often served at Christmas markets. *Gans* (stuffed goose) is a Martinmas tradition (11 November) and also popular at Christmas time.

Fast-Food Faves

International fast-food chains are ubiquitous, of course, but there's plenty of home-grown fast food as well. If there ever was a snack food with cult status, it must be Berlin's humble Currywurst. To the uncouth or uninitiated, we're talking about a smallish fried or grilled wiener sliced into bite-sized ringlets, swimming in a spicy tomato sauce, dusted with curry powder and served on a flimsy paper plate with a plastic toothpick for stabbing. The wurst itself is

NEED TO KNOW

Price Ranges

The symbol below indicates the average cost per main course at the restaurant in question.

€€€	over €18
€€	€8–18
€	under €8

Opening Hours

As a guideline, figure on cafes being open from 8am to 8pm, restaurants from 11am to 11pm and fast-food joints from 11am until midnight or later.

Bills & Tipping

➡ It's customary to add between 5% and 10% for good service.

➡ Tip as you hand over the money, rather than leaving it on the table. For example, say '*30, bitte*' if your bill comes to €28 and you want to give a €2 tip. If you have the exact amount, just say '*Stimmt so*' (that's fine).

Reservations

Reservations are essential at the top eateries and recommended for midrange restaurants – especially at dinner-time and at weekends. Berliners tend to linger at the table, so if a place is full at 8pm it's likely that it will stay that way for a couple of hours.

Late-Night & Sunday Shopping

➡ One handy feature of Berlin culture is the *Spätkauf* (*Späti* in local vernacular), which are small neighbourhood stores stocked with the basics and open from early evening until 2am or later. They're especially prevalent in areas with busy streetlife or nightlife.

➡ Some supermarkets stay open until midnight; a few even through the night.

➡ Shops and supermarkets in major train stations (Hauptbahnhof, Ostbahnhof, Friedrichstrasse) are open late and on Sundays.

➡ Petrol stations also stock some supplies.

Eating by Neighbourhood

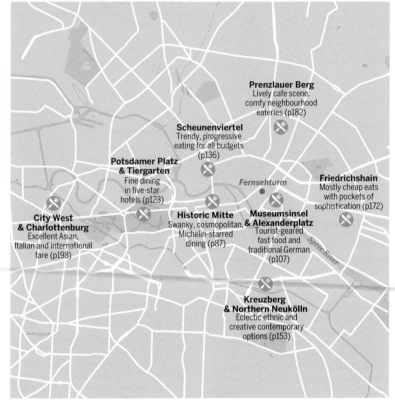

subtly spiced and served with or without its crunchy epidermis.

The people of Hamburg might disagree, but Berliners know that their city is the true birthplace of this beloved calorie bomb. The first sausage started its triumphant course to snack stands across the nation from the steaming Imbiss (snack bar) of Herta Heuwer on 4 September 1949.

What exactly went into Herta's sauce will never be known, as in 1999 she took the secret to her grave. Her contribution to culinary history has garnered her a **memorial plaque** (Map p334; Kantstrasse 101; S Wilmersdorfer Strasse) where her *Imbiss* once stood.

There's always a healthy debate about where to find the best dog in town, but we're going to stick our necks out and share our very own favourite top three: Curry 36 (p154) in Kreuzberg, Konnopke's *Imbiss*

(p185) in Prenzlauer Berg and **Witty's** (☎211 9494; www.wittys-berlin.de; Wittenbergplatz 5, cnr Ansbacher Strasse; snacks €3-6; ☺11am-1am; Wittenbergplatz) organic wieners in Schöneberg. Pair 'em with *pommes rot-weiss* (fries with ketchup and mayo).

The Currywurst competes with the *Döner* (doner kebab) for title of best hangover cure or prevention. The ultimate 'Turkish delight' is a lightly toasted bread pocket stuffed with thinly shaved spit-roasted veal or chicken, copious amounts of fresh salad and doused with your choice of sauce. Three sauces are standard: *Kräuter* (herb), *scharf* (hot) and *Knoblauch* (garlic). Specify which when ordering or select a combination or all three. A less messy version is called *Dürum Döner* and contains the same ingredients wrapped up in a tortilla-style flatbread. Spit-roasted meat may have been around forever, but the idea of serving it this way is a local tradition conceived in 1971 by Mehmed Aygün, owner of the Hasir mini-chain of Berlin restaurants. Today, there are more than 1500 *Döner* shops all over town, especially in Kreuzberg and northern Neukölln.

Berlin polyglot society has also been introduced to Lebanese felafel, Californian burritos and Vietnamese *bánh mì* sandwiches, while local burger joints have given the big global players a run for their money.

Ethnic Delights

Berlin's multicultural tapestry has brought the world's food to town, from Austrian schnitzel to Zambian zebra steaks. Sushi is hugely popular and Mexican and Korean restaurants have also become all the rage. Reflecting the trend towards tasty and healthy food is the abundance of Asian eateries, especially Vietnamese and Thai, along with various fusion establishments blending several cuisines.

Vegetarians & Vegans

Berlin was slow in coming but is now embracing meat-free fare with the fervour of a religious convert. Health-conscious cafes and restaurants have been sprouting faster than alfafa and serve up inspired menus that leave the classic veggie or tofu burger in the dust. With dishes like sweet potato saltimbocca, tandoori seitan, pearl barley strudel with chanterelles, or parmesan dumplings, chefs strive to push the creative envelope.

Even veganism has made significant inroads: **Veganz** (☎4403 6048; www.veganz.de; Schivelbeiner Strasse 34; ⏲8am-9pm Mon-Sat; [S]Schönhauser Allee, 🚋M1, 🚆Schönhauser Allee), Germany's first all-vegan supermarket, opened in Berlin in 2011, followed by the city's first vegan gourmet restaurant, Kopps (p138), the same year. Even many non-vegetarian restaurants now offer more than the token vegetable lasagne. For a comprehensive list of vegan and vegetarian restaurants in Berlin, see www.happycow.net/europe/germany/berlin.

Breakfast & Brunch

Berliners are big on *Frühstück* (breakfast), which is usually a sweet and savoury spread of various breads and rolls, cheeses, cold cuts, preserves, yoghurt and muesli, perhaps accompanied by a boiled or fried egg. It's something of a carbo-overload but ideal for mopping up the excesses of the night before or for getting ready for a long day of sightseeing.

In most hotels, breakfast is served in the form of an all-you-can-eat buffet until at least 10am, although trendier joints will keep it open until 11am or noon. But don't worry if you've overslept: most self-respecting Berlin cafes serve breakfast until well into the afternoon. All-you-can-eat Sunday brunch buffets are a social institution in their own right, easily lasting a couple of hours, and provide an ideal excuse to recap Saturday night's shenanigans at leisure.

Where to Eat

Restaurants are often formal places with full menus, crisp white linen and high prices. Some restaurants are open for lunch and dinner only but more casual places tend to be open all day. Same goes for cafes, which usually serve both coffee and alcohol, as well as light meals, although ordering food is not obligatory. Many cafes and restaurants offer inexpensive weekday 'business lunches' that usually include a starter, main course and drink for under €10.

English menus are quite common now and, in fact, some places, especially those owned by neo-Berliners from the US, UK or around Europe, don't even bother with German menus any longer. When it comes to paying, sometimes the person who invites pays, but generally Germans go Dutch and split the bill. This might mean everyone chipping in at the end of a meal or asking the server to pay separately (*getrennte Rechnung*).

Handy speed-feed shops, called *Imbiss*, serve all sorts of savoury fodder, from sausage-in-a-bun to *Döner* and pizza. Many bakeries serve sandwiches alongside pastries.

Supper Clubs

There's no telling how much longer the global supper-club trend will last, but for now there are still quite a few Berlin locals (usually transplants from other countries) that throw open their homes to turn perfect strangers into friends over home-cooked meals. Recommending a supper club can be tricky, since these below-the-radar restaurants are rarely permanent. The best we can suggest is to Google

'Berlin supper clubs' and see what pops up. The **Ghetto Gourmet** (www.theghet.com) keeps a finger on the pulse of the scene.

Self-Catering

Several supermarket chains compete for shoppers throughout Berlin. More up-market chains like Kaiser's and Reichelt have fresh meat, cheese and deli counters, and usually an attached bakery. Discount chains include Aldi, Lidl, Netto and Penny Markt, which all offer decent quality and selection, albeit in a rather helter-skelter, warehouse-style setting. For the ultimate selection, the food hall of the KaDeWe (p202) department store is simply unbeatable, but the prices reflect this. Farmers markets and small Turkish corner stores are also good food sources. 'Bio stores' that specialise in natural, organic, hormone-free and sustainable food have become ubiquitous in most of the central neighbourhoods.

Farmers Markets

Practically every Berlin *Kiez* (neighbourhood) has its own weekly or biweekly farmers market, but these are our favourites:

Türkenmarkt (p164) Bazaar-like canalside market with bargain-priced produce and a bonanza of Mediterranean deli fare (olives, feta etc).

Kollwitzplatzmarkt (p189) Posh player with velvety gorgonzola, juniper-berry smoked ham, homemade pesto and other exquisite morsels. The Thursday market is smaller and all organic. Kids' playground nearby.

Ökomarkt Chamissoplatz (Map p322) One of the oldest and largest organic farmers markets in Berlin (operating since 1994) on a pretty square in the Bergmannkiez with adjacent playground.

Winterfeldtmarkt (p122) Local institution with quality produce alongside artsy-crafty stuff and global snack stands.

Karl-August-Platz Markt (p334) Fresh fruit and veg plus artisanal cheeses, pesto etc, on a beautiful square around a neo-Gothic church.

I Scream Ice Cream

Berlin is nirvana for ice-cream lovers with countless home-grown parlours popping up as soon as the last winter winds have died down. With locals being increasingly healthy and carb-conscious, frozen-yoghurt shops have finally made some major inroads as well. Everyone's got their favourite stop for frozen delights; here are some of ours:

Caffe e Gelato (Map p316) Traditional Italian-style ice cream gets a 21st-century twist at this huge space on the upper floor of the Potsdamer Platz Arkaden mall. Aside from creamy concoctions, there are also organic, lactose- and sugar-free varieties, all of them delicious.

Die Kleine Eiszeit (Map p330) Brave the inevitable line to choose from a couple of dozen homemade flavours made only with fresh ingredients in this Prenzlauer Berg favourite since GDR days.

Fräulein Frost (Map p324) This pink-and-white parlour is all about experimentation. GuZiMi, which stands for *Gurke-Zitrone-Minze* (cucumber-lemon-mint), is the perennial bestseller.

Wonderpots (Map p314) Guilt-free frozen yoghurt handmade daily from organic, low-fat cultures is the winning formula here. Toppings range from fresh fruit to brownie chips and apple sauce.

Lonely Planet's Top Choices

Cafe Jacques (p154) Candlelit cocoon of killer Mediterranean food and wine.

Oderquelle (p182) Inspired port of call for modern German.

Defne (p154) Turkish delights beyond the doner kebab.

Cookies Cream (p87) Cool but comfortable hidden herbi-vore haven.

Lavanderia Vecchia (p157) Top-flight Italian in up-and-coming Neukölln.

Uma (p87) Tummy-tantalising sushi, grills and Japanese classics.

Best By Budget

€
Ishin (p87)

Susuru (p136)

Rosenthaler Grill- und Schlemmerbuffet (p140)

Dolores (p107)

Curry 36 (p154)

Côcô (p140)

€€
Frau Mittenmang (p182)

Schneeweiss (p172)

Der Fischladen (p184)

Der Hahn ist tot! (p182)

Bar Raval (p154)

€€€
Katz Orange (p139)

Brooklyn Beef Club (p109)

Pauly Saal (p138)

Restaurant Tim Raue (p89)

Best By Cuisine

Berlin
Zur Letzten Instanz (p107)

Max und Moritz (p156)

Dicke Wirtin (p200)

German
Spätzle & Knödel (p172)

Henne (p156)

Schwarzwaldstuben (p136)

Asian
Mr Hai Kabuki (p200)

Chèn Chè (p136)

Good Friends (p200)

Kimchi Princess (p156)

Italian
Hartweizen (p139)

Osteria Centrale (p199)

A Magica (p185)

Vegetarian
Lucky Leek (p184)

Kopps (p138)

Cookies Cream (p87)

International
Tomasa (p153)

Spindler & Klatt (p157)

Zagreus Projekt (p139)

Austrian
Horváth (p156)

Ottenthal (p201)

Austria (p153)

Deli
Mogg & Melzer (p138)

Rogacki (p199)

Barcomi's Deli (p136)

French
La Raclette (p156)

Gugelhof (p184)

Brel (p200)

Spanish
Bar Raval (p154)

Mariamulata (p157)

Tapitas (p184)

Turkish/Arabic
Hasir Kreuzberg (p156)

Maroush (p157)

City Chicken (p157)

Best Gourmet Shopping

KaDeWe Food Hall (p202)

Goldhahn & Sampson (p189)

Rogacki (p199)

Best for Trendy Dining

Katerschmaus (p157)

Grill Royal (p139)

Pauly Saal (p138)

Ula Berlin (p185)

Backroom Cantina (p87)

Best for Quirk Factor

Sauvage (p157)

Zagreus Projekt (p139)

W- der Imbiss (p185)

White Trash Fast Food (p139)

Best for Burgers

White Trash Fast Food (p139)

Bird (p184)

Burgermeister (p157)

Berlin Burger International (p157)

Bar at Badeschiff (p154)

Drinking & Nightlife

Snug pubs, riverside beach bars, clubs, beer gardens, underground dives, DJ bars, snazzy hotel lounges, cocktail caverns – with such variety, finding a party to match your mood is not exactly a tall order. Be aware that Berliners sure know how to have a good time, so you'd better pack some stamina if you want to join them.

Enjoying a drink at a Berlin bar

Bars & Pubs

With no curfew, Berlin is a notoriously late city where bars stay packed from dusk to dawn and beyond, and some clubs don't hit their stride until 4am. Generally, the emphasis is on style and atmosphere, and some proprietors have gone to extraordinary lengths to come up with unique design concepts.

You'll tend to find edgier, more underground venues on the east side of the city, with places out west being more suited for date nights than dedicated drinking.

The line between cafe and bar is often blurred, with many places changing stripes as the hands move around the clock, although alcohol is served pretty much all day. Some bars have happy hours, especially in tourist-thick Mitte and student-flavoured Friedrichshain.

ETIQUETTE

Table service is common, and you shouldn't order at the bar unless you intend to hang out there or there's a sign saying *Selbst-bedienung* (self-service). It's customary to keep a tab instead of paying for each round separately. Note that in bars with live DJs €1 or €2 is usually added to the cost of your first drink. Tip bartenders about 5%, servers 10%. Drinking in public is legal and widely practised, but be civilised about it. No puking on the U-Bahn, please!

COCKTAIL BARS

Cocktail culture is booming in Berlin. No matter whether you're into American-style bars, cosmopolitan hotel bars, hidden speakeasies or trendy lounges, you'll find a place for some quality imbibing. A recent

NEED TO KNOW

Opening Hours

➡ Many pubs also serve food and tend to be open from noon.

➡ Regular bars start up around 6pm and close at 1pm or 2pm the next day, later on weekends.

➡ Trendy places and cocktail bars don't open until 8pm or 9pm and stay open until the last tippler leaves.

➡ Clubs open at 11pm or at midnight but don't fill up until 1am or 2am, reaching their peak between 4am and 6am. Many open only Friday and Saturday nights.

Costs

Big clubs like Berghain/Panorama Bar or Watergate will set you back €12 to €15 admission, but there are plenty of others that charge between €5 and €10. Places that open a bit earlier don't charge admission until a certain hour, usually 11pm or midnight. Student discounts are virtually unheard of, but some clubs run Ladies Night when women don't have to pay.

Dress Code

Berlin's clubs are very relaxed. In general, individual style almost always beats high heels and Armani. Cocktail bars and some clubs like Felix and Puro Skylounge may prefer a more glam look, but in pubs anything goes.

What's On?

For the latest scoop, scan the listings magazines *Zitty* (www.zitty.de), *Tip* (www.tip-berlin.de) or *030;* sift through flyers in shops, cafes, clubs and bars; and check internet platforms such as **Resident Advisor** (www.residentadvisor.net).

trend are 'cuisine-style' cocktails which incorporate herbs and spices like saffron, basil or chili. A good cocktail will set you back between €10 and €15.

Alongside old-school places that have been pouring for decades are sassy newcomers that have the creative in-crowd in a headlock. Here, the patrons are generally younger, the vibe is more exuberant and there may even be a small dance floor.

(Top) Outdoor bar on the Spree River
(Left) Sunset at a beach bar

TRAVELSTOCK44 / ALAMY ©

Drinking by Neighbourhood

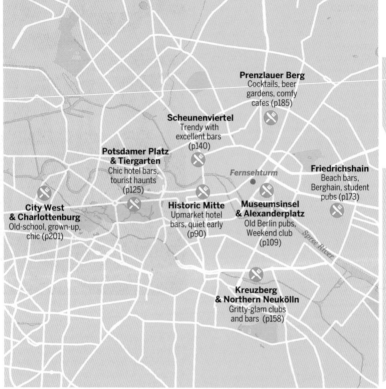

Prenzlauer Berg
Cocktails, beer
gardens, comfy
cafes (p185)

Scheunenviertel
Trendy with
excellent bars
(p140)

Potsdamer Platz & Tiergarten
Chic hotel bars,
tourist haunts
(p125)

Fernsehturm

Friedrichshain
Beach bars,
Berghain, student
pubs (p173)

City West & Charlottenburg
Old-school, grown-up,
chic (p201)

Historic Mitte
Upmarket hotel
bars, quiet early
(p90)

Museumsinsel & Alexanderplatz
Old Berlin pubs,
Weekend club
(p109)

Spree River

Kreuzberg & Northern Neukölln
Gritty-glam clubs
and bars (p158)

Dedicated cocktail bars tend to be elegant cocoons with mellow lighting and low sound levels, helmed by mix-meisters capable of whipping up anything from classic martinis to creative house concoctions.

There are also many casual bars that serve cocktails, although these tend to be of the Sex on the Beach and Cosmopolitan variety. Prices are lower (between €6 and €8) but quality can be hit or miss as sometimes inferior spirits are used.

BEACH BARS

Paris may claim to have invented the beach bar, and other landlocked cities have also jumped on the 'sandwagon', but with lots of outdoor boozing grounds Berlin has definitely got the edge. Daytime chilling is often followed by alfresco parties that go till sunrise and beyond. Most are open from May to September, although exact timings depend on the weather.

Clubbing

The sun may not be shining, the weather may not be sweet, but if you just want to move those dancing feet, Berlin is all you could ever want or need. Taste is no barrier to enjoyment either – whether you're into hardcore techno, high-speed drum and bass, kick-ass punk, sweet Britpop, fist-pumping hip hop, beat-free ambient or even swing and tango, you can find a place to party any night of the week.

With so many top electro DJs living in Berlin – and others happy to visit – the city is a virtual musical testing lab. Line-ups are often amazing. DJ royalty to watch out for include André Galluzzi, Ellen Allien, Kiki, Sascha Funke, Ricardo Villalobos, Paul Kalkbrenner, Modeselektor, Apparat, M.A.N.D.Y, Tiefschwarz, Gudrun Gut, Booka Shade, Richie Hawtin and too many more to mention.

To determine which clubs best match your style, go to www.clubmatcher.de.

WHEN TO GO

Whatever club or party you're heading for, don't bother showing up before 1am unless you want to have a deep conversation with a bored bartender. And don't worry about closing times – Berlin's famously long nights have gotten even later of late and, thanks to a growing number of after parties and daytime clubs, not going home at all is definitely an option at weekends. In fact, many folks put in a good night's sleep, then hit the dance floor when other people head for Sunday church.

AT THE DOOR

Doors are tough at top clubs such as Berghain/Panorama Bar, Watergate and Cookies, but overall making it past the bouncer is still easier in Berlin than in other European capitals. There's generally no need to dress up, and sometimes flaunting fancy labels and glam cocktail dresses can get in the way of your getting in. And if your attitude is right, age rarely matters. If you have to queue, be respectful, don't drink and don't talk too loudly. Don't arrive wasted. If you do get turned away, don't argue. And don't worry, there's always another party somewhere...

Cold beer, Berliner Kindl-Schultheiss Brauerei

Drinks

Predictably, beer is big in Berlin and served (and consumed) almost everywhere all day long. Most places pour a variety of local, national and imported brews, including at least one draught beer (*vom Fass*) served in 300mL or 500mL glasses.

Beer has been brewed in Berlin since the Middle Ages, reaching its peak in the 19th century when there used to be hundreds of breweries, especially in Prenzlauer Berg. Today, the only one left is the **Berliner Kindl-Schultheiss Brauerei** (www.schultheiss. de; Indira-Gandhi-Strasse 66-69; tours €5, with beer tasting €7; ☉ tours 10am, 2pm & 5.30pm Mon-Thu; 🚇M13 to Betriebshof Indira-Gandhi-Strasse), located on the far eastern edge of Prenzlauer Berg, which produces the Berliner Pilsner, Schultheiss, Berliner Kindl and Berliner Bürgerbräu brands. For a behind-the-scenes look, book a guided tour (in German) – preferably followed by a beer tasting – via the website.

Other German and imported beers are widely available. Aside from the ubiquitous Beck's and Heineken, look for Jever Pilsener from northern Germany, Rothaus Tannenzäpfle from the Black Forest, and Krušovice and Budweiser from the Czech Republic. American Budweiser is practically nonexistent here.

Flavoured beers such as Beck's Green Lemon or Schöfferhofer Grapefruit have made some inroads. Nonalcoholic Clausthaler and Beck's are common, and you can drink your lager as an Alster, Radler or Diesel (mixed with Fanta, Sprite or Coke, respectively).

Several noteworthy microbreweries include Hops & Barley and Schalander in Friedrichshain, Brauhaus Georgbräu near Museumsinsel, Rollberg Brauerei in Neukölln and Brauhaus Lemke in Charlottenburg.

Also keep your eyes open for a Berlin-made bottled beer simply labelled 'Bier.'

BEER VARIETIES

The most common brews include the following:

Pils (pilsner) Bottom-fermented beer with a pronounced hop flavour and a creamy head.

Weizenbier/Weissbier (wheat beer) Top-fermented wheat beer that's fruity and refreshing. Comes bottled either as *Hefeweizen*, which has a stronger shot of yeast, or the filtered and fizzier *Kristallweizen*.

Berliner Weisse This cloudy, slightly sour wheat beer is typically sweetened with a *Schuss* (shot) of woodruff or raspberry syrup. It's quite refreshing on a hot day but few locals drink it.

Schwarzbier (black beer, like porter) This full-bodied dark beer is fermented using roasted malt.

Bockbier Strong beer with around 7% alcohol; brewed seasonally. Maibock shows up in May, Weihnachtsbock around Christmas.

WINE & NONALCOHOLIC DRINKS

Sparkling wine is served in 100ml flutes. Depending on where a place sees itself on the trendiness scale, it will serve German *Sekt*, Italian *prosecco* or French *cremant*. In clubs it's often served on the rocks (*Sekt auf Eis*).

The quality of wine served in most pubs and bars ranges from drinkable to abysmal, which is probably why so many Germans drink it with fizzy water, called a *Weinschorle*. Cider is also sometimes available;

OBC, or Original Berliner Cidre, is a dry local label.

If you're not boozing, a *Saftschorle* (fizzy water and juice) is a refreshing alternative. A local speciality that's been making a comeback is *Fassbrause* (literally, keg brew), a beer-coloured but nonalcoholic drink made from fruit, spice and malt extract.

If you need a caffeine kick, there's Red Bull but locals tend to prefer Club-Mate as well as fritz-kola, which is less sweet and has lots more caffeine than regular coke. It also comes as lemonade – the apple-cherry-elderberry is hard to beat.

Also made locally in Kreuzberg is Wostok, an alcohol-free lemonade flavoured with eucalyptus and ginseng.

Party Miles
SCHEUNENVIERTEL

Torstrasse A globe-spanning roster of shiny, happy hipsters populates the shabby-chic drinking dens lining this noisy thoroughfare.

Oranienburger Strasse Major tourist zone where you have to hopscotch around sex workers and pub crawlers to drown your sorrows at pricey bars.

Beer garden, Prater (p185)

KREUZBERG & NORTHERN NEUKÖLLN

Weserstrasse The party drag in Berlin's newest 'It neighbourhood' is packed with delightfully divey, improvised living-room-style bars and pubs.

Kottbusser Tor & Oranienstrasse Grunge-tastic area best suited for dedicated drink-a-thons. The closest music and dance venue is the legendary SO36.

Schlesische Strasse Freestyle strip where you could kick off with cocktails at Badeschiff, catch a band at Magnet Club, dance till breakfast time at Watergate followed by daytime chilling at Club der Visionäre.

Köpenicker Strasse Industrial-flavoured riverside strip where nights might start with supper and drinks at chic Spindler & Klatt, then move on to first-hour techno temple Tresor, the libidinous KitKatClub or the hypertrendy Kater Holzig playground.

FRIEDRICHSHAIN

Revaler Strasse The skinny-jeanster set invades the gritty clubs and bars along this 'techno strip' set up in a former train-repair station. Live concerts at Astra Kulturhaus, techno-electro at Suicide Circus, or a potpourri of sounds at Cassiopeia.

Ostkreuz Draw a bead on this cool party zone by staggering through the dark trying to find the entrance to Salon zur Wilden Renate or ://about blank.

Mühlenstrasse Paralleling the Spree, this strip is perfect for an extended beach-bar hop with stops at Oststrand and Strandgut Berlin as a warm-up for hardcore partying at Berghain/Panorama Bar.

Simon-Dach-Strasse If you need a cheap buzz, head to this well-trodden booze strip popular with field-tripping school groups and stag parties. Locals? Not so much.

(Top) Beergarden at Clärchens Ballhaus (p140)
(Middle) Partying at Felix (p90)
(Bottom) Evening drinks at Club der Visionäre (p161)

Lonely Planet's Top Choices

Berghain/Panorama Bar
(p175) Hyped but still happening Holy Grail of techno clubs with DJ royalty every weekend.

Clärchens Ballhaus (p140) Hipsters mix it up with grannies for tango and jitterbug in a kitsch-glam 1913 ballroom.

Club der Visionäre (p159) Summers wouldn't be the same without chilling and dancing in this historic canalside boat shed.

Cookies (p90) Sassy temple to good times with top DJs and unexpected nooks and crannies.

Prater (p185) Berlin's oldest beer garden still rocks beneath the chestnuts after 175 years in business.

Würgeengel (p158) Fun crowd keeps the cocktails and conversation flowing in a genuine '50s setting.

Best Techno-Electro Clubs

Watergate (p159)

Suicide Circus (p173)

://about blank (p174)

Salon zur Wilden Renate (p174)

Kater Holzig (p159)

Best Nontechno Clubs

Kaffee Burger (p141)

Felix (p90)

Gretchen (p158)

Prince Charles (p159)

S036 (p161)

Best Hipster Bars

Neue Odessa Bar (p141)

King Size Bar (p141)

August II (p141)

Tausend (p90)

Drayton Bar (p90)

Best Bars with a View

Solar (p125)

Bebel Bar (p90)

Puro Skylounge (p201)

Amano Bar (p140)

Weekend (p109)

Best DJ Bars

Monarch Bar (p159)

Madame Claude (p159)

Süss War Gestern (p174)

Soju Bar (p159)

Best Outdoor Bars

Strandgut Berlin (p175)

Oststrand (p175)

Deck 5 (p187)

Strandbar Mitte (p140)

Best Cocktail Bars

Buck & Breck (p141)

Becketts Kopf (p186)

Curtain Club (p125)

Bebel Bar (p90)

Shōchū (p90)

Best Brewpubs

Hops & Barley (p174)

Schalander (p172)

Rollberg Brauerei (p160)

Brauhaus Georgbräu (p109)

Brauhaus Lemke (p198)

Best for a Kottbusser Tor Bar-Hop

Monarch Bar (p159)

Möbel Olfe (p158)

Luzia (p159)

Roses (p159)

Best Beer Gardens

Café am Neuen See (p125)

Mauersegler (p187)

Golgatha (p158)

Best Cafes

Café Bravo (p140)

Tadschikische Teestube (p90)

St Gaudy Cafe (p186)

Aunt Benny (p176)

Mein Haus am See (p141)

Best Designer Dens

Shōchū (p90)

Drayton Bar (p90)

Amano Bar (p140)

Spindler & Klatt (p157)

PLAN YOUR TRIP DRINKING & NIGHTLIFE

⭐ Gay & Lesbian Berlin

Berlin's legendary liberalism has spawned one of the world's biggest, most divine and diverse GLBT playgrounds. Anything goes in 'Homopolis' (and we do mean anything!), from the highbrow to the hands-on, the bourgeois to the bizarre, the mainstream to the flamboyant. Except for the most hardcore places, gay spots get their share of opposite-sex and straight patrons.

Gay in Berlin

Generally speaking, Berlin's gayscape runs the entire spectrum from mellow cafes, campy bars and cinemas to saunas, cruising areas, clubs with darkrooms and all-out sex venues. In fact, sex and sexuality are entirely everyday matters to the unshockable city folks and there are very few, if any, itches that can't be quite openly and legally scratched. As elsewhere, gay men have more options for having fun, but grrrrls – from lipstick lesbians to hippie chicks to bad-ass dykes – won't feel left out either. For gay-geared lodging, see p226.

History

Berlin's emergence as a gay capital was kick-started by sexual scientist Magnus Hirschfeld who, in 1897, paved the way for gay liberation with the founding of the Scientific Humanitarian Committee, the world's first homosexual advocacy group. Gay life thrived in the wild and wacky 1920s, driven by a demimonde that drew and inspired writers like Christopher Isherwood, until the Nazis put an end to the fun in 1933. Postwar recovery came slowly, but by the 1970s the scene was firmly re-established, at least in the western city. Since 2001, Berlin has been governed by an openly gay mayor, Klaus Wowereit, who was not shy about saying the now famous words: 'I'm gay, and that's a good thing'. To learn more about Berlin's queer history, visit the Schwules Museum (p151).

Gay Rights

Berliners are very tolerant of gays (*Schwule*) and lesbians (*Lesben*), although that does not rule out the occasional homophobic outburst. Protection from discrimination is enshrined in law, and registered life partnerships (civil unions) give gays and lesbians most of the same rights, duties and protections as their married heterosexual counterparts. They do not, however, give them the same tax benefits. In June 2012 a motion by the Green Party in favour of legalising same-sex marriage was shot down by the ruling coalition of the conservative CDU/CSU and FDP parties in the *Bundestag* (German parliament).

Clubbing

Some of the best club nights are independent of the venues they use and may move around, although most have some temporary residency. Berlin's scene is especially fickle and venues and dates may change at the drop of a hat, so make sure you always check the websites or the listings magazines for the latest scoop. Unless noted, these parties are geared towards men.

Cafe Fatal All comers descend on SO36 (p161) for the ultimate rainbow tea dance that goes from 'strictly ballroom' to 'dirty dancing' in a flash. If you can't tell a waltz from a foxtrot, come at 7pm for free lessons. Sundays.

Chantals House of Shame Trash diva Chantal's louche lair at Bassy (p187) is a beloved institution, not so much for the glam factor as for the over-the-top transvestite shows and the hotties who love 'em. Thursdays.

Girls Town (www.girlstown-berlin.de) This busy and buzzy girl-fest takes over the vintage Kino International (p176) with down-and-dirty dance music in the foyer and cocktails-with-a-view in the upstairs bar. Second Saturday of every other month.

L-Tunes (www.ltunes.de) Lesbians get their groove on with Pink, Madonna and Melissa Etheridge in the dimly lit dancing pit of SchwuZ (p158). Last Saturday of the month.

Gayhane Geared towards gay Muslims but everyone's welcome to rock the kasbah when this 'homoriental' party takes over SO36 (p161) with Middle Eastern beats and belly dancing. Last Saturday of the month.

GMF Berlin's premier Sunday club, currently at Weekend (p109), is known for excessive SM (standing and modelling) with lots of smooth surfaces – and that goes for both the crowd and the setting. Predominantly boyz, but girls OK.

Irrenhaus (www.ninaqueer.com) The name means 'insane asylum' and that's no joke. Trash queen Nina Queer puts on nutty, naughty shows at Kreuzberg's **Comet Club** (Falckensteinstrasse 47) that are not for the faint-of-heart. Expect the best. Fear the worst. Third Saturday of the month.

Klub International (www.klub-international.com) Up to 1500 boyz-to-men come out to the glamorous Kino International (p176) to work three sizzling dance floors presided over by trash royalty like Biggy van Blond, Nina Queer and Ades Zabel. First Saturday of the month.

Pet Shop Bears This party attracts a *Butt* magazine type international crowd of lean but hairy 30- and 40-somethings who come for kicking electropop. At Berghain Kantine, next door to Berghain (p175). Usually last Friday of the month.

Pork (www.ficken3000.com) A down-at-heel sex club during the week, **Ficken 3000** (Urbanstrasse 70) truly hits its stride on Sundays for this polysexual arty-trash party. Dancing upstairs, orgy downstairs.

Propaganda (www.propaganda-party.de) In the sexy old Metropol Theatre on Nollendorfplatz, this New York–style house and electro party-and-a-half draws fashionable see-and-be-scenesters with its buff and bronzed go-go dancers, big sound and gyrating on two dance floors. Second Saturday of the month.

NEED TO KNOW

Magazines

➡ **Blu** (www.blu.fm) Print and online magazine with searchable, up-to-the-minute location and event listings.

➡ **L-Mag** (www.-mag.de) Bimonthly magazine for lesbians.

➡ **Out in Berlin** (www.gay-berlin.net) Up-to-date free English/German booklet and website, often found at the tourist offices.

➡ **Siegessäule** (www.siegessaeule.de) Free weekly lesbigay 'bible'.

Websites

➡ **Berlin Gay Web** (http://berlin.gay-web.de)

➡ **Discodamaged** (www.discodamaged.net)

➡ **Gay Berlin 4u** (www.gayberlin4u.com)

➡ **Gay Romeo** (www.gayromeo.com) Berlin's gay online dating site of choice.

➡ **Patroc Gay Guide** (www.patroc.de/berlin)

Help

➡ **Mann-O-Meter** (☎216 8008; www.mann-o-meter.de; Bülowstrasse 106; ⏲5-10pm Tue-Fri, 4-8pm Sat & Sun; [S]Nollendorfplatz) Gay men's information centre.

➡ **Maneo** (www.maneo.de) Gay victim support centre, gay-attack hotline.

➡ **Lesbenberatung** (www.lesbenberatung-berlin.de) Lesbian resource centre.

Tours

➡ **Berlinagenten** (p289) Customised gay-lifestyle tours (nightlife, shopping, luxury, history, culinary).

➡ **Lügentour** (www.luegentour.de) Interactive and humorous walking tour takes you back to the lesbigay scene in 1920s Schöneberg; alas in German only.

➡ **Schröder Reisen** (www.comedy-im-bus.de) Outrageous comedy bus tours led by trash drag royalty and self-styled 'VIP housewife on the dole' Edith Schröder and friends.

SpyClub (www.spyclub.de) Dress up! is the motto and they mean it, so get your glam on to get past the door standing between you and Berlin's most fashionable house and electro party at Cookies (p90). Fourth Saturday of the month.

Festivals & Events

Leather & Fetish Week Europe's biggest fetish fest whips the leather, rubber, skin and military sets out of the dungeons and into the Berlin clubs over the long Easter weekend. It culminates with the crowning of the 'German Mr Leather'.

Lesbisch-Schwules Strassenfest The Lesbigay Street Festival takes over the Schöneberg rainbow village in June, with bands, food, info booths and partying.

Christopher Street Day Later in June, hundreds of thousands people of various sexual persuasions paint the town pink with a huge parade and more queens than at a royal wedding.

Transgenialer CSD On the same day as the CSD, Kreuzberg celebrates this alternative version.

Ladyfest This community festival in August brings out creative and artistic feminists, lesbians and their friends for four days of music, art, performance and workshops.

Lesbischwules Parkfest Also in August, the gay community takes over the Volkspark Friedrichshain for this delightfully noncommercial festival.

Folsom Europe The leather crowd returns in early September for another weekend of kinky partying.

Hustlaball Things wrap up in October with a weekend of debauched partying in the company of porn stars, go-gos, trash queens, stripping hunks and about 3000 other men who love 'em.

Gay & Lesbian by Neighbourhood

➡ **Schöneberg** (p123) The area around Nollendorfplatz (Motzstrasse and Fuggerstrasse especially) has been a gay mecca since the 1920s and is still the closest Berlin has to a 'gay village'. Old-school institutions like Tom's, Connection and Hafen pull in the punters night

---

GAY MEMORIALS

The gay community suffered tremendously under the Nazis. Male homosexuals were humiliated and legally and socially ostracised. Some 54,000 were deported to concentration camps where they were outed by a pink triangle affixed to their prison garb; scores persished. Two memorials train the spotlight on the plight of these men: a **pink-granite triangle** on the south facade of Nollendorfplatz U-Bahn station and the Denkmal für die im Nationalsozialismus verfolgten Homosexuellen (p82) on the eastern edge of Tiergarten park.

---

after night, and there's also plenty of nocturnal action for the leather and fetish set.

➡ **Scheunenviertel** (p127) Gets a mixed crowd, but its stylish and trendy bars and cafes also draw a sizeable contingent of queer customers. Sunday's GMF is one of the best weekly lesbigay parties in town.

➡ **Kreuzberg & Northern Neukölln** (p146) These districts are current hipster central. Things are still comparatively subdued in the cafes and bars along Mehringdamm, the main strip in western Kreuzberg (Bergmannkiez). Around Kottbusser Tor and along Oranienstrasse the crowd skews younger, wilder and more alternative and key venues stay open till sunrise and beyond. For a DIY subcultural vibe, head across the canal to northern Neukölln, which also has a couple of outrageously offbeat theatres.

➡ **Friedrichshain** (p166) Across the river, Friedrichshain has few gay bars but is still a de rigeur stop on the gay nightlife circuit thanks to clubs like Berghain and the hands-on Lab.oratory, and monthly parties at Kino International.

➡ **Prenzlauer Berg** (p178) This was East Berlin's pink hub before the fall of the Wall and there are still a couple of relics from back then. Otherwise, mellow cafes and lounges draw a grown-up hipster crowd, and there's also a couple of popular cruising dens and fun stations for the fetish set.

Lonely Planet's Top Choices

GMF (p109) Glamtastic Sunday club with pretty people and head-spinning city views.

Roses (p159) Plush, pink, campy madhouse is an essential experience.

Möbel Olfe (p158) Old furniture store recast as busy drinking den.

Chantals House of Shame (p187) Eponymous trash-drag diva's parties run wild and wicked.

Best Venues by Day of the Week

Monday Monster Ronson's Ichiban Karaoke (p175)

Tuesday Cookies (p90)

Wednesday Marietta (p186), Zum Schmutzigen Hobby (p174)

Thursday Möbel Olfe (p158), Chantals House of Shame (p187), Monster Ronson's Ichiban Karaoke (p175)

Friday SchwuZ (p158)

Saturday SchwuZ (p158), Berghain (p175)

Sunday GMF (p109), Pork (p59), Cafe Fatal (p58)

Best Gay Bars

Zum Schmutzigen Hobby (p174)

Möbel Olfe (p158)

Hafen

Himmelreich (p175)

Best Sex Clubs/ Darkrooms

Lab.oratory (p176)

Greifbar (p188)

KitKatClub (p162)

Candlelit party, Clärchens Ballhaus (p140)

Entertainment

Berlin's cultural scene is lively, edgy and the richest and most varied in the German-speaking world. With three state-supported opera houses, five major orchestras – including the world-class Berliner Philharmoniker – scores of theatres, cinemas, cabarets and concert venues, you've got enough entertainment options to last you a lifetime.

Classical Music

Classical music fans are truly spoilt in Berlin. Not only is there a phenomenal range of concerts throughout the year, but most of the major concert halls are architectural (and acoustic) gems of the highest order. A trip to the Philharmonie or the Konzerthaus is a particular treat, and regular concerts are also organised in many churches and palaces such as Schloss Charlottenburg and Schloss Köpenick.

Top of the pops is, of course, the world-famous Berliner Philharmoniker, which was founded in 1882 and counts Hans Bülow, Wilhelm Furtwängler and Herbert von Karajan among its music directors. Since 2002, Sir Simon Rattle has continued the tradition.

Though not in the same league, the other orchestras are no auditory slouches either. Look for concerts by the Berliner Symphoniker, the Deutsches Symphonie-Orchester, the Konzerthausorchester and the Rundfunk-

Sinfonieorchester Berlin. Note that most venues take a summer hiatus (usually July and August).

OPERA

Not many cities afford themselves the luxury of three state-funded opera houses, but then opera has been popular in Berlin ever since the first fat lady loosened her lungs. Fans can catch some of Germany's biggest and best performances here. Leading the pack in the prestige department is the Staatsoper Unter den Linden (p202), the oldest among the three, founded by Frederick the Great in 1743. The hallowed hall hosted many world premieres, including Carl Maria von Weber's *Der Freischütz* and Alban Berg's *Wozzeck*. Giacomo Meyerbeer, Richard Strauss and Herbert von Karajan were among its music directors. Since reunification, Daniel Barenboim has swung the baton.

The Komische Oper (Comic Opera) opened in 1947 with *Die Fledermaus* by Johann Strauss and still champions light opera, operettas and dance theatre. Across town in Charlottenburg, the Deutsche Oper Berlin entered the scene in 1912 with Beethoven's *Fidelio*. It was founded by local citizens keen on creating a counterpoint to the royal Staatsoper.

SUNDAY SOUNDS

Wind down the weekend with a classical **Sonntagskonzerte** (Map p320; ☎5268 0256; www.sonntagskonzerte.de; Auguststrasse 24; ⌚Sep-Jun; [S]Oranienburger Tor, 🚋M1, 🚆Oranienburger Strasse) held in one of the most unusual spaces in Berlin: the Spiegelsaal (Mirror Hall) upstairs at Clärchens Ballhaus, a 19th-century ballroom right in the heart of the Scheunenviertel. On Sundays at 7pm, a small crowd of clued-in fans gathers amid the faded elegance of this historic room to listen to piano concerts, opera recitals, string quartets and other musical offerings.

With its cracked and blinded mirrors, elaborate chandeliers and old-timey wallpaper, it recalls the decadence of past epochs when it was the domain of the city's elite while the common folks hit the planks in the ballroom downstairs.

For upcoming concerts, check the website or call ahead. It's possible to make reservations but there are no assigned seats, so come early.

NEED TO KNOW

Tickets

➡ It's always advisable to buy tickets in advance, but essential in the case of the Berliner Philharmoniker, the Staatsoper and big-name concerts.

➡ Credit-card bookings by telephone, or online through a venue's box office, are now fairly common but usually come with a small service charge. Some places, though, take only reservations, requiring you to pick up tickets in person before the performance.

➡ Ticket agencies (*Theaterkasse*) may still have tickets when the theatre's own contingent is sold out. These are commonly found in shopping malls. Service fees can be hefty. The main online agency is **Eventim** (www.eventim.de).

➡ **Hekticket** (www.hekticket.de) sells half-price tickets after 2pm for select same-day performances online and in person at its outlets near Zoo Station and Alexanderplatz.

➡ Some theatres sell unsold tickets at a discount starting 30 minutes or an hour before curtain. Some restrict this courtesy to students.

➡ It's fine to buy spare tickets from other theatregoers, though you might want to make sure they're legit (eg by showing them to an usher or the box office clerk) before forking over any cash.

➡ For indie concerts and events, the best agency is Koka 36 in Kreuzberg.

➡ Classical-music aficionados under 30 can get cheaper tickets by buying the Classic Card.

Useful Magazines

➡ **Zitty** (www.zitty.de) Biweekly listings magazine, more alternative than *Tip*.

➡ **Tip** (www.tip.de) Biweekly listings magazine.

➡ **Ex-Berliner** (www.ex-berliner.de) Expat-oriented English-language monthly.

In July and August performances are free and take place outdoors against the glorious backdrop of the Bodemuseum on Museumsinsel (8.30pm, weather permitting).

Film

Berliners keep a wide array of theatres in business, from indie art houses and tiny neighbourhood screens to stadium-style megaplexes. Mainstream Hollywood movies are dubbed into German, but a growing number of theatres also show flicks in their original language, denoted in listings by the acronym 'OF' (*Originalfassung*) or 'OV' (*Originalversion*); those with German subtitles are marked 'OmU' (*Original mit Untertiteln*). The Cinestar Original (p126) at the Sony Center in Potsdamer Platz only screens films in English.

Food and drink may be taken inside the auditoriums, although you are of course expected to purchase your beer and popcorn (usually at inflated prices) in the theatre. Almost all cinemas also add a sneaky *Überlängezuschlag* (overrun supplement) of €0.50 to €1.50 for films longer than 90 minutes. Seeing a flick on a *Kinotag* (film day, usually Monday or Tuesday) can save you a couple of euros.

From May to September, alfresco screenings are a popular tradition, with classic and contemporary flicks spooling off in *Freiluftkinos* (open-air cinemas). Come early to stake out a good spot and bring pillows, blankets and snacks. Films are usually screened in their original language, with German subtitles, or in German with English subtitles. Here are some of our favourites:

Freiluftkino Insel im Cassiopeia With free blankets.

Freiluftkino Friedrichshain (Map p328) In the open-air amphitheatre inside the park.

Freiluftkino Kreuzberg (p324) At Bethanien.

Freiluftkino Mitte In the courtyard of Haus Schwarzenberg.

Berlin also hosts most German and international movie premieres and, in February, stages the most important event on Germany's film calendar, the Berlin International Film Festival. Better known as the **Berlinale** (www.berlinale.de), it was founded in 1951 on the initiative of the Western Allies. Around 400 films are screened in theatres around town, with some of them competing for the Golden and Silver Bear trophies.

Dozens of other film festivals take place throughout the year, including 'Achtung Berlin', featuring movies made in Berlin and, yes, the 'Porn Film Festival'. For the entire schedule, see http://berliner-film festivals.de. See p258 for additional information on film in Berlin.

Live Rock, Pop, Jazz & Blues

Berlin's live-music scene is as diverse as the city itself. There's no Berlin sound as such, but many simultaneous trends, from punk rock to hardcore rap and hip hop, reggae to sugary pop and downtempo jazz. With three top clubs – Magnet (p161), **Comet** (Falckensteinstrasse 48, Kreuzberg) and Lido (p161) – the area around Schlesisches Tor U-Bahn station in Kreuzberg is a hub of the scene. Another venue, the Astra Kulturhaus (p176), is just across the river in Friedrichshain. Some venues turn into dance clubs after the concerts. With scores of pubs and bars also hosting concerts, you're never far from a musical good time.

International top artists perform at various venues around town, the most important of which are:

Arena The midsized Arena easily holds its own against larger venues, particularly when the open riverside area is being used. The adjacent Glashaus hosts smaller gigs and some theatre; the Badeschiff and Hoppetosse restaurant club are also part of the complex.

C-Halle C-Halle started out as a US air-force gym and now hosts up to 3500 fans, primarily for hardcore rock concerts (eg Limp Bizkit, Apocalyptica).

Kindl-Bühne Wuhlheide This 17,000-seat outdoor amphitheatre in the deep east was built in the early 1950s from war debris and is much beloved for its vibe and variety.

O2 World The jewel among Berlin's multiuse venues, this 17,000-seat arena has welcomed entertainment royalty (Tina Turner, Lady Gaga) and is also home turf for the city's professional ice-hockey team, the Eisbären Berlin, and basketball team, Alba Berlin.

Olympiastadion Not even Madonna managed to fill the 74,400 seats of the historic Olympic stadium that's also home to Berlin soccer team Hertha BSC.

Tempodrom The white, tent-shaped Tempodrom has super-eclectic programming that may feature a salsa congress, a Steve Winwood concert and the German snooker masters all in the same month.

Waldbühne Summers in Berlin just wouldn't be the same without this chill spot for symphonies under the stars, big-name rock, jazz and comedy acts and film presentations. The 22,000-seat open-air amphitheatre in the woods has been around since 1936 and has exceptional acoustics.

See p257 for background information on Berlin music.

Theatre

Get ready to smell the greasepaint and hear the roar of the crowd; with over 100 stages around town, theatre is a mainstay of Berlin's cultural scene. Add in a particularly active collection of roaming companies and experimental outfits and you'll find there are more than enough offerings to satisfy all possible tastes. Kurfürstendamm in Charlottenburg and the area around Friedrichstrasse in Mitte (the 'East End'), are Berlin's main drama drags.

Most plays are performed in German, naturally, but of late several of the major stages have started using English surtitles in some of their productions. There's also the English Theatre Berlin (p162), which has some pretty innovative productions.

Many theatres are closed on Mondays and from mid-July to late August.

The **Berliner Theatertreffen** (Berlin Theatre Gathering; www.theatertreffen-berlin.de), in May, is a three-week-long celebration of new plays and productions and brings together top ensembles from Germany, Austria and Switzerland.

Cabaret

The light, lively and lavish variety shows of the Golden Twenties have been undergoing a sweeping revival in Berlin. Get ready for an evening of dancing and singing, jugglers, acrobats and other entertainers. A popular venue is the Bar Jeder Vernunft (p202); its occasional reprise of the musical *Cabaret* plays to sell-out audiences. Across town, the Friedrichstadtpalast (p143) is Europe's largest revue theatre and the realm of leggy, feather-clad dancers. The nearby Chamäleon Varieté (p142) is considerably more intimate. Another wonderful venue is the **Wintergarten Varieté** (☑ 2500 8888; www.wintergarten-variete.de; Potsdamer Strasse 96; tickets €22-67; Kurfürstenstrasse), which is used by travelling shows.

These 'cabarets' should not be confused with *Kabarett,* which are political and satirical shows with monologues and skits.

Dance

With independent choreographers and youthful companies consistently promoting experimental choreography, Berlin's independent dance scene is thriving as never before. The biggest name in choreography is Sasha Waltz, whose company Sasha Waltz & Guests has a residency at the cutting-edge Radialsystem V (p176). Other indie venues include the Sophiensaele (p142) in Mitte, Dock 11 (p188) in Prenzlauer Berg and Hebbel am Ufer (p162) in Kreuzberg. The latter, in cooperation with Tanzwerkstatt Berlin, organises **Tanz im August** (www.tanzimaugust.de), Germany's largest contemporary dance festival, which attracts loose-limbed talent and highly experimental choreography from around the globe.

In the mainstream, the Staatsballett Berlin (Berlin State Ballet) performs both at the Staatsoper Unter den Linden and the Deutsche Oper Berlin. Note that Staatsoper performances take place at the Schiller Theater in Charlottenburg while its historic venue on Unter den Linden is undergoing restoration, probably until 2014.

Comedy Clubs

From stand-up to sketch and musical comedy, there are many ways to have your funny bones tickled in Berlin, although it helps if you understand German. The Kookaburra (p188) comedy club does regular English-language shows, including those by the hilarious improv troupe Comedy Sportz Berlin.

Entertainment by Neighbourhood

➡ **Historic Mitte** (p74) Tops for classical music and opera.

➡ **Potsdamer Platz & Tiergarten** (p111) State-of-the-art multiplexes, casino.

➡ **Scheunenviertel** (p142) Cabaret, comedy, cinema and the 'East End' theatre district.

➡ **Kreuzberg & Northern Neukölln** (p161) Live music, off-theatre, small cinemas.

➡ **Friedrichshain** (p176) Live music, outdoor cinema.

➡ **Prenzlauer Berg** (p188) Live music.

➡ **City West & Charlottenburg** (p190) Theatre, opera, jazz and indie screens.

Lonely Planet's Top Choices

Berliner Philharmonie (p126) One of the world's top orchestras within its own 'cathedral of sound'.

Radialsystem V (p176) Earns bragging rights for its cutting-edge, genre-defying productions, especially in dance.

Staatsoper Unter den Linden Point your high-brow compass to this top-ranked opera house.

Babylon (p142) Diverse and intelligent film programming in a 1920s building.

Astra Kulturhaus (p176) Head-bobbing platform for indie bands, big names included.

Best for Classical Music

Hochschule für Musik Hanns Eisler (p91)

Konzerthaus Berlin (p91)

Sonntagskonzerte (p63

Best for Theatre

English Theatre Berlin (p162)

Volksbühne am Rosa-Luxemburg-Platz (p142)

Berliner Ensemble (p142)

Deutsches Theater (p143)

Maxim Gorki Theater (p91)

Amphitheater (p142)

Best for Dance

Radialsystem V (p176)

Hebbel am Ufer (p162)

Sophiensaele (p142)

Dock 11 (p188)

Best Live-Music Venues

Magnet Club (p161)

Lido (p161)

Festsaal Kreuzberg (p163)

O2 World (p64)

Arena (p64)

Tempodrom (p64)

C-Halle (p64)

Best for Live Jazz & Blues

b-flat (p142)

A-Trane (p202)

Quasimodo (p202)

Yorckschlösschen (p162)

Best Pubs for Live Music

Madame Claude (p159)

Kaffee Burger (p141)

Ä (p159)

Best Cinemas

Babylon (p142)

Cinestar Original (p126)

Kino International (p176)

Arsenal (p126)

Astor Film Lounge (p202)

Best for Opera

Staatsoper Unter den Linden

Deutsche Oper (p202)

Komische Oper (p91)

Best for Cabaret

Bar Jeder Vernunft (p202)

Chamäleon Varieté (p142)

Tipi am Kanzleramt (p91)

Friedrichstadtpalast (p143)

Best for Cutting-Edge Performance

Radialsystem V (p176)

Hebbel am Ufer (p162)

Volksbühne am Rosa-Luxemburg-Platz (p142)

Best Open-Air Venues

Waldbühne (p64)

Amphitheater (p142)

Kindl-Bühne Wuhlheide (p64)

Freiluftkino Friedrichshain (Map p328)

Best Free Entertainment

Bearpit Karaoke at Mauerpark (p180)

Tuesday lunchtime concerts at Berliner Philharmonie (p126)

Recitals at Hochschule für Musik Hanns Eisler (p91)

Monday jam session at A-Trane (p202)

Wednesday jam sessions at Quasimodo (p202) and b-flat (p142)

Weekend concerts at Teehaus im Englischen Garten (p125)

Best for Punk & Heavy Rock

SO36 (p161)

Wild at Heart (p161)

K17 (p176)

Shopping

Berlin is a great place to shop, and we're definitely not talking malls and chains. The city's appetite for the individual manifests in small neighbourhood boutiques and buzzing markets that are a pleasure to explore. Shopping here is as much about visual stimulus as it is about actually spending your cash, no matter whether you're frugal or a power-shopper.

Where to Shop

The closest Berlin comes to having a shopping boulevard is Kurfürstendamm (Ku'damm) and its extension, Tauentzienstrasse. They're largely the purview of the mainstream retailers you probably know from back home, such as Mango, H&M, Levi's and Esprit. You'll find more of the same in such malls as Alexa (p110) and Potsdamer Platz Arkaden (p126).

Getting the most out of shopping in Berlin, though, means venturing off the high street and into the *Kieze* (neighbourhoods). This is where you'll discover a cosmopolitan cocktail of indie boutiques stirred by the city's zest for life, envelope-pushing energy and entrepreneurial spirit.

Each *Kiez* comes with its own flair, identity and mix of stores calibrated to the needs, tastes and bank accounts of local residents.

Local Designers

In a city where individualism trumps conformity, it's not surprising that home-grown fashions and accessories are an expression of this idiosyncratic spirit. The Berlin look is down to earth, often practical (even when painstakingly crafted) and often irreverent.

Discover fashion-forward local designers such as C.Neeon, C'est Tout, Claudia Skoda, Kostas Murkudis, Esther Perbrandt, Kaviar Gauche, Kilian Kerner, Potipoti, Nanna Kuckuck, LalaBerlin and presque fini who walk the line between originality and contemporary trends in a way that more mainstream labels do not.

Key streetwear labels include Irie Daily, Hasipop and Butterflysoulfire. Fishbelly is an internationally renowned local underwear label. When it comes to accessories, look for eyewear by ic! Berlin, Mykita and Lunettes, bags by Ta(u)sche and hats by Fiona Bennett.

Reflecting a general trend, Berliners have also jumped on the green-label bandwagon. Fashion designers with eco-cred include Slomo, Mikenke and Caro.E.

Flea Markets

Flea markets are like urban archaeology: you'll need plenty of patience and luck when sifting through other people's cast-offs, but oh the thrill when finally unearthing a piece of treasure! Berlin has plenty of such hunting grounds, which set up on weekends (usually Sundays) year-round – rain or shine – and are the perfect antidote to cookie-cutter high-street shopping. Many are also now the purview of emerging local designers who use them to test the market for their jewellery pieces, bags, T-shirts and other clothing and accessories. The most famous market is the weekly Flohmarkt am Mauerpark (p180) in Prenzlauer Berg, which is easily combined with nearby Flohmarkt am Arkonaplatz (p188).

NEED TO KNOW

Opening Hours

➡ Shopkeepers may set their opening hours from Monday to Saturday. In practice, only department stores, supermarkets, shops in major commercial districts (such as the Kurfürstendamm), and those in malls take full advantage of this. These stores usually open around 9.30am and close at 8pm or later.

➡ Boutiques and other smaller shops keep flexible hours, opening some time mid-morning and generally closing at 7pm or 8pm, sometimes an hour or two earlier on Saturday.

➡ Stores are closed on Sunday, except for some bakeries, flower shops, souvenir shops and supermarkets in major train stations, including Hauptbahnhof, Friedrichstrasse and Ostbahnhof. Shops may also open from 1pm to 8pm on two December Sundays before Christmas and on a further six Sundays throughout the year, the latter being determined by local government.

➡ Note that most stores, especially smaller ones, do not accept credit cards.

Taxes & Refunds

If your permanent residence is outside the EU, you may be able to partially claim back the 19% value-added tax (VAT, *Mehrwertsteuer*) you have paid on purchased goods. The rebate applies only to items purchased in stores displaying the 'Tax-Free for Tourists' sign. Obtain a tax-free form from the sales clerk, then show this form, your unused goods and the receipt to a customs official at the airport before checking your luggage. The customs official will stamp the form, which you can then take straight to the cash refund office at the airport.

Vintage

From glamour gowns to faded T-shirts, Berlin's idiosyncratic fashion style goes well with vintage and secondhand clothing and there is hardly anyone who doesn't have a 'pre-owned' piece in their wardrobe. Stores run the gamut from warehouse-sized spaces selling threads by weight to couture emporia stocked with Gucci and Paco Rabanne. There are even vintage shoe boutiques in case you need a pair of wingtips or '70s platform shoes to complete your retro look.

Shopping by Neighbourhood

➡ **Historic Mitte** (p74) Tacky souvenir shops meet big-label glamour haunts and top-flight galleries along Friedrichstrasse and Unter den Linden.

➡ **Museumsinsel & Alexanderplatz** (p93) Eastern Berlin's mainstream shopping hub, plus a weekend antiques market next to the museums.

➡ **Potsdamer Platz & Tiergarten** (p111) Big indoor mall and a weekend flea market on the park's northwestern edge.

➡ **Scheunenviertel** (p127) Boutique haven with Berlin-made fashions and accessories; also a high-end international designers and gallery quarter.

➡ **Kreuzberg & Northern Neukölln** (p146) Epicentre of vintage fashion and streetwear along with music and accessories, all in indie boutiques.

➡ **Friedrichshain** (p166) Up-and-coming area centred around Boxhagener Platz, site of a Sunday flea market; antiques market at Ostbahnhof.

➡ **Prenzlauer Berg** (p178) Berlin-made fashions, niche boutiques, anything for children and a fabulous flea market.

➡ **City West & Charlottenburg** (p190) Mainstream and couture on Kurfürstendamm, indie boutiques in the side streets, homewares on Kantstrasse.

Lonely Planet's Top Choices

KaDeWe (p202) The ultimate consumer temple.

Flohmarkt am Mauerpark (p180) Bargain-hunting at its best.

Galeries Lafayette (p92) French 'je ne sais quoi'.

Dussmann - Das Kulturkaufhaus (p91) Mother lode of books and music.

Flagshipstore (p188) Hand-picked Berlin fashion and accessories.

Fassbender & Rausch (p92) Palace of pralines and chocolates.

HardWax (p164) Key music stop for electro heads.

Best Bookshops

Berlin Story (p92)

Another Country (p163)

Hundt Hammer Stein (p144)

Pro QM (p144)

Best Quirky Stores

Luxus International (p188)

Killerbeast (p164)

Mondos Arts (p177)

Ampelmann Galerie (p145)

1. Absinth Depot Berlin (p144)

Best Gastro Delights

KaDeWe food hall (p202)

Marheineke Markthalle (p163)

Markthalle IX (p163)

Goldhahn & Sampson (p189)

Ritter Sport Bunte Schokowelt (p92)

Best Music Shops

Space Hall (p163)

Rotation Records (p144)

Best Fashion Shops

VOO Store (p164)

UVR Connected (p164)

Thatchers (p189)

Berlin Fashion Network (p143)

Prachtmädchen (p177)

Overkill (p164)

Best Malls & Department Stores

Galeries Lafayette (p92)

Galeria Kaufhof (p110)

Potsdamer Platz Arkaden (p126)

Alexa (p110)

Best Flea Markets

Flohmarkt am Mauerpark (p180)

Neukoelln Flowmarkt (p165)

Antikmarkt am Ostbahnhof (p177)

Flohmarkt am Arkonaplatz (p188)

Best Made in Berlin

ic! Berlin (p143)

Ausberlin (p110)

Bonbonmacherei (p144)

Ach Berlin (p92)

Lala Berlin (p144)

Ta(u)sche (p188)

Best Erotica

Hautnah (p203)

Schwarzer Reiter (p145)

Fun Factory (p143)

Best Gifts

Ampelmann Galerie (p145)

Herrlich (p163)

Käthe Wohlfahrt (p203)

VEB Orange (p189)

Best Antiques

Antikmarkt am Ostbahnhof (p177)

Kunst- & Nostalgiemarkt (p92)

Best for Kids

Ratzekatz (p189)

Steiff Galerie in Berlin (p203)

Best Shopping Strips

Alte & Neue Schönhauser Strasse & Münzstrasse, Scheunenviertel (p127)

Friedrichstrasse, Historic Mitte (p74)

Kastanienallee, Prenzlauer Berg (p178)

Kurfürstendamm & Tauentzienstrasse, City West & Charlottenburg (p190)

Bergmannstrasse, Kreuzberg (p163)

Oranienstrasse, Kreuzberg (p163)

Explore Berlin

BERLIN'S TOP SIGHTS

Neighbourhoods at a Glance

1 Historic Mitte (p74)

With the mother lode of sights clustered within a walkable area, this part of the city should be your first port of call. Book ahead for access to the Reichstag dome, then check off the Brandenburg Gate, the Holocaust Memorial, Unter den Linden boulevard and splendid Gendarmenmarkt on an easy stroll. Head to Friedrichstrasse for upmarket shopping and entertainment.

2 Museumsinsel & Alexanderplatz (p93)

Museum lovers hit the jackpot on this little Spree island with its five world-class museums, including the unmissable Pergamonmuseum, and the majestic Berliner Dom watching over it all. Catch the lift up the iconic Fernsehturm on socialist-style Alexanderplatz, discover Berlin's birthplace in the

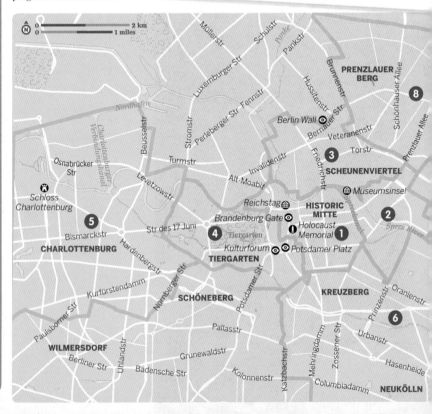

Nikolaiviertel and learn about life under socialism at the DDR Museum.

❸ Scheunenviertel (p127)

With its narrow streets and charming courtyards like the Hackesche Höfe, the Scheunenviertel is fashionista central and also teems with hip bars and restaurants. Come face to face with the quarter's Jewish roots on a visit of the Neue Synagoge, then check out the galleries along Auguststrasse.

❹ Potsdamer Platz & Tiergarten (p111)

This new quarter, forged from ground once bisected by the Berlin Wall, is a showcase of fabulous contemporary architecture. Art lovers should not skip the nearby Kulturforum museums, especially the Gemäldegalerie and the Neue Nationalgalerie, both neighbours of the world-class Berliner Phil-

harmonie. The leafy Tiergarten, with its rambling paths and hidden beer gardens, makes for a perfect sightseeing break.

❺ City West & Charlottenburg (p190)

Charlottenburg has a distinct bourgeois vibe. Its main artery, the grand Kurfürstendamm, is nirvana for shopaholics and spills into leafy side streets teeming with boutiques, galleries, cafes and restaurants. Sightseeing must-sees include Schloss Charlottenburg and the landmark Kaiser-Wilhelm-Gedächtniskirche, a church ruin turned antiwar memorial. The area around here is undergoing a massive facelift.

❻ Kreuzberg & Northern Neukölln (p146)

Kreuzberg and adjacent northern Neukölln are epicentres of free-wheeling, multicultural and alternative Berlin. Spend the day hunting down vintage threads and street art, chill in a cafe or an airport-turned-public park, then plunge headlong into the city's most vibrant nightlife. A more grown-up vibe rules around Bergmannstrasse in no less charismatic western Kreuzberg, home to the district's main sight, the Jüdisches Museum.

❼ Friedrichshain (p166)

Student-flavoured Friedrichshain is tailor-made for soaking up Berlin's relaxed vibe and great for nightlife explorations and chilling in riverside bars next to the East Side Gallery, the largest surviving section of Berlin Wall. Another place to connect with the district's socialist past is the monumental Karl-Marx-Allee.

❽ Prenzlauer Berg (p178)

Splendidly well groomed, Prenzlauer Berg is one of Berlin's most pleasant residential neighbourhoods and a joy to explore on foot. On Sundays, the city descends on its Mauerpark for flea marketeering, outdoor karaoke and chilling in the sun.

Historic Mitte

GOVERNMENT QUARTER | PARISER PLATZ | UNTER DEN LINDEN | GENDARMENMARKT | CHECKPOINT CHARLIE

Neighbourhood Top Five

1 Standing in awe of history at the **Reichstag** (p76), then taking in the views from its landmark dome.

2 Soaking in the stillness and presence of uncounted souls at the **Holocaust Memorial** (p79).

3 Indulging in a gourmet meal at one of the stellar restaurants surrounding **Gendarmenmarkt** (p87).

4 Confronting the horrors of Nazi Germany at the haunting **Topographie des Terrors** (p86) exhibit.

5 Catching cabaret, comedy, musicals or concerts at the historic **Admiralspalast** (p91).

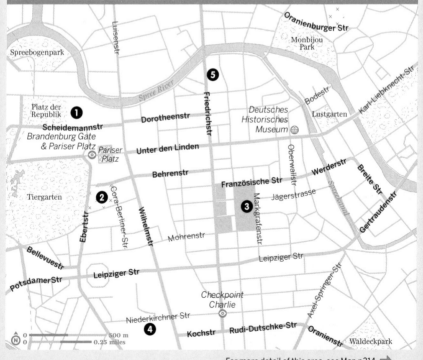

For more detail of this area, see Map p314 ➡

Explore: Historic Mitte

A cocktail of culture, commerce and history, Historic Mitte packs it in when it comes to blockbuster sights: the Reichstag, the Brandenburg Gate, the Holocaust Memorial and Checkpoint Charlie are all within its confines. Cutting through it all is Unter den Linden, a chic boulevard stretching from Pariser Platz past a phalanx of imposing structures built under various Prussian kings and reflecting the one-time grandeur of the royal family.

Alas, Unter den Linden is pretty deserted after dark; fortunately there is some action along Friedrichstrasse, which bisects it. Since reunification, this strip has reclaimed its role as a trendy shopping, drinking and dining hub. In fact, Friedrichstrasse and Gendarmenmarkt, Berlin's most beautiful square one block east, boast the greatest density of fancy restaurants (several with a Michelin star or two) in town.

Walking is the best way to get around this area, although buses 100 and 200, which run along Unter den Linden, can come in handy if your feet are sore.

Local Life

➡ **Glamour Shopping** Brand-name bunnies flock to Friedrichstrasse to give their credit cards a serious workout. Aside from boutiques, the Friedrichstadtpassagen, led by the stunningly designed Galeries Lafayette (p92), beckon with top-flight Berlin and international designers.

➡ **High-Brow Culture** Music and theatre fans especially regularly flock to this part of town to treat their ears to concerts at the Konzerthaus Berlin (p91), theatre at the Maxim Gorki (p91) and opera at the Komische Oper (p91).

➡ **Power of Words** What's better than spending a night off in front of the TV? Spending it browsing around a bookstore, of course. Open until 11pm, Dussmann (p91), the self-titled 'cultural department store', is an eldorado for bookworms and also has a huge music selection.

Getting There & Away

➡ **Bus** Nos 100 and 200 run along Unter den Linden from Alexanderplatz.

➡ **S-Bahn** S1 and S2/25 stop at Brandenburger Tor and at Friedrichstrasse.

➡ **Tram** The M1 travels from Museumsinsel to Prenzlauer Berg via Friedrichstrasse.

➡ **U-Bahn** Stadtmitte (U2, U6), Französische Strasse (U6) and Hausvogteiplatz (U2) are all convenient for Gendarmenmarkt. For Unter den Linden, get off at Brandenburger Tor (U55), Friedrichstrasse (U6) or Französische Strasse (U6).

Lonely Planet's Top Tip

For an engaging overview of the Berlin Wall and related key Cold War sites scattered around the city, visit the Mauerinformation exhibit in the Brandenburger Tor U-Bahn station. Aside from photographs and an aerial map, it presents a film about the border installations and an opportunity to rent a Berlin Wall audioguide for a more in-depth experience.

HISTORIC MITTE

✕ Best Places to Eat

➡ Uma (p87)
➡ Restaurant Tim Raue (p89)
➡ Augustiner am Gendarmenmarkt (p87)
➡ Ishin (p87)

For reviews, see p87 ➡

🍷 Best Places to Drink

➡ Drayton Bar (p90)
➡ Tausend (p90)
➡ Berliner Republik (p90)

For reviews, see p90 ➡

⊙ Best Landmarks

➡ Brandenburger Tor (p78)
➡ Reichstag (p76)
➡ Holocaust Memorial (p79)
➡ Gendarmenmarkt (p84)

For reviews, see p81 ➡

TOP SIGHTS
REICHSTAG

It's been burned, bombed, rebuilt, buttressed by the Berlin Wall, wrapped in fabric and finally turned into the modern home of the German parliament: the Reichstag, one of Berlin's most iconic buildings. Its most eye-catching feature is the glistening glass dome, which draws more than three million visitors each year. The grand old structure was designed by Paul Wallot and completed in 1894 when Germany was still a constitutional monarchy known as the Deutsches Reich (German Empire), hence the building's name.

Home of the Bundestag

Today, the Reichstag is the historic anchor of the new federal government quarter built after reunification. The Bundestag, Germany's parliament, has hammered out its policies here since moving from the former German capital of Bonn to Berlin in 1999. The parliament's arrival followed a complete architectural revamp masterminded by Lord Norman Foster who preserved only the building's 19th-century shell while adding the landmark glass dome. It is accessible by lift with prior reservation (see Visiting the Dome).

Dome

Resembling a giant glass beehive, the sparkling cupola is open at the top and bottom and sits right above the plenary chamber as a visual metaphor for transparency and openness in politics. A lift whisks you to the rooftop terrace from where you can easily pinpoint such sights as the curvaceous House of World Cultures and the majestic Berliner Dom (Berlin Cathedral) or marvel at the enormous dimensions of Tiergarten park. To learn more about these landmarks, the Reichstag building and the workings of parliament, pick up a free multilingual audioguide as you exit the lift. The commentary starts automatically as you

DON'T MISS...

➡ The dome
➡ The facade

PRACTICALITIES

➡ Map p314
➡ www.bundestag.de
➡ Platz der Republik 1
➡ ⊗8am-midnight, last admission 10pm
➡ 🚌100, Ⓢ Bundestag

mosey up the glass dome's 230m-long ramp, which spirals around a mirror-clad cone that deflects daylight down into the plenary chamber.

Main Facade

Stylistically, the monumental, west-facing main facade borrows heavily from the Italian Renaissance with a few neo-baroque elements thrown into the mix. A massive staircase leads up to a portico curtained by six Corinthian columns and topped by the dedication Dem Deutschen Volke (To the German People), which wasn't added until 1916. The bronze letters were designed by Peter Behrens, one of the fathers of modern architecture, and cast from two French cannons captured during the Napoleonic Wars of 1813–15. The original dome, made of steel and glass and considered a high-tech marvel at the time, was destroyed during the Reichstag fire in 1933.

Historic Milestones

Home of the German parliament from 1894 to 1933 and again since 1999, the hulking Reichstag will likely give you more flashbacks to high-school history than any other Berlin landmark. On 9 November 1919, parliament member Philipp Scheidemann proclaimed the German republic from one of its windows. In 1933, the Nazis used a mysterious fire as a pretext to seize dictatorial powers. A dozen years later, victorious Red Army troops raised the Soviet flag on the bombed-out building, which stood damaged and empty on the western side of the Berlin Wall throughout the Cold War. In the late 80s, megastars including David Bowie, Pink Floyd and Michael Jackson performed concerts on the lawn in front of the building.

The Wall collapsed soon thereafter, paving the way to German reunification which was enacted here in 1990. Five years later the Reichstag made headlines once again when the artist couple Christo and Jeanne-Claude wrapped the massive structure in silvery fabric. It had taken an act of the German parliament to approve the project, which was intended to mark the end of the Cold War and the beginning of another era. For two weeks starting in late June 1995, visitors from around the world flocked to Berlin to admire this unique sight. Shortly after the fabric came down, Lord Norman Foster set to work.

An extensive photographic exhibit at the bottom of the dome captures many of these historic moments.

VISITING THE DOME

Free reservations for Reichstag dome visits must be made online at www.bundestag.de. Book early, especially in summer, and prepare to show ID, go through a metal detector and have your belongings X-rayed. Guided tours and lectures can also be booked via the website.

It was the night of 27 February 1933: the Reichstag was ablaze. When the flames were extinguished, the plenary hall lay in ashes and a Dutch anarchist named Marinus van der Lubbe had been arrested for arson. Although there was never conclusive proof of who actually started the fire, historians regard the incident as a key factor in Hitler's total power grab. Claiming that the fire was part of a large-scale communist conspiracy, the Nazis pushed through the 'Reichstag Fire Decree' just one day after the conflagration, quashing civil rights and triggering the persecution of political opponents. The true events of that night remain a mystery. Its impact on history does not.

TOP SIGHTS
REICHSTAG

JON ARNOLD / GETTY IMAGES ©

TOP SIGHTS
BRANDENBURGER TOR & PARISER PLATZ

A symbol of division during the Cold War, the landmark Brandenburger Tor (Brandenburg Gate) now epitomises German reunification and often serves as a photogenic backdrop for festivals, concerts and New Year's Eve parties. Carl Gotthard Langhans found inspiration in the Acropolis in Athens for the elegant triumphal arch, completed in 1791 as the royal city gate. It stands sentinel over Pariser Platz, a harmoniously proportioned square once again framed by banks as well as the US, British and French embassies, just as it was during its 19th-century heyday.

Crowning the Brandenburger Tor is the **Quadriga**, Johann Gottfried Schadow's sculpture of the winged Goddess of Victory piloting a chariot drawn by four horses. After trouncing Prussia in 1806, Napoleon kidnapped the lady and held her hostage in Paris until she was freed by a gallant Prussian general in 1815.

The first building to be reconstructed on Pariser Platz was a near-replica of the 1907 Hotel Adlon, Berlin's poshest caravanserai that allegedly inspired the 1932 movie *Grand Hotel,* starring Greta Garbo. Now called **Hotel Adlon Kempinski**, it's still a celebrity favourite. Remember Michael Jackson dangling his baby out the window? It happened at the Adlon.

If the doors are open, pop into the Frank Gehry–designed **DZ Bank** on the square's south side to catch a glimpse of the glass-covered atrium with its bizarre free-form sculpture that's actually a conference room.

The only building on Pariser Platz with a glass facade is the **Akademie der Künste** (Academy of Arts; Map p314; ☎200 570; www.adk.de; Pariser Platz 4; Ⓢ Brandenburger Tor, Ⓡ Brandenburger Tor) at No 4, designed by Günter Behnisch. This is one of Berlin's oldest cultural institutions, founded by King Friedrich I in 1696 as the Prussian Academy of Arts. Come here for readings, lectures, workshops and exhibits, many of them free.

DON'T MISS...

➡ Quadriga
➡ Hotel Adlon Kempinski

PRACTICALITIES

➡ Map p314
➡ Pariser Platz
➡ Ⓢ Brandenburger Tor, Ⓡ Brandenburger Tor

TOP SIGHTS
HOLOCAUST MEMORIAL

It took 17 years of discussion, planning and construction, but on 10 May 2005 the Denkmal für die ermordeten Juden Europas (Memorial to the Murdered Jews of Europe) was officially dedicated. Colloquially known as the Holocaust Memorial, it's Germany's central memorial to the Nazi-planned genocide during the Third Reich. For the football-field-sized space, New York architect Peter Eisenman created 2711 sarcophagi-like concrete stelae (slabs) of equal size but various heights, rising up in sombre silence from undulating ground.

You're free to access this massive concrete maze at any point and make your individual journey through it. At first it may seem austere, even unemotional. But take time to feel the coolness of the stone and contemplate the interplay of light and shadow, then stumble aimlessly among the narrow passageways and you'll soon connect with a metaphorical sense of disorientation, confusion and claustrophobia. Guided tours run at 4pm on Sunday in English and at 11am and 2pm on Saturday and Sunday in German.

For context, visit the subterranean Ort der Information (information centre), which movingly lifts the veil of anonymity from the six million Holocaust victims. A graphic timeline of Jewish persecution during the Third Reich is followed by a series of rooms documenting the fates of individuals and families. The most visceral is the darkened **Room of Names**, where the names and years of birth and death of Jewish victims are projected onto all four walls while a solemn voice reads their short biographies. Poignant and heart-wrenching, these exhibits will leave no one untouched.

DON'T MISS...

- Field of Stelae
- Ort der Information
- Room of Names

PRACTICALITIES

- Map p314
- ☎2639 4336
- www.stiftung-denkmal.de
- Cora-Berliner-Strasse 1
- admission free, audioguide €3
- 🕒field 24hr, information centre 10am-8pm Tue-Sun, last entry 7.15pm Apr-Sep, 6.15pm Oct-Mar
- [S]Brandenburger Tor, 🚇Brandenburger Tor

TOP SIGHTS
DEUTSCHES HISTORISCHES MUSEUM

If you're wondering what the Germans have been up to for the past 2000 years, take a spin around this engaging museum in the baroque Zeughaus, formerly the Prussian arsenal and now home of the German Historical Museum. Upstairs, displays concentrate on the period from the 1st century AD to the end of WWI in 1918, while the ground floor tracks the 20th century all the way through to German reunification.

DON'T MISS...

→ Nazi globe
→ Schlüter's sculptures in the courtyard
→ IM Pei Exhibition Hall

PRACTICALITIES

→ Map p314
→ ☑203 040
→ www.dhm.de
→ Unter den Linden 2
→ adult/concession €8/4
→ ☉10am-6pm
→ 🚌100, 200, 🚊Alexanderplatz, Hackescher Markt

Permanent Exhibit

All the major milestones in German history are dealt with in a European context. The timeline begins with the Roman occupation and moves on to the coronation of Charlemagne, the founding of the Holy Roman Empire and everyday life in the Middle Ages. It then jumps ahead to Martin Luther and the Reformation and the bloody Thirty Years' War and its aftermath, addresses Napoleon and the collapse of the Holy Roman Empire in 1806 and the founding of the German Empire in 1871. World War I, which brought the end of the monarchy and led to the Weimar Republic, is a major theme, as are of course the Nazi era and the Cold War. The exhibit ends in 1994 with the withdrawal of Allied troops from German territory.

Displays are a potpourri of documents, paintings, books, dishes, textiles, weapons, furniture, machines and other objects ranging from the sublime to the trivial. One of the oldest objects is a 3rd century Roman milestone. There's also splendid medieval body armour for horse and rider and a felt hat once worn by Napoleon I. Among the more unusual objects is a pulpit hourglass, which was introduced after the Reformation to limit the length of sermons to one hour. A startling highlight is a big globe that originally stood in the Nazi Foreign Office with a bullet hole where Germany should be. Among the newer objects is a 1985 Robotron, the first PC made in East Germany.

The Building

The rose-coloured Zeughaus, which was used as a weapons depot until 1876, was a collaboration of three architects: Johann Arnold Nering, Martin Gruenberg and Andreas Schlüter. Completed in 1730, it is the oldest building along Unter den Linden and a beautiful example of secular baroque architecture. This is in no small part thanks to Schlüter's magnificent sculptures, especially those in the glass-covered courtyard whose facades are festooned with heads of dying soldiers, their faces contorted in agony. Although intended to represent vanquished Prussian enemies, they actually make more of a pacifist statement for modern viewers.

IM Pei Exhibition Hall

High-calibre temporary exhibits take up a modern annexe designed by IM Pei and hence called IM Pei Bau. Fronted by a glass spiral, it's an uncompromisingly geometrical space, made entirely from triangles, rectangles and circles, yet imbued with a sense of lightness achieved through an airy atrium and generous use of glass.

SIGHTS

Government Quarter

REICHSTAG HISTORIC BUILDING

See p76.

BUNDESKANZLERAMT BUILDING

Map p314 (Federal Chancellery; Willy-Brandt-Strasse 1; ⏲closed to public; 🚌100, [S]Bundestag) Located across the big lawn just west of the Reichstag, Germany's 'White House' is the Federal Chancellery, a sparkling, modern design by Axel Schultes and Charlotte Frank. The H-shaped compound consists of two long office blocks flanking a central white cube where current Chancellor Angela Merkel keeps her desk. Eduardo Chillida's rusted-steel *Berlin* sculpture graces the eastern forecourt. The best views of the entire building are from the Moltkebrücke (bridge) or the northern river promenade.

PAUL-LÖBE-HAUS BUILDING

Map p314 (Konrad-Adenauer-Strasse; 🚌100, [S]Bundestag, 🚆Hauptbahnhof) The glass-and-concrete Paul-Löbe-Haus houses offices for the Bundestag's parliamentary committees. From above it looks like a double-sided comb and on the inside there's an atrium long enough to be a bowling alley for giants. It's linked by a double footbridge to the Marie-Elisabeth-Lüders-Haus across the Spree in a visual symbol of reunification. Opening hours vary, depending on parliamentary use.

[FREE] **MARIE-ELISABETH-LÜDERS-HAUS** BUILDING

Map p314 (www.bundestag.de; Schiffbauerdamm; ⏲main building closed to public, galleries 11am-5pm Tue-Sun; [S]Bundestag, 🚆Hauptbahnhof) Home to the parliamentary library, the Marie-Elisabeth-Lüders-Haus is an extravagant structure with a massive tapered stairway, a flat roofline jutting out like a springboard and giant circular windows. Two art spaces are accessible from the river promenade: the **Wall Installation by Ben Wagin** (Map p314; Konrad-Adenauer-Strasse; admission free; ⏲1-7pm Fri-Sun) and the **Kunst-Raum** (Map p314; ☎2273 2027; admission free; ⏲11am-5pm Tue-Sun), which presents contemporary art infused with a political slant.

PARLAMENT DER BÄUME MEMORIAL

Map p314 (Parliament of Trees; cnr Schiffbauerdamm & Adele-Schreiber-Krieger-Strasse; [S]Bundestag) Created by Ben Wagin, the Parliament of Trees is an art installation commemorating the victims of the Berlin Wall. Standing near where the Wall once ran, it consists not only of trees but also of original sections of the barrier, memorial stones, pictures and text. The names of 258 victims are inscribed on slabs of granite.

STRASSE DES 17 JUNI STREET

Map p314 (Strasse des 17 Juni; [S]Brandenburger Tor, 🚆Brandenburger Tor) The broad boulevard bisecting Tiergarten was named Street of 17 June in honour of the victims of the bloodily quashed 1953 workers' uprising in East Berlin. With origins in the 16th century, it originally linked two royal palaces and was doubled in width and turned into a swastika-lined triumphal road under Hitler.

The section between the Brandenburger Tor and the Siegessäule (Victory Column, located 2km west of Brandenburg Gate) turns into a mega-party zone on New Year's Eve and for such festivals as Christopher Street Day (p23).

SOWJETISCHES EHRENMAL TIERGARTEN MEMORIAL

Map p314 (Soviet War Memorial; Strasse des 17 Juni; [S]Brandenburger Tor, 🚆Brandenburger Tor) The imposing Soviet War Memorial overlooks Strasse des 17 Juni and is flanked by two Russian T-34 tanks said to have been the first to enter the city in 1945. It was built by German workers on order of the Soviets and completed just months after the end of the war. More than 2000 Red Army soldiers are buried behind the colonnade.

HAUS DER KULTUREN DER WELT CULTURAL BUILDING

Map p314 (House of World Cultures; ☎397 870; www.hkw.de; John-Foster-Dulles-Allee 10; admission varies; ⏲exhibits 11am-7pm Wed-Mon; 🚌100, [S]Bundestag) The highly respected House of World Cultures is a centre for international cultural exchange. It showcases contemporary non-European art, music, dance, literature, films and theatre, and is also a discussion forum on Zeitgeist-reflecting issues. The extravagant building, designed by Hugh Stubbins as the American contribution to the 1957 architectural exhibition, is topped by a gravity-defying parabolic roof.

The curvaceous reflecting pool features Henry Moore's sculpture called *Large Divided Oval: Butterfly*, whose shape echoes the building's. Computerised chime concerts ring out at noon and 6pm daily from the nearby 68-bell carillon and live concerts take place Sundays at 3pm from May to September (also at 2pm in December). The building is 750m due west of the Reichstag via Scheidemannstrasse and John-Foster-Dulles-Allee.

DENKMAL FÜR DIE IM NATIONALSOZIALISMUS VERFOLGTEN HOMOSEXUELLEN MEMORIAL

Map p314 (Memorial to the Homosexuals Persecuted under the Nazi Regime; Ebertstrasse; ⏰24hr; [S]Brandenburger Tor, Potsdamer Platz, [U]Brandenburger Tor, Potsdamer Platz) The Memorial to the Homosexuals Persecuted under the Nazi Regime trains the spotlight on the tremendous suffering of Europe's gay community under the Nazis. Across from the Holocaust Memorial, it's a freestanding, 4m-high, off-kilter concrete cube designed by Danish-Norwegian artists Michael Elmgreen and Ingar Dragset. A looped video plays through a warped, narrow window.

Pariser Platz & Unter den Linden

BRANDENBURGER TOR & PARISER PLATZ LANDMARK

See p78.

HOLOCAUST MEMORIAL MEMORIAL

See p79.

DEUTSCHES HISTORISCHES MUSEUM MUSEUM

See p80.

[FREE] HITLER'S BUNKER HISTORIC SITE

Map p314 (cnr In den Ministergärten & Gertrud-Kolmar-Strasse; ⏰24hr; [S]Brandenburger Tor, [U]Brandenburger Tor) Berlin was burning and Soviet tanks advancing relentlessly when Adolf Hitler committed suicide on 30 April 1945 alongside Eva Braun, his long-time female companion, hours after their marriage. Today, a parking lot covers the site, revealing its dark history only via an information panel with a diagram of the vast bunker network and information on its construction and post-WWII history.

LOCAL KNOWLEDGE

ART & CARS

It's shiny cars galore at the **Automobil Forum Unter den Linden** (Map p314; ☎2092 1200; www.volkswagenag.com/content/afb/content/de/homepage.html; Unter den Linden 21; ⏰10am-8pm; 🚌100, 200, [S]Französische Strasse, Friedrichstrasse), an ode to the auto where Volkswagen, Bugatti, Bentley and other manufacturers showcase their latest wheels. But even if you can't tell a piston from a carburettor, look for free art exhibits in the basement. Frequent shows spotlight various media, from photographs to paintings to electronic arts and music.

MADAME TUSSAUDS MUSEUM

Map p314 (☎01805-545 800; www.madametussauds.com/berlin; Unter den Linden 74; adult/child €23/16; ⏰10am-7pm, last admission 6pm; 🚌100, [S]Brandenburger Tor, [U]Brandenburger Tor) No celebrity in town to snare your stare? Don't fret: at this legendary wax museum, Lady Gaga, Obama and Marilyn stand still – very still – for you to snap their picture. Best of all, you're free to touch all 82 figures, give them a kiss or whatever other silliness you can dream up. Check the website for discounted online tickets.

Sure, it's an expensive haven of kitsch and camp but where else can you cuddle with Robbie Williams or hug the Pope? There are dozens of German and international stars from politics (Marx, Dalai Lama), culture (Marlene Dietrich), sports (Muhammad Ali, Boris Becker), music (the Beatles, Michael Jackson) and Hollywood (George Clooney, Nicole Kidman). The most controversial figure is the waxen likeness of Adolf Hitler, depicted as a beaten man hunkered in the bunker during his final days. On opening day, the 'Führer' lost his head when a local man tore it off, not in protest it turned out, but to fulfil a beer bet. It was quickly reattached. You can learn how in the section detailing the process of making these figures.

[FREE] TRÄNENPALAST MUSEUM

Map p314 (☎4677 7790; www.hdg.de; Reichstagsufer 17; ⏰9am-7pm Tue-Fri, 10am-6pm Sat & Sun; [S]Friedrichstrasse, 🚌100) During the Cold War, tears flowed copiously in this glass-and-steel border crossing pavilion where East Berliners had to bid adieu to family visiting from West Germany – hence its moniker 'Palace of Tears'. The exhibit uses original objects (including the claustrophobic passport control booths and an auto-firing system), photographs and historical footage to grippingly document the division's social impact on the daily lives of Germans on both sides of the border.

BEBELPLATZ MEMORIAL

Map p314 (Bebel Square; 🚇100, 200, Ⓢ Französische Strasse, Hausvogteiplatz) On this treeless square, books by Brecht, Mann, Marx and other 'subversives' went up in flames during the first full-blown public book burning, staged by the Nazi German Student League in 1933. Michael Ullmann's underground installation, *Empty Library*, beneath a glass pane at the square's centre, poignantly commemorates the event.

Named for August Bebel, the cofounder of the Social Democratic Party (SPD), it was called Opernplatz (Opera Square) when first laid out in the mid-18th century as part of the Forum Fridericianum, a cultural centre envisioned by Frederick the Great. Money woes meant that only some of the buildings could be realised: the Staatsoper Unter den Linden (National Opera House, closed for restoration until 2014), the Alte Königliche Bibliothek (Old Royal Library), a palace for Fritz' brother Heinrich (now the Humboldt Universität) and the copperdomed Sankt-Hedwigs-Kathedrale.

SANKT-HEDWIGS-KATHEDRALE CHURCH

Map p314 (📞203 4810; www.hedwigs-kathedrale .de; Behrenstrasse 39; ⊙10am-5pm Mon-Sat, 1-5pm Sun; 🚇100, 200, Ⓢ Französische Strasse, Hausvogteiplatz) This copper-domed church (1773) was designed by Knobelsdorff, inspired by the Pantheon in Rome and named for the patron saint of Silesia. It was Berlin's only Catholic house of worship until 1854. Blown to bits during WWII, the church now has a circular, modern interior, lidded by a ribbed dome and accented with Gothic sculpture and a copy of Michelangelo's *Pietà*.

During WWII St Hedwig was a centre of Catholic resistance led by Bernard Lichtenberg, who died en route to the Dachau concentration camp in 1943 and is buried in the crypt.

FREE NEUE WACHE MEMORIAL

Map p314 (Unter den Linden 4; ⊙10am-6pm; 🚇100, 200, Ⓢ Hausvogteiplatz) This columned,

templelike structure, designed by Karl Friedrich Schinkel in 1818, was originally a Prussian royal guardhouse and is now an antiwar memorial. At its centre is Käthe Kollwitz' heart-wrenching sculpture of a mother cradling her dead soldier son. Buried beneath are the remains of an unknown soldier, a Nazi resistance fighter and soil from nine European battlefields and concentration camps.

FREE FRIEDRICHSWERDERSCHE KIRCHE MUSEUM

Map p314 (📞266 424 242; www.smb.museum /fwk; Werderscher Markt; ⊙10am-6pm; 🚇100, 200, Ⓢ Hausvogteiplatz) This perkily turreted church is a rare neo-Gothic design by Schinkel (1830) and cuts a commanding presence on the Werderscher Markt. The softly lit nave now functions as a museum of 19th-century German sculpture featuring works by such period heavyweights as Johann Gottfried Schadow, Christian Daniel Rauch and Christian Friedrich Tieck. Upstairs is an exhibit on Schinkel's life and achievements.

The postmodern hulk next to the church is the German Foreign Office.

⊙ Gendarmenmarkt

FRIEDRICH-STADTPASSAGEN SHOPPING CENTRE

Map p314 (Friedrichstrasse btwn Französische Strasse & Mohrenstrasse; ⊙10am-8pm Mon-Sat; Ⓢ Französische Strasse, Stadtmitte) Even

---

ℹ️ VIEWS WITH A THRILL

Drift up but not away for about 15 minutes with the **Berlin Hi-Flyer** (Map p314; 📞5321 5321, for wind conditions 226 678 811; www.air-service-berlin.de; cnr Wilhelmstrasse & Zimmerstrasse; adult/concession €19/13; ⊙10am-10pm Apr-Oct, 11am-6pm Nov-Mar, closed 20 Dec-2 Jan; Ⓢ Kochstrasse), a heliumfilled balloon that remains tethered to the ground as it lifts you noiselessly 150m into the air for panoramas of the historic city centre. Your pilot will help you pinpoint all the key sights. Confirm ahead as there are no flights in windy conditions.

TOP SIGHTS
GENDARMENMARKT

The Gendarmenmarkt area is Berlin at its ritziest. The graceful square was named after the Gens d'Armes, an 18th-century Prussian regiment recruited from Huguenots. Their main house of worship – the **Französischer Dom** (French Cathedral; Map p314; ☎229 1760; www.franzoesischer-dom.de; Gendarmenmarkt; church free, museum adult/concession €2/1, tower adult/child €2.50/1; 🕐church & museum noon-5pm Tue-Sun, tower 10am-7pm; [S]Französische Strasse) – consists of a soaring domed **tower**, whose viewing platform is reached via 284 steps, and the **French Church**, which hosts concerts and free 20-minute organ recitals at 12.30pm Tuesday to Friday. The French Cathedral is a spitting image of the **Deutscher Dom** (German Cathedral; Map p314; ☎2273 0431; Gendarmenmarkt 1; admission & tours free; 🕐10am-7pm Tue-Sun May-Sep, to 6pm Oct-Apr; [S]Französische Strasse, Stadtmitte) opposite, which is now home to an exhibit about Germany's path to parliamentary democracy.

Completing the trio is Karl Friedrich Schinkel's grandly porticoed **Konzerthaus** (concert hall). In front is a **memorial** to one of Germany's most revered 18th-century poets and playwrights, Friedrich Schiller.

DON'T MISS...

- An organ recital in the French Church
- Climbing the tower of the Französischer Dom

PRACTICALITIES

- Map p314
- 🕐24hr
- [S]Französische Strasse, Stadtmitte

if you're not part of the Gucci and Prada brigade, the wow factor of this trio of shopping complexes (called *Quartiere*) linked by a subterranean passageway is undeniable. Highlights are Jean Nouvel's shimmering glass funnel inside the Galeries Lafayette, the dazzlingly patterned art-deco-style Quartier 206 and John Chamberlain's tower made from crushed automobiles in Quartier 205.

[FREE] MAX PLANCK SCIENCE GALLERY — GALLERY

Map p314 (☎4990 5630; www.max-planck-science-gallery.de; Markgrafenstrasse 37; 🕐10am-6pm Mon-Wed & Fri, 10am-8pm Thu; [S]Hausvogteiplatz) Cutting-edge science discovered or developed by the smart folks of the Max Planck Society research institute is introduced to the non-geek public at this digital gallery. The boundaries between real and virtual worlds are blurred at 3D interactive stations in the minimalist cool one-room space. Exhibits change every few months.

EMIL NOLDE MUSEUM — MUSEUM

Map p314 (☎4000 4690; www.nolde-stiftung.de; Jägerstrasse 55; adult/concession €8/3, audioguide €4; 🕐10am-7pm; [S]Französische Strasse, Hausvogteiplatz) Bright flowers, stormy seas and red-lipped women with jaunty hats – the paintings and watercolours of Emil Nolde (1867–1956) are intense, sometimes melancholic and lyrically captivating. Admire a rotating selection of works by this key figure of German expressionism – and member of the artist group Die Brücke (The Bridge) – presented in a brightly converted 19th-century bank building.

Nolde was closely connected with Berlin and spent many winters here with his wife Ada, starting in 1905. Although somewhat sympathetic to the Nazis, the regime deemed him a 'degenerate artist' and forbade him from painting. In defiance, he nevertheless secretly produced some 1300 'unpainted pictures' at his main home in Seebüll in the northern German countryside.

[FREE] MENDELSSOHN EXHIBIT — MUSEUM

Map p314 (☎8170 4726; www.jaegerstrasse.de; Jägerstrasse 51; donations welcome; 🕐noon-6pm; [S]Hausvogteiplatz, Französische Strasse) The Mendelssohns are one of the great German family dynasties, starting with the *pater familias,* Jewish Enlightenment philosopher Moses Mendelssohn (1729–86). An exhibit in the private banking house founded in 1815 by two of his sons now traces the fate and history of this influential family, who was forced into bankruptcy by the Nazis, prompting many to flee the country.

Other personalities associated with Jägerstrasse include Alexander von Humboldt, who was born at No 22, and the painter Georg Grosz, who lived at No 63. Rahel Varnhagen held her intellectual salons at No 54, now the restaurant Vau.

Checkpoint Charlie

BERLIN WALL PANORAMA GALLERY

Map p314 (www.asisi.de; cnr Friedrichstrasse & Zimmerstrasse; [S]Kochstrasse) For most of us it's hard to visualise what Berlin looked like during the Cold War. Yadegar Asisi can fix that. The Berlin artist specialises in creating monumental and bafflingly detailed 360-degree panoramas. His latest venture, housed in a custom-made steel rotunda at Checkpoint Charlie, vividly captures a scene from daily life on both sides of the Berlin Wall. It shows dilapidated buildings, playing children and patrolling border guards.

MAUERMUSEUM MUSEUM

Map p314 (Haus am Checkpoint Charlie; ☎253 7250; www.mauermuseum.de; Friedrichstrasse 43-45; adult/concession €12.50/9.50; 🕘9am-10pm; [S]Kochstrasse) The Cold War years are engagingly, if haphazardly, documented in this privately run tourist magnet. The best bits are about ingenious escapes to the West in hot-air balloons, tunnels, concealed car compartments and even a one-man submarine. Other galleries (all are multilingual) focus on such milestones as the Berlin Airlift, the 1953 East German workers' uprising, the Wall construction and reunification.

A new exhibit shines the spotlight on Raoul Wallenberg, a Swedish diplomat who rescued over 100,000 Jews living in Budapest from the concentration camps.

[FREE] **STASI AUSSTELLUNG** MUSEUM

Map p314 (☎2324 7951; www.bstu.bund.de; Zimmerstrasse 90; 🕘10am-6pm; [S]Kochstrasse, Stadtmitte) For 40 years, the East German Ministry of State Security (Stasi) controlled,

TOP SIGHTS CHECKPOINT CHARLIE

Checkpoint Charlie was the principal gateway for foreigners and diplomats between the two Berlins from 1961 to 1990. Since it was the third Allied checkpoint to open, it was named 'Charlie' in reference to the third letter in the Nato phonetic alphabet (alfa, bravo, charlie...). The only direct Cold War–era confrontation between the US and the Soviet Union took place in this very spot when tanks faced off shortly after the Wall went up.

Unfortunately, this potent symbol of the Cold War is now a tacky tourist trap. Near the famous sign warning 'You are now leaving the American sector', souvenir shops hawk faux Wall pieces and plastic Trabant cars. Uniformed actors issue 'genuine GDR visas' or pose for tips in front of a replica guardhouse. Although hugely popular, the privately financed Mauermuseum (p85) is more a labour of love than a properly curated exhibit. One redeeming aspect around here is the free **open-air gallery** that uses photos and documents to illustrate milestones in Cold War history. New since September 2012 is Yadegar Asisi's Berlin Wall Panorama (p85). An official **Cold War Museum** is in the planning stages and may open by 2015. Until then, a 'Blackbox' offers a preview.

DON'T MISS...

- Berlin Wall Panorama
- Open-air gallery
- Mauermuseum

PRACTICALITIES

- Map p314
- cnr Zimmerstrasse & Friedrichstrasse
- 🕘24hr
- [S]Kochstrasse, Stadtmitte

TOP SIGHTS
TOPOGRAPHIE DES TERRORS

On the site of the most feared institutions of Nazi Germany – including the Gestapo headquarters and the Schutzstaffel (SS) central command – this compelling exhibit dissects the anatomy of the Nazi state. By tracing the stages of terror and persecution, it puts a face on the perpetrators and documents the impact these brutal institutions had on all of Europe. From their desks, top Nazi commanders like Himmler and Heydrich hatched Holocaust plans and organised the systematic persecution of political opponents, many of whom suffered torture and death in the Gestapo prison.

To complement the exhibit, borrow a free audioguide and take a self-guided tour of the historic grounds, which take you past 15 information stations with photos, documents and 3D graphics. From spring to autumn, another exhibit called 'Berlin 1933–1945: Between Propaganda & Terror' opens up in a trench against the glassed-in foundations of the Gestapo prison cells. It zeroes in on the role of Berlin during the Third Reich and how life changed for local residents after the city had become the Nazi leadership's political power nexus. A 200m stretch of the Berlin Wall along Niederkirchner Strasse hems in part of the grounds.

DON'T MISS...

- Model of the grounds
- Diagram of the concentration camp system
- Outdoor trench exhibit

PRACTICALITIES

- Topography of Terror
- Map p314
- ☎2548 6703
- www.topographie.de
- Niederkirchner Strasse 8
- ⏰10am-8pm May-Sep, to dusk Oct-Apr
- 👪
- [S]Potsdamer Platz, [U]Potsdamer Platz

manipulated and repressed its own people with the goal of ridding itself of any 'hostile negative elements' that could threaten the government's existence. Using original objects and documents and informative panels, this compact exhibit is divided into nine sections that document the history of the Stasi and the organisation's all-out zeal. It sheds light on how the Stasi was structured, how people were spied on and by whom, and how the Stasi affected people's daily lives when it came to travel, worship, education or even sports.

MUSEUM FÜR KOMMUNIKATION BERLIN — MUSEUM

Map p314 (☎202 940; www.mfk-berlin.de; Leipziger Strasse 16; adult/concession €3/1.50; ⏰9am-8pm Tue, to 5pm Wed-Fri, 10am-6pm Sat & Sun; [S]Mohrenstrasse, Stadtmitte) Three cheeky robots welcome you to this elegant, neo-baroque museum, which takes you on an entertaining romp through the evolution of communication technology – smoke signals to computers. Admire such rare items as a Blue Mauritius stamp, test time-honoured communication techniques or ponder how information technology has changed our daily lives. A multimedia iPod touch guide (€1.50) provides the full low-down.

DEUTSCHES CURRYWURST MUSEUM — MUSEUM

Map p314 (☎8871 8630; www.currywurstmuseum.de; Schützenstrasse 70; adult/concession €11/8; ⏰10am-10pm, last admission 8pm; [S]Stadtmitte, Kochstrasse) The Currywurst, Berlin's beloved cult snack, now has its own museum. Sniff out curry secrets in the Spice Chamber, find out what kind of curry type you are, learn about the wurst's history and watch a movie about one woman's quest for the best Currywurst. A bit silly? Perhaps. But somehow also colourful, experiential and fun.

FORMER REICHSLUFTFAHRT-MINISTERIUM — HISTORIC BUILDING

Map p314 (Reich Aviation Ministry; Leipziger Strasse 5-7; ⏰closed to the public; [S]Kochstrasse) Designed by Ernst Sagebiel, the Reich Aviation Ministry was Hermann Göring's massive power centre and a rare Nazi-era architectural relic still standing. After the war, it was used by several GDR ministries and is now the home of the Federal Finance Ministry. With over 2000 rooms, it's Europe's largest office building. In 2007, scenes from the movie *Valkyrie* were filmed outside the ministry.

🍴 EATING

Mitte is awash with swanky restaurants where the decor is fabulous, the crowds cosmopolitan and menus stylish. Sure, some places may be more sizzle than substance, but the see-and-be-seen punters don't seem to mind. The area also has the greatest density of Berlin's Michelin-starred restaurants.

🍴 Government Quarter

BERLIN PAVILLON INTERNATIONAL €
Map p314 (☎2065 4737; www.berlin-pavillon.de; Scheidemannstrasse 1; mains €2.50-9; 🚌100, [S]Bundestag, Brandenburger Tor, 🚆Brandenburger Tor) For quick feeds this tourist-geared, self-service cafeteria on the edge of Tiergarten comes in rather handy for breakfast, cakes and simple hot dishes. In summer, the beer garden offers shaded respite.

🍴 Pariser Platz & Unter den Linden

[TOP CHOICE] **UMA** ASIAN €€€
Map p314 (☎301 117 324; www.uma-restaurant.de; Behrenstrasse 72; mains €16-55; ⏰dinner Mon-Sat; 🚌100, [S]Brandenburger Tor, 🚆Brandenburger Tor) Japanese for horse, Uma raises the bar for luxury with its exquisite decor, eye-catching artwork and Euro-inflected Asian dishes that weave flavours together like fine tapestries. Aside from sushi and sashimi, there are meaty mains from the *robata* (charcoal) grill and such tasty morsels as Korean fried octopus and wasabi-infused soft-shell crab meant for sharing.

ISHIN – MITTELSTRASSE JAPANESE €€
Map p314 (www.ishin.de; Mittelstrasse 24; platter €7-18; ⏰Mon-Sat; [S]Friedrichstrasse, 🚆Friedrichstrasse) Look beyond the cafeteria-style get-up to sushi glory for minimal wallets. Combination platters are ample and affordable, especially during happy hour (all day Wednesday and Saturday, until 4pm on other days). If you're not in the mood for raw fish, tuck into a steaming rice bowl topped with meat and/or veg. Nice touch: the unlimited free green tea. There's another branch near **Checkpoint Charlie** (Map p314; Charlottenstrasse 16; [S]Kochstrasse).

COOKIES CREAM VEGETARIAN €€€
Map p314 (☎2749 2940; www.cookiescream.com; Behrenstrasse 55; mains €20, 3-course menu €36; ⏰dinner Tue-Sat; 🍷; [S]Französische Strasse) Kudos if you can locate this chic herbivore haven right away. Hint: it's upstairs past a giant chandelier in the service alley of the Westin Grand Hotel. Ring the bell to enter an elegantly industrial loft for flesh-free, flavour-packed dishes from current-harvest ingredients. Dining here gets you free admission to the attached nightclub.

BACKROOM CANTINA FUSION €€€
Map p314 (☎2758 2070; www.tausendberlin.com; Schiffbauerdamm 11; mains €15-30; ⏰dinner Tue-Sat; [S]Friedrichstrasse, 🚆Friedrichstrasse) Magic is happening in the backroom of the stylish Tausend bar, and foodies are all over it. Head chef Duc Ngo creates culinary alchemy by effortlessly blending Japanese, Mediterranean and South American flavours. Think seared tuna paired with foie gras and risotto, and crème brûlée infused with sweetened Asian azuki beans.

🍴 Gendarmenmarkt

AUGUSTINER AM GENDARMENMARKT GERMAN €€
Map p314 (☎2045 4020; www.augustiner-braeu-berlin.de; Charlottenstrasse 55; mains €6-19; ⏰10am-1am; [S]Französische Strasse) Tourists, concert-goers and hearty-food lovers rub shoulders at rustic tables in this surprisingly authentic Bavarian beer hall. Soak up the down-to-earth vibe right along with a mug of full-bodied Augustiner brew. Sausages, roast pork and pretzels provide rib-sticking sustenance, but there's also plenty of lighter (even meat-free) fare as well as good-value lunch specials.

CHIPPS INTERNATIONAL €€
Map p314 (☎3644 4588; www.chipps.eu; Jägerstrasse 35; mains €11-17; ⏰8am-11pm Mon-Fri, 9am-10pm Sat & Sun; [S]Hausvogteiplatz) The

START BERLINER DOM
END BEBELPLATZ
DISTANCE 650M
DURATION 20 MINUTES

Neighbourhood Walk
Royal Berlin

With the reconstruction of the Berlin City Palace imminent, this tour takes in existing vestiges of Prussian grandeur lined up along Unter den Linden. The walk starts at the ❶ **Schlossbrücke**, which would be just any old bridge were it not decorated with marvellous Karl Friedrich Schinkel–designed marble sculptures. On your right, the ❷ **Zeughaus** is the former royal arsenal turned history museum.

Opposite, the froufrou baroque ❸ **Kronprinzenpalais** was the residence of Crown Prince Frederick before he became 'the Great'. In the 1920s the National Gallery presented contemporary art here until it was deemed 'degenerate' and shut down by the Nazis. In 1990 the formal German reunification treaty was signed here. Next door, the ❹ **Prinzessinnenpalais** started out as the Prussian treasurer's pad before becoming the residence of the crown princesses. Across the street, the ❺ **Neue Wache** is a former royal guardhouse turned antiwar memorial.

Next up, the opulent ❻ **Staatsoper Unter den Linden** (National Opera House), designed by Knobelsdorff, has graced Bebelplatz since 1743 but is currently closed for renovation. The west side of Bebelplatz is adorned with the ❼ **Alte Königliche Bibliothek** (Old Royal Library), a handsome baroque building nicknamed *Kommode* (chest of drawers) because of its curvaceous facade. It's now part of the law school of the ❽ **Humboldt Universität**, Berlin's oldest university founded in 1810 across the street in a former royal palace. Marx and Engels studied here, while the faculty included the Brothers Grimm and Albert Einstein. At last count, it had produced 29 Nobel Prize winners.

Seemingly surveying his domain, Frederick the Great cuts a commanding figure on horseback in the famous 1850 ❾ **Reiterdenkmal Friedrich des Grossen**. The monument kept Christian Daniel Rauch busy for a dozen years. The plinth is decorated with German military men, scientists, artists and thinkers.

people behind the Cookies club and Cookies Cream restaurant have done it again. Their latest venture, a crisp spot with show kitchen and panorama windows in a quiet side street, turns heads with yummy cooked breakfasts, giant salads and hot meals that spin regional, seasonal ingredients into taste-bud magic. Meat and fish are served on the side only.

BORCHARDT FRENCH, GERMAN €€€

Map p314 (☎8188 6262; Französische Strasse 47; mains €20-40; ⏰11.30am-1am; [S]Französische Strasse) A Berlin institution, this high-ceilinged brasserie is as famous for its succulent Wiener schnitzel as it is for its guest roster of international power players, A-list babes and pasty-faced politicians. The neo-baroque setting with its soaring pillars oozes tradition rooted in 1853 when the business was founded by August FW Borchardt, chief caterer to the Prussian royal court.

FISCHERS FRITZ INTERNATIONAL €€€

Map p314 (☎2033 6363; www.fischersfritzberlin.com; Charlottenstrasse 49; mains €50-90, menu from €105; ⏰lunch & dinner; [S]Französische Strasse) Even those shunning hotel restaurants on principle must concede that Christian Lohse has earned his two Michelin stars by jazzing up superb fish, meat and seafood into a carnival of flavours. Based at the Regent, it's as fancy and formal as Berlin gets, so shine your shoes and pack your manners. The three-course set lunch for €47 is practically a steal.

VAU INTERNATIONAL €€€

Map p314 (☎202 9730; www.vau-berlin.de; Jägerstrasse 54/55; mains lunch €18, dinner €40, 5-course menu €120; ⏰noon-2.30pm & 7-10.30pm Mon-Sat; [S]Hausvogteiplatz) In the same locale that Rahel Varnhagen held her literary salons a couple of centuries ago, Michelin-starred chef Kolja Kleeberg now pampers a Rolls Royce crowd with fanciful gourmet creations. In fine weather the courtyard tables beckon, although the interior – a cocktail of glass, steel, slate and wood by Meinhard von Gerkan – is a visual treat as well.

CHA CHÃ THAI €€

Map p314 (☎206 259 613; www.eatchacha.com; Friedrichstrasse 63; ⏰11.30am-10pm Mon-Fri, noon-10pm Sat, 12.30-9pm Sun; 🚭; [S]Stadtmitte) Feeling worn out from sightseeing or power-shopping? No problem: a helping of massaman curry should quickly return you to top form for, according to the menu of this Thai nosh spot, the dish has an 'activating' effect. In fact, all menu items here are described as having a 'positive eating' benefit, be it vitalising, soothing or stimulating. Gimmicky? Perhaps, but darn tasty too.

GOOD TIME THAI €€

Map p314 (☎2007 4870; www.goodtime-berlin.de; Hausvogteiplatz 11a; mains €10-19; ⏰noon-midnight; 🚭; [S]Hausvogteiplatz) Sweep on down to this busy dining room with a garden courtyard for fragrant Thai and Indonesian dishes. Creamy curries, succulent shrimp, roast duck or an entire *rijstafel* spread (an elaborate buffet-style meal) – everything tastes flavourful and fresh, if a bit easy on the heat to accommodate German stomachs.

SAGRANTINO ITALIAN €€

Map p314 (☎2064 6895; www.sagrantino-winebar.de; Behrenstrasse 47; mains €10-16; ⏰7.30am-midnight Mon-Fri, 9am-noon & 5pm-midnight Sat; [S]Französische Strasse) The ambience here is so classically Italian you'd half expect to see a sprawling vineyard out the window. That would be a vineyard in Umbria, for that's the region showcased at this little trattoria. At lunchtime, the pasta-salad (or soup) combos go for a mere €6.50.

🍴 Checkpoint Charlie

RESTAURANT TIM RAUE ASIAN €€€

Map p314 (☎2593 7930; www.tim-raue.com; Rudi-Dutschke-Strasse 26; 2-/3-course lunch €28/38, 4-/6-course dinner €110/140; ⏰Tue-Sat; [S]Kochstrasse) Now here's a Michelin-starred restaurant we can get our mind around. Unstuffy ambience and subtly sophisticated design pair perfectly with Raue's brilliant Asian-inspired cuisine that looks like art on a plate and launches a taste explosion in your mouth. The menu changes weekly, but his personal spin on Peking duck and creatively stuffed dim sum are perennial bestsellers. The selection of koshu (aged sake) is tops.

TAZ CAFE CAFE €

Map p314 (☎2590 2164; www.taz.de; Rudi-Dutschke-Strasse 23; mains €6-7; ⏰8am-8pm; 📶; [S]Kochstrasse) Join *taz* newspaper staffers at fire-engine red tables for daily-changing lunches with global pizzazz and prepared with seasonal vegetables and free-range meats. Afternoons bring cakes, snacks and delicious fair-trade house espresso.

 DRINKING & NIGHTLIFE

Government Quarter

BERLINER REPUBLIK   PUB

Map p314 (www.die-berliner-republik.de; Schiffbauerdamm 8; ⊙10am-6am; ⓢFriedrichstrasse, ⓡFriedrichstrasse) Just as in a mini–stock exchange, the cost of drinks fluctuates with demand at this raucous riverside pub. Everyone goes Pavlovian when a heavy brass bell rings, signalling rock-bottom prices. You won't be hoisting mugs with many Berliners here, but it's a fun spot nonetheless.

TAUSEND   BAR

Map p314 (www.tausendberlin.com; Schiffbauerdamm 11; ⊙from 7.30pm Tue-Sat; ⓢFriedrichstrasse, ⓡFriedrichstrasse) No sign, no light, no bell, just an anonymous steel door tucked under a railway bridge leads to one of Berlin's chicest bars. Behind it, flirty frocks sip raspberry mojitos alongside London Mule–cradling three-day stubbles. The eye-catching decor channels 80s glam while DJs and bands fuel the vibe. Hungry? Proceed to Backroom Cantina (p87). Selective door.

Pariser Platz & Unter den Linden

COOKIES   CLUB

Map p314 (www.cookies.ch; cnr Friedrichstrasse & Unter den Linden; ⊙from midnight Tue, Thu & Sat; ⓢFranzösische Strasse) Heinz Gindullis, aka Cookies, has done it again: for the eighth time he's reinvented his club, this time creating an indoor playground complete with wicked little theme rooms like a mirror cabinet, a 'toy' shop and even a wedding chapel. Upstairs, top local and international electro DJs heat up the sexy crowd on the mosaic dance floor that segues smoothly into the Drayton Bar.

DRAYTON BAR   BAR

Map p314 (☑280 8806; www.draytonberlin.com; Behrensstrasse 55; ⊙Tue-Sat; ⓢFranzösische Strasse) This glamour vixen of a bar oozes 1920s-inspired sophistication from every dimly lit corner. Oversized gilded peacock lamps flank the bar where Christian Gentemann creates classic and 'cuisine-style' cocktails from homemade syrups, infusions, fresh herbs and selected spices. The entrance is via Cookies Cream restaurant. At midnight on Tuesdays, Thursdays and Saturdays, the bar expands into the Cookies (p90) club.

BEBEL BAR   BAR

Map p314 (www.hotelderome.com; Behrenstrasse 37; ⊙from 9am; ⓠ100, 200, ⓢFranzösische Strasse, Hausvogteiplatz) Channel your inner George Clooney when you belly up to the bar of this elegant, mood-lit thirst parlour at the Hotel de Rome. Top-label cocktails here have a progressive, sexy edge thanks to bold ingredients, including balsamic vinegar and basil. Even the virgin drinks pack a flavour punch. On summery nights, head to the rooftop terrace bar.

SHŌCHŪ   BAR

Map p314 (☑301 117 328; www.shochubar.de; Behrenstrasse 72; ⊙Mon-Sat; ⓢBrandenburger Tor, ⓡBrandenburger Tor) Banter quietly away in this dimly lit deluxe drinking den specialising in cocktails based on shōchū, a traditional Japanese spirit. Look on as bartenders whip up libational flights of fancy infused with saffron, bergamot, jasmine and other tantalising aromas.

FELIX   CLUB

Map p314 (www.felix-clubrestaurant.de; Behenstrasse 72; ⊙Mon & Thu-Sat; ⓢBrandenburger Tor, ⓡBrandenburger Tor) Once past the rope of this swanky club at the Hotel Adlon, you too can shake your booty to high-octane hip hop, dance and disco beats, sip champagne cocktails and flirt up a storm. Women get free entry and a glass of prosecco on Mondays, while the worker-bee brigade kicks loose on after-work Thursdays.

TADSCHIKISCHE TEESTUBE   CAFE

Map p314 (www.restaurant-trofeo.de; Am Festungsgraben 1; ⊙5pm-midnight Mon-Fri, from 3pm Sat & Sun; ⓠ100, 200, ⓢFriedrichstrasse, ⓡFriedrichstrasse) Sip steaming tea poured from silvery samovars while reclining amid plump pillows, hand-carved sandalwood pillars and heroic murals in this original Tajik tearoom. A 1974 gift from the Soviets to the East German government, it is tucked upstairs in an elegant 18th-century town palace that was once a German–Soviet cultural centre.

 Gendarmenmarkt

ASPHALT
CLUB

Map p314 (📞2200 2396; www.asphalt-berlin.com; Mohrenstrasse 30; ⊙from 8pm Thu-Sat; ⓈStadtmitte) Not so modestly considering itself as the 'future of progressive clubbing', Asphalt lures mostly cashed-up, grown-up weekend warriors to its Hilton-based party boîte, whose low lighting somehow makes everyone more mysterious and attractive. Musically, it's whatever makes the dance floor hum, mostly hip hop, disco and pop.

⭐ ENTERTAINMENT

KONZERTHAUS BERLIN
CLASSICAL MUSIC

Map p314 (📞tickets 203 092 101; www.konzerthaus.de; Gendarmenmarkt 2; ⓈStadtmitte, Französische Strasse) This top-ranked concert hall – a Schinkel design from 1821 – counts the Konzerthausorchester as its 'house band' but also hosts international soloists, thematic concert cycles, children's events and performances by the Rundfunk-Sinfonieorchester Berlin.

ADMIRALSPALAST
PERFORMING ARTS

Map p314 (📞4799 7499; www.admiralspalast.de; Friedrichstrasse 101-102; ⓈFriedrichstrasse, ℝFriedrichstrasse) This beautifully restored 1920s 'palace' stages crowd-pleasing plays, concerts and musicals in its elegant, historic hall. More intimate shows – including comedy, readings, dance, concerts and theatre – are presented on two smaller stages. Programming is international and usually of high calibre.

TIPI AM KANZLERAMT
CABARET

Map p314 (📞3906 6550; www.tipi-am-kanzleramt.de; Grosse Querallee; ⓈBundestag, ℝHauptbahnhof) Between the Chancellory and the House of World Cultures is Tipi, a vast permanent tent that presents a year-round program of high-calibre cabaret, dance, *chanson*, acrobatics, musical comedy and magic shows starring German and international artists. It's about 500m west of the Reichstag via Paul-Löbe-Allee.

KOMISCHE OPER
OPERA

Map p314 (📞4799 7400; www.komische-oper-berlin.de; Behrenstrasse 55-57; ⓈLinie100, 200, ⓈFranzösische Strasse) Musical theatre, light opera, operetta and dance theatre from many periods are the bread and butter of the high-profile Comic Opera venue with its opulent neo-baroque auditorium. Seats feature an ingenious subtitling system that gives you the option of reading along in German, English, French or Turkish. The **box office** (Map p314; 📞4799 7400; Unter den Linden 41; ⊙11am-7pm Mon-Sat, 1-4pm Sun; ⓈLinie100, 200, ⓈFranzösische Strasse, Friedrichstrasse) is located at Unter den Linden.

MAXIM GORKI THEATER
THEATRE

Map p314 (📞2022 1115; www.gorki.de; Am Festungsgraben 2; ⓈLinie100, 200, ⓈFriedrichstrasse, ℝFriedrichstrasse) The Gorki was founded in 1952 as a key exponent of Soviet-style Socialist Realism. Naturally, it's mellowed a lot since and now stages contemporary interpretations of the classics as well as plays dealing with local and regional themes. Some performances have English surtitles.

HOCHSCHULE FÜR MUSIK HANNS EISLER
CLASSICAL MUSIC

Map p314 (📞688 305 700; www.hfm-berlin.de; Charlottenstrasse 55; ⓈStadtmitte, Französische Strasse) The gifted students at Berlin's top-rated music academy populate several orchestras, a choir and a big band, which collectively stage as many as 400 performances annually, most of them in the Neuer Marstall (p107) on Schlossplatz, where the Prussian royals once kept their coaches and horses. Many concerts are free or low-cost.

🛍 SHOPPING

For fancy fashion and accessories, make a beeline to Friedrichstrasse with its dazzling Friedrichstadtpassagen and Galeries Lafayette.

DUSSMANN – DAS KULTURKAUFHAUS
BOOKS, MUSIC

Map p314 (📞2025 1111; www.kulturkaufhaus.de; Friedrichstrasse 90; ⊙10am-midnight Mon-Fri, to 11.30pm Sat; ⓈFriedrichstrasse, ℝFriedrichstrasse) It's easy to lose track of time in this cultural playground with wall-to-wall books, DVDs and CDs, leaving no genre unaccounted for. Bonus points for the free reading-glass rentals, on-site cafe and a performance space used for concerts, political discussions and high-profile book readings and signings.

GALERIES LAFAYETTE DEPARTMENT STORE

Map p314 (☎209 480; www.galerieslafayette.de; Friedrichstrasse 76-78; [S]Französische Strasse) Part of the Friedrichstadtpassagen shopping centre, the Berlin branch of the exquisite French emporium is centred on a glass cone shimmering with kaleidoscopic intensity. From here, three floors of concentric circles rise up. Aside from racks packed with Prada & Co, you can get your mitts on edgy Berlin fashions and gourmet treats in the food hall.

FASSBENDER & RAUSCH FOOD

Map p314 (☎2045 8443; www.fassbender-rausch.com; Charlottenstrasse 60; ⏲10am-8pm Mon-Sat, 11am-8pm Sun; [S]Stadtmitte) If the Aztecs thought of chocolate as the elixir of the gods, then this emporium of truffles and pralines must be heaven. Bonus: the chocolate volcano and giant replicas of Berlin landmarks. The upstairs cafe serves sinful drinking chocolates and cakes, and has views of Gendarmenmarkt.

ACH BERLIN GIFTS, SOUVENIRS

Map p314 (☎9212 6880; www.achberlin.de; Markgrafenstrasse 29; [S]Hausvogteiplatz, Französische Strasse) Brandenburg Gate cookie cutters, TV Tower wall hooks, street-art-style wallets, the Berlin skyline on a pillow – there's no limit to the imagination of local designers when it comes to turning the Berlin brand into fun and creative souvenirs. This classy gallerylike space stocks a great assortment and also incorporates a small cafe.

BERLIN STORY BOOKS

Map p314 (www.berlinstory.de; Unter den Linden 40; ⏲10am-7pm Mon-Sat, to 6pm Sun; 🚌100, 200, [S]Friedrichstrasse, Französische Strasse, 🚆Friedrichstrasse) Never mind the tacky souvenirs, this store's ammo is its broad selection of Berlin-related books, maps, DVDs, CDs and magazines, in English and a dozen other languages, some published in-house. For a primer on Berlin's vivid history, visit the in-store **museum** (admission €5).

KUNST- & NOSTALGIEMARKT ANTIQUES

Map p314 (Am Kupfergraben; ⏲10am-4pm Sat & Sun; [S]Friedrichstrasse, 🚆Friedrichstrasse) This art and collectible market gets high marks for its scenic Museum Island–adjacent location. Antique book collectors have plenty of boxes to sift through and there's also a good sampling of furniture, bric-a-brac and small-scale Eastern Bloc detritus.

NIVEA HAUS BEAUTY

Map p314 (☎2045 6160; http://shop.nivea.de; Unter den Linden 28; 🚌100, 200, [S]Friedrichstrasse, Brandenburger Tor, 🚆Friedrichstrasse, Brandenburger Tor) *Nivea* is Latin for Snow White whose 'castle' sits right on prestigious Unter den Linden. At the flagship store of this German beauty purveyor you can peruse the entire product palette, sign up for a consultation or get a quick pick-me-up facial or massage (no reservation; from €12 for a 10-minute massage).

FRAU TONIS PARFUM BEAUTY

Map p314 (☎2021 5310; www.frau-tonis-parfum.com; Zimmerstrasse 13; ⏲10am-6pm Mon-Sat; [S]Kochstrasse) Follow your nose to this scent-sational made-in-Berlin perfume boutique. Try Marlene Dietrich's favourite (a bold violet) or ask staff to whip up a customised fragrance.

RITTER SPORT BUNTE SCHOKOWELT FOOD

Map p314 (☎2009 5080; www.ritter-sport.de; Französische Strasse 24; ⏲10am-7pm Mon-Wed, to 8pm Thu-Sat, to 6pm Sun; 👪; [S]Französische Strasse) Fans of the colourful square chocolate bars can pick up limited edition, organic and diet varieties in addition to all the classics at Ritter Sport's flagship store. Upstairs, a free **exhibit** explains the journey from cocoa bean to finished product, but we're especially fond of the chocolate station where you can create your personalised bars.

BOXOFFBERLIN GIFTS, SOUVENIRS

Map p314 (☎4470 1555; www.boxoffberlin.de; Zimmerstrasse 11; ⏲11am-8pm Mon-Sat; [S]Kochstrasse) A great souvenir store if the TV Tower fridge magnets or Reichstag snow globes don't appeal. Owners Torsten and Stephan ('the Bobs') have put together an assortment of quality Berlin souvenirs that ranges from hand-crocheted Berlin bears to Trabi T-shirts. Cap off a browse with a cup of fair-trade coffee.

Museumsinsel & Alexanderplatz

ALEXANDERPLATZ | NIKOLAIVIERTEL | SCHLOSSPLATZ

Neighbourhood Top Five

1 Time-travelling through ancient Greece and Babylon to the Middle East at the glorious **Pergamonmuseum** (p96).

2 Making a date with Nefertiti and her royal entourage at the stunningly rebuilt **Neues Museum** (p98).

3 Letting the sights drift by while enjoying cold drinks on a riverboat deck (p109).

4 Finding out about life across the Berlin Wall at the interactive **DDR Museum** (p104).

5 Getting high from the knock-out views from the top of the **Fernsehturm** (p103), Germany's tallest structure.

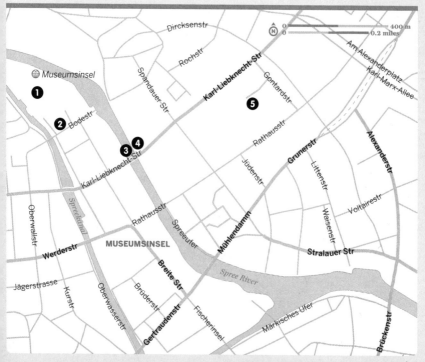

For more detail of this area, see Map p318 ➡

Lonely Planet's Top Tip

It would take superhuman stamina to visit all five museums on Museumsinsel in one day, so don't even try; concentrate your energy on those that interest you most. Skip the worst crowds on Museumsinsel by arriving first thing in the morning, late in the afternoon or on Thursdays, when all museums stay open later than usual.

✕ Best Places to Eat

→ Brooklyn Beef Club (p109)

→ .HBC (p107)

→ Dolores (p107)

→ Zur Letzten Instanz (p107)

For reviews, see p107 →

🍷 Best Places to Drink

→ Weekend (p109)

→ .HBC (p109)

For reviews, see p109 →

◉ Best Non-Museums Sights

→ Berliner Dom (p106)

→ Fernsehturm (p103)

→ Humboldt-Box (p106)

→ Marienkirche (p103)

→ Nikolaiviertel (p109)

For reviews, see p103 →

Explore: Museumsinsel – Alexanderplatz Area

Noisy and chaotic, Alexanderplatz (Alex for short) was the transport and commercial hub of East Berlin and not the place to linger. Despite attempts to temper the 1960s socialist look, it remains an oddly cluttered, soulless, concrete square. Confusingly cut by roads, train and tram tracks and traffic, its main redeeming feature is the soaring TV Tower, which delivers great views from the top and is handy for orientation from below.

Fans of antique treasures and fine art, meanwhile, will feel as though they've hit the jackpot at nearby Museumsinsel (Museum Island), the main attraction in these parts. Opposite the museums, the rebuilding of the Berlin City Palace is set to begin in 2014. An information centre called Humboldt-Box provides historical perspective and a preview of what will be inside. They're big on reconstruction in this part of town, another example being the nearby Nikolaiviertel, a medieval-looking quarter built in 1987 that seeks to replicate Berlin's medieval birthplace. For an original remnant of the 13th-century town wall, head to the historic area around Klosterstrasse U-Bahn station.

Local Life

→ **Late-night Openings** Clued-in locals know that the best time to see the Museumsinsel collections without the crowds is on Thursday night when all five of them stay open as late as 10pm.

→ **Shopping** Big shopping centres are scarce in central Berlin, which probably explains the enormous local popularity of the Alexa mega-mall, which harbours practically every franchise under the sun and stays open until 9pm.

→ **Drinks with a View** There are few better places for summertime sunset cocktails than the rooftop terrace of the Weekend (p109) club with the entire glittering city at your feet.

Getting There & Away

→ **Bus** M48 links Alexanderplatz with Potsdamer Platz; bus 248 goes to the Märkisches Museum via Nikolaiviertel.

→ **S-Bahn** S5, S7/75 and S9 all converge at Alexanderplatz.

→ **Tram** M4, M5 and M6 connect Alexanderplatz with Marienkirche.

→ **U-Bahn** U2, U5 and U8 stop at Alexanderplatz. Other main stops are Klosterstrasse and Märkisches Museum (U2) and Jannowitzbrücke (U8).

BJORN HOLLAND / GETTY IMAGES ©

TOP SIGHTS
MUSEUMSINSEL

Walk through ancient Babylon, meet an Egyptian queen, clamber up a Greek altar or be mesmerised by Monet's ethereal landscapes. Welcome to Museumsinsel (Museum Island), Berlin's most important treasure trove spanning 6000 years' worth of art, artefacts, sculpture and architecture from Europe and beyond. Spread across five grand museums built between 1830 and 1930, the complex takes up the entire northern half of the little Spree Island where Berlin's settlement began in the 13th century.

Berlin's 'Louvre'

The first repository to open was the **Altes Museum** (Old Museum), completed in 1830 next to the Berlin Cathedral and the Lustgarten park. Today it presents Greek, Etruscan and Roman antiquities. Behind it, the **Neues Museum** (New Museum) showcases the Egyptian collection, most famously the bust of Queen Nefertiti, and also houses the Museum of Pre- and Early History. The templelike **Alte Nationalgalerie** (Old National Gallery) trains the focus on 19th-century European art. The island's top draw, though, is the **Pergamonmuseum**, with its monumental architecture from ancient worlds, including the namesake Pergamonaltar. The **Bodemuseum** at the island's northern tip, meanwhile, is famous for its sculptures.

Museumsinsel Masterplan

In 1999 the Museumsinsel repositories collectively became a Unesco World Heritage Site. The distinction was at least partly achieved because of a master plan for the renovation and modernisation of the complex, which is expected to be

DON'T MISS...

- Pergamonaltar
- Ishtar Gate
- Bust of Nefertiti
- Berlin Goldhut
- *Praying Boy*
- Sculpture by Tilman Riemenschneider

PRACTICALITIES

- Map p97
- ☎ all museums 2090 5577
- www.smb.museum
- adult/concession varies per museum, combined ticket for all museums €14/7
- 🕐10am-6pm Tue-Sun, to 8-10pm Thu
- 🚌100, 200, [S]Hackescher Markt, Friedrichstrasse

TOP TIP

Arrive early or late on weekdays or skip the queues by purchasing your ticket online at least one day in advance. An excellent multilanguage audioguide is included in the admission price.

Museumsinsel is the product of a late-18th and early 19th-century fad among European royalty to open their private collections to the public. The Louvre in Paris, the Prado in Madrid and the Glyptothek in Munich all date from this period. In Berlin, King Friedrich Wilhelm III and his successors followed suit.

A ROYAL CAPITAL

Pergamon was the capital of the Kingdom of Pergamon, which reigned over vast stretches of the eastern Mediterranean in the 3rd and 2nd century BC. The Attalids, rulers of Pergamon, turned their royal residence into a major cultural and intellectual centre. Draped over a 330m-high ridge were grand palaces, a library, a theatre and glorious temples dedicated to Trajan, Dionysus and Athena. The scale model next to the Pergamonaltar illustrates how all the buildings fit together.

completed in 2025 under the aegis of British architect David Chipperfield. Except for the Pergamon, whose exhibits will be partly reorganised in the coming years, the restoration of the museums themselves has been completed. At press time, construction had begun on the **James-Simon-Galerie**, a colonnaded modern foyer named for an early-20th-century German-Jewish philanthropist. It will serve as the central entrance to four of the five museums and also harbour a cafe and other service facilities. Another master plan key feature is the subterranean 'Archaeological Promenade' that will eventually link the four archaeological museums. For more details see www.museumsinsel-berlin.de.

Pergamonmuseum

Berlin's top tourist attraction, the **Pergamonmuseum** (Map p318; ☎266 424 242; www.smb.museum; Am Kupfergraben 5; adult/concession €8/4; ◷10am-6pm Fri-Wed, to 9pm Thu; ▯100, ▣Hackescher Markt, Friedrichstrasse) opens up a fascinating window onto the ancient world. Completed in 1930, the palatial three-wing complex presents a rich feast of classical sculpture and monumental architecture from Greece, Rome, Babylon and the Middle East in three collections: the Collection of Antiquities, the Museum of Near Eastern Antiquities and the Museum of Islamic Art. Most of the pieces were excavated and spirited to Berlin by German archaeologists around the turn of the 20th century.

Antikensammlung

The undisputed highlight of the Antikensammlung (Collection of Antiquities), which presents artworks from ancient Greece and Rome here and in the Altes Museum, is the massive **Pergamonaltar** (Pergamon Altar). The Greek marble shrine was built during the reign of King Eumenes II (197–59 BC) in today's Bergama in Turkey. Its pedestal was once decorated with a brightly painted sculpted frieze showing the gods locked in epic battle with the giants; remaining sections of the frieze have been reassembled on the exhibit hall's walls. The anatomical detail, the emotional intensity and the dramatic composition of the figures show Hellenic art at its finest. To see the actual sacrificial altar, climb up the steep staircase to a colonnaded courtyard where another frieze depicts episodes from the life of Telephos, Pergamon's mythical founder.

A small door to the right of the Pergamonaltar leads to the **Market Gate of Miletus** (2nd century AD). Merchants and customers once flooded through the splendid 17m-high gate into the bustling market square of this wealthy Roman trading

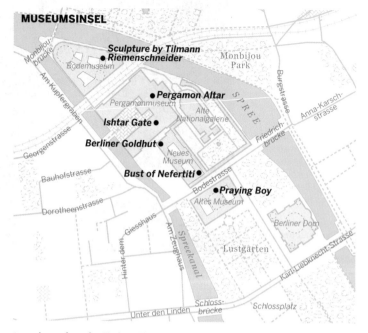

town in modern-day Turkey. The richly decorated marble gate blends Greek and Roman design features and is the world's single largest monument ever to be reassembled in a museum.

Vorderasiatisches Museum

Step through the Gate of Miletus and travel back 800 years to yet another culture and civilisation: Babylon during the reign of King Nebuchadnezzar II (604–562 BC). You're now in the Museum of the Ancient Near East, where it's impossible not to be awed by the magnificence of the **Ishtar Gate**, the **Processional Way** leading up to it and the facade of the **king's throne hall**. All are sheathed in radiant blue glazed bricks and adorned with ochre reliefs of strutting lions, bulls and dragons representing Babylonian gods. They're so striking, you can almost imagine hearing the roaring and fanfare as the procession rolled into town.

Other treasures from the collection include the colossal statue of the weather god Hadad (775 BC, room 2) from Syria and the nearly 5000-year-old cone mosaic temple facade from Uruk (room 5).

Museum für Islamische Kunst

Top billing in the Museum of Islamic Art upstairs belongs to the facade from the **caliph's palace of Mshatta** (8th century, room 9) in today's Jordan, which was a gift to Kaiser Wilhelm II from Ottoman Sultan Abdul Hamid II. A masterpiece of early Islamic art, it depicts animals and mythical creatures frolicking peacefully amid a riot of floral motifs in an allusion to the Garden of Eden.

Other rooms feature fabulous ceramics, carvings, glasses and other artistic objects as well as the bright turquoise 11th-century **prayer niche** from a mosque in Konya, Turkey, and an intricately patterned cedar-and-poplar ceiling from the Alhambra in Spain's Granada.

TAKE A BREAK

The Cafe Pergamon in the museum's north wing serves regional and international fare, plus coffee and home-made cakes. A few steps away, **Zwölf Apostel** (Map p314; www.12-apostel.de; Georgenstrasse 2; mains €8-16; ⬛M1, ⬛Friedrich-strasse, Friedrichstrasse) has lunchtime pizza specials at heavenly prices.

The Pergamonmu-seum was purpose-built between 1910 and 1930 to house the massive amounts of ancient art and archaeological treas-ures excavated by German scientists in such sites as Baby-lon, Assur, Uruk and Miletus. Designed by Alfred Messel, the building was constructed after his death by his close friend Ludwig Hoff-mann and badly pum-melled in WWII. Many objects were whisked to the Soviet Union as war booty but most were returned in 1958.

Egyptian courtyard at Neues Museum

Capping a tour of the museum is the **Aleppo Room** (room 16). Guests arriving in this richly painted, wood-panelled reception room would have had no doubt as to the wealth and power of its own-er, a Christian merchant in 17th-century Aleppo, Syria, which was an important trading town even back then. The beautiful, almost dizzying, decora-tions combine Islamic floral and geometric motifs with courtly scenes and Christian themes.

Neues Museum

David Chipperfield's reconstruction of the bombed-out **Neues Museum** (New Museum; Map p318; ✆266 424 242; www.smb.museum; adult/concession €10/5; ⊙10am-6pm Sun-Wed, to 8pm Thu-Sat; ⬛100, 200, ⬛Hackescher Markt) is the new home of the show-stopping **Ägyptisches Museum** (Egyptian Museum), headlined by Queen Nefertiti, and the equally enthralling **Museum für Vor- und Früh-geschichte** (Museum of Pre- and Early History). Like a giant jigsaw puzzle, the British star architect incorporated every original shard, scrap and brick he could find into the new structure. This brilliant blend of the historic and modern creates a dynamic space that beautifully juxtaposes massive stairwells, domed rooms, muralled halls and high ceilings. Mu-seum tickets are only valid for admission during a designated half-hour time slot. Skip the queue by buying advance tickets online.

Ägyptisches Museum

Most visitors come to the Neues Museum for an audience with Berlin's most beautiful woman, the 3330-year-old Egyptian queen **Nefertiti** – she of the long graceful neck and timeless good looks. The extremely well preserved sculpture was part of the treasure trove unearthed around 1912 by a Berlin expedition of archaeologists while sifting through the sands of Armana, the royal city built by Nefertiti's husband, King Akhenaten (r 1353–1336 BC).

Another famous work is the so-called Berlin **Green Head** – the bald head of a priest carved from smooth green stone. Created around 400 BC in the Late Egyptian Period, it shows Greek influence and is unusual in that it is not an actual portrait of a specific person but an idealised figure meant to exude universal wisdom and experience.

Museum für Vor- und Frühgeschichte

Within this collection, pride of place goes to the **Trojan antiquities** discovered by archaeologist Heinrich Schliemann in 1870 near Hisarlik in modern-day Turkey. However, most of the elaborate jewellery, ornate weapons and gold mugs on display are replicas since the originals became Soviet war booty after WWII and remain in Moscow to this day. Exceptions are the three humble-looking 4500-year-old silver jars that are proudly displayed in their own glass case.

One floor up the grand staircase, just past Nefertiti and the museum's precious **papyrus collection** (room 211), is another head turner: the bronze **Xanten Youth** (room 202), which served as a dumb waiter in a Roman villa. The massive sculpture of the **sun god Helios** in the south dome (room 203) also has its admirers.

The most fascinating item on the top floor is the 3000-year-old **Berliner Goldhut** (Berlin Gold Hat, room 205). Resembling a wizard's hat, it must indeed have struck the Bronze Age people as something magical. The entire cone is swathed in elaborate bands of astrological symbols believed to have helped priests calculate the movements of sun and moon and thus predict the best times for planting and harvesting. It's one of only four of its kind unearthed thus far.

Altes Museum

Schinkel pulled out all the stops for the grand neoclassical **Altes Museum** (Old Museum; Map p318; ☑266 424 242; www.smb.museum; Am Lustgarten; adult/concession €8/4; ☉10am-6pm Fri-Wed, to 8pm Thu; ☐100, 200, ☒Friedrichstrasse) which was the first exhibition space to open on Museumsinsel in 1830. A curtain of fluted columns gives way to a Pantheon-inspired rotunda that's the focal point of a prized antiquities collection. In the downstairs galleries, sculptures, vases, tomb reliefs and jewellery shed light on various facets of life in ancient Greece, while upstairs the focus is on the Etruscans and Romans. Top draws include the *Praying Boy* bronze sculpture, Roman silver vessels and portraits of Caesar and Cleopatra.

Greeks

This chronologically arranged exhibit spans all periods in ancient Greek art from the 10th to the 1st century BC. Among the oldest items is a collection of bronze helmets, but it's the monumental statues and elaborate vases that show the greatest artistry.

Among the first eye-catchers (in room 2) is the strapping **Kouros**, a nude male with a Mona Lisa smile and a great mop of hair. In the next gallery, all eyes are on the **Berlin Goddess**, a beautifully preserved funerary statue of a wealthy young woman in a fancy red dress. The finely carved **Seated Goddess of Tarent** (room 9) is another highlight. Ancient Greece's 'Next Top Model', though, is the **Praying Boy** (room 5), a life-size 3rd-century bronze statue from Rhodes that is the epitome of physical perfection.

MUSEUMSINSEL & ALEXANDERPLATZ MUSEUMSINSEL

BOWLED OVER

Looking like a baptismal font for giants, the massive granite basin outside the Altes Museum was designed by Karl Friedrich Schinkel and carved from a single slab by Christian Gottlieb Cantian. It was considered an artistic and technical feat back in the 1820s. The original plan to install it in the museum's rotunda had to be ditched when the bowl ended up being too massive to fit its dimensions. Almost 7m in diameter, it was carved in situ from a massive boulder in Brandenburg and transported via a custom-built wooden railway running to the Spree and from there by barge to Berlin.

For more 19th-century sculpture, visit Friedrichswerdersche Kirche (p83), one of six pillars of the National Gallery. The remaining five are the Alte Nationalgalerie, renowned for its romantic art; the Museum Berggruen with modernist works by Picasso and Klee; the Neue Nationalgalerie showcasing 20th-century art; the Sammlung Scharf-Gerstenberg Collection of surrealist art; and the Hamburger Bahnhof, which specialises in contemporary art.

The *Praying Boy* overlooks the soaring **rotunda** that's lidded by a grand coffered and frescoed ceiling. Light filters through a central skylight illuminating 20 large-scale statues representing a who's who among antique gods, including Nike, Zeus and Fortuna.

Etruscans & Romans

February 2011 marked the first time the Etruscan collection – one of the largest outside Italy – got airplay since 1939. Admire a circular shield from the grave of a warrior alongside amphorae, jewellery, coins and other items from daily life dating back as far as the 8th century BC. Learn about Etruscan language by studying the **tablet from Capua** and about funerary rites by examining the highly decorated **cinerary urns** and sarcophagi.

Ensuing rooms are dedicated to the Romans. There's fantastic sculpture, a superb 70-piece silver table service called the **Hildesheim Treasure** and busts of Roman leaders, including Caesar and Cleopatra. An adults-only **erotic cabinet** (behind a closed door, no less) brims with not so subtle depictions of satyrs, hermaphrodites and giant phalli.

Bodemuseum

Mighty and majestic, the **Bodemuseum** (Map p318; ☎266 424 242; www.smb.museum; Monbijoubrücke; adult/concession €8/4; ☉10am-6pm Tue, Wed & Fri-Sun, to 10pm Thu; ⓡHackescher Markt) has pushed against the northern tip of Museumsinsel like a proud ship's bow since 1904. The gloriously restored neo-baroque beauty presents several collections in mostly naturally lit galleries with marble floors and wood-panelled ceilings.

The building was designed by Ernst von Ihne and originally named Kaiser-Friedrich-Museum before being renamed for its first director, Wilhelm von Bode, in 1956. It's a beautifully proportioned architectural composition built around a central axis. Sweeping staircases, interior courtyards, frescoed ceilings and marble floors give the museum the grandeur of a palace.

The tone is set in the grand domed entrance hall where visitors are greeted by Andreas Schlüter's monumental sculpture of Great Elector Friedrich Wilhelm on horseback. From here head straight to the central Italian Renaissance–style basilica where all eyes are on colourfully glazed terracotta sculpture by Luca della Robbia. This leads to a smaller domed, rococo-style hall with marble statues of Frederick the Great and his generals. The galleries radiate out from both sides of this axis and continue upstairs.

Skulpturensammlung

The majority of rooms showcase the Bode's Sculpture Collection, which British Museum director Neil MacGregor hailed as 'the most comprehensive display of European sculpture anywhere'. Works here span the arc of artistic creativity from the early Middle Ages to the late 18th century, with a special focus on the Italian Renaissance. There are priceless masterpieces like Donatello's **Pazzi Madonna**, Giovanni Pisano's **Man of Sorrows** relief, and the portrait busts of Desiderio da Settignano. Staying on the ground floor, you can cruise from the Italians to the Germans when admiring the 12th-century **Gröninger Empore**, a church gallery from a former monastery that is considered a major work of the Romanesque period.

Most of the German sculptures, though, are upstairs, with an entire room dedicated to late-Gothic master carver Tilman Riemenschneider. Highlights here include the exquisite **St Anne and Her Three Husbands** as well as the **Four Evangelists**. In the next room, you can compare Riemenschneider's emotiveness to his contemporaries Hans Multscher and Nicolaus Gerhaert van Leyden. The monumental **knight-saints** from the period of the Thirty Years' War are another impressive standout on this floor.

Museum für Byzantische Kunst

Before breaking for coffee at the elegant cafe, pop back down to the ground floor where the Museum of Byzantine Art takes up just a few rooms off the grand domed foyer. Its focus lies on western Roman and Byzantine art from the 3rd to the 15th century. The elaborate Roman sarcophagi, the ivory carvings and the mosaic icons collectively reveal the high level of artistry in these early days of Christianity.

Münzsammlung

Coin collectors will get a kick out of the Numismatic Collection on the 2nd floor. With half a million coins – and counting – it's one of the largest of its kind in the world, even if only a small fraction can be displayed at one time. The oldest farthing is from the 7th century BC and displayed in a special case alongside the smallest, largest, fattest and thinnest coins.

MUSEUMSINSEL & ALEXANDERPLATZ MUSEUMSINSEL

THE MYSTERY OF PRIAM'S TREASURE

Heinrich Schliemann (1822–90) was not a particularly careful or skilled archaeologist but he was certainly one of the luckiest. Obsessed with the idea of uncovering Homer's Troy, he hit the mother lode in 1873 near Hissarlik in today's Turkey, putting paid to the belief that the town mentioned in the *Iliad* was mere myth. He also famously unearthed a hoard of gold and silver vessels, vases and jewellery, which he believed had once belonged to King Priam. The fact that it later turned out to be a good thousand years older than Homer's Troy doesn't make the find any less spectacular.

Schliemann illegally smuggled the cache to Berlin, had to pay a fine to the Ottoman Empire and eventually donated it to Berlin's ethnological museum. In a strange twist of fate, the treasure was carted off after WWII as war booty by the Soviets, who remained mum about its whereabouts until 1993. It remains at the Pushkin Museum in Moscow to this day, leaving only replicas in Berlin.

THE LUSTGARDEN

The patch of green fronting the Altes Museum has seen almost as many makeovers as Madonna. It started as a royal kitchen garden and became a military exercise ground before being turned into a pleasure garden by Schinkel. The Nazis held mass rallies here, the East Germans ignored it. Restored to its Schinkel-era appearance, it's now a favourite resting spot for sunbathers and foot-weary tourists.

The banker JHW Wagener was an avid collector of art and a generous man who, in 1861, bequeathed his entire collection of 262 paintings to the Prussian state to form the basis of a national gallery. Just one year later, William I commissioned Friedrich August Stüler to design a suitable museum. He came up with the Alte Nationalgalerie, an imposing templelike structure perched on a pedestal and fronted by a curtain of Corinthian columns. The entrance is reached via a sweeping double staircase crowned by a statue of King Friedrich Wilhelm IV on horseback.

Dome and staircase, Bodemuseum (p100)

Alte Nationalgalerie

The **Alte Nationalgalerie** (Old National Gallery; Map p318; ☎266 424 242; www.smb.museum; Bodestrasse 1-3; adult/concession €8/4; ⊙10am-6pm Fri-Wed, to 10pm Thu; ☐100, 200, ☒Hackescher Markt) shows first-rate 19th-century European art. It was a tumultuous century that saw profound changes in society. Artists reacted in different ways. While German Romantics like Caspar David Friedrich sought solace in nature, the epic canvases of Adolf Menzel and Franz Krueger glorified moments in Prussian history, and the impressionists focused on aesthetics and beauty.

Johann Gottfried Schadow's **Statue of Two Princesses** and a bust of Johann Wolfgang von Goethe are standout sculptures on the ground floor. In the next galleries, Adolf Menzel gets the star treatment, look for his famous **A Flute Concert of Frederick the Great at Sanssouci**, showing the king playing the flute at Potsdam palace.

The 2nd floor shows impressionist paintings by such famous Frenchmen as Monet, Degas, Cezanne, Renoir and Manet, whose **In the Conservatory** is considered a masterpiece. Among the Germans, there's Arnold Böcklin's **Isle of Death** and several canvases by Max Liebermann.

Romantics rule the top floor with Caspar David Friedrich's mystical landscapes as well as the Gothic fantasies of Karl Friedrich Schinkel. Also look for key works by Carl Blechen and portraits by Philip Otto Runge and Carl Spitzweg.

TOP SIGHTS
MUSEUMSINSEL

◉ SIGHTS

◉ Alexanderplatz

MARIENKIRCHE   CHURCH

Map p318 (www.marienkirche-berlin.de; Karl-Liebknecht-Strasse 8; ⊙10am-6pm; 🚌100, 200, ⓇHackescher Markt, Alexanderplatz) This Gothic brick gem has welcomed worshippers since the 13th century, making it one of Berlin's oldest surviving churches. A faded *Dance of Death* fresco inspired by the plague of 1486 in the vestibule leads to a relatively plain interior enlivened by elaborate epitaphs and a baroque alabaster pulpit by Andreas Schlüter (1703).

NEPTUNBRUNNEN   FOUNTAIN

Map p318 (ⓈAlexanderplatz, ⓇAlexanderplatz) This elaborate fountain was designed by Reinhold Begas in 1891 and depicts Neptune holding court over a quartet of buxom beauties symbolising the rivers Rhine, Elbe, Oder and Vistula. Kids gets a kick out of the water-squirting turtle, seal, crocodile and snake.

ROTES RATHAUS   HISTORIC BUILDING

Map p318 (Rathausstrasse 15; ⊙closed to the public; ⓈAlexanderplatz, Klosterstrasse, ⓇAlexanderplatz) The hulking Rotes Rathaus is the office of Berlin's Senate and governing mayor. The moniker 'red', by the way, was inspired by the colour of its bricks and not (necessarily) the political leanings of its occupants. The structure blends Italian Renaissance elements with northern German brick architecture and is framed by a terracotta frieze that illustrates milestones in Berlin history until 1871.

SEALIFE BERLIN   AQUARIUM

Map p318 (www.visitsealife.com; Spandauer Strasse 3; adult/child €17.50/12.50; ⊙10am-7pm, last admission 6pm; 🚌100, 200, ⓇHackescher Markt, Alexanderplatz) Sharks dart, moray eels lurk and spidercrabs crawl in this small but entertaining aquarium where crowd favourites include smile-inducing seahorses, ethereal jellyfish, Ophira the Octopus and an ocean tank patrolled by eagle rays. Visits conclude with a slow lift ride through the **Aquadom**, a 16m-tall cylindrical tropical fish tank that can be previewed for free from the lobby of the Radisson Blu Hotel.

All in all, some 5000 creatures inhabit 35 tanks as well as an interactive rock pool where you can enjoy close encounters with starfish and crabs. All labelling is in English and German. The website has an online booking function, the occasional ticket deal and discounted combination tickets with

MUSEUMSINSEL & ALEXANDERPLATZ SIGHTS

◉ TOP SIGHTS
FERNSEHTURM

No matter where you are in Berlin, simply look up and chances are that you will see the Fernsehturm (TV Tower). Germany's tallest structure, which is as iconic to the city as the Eiffel Tower is to Paris, has been soaring 368m high since 1969 (including the antenna). Come early to beat the queue for the lift to the panorama platform at 203m, where views are stunning on clear days. Pinpoint city landmarks from here or from the lovably stuffy cafe, which makes one revolution in 30 minutes.

The tower was supposed to demonstrate the GDR's strength and technological prowess but became a bit of a laughing stock when it turned out that, when struck by the sun, the steel sphere below the antenna produces the reflection of a giant cross. And this coming from a country where atheism was the new religion! West Berliners gleefully dubbed the phenomenon 'the Pope's revenge'.

Holders of VIP tickets, early-bird tickets and late-night tickets, which must be prepurchased online and printed out, can jump the queue.

DON'T MISS...

➡ Sunset cocktails with a view

PRACTICALITIES

➡ Map p318

➡ www.tv-turm.de

➡ Panoramastrasse 1a

➡ adult/child €12/7.50, VIP tickets €19.50/11.50

➡ ⊙9am-midnight Mar-Oct, from 10am Nov-Feb

➡ ⓈAlexanderplatz, ⓇAlexanderplatz

Madame Tussauds (p82) and the Legoland Discovery Centre (p114).

LOXX MINIATUR WELTEN BERLIN MUSEUM

Map p318 (www.loxx-berlin.de; Grunerstrasse 20, 3rd fl, Alexa shopping mall; adult/concession €12/11; ⏲10am-8pm Apr–mid-Oct, to 7pm mid-Oct–Mar, last admission 1hr before closing; [S]Alexanderplatz, 🚆Alexanderplatz) If you want to see Dad turn into a little kid, take him to this huge model railway where digitally controlled trains zip around central Berlin en miniature. Landmarks from the Brandenburg Gate to the TV Tower have been recreated on a scale of 1:87; more are added all the time. Potsdamer Platz was 'under construction' when we visited.

Nikolaiviertel

NIKOLAIKIRCHE MUSEUM

Map p318 (www.stadtmuseum.de; Nikolaikirchplatz; adult/concession incl audioguide €5/3; ⏲10am-6pm; 🚌100, 200, [S]Alexanderplatz) The lofty late-Gothic Church of St Nicholas (1230) is Berlin's oldest surviving building and now a museum documenting the architecture and history of the church. Grab the free audioguide for the scoop on the octagonal baptismal font and the late-Gothic triumphal cross or find out why the building is nicknamed 'pantheon of prominent Berliners'. Getting buried here, by the way, cost a nobleman 80 thalers, an 'old person' 50 thalers.

Head up the gallery for close-ups of the organ, a sweeping view of the interior and a chance to listen to recorded church hymns.

MÄRKISCHES MUSEUM MUSEUM

Map p318 (www.stadtmuseum.de; Am Köllnischen Park 5; adult/concession €5/3; ⏲10am-6pm Tue-Sun; [S]Märkisches Museum) This old-school history museum is a rewarding stop for anyone keen on learning how the tiny trading village of Berlin-Cölln evolved into today's metropolis. Official documents, weapons, sculptures and objects from daily life are thematically arranged, often in opulent historic rooms such as the Gothic chapel and the Great Hall.

TOP SIGHTS
DDR MUSEUM

How did regular East German Joes and Janes spend their day-to-day lives? The 'touchy-feely' DDR Museum does an entertaining job at pulling back the iron curtain on an extinct society. In hands-on fashion, you'll learn how, under socialism, kids were put through collective potty training, engineers earned little more than farmers and everyone, it seems, went on nudist holidays. You get to rummage through schoolbags, open drawers and cupboards or watch TV in a 1970's living room. It's not only kids who love squeezing behind the wheel of a Trabant (Trabi) car for a virtual drive through a concrete-slab housing estate.

The more sinister sides of life in the GDR are also addressed, including chronic supply shortages, surveillance by the Stasi (secret police) and the SED party power monopoly. You can stand in a recreated prison cell or imagine what it was like to be in the cross hairs of a Stasi officer by sitting on the victim's chair in a tiny, windowless interrogation room.

For a literal taste of the GDR, drop by the museum restaurant to try a *Grilletta*, *Ketwurst* or *Broiler*, as burger, hot dogs and chicken were called in East Germany.

DON'T MISS...

- Trabi ride
- Stasi interrogation room
- *Grilletta* in the restaurant

PRACTICALITIES

- GDR Museum
- Map p318
- ☎847 123 731
- www.ddr-museum.de
- Karl-Liebknecht-Strasse 1
- adult/concession €6/4
- ⏲10am-8pm Sun-Fri, to 10pm Sat
- 👪
- 🚌100, 200, 🚆Hackescher Markt

THE BRAVE WOMEN OF ROSENSTRASSE

Rosenstrasse is a small, quiet and nondescript street where, in 1943, one of the most courageous acts of civilian defiance against the Nazis took place. It was at Nos 2–4, outside a Jewish welfare office, where hundreds of local women gathered in freezing rain in the middle of winter. They all had one thing in common: they were Christians whose Jewish husbands had been locked up inside for deportation to Auschwitz. Until that time, Jews married to non-Jewish Germans had enjoyed a certain degree of protection – but no more. 'Give us our husbands back', the women shouted – unarmed, unorganised and leaderless but with one voice. When the police threatened to shoot them, they shouted even louder. It took several weeks, but eventually they were heard. Propaganda minister Joseph Goebbels personally ordered the release of every single prisoner.

Today a pale-pink sandstone memorial called **Block der Frauen** (Block of Women; Map p318; Rosenstrasse; S Alexanderplatz, R Hackescher Markt, Alexanderplatz) by the late Jewish-German artist Inge Hunzinger marks the site of the building while information pillars provide further background. The incident was movingly recounted in Margarethe von Trotta's 2003 feature film *Rosenstrasse*.

Scale models help visualise the city's physical growth. Crowd favourites include the 19th-century *Kaiserpanorama*, basically a 3D slide show that was a form of mass entertainment back then. A good time to visit is around 3pm on Sundays when the historic mechanical musical instruments are launched on their cacophonous journey (adult/concession €2/1).

The museum building itself, by the way, is a hotchpotch of replicas of actual buildings in the surrounding region of Brandenburg. The tower, for instance, is modelled after that of the bishop's palace in Wittstock, while St Catherine's Church in Brandenburg town inspired the Gothic gables. A copy of the Roland statue, a medieval symbol of civic liberty and freedom, guards the museum entrance.

EPHRAIM-PALAIS   MUSEUM

Map p318 (www.stadtmuseum.de; Poststrasse 16; adult/concession €5/3; ⊙10am-6pm Tue & Thu-Sun, noon-8pm Wed; S Klosterstrasse) Once the residence of the court jeweller and coin minter Veitel Heine Ephraim, this pretty, pint-sized 1766 town palace now presents changing exhibits focusing on aspects of Berlin's artistic and cultural legacy. It's hard to tell that this building is in fact a replica, the original having been destroyed during the construction of the Mühlendamm bridge in 1935.

Only the curved rococo facade with its gilded ironwork balconies and sculptural ornamentation was saved and stored in what later became West Berlin. In 1984, it

was returned to East Berlin so that it could be used in the construction of the Nikolaiviertel. Inside, architectural highlights include the oval staircase and the *Schlüterdecke*, an ornate ceiling, on the 1st floor.

FREE KNOBLAUCHHAUS   MUSEUM

Map p318 (www.stadtmuseum.de; Poststrasse 23; ⊙10am-6pm Tue & Thu-Sun, noon-8pm Wed; S Klosterstrasse) The oldest residential building in the Nikolaiviertel (1761) is the former home of the Knoblauch family, which included politicians, architects and patrons of the arts who enjoyed tea and talk with Schinkel, Schadow and other luminaries of the day. The period rooms impart a sense of how the well-to-do lived, dressed and made their money during the early 19th-century Biedermeier period.

ZILLE MUSEUM   MUSEUM

Map p318 (www.heinrich-zille-museum.de; Propststrasse 11; adult/concession €6/5; ⊙11am-7pm Apr-Oct, to 6pm Nov-Mar; S Klosterstrasse) Like no other artist of his time, Heinrich Zille (1859–1929) managed to capture the hardships of working-class life in the age of industrialisation with empathy and humour. This small private museum in the Nikolaiviertel preserves his legacy with a selection of drawings, photographs and graphic art. There's also an interesting video on his life, though in German only.

Afterwards, you can channel Zille's ghost over a beer at the nearby **Zum Nussbaum** (Map p318) pub, his rather authentically re-created favourite watering hole.

HANF MUSEUM MUSEUM

Map p318 (☎242 4827; www.hanfmuseum.de; Mühlendamm 5; adult/concession €4.50/3; ⏰10am-8pm Tue-Fri, noon-8pm Sat & Sun; [S]Klosterstrasse, Märkisches Museum) One of only four in the world devoted to the subject of hemp, the small Hemp Museum gives hobby botanists a chance to expand their knowledge about this versatile plant by studying its cultural, medicinal and religious significance. There are exhibits about the commercial uses of hemp as well as displays on the discussion about the legalisation of marijuana.

Schlossplatz

BERLINER DOM CHURCH

Map p318 (Berlin Cathedral; ☎2026 9110; www.berlinerdom.de; Am Lustgarten; adult/concession €7/4; ⏰9am-8pm Mon-Sat, noon-8pm Sun Apr-Sep, to 7pm Oct-Mar; 🚌100, 200, 🚆Hackescher Markt) Pompous yet majestic, the Italian Renaissance-style former royal court church (1905) does triple duty as house of worship, museum and concert hall. Inside it's gilt to the hilt and outfitted with a lavish marble-and-onyx altar, a 7269-pipe Sauer organ and elaborate royal sarcophagi. Climb up the 267 steps to the gallery for glorious city views.

For more dead royals, albeit in less extravagant coffins, drop down below to the crypt. Skip the cathedral museum unless you're interested in the building's construction. The sanctuary has great acoustics and is often used for concerts, sometimes played on the huge and famous Sauer organ.

Admission to the Dom is free during the short prayer services at noon Monday to Saturday and 6pm Monday to Friday. The service at 6pm on Thursday is in English. Last paid admission is one hour before closing.

STAATSRATSGEBÄUDE HISTORIC BUILDING

Map p318 (Schlossplatz 1; 🚌100, 200, [S]Hausvogteiplatz) The hulking 1960 State Council Building is the only remaining Schlossplatz structure from the GDR era. It integrates an arched portal from the demolished Berlin City Palace from whose balcony Karl Liebknecht proclaimed a socialist republic on 9 November 1918.

The foyer sports a kaleidoscopic glass window by the artist Walter Womacka that depicts the 'historical evolution' of the GDR from its 1918–19 revolutionary days to the founding of the state in 1949. The portraits in the centre show Liebknecht and Rosa

BERLIN CITY PALACE 2.0

Nothing of today's Schlossplatz evokes memories of the **Berliner Stadtschloss** (Berlin City Palace), the grand residence where the Prussian royal family made its home for 500 years. Despite international protests, the East German government razed the barely war-damaged structure in 1951 and replaced it with a multipurpose hall called **Palast der Republik** (Palace of the Republic). Behind its orange-tinted mirrored facade, the East German parliament hammered out policy and common folk came to hear Harry Belafonte sing or to party on New Year's Eve. By all accounts, the interior was both impressive and a study in ostentation, exemplified by the foyer with its hundreds of dangling lamps, resulting in the nickname 'Erich's Lampenladen' (Erich's lamp shop, the Erich in question being East Germany's leader, Erich Honecker).

After the fall of the Wall, the Palast closed instantly because of asbestos contamination. Years of debate resulted in the demolition of the behemoth. Then came the plan to build a replica of the Prussian palace shell – but with a modern interior. To be called **Humboldtforum**, it would be the new home of the Museum of Ethnology and the Museum of Asian Art – both currently in Museen Dahlem (p213) – as well as a library. Alas, it all comes with a price tag of €700 million, no small change in times of fiscal belt-tightening.

In the meantime, though, the oddly shaped **Humboldt-Box** (☎0180 503 0707; www.humboldt-box.com; Schlossplatz; adult/concession €4/2.50; 10am-8pm; 🚌100, 200, 🚆Alexanderplatz, Hackescher Markt) on Schlossplatz offers a sneak preview of the planned reconstruction by displaying teaser exhibits from each future resident along with a fantastically detailed model of the historic city centre. There are great views of Museumsinsel and the construction grounds from the top-floor terrace. Nearby, a small sample section of the historic palace facade provides a hint as to what it'll look like upon completion.

Luxemburg, cofounders of the German Communist Party. Somewhat ironically, the building is now used by a private international business school financed by such blue-chip corporations as Bayer, Deutsche Bank and Siemens.

NEUER MARSTALL HISTORIC BUILDING

Map p318 (Breite Strasse; 🚌100, 200, ⓈSpittelmarkt) The 1901 neo-baroque Neuer Marstall (New Stables) by Ernst von Ihne once sheltered royal horses and carriages. In 1918, revolutionaries hatched plans to topple the Prussian monarchy here; a GDR-era bronze relief on the (north) facade facing Schlossplatz shows Karl Liebknecht proclaiming a German socialist republic that same year. The building now hosts concerts of the **Hochschule für Musik Hanns Eisler**, a prestigious music academy.

The Neuer Marstall is an extension of the 1670 **Alter Marstall** (Old Stables), which is Berlin's oldest baroque building. It rubs shoulders with the **Ribbeckhaus**, the city's only surviving Renaissance structure. Both harbour public libraries.

🍴 EATING

With its abundant fast-food outlets, Alexanderplatz itself is not exactly a foodie haven, although there is a respectable self-service cafeteria in the Galeria Kaufhof. Otherwise, try the food court in the Alexa mall, the traditional German restaurants in the Nikolaiviertel or head straight to the Scheunenviertel for better options.

🍴 Alexanderplatz

DOLORES CALIFORNIAN €

Map p318 (🕿2809 9597; www.dolores-online .de; Rosa-Luxemburg-Strasse 7; burrito €4-6; ⊙11.30am-10pm Mon-Fri, 1-10pm Sun; 🛜🖊; 🚌100, 200, ⓈAlexanderplatz, 🚉Alexanderplatz) Dolores is a bastion of California-style burritos – fresh, authentic and priced to help you stay on budget. Select your preferred combo of marinated meats (the lime coriander chicken is yummy) or tofu, rice, beans, veggies, cheese and salsa, and the cheerful staff will build it on the spot. Great homemade lemonade, too.

ZUR LETZTEN INSTANZ GERMAN €€

Map p318 (🕿242 5528; www.zurletzteninstanz .de; Waisenstrasse 14-16; mains €9-18; ⓈKlosterstrasse) Oozing folksy Old Berlin charm, this rustic eatery has been an enduring hit since 1621 and has fed everyone from Napoleon to Beethoven to Angela Merkel. Although now tourist-geared, food quality is still pretty high when it comes to such local rib-stickers as *Grillhaxe* (grilled pork knuckle) and *Bouletten* (meat patties).

HOFBRÄUHAUS BERLIN GERMAN €€

Map p318 (www.berlin-hofbraeu.de; Karl-Liebknecht-Strasse 30; mains €4-18; ⊙10am-2am Thu-Sat, to 1am Sun-Wed; 🚌100, 200, ⓈAlexanderplatz, 🚉Alexanderplatz) A favourite with coach tourists and field-tripping teens, this giant beer hall serves the same litre-sized mugs of beer and big plates of rib-sticking German fare as the Munich original. A brass band and dirndl- and lederhosen-clad servers add further faux authenticity. The lunch specials for €5 are a steal.

RESTAURANT WANDEL INTERNATIONAL €

Map p318 (🕿2404 7230; www.wandel-berlin.de; Bernhard-Weiss-Strasse 6; ⊙7am-7pm Mon-Fri; ⓈAlexanderplatz, 🚉Alexanderplatz) Prices are hard to beat in this stylish cafeteria where German-French-Asian-peppered mains top out at €4.90. The place drowns with office drones at lunchtime, but is a relaxed spot just before and after the rush. Waist-watchers will welcome the salad buffet. Respectable coffee to boot.

.HBC INTERNATIONAL €€€

Map p318 (🕿2434 2920; www.hbc-berlin.de; Karl-Liebknecht-Strasse 9; mains €15-25; ⊙dinner

START U-BAHN STATION
KLOSTERSTRASSE
END NIKOLAIVIERTEL
DISTANCE 1.3KM
DURATION ONE HOUR

Neighbourhood Walk
Back to the Roots

This tour charts Berlin history from its medieval beginnings to the early 20th century. From U-Bahn station Klosterstrasse walk east on Parochialstrasse. Note the historic restaurant **1 Zur Letzten Instanz**, then turn left on Littenstrasse and stop at a crude 8m-long pile of boulders and bricks. It's what's left of **2 Stadtmauer**, the wall built around 1250 to protect the city's first settlers from marauders. Looming above is the monumental **3 Justizgebäude Littenstrasse**, a 1912 courthouse with a graceful art nouveau foyer.

On your left, the Gothic **4 Franziskaner Klosterkirche** (Franciscan Monastery Church) was once a prestigious school for such luminaries as Schinkel and Bismarck and is now used for outdoor art exhibits and concerts. Follow Littenstrasse north, turn left on Grunerstrasse and left again on Klosterstrasse. The big building on your right is **5 Altes Stadthuas** (Old City Hall), whose distinctive 87m-high domed tower is crowned by the goddess Fortuna. Keep

going on Klosterstrasse to the 17th-century **6 Parochialkirche**, which manages to be both graceful and monumental at once. Designed by the same architect as Schloss Charlottenburg, it burnt out in WWII and, though restored, deliberately still reveals the scars of war.

Turn right on Stralauer Strasse, which leads to **7 Molkenmarkt**, Berlin's oldest square and one-time thriving marketplace. The ornate building at No 2 is the historic **8 Alte Münze**, the old mint turned event location. Reichsmark, GDR Mark, Deutsche Mark and even euro coins were all minted here until 2006. Note the decorative frieze depicting the evolution of metallurgy and coin minting.

Across the street, the **9 Nikolaiviertel** may look medieval, but don't be fooled: it's a product of the 1980s, built by the East German government to celebrate Berlin's 750th birthday. The 1230 Nikolaikirche and a handful of small museums are worth a quick look.

Mon-Sat; 🚌100, 200, Ⓢ Alexanderplatz, Ⓡ Alexanderplatz) This bar-gallery-concert-party venue in the former Hungarian culture centre also has a well-regarded restaurant which lures adventurous eaters with exciting flavour pairings. Meat and fish sharing a plate (think pork belly with scallops or shrimp-stuffed quail) are no rarity and usually harmonise beautifully. Soak up the charmingly socialist retro ambience while glimpsing the TV Tower through the picture windows.

✕ Nikolaiviertel

BRAUHAUS GEORGBRÄU GERMAN €€
Map p318 (www.georgbraeu.de; Spreeufer 4; mains €10-14; Ⓢ Alexanderplatz, Ⓡ Alexanderplatz) Tourist-geared but cosy, this brewpub is the only place where you can guzzle the local St Georg pilsner. In winter the woodsy beer hall is perfect for tucking into hearty Berlin-style goulash or *Eisbein* (boiled pork knuckle), while in summer the riverside beer garden beckons.

BROOKLYN BEEF CLUB AMERICAN €€€
Map p318 (☑2021 5820; www.brooklynbeefclub.com; Köpenicker Strasse 92; mains €50-100; ☉dinner Mon-Sat; Ⓢ Märkisches Museum) You'll have a fine time spiking your cholesterol count with the flavourful, melt-in-your mouth Angus-certified meats served in this former Stasi hang-out turned classic American steakhouse. Blood-red walls, vaulted ceilings and historic black-and-white photographs bring *noir* flair to the rear room, while the more contemporary one in front is dominated by a bar stocked with some 160 whisky varieties.

STEELSHARK JAPANESE €€
Map p318 (☑2576 2461; www.steelshark.de; Propststrasse 1; nigiri €1.60-3.50, platters €3.50-15; ☉11.30am-10pm Mon-Sat, 3-10pm Sun; Ⓢ Alexanderplatz, Ⓡ Alexanderplatz) At this hole-in-the-wall tucked into a hidden corner in the Nikolaiviertel, all morsels are carefully assembled and feature thick cuts of fresh fish and perfectly cooked rice. The selection is mostly classic, but there's also 'Italian-style sushi' featuring rolls filled with such things as marinated artichokes, mozzarella, rucola and figs. Best of all: it delivers. Order by phone or online.

GRILLWALKERS: MOBILE WURST

At first they were only on Alexanderplatz, but now they've spread into other parts of town – the Grillwalkers or, what we cheekily call 'Self-Contained Underpaid Bratwurst Apparatus', aka SCUBA. Picture this: young guys with a mobile gas grill strapped around their bellies where sizzling bratwursts wait for customers. At €1.35 a pop, squished into a roll and slathered with mustard or ketchup, they're going fast.

🍷 DRINKING & NIGHTLIFE

.HBC CLUB, LIVE MUSIC
Map p318 (☑2434 2930; www.hbc-berlin.de; Karl-Liebknecht-Strasse 9; ☉Mon-Sat; 🚌100, 200, Ⓢ Alexanderplatz, Ⓡ Alexanderplatz) In the rambling former Hungarian Culture Center, this multitasking venue strives to put the finger on the pulse of current creative trends in art, music, film, literature, fashion and performance. This translates into a mind-bogglingly eclectic schedule of parties, screenings, concerts, exhibits and genre-defying events held in the foyer, the bar, the old cinema or the 'secret' Pink Room.

GOLDEN GATE CLUB
Map p318 (Schicklerstrasse 4; cover €4-8; ☉from midnight Thu-Sat; Ⓢ Jannowitzbrücke) If you yearn for the rough sound and aesthetics of '90s Berlin, you'll break into a sweaty flashback at this grimy club in a graffiti-slathered crumbler beneath the Jannowitzbrücke train tracks. Dedicated hedonists, dressed down for business, slam the dance floor for 24-hour technofests. Cool crowd, great music, scary toilets. Best time: Friday in the am.

WEEKEND CLUB
Map p318 (www.week-end-berlin.de; Am Alexanderplatz 5; ☉Thu-Sat; Ⓢ Alexanderplatz, Ⓡ Alexanderplatz) This house and electro den has seen hipper times, but thanks to its unbeatable location with panoramic views of Alexanderplatz (in summer from the rooftop terrace) it's still a popular destination for an international cadre of shiny, happy hotties. Prices are hefty, door is middling.

BEARMANIA

The bear has graced Berlin's official flag since 1280, so it's only fitting that the city also has an official 'city bear'. The honour currently falls to a female brown bear named Schnute, who resides with her daughter Maxi in an **open-air bear pit and enclosure** (Map p318; ⏲from 7.30am May-Sep, 8am Oct-Apr; [S]Märkisches Museum) in the Köllnischer Park behind the Märkisches Museum. The ladies theoretically receive visitors from 7.30am, although there's no guarantee they'll actually show up, especially in winter when they seem to prefer hanging out in their enclosure. Brown bears have made their home here since 1939 after four of them were donated to the Märkisches Museum. Berlin even celebrates the 'Day of the Berlin Bear' on 22 March. For more information, see the website of the Friends of the Berlin Bears (www.berliner-baerenfreunde.de).

☆ ENTERTAINMENT

THEATERDISCOUNTER THEATRE

Map p318 (☎2809 3062; www.theaterdiscounter.de; Klosterstrasse 44; [S]Klosterstrasse) Now in permanent digs on the 2nd floor of the former East Berlin telephone exchange, this indie troupe constantly pushes the envelope when it comes to theatrical format. Plays have minimal rehearsal times, a rapid turnover and tickets are cheap. Look here for brand-new experimental plays.

🛍 SHOPPING

GALERIA KAUFHOF DEPARTMENT STORE

Map p318 (www.galeria-kaufhof.de; Alexanderplatz 9; ⏲9.30am-8pm Mon-Wed, to 10pm Thu-Sat; [S]Alexanderplatz, [R]Alexanderplatz) A total renovation by John P Kleihues turned this former GDR-era department store into a retail cube fit for the 21st century, complete with a glass-domed light court and a sleek travertine skin that glows green at night. There's little you won't find on the five football-field-sized floors, including a gourmet supermarket on the ground floor.

AUSBERLIN GIFTS, SOUVENIRS

Map p318 (www.ausberlin.de; Karl-Liebknecht-Strasse 17; 🚌100, 200, [S]Alexanderplatz, [R]Alexanderplatz) 'Made in Berlin' is the motto of this low-key store where you can pick up the latest BPitch or Ostgut CD, witty Kotty D'Azur T-shirts by Muschi Kreuzberg, a Bar 25 pillow and all sorts of other hot-label mementoes designed right here in this fair city.

ALEXA SHOPPING CENTRE

Map p318 (www.alexacentre.com; Grunerstrasse 20; ⏲10am-9pm Mon-Sat; [S]Alexanderplatz, [R]Alexanderplatz) Power shoppers love this XXL-sized mall that cuts a rose-hued presence near Alexanderplatz. The predictable range of high street retailers is here, plus a few more upmarket stores like Swarovski, Crumpler, Adidas Neo and Triumph. Good food court for a bite on the run.

Potsdamer Platz & Tiergarten

POTSDAMER PLATZ | KULTURFORUM | TIERGARTEN | DIPLOMATENVIERTEL

Neighbourhood Top Five

1 Feeling your spirit soar while studying an Aladdin's cave of Old Masters at the magnificent **Gemäldegalerie** (p116).

2 Getting lost amid the lawns, trees and leafy paths of the **Tiergarten park** (p125), followed by guzzling a cold one in a beer garden.

3 Stopping for coffee and people-watching beneath the magnificent canopy of the svelte glass-and-steel **Sony Center** (p113).

4 Learning about the brave people who stood up to the Nazis and often paid the ultimate price at the **Gedenkstätte Deutscher Widerstand** (p121).

5 Catching Europe's fastest lift to the **Panoramapunkt** (p114) to admire Berlin's impressive cityscape.

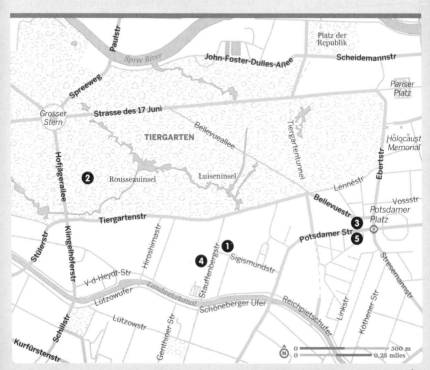

For more detail of this area, see Map p316 ➡

Lonely Planet's Top Tip

From July to September, the lovely thatch-roofed Teehaus im Englischen Garten (p125) presents free concerts at 4pm and 7pm every Saturday and Sunday.

✖ Best Places to Eat

➡ Restaurant Gropius (p125)

➡ Facil (p125)

➡ Joseph-Roth-Diele (p123)

For reviews, see p123 ➡

🍷 Best Places to Drink

➡ Victoriabar (p126)

➡ Solar (p125)

➡ Café am Neuen See (p125)

For reviews, see p125 ➡

◉ Best for Architecture

➡ Philharmonie (p120)

➡ Bauhaus Archiv (p122)

➡ Sony Center (p113)

For reviews, see p119 ➡

Explore: Potsdamer Platz & Tiergarten

Despite the name, Potsdamer Platz is not just a square but Berlin's newest quarter, born in the '90s from terrain once bifurcated by the Berlin Wall. A collaborative effort by the world's finest architects, it is a vibrant showcase of urban renewal. The area itself is rather compact and quickly explored if you don't linger in the shopping mall, have a restorative coffee in the Sony Center plaza, see Berlin from above from the Panoramapunkt or dive into German film history at the Museum für Film und Fernsehen.

At the nearby Kulturforum cultural complex, you can mingle with masters old and modern in five museums and take in a concert at the renowned Berliner Philharmonie, all master planned in the 1950s by architectural wizard Hans Scharoun. Further west, black limousines are a common sight in the Diplomatenviertel (Diplomatic Quarter), which is also distinguished by some fine contemporary architecture. And if your head is spinning after all that cultural stimulus, the leafy paths of the vast Tiergarten, Berlin's equivalent of New York's Central Park, will likely prove to be a restorative antidote.

Local Life

➡ **Museums** Berliners are passionate about art, and they especially love the blockbuster international exhibits that periodically land at the Neue Nationalgalerie (p119). When New York City's Museum of Modern Art came by, art devotees waited an average of three hours to score a ticket. Some even camped out overnight.

➡ **Concerts** Empty seats are a rare sight at the Berliner Philharmonie (p126), especially when Sir Simon Rattle swings the baton. The free lunchtime concerts lure plenty of onlookers, from students to tourists and desk-jockeys.

➡ **Tiergarten** When the sun is out, Berliners just want to get outdoors to the sweeping lawns, shady paths and romantic corners of the Tiergarten park, followed by a cold beer and pizza at the beer garden of Café am Neuen See (p125).

Getting There & Away

➡ **Bus** No 200 comes through from Zoologischer Garten and Alexanderplatz, M41 links the Hauptbahnhof with Kreuzberg and Neukölln via Potsdamer Platz, and the M29 comes in from Checkpoint Charlie.

➡ **S-Bahn** S1 and S2 link Potsdamer Platz with Unter den Linden and the Scheunenviertel.

➡ **U-Bahn** U2 stops at Potsdamer Platz and Mendelssohn–Bartholdy–Park.

BUENA VISTA IMAGES / LGETTY IMAGES ©

Potsdamer Platz 2.0 was built in the 1990s and is essentially a modern reinterpretation of the historic original. It's divided into three slices. South of Potsdamer Strasse, DaimlerCity is home to a large shopping mall, public art and high-profile entertainment venues. The Sony Center in the middle is the flashiest and most visitor-friendly of the trio with a central plaza canopied by a glass roof that erupts in a light show of changing colours after dark. Finally, there's the comparatively subdued Beisheim Center, whose design is an homage to classic American skyscrapers. The Ritz-Carlton Hotel, for instance, is modelled on the Rockefeller Center in New York City.

More than a decade after its completion, the new quarter has become an integral part of the city landscape. Up to 100,000 people barrel through its streets and squares daily, drawn by the shops of the Potsdamer Platz Arkaden mall, the roulette tables of the Spielbank Berlin, or the multiplex cinemas, including the all-English Cinestar at the Sony Center.

In February, when the Berlinale film festival comes to town, stars and starlets flock to glamorous movie premieres at the Theater am Potsdamer Platz.

DON'T MISS...

➡ Panoramapunkt
➡ Sony Center
➡ Berlin Wall remnants

PRACTICALITIES

➡ Map p316
➡ 🚌200, Ⓢ Potsdamer Platz, Ⓡ Potsdamer Platz

Sony Center

Designed by Helmut Jahn, the visually dramatic **Sony Center** (Map p316) is fronted by a 26-floor, glass-and-steel tower that's the highest building on Potsdamer Platz. It integrates rare relics from the prewar era, such as a section of the facade of the Hotel Esplanade (visible from Bellevuestrasse) and the opulent Kaisersaal, whose 75m move to its current location required some wizardly technology. The heart of the Sony Center, though, is a central plaza dramatically canopied by a tentlike glass roof with supporting beams radiating out like spokes of a bicycle. The plaza and its many cafes are great for hanging out and people-watching.

VIEW FROM THE TOP

Europe's fastest lift, **Panoramapunkt** (Map p316; ☑2593 7080; www.panoramapunkt.de; Potsdamer Platz 1; adult/concession €5.50/4; ☉10am-8pm, last ride 7.30pm, shorter hours in winter; ☐M41, 200, ⓈPotsdamer Platz, ⒭Potsdamer Platz) yo-yos up and down the red-brick postmodern Kollhof Building. From the viewing platform at a lofty 100m, a stunning panorama reveals the city landmarks. After savouring the views, study key moments in Potsdamer Platz history by visiting the exhibit, then relax over coffee at the on-site cafe.

WWII sucked all life out of Potsdamer Platz, which suffered 80% destruction and plunged into a coma before being bisected by the Berlin Wall in 1961. Today, a double row of cobblestones shows the course of the Wall, and a few Berlin Wall sections (Map p316) outside the Potsdamer Platz train station entrance feature explanatory texts about other memorial sites and future Wall-related projects. An original GDR border watchtower (Map p316) is just a short walk away on Erna-Berger-Strasse (off Stresemannstrasse).

Museum für Film und Fernsehen

From silent movies to sci-fi, the **Museum für Film und Fernsehen** (Map p316; ☑300 9030; www.deutsche-kinemathek.de; Potsdamer Strasse 2; adult/concession €6/4.50; ☉10am-6pm Tue, Wed & Fri-Sun, to 8pm Thu; ☐200, ⓈPotsdamer Platz, ⒭Potsdamer Platz) in the Sony Center charts major milestones in German film and broadcast history. Be sure to make use of the excellent free audioguide as you work your way through various themed galleries.

The tour kicks off with an appropriate sense of drama with a dizzying mirrored walkway that conjures visions of *The Cabinet of Dr Caligari*. Major themes include pioneers and early divas, silent-era classics such as Fritz Lang's *Metropolis*, Leni Riefenstahl's ground-breaking Nazi-era documentary *Olympia*, German exiles in Hollywood and post-WWII movies. Stealing the show as she did in real life, though, is femme fatale Marlene Dietrich whose glamour lives on through her original costumes, photographs and documents. The last gallery looks at East German films of the 1980s that foreshadowed the regime's downfall and also at the generation of postreunification film makers who had international success with movies addressing German 20th-century history, such as the Third Reich, domestic terrorism and the fall of the Berlin Wall.

Unless you're familiar with German TV, the **Fernsehmuseum** will probably be of less interest. Its centrepiece is the Hall of Mirrors where snippets from five decades of seminal TV shows in both Germanys are projected onto an 8m-high wall. Afterwards, head upstairs to access an archive of favourite shows at private viewing consoles. If you ever wondered what people were watching in East Germany or what *Star Trek* sounds like in German, this is your chance.

Legoland Discovery Centre

The world's first indoor **Legoland** (Map p316; ☑01805-6669 0110; www.legolanddiscoverycentre.de/berlin; Potsdamer Strasse 4; admission €16; ☉10am-7pm, last admission 6pm; ☐200, ⓈPotsdamer Platz, ⒭Potsdamer Platz) is a fantasy environment made entirely of those little coloured plastic building blocks. It's very cute but quite low-tech and best suited for kids aged three to eight. It's also pretty commercial, starting with an animated introductory film about the making of Lego bricks, which happens next door in the Lego Factory. Then children can build their own structures and test them for 'earthquake safety'.

More high-tech adventure stations include Ninjago, where they can channel their inner ninja when battling snakes and braving a laser labyrinth. Elsewhere, they can become a Merlin apprentice and 'fly' through a magical potion room. Other 'thrills' include the 4D cinema (with tactile special effects), a ride through the Dragon's Castle (top speed: 10km/h), and a medieval world inhabited by knights and dragons and outfitted with a 'torture-tickle chamber'. You can marvel at a Berlin in miniature at Miniland, which uses over two million Lego bricks to recreate major landmarks.

Check the website for ticket deals and combination tickets with SeaLife (p103) and Madame Tussauds (p82).

Weinhaus Huth & Daimler Contemporary

Looking a bit lost amid all the postmodern skyscrapers, the 1912 **Weinhaus Huth** (Map p316; Alte Potsdamer Strasse 5, Potsdamer Platz) was one of the first steel-frame buildings in town and the only Potsdamer Platz structure that survived WWII intact. On the top floor is the **Daimler Contemporary** (Map p316; ☎2594 1420; www.sammlung.daimler.com; 4th fl, Weinhaus Huth, Alte Potsdamer Strasse 5; admission free; 🕑11am-6pm; 🚌200, [S]Potsdamer Platz, 🚆Potsdamer Platz), a loft-style gallery showcasing first-rate international abstract, conceptual and minimalist art. Andy Warhol, Jonathan Monk – you never know who's on view. Ring the bell to be buzzed in.

Boulevard der Stars

Every February, celebs sashay down the red carpet to the Theater am Potsdamer Platz, the main venue of the Berlinale. To bring year-round glamour to the neighbourhood, Berlin now has its own version of Hollywood's Walk of Fame, the **Boulevard der Stars** (Boulevard of the Stars; Map p316; www.boulevard-der-stars-berlin.de; Potsdamer Strasse; 🕑24hr; 🚌200, [S]Potsdamer Platz, 🚆Potsdamer Platz). Several dozen brass stars embedded in the red asphalt carpet along the centre strip of Postdamer Strasse honour famous actors and directors from German film and TV. Some even achieved international fame, such as Marlene Dietrich, Werner Herzog, Romy Schneider and Armin Mueller-Stahl. Each star bears the engraved names, biographical data, profession and autograph of the honouree. Fans can sometimes be seen making a brass rubbing of the signature. Another gimmick are the 'star gazers' which provide a holographic image of the celebrity hovering above their brass star. You can even take a photograph through this special camera or have a photo taken with your favourite star. There are currently 61 stars, with new ones added all the time.

DaimlerCity Public Sculpture Tour

DaimlerCity is not only a postmodern urban landscape but also an exquisite outdoor gallery. Large-scale abstract sculptures by blue-chip artists like Keith Haring and Robert Rauschenberg explore the relationship between art and urban space and inject much-needed visual appeal into the otherwise fairly austere environment.

Start with Keith Haring's **Boxers**, near the corner of Eichhornstrasse and Postdamer Strasse. Two huge stick figures made of cut steel – one blue, one red – seem to punch each other out, although they may also be embracing each other. Walk south to Marlene-Dietrich-Platz to ponder Frank Stella's otherworldly **Prince Frederick Arthur of Homburg, General of Cav**. Made of white-silver aluminium, carbon and fibreglass, it explores the relationship of space, colour and form in a three-dimensional setting. Just beyond, in the middle of a pond, is Mark Di Suvero's **Galileo**, an abstract jumble of rusted steel T-beams assembled into a surprisingly fragile-looking sculpture.

You need to crane your neck to spot Auke de Vries's **Gelandet** (Landed) on the edge of the roof of the DaimlerServices building on Schellingstrasse (look for the square tower with the green top). Finally, north of here, on Fontaneplatz, Robert Rauschenberg's **Riding Bikes** consists of two recycled bicycles illuminated by multicoloured neon tubes, which reflects his decade-long approach to turn reality into art while creating as little wastage as possible.

STEFANO AMANTINI / SIME / 4CORNERS ©

TOP SIGHTS GEMÄLDEGALERIE

The Gemäldegalerie (Picture Gallery) ranks among the world's finest and most comprehensive collections of European art from the 13th to the 18th centuries. Its opening in a custom-built Kulturforum space in 1998 marked the happy reunion of a collection separated by the Cold War for half a century. Some works had remained at the Bodemuseum in East Berlin, the rest went on display in the West Berlin suburb of Dahlem. Today, about 1500 works span the arc of artistic vision over five centuries. Dutch and Flemish painters, including Rembrandt, are especially well represented, as are exponents of the Italian Renaissance. Another focus is on German artists from the late Middle Ages, and there's also a sprinkling of British, French and Spanish masters. Expect to feast your eyes on masterpieces by Titian, Goya, Botticelli, Holbein, Gainsborough, Canaletto, Hals, Rubens, Vermeer and other heavy hitters.

Rooms radiate out from the football-field-sized central foyer. The following overview highlights some of the key canvases, but you'll likely find your own favourites as you explore the dozens of galleries, many of them beautifully lit by muted daylight.

East Wing: German, Dutch & Flemish Masters

The exhibit kicks off with religious paintings from the Middle Ages but moves quickly to the Renaissance and works by two of the era's most famous artists: Albrecht Dürer and Lucas Cranach the Elder. A standout in room 2

DON'T MISS...

- Rembrandt Room (Room X)
- Amor Victorius (Room XIV)
- Dutch Proverbs (Room 7)
- Fountain of Youth (Room III)

PRACTICALITIES

- Map p316
- ☎266 424 242
- www.smb.museum/gg
- Matthäikirchplatz 8
- adult/concession €8/4
- 🕐10am-6pm Tue, Wed & Fri-Sun, to 10pm Thu
- 🚌M29, M41, 200, [S]Potsdamer Platz, 🚆Potsdamer Platz

is Dürer's **Portrait of Hieronymus Holzschuher** (1526), a Nuremberg patrician, career politician and strong supporter of the Reformation. Note how the artist brilliantly lasers in on his friend's features with utmost precision, down to the furrows, wrinkles and thinning hair.

One of Cranach's finest works is **Fountain of Youth** (1546) in Room III, which illustrates humankind's yearning for eternal youth. Old crones plunge into a pool of water and emerge as dashing hotties – this fountain would surely put plastic surgeons out of business. The transition is also reflected in the landscape, which is stark and craggy on the left and lush and fertile on the right.

A main exponent of the Dutch Renaissance was Peter Bruegel the Elder who here is represented with the stunning **Dutch Proverbs** (1559) in Room 7. The moralistic yet humorous painting crams over 100 proverbs and idioms into a single seaside village scene. While some point up the absurdity of human behaviour, others unmask its imprudence and sinfulness. Some sayings are still in use today, among them 'swimming against the tide' and 'armed to the teeth'.

North Wing: Dutch 17th-Century Paintings

The first galleries in the north wing feature some exceptional portraits, most notably Frans Hals' **Malle Babbe** (1633) in Room 13. Note how Hals ingeniously captures the character and vitality of his subject 'Crazy Barbara' with free-wielding brushstrokes. Hals met the lady with the almost demonic laugh in the workhouse for the mentally ill where his son Pieter was also a resident. The tin mug and owl are symbols of Babbe's fondness for tipple.

Another eye-catcher is **Woman with a Pearl Necklace** (1662–64) in Room 18, one of the most famous paintings by Dutch Realist Jan Vermeer. It depicts a young woman studying herself in the mirror while fastening a pearl necklace around her neck, an intimate moment beautifully captured with characteristic soft brushstrokes.

The real highlight of the north wing awaits in the octagonal Room X, which is dedicated to Rembrandt and dominated by the large-scale **Mennonite Minister Cornelius Claesz Anslo** (1641), which shows the preacher in conversation with his wife. The huge open Bible and his gesturing hand sticking out in almost 3D-style from the centre of the painting are meant to emphasise the strength of his religious convictions. Also note Rembrandt's small self-portrait next to it.

FURTHER INFORMATION

Be sure to pick up a free map from the ticket counter and also take advantage of the excellent free audioguide to get the low-down on selected works. The room numbering system is quite confusing as both Latin (I, II, III) and Arabic numbers (1, 2, 3) are used. A tour of all 72 rooms covers almost 2km, so budget at least a couple of hours for your visit. A ticket to the Gemäldegalerie is also good for same-day admission to the permanent collections of the other Kulturforum museums. Admission is free to anyone under 18.

Three small rooms in the gallery's northwest corner present a smattering of English and French works, including Thomas Gainsborough's *Portrait of John Wilkinson*. Works by Gainsborough are rarely seen outside the UK, which is what makes this portrait of the British industrialist so special. Nicknamed 'Iron Mad Wilkinson' for pioneering the making and use of cast iron, he is – somewhat ironically – shown in a natural setting, almost blending with his surroundings.

POTSDAMER PLATZ & TIERGARTEN GEMÄLDEGALERIE

GEMÄLDEGALERIE

Woman with a
Pearl Necklace
Portrait of   Room XVIII   Room XIII
John   ● Malle Babbe
Wilkinson
Room XX   Room X

Il Campo   ● Cornelius Claesz
di Rialto   Anslo

Room XII   Dutch
                            Proverbs
Amor ●   Room VII
Victorius
    Room XIV

— Room XVI
Leda with ●   Fountain of ● Room III ● Portrait of
the Swan   Youth   Room II Hieronymus
                                    Holzschuher

            Room
Madonna with ● XVIII
Child and Singing
    Angels   Gallery
                Entrance

West Wing: Italian Masterpieces

The first galleries in the west wing stay in the 17th and 18th centuries. Crowds often form before Canaletto's **Il Campo di Rialto** (1758–63) in Room XII, which depicts the arcaded main market square of the artist's hometown Venice with stunning precision and perspective. Note the goldsmith shops on the left, the wig-wearing merchants in the centre and the stores selling paintings and furniture on the right.

Older by 150 years is Caravaggio's delightful **Amor Victorius** (1602/3) in Room XIV. Wearing nothing but a mischievous grin, a pair of black angel wings and a fistful of arrows, this cheeky Amor means business. Note the near-photographic realism achieved by the almost theatrical use of light and shadow.

The next galleries travel back to the Renaissance when Raphael, Titian and Correggio dominated Italian art. The latter's **Leda with the Swan** (1532) in Room XVI is worth a closer look. Judging by her blissed-out expression, Leda is having a fine time with that swan who, according to Greek mythology, is none other than Zeus himself. The erotically charged nature of this painting apparently so incensed Louis, Duke of Orleans, that he cut off Leda's head with a knife. It was later restored.

Lest you think that all West Wing paintings have a naughty subtext, let us draw your attention to Sandro Botticelli's **Madonna with Child and Singing Angels** (1477) in Room XVII. This circular painting (a format called a tondo) shows Mary flanked by two sets of four wingless angels. It's an intimate moment that shows the Virgin tenderly embracing – perhaps even about to breastfeed – her child. The white lilies are symbols of her purity.

SIGHTS

◉ Potsdamer Platz

POTSDAMER PLATZ NEIGHBOURHOOD

See p113 for Potsdamer Platz and Sony Center, Museum für Film und Fernsehen, Legoland Discovery Centre, Weinhaus Huth, Daimler Contemporary, Boulevard der Stars and DaimlerCity.

MARTIN-GROPIUS-BAU GALLERY

Map p316 (☏254 860; www.gropiusbau.de; Niederkirchner Strasse 7; admission varies; ☉10am-7pm Wed-Mon; Ⓢ Potsdamer Platz, Ⓡ Potsdamer Platz) With its mosaics, terracotta reliefs and airy atrium, this exhibit space is a high-calibre showcase for crème-de-la-crème travelling shows. No matter whether it's a Diane Arbus retrospective, a survey of art from Los Angeles since the 1950s or an ethnological exhibit on the mysteries of Angkor Wat, it's bound to be well curated and utterly fascinating.

The 1881 three-storey cube exudes the majesty of an Italian Renaissance palace, a design that sprang from the fevered brow of Martin Gropius (Walter's great-uncle). After WWII, the pretty building stood neglected just west of the Berlin Wall (there's still a short stretch of it running east along Niederkirchner Strasse), patiently awaiting its restoration.

The Berlin state parliament convenes in the stately neo-Renaissance structure across the street.

DALÍ – DIE AUSSTELLUNG GALLERY

Map p316 (☏0700 3254 237 546; www.dali berlin.de; Leipziger Platz 7; adult/concession €11/9; ☉noon-8pm Mon-Sat, 10am-8pm Sun; ☐200, Ⓢ Potsdamer Platz, Ⓡ Potsdamer Platz) If you

BARGAIN BOX

A ticket to any one Kulturforum museum entitles you to same-day admission to the permanent collection of the other four, as well as to the Kunstgewerbemuseum in Köpenick. Participating museums are Gemäldegalerie, Neue Nationalgalerie, Kunstgewerbemuseum and Kupferstichkabinett. Admission is free to anyone under 18. Special exhibits cost extra.

only know Salvador Dalí as the painter of melting watches, burning giraffes and other surrealist imagery that plumbs the depths of the unconscious, this privately owned museum will likely offer new perspectives on the man. The more than 400 works focus primarily on his graphics, illustrations, sculptures, drawings and films.

Highlights include the etchings on the theme of Tristan and Isolde, epic sculptures like *Surrealist Angel* and the *Don Quixote* lithographs. As the museum does not receive public subsidies admission is steep.

◉ Kulturforum

GEMÄLDEGALERIE GALLERY

See p116.

NEUE NATIONALGALERIE GALLERY

Map p316 (☏266 2951; www.neue-national galerie.de; Potsdamer Strasse 50; adult/concession €10/5; ☉10am-6pm Tue, Wed & Fri, to 10pm Thu, 11am-6pm Sat & Sun; Ⓢ Potzdamer Platz, Ⓡ Potsdamer Platz) The first of the Kulturforum museums to open in 1968, the New National Gallery is also the most spectacular, architecturally speaking. All glass and steel, squatting on a raised platform, this late masterpiece of Ludwig Mies van der Rohe resembles a postmodern Buddhist temple; it presents paintings and sculpture created by 20th-century European artists working until 1960 in changing exhibits mostly drawn from its own collection.

All major genres are represented, including cubism (Pablo Picasso, Gris Leger), surrealism (Salvador Dalí, Joan Miró, Max Ernst), new objectivity (Otto Dix, George Grosz) and Bauhaus (Paul Klee, Wassily Kandinsky). Most impressive, though, is the German expressionist collection. The warped works of Otto Dix (eg *Old Couple*, 1923), the 'egghead' figures of George Grosz, and Ernst Ludwig Kirchner's chaotic *Potsdamer Platz* (1914) – peopled by a demimonde of prostitutes and revellers – are all stand-outs. Of special significance is the group of 11 Max Beckmann paintings, which trace the artist's development between 1906 and 1942.

The space is also used to host blockbuster travelling exhibitions that often meet with exceptional interest. The selection of art from New York's Museum of Modern Art, for instance, had people camp out overnight for tickets.

BERLINER PHILHARMONIE ARCHITECTURE

Map p316 (☎2548 8156; www.berliner-philharmoniker.de; Herbert-von-Karajan-Strasse 1; tours adult/concession €3/2; ⏰tour 1.30pm; 🚌200, [S]Potsdamer Platz, [U]Potsdamer Platz) Hans Scharoun's 1963 iconic concert venue, with its distinctive outline and honey-coloured facade, is a masterpiece of organic architecture and home base of the prestigious Berliner Philharmoniker. The auditorium feels like the inside of a finely crafted instrument and boasts supreme acoustics and excellent sightlines from every seat. It's an imposing yet intimate hall with terraced and angled 'vineyard' seating wrapped around a central orchestra stage. Try catching a concert here or join the daily guided tour (in German) which meets at the artist entrance across the parking lot facing Potsdamer Strasse.

The adjacent **Kammermusiksaal** (Chamber Music Hall; Map p316), also based on a design by Scharoun, is essentially a more compact riff on the Philharmonie.

KUNSTGEWERBEMUSEUM MUSEUM

Map p316 (Museum of Decorative Arts; ☎266 424 242; www.smb.museum; Matthäikirchplatz; 🚌200, [S]Potsdamer Platz, [U]Potsdamer Platz) From medieval gem-encrusted crosses to art deco ceramics and modern appliances, the cavernous Museum of Decorative Arts harbours a mind-boggling survey of precious arts and crafts through the ages. Alas, it remains closed for renovation and reorganisation until at least mid-2014.

MUSIKINSTRUMENTEN-MUSEUM MUSEUM

Map p316 (Musical Instruments Museum; ☎254 810; www.mim-berlin.de; Tiergartenstrasse 1, enter via Ben-Gurion-Strasse; adult/concession €4/2; ⏰9am-5pm Tue, Wed & Fri, to 10pm Thu, 10am-5pm Sat & Sun; 🚌200, [S]Potsdamer Platz, [U]Potsdamer Platz) Packed with fun, precious and rare sound machines, the Musical Instruments Museum shares a building with the Philharmonie. There are plenty of old trumpets, bizarre bagpipes and even a talking walking stick as well as a handful of 'celebrity instruments': the glass harmonica invented by Ben Franklin, a flute played by Frederick the Great and Johann Sebastian Bach's cembalo. Stop at the listening stations to hear what some of the more obscure instruments sound like.

A crowd favourite is the Mighty Wurlitzer (1929), an organ with more buttons and keys than a troop of beefeaters that's cranked up at noon on Saturday. Classical concerts, many free, take place year-round (ask for a free schedule or check the website).

KUPFERSTICHKABINETT GALLERY

Map p316 (Museum of Prints and Drawings; ☎266 424 242; www.smb.museum/kk; Matthäikirchplatz; adult/concession €8/4; ⏰10am-6pm Tue-Fri, 11am-6pm Sat & Sun; 🚌200, [S]Potsdamer Platz, [U]Potsdamer Platz) Botticelli's original illustrations for Dante's *Divine Comedy* are among the prized possessions of art on paper held by the Museum of Prints and Drawings. This is one of the world's largest and finest collections of its kind, a bonanza of hand-illustrated books, illuminated manuscripts, drawings and prints produced mostly in Europe from the 14th century onward – Dürer to Rembrandt to Schinkel, Picasso to Giacometti to Warhol.

The works don't do well under light, which is why only a tiny fraction of the collection is shown on a rotating basis.

[FREE] **MATTHÄUSKIRCHE** CHURCH

Map p316 (Church of St Matthews; ☎262 1202; www.stiftung-stmatthaeus.de; Matthäikirchplatz; ⏰noon-6pm Tue-Sun; 🚌200, [S]Potsdamer Platz, [U]Potsdamer Platz) Standing a bit lost and forlorn within the Kulturforum, the Stüler-designed Matthäuskirche (1846) is a beautiful neo-Romanesque confection with alternating bands of red and ochre brick and a light-flooded, modern sanctuary that doubles as a gallery. Climb the tower for good views of the Kulturforum and Potsdamer Platz. A nice time to visit is for the free 20-minute organ recitals at 12.30pm Tuesday to Sunday.

German resistance fighter Dietrich Bonhoeffer was ordained a Lutheran minister here in 1931. A few years later the church was scheduled to be transplanted to Spandau to make room for Albert Speer's Germania. Fortunately the war – and history – took a different turn. Bonhoeffer was executed by the Nazis on 9 April 1945, a day after V-E Day.

⊙ Tiergarten & Diplomatenviertel

Berlin's rulers used to hunt boar and pheasants in the rambling **Tiergarten** (🚌200, [U]Potsdamer Platz) until Peter Lenné landscaped the grounds in the 18th century. Today, one of the world's largest urban parks is a popular place for strolling, jogging, picnicking, frisbee tossing, barbecuesand, yes, nude tanning and gay cruising (especially around the Löwenbrücke). It is bisected by a major artery, the Strasse des 17 Juni. Walking across the entire park takes about an hour, but even a shorter stroll has its rewards. See the Neighbourhood Walk (p124) for inspiration.

SIEGESSÄULE MONUMENT

Map p316 (Victory Column; Grosser Stern; 🚌100, 200) Like arms of a starfish, five roads merge into the roundabout called Grosser Stern at the heart of the Tiergarten. At its centre is the landmark Victory Column, built to celebrate 19th-century Prussian military triumphs and now a symbol of Berlin's gay community.

The gilded lady on top – irreverently called Goldelse – represents the Goddess of Victory. Film buffs might remember her from a key scene in Wim Wenders' 1985 flick *Wings of Desire*. You can climb just below her skirt for views of Tiergarten park.

The column originally sto… the Reichstag until the Nazis mo… in 1938 to make room for their utopi… mania urban planning project. The p… estal was added at the time, bringing the column height to 67m.

SCHLOSS BELLEVUE HISTORICAL BUILDING

Map p316 (Spreeweg 1; 🕒closed to public; 🚆Bellevue) The German president makes his home in snowy white Schloss Bellevue. The neoclassical palace was built in 1785 by Philipp Daniel Boumann for the youngest brother of Frederick the Great, then became a school under Kaiser Wilhelm II and a museum of ethnology under the Nazis. The president is supported by the *Bundespräsidialamt* (Office of the Federal President) based in the oval modern building south of the palace.

AKADEMIE DER KÜNSTE GALLERY

Map p316 (☎200 572 000; www.adk.de; Hanseatenweg 10; 🕒exhibits 11am-8pm Tue-Sun; [S]Hansaplatz, 🚆Bellevue) The Academy of Arts has

TOP SIGHTS
GEDENKSTÄTTE DEUTSCHER WIDERSTAND

If you've seen the movie *Valkyrie* you're well aware of Claus Schenk Graf von Stauffenberg, the poster boy of the German resistance against Hitler and the Third Reich. The very rooms where a group of senior army officers, led by Stauffenberg, plotted the bold but ill-fated assassination attempt on the Führer on 20 July 1944 are now part of the German Resistance Memorial Centre. The building itself, the historic Bendlerblock, harboured the Wehrmacht high command from 1935 to 1945 and today is the secondary seat of the German defence ministry (the primary is still in Bonn).

The centre also documents the efforts of many other Germans who risked their lives opposing the Third Reich for ideological, religious or military reasons. Most were just regular folks, such as the students Hans and Sophie Scholl or the craftsman Georg Elser; others were prominent citizens like the artist Käthe Kollwitz and the theologian Dietrich Bonhoeffer.

In the yard, a statue marks the spot where Stauffenberg and three of his co-conspirators were executed on 20 July 1944.

DON'T MISS...

- Stauffenberg exhibit
- Stauffenberg memorial statue
- Jewish resistance exhibit

PRACTICALITIES

- German Resistance Memorial Center
- Map p316
- ☎2699 5000
- www.gdw-berlin.de
- Stauffenbergstrasse 13-14
- 🕒9am-6pm Mon-Wed & Fri, to 8pm Thu, 10am-6pm Sat & Sun
- 🚌M29, [S]Potsdamer Platz, Kurfürstenstrasse, 🚆Potsdamer Platz

…n Kreuzberg and Charlottenburg, residential Schöneberg has a radical …in the squatter days of the '80s but now flaunts a mellow middle-class …some 19th-century townhouses line many of its quiet, leafy side streets, …eezed tight with boho cafes and indie boutiques. It's perfect for exploring …stance, start at Nollendorfplatz U-Bahn station and head south to ethnic-flav… …uptstrasse, via Maassenstrasse, Goltzstrasse and Akazienstrasse. The best day to visit is Saturday, when a farmers market takes over Winterfeldtplatz.

Nollendorfplatz & the 'Gay Village'

In the early 20th century, Nollendorfplatz was a bustling urban square filled with cafes, theatres and people on parade. Then as now, it was also the gateway to the city's historic gay quarter, whose notorious bars were the haunt of a demimonde along with Marlene Dietrich, Claire Waldorff and British writer Christopher Isherwood. The latter penned his novellas, *Berlin Stories*, which inspired the film and musical *Cabaret*, while living at Nollendorfstrasse 17. Rainbow flags still fly proudly above bars and businesses, especially along Motzstrasse and Fuggerstrasse, home to bars, clubs and cruising dens. A triangular memorial plaque affixed to the south entrance of Nollendorfplatz U-Bahn station commemorates homosexual victims of the Nazi era.

Farmers Market

On Wednesday or Saturday morning, a lively market sets up on otherwise ho-hum Winterfeldtplatz (square). Along with farm-fresh seasonal produce, you'll find handmade cheeses, cured meats, local honey and plenty more foodie staples and surprises. The Saturday edition also has artsy-craftsy stalls. Food stands feed hunger pangs and there's more cafes and eating options surrounding the square, including soul-sustaining felafels from **Habibi** (Goltzstrasse 24; snacks €2.50-5; ⏰11am-3am Sun-Thu, to 5pm Fri & Sat; [S]Nollendorfplatz).

Shopping on Goltzstrasse & Akazienstrasse

Shopping is one of life's little pleasures and a charming place for it is Goltzstrasse and its continuation, Akazienstrasse. Both offer charming boutiques where you can nose

a pedigree going back to 1696 but its programming is solidly rooted in the here and now. It covers all forms of artistic expression, from architecture to literature to music, theatre and digital media, and also stages high-profile exhibits.

A sculpture by Henry Moore fronts the late-1950s building by Werner Düttmann, a student of Hans Scharoun and a key post-WWII modernist architect.

DIPLOMATENVIERTEL NEIGHBOURHOOD

Map p316 (Diplomatic Quarter; 🚌200, [S]Potsdamer Platz, 🚋Potsdamer Platz) The Brothers Grimm were among the 19th-century intellectuals living in the quiet colony south of the Tiergarten, which evolved into an embassy quarter starting in the 1920s. After WWII the obliterated area remained in a state of quiet decay while the embassies all set up in Bonn, now the capital of West Germany. After reunification, many countries rebuilt on their historic lots, accounting for some of Berlin's boldest new architecture that's easily explored on a DIY wander.

BAUHAUS ARCHIV MUSEUM

Map p316 (☎254 0020; www.bauhaus.de; Klingelhöferstrasse 14; adult/concession Sat-Mon €7/4, Wed-Fri €6/3; ⏰10am-5pm Wed-Mon; [S]Nollendorfplatz) Bauhaus founder Walter Gropius himself designed the avant-garde building that now houses the Bauhaus archive and museum with its distinctive white shed roofs. Inside, changing exhibits using study notes, workshop pieces, photographs, blueprints, models and other objects and documents illustrate the Bauhaus theories.

Highlights include material relating to Gropius' 1925 Bauhaus buildings in Dessau and Lázló Moholy-Nagy's clever kinetic sculpture called *Light-Space-Modulator*. Nice cafe and cool shop stocked with Bauhaus-inspired gewgaws.

around for vintage clothing, antique books, handmade jewellery or exotic teas. Wedged in between are plenty of cafes and eateries to restore energies, including the award-winning **Double Eye** (Akazienstrasse 22; ⊘9am-6.30pm Mon-Fri, to 6pm Sat; ⓈEisenacher Strasse) and, at dinnertime, the always-packed Greek ouzeria **Ousies** (⌨216 7957; www.taverna -ousies.de; Grunewaldstrasse 16; small plates €4-9, mains €10-18; ⊘dinner; ⓈEisenacher Strasse).

Hauptstrasse
Chic cafes gradually give way to grocers and snack bars dishing up doner kebab instead of quiche. The main artery of this multiculti section of Schöneberg is bustling Hauptstrasse, home to **Öz-Gida** (www.ozgida.de; Hauptstrasse 16; ⓈKleistpark, Eisenacher Strasse), a huge Turkish supermarket known citywide for its olive selection, cheese spreads and quality meats. David Bowie and Iggy Pop used to share a pad at Hauptstrasse 155.

Rathaus Schöneberg
Follow Hauptstrasse west to **Rathaus Schöneberg** (John-F-Kennedy-Platz; ⓈRathaus Schöneberg), the district town hall, which served as the seat of the West Berlin government between 1948 and 1990. It was from these steps in 1963 that US President John F Kennedy gave his famous 'Ich bin ein Berliner' speech. A flea market takes over the square at weekends.

Cocktail Culture
Schöneberg has of late emerged as a hotbed for dapper drinking with some of the best bars handily clustered within stumbling distance of each other. Skip the cookie-cutter drinking dens on Maassenstrasse and head straight to **Stagger Lee** (⌨2903 6158; www .staggerlee.de; Nollendorfstrasse 27; ⓈNollendorfplatz), a sophisticated saloon complete with swing door and heavy leather sofas. Around the corner, **Green Door** (⌨215 2515; www .greendoor.de; Winterfeldtstrasse 50; ⊘6pm-3am; ⓈNollendorfplatz), the neighbourhood classic, has been pouring potent libations since 1995. Nearby **Voima** (www.voima.de; Winterfeldtstrasse 22; ⊘Wed-Sun; ⓈNollendorfplatz), named after a Finnish icebreaker, is a relative newcomer and uses Finnish liqueur to whip up many of its cool cocktails.

✖ EATING

For a quick nibble, head to the basement food court in the Potsdamer Platz Arkaden (p126) mall. Eating options in Tiergarten park and the Diplomatenviertel are scarce.

✖ Potsdamer Platz

VAPIANO
ITALIAN €€
Map p316 (⌨2300 5005; www.vapiano.de; Potsdamer Platz 5; mains €5.50-9; ⊘11am-midnight Mon-Sat, to 11pm Sun; ⌨200, ⓈPotsdamer Platz, ⍗Potsdamer Platz) Matteo Thun's jazzy decor is a great foil for the tasty Italian fare at this successful German self-service chain. Mix-and-match pastas, creative salads and crusty pizzas are all prepared right before your eyes, and there's fresh basil on the table. Your order is recorded on a chip card and paid for upon leaving. There's another branch in **Charlottenburg** (Map p334; ⌨8871 4195; www.vapiano.de; Augsburger Strasse 43; €5.50-9; ⊘10am-1am Mon-Sat, to midnight Sun; ⓈKurfürstendamm).

WEILANDS WELLFOOD
INTERNATIONAL €
Map p316 (⌨2589 9717; www.weilands-wellfood .de; Marlene-Dietrich-Platz 1; mains €4-9; ⊘10am-10pm; ⊛✍; ⓈPotsdamer Platz, ⍗Potsdamer Platz) The whole-wheat pastas, vitamin-packed salads and fragrant wok dishes at this upbeat self-service bistro are perfect for health- and waist-watchers but don't sacrifice a lick to the taste gods. Sit outside by the little pond, ideally outside the office-jockey lunch rush.

JOSEPH-ROTH-DIELE
GERMAN €
Map p316 (⌨2636 9884; www.joseph-roth -diele.de; Potsdamer Strasse 75; dishes €4-9; ⊘10am-midnight Mon-Fri; ⓈKurfürstenstrasse) Named for an Austrian Jewish writer, this wood-panelled saloon time-warps you back to the 1920s, when Roth used to live next

START POTSDAMER PLATZ
END TIERGARTEN S-BAHN
STATION
DISTANCE 5KM
DURATION 2 TO 2½ HOURS

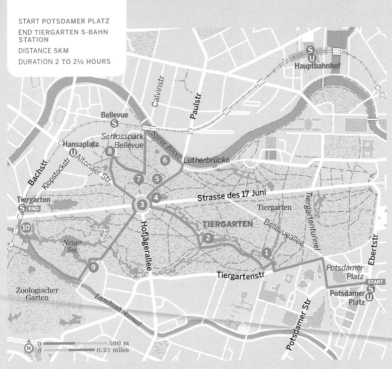

Neighbourhood Walk

Traipsing Around the Tiergarten

A ramble around Tiergarten delivers a relaxing respite from the tourist track. From Potsdamer Platz, make your way to **1 Luiseninsel**, an enchanting gated garden dotted with statues and seasonal flower beds. Not far away is **2 Rousseauinsel**, a memorial to 18th-century French philosopher Jean-Jacques ('Back to Nature') Rousseau. On a teensy island, it was modelled after his actual burial site near Paris. Look for the weathered stone pillar.

At the heart of the park, engulfed by traffic, the imposing **3 Siegessäule** (Victory Column) commemorates Prussian military triumphs enforced by Iron Chancellor Otto von Bismarck. Nearby, the colossal **4 Bismarck Denkmal**, a monument to the man, shows him flanked by statues of Atlas (with the world on his back), Siegfried (wielding a sword) and Germania (stomping a panther).

Following Spreeweg north takes you past the oval **5 Bundespräsidialamt**, the offices of the German president, to his residence in **6 Schloss Bellevue**, a former royal palace. Follow the path along the Spree, then turn left into the **7 Englischer Garten** (English Garden) created in the '50s in commemoration of the 1948 Berlin Airlift. At its heart, overlooking a pretty pond, the thatched-roof teahouse serves food and refreshments and hosts free summer concerts. Afterwards, check out the latest exhibit at the nearby **8 Akademie der Künste**, on the edge of the Hansaviertel, a quarter borne from a 1957 international building exhibition.

Walk south back through the park, crossing Altonaer Strasse and Strasse des 17 Juni, to arrive at the Neuer See with **9 Café am Neuen See** at its south end. From here, saunter north along the Landwehrkanal via the **10 Gaslaternenmuseum**, an open-air collection of 90 historic gas lanterns, and wrap up your tour at Tiergarten S-Bahn station.

door. Walls decorated with bookshelves and quotes from his works draw a literary, intellectual crowd. Come here for a quick lunch, cakes or a leisurely drink.

RESTAURANT GROPIUS INTERNATIONAL **€€**

Map p316 (☎2548 6406; www.mosaik-berlin.de/restaurant-gropius; Martin-Gropius-Bau, Niederkirchner Strasse 7; mains €7-18; ⏰10am-7pm Wed-Mon; 🚌M41, 200, [S]Potsdamer Platz, 🚆Potsdamer Platz) Even without seeing an exhibit, stop by the restaurant of the Martin-Gropius-Bau for delicious dishes inspired by a current show. When California art was the focus, for instance, the menu featured tacos and quesadillas. Dine beneath crystal chandeliers in the elegant dining room or the tree-shaded garden. Also good just for coffee and cake.

FACIL INTERNATIONAL **€€€**

Map p316 (☎590 051 234; www.facil.de; Mandala Hotel, Potsdamer Strasse 3; 1-/2-/3-course lunch €19/29/39, dinner mains €16-55, 4-/8-course dinner €86/146; ⏰noon-3pm & 7-11pm Mon-Fri; 🚌200, [S]Potsdamer Platz, 🚆Potsdamer Platz) Michael Kempf's Michelin-starred fare is hugely innovative yet deliciously devoid of unnecessary flights of fancy. Enjoy it while draped in a sleek Donghia chair in the glass-enclosed dining chamber at the Mandala Hotel. Budget-savvy gourmets take advantage of the lunchtime menu.

QIU INTERNATIONAL **€€**

Map p316 (☎590 051 230; www.qiu.de; Mandala Hotel, Potsdamer Strasse 3; 2-course lunch €14; ⏰lunch Mon-Fri; 🚌200, [S]Potsdamer Platz, 🚆Potsdamer Platz) The two-course business lunch at this stylish lounge at the Mandala Hotel is a virtual steal, while at night the sensuous setting amid mood-lit fringe lamps and golden mosaic waterfall is great for predinner or postshow cocktails.

DESBROSSES FRENCH **€€€**

Map p316 (☎337 776 340; www.desbrosses.de; Ritz-Carlton Berlin, Potsdamer Platz 3; mains €23-36; ⏰breakfast, lunch & dinner; 🚌200, [S]Potsdamer Platz, 🚆Potsdamer Platz) This 1875 brasserie was moved piece by piece from the south of France to the Ritz-Carlton Berlin and is now anchored by an open kitchen where toqued chefs turn out up-market French country classics – steak frites, *boudin noir* (blood sausage) and *boeuf bourguignon*. Be sure not to OD on the crusty breads made in the on-site *boulangerie* (bakery). Weekday lunch specials go for €14.

🍴 Tiergarten

CAFÉ AM NEUEN SEE INTERNATIONAL **€€**

Map p316 (☎254 4930; www.cafe-am-neuen-see.de; Lichtensteinallee 2; pizza €9-12.50, mains €10-26; ⏰9am-11pm; 🚌100, 200) This lakeside Tiergarten restaurant serves pizza and German fare year-round, but really the time to visit is during beer garden season when it's like a microvacation from the city bustle. Balance the cold beers with hearty snacks. Romantics can even rent a boat and take their sweetie for a spin. The cafe is in the southwestern section of Tiergarten. From the Victory Column, follow the Fasanenallee walkway 500m through the park.

TEEHAUS IM ENGLISCHEN GARTEN INTERNATIONAL **€€**

Map p316 (☎3948 0400; www.teehaus-tiergarten.com; Altonaer Strasse 2; mains €7.50-16.50; ⏰10am-11pm; 🚌100, 🚆Bellevue) The gastronomic anchor of the English Garten in the northwestern corner of Tiergarten park, this thatched-roof teahouse with outdoor terrace is a peaceful spot, not just for tea but for a global roster of simple but tasty dishes – quiche to schnitzel to chilli con carne.

🍷 DRINKING & NIGHTLIFE

🍷 Potsdamer Platz

SOLAR BAR

Map p316 (☎0163 765 2700; www.solar-berlin.de; Stresemannstrasse 76; ⏰6pm-2am Sun-Thu, to 4am Fri & Sat; 🚆Anhalter Bahnhof) Views of the skyline are truly impressive at this chic 17th-floor sky lounge above a posh restaurant (mains €18 to €29). With its dim lighting and soft black leather couches, it's a great spot for a date or sunset drinks. Even getting there aboard an exterior glass lift is half the fun. Enter via the chunky high-rise behind the Pit Stop auto shop.

CURTAIN CLUB BAR

Map p316 (☎337 776 196; www.ritzcarlton.de; Ritz-Carlton Berlin, Potsdamer Strasse 3; ⏰from

6pm; 🖥200, Ⓢ Potsdamer Platz, Ⓡ Potsdamer Platz) Every night at 6pm sharp, it's showtime at the Ritz-Carlton Berlin: a uniformed former beefeater (Tower of London guard) ceremoniously pulls back the heavy curtains on this elegant, wood-panelled bar presided over by cocktail-meister Arnd Heissen. His speciality is cocktails inspired by the world of perfumes.

VICTORIABAR   BAR

(☑030 2575 9977; www.victoriabar.de; Potsdamer Strasse 102; ⊘6.30pm-3am Sun-Thu, to 4am Fri & Sat; Ⓢ Kurfürstenstrasse) Original art decorates this discreet cocktail lounge favoured by a grown-up crowd that's like a two-inch heel – chic but sensible. Try the Ramos Gin Fizz, bar owner Stefan Weber's favourite libation. Budget boozers invade for happy hour before 9.30pm. It's about 750m south of the Kulturforum via Potsdamer Strasse.

⭐ ENTERTAINMENT

BERLINER PHILHARMONIE   CLASSICAL MUSIC

Map p316 (☑2548 8999; www.berliner-philharmoniker.de; Herbert-von-Karajan-Strasse 1; 🖥200, Ⓢ Potsdamer Platz, Ⓡ Potsdamer Platz) This world-famous concert hall has excellent acoustics and, thanks to Hans Scharoun's clever terraced vineyard design, not a bad seat in the house. It's the home base of the Berliner Philharmoniker, currently led by Sir Simon Rattle. Concerts are also at the adjacent **Kammermusiksaal**.

CINESTAR ORIGINAL   CINEMA

Map p316 (☑2606 6400; www.cinestar.de; Sony Center, Potsdamer Strasse 4; Ⓢ Potsdamer Platz, Ⓡ Potsdamer Platz) A favourite among English-speaking expats and anglophile Germans, this state-of-the-art cinema with big screens, comfy seats and ear-popping surround-sound shows the latest Hollywood blockbusters, all in English, all the time.

ARSENAL   CINEMA

Map p316 (☑2695 5100; www.arsenal-berlin.de; Sony Center, Potsdamer Strasse 21; Ⓢ Pots-

damer Platz, Ⓡ Potsdamer Platz) The antithesis of popcorn culture, this artsy twin-screen cinema features a bold global flick schedule that hopscotches from Japanese satire to Brazilian comedy and German road movies. Many films have English subtitles.

BLUE MAN GROUP   THEATRE

Map p316 (☑0180 54444; www.bluemangroup.de; Marlene-Dietrich-Platz 4; tickets €60; Ⓡ Potsdamer Platz) This musical and visual extravaganza, starring slightly nutty and energetic guys dipped in Smurf-blue latex suits, performs at its own permanent theatre, a converted IMAX now called Bluemax.

THEATER AM POTSDAMER PLATZ   MUSICALS

Map p316 (☑259 2290, tickets 01805 4444; www.stage-entertainment.de; Marlene-Dietrich-Platz 1; ticket price varies; Ⓢ Potsdamer Platz, Ⓡ Potsdamer Platz) Big-name touring musicals are showcased at this up-in-lights location designed by Renzo Piano. Inside, there's seating for 1800 and a sense of occasion.

SPIELBANK BERLIN   CASINO

Map p316 (☑255 990; www.spielbank-berlin.de; Marlene-Dietrich-Platz 1; admission €2.50; ⊘slots 11am-3am, tables 3pm-3am, poker 7pm-3am Mon-Fri, 3pm-3am Sat & Sun; Ⓢ Potsdamer Platz, Ⓡ Potsdamer Platz) Vegas it ain't, but there are still plenty of opportunities to challenge Lady Luck over a game of poker, roulette or black jack at this casino. Slot machines in the basement, poker on the ground floor, and roulette, black jack and poker upstairs. Bring ID. No entry under 18.

🛍 SHOPPING

POTSDAMER PLATZ ARKADEN   SHOPPING MALL

Map p316 (☑255 9270; www.potsdamer-platz-arkaden.de; Alte Potsdamer Strasse 7; ⊘10am-9pm Mon-Sat; Ⓢ Potsdamer Platz, Ⓡ Potsdamer Platz) You'll find all your basic shopping cravings met at this attractive indoor mall. The basement has two supermarkets and numerous fast-food outlets. There's a post office at street level and decadent ice cream upstairs.

Scheunenviertel

HACKESCHER MARKT | HAUPTBAHNHOF | ORANIENBURGER TOR | TORSTRASSE

Neighbourhood Top Five

❶ Coming to grips with the absurdity of a divided city at the **Gedenkstätte Berliner Mauer** (p130), Germany's central memorial to the victims of the Berlin Wall.

❷ Glimpsing high drama, abstract mind-benders and glowing colour among the contemporary artworks at **Sammlung Boros** (p134).

❸ Exploring idiosyncratic shops, galleries and cafes in the charismatic maze of the **Hackesche Höfe** (p132).

❹ Swinging your legs to salsa, tango, ballroom, waltz and swing at the grand retro ballroom Clärchens Ballhaus or, in summer, at **Strandbar Mitte** (p140).

❺ Sizing yourself up next to giant dinos at Berlin's own Jurassic Park, the **Museum für Naturkunde** (p133).

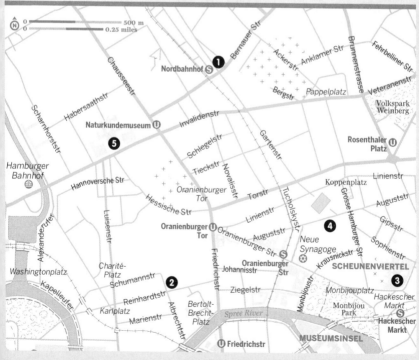

For more detail of this area, see Map p319 and p320 ➡

Lonely Planet's Top Tip

To get a better understanding of the Scheunenviertel's role in Berlin's Jewish history, rent a multimedia iGuide from the Anne Frank Zentrum (p135) for €5 (concession €2.50). Available in English and German, it takes you to key sites around the Scheunenviertel and uses photographs and interviews to add dimension and depth.

✖ Best Places to Eat

➡ Hartweizen (p139)
➡ Chèn Chè (p136)
➡ Katz Orange (p139)
➡ Schwarzwaldstuben (p136)

For reviews, see p136 ➡

🍷 Best Places to Drink

➡ Buck & Breck (p141)
➡ Neue Odessa Bar (p141)
➡ Mein Haus am See (p141)
➡ Amano Bar (p140)

For reviews, see p140 ➡

⊙ Best Jewish History Sites

➡ Neue Synagoge (p131)
➡ Gedenkstätte Stille Helden (p135)
➡ Alter Jüdischer Friedhof (p137)
➡ Museum Blindenwerkstatt Otto Weidt (p135)

For reviews, see p132 ➡

Explore: Scheunenviertel

The Scheunenviertel, or Barn Quarter, packs bunches of charisma into its relatively compact frame. Its greatest charms are in the labyrinth of quiet lanes fanning out from its main drags, Oranienburger Strasse and Rosenthaler Strasse. Just wander and you'll constantly stumble upon the unexpected here, an idyllic courtyard or bleeding-edge art gallery, a fashion-forward boutique, a shabby-chic bar or a glam belle époque ballroom. A distinctive feature of the quarter is its *Höfe* – interlinked courtyards filled with cafes, stores and party venues.

Since reunification, the Scheunenviertel has also reprised its historic role as Berlin's main Jewish quarter, with the Neue Synagoge as its shining beacon. Gritty Torstrasse, meanwhile, delivers a roll call of trendy restaurants and bars that lure a cashed-up creative crowd of locals and visitors.

Although technically no longer part of the historic Scheunenviertel, this chapter also covers the area west of Friedrichstrasse/Chausseestrasse, which harbours two of Berlin's contemporary arts highlights, the Hamburger Bahnhof and the Sammlung Boros. The area's other major drawcard is the Gedenkstätte Berliner Mauer, Germany's central memorial to the Berlin Wall.

Local Life

➡ **Shopping** Find out what keeps Berlin designers' sewing machines humming by prowling the back streets for fashion-forward local label stores.

➡ **Bar-Hopping** Play it cool when joining hotties and hopefuls on their quest for a classy buzz in Torstrasse's doorstaff-guarded booze burrows.

➡ **Monbijoupark** Grab a picnic, guzzle a beer in Strandbar Mitte (p140), Berlin's first beach bar, or catch a concert or play in the outdoor Amphitheater (p142) of this riverfront park.

Getting There & Away

➡ **Bus** No 142 runs along Torstrasse.

➡ **S-Bahn** Hackescher Markt (S5, S7 and S9) and Oranienburger Strasse (S2) stations are both good jumping-off points.

➡ **Tram** M1 runs from Museumsinsel (Museum Island) to Prenzlauer Berg and makes key stops within the Scheunenviertel.

➡ **U-Bahn** Weinmeisterstrasse (U8) is the most central station. Rosenthaler Platz (U8), Rosa-Luxemburg-Platz (U2) and Oranienburger Tor (U6) are closer to Torstrasse and the northern Scheunenviertel.

Berlin's main museum of contemporary art opened in 1996 in the former Hamburger Bahnhof railway station, whose loft and grandeur perfectly lend themselves to showcasing this Aladdin's cave of paintings, installations, sculptures and video art. Most of the museum's inventory is based on permanent loans from two collectors, Erich Marx and Friedrich Christian Flick, and spans the entire arc of post-1950 artistic movements – conceptual art, pop art, minimal art, arte povera and fluxus. Seminal works by such major players as Andy Warhol, Cy Twombly and Bruce Nauman are presented in changing configurations in both the main museum and the adjacent Rieckhallen, a 300m-long warehouse open since 2004.

There are free guided **English tours** at noon on Saturday and Sunday. Tours in German are offered at noon and 4pm Tuesday to Friday and at 6pm Saturday and 2pm Sunday. Wrap up your visit with a browse through the excellent **bookshop** and coffee or a meal at Berlin's smartest museum restaurant, Sarah Wiener im Hamburger Bahnhof (p139).

The Building
Trains first rolled through the Hamburger Bahnhof in 1874, but after only 32 years the station had become too small and was turned into a traffic museum. After WWII, the building stood empty until Josef Paul Kleihues was hired in 1989 to create a modern exhibition space. He kept the elegant exterior, which at night is bathed in the mystical blues and greens of a Dan Flavin light installation. The interior, though, was gutted and turned into modern minimalist galleries that orbit the lofty central hall with its exposed iron girders.

Marx Collection
Erich Marx is an entrepreneur with a Midas touch and a passion for modern art, especially choice works by Joseph Beuys, Anselm Kiefer, Robert Rauschenberg, Cy Twombly and Andy Warhol. The collection includes such iconic paintings as Warhol's portrait of Mao Zedong and Rauschenberg's *Pink Door*. Works by Beuys, the ultimate artistic boundary-pusher, fill the entire ground floor of the western wing. And since we're name-dropping, there are also seminal works by Roy Lichtenstein, Keith Haring, Jeff Koons and Georg Baselitz, along with the stellar photographs of Cindy Sherman and Andreas Gursky. And yes, we could go on...

Flick Collection
The Rieckhallen (Rieck Halls) present changing exhibits from the collection of German industrialist Friedrich Christian Flick, who has a special penchant for Bruce Nauman, Paul McCarthy, Rodney Graham and Jason Rhoades. With regard to paintings, though, the collection is especially strong when it comes to German artists, such as Sigmar Polke, Gerhard Richter, Neo Rauch.

DON'T MISS...
⇒ Andy Warhol's *Chairman Mao* (1975)
⇒ Anselm Kiefer's *Volkszählung* (Census, 1991)
⇒ Joseph Beuys' *The End of the Twentieth Century* (1983)
⇒ Robert Rauschenberg's *Pink Door* (1954)

PRACTICALITIES
⇒ Map p319
⇒ ☎266 424 242
⇒ www.hamburger bahnhof.de
⇒ Invalidenstrasse 50-51
⇒ adult/concession €8/4
⇒ ⊙10am-6pm Tue-Fri, 11am-8pm Sat, 11am-6pm Sun
⇒ Ⓢ Hauptbahnhof, Ⓡ Hauptbahnhof

SCHEUNENVIERTEL HAMBURGER BAHNHOF – MUSEUM FÜR GEGENWART

TOP SIGHTS
GEDENKSTÄTTE BERLINER MAUER

Stretching along Bernauer Strasse between Gartenstrasse and Brunnenstrasse, the Berlin Wall Memorial is the central memorial site of German division. It incorporates a stretch of original Wall along with vestiges of the border installations, exhibits, a chapel and a monument. This is the only place where you can see how all the elements of the Wall and the death strip fit together and how the border was enlarged and perfected over time.

The memorial extends for about 1km and is divided into four sections, of which three were completed at press time. Multimedia stations, 'archaeological windows' and markers sprinkled throughout provide detailed background.

For an overview and to pick up a free map, drop by the **visitors centre** at the corner of Gartenstrasse and Bernauer Strasse, which also screens a short documentary on the Wall.

Window of Remembrance
This wall of portraits in Area A gives identity to some of the people who lost their lives at the Berlin Wall, one of them only six years young. The parklike area surrounding the installation was once part of the adjacent cemetery.

National Monument
East of the Window of Remembrance looms the National Monument, which consists of a 70m section of original wall bounded by two rusted steel flanks. Behind is a reconstructed death strip complete with a security patrol path, the lamps that bathed it in fierce light at night and a guard tower.

Documentation Centre
For a sweeping overview of the memorial, climb up the viewing tower of the Documentation Centre at the corner of Ackerstrasse. Inside, a small exhibit uses photographs, original recordings and archival documents to detail the events leading up to that day in August 1961 when the first spools of barbed wire were uncoiled.

Chapel of Reconciliation
Just past Ackerstrasse, the modern Chapel of Reconciliation stands in the spot of an 1894 brick church which was blown up in 1985 to make room for a widening of the border strip. A 15-minute remembrance service for Wall victims is held at noon Tuesday to Friday.

Ghost Stations Exhibit
The Wall also divided the city's transportation system. Three lines with stations in West Berlin used tracks that ran through the eastern sector to return to stations back on the western side. Stations on East Berlin turf were closed and patrolled by GDR guards. Nordbahnhof S-Bahn station, on Gartenstrasse, was one of these so-called 'ghost stations'; an on-site exhibit provides a chronicle.

DON'T MISS...
- View of the National Monument from the Documentation Centre
- Remembrance service at the Chapel of Reconciliation
- Ghost Station exhibit

PRACTICALITIES
- Map p319
- 467 986 666
- www.berliner-mauer-gedenkstaette.de
- Bernauer Strasse btwn Gartenstrasse & Brunnenstrasse
- 9.30am-7pm Apr-Oct, to 6pm Nov-Mar, open-air exhibit 24hr, Ghost Station exhibit during S-Bahn operation
- Brunnenstrasse, Nordbahnhof

SCHEUNENVIERTEL GEDENKSTÄTTE BERLINER MAUER

TOP SIGHTS
NEUE SYNAGOGE

The gleaming gold dome of the Neue Synagoge is the most visible symbol of Berlin's revitalised Jewish community. Architect Eduard Knobloch looked to the Alhambra in Granada for inspiration, which explains the exotic Moorish-Byzantine design elements, including the elaborate facade and the shiny dome. When Knobloch fell sick, his close friend Friedrich August Stüler took over the job so that the building could be consecrated on Rosh Hashanah in 1866 in the presence of Otto von Bismarck and other Prussian dignitaries. Seating 3200 people, it was Germany's largest synagogue.

Non-landowning Jews were the first people to settle in the Scheunenviertel by order of King Friedrich Wilhelm I in 1737. The community grew significantly in the 19th century and again in the early 20th when the quarter absorbed huge numbers of Jewish immigrants from Eastern Europe, and streets and shops soon rang with the sounds of Yiddish. Most newcomers were Hasidic Jews who had trouble assimilating with the more liberal existing Jewish community.

DON'T MISS...

- The facade
- The dome

PRACTICALITIES

- Map p320
- ☎8802 8300
- www.cjudaicum.de
- Oranienburger Strasse 28-30
- adult/concession €3/2
- ⏰10am-8pm Sun & Mon, to 6pm Tue-Thu, to 5pm Fri, reduced hr Nov-Apr
- [S]Oranienburger Tor, [R]Oranienburger Strasse

The Story of Wilhelm Krützfeld

Although Berlin's Jewish community was essentially eradicated during the Third Reich, the synagogue itself was destroyed not by Nazis but by Allied bombs in 1943. Not that the Nazis didn't try. In fact, during the countrywide Kristallnacht pogroms (Night of Broken Glass) on the night of 9 November 1938, a gang of SA (Sturmabteilung, a parliamentary group within the Nazi party) attempted to set the building on fire. Their efforts, however, were thwarted by courageous local police commander Wilhelm Krützfeld who reminded them that the building was, by law, a protected monument. He even managed to convince the fire brigade to come out and extinguish the flames, even though they were under orders not to do so for Jewish buildings. Miraculously, the following day Krützfeld did not get into hot water with the Nazis and was only reprimanded for his actions. A plaque affixed to the main facade commemorates this act of courage.

Today's Centrum Judaicum

After the war, the ruined synagogue was left to linger until the mid-1980s. Reconstruction began in 1988 on the 50th anniversary of Kristallnacht and continued after the fall of the Wall. Rededicated in 1995, today's synagogue is not so much a house of worship (although prayer services do take place) but a museum and place of remembrance called **Centrum Judaicum**. In addition to temporary presentations, a permanent exhibit features architectural fragments and objects recovered from the ruins of the building before its reconstruction. They include a Torah scroll and an eternal lamp and help tell the history of the building and the lives of the people associated with it. A **multilingual audioguide** (€3) also helps bring the past to life. Behind the new building a glass-and-steel mantle props up the remaining ruins of the sanctuary and a stone band in the ground traces the outline of the original synagogue. Note that this section is only accessible on a guided tour; call the synagogue for times. The dome can be climbed.

SIGHTS

Hackescher Markt Area

NEUE SYNAGOGE SYNAGOGUE
See p131.

HECKMANNHÖFE HISTORIC SITE
Map p320 (Oranienburger Strasse 32; 🚇M1, 🚉Oranienburger Strasse) For a retreat from the urban frenzy, skip on over to this idyllic courtyard complex linking Oranienburger Strasse with Auguststrasse. Kick back with cake and cappuccino in one of the cafes or browse around some unique shops like the Bonbonmacherei (p144), an old-fashioned candy kitchen, and Sterling Gold, which specialises in retro ball gowns.

C/O BERLIN GALLERY
Map p320 (📞2844 4160; www.co-berlin.info; Oranienburger Strasse 35/36; ⏰11am-8pm; 🚉Oranienburger Tor, 🚇M1, 🚉Oranienburger Strasse) It's always worth checking out the latest exhibit at C/O, which has put on contemporary photography shows in the Postfuhramt, an elegant 19th-century postal station, since 2000. Top dogs of the genre, including Robert Mapplethorpe, James Nachtwey and Annie Leibovitz, have all been featured. Note that the building was sold to a new investor in 2012, making the gallery's future in this location uncertain. Call ahead or check the website for the latest information.

KUNSTHAUS TACHELES LANDMARK
Map p319 (Oranienburger Strasse 54-56; 🚉Oranienburger Tor, 🚉Oranienburger Strasse) After the fall of the Wall, this graffiti-slathered art squat became a permanent fixture on Oranienburger Strasse, drawing locals and tourists to its galleries, cultural venues, bizarre sculptures and beer garden. Although over time it lost much of its anarchic edge, it was still one of the few bastions of alternative spirit in this heavily gentrified area. Now the Tacheles too has fallen victim to development, starting in 1998 when the land was sold to property investors. The group went bankrupt and the creditor bank decided to recoup its losses by auctioning off the plot. Initial attempts to evict the artists and clear the space in summer 2010 failed, in part because of backing by the Berlin Senate. But in mid-2012, after years of a legal tug of war, the last of the artists left. The structure itself enjoys protected status, but its future and that of the empty land surrounding it remains uncertain.

⊙ TOP SIGHTS
HACKESCHE HÖFE

The Hackesche Höfe is the largest and most famous of the courtyard ensembles peppered throughout the Scheunenviertel. Built in 1907, it links Rosenthaler Strasse with Sophienstrasse and lingered through the city's division until being acquired by West German investors in 1994. After a total makeover, the complex of eight interlinked courtyards reopened to great fanfare in 1996 with a congenial mix of cafes, galleries, boutiques and entertainment venues.

Fronted by a beautiful art deco facade, the main entrance off Rosenthaler Strasse leads you to **Court I**, prettily festooned with patterned tiles by art nouveau architect August Endell. One of Berlin's best cabarets, the Chamäleon Varieté (p142), is located here, as is an arthouse cinema. Shoppers can look forward to plenty of flagship stores by Berlin designers. If you're a fan of the little characters on Berlin traffic lights, stock up on souvenirs in the Ampelmann Galerie (p145). Court VII leads off to the **Rosenhöfe**, a fanciful art nouveau–inspired courtyard with a sunken rose garden and tendril-like balustrades.

DON'T MISS...

➡ The art nouveau facade in Court I
➡ Berlin designer boutiques
➡ Rosenhöfe

PRACTICALITIES

➡ Map p320
➡ 📞2809 8010
➡ www.hackesche-hoefe.com
➡ Rosenthaler Strasse 40/41, Sophienstrasse 6
➡ 🚇M1, 🚉Hackescher Markt

SCHEUNENVIERTEL SIGHTS

TOP SIGHTS
MUSEUM FÜR NATURKUNDE

Fossils and minerals don't quicken your pulse? Well, how about a 12m-high brachiosaurus, the Guinness Book–certified world's largest mounted dino? This giant is joined by a dozen Jurassic buddies, including the ferocious allosaurus and a spiny-backed kentrosaurus, all about 150 million years old and from Tanzania. Clever 'Juraskopes' bring half a dozen of them back to virtual flesh-and-bone life. The same hall also sports an ultra-rare fossilised archaeopteryx.

Beyond here you can journey deep into space or clear up such age-old mysteries as why zebras are striped and why peacocks have such beautiful feathers. Surprises include massively magnified insect models; wait until you see the mindboggling anatomy of an ordinary house fly! A newish highlight is the wet collection: 276,000 glass jars containing over one million ethanol-preserved animals and displayed in a huge glowing glass cube in its own darkened hall.

A crowd favourite among the stuffed animals is Bobby, the gorilla, although he'll soon be eclipsed by the late polar bear celebrity Knut.

DON'T MISS...

- Brachiosaurus
- Archaeopteryx
- Insect models

PRACTICALITIES

- Museum of Natural History
- Map p319
- ☎2093 8591
- www.naturkundmuseum-berlin.de
- Invalidenstrasse 43
- adult/concession incl audioguide €6/3.50,
- ⏰9.30am-6pm Tue-Fri, 10am-6pm Sat & Sun
- [S]Naturkundemuseum

[FREE] JÜDISCHE MÄDCHENSCHULE HISTORIC BUILDING

Map p320 (www.maedchenschule.org; Auguststrasse 11-13; ⏰hours vary; [S]Oranienburger Tor, 🚋M1, 🚉Oranienburger Strasse) After languishing for years, the 1920s former Jewish Girls' School reopened in 2012 as the new home of three renowned Berlin galleries – Eigen+Art, Camera Work and Michael Fuchs – and three eateries, including a deli, a kosher restaurant and the elegant Pauly Saal. Camera Work also operates the Museum The Kennedys on the 2nd floor.

The entire project is the brainchild of Michael Fuchs, who negotiated a 30-year lease of the protected red-brick building with its owner, Berlin's Jewish community, and then put it through a sensitive but thorough one-year restoration. Plenty of original design features have survived, including the tiles in the entrance and the classroom lights.

MUSEUM THE KENNEDYS MUSEUM

Map p320 (www.thekennedys.de; Auguststrasse 11-13; ⏰11am-7pm; [S]Oranienburger Tor, 🚋M1, 🚉Oranienburger Strasse) Set up like a walk-through family album, this intimate exhibit trains the spotlight on US president John F Kennedy who has held a special place in German hearts since his '*Ich bin ein Berliner*!' solidarity speech in 1963. Family history, the Berlin visit and the President's assassination are among the topics addressed through photographs, documents and relics. There's even a hilarious Superman comic book edition starring the President. At press time, the museum was set to move from its original Pariser Platz location and reopen in the Jüdische Mädchenschule in November 2012. Check the website for admission prices.

KW INSTITUTE FOR CONTEMPORARY ART GALLERY

Map p320 (☎243 4590; www.kw-berlin.de; Auguststrasse 69; adult/concession €6/4; ⏰noon-7pm Tue, Wed & Fri-Sun, to 9pm Thu; [S]Oranienburger Strasse, 🚋M1, 🚉Oranienburger Tor) In an old margarine factory, nonprofit KW helped chart the fate of the Scheunenviertel as Berlin's original post-Wall art district. It still stages ground-breaking shows reflecting the latest – and often radical – trends in contemporary art. Its founder, Klaus Biesenbach, was also the engine behind the **Berlin Biennale** (www.berlinbiennale.de) art fair, inaugurated in 1990. The courtyard Café Bravo (p140) makes for a stylish coffee break.

ME COLLECTORS ROOM   GALLERY
Map p320 (☎8600 8510; www.me-berlin.com; Auguststrasse 68; adult/concession €6/4; ⊙noon-6pm Tue-Sun; ☎; ⏣M1, ⏣Oranienburger Strasse) Thomas Olbricht collects art from the 16th century to today and invites curators to put together changing exhibits that reflect such existential human themes as life, love, sexuality, transience and death. The collection includes works by Gerhard Richter, Thomas Demand and Cindy Sherman along with many lesser-known artists. Upstairs is a *Wunderkammer*, a 'cabinet of curiosities' with wondrous objects from around the world.

The on-site Me Cafe is a pleasant spot to reflect upon it all.

SAMMLUNG HOFFMANN   GALLERY
Map p320 (☎2849 9120; www.sammlung-hoffmann.de; Sophienstrasse 21; tours €10; ⊙11am-4pm Sat by appointment only; ⏣Weinmeisterstrasse) Blink and you'll miss the plain doorway leading to the Sophie-Gips-Höfe, an artsy trio of 19th-century courtyards linking Sophienstrasse and Gipsstrasse. The former sewing-machine factory now harbours stores, offices, flats and the Sammlung Hoffmann, the private contemporary art collection assembled by Erika Hoffmann and her late husband Rolf. On Saturdays between 11am and 4pm, Ms Hoffmann shows small groups of art fans around her two-storey apartment, which brims with works by such luminaries as

Gerhard Richter, Frank Stella, Jean-Michel Basquiat and AR Penck. Registration for the tours should be made at least several days in advance.

RAMONES MUSEUM   MUSEUM
Map p320 (☎7552 8889; www.ramonesmuseum.com; Krausnickstrasse 23; admission €3.50; ⊙noon-8pm Sun-Thu, to 10pm Fri & Sat; ☎; ⏣Oranienburger Strasse) They sang 'Born to Die in Berlin' but the legacy of punk pioneers the Ramones is kept very much alive in the German capital, thanks to this eclectic collection of memorabilia. Look for Marky Ramone's drumsticks and Johnny Ramone's jeans amid signed album covers, posters, flyers, photographs and other flotsam and jetsam. The on-site cafe also hosts the occasional concert.

⦿ Hauptbahnhof & Oranienburger Tor

HAMBURGER BAHNHOF –
MUSEUM FÜR GEGENWART   GALLERY
See p129.

GEDENKSTÄTTE BERLINER MAUER MEMORIAL
See p130.

SAMMLUNG BOROS   GALLERY
Map p319 (☎2759 4065; www.sammlung-boros.de; Reinhardtstrasse 20; adult/concession €10/6; ⊙2-6pm Fri, 10am-6pm Sat & Sun; ⏣Oranienburger Tor, Friedrichstrasse, ⏣M1, ⏣Friedrichstrasse) The vibe of war, vegetables and whips still hangs over the 80 rooms of this Nazi-era bunker turned shining beacon of art. It's all thanks to the vision of Christian Boros, advertising guru and collector of art by practitioners currently writing history,

---

BEYOND THE SCHEUNENVIERTEL: LESSER-KNOWN JEWISH SITES

The Holocaust Memorial, the Neue Synagoge and the Jüdisches Museum are Berlin's flagship Jewish sites, but there are plenty of other important places of remembrance. Here's a top five:

➡ **Gleis 17** (Platform 17; Am Bahnhof Grunewald; ⏣Grunewald) Trains departed for the concentration camp from these tracks.

➡ **Haus der Wannsee-Konferenz** (p214) The villa where Nazi leaders planned the 'Final Solution'.

➡ **Mendelssohn Exhibit** (p84) An homage to one of Berlin's most prominent Jewish families.

➡ **Jüdischer Friedhof Schönhauser Allee** (p181) Final resting place for famous Jewish Berliners.

➡ **Block der Frauen** (p105) Memorial to a successful act of Nazi resistance.

HAUS SCHWARZENBERG

In blatant contrast to the luxe boutiques and trendy cafes typical of the Scheunen-viertel, **Haus Schwarzenberg** (Map p320) at Rosenthaler Strasse 39 is a flashback to the early 1990s when most of the quarter's buildings looked just as grimy and dilapidated. In recent years, the building has been stabilised but there are no plans for its beautification. Quite the opposite. Instead, the goal is to retain an unpretentious, authentic space where art and creativity can flourish beyond mainstream and commerce. Festooned with street art and bizarre metal sculptures, the courtyard gives access to studios, offices, a surreal 'amusement park', an edgy-arty bar, an arthouse cinema and three small exhibits dealing with Jewish persecution during the Third Reich.

Museum Blindenwerkstatt Otto Weidt (Map p320; ⏹2859 9407; www.museum -blindenwerkstatt.de; Rosenthaler Strasse 39; admission free; ☉10am-8pm; ☒Hackescher Markt, Weinmeisterstrasse) Otto Weidt was a broom and brush maker who risked his life protecting his blind and deaf Jewish workers from the Nazis. The exhibit is inside the very workshop where he hid an entire family in a room behind a cabinet, provided food and false papers and bribed Gestapo officials into releasing Jews scheduled for deportation. A highlight is an emotional video in which survivors recall Weidt's efforts to save their lives.

Anne Frank Zentrum (Map p320; ⏹288 865 610; www.annefrank.de; Rosenthaler Strasse 39; adult/concession/child €5/2.50/free; ☉10am-6pm Tue-Sun; Ⓢ Weinmeisterstrasse, ☒Hackescher Markt) This exhibit uses artefacts and photographs to tell the extraordinary story of a girl who needs no introduction. Who hasn't read the diary of Anne Frank penned while in hiding from the Nazis in Amsterdam? Frank perished from typhus at Bergen-Belsen concentration camp just days before her 16th birthday. A room is devoted to her diary and its profound impact on postwar generations.

Gedenkstätte Stille Helden (Silent Heroes Memorial Exhibit; Map p320; ⏹2345 7919; www.gedenkstaette-stille-helden.de; Rosenthaler Strasse 41; ☉10am-8pm) The Silent Heroes Memorial Exhibit is dedicated to ordinary Germans who found the courage to hide and help their persecuted Jewish neighbours, just as Otto Weidt had done. Interactive media tables provide themed background information, while upstairs multimedia information pillars document the fate of individuals, both from the point of view of the helpers and of the persecuted.

Monsterkabinett (www.monsterkabinett.de; Haus Schwarzenberg, Rosenthalar Strasse 39, 2nd courtyard; adult/concession €8/5; ☉6-10pm Thu, 4-10pm Fri & Sat; Ⓢ Weinmeister-strasse, ☒Hackescher Markt) If you want to meet 'Püppi' the techno-loving go-go dancer' or 'Orangina' the twirling six-legged doll, you need to descend a steep spiralling staircase into Hannes Heiner's surrealist underground world. Inspired by his dreams, the artist has fashioned a menagerie of animated mechanical monsters and assembled them in a computer-controlled art and sound installation that will entertain, astound and perhaps even frighten you just a little bit.

Olafur Eliasson, Damien Hirst, Sarah Lucas and Wolfgang Tilmanns among them. A selection of his treasures can be viewed on guided tours (also in English). Book online as early as possible.

During the tour you'll also pick up fascinating nuggets about the war-scarred shelter that preserves the original fittings, pipes, steel doors and vents. Built for 2000 people, its dank rooms crammed in twice as many during the heaviest air raids towards the end of the war. Afterwards, the Soviets

briefly used it as a POW prison before it assumed a more benign role as a fruit and vegetable storeroom in GDR times, which spawned the nickname 'Banana Bunker'. In the 1990s, the claustrophobic warren saw some of Berlin's naughtiest techno raves and fetish parties. Boros finally snapped it up in 2003.

BRECHT-WEIGEL GEDENKSTÄTTE MEMORIAL
Map p319 (www.adk.de/de/archiv/gedenksta etten; Chausseestrasse 125; tours adult/

concession €5/2.50; ⊙tours half-hourly 10-11.30am & 2-3.30pm Tue, 10-11.30am Wed & Fri, 10-11.30am & 5-6.30pm Thu, 10am-3.30pm Sat, hourly 11am-6pm Sun; ⓢOranienburger Tor, Naturkundemuseum) Playwright Bertolt Brecht lived in this house from 1953 until his death in 1956. Guides take you inside his office, a large library and the tiny bedroom where he died. Decorated with Chinese artwork, it's been left as though he'd briefly stepped out, leaving his hat and woollen cap hanging on the door. Downstairs are the cluttered quarters of his actress wife Helene Weigel.

The couple are buried on the adjacent **Dorotheenstädtischer Friedhof**. Tours are in German and limited to eight persons. The basement restaurant, Brechtkeller, serves Austrian food prepared from Weigel's recipes, amid family pictures and original set models from Brecht's productions.

FREE DOROTHEENSTÄDTISCHER
FRIEDHOF CEMETERY
Map p319 (Chausseestrasse 126; ⊙8am-dusk; ⓢOranienburger Tor, Naturkundemuseum, 🚋M1) This compact cemetery is the place of perpetual slumber for a veritable roll call of famous Germans and dotted with artistic tombstones. Karl Friedrich Schinkel, in fact, designed his own. Brecht, who lived next door, chose to be buried here, allegedly to be close to his philosopher idols Hegel and Fichte. Dramatist Heiner Müller is a recent addition; fans still leave cigars for him. A map by the entrance shows grave locations.

BERLINER MEDIZINHISTORISCHES
MUSEUM MUSEUM
Map p319 (☏450 536 156; www.bmm-charite.de; Charitéplatz 1; adult/concession €7/3.50; ⊙10am-5pm Tue, Thu, Fri & Sun, to 7pm Wed & Sat; ⓢHauptbahnhof, 🚉Hauptbahnhof) Affiliated with the Charité Hospital, this museum chronicles 300 years of medical history in an anatomical theatre, a pathologist's dissection room, a laboratory and a historical patients' ward. The heart of the exhibit, though, is the grisly pathology collection that's essentially a 3D medical textbook on human disease and deformities. Definitely not for the squeamish. In fact, those under 16 must be accompanied by an adult.

Monstrous tumours, inflamed organs, a colon the size of an elephant's trunk and two-headed foetuses are all pickled in formalin and neatly displayed in glass jars. Changing exhibits are shown on the 2nd floor. The basis of the specimen collection was assembled by Rudolf Virchow (1821–1902), a famous doctor, researcher and professor. Also have a look at his lecture hall – a preserved ruin – that is used for special events.

✗ EATING

✗ Hackescher Markt Area

SCHWARZWALDSTUBEN GERMAN €€
Map p320 (☏2809 8084; Tucholskystrasse 48; dishes €7-14; 🚉Oranienburger Strasse) In the mood for a Hansel and Gretel moment? Then join the other 'lost kids' in this send-up of the Black Forest complete with plastic pines and baseball-capped Bambi heads. We can't get enough of the *geschmelzte Maultaschen* (sautéed ravioli-like pasta) and the giant schnitzel. Everything goes down well with a glass of Rothaus Tannenzäpfle beer, straight from the Black Forest.

SUSURU JAPANESE €
Map p320 (www.susuru.de; Rosa-Luxemburg-Strasse 17; mains €6.50-9; 🖳📠; ⓢRosa-Luxemburg-Platz) Go ye forth and slurp! *Susuru* is Japanese for slurping and, quite frankly, that's the best way to deal with the oodles of noodles at this soup parlour, which looks as neat and stylish as a bento box.

CHÈN CHÈ VIETNAMESE €€
Map p320 (www.chenche-berlin.de; Rosenthaler Strasse 13; dishes around €8; 📠; ⓢRosenthaler Platz, 🚋M1) Smouldering joss sticks point the way to this exotic Vietnamese teahouse at the back of a quiet courtyard. Settle down in the charming Zen garden or beneath the chandelier and pick from the small menu of steaming *pho* (soups), curries and noodle dishes served in traditional clay pots. Exquisite tea selection and small store.

BARCOMI'S DELI CAFE €
Map p320 (www.barcomis.de; 2nd courtyard, Sophie-Gips-Höfe, Sophienstrasse 21; dishes €2-11; ⊙9am-9pm Mon-Sat, 10am-9pm Sun; ⓢWeinmeisterstrasse) Join latte-rati, families and expats at this New York–meets-Berlin deli for custom-roasted coffee, wraps, bagels

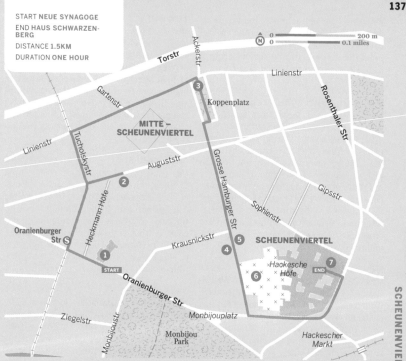

START NEUE SYNAGOGE
END HAUS SCHWARZEN-
BERG
DISTANCE 1.5KM
DURATION ONE HOUR

Neighbourhood Walk
Traces of Jewish Life in the Scheunenviertel

This easy walk takes you past vestiges, memorials and revitalised sites of Jewish life throughout the Scheunenviertel. It starts at the imposing **1** **Neue Synagoge**, inaugurated in 1866 as Germany's largest Jewish house of worship and now a museum and community centre. Turn right on Tucholskystrasse and right again on Auguststrasse to find yourself at the **2** **Jüdische Mädchenschule** (Jewish Girls' School), which reopened in 2012 as a vaunted gallery and restaurant space.

Continue north on Tucholskystrasse, then follow Linienstrasse east to **3** **Der Verlassene Raum** (The Deserted Room). Karl Biedermann's art installation consists of a table and two chairs, one knocked over as a symbol of Jewish residents being forced to flee suddenly from their homes.

Continue south on Grosse Hamburger Strasse and look for the **4** **Missing House**, Christian Boltanski's 1990 memorial installation on the site of a bombed-out apartment building. Signs bearing the names of its former residents are affixed to the facades of the adjacent buildings. The structure opposite, at No 27, was a **5** **Jewish Boys' School** founded in 1788. The Nazis closed it down but it survived the war intact. Since 1993 both boys and girls – Jewish and not – have once again hit the books here. A few steps south, the **6** **Alter Jüdischer Friedhof** was Berlin's first Jewish cemetery. Some 12,000 people were buried here between 1672 and 1827, including Enlightenment philosopher Moses Mendelssohn. His replica tombstone stands representative for all six-feet-under residents.

The tour concludes at **7** **Haus Schwarzenberg**, which houses three small museums dealing with the fate of Jews under the Nazis: the workshop of a broom maker who saved many of his workers, a museum about Anne Frank and a memorial site honouring ordinary Germans who hid and helped their Jewish neighbours.

with lox (smoked salmon), soups, salads and possibly the best brownies and cheesecake this side of the Hudson River. Bonus points for the charming and quiet setting in a classic Scheunenviertel courtyard.

PAULY SAAL
GERMAN €€€

Map p320 (☑3300 6070; www.paulysaal.com; Auguststrasse 11-13; mains lunch €15-20, dinner €30-38; ◷noon-11pm; ⓢOranienburger Tor, ◪M1, ◪Oranienburger Strasse) In the former gym of a Jewish Girls' School, chef Siegfried Danler gives classic, earthy German dishes a modern, lighter spin by using only top-flight organic and regional ingredients. Dine amid such conversation-inspiring art as Daniel Richter's stuffed and bandaged foxes and Cosima von Bonin's giant rocket or retreat to the old schoolyard canopied by umbrellas and a leafy old tree.

MOGG & MELZER
DELI €€

Map p320 (www.moggandmelzer.com; Auguststrasse 11-13; mains €7-15; ◷8am-11pm Mon-Fri, 10am-11pm Sat; ◪M1, ◪Oranienburger Strasse) Pastrami lovers rejoice behind big windows in the former Jewish Girls' School, for this is Berlin's first genuine New York-style Jewish deli. The juicy sandwiches come in two sizes on rye and are topped with melted Swiss cheese and paired with salted pickles. The arty 1930s-inspired surrounds, featuring purple-topped benches and Finnish designer chairs, are very Berlin indeed.

TRANSIT
ASIAN €

Map p320 (☑2478 1645; www.transit-restaurants.com; Rosenthaler Strasse 68; dishes €3; ◷11am-1am; ⓢRosenthaler Platz) Fill up on Asian tapas at this tunnel-shaped casual eatery with its colourful paper lanterns. There's a sister branch in Friedrichshain (p172).

MONSIEUR VUONG
ASIAN €€

Map p320 (☑9929 6924; www.monsieurvuong.de; Alte Schönhauser Strasse 46; mains around €8; ◷noon-midnight; ⓢWeinmeisterstrasse, Rosa-Luxemburg-Platz) Berlin's 'godfather' of upbeat Indochina nosh-stops, Monsieur has been copied many times – the concept is just that good. Pick from a compact menu of flavour-packed soups and two or three oft-changing mains, then sit back and enjoy your leftover money. Amazingly, the quality hasn't come down despite the never-ending queue. Come in the afternoon to avoid the frenzy.

YAM YAM
KOREAN €

Map p320 (www.yamyam-berlin.de; Alte Schönhauser Strasse 6; mains €4.50-8; ⓢRosa-Luxemburg-Platz) In a dashing move of career derring-do, Sumi Ha morphed her fancy fashion boutique into a stylish self-service bijou where the spicy *bibimbap* (a hot pot rice dish), fresh *gimbab* (seaweed rolls), steamy *mandu* (dumplings) and other fancified Korean street food all pass the authenticity test.

CAFÉ NORD-SUD
FRENCH €

Map p320 (Auguststrasse 87; 3-course menu €7.50; ◷lunch & dinner Mon-Sat; ⓢOranienburger Tor, ◪Oranienburger Strasse) In his humble cafe, owner Jean-Claude Malfoy takes on the roles of greeter, server, sommelier and cook in what amounts to a Peter Sellers–worthy performance. Portions are not huge or super-fancy but at €7.50 for a set three-course meal, all we can say is oh là là!

DADA FALAFEL
MIDDLE EASTERN €

Map p319 (www.dadafalafel.de; Linienstrasse 132; dishes €3.50-7; ◷10am-2am; ⓢOranienburger Tor) 'Eating is a necessity, but to eat intelligently is an art.' This quote by 17th-century French author François de La Rochefoucauld is the motto of this teensy exotic takeaway with attached gallery. One bite of Dada's freshly prepared felafel doused with a tangy homemade sauce and you too will understand why there's always a queue of local loyalists, despite usually perfunctory service.

KOPPS
VEGAN €€

Map p320 (☑4320 9775; www.kopps-berlin.de; Linienstrasse 94; mains €12-16; ◷8.30am-midnight; ☑; ⓢRosenthaler Platz, ◪M1) 'German vegan' may seem like an oxymoron but not at Kopps, which dishes up delicious goulash, rouladen (beef olives) and schnitzel *sans* animal products. The space is sparse but stylish, with bluish-grey walls and recycled doors and mirrors in unexpected places. Excellent breakfasts, bursting weekend brunch and DJs after 10pm on weekends.

PAN ASIA
ASIAN €€

Map p320 (☑8188 6230; www.panasia.de; Rosenthaler Strasse 38; mains €7-17; ◷Sun-Thu noon-midnight, Fri noon-1am; ◪Hackescher Markt) Manga films, light projections and long communal tables account for the hipster quotient at this high-energy restaurant next to the Hackesche Höfe. The menu predictably hopscotches from Thailand to China, via Japan and Vietnam, and back. Fresh ingredients and healthy, low-fat cooking techniques make it a favourite with waist-watchers.

🍴 Hauptbahnhof & Oranienburger Tor

GRILL ROYAL STEAKHOUSE **€€€**

Map p319 (☎2887 9288; www.grillroyal.com; Friedrichstrasse 105b; mains €16-39, steaks €18-55; 🕒dinner; [S]Friedrichstrasse, [R]Friedrichstrasse) A platinum card is a handy accessory at this 'look-at-me' temple where A-listers, power politicians, pouty models and 'trust-afarians' can be seen slurping oysters and tucking into their prime cuts, including superb regionally raised organic Angus cattle. No complaints about the food quality, the sensibly sensuous decor or the people-watching potential. Service, alas, can be snooty. Riverside tables beckon in fine weather.

SARAH WIENER IM HAMBURGER BAHNHOF AUSTRIAN **€€**

Map p319 (☎7071 3650; www.sarahwiener.de; Invalidenstrasse 50-51; mains €11-22; 🕒10am-6pm Tue-Fri, 11am-8pm Sat, 11am-6pm Sun; [S]Hauptbahnhof, [R]Hauptbahnhof) Berlin's smartest museum cafe is the domain of culinary star Sarah Wiener, famous as much for her classic veal schnitzel as for her tasty *Sachertorte* (Sacher cake) and other Austrian cakes. The huge, high-ceilinged room gets texture from a long bar, patterned stone floor, dimmed lights and various conversation corners where artsy types discuss the latest museum exhibit.

🍴 Torstrasse

[TOP CHOICE] **KATZ ORANGE** INTERNATIONAL **€€€**

Map p320 (☎983 208 430; www.katzorange.com; Bergstrasse 22; mains €13-22; 🕒dinner Tue-Sat year-round, lunch May-Sep; [S]Rosenthaler Platz) Wits its gourmet organic farm-to-table menu, feel-good country styling and swift and smiling servers, the 'Orange Cat' hits a gastro grand slam. Owner Ludwig Cramer-Klett regards his restaurant as a 'spiritual project' and a space that allows patrons to connect to each other while respecting the food they eat. The setting in a castle-like former brewery is stunning, especially in summer when the patio opens.

STUMBLING UPON HISTORY

If you lower your gaze, you'll see them everywhere, but especially in the Scheunenviertel: small brass paving stones engraved with names and placed in front of house entrances. Called *Stolpersteine* (stumbling blocks), they are part of a nationwide project by Berlin-born artist Gunter Demnig and are essentially mini-memorials honouring the people (usually Jews) who lived in that house before being killed by the Nazis.

ZAGREUS PROJEKT INTERNATIONAL **€€€**

Map p320 (☎2809 5640; www.zagreus.net; Back courtyard, Brunnenstrasse 9a; 4-course dinner €36; [S]Rosenthaler Platz, 🚋M1) Art meets food in this project space headed by chef-artist-gallery-owner Ulrich Krauss. Every other month, Krauss invites different artists to create a site-specific installation, then composes a menu inspired by the artwork and serves it to a small group of diners at a communal table right in the gallery. Great for art-loving foodies and food-loving artists. Reservations required as hours vary.

HARTWEIZEN ITALIAN **€€**

Map p320 (☎2849 3877; www.hartweizen.com; Torstrasse 96; mains €11-24; 🕒dinner Mon-Sat; [S]Rosenthaler Platz) With its simple wooden tables, panorama windows and bright bulbs, Hartweizen is eons away from Chianti-bottle kitsch. Instead, it is quite simply a top Italian restaurant focused on the feisty flavours of the Puglia region. The most creativity goes into the appetisers, but fish and meat are also first-rate, the pastas homemade and the wines fairly priced.

WHITE TRASH FAST FOOD AMERICAN **€€**

Map p320 (☎5034 8668; www.whitetrashfastfood.com; Schönhauser Allee 6-7; mains €8-20; 🕒from noon Mon-Fri, from 6pm Sat & Sun; [S]Rosa-Luxemburg-Platz) Wally Potts – city cowboy, California import and Berlin's coolest bar owner – has spun this ex-Irish pub with Chinese flourishes into a culinary punk-hole complete with in-house tattoo parlour. On some nights, DJs and bands make conversation a challenge, thus helping you focus on the manly burgers and steaks flown in straight from the US of A. More music downstairs in the cavernous Diamond Lounge.

LOCAL KNOWLEDGE

ROSENTHALER PLATZ: SNACK CENTRAL

For feeding hunger pangs on the quick and cheap, choices could not be greater than the area around Rosenthaler Platz. Here's our personal hit list:

Fleischerei Imbiss (Map p320; Torstrasse 116; snacks from €2.50; ⏰11am-2am Mon-Sat, 2pm-midnight Sun; [S]Rosenthaler Platz, 🚋M1 to Rosenthaler Platz) For divine Currywurst with bubbly.

Rosenthaler Grill- und Schlemmerbuffet (Map p320; ☎283 2153; Torstrasse 125; dishes €2.50-7; ⏰24hr; [S]Rosenthaler Platz) For Oscar-worthy doner kebabs.

Rosenburger (Map p320; ☎2408 3037; Brunnenstrasse 196; burgers from €2.90; ⏰from 11am; [S]Rosenthaler Platz) For freshly made organic burgers.

Côcô (Map p320; Rosenthaler Strasse 2; sandwiches €4.20-5.50; ⏰11am-10pm Mon-Thu, 11am-midnight Fri & Sat, noon-10pm Sun; [S]Rosenthaler Platz) For bulging *bánh mì* (Vietnamese sandwiches).

MANI MEDITERRANEAN €€€

Map p320 (☎0163 635 9464; www.mani-restaurant.com; Torstrasse 136; small plates €4-12.50, mains €16.50-22; ⏰lunch Mon-Fri, dinner Tue-Sat; [S]Rosenthaler Platz, 🚋M1) This modernist design jewel presents a richly flavoured menu that jets your taste buds from Paris to Tel Aviv. Perched at a shiny black table, perhaps near the fireplace, you can watch the kitchen staff churn out such richly nuanced morsels as venison tartare or their signature truffled foie gras burger. Extra kudos for the inspired wine selection and value-priced two-course business lunches.

DRINKING & NIGHTLIFE

Hackescher Markt Area

CLÄRCHENS BALLHAUS CLUB

Map p320 (☎282 9295; www.ballhaus.de; Auguststrasse 24; ⏰restaurant 12.30-11.30pm, dancing nightly; 🚋M1, 🚆Oranienburger Strasse) Yesteryear is now at this late, great 19th-century dance hall where groovers and grannies hoof it across the parquet without even a touch of irony. There's different sounds nightly – salsa to swing, tango to disco – and a live band on Saturday. The later it gets, the younger the crowd.

Dance classes, dinner and concerts are held upstairs in the *Spiegelsaal* (Mirror Hall). Pizza and German staples provide sustenance all day long, in summer in the pretty garden (pizza €5 to €10, mains €10 to €16).

AMANO BAR BAR

Map p320 (www.bar.hotel-amano.com; Auguststrasse 43; ⏰from 4pm; [S]Rosenthaler Platz) The same bar baron that's behind Tausend has dreamed up this glamour vixen at the budget-hip Hotel Amano. The L-shaped lounge with its marble bar, cubistic furnishings and warm chocolate hues attracts chatty sophisticates with such stellar cocktails as the Fat Julep and the Yoshitaka Amano. In summer, the action moves to the rooftop terrace.

BAR 3 BAR

Map p320 (Weydinger Strasse 20; ⏰from 9pm Tue-Sat; [S]Rosa-Luxemburg-Strasse) With its wrap-around glass windows, black decor and dim lighting, this stylish, minimalist bar seems to be jostling for *Wallpaper* coverage but is actually a laid-back lair for local lovelies, artists and actors from the nearby Volksbühne theatre. Scope out the action huddled around the U-shaped bar and guzzling cold Kölsch beer from Cologne.

STRANDBAR MITTE BAR

Map p320 (☎2838 5588; www.strandbar-mitte.de; Monbijoustrasse 1-3; ⏰from 10am May-Sep; 🚋M1, 🚆Oranienburger Strasse) With a full-on view of the Bodemuseum, palm trees and a relaxed ambience, this riverside playground is great for balancing a surfeit of sightseeing stimulus with a revivifying drink. After 7pm there's dancing under the stars with tango, cha cha, waltz and salsa.

CAFÉ BRAVO CAFE

Map p320 (☎2345 7777; Auguststrasse 69; €4-12; ⏰9am-8pm Mon, to 1am Tue-Thu, to 2am Fri & Sat, 10am-8pm Sun; 🚆Oranienburger Strasse) Is it art? Is it a cafe? Answer: it's both. The glass-and-chrome cube in the quiet and pretty courtyard of the KW Institute for Contemporary Art (p133) was dreamed up by US artist Dan Graham and is a suitably edgy refuelling stop on any Scheunenviertel saunter. The food's quality is uneven, so stick with liquids.

KING SIZE BAR — BAR

Map p319 (www.kingsizebar.de; Friedrichstrasse 112b; ⏰9pm-7am Wed-Sat; [S]Oranienburger Tor) Good things come in small packages at this self-ironically named and well-stocked hole-in-the-wall. A local favourite of boho-bourgeois elite, it's at its raucous best after 1am when the space before the toilet turns into an impromptu dance floor. Join in or watch the action sipping a signature Moscow Mule, served – as are all drinks – in cut-crystal whisky tumblers. Smoking allowed.

AUGUST II — BAR

Map p320 (www.augustthesecond.de; Auguststrasse 2; ⏰from 9pm Thu-Sat; [S]Oranienburger Tor, 🚋M1) Another entry in the trend towards tiny bar-club combos, August II seduces the locals' three-day stubble, ironic tees and Sinatra hat hipsters. The vibe is funky-glam thanks to complexion-friendly chandelier lighting and first-rate pours. Handily within stumbling distance of the similar bars.

FLAMINGO — CLUB

Map p320 (www.flamingoberlin.com; Am Monbijou Park, S-Bahn arch 157/158; 🚋M1, 🚆Hackescher Markt) The S-Bahn rushes above, but the global scenesters mingling inside this nightspot are too busy flirting, dancing and swilling surprisingly well-mixed libations to notice. Golden palm lamps add a cosy-sexy touch to the otherwise rather stark black and minimalist venue with separate bar, lounge and dance floor.

🍷 Torstrasse

BUCK AND BRECK — BAR

Map p320 (☎0176 3231 5507; www.buckandbreck.com; Brunnenstrasse 177; ⏰from 8pm; [S]Rosenthaler Platz) After stints around town, charismatic Berlin barmeister Gonçalo de Sousa Monteiro is finally flying solo and treating clued-in patrons to his libational flights of fancy in an intimate cocktail salon behind a nameless door. Historical concoctions are his strength, including the eponymous Buck and Breck, a potent blend of cognac, bitters, absinthe and champagne. Call ahead as space is limited.

BUTCHER'S — BAR

Map p320 (Torstrasse 116; ⏰9pm Wed-Sat; [S]Rosenthaler Platz, 🚋M1) Shhhh... The newest venture by cocktail whisperer David Wiedemann is a 1920s-style speakeasy tucked into a butchershop behind a sausage parlour called Fleischerei. Drinks are expertly mixed and the ambience is refined, even if meat hooks, a leather bar and red light channel the place's early incarnation. The entrance is inside through the red phone booth.

MEIN HAUS AM SEE — CAFE, BAR

Map p320 (www.mein-haus-am-see.blogspot.de; Brunnenstrasse 197/198; ⏰from 9am; [S]Rosenthaler Platz, 🚋M1) This 'House by the Lake' is nowhere near anything liquid, unless you count the massive numbers of beverages consumed at this chill boho hangout that multitasks as a cafe-bar, gallery, performance space and club. Plop down onto grandma's sofa for intimate chats or grab a seat on the broad staircase for some quality people-watching. Best of all, it's almost always open.

NEUE ODESSA BAR — BAR

Map p320 (Torstrasse 89; [S]Rosenthaler Platz) Rub shoulders with a global mix of grown-ups with a hot fashion sense at this comfy-chic and always busy Torstrasse staple. The patterned wallpaper, velvet sofas and smart lamps create cosy ambience, no matter if your taste runs towards Krusovice or cocktails. Smoking allowed.

KAFFEE BURGER — CLUB

Map p320 (☎2804 6495; www.kaffeeburger.de; Torstrasse 60; [S]Rosa-Luxemburg-Platz) Nothing to do with either coffee or meat patties, this sweaty cult club with lovingly faded Commie-era decor is the famous home of

LOCAL KNOWLEDGE

TRENDY TORSTRASSE

Though loud and heavily trafficked, Torstrasse is booming, and not just since Brangelina were rumoured to have bought a flat nearby. With surprising speed, this main thoroughfare has turned into a hip strip where trendy eats pop up with the frequency of fruit-fly births, gritty-glam bars pack in night crawlers and indie boutiques lure the fashion-savvy.

the twice-monthly Russendisko that even Madonna could not resist. But even without a tabloid-regular in sight, it's always a fun-for-all concert and party pen with a sound policy that swings from indie and electro to klezmer punk without missing a beat.

🍷 Hauptbahnhof & Oranienburger Tor

MELODY NELSON BAR

Map p319 (Novalisstrasse 2; ⏱Tue-Sat; [S]Oranienburger Tor) Everything about this hushed bar speaks of refinement but without an iota of stuffiness: the dim lighting, the plush seating, the carpeted floors. It helps that sexy siren Jane Birkin is winking at you from behind the bar. The cocktails rock, especially the self-styled 'Black Mojito'. Good for quiet tête-à-têtes during the week and preparty on weekends.

☆ ENTERTAINMENT

CHAMÄLEON VARIETÉ CABARET

Map p320 (☎400 0590; www.chamaeleonberlin.com; Rosenthaler Strasse 40/41; 🚊M1, 🚆Hackescher Markt) A marriage of art nouveau charms and high-tech theatre trappings, this intimate 1920s-style cabaret in an old ballroom presents classy variety shows – comedy, juggling acts and singing – often in sassy, sexy and unconventional fashion.

BABYLON CINEMA

Map p320 (☎242 5969; www.babylonberlin.de; Rosa-Luxemburg-Strasse 30; [S]Rosa-Luxemburg-Platz) This top-rated indie screens a well-curated potpourri of new German films, international arthouse flicks, themed retrospectives and other stuff you'd never catch at the multiplex. For the silent movies, the original theatre organ is put through its paces. It's in a fantastic protected 1920s building by new objectivity wizard Hans Poelzig.

AMPHITHEATER THEATRE

Map p320 (www.amphitheater-berlin.de; Monbijouplatz 1-3; ⏱May-Sep; 🚊M1, 🚆Oranienburger Strasse) Every summer, the Hexenkessel Hoftheater presents classic crowd-pleasers from Shakespeare to Molière to an adoring public in an outdoor theatre that borrows a page from London's Shakespeare's Globe. On Mondays, live concerts take over the space.

VOLKSBÜHNE AM ROSA-LUXEMBURG-PLATZ THEATRE

Map p320 (☎2406 5777; www.volksbuehne-berlin.de; Rosa-Luxemburg-Platz; [S]Rosa-Luxemburg-Platz) Nonconformist, radical and provocative: performances at the 'People's Stage' are not for the squeamish. Since 1992, the theatre has been led by enfant terrible Frank Castorf who regularly tears down the confines of the proscenium stage with Zeitgeist-critical productions that are somehow both populist and elitist all at once.

SOPHIENSAELE PERFORMING ARTS

Map p320 (☎283 5266; www.sophiensaele.com; Sophienstrasse 18; [S]Weinmeisterstrasse, 🚆Hackescher Markt) Back in the 1990s, Sascha Waltz transformed the Sophiensaele into Berlin's number-one spot for experimental and avant-garde dance. Dance is still big, but the program now extends to contemporary theatre, music and performance art, often presented by young artists exploring non-conventional concepts and new forms of expression.

B-FLAT LIVE MUSIC

Map p320 (☎283 3123; www.b-flat-berlin.de; Rosenthaler Strasse 13; ⏱from 8pm Sun-Thu, from 9pm Fri & Sat; [S]Weinmeisterstrasse, Rosenthaler Platz, 🚊M1) Cool cats of all ages come out to this intimate venue, where the audience sits quite literally within spitting distance of the performers. The emphasis is on acoustic music; mostly jazz, world beats, Afro-Brazilian and other soundscapes. Wednesday's free jam session often brings down the house.

BERLINER ENSEMBLE THEATRE

Map p319 (☎information 284 080, tickets 2840 8155; www.berliner-ensemble.de; Bertolt-Brecht-Platz 1; [S]Friedrichstrasse, [S]Oranienburger Tor) The company founded by Bertolt Brecht in 1949 is based at the neo-baroque theatre where his *Threepenny Opera* premiered in 1928. Since 1999, artistic director Claus Peymann has kept the master's legacy alive while also peppering the repertory with works by Kleist, Shakespeare, Beckett and other European playwrights. Tickets are cheap and performances often sell out.

DEUTSCHES THEATER
THEATRE

Map p319 (☎2844 1225; www.deutschestheater.de; Schumannstrasse 13a; [S]Oranienburger Tor) Steered by the seminal Max Reinhardt from 1905 until 1932, the DT is still among Berlin's top stages. Now under artistic director Ulrich Khuon, the repertory includes both classical and bold new plays that usually reflect the issues and big themes of today. Plays are also performed in the adjacent *Kammerspiele* and at the 80-seat Box + Bar.

FRIEDRICHSTADTPALAST
CABARET

Map p319 (☎2326 2326; www.show-palace.eu; Friedrichstrasse 107; [S]Oranienburger Tor, 🚋M1) Europe's largest revue theatre has a tradition going back to the 1920s and is famous for glitzy Vegas-style productions with leggy showgirls, a high-tech stage, mind-boggling special effects and plenty of artistry.

SHOPPING

Label hounds addicted to staying ahead of the fashion curve and seekers of the latest Berlin fashions should concentrate their browsing along and around Alte Schönhauser Strasse, Neue Schönhauser Strasse, Münzstrasse and inside the Hackesche Höfe. Cutting-edge galleries line Linienstrasse and Auguststrasse and their side streets.

BERLIN FASHION NETWORK
FASHION

Map p320 (www.berlinfashionnetwork.com; Court III, Hackesche Höfe; ⏲11am-8pm Mon-Sat; 🚋M1, 🚆Hackescher Markt) Keen on impressing your friends back home with the latest Berlin brands? At this stylish concept store, you can browse two floors of homegrown his-and-her fashions, accessories, music and more, all with that urban, cheeky and fresh capital twist. Both new and established designers get rack space, including German Garment, ichJane, NIX and Mio Animo.

IC! BERLIN
ACCESSORIES

Map p320 (☎2472 7200; www.ic-berlin.de; Max-Beer-Strasse 17; ⏲11am-8pm Mon-Sat; [S]Weinmeisterstrasse) What looks like a bachelor pad, with worn sofas, wacky art and turntables, is the flagship store of this internationally famous eyewear maker. The feather-light frames with their klutz-proof, screwless hinges are stored in retro airline serving trolleys and have added 'spec appeal' to celebs from Madonna to the king of Morocco.

CLAUDIA SKODA
FASHION

Map p320 (☎280 7211; www.claudiaskoda.com; Alte Schönhauser Strasse 35; ⏲noon-7pm Mon-Sat; [S]Weinmeisterstrasse) Berlin-born Claudia Skoda has been a local design icon since the 1970s, when she used to party with David Bowie and Iggy Pop. Fashionistas from around town make regular visits to this gorgeous boutique to check out her latest figure-hugging knitted couture, from bold, but classy, dresses to colour-happy wrist warmers and snug sweaters, all made from top-quality yarns.

C'EST TOUT
FASHION

Map p320 (www.cesttout.de; Mulackstrasse 26; ⏲noon-7pm; [S]Weinmeisterstrasse) Katja Will, a one-time head of style at MTV, is the creative brains behind this Berlin label for women. Her signature piece is the unfussy yet elegant and form-flattering dress made from soft fabrics like silk and jersey that transitions well from office to opera.

FUN FACTORY
ACCESSORIES

Map p320 (☎2804 6366; www.funfactory-store.com; Oranienburger Strasse 92; ⏲11am-8pm Mon-Thu, to 9pm Fri & Sat; 🚆Hackescher Markt)

LOCAL KNOWLEDGE

THE SCHEUNENVIERTEL: FROM HAY TO HIP

The Scheunenviertel's odd name, Barn Quarter, hearkens back centuries to the days of wooden houses, frequent fires and poor fire-fighting techniques, which is why the Prussian king ordered all barns containing flammable crops to be stored outside the city walls. In the early 20th century, the quarter absorbed huge numbers of poor Eastern European Jewish immigrants, many of whom were later killed by the Nazis. After the war, the Scheunenviertel gradually deteriorated into a down-at-heel East Berlin barrio but has catapulted from drab to fab since reunification. Now a creative-class darling, its cafes and bars brim with iPad-toters, sassy fashionistas and bearded hipsters.

New York designer Karim Rashid dreamed up the design of this high-tech flagship store for of the purveyor of 'Patchy Paul' and 'Dildo Dolphin'. There are two floors of goodies linked by the 'stairs of passion': lingerie and body potions downstairs, and dildos, vibes and other 'lifestyle' sex toys plus literature upstairs.

ROTATION RECORDS — MUSIC

Map p320 (☎2532 9116; www.rotation-records.de; Weinbergsweg 3; 🕒noon-7pm; [S]Rosenthaler Platz, 🚋M1) Click, click, click… is the sound of electro-heads flipping through the vinyl selection in what many consider Berlin's best store for electronic dance music, mainly house and techno, both new and used. Also stocks hand-picked street fashion, some by Berlin designers or DJs like Ellen Allien, along with useful and clever gadgets and accessories.

EAST BERLIN — FASHION

Map p320 (☎2472 4189; www.eastberlinstore.com; Alte Schönhauser Strasse 33/34; 🕒11am-8pm Mon-Sat; [S]Weinmeisterstrasse) An outgrowth of the techno scene, East Berlin has kept girls and boys looking good in their signature TV Tower–emblazoned tees and hoodies since the early 1990s. These days, their expanded label selection includes the latest streetwear by Adelheid, Minikum, Nikita and about a dozen other style makers. Cute jewellery, too.

LALA BERLIN — FASHION

Map p320 (☎6579 5466; www.lalaberlin.com; Mulackstrasse 7; 🕒noon-8pm Mon-Sat; [S]Rosa-Luxemburg-Platz) Former MTV editor Leyla Piedayesh makes top-flight women's fashion that flatters both the twig-thin and the well upholstered. Check out the elegant knitwear in jewel-like hues or her witty takes on logo obsession. Her celebrity fan base includes Claudia Schiffer.

GROBER UNFUG — BOOKS

Map p320 (☎281 7331; www.groberunfug.de; Torstrasse 75; 🕒11am-7pm Mon-Wed, to 8pm Thu & Fri, to 6pm Sat; [S]Rosenthaler Platz) Fans of international comics and graphic novels can easily lose a few hours in this very cool repository of books, DVDs, soundtracks and knick-knacks. There's a mega-selection of indie and mainstream imports from the US, Japan and elsewhere. Exhibits, auctions, signings and performances take over the adjacent gallery space. There's a smaller branch in **Kreuzberg** (Map p322; ☎6940 1490; www.groberunfug.de; Zossener Strasse 33; 🕒11am-7pm Mon-Fri, to 6pm Sat; [S]Gneisenaustrasse).

HUNDT HAMMER STEIN — BOOKS

Map p320 (www.hundthammerstein.de; Alte Schönhauser Strasse 23/24; 🕒11am-7.30pm Mon-Fri, to 7pm Sat; [S]Weinmeisterstrasse) Kurt Hammerstein has a nose for good books beyond the bestseller lists. Feel free to browse through this tidy and well-curated lit lair with word candy from around the world or ask the affable owner to match a tome to your taste. There's a sizeable English selection, quality books for tots and a sprinkling of travel guides as well.

HERR VON EDEN — FASHION

Map p320 (☎2404 8682; www.herrvoneden.com; Alte Schönhauser Strasse 14; 🕒10.30am-8pm Mon-Fri, 10am-7pm Sat; [S]Weinmeisterstrasse) Bent Angelo Jensen has made sure that Berlin's dandies look the part for over a decade. Fabrics, cuts, colours, details – all are designed to release the inner peacock and help you strut your stuff in style. Prices are high, but so are the standards. There's also a women's line.

PRO QM — BOOKS

Map p320 (www.pro-qm.de; Almstadtstrasse 48; 🕒11am-8pm Mon-Sat; [S]Rosa-Luxemburg-Platz) This treasure trove of the printed word is squarely focused on design, art, architecture, pop and photography with a sprinkling of political and philosophical tomes (many in English) and a broad selection of obscure mags from around the world. With floor-to-ceiling shelves and stacks of books throughout, it's a browser's paradise.

BONBONMACHEREI — FOOD

Map p320 (☎4405 5243; www.bonbonmacherei.de; Oranienburger Strasse 32, Heckmann Höfe; 🕒noon-8pm Wed-Sat Sep-Jun; 🚋M1, [R]Oranienburger Strasse) The aroma of peppermint and liquorice wafts through this old-fashioned basement candy kitchen whose owners use antique equipment and time-tested recipes to churn out such tasty treats as their signature leaf-shaped Berliner Maiblätter.

1. ABSINTH DEPOT BERLIN — FOOD, DRINK

Map p320 (☎281 6789; www.absinth-berlin.de; Weinmeisterstrasse 4; 🕒2pm-midnight Mon-Fri, 1pm-midnight Sat; [S]Weinmeisterstrasse) Van Gogh, Toulouse-Lautrec and Oscar Wilde were among the *fin-de-siècle* artists who drew inspiration from the 'green fairy', as absinthe is also known. This quaint little shop has over 100 varieties of the potent stuff and an expert owner who'll happily help you pick out the perfect bottle for your own mind-altering rendezvous.

AMPELMANN GALERIE   SOUVENIRS
Map p320 (⏹4472 6438; www.ampelmann.de; Court V, Hackesche Höfe, Rosenthaler Strasse 40-41; ⊗9.30am-10pm Mon-Sat, 10am-7pm Sun; ⏹M1, ⏹Hackescher Markt) It took a vociferous grassroots campaign to save the little Ampelmann, the endearing fellow on East German pedestrian traffic lights. Now the beloved cult figure and global brand graces an entire store worth of T-shirts, fridge magnets, pasta, onesies, umbrellas and other knick-knacks. Other branches include **DomAquarée** (Map p318; ⏹2758 3238; Karl-Liebknecht-Strasse 5; ⊗9.30am-9pm; ⏹Alexanderplatz, ⏹Alexanderplatz) and in the **Potsdamer Platz Arkaden** (Map p316; ⏹2592 5691; Alte Potsdamer Strasse 7; ⊗10am-9pm Mon-Sat, 1-7pm Sun; ⏹Potsdamer Platz, ⏹Potsdamer Platz) and **Gendarmenmarkt** (Map p314; ⏹4003 9095; Markgrafenstrasse 37; ⊗9.30am-8pm; ⏹Hausvogteiplatz).

HAPPY SHOP   FASHION, ACCESSORIES
Map p320 (⏹2900 9500; www.happyshop-berlin.com; Torstrasse 67; ⊗11am-7pm Tue-Sat; ⏹Rosa-Luxemburg-Platz) Fun, colourful fashion beyond the mainstream is the mojo of

Happy Shop, in an artsy wooden pavilion with striped facade and pink doors. Racks and mannequins are suspended from the ceiling and lowered by pushing a button. Aside from owner-designer Micha Woeste's own Smeilinener label, the global line-up includes Belgian eccentric Bernhard Willhelm and Japanese wunderkind Mihara Yasuhiro. Ring the bell to enter.

SCHWARZER REITER   FASHION, ACCESSORIES
Map p320 (⏹4503 4438; www.schwarzer-reiter.de; Torstrasse 3; ⊗noon-8pm Mon-Sat; ⏹Rosa-Luxemburg-Platz) If you worship at the altar of hedonism, you'll find a wide range of accessories in this classy store decked out in sensuous black and purple. Beginner and advanced pleasure needs can be fulfilled, from rubber duckie vibrators, feather teasers and furry blindfolds to unmentionable hardcore stuff. There are plenty of cool gadgets girls and boys with imagination might need for a night of naughtiness.

NO 74 BERLIN   FASHION
Map p320 (⏹5306 2513; www.no74-berlin.com; Torstrasse 74; ⊗noon-8pm Mon-Sat; ⏹Rosenthaler Platz) Sleek, minimalist and gallery-style, No 74 is the holy grail for kool kids in search of the latest streetwear threads and accessories by adidas lines Y-3, SLVR and adidas by Stella McCartney along with limited sneaker editions by adidas Originals.

Kreuzberg & Northern Neukölln

BERGMANNKIEZ | KOTTBUSSER TOR & THE LANDWEHRKANAL | NORTHERN NEUKÖLLN |
SCHLESISCHES TOR & THE SPREE

Neighbourhood Top Five

❶ Challenging your party stamina by catching tomorrow's headliners at **Magnet Club** (p161), then dancing till breakfast at **Watergate** (p159) and wrapping up with a dedicated chill session at **Club der Visionäre** (p159).

❷ Stepping back into the long, tumultuous and fascinating history of Jews in Germany at the **Jüdisches Museum** (p148).

❸ Soaking up the punky-funky alt-feel of eastern Kreuzberg or northern Neukölln in search of your favourite **drinking den** (p158).

❹ Foraging for unusual gifts for you and yours in the charming boutiques along **Bergmannstrasse** (p163).

❺ Immersing yourself in multicultural bounty on a crawl through the bustling **Türkenmarkt** (p164).

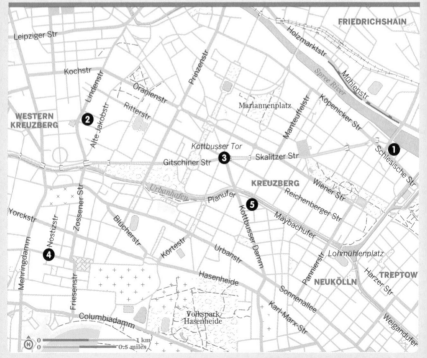

For more detail of this area, see Map p324

Explore: Kreuzberg & Northern Neukölln

Kreuzberg gets its street cred from being delightfully edgy, bipolar, wacky and, most of all, unpredictable. While the western half around Bergmannstrasse has an upmarket, genteel air, eastern Kreuzberg (still nicknamed SO36, after its prereunification postal code) is a multicultural mosaic, a bubbly hodgepodge of tousled students, aspiring creatives, shisha-smoking Turks and Arabs, and international life artists. Spend a day searching for great street art, scarfing a shawarma, browsing vintage stores and hanging by the canal, then find out why Kreuzberg is also known as a night-crawler's paradise.

All that hipness has spilled across the Landwehrkanal (canal) to the northern part of Neukölln, also known as Kreuzkölln. Once making headlines for its crime and poor schools, the district has catapulted from ghetto-gritty to funkytown-hip in no time. At least partly thanks to an influx of young, creative neo-Berliners (including many from Italy, Spain and England), the quarter sees trash-trendy bars, performance spaces and galleries coming on-line almost daily. Come now for a fun offbeat experience: turbo-gentrification is just waiting in the wings.

Local Life

➡ **Bar-hopping** Kreuzberg and Kreuzkölln deliver some of the city's most hot-stepping night-time action, especially around Kottbusser Tor, along Schlesische Strasse and on Weserstrasse.

➡ **Shopping** Delightfully devoid of high-street chains, shopping in Kreuzberg is all about individual style. Join locals in putting together that inimitable outfit from vintage shops, local designers and streetwear boutiques.

➡ **Chilling** Locals don't live to work, heck, they may not work at all, which is why they have plenty of time to chill in green oases like Viktoriapark or Görlitzer Park or to count the boats floating by on the Landwehrkanal or Spree River.

Getting There & Away

➡ **Bus** M29 links Potsdamer Platz with Oranienstrasse via Checkpoint Charlie; the M41 hits the Bergmannkiez before trudging down to Neukölln via Hermannplatz.

➡ **U-Bahn** Getting off at Kottbusser Tor puts you in the thick of eastern Kreuzberg, although Görlitzer Bahnhof and Schlesisches Tor are also handy. For northern Neukölln, Schönleinstrasse, Hermannplatz and Rathaus Neukölln are key stops. For the Bergmannkiez area, head to Mehringdamm or Gneisenaustrasse.

Lonely Planet's Top Tip

For the ultimate 'Turkish Delight', head for **Sultan Hamam** (www.sultan hamamberlin.de; 2175 3375; Bülowstrasse 57; noon-11pm; 3/5hr session €16/21; Yorckstrasse), where a traditional Turkish bath house meets modern spa culture. Relax in the richly tiled sauna and steam room, then treat yourself to a soapy scrub and kese (full body peeling with silken gloves). It's mostly for women, although men are welcome on Sundays and Mondays.

Best Places to Eat

➡ Cafe Jacques (p154)
➡ Henne (p156)
➡ Horváth (p156)
➡ Defne (p154)

For reviews, see p153 ➡

Best Places to Drink

➡ Möbel Olfe (p158)
➡ Würgeengel (p158)
➡ Luzia (p159)
➡ Club der Visionäre (p159)

For reviews, see p158 ➡

Best Places to Dance

➡ Watergate (p159)
➡ Ritter Butzke (p159)
➡ Horst Krzbrg (p158)
➡ Loftus Hall (p160)

For reviews, see p158 ➡

KREUZBERG & NORTHERN NEUKÖLLN

TOP SIGHTS
JÜDISCHES MUSEUM

In a landmark building by Daniel Libeskind, Berlin's Jewish Museum offers a chronicle of the trials and triumphs in 2000 years of Jewish history in Germany. The exhibit smoothly navigates through all major periods, from the Middle Ages via the Enlightenment to the community's current renaissance. Find out about Jewish cultural contributions, holiday traditions, the difficult road to emancipation and outstanding individuals such as the philosopher Moses Mendelssohn, jeans inventor Levi Strauss and the painter Felix Nussbaum.

The Building

Libeskind's architectural masterpiece is essentially a 3D metaphor for the tortured history of the Jewish people. Its zigzag outline symbolises a broken Star of David; its silvery titanium-zinc walls are sharply angled, and instead of windows there are only small gashes piercing the building's gleaming facade.

The Axes

The building's visual allegory continues on the inside. Exhibits are accessed through an adjoining baroque structure that once housed the Prussian supreme court. A steep staircase descends to the museum basement where three intersecting walkways – called 'axes' – represent the fates of Jews during the Nazi years. The **Axis of Emigration** leads to a disorienting 'garden' of 49 tilted concrete columns; oleaster, a symbol of hope, sprouts from each. The **Axis of the Holocaust** ends in the tomb-like 'void' that stands for the loss of Jewish life, culture and humanity in Europe. Only the **Axis of Continuity**, which represents the present and the future, leads

DON'T MISS...

➡ Axis of the Holocaust

➡ Shalechet – Fallen Leaves art installation

➡ Moses Mendelssohn Exhibit

PRACTICALITIES

➡ Jewish Museum

➡ Map p322

➡ ☑2599 3300

➡ www.jmberlin.de

➡ Lindenstrasse 9-14

➡ adult/concession €5/2.50

➡ ⏰10am-10pm Mon, to 8pm Tue-Sun, last admission 1hr before closing

➡ ⓢHallesches Tor, Kochstrasse

to the actual exhibits, but it too is a cumbersome journey up a sloping walkway and several steep flights of stairs.

The Exhibit

The permanent exhibit portrays facets and milestones of German-Jewish life and culture through art, daily objects, photographs and letters, media stations and interactive displays. One of the 13 sections is dedicated to the philosopher Moses Mendelssohn (1729–86), a key figure in the Jewish Enlightenment. His progressive thinking and lobbying paved the way for the Emancipation Edict of 1812, which made Jews full citizens with equal rights and duties. Elsewhere you can learn about Jewish holiday traditions, what it means to live kosher or how people such as composer Arnold Schönberg, writer Walter Benjamin or artist Max Liebermann influenced global culture from their Berlin base. The subject of anti-Semitism pops up throughout, culminating in the 'National Socialism' section. However, the exhibit ends on a more uplifting note, charting the revival of German-Jewish life in Germany, especially in the years since the fall of the Wall.

Art Installations

The Jewish Museum is peppered with art installations, of which Menashe Kadishman's **Shalechet – Fallen Leaves** is among the most poignant. More than 10,000 open-mouthed faces cut from rusty iron plates lie arbitrarily scattered on the floor in an ocean of silent screams. The haunting effect is exacerbated by the space itself, another cold and claustrophobic 'void'. Also note Dresden-born artist Via Lewandowsky's **Gallery of the Missing**, which consists of black glass sculptures erected near three of these voids. Each contains acoustic descriptions of missing or destroyed objects relating to German-Jewish culture, such as the *Encyclopaedia Judaica*, whose completion came to a sudden halt in 1934.

The Future

An extension to the Jewish Museum opposite the main building should have opened by the time you're reading this. The so-called **Jewish Museum Academy** occupies Berlin's former central flower market. Another Libeskind design, it is based on a house-in-house concept made up of three cubes – an entrance cube, a library cube and an auditorium – which are flanked by offices. The hall space between the buildings will become the 'Diaspora Garden'.

FURTHER INFORMATION

Budget at least two hours to visit the museum, plus extra time to go through the airport-style security checks before entering. For a more in-depth experience, rent an audio guide for €3. Tours take place at 11am on Saturdays and Sundays but are in German only.

Tickets to the Jewish Museum are also good for reduced admission on the same day and the following two days to the Berlinische Galerie (p150), located just 500m away.

TAKE A BREAK

For a refuelling stop, pop by the museum's **Café Schmus** (10am-10pm Mon, 10am-8pm Tue-Sun, dishes €5.50-8) for modern takes on traditional Jewish cuisine. Dishes are not kosher but don't feature pork or shellfish. On sunny days, the glass courtyard or the garden are pleasant relaxation spots.

KREUZBERG & NORTHERN NEUKÖLLN JÜDISCHES MUSEUM

SIGHTS

Bergmannkiez

One of Berlin's most charismatic neighbourhoods, the Bergmannkiez in western Kreuzberg is bisected by the Bergmannstrasse, which is chock-a-block with people-watching cafes and quirky shops. Nearby, the decommissioned Tempelhof Airport saw its finest hour during the 1948 Berlin Airlift. Above it all 'soars' the Kreuzberg hill, Berlin's highest natural elevation and a wonderful summertime play zone.

JÜDISCHES MUSEUM — MUSEUM

See p148.

BERLINISCHE GALERIE — GALLERY

Map p322 (☎7890 2600; www.berlinischegalerie.de; Alte Jakobstrasse 124; adult/concession/child €8/5/free; ⌚10am-6pm Wed-Mon; [S]Kochstrasse, Hallesches Tor) Berlin may be all hip and hot in today's art circles but fact is the city has long inspired creatives from around the world. The Berlin Gallery, in a converted glass warehouse around the corner from the Jüdisches Museum, is a superb spot for taking stock of what the local scene has been up to for, oh, the past century or so. The stark, whitewashed hall, anchored by two intersecting floating stairways, presents edgy works from major artistic periods – Berlin Secessionism (Lesser Ury, Max Liebermann) to New Objectivity (Otto Dix, George Grosz) and contemporary art by such 'Junge Wilde' (Young Wild Ones) members as Salomé and Rainer Fetting. Temporary exhibits inject additional 'impulses, as do the occasional lecture or movie screening. Jüdisches Museum ticket holders qualify for reduced admission on the same day and the following two days, and vice versa.

DEUTSCHES TECHNIKMUSEUM — MUSEUM

Map p322 (German Museum of Technology; ☎902 540; www.dtmb.de; Trebbiner Strasse 9; adult/concession €6/3, after 3pm if under 18 yr free, audioguide €2/1; ⌚9am-5.30pm Tue-Fri, 10am-6pm Sat & Sun; 👪; [S]Gleisdreieck) A roof-mounted 'candy bomber' (the plane used in the 1948 Berlin Airlift) is merely the overture to the enormous and hugely engaging German Museum of Technology. Fantastic for kids, this giant shrine to technology counts the world's first computer, an entire hall of vintage locomotives and extensive exhibits on aviation and navigation among its top attractions. The adjacent **Spectrum Science Centre**, where kids can participate in hands-on experiments, is closed for renovation until at least mid-2013.

TEMPELHOFER PARK — PARK

Map p322 (☎2801 8162; www.tempelhoferfreiheit.de; enter via Oderstrasse, Tempelhofer Damm or Columbiadamm; ⌚sunrise to sunset; [S]Paradestrasse, Boddinstrasse, Leinestrasse) The airport that so gloriously handled the Berlin Airlift of 1948–49 was repurposed as a public park after flight operations ceased in 2008. Now you can ponder the past while cycling, blading or strolling along the vast tarmacs. It's a wonderfully noncommercial, creative and wide-open space dotted with barbecue lawns, dog parks, an artsy mini_golf course, a beer garden, art installations, abandoned airplanes and urban gardening.

AN AVIATION LEGEND: TEMPELHOF AIRPORT

In Berlin history, Tempelhof Airport is a site of legend. Aviation pioneer Orville Wright put on flight shows over its grassy field as early as 1903, the first Zeppelin landed in 1909 and Lufthansa ran its first scheduled flights from here in 1926. The Nazis turned it into a massive compound that is still reportedly the world's second-largest building after the Pentagon. After the war, in 1948–49, the airport saw its finest hours during the Berlin Airlift. British architect Lord Norman Foster once called it 'the mother of all airports'. Flight operations stopped in 2008 after much brouhaha and against the wishes of many Berliners. The massive compound is now open for touring and hosts special events like rave parties and trade fairs like the Bread & Butter street fashion show. Guided **tours** (Map p322; ☎200 037 441; www.tempelhoferfreiheit.de; Platz der Luftbrücke; tours adult/child €12/6; ⌚2½-hour tours 4pm Mon-Fri, 1pm Fri, 11am & 2pm Sat & Sun; [S]Platz der Luftbrücke) of the airport building are available. The airfield, meanwhile, has been recast as the Tempelhofer Park (p150).

LOCAL KNOWLEDGE

A 'ROYAL' GARDEN FOR THE PEOPLE

Urban gardening is taking root all over the world, and in Berlin a site on Moritzplatz – once sitting abandoned in the shadow of the Berlin Wall for over 60 years – has been transformed into one of these delightful oases, the **Prinzessinnengärten** (Princess Gardens; Map p324; www.prinzessinnengarten.net; Prinzenstrasse 35-38, Moritzplatz; [S]Moritzplatz). In 2009, founders Robert Shaw and Marco Clausen inspired a small army of volunteers to help turn wasteland into farmland. It's become a bright and thriving space where anyone can get their hands dirty planting and tending over 400 varieties of organic herbs, vegetables and flowers. There are workshops on gardening and beekeeping, activities for kids and, of course, a **Gartencafe** (Map p324; mains €5-8; 🕘noon-10pm May-Sep; [S]Moritzplatz) where meals are prepared with the homegrown crops. But like so many things in Berlin, the garden's future is uncertain and Shaw and Clausen, who rent the land from the city, expect they'll be moved out eventually. But in the meantime, this little slice of utopia is allowed to sprout. So to speak.

New projects seem to go live almost overnight. Call ahead if you're interested in guided tours of the grounds.

LUFTBRÜCKENDENKMAL MEMORIAL

Map p322 (Berlin Airlift Memorial; Platz der Luftbrücke; [S]Platz der Luftbrücke) Nicknamed *Hungerharke* (Hunger Rake), the Berlin Airlift Memorial right outside the former Tempelhof Airport honours those who participated in keeping the city fed and free during the 1948 Berlin Blockade. The trio of spikes represents the three air corridors used by the Western Allies, while the plinth bears the names of the 79 people who died in this colossal effort.

VIKTORIAPARK PARK

Map p322 (btwn Kreuzbergstrasse, Methfesselstrasse, Dudenstrasse & Katzbachstrasse; [S]Platz der Luftbrücke) Take a break in this unruly, rambling park draped over the 66m-high Kreuzberg hill, Berlin's highest natural elevation. It's home to a vineyard, a waterfall and – at the top – a pompous 19th-century Karl Friedrich Schinkel memorial commemorating Napoleon's 1815 defeat. In summer, locals arrive to chill, tan or have a beer at the Golgatha (p158) beer garden.

CHAMISSOPLATZ SQUARE

Map p322 ([S]Platz der Luftbrücke) On Saturday mornings, the entire neighbourhood turns out for Berlin's longest-running **organic farmers market** held on this pretty square framed by stately 19th-century townhouses. With cobbled streets, old-timey lanterns and even an octagonal pissoir, the entire square looks virtually unchanged a century on. No surprise that movie directors favour it as an outdoor set for Old Berlin.

SCHWULES MUSEUM MUSEUM

Map p322 (Gay Museum; ☎6959 9050; www.schwulesmuseum.de; Mehringdamm 61; adult/concession €5/3; 🕘2-6pm Wed-Mon, to 7pm Sat; [S]Mehringdamm) Museum, archive and community centre all in one, the nonprofit Gay Museum is a great place to learn about milestones over the last 200 years of Berlin's queer history. Temporary exhibits keep things dynamic and often focus on gay icons, artists or historical themes. Enter via the courtyard behind the Melitta Sundström cafe.

Kottbusser Tor & the Landwehrkanal

[FREE] **KÜNSTLERHAUS BETHANIEN** GALLERY

Map p324 (☎616 9030; www.bethanien.de; Kottbusser Strasse 10; 🕘2-7pm Tue-Sun; [S]Kottbusser Tor) Even after moving to bigger digs, this seminal Kreuzberg art space has kept its mission intact: to be an artistic sanctuary and creative cauldron for emerging artists from around the globe. With studio space for 25 of them, it's among Germany's largest residency programs. Exhibits showcase their work, as well as that of former residents and other artists.

[FREE] **KREUZBERG MUSEUM** MUSEUM

Map p324 (☎5058 5233; www.kreuzbergmuseum.de; Adalbertstrasse 95a; 🕘noon-6pm Wed-Sun; [S]Kottbusser Tor) The ups and downs of one

WORTH A DETOUR

TREPTOW PARK & THE SOVIET WAR MEMORIAL

Southeast of Kreuzberg, the former East Berlin district of Treptow gets its character from the Spree River and two parks, the Treptower Park and the Plänterwald. Both are vast sweeps of expansive lawns, shady woods and tranquil riverfront and have been popular for chilling, tanning, picnicking, jogging or just strolling around for well over a century. In summer, **Stern und Kreisschiffahrt** (☎536 3600; www.sternundkreis.de; [S]Treptower Park) operate cruises from landing docks just south of the Treptower Park S-Bahn station. A bit further south, you can scarf a sausage or swill a beer at **Zenner-Eierschale** (☎533 7370; Alt-Treptow 14-17; mains €6-12; ⏰10am-midnight; [S]Treptower Park, [S]Plänterwald), a historic restaurant and beer garden with an integrated Burger King. From the terrace, you'll have a lovely view of the **Insel der Jugend** (www.inselberlin.de; Alt-Treptow 6; [S]Plänterwald, Treptower Park), a pint-sized island reached via a 1915 steel bridge that was the first of its kind in Germany at the time. In summer, there's a cafe, boat rentals and cultural events.

Nearby awaits Treptower Park's main sight: the gargantuan **Sowjetisches Ehrenmal Treptow** (Soviet War Memorial; Treptower Park; admission free; ⏰24hr; [S]Treptower Park), which stands above the graves of 5000 Soviet soldiers killed in the 1945 Battle of Berlin. Inaugurated in 1949, it's a bombastic and sobering testament to the immensity of Russia's wartime losses. Coming from the S-Bahn station, you'll first be greeted by a **statue of Mother Russia** grieving for her dead children. Beyond, two mighty walls fronted by soldiers kneeling in sorrow flank the gateway to the memorial itself; the red marble used here was supposedly scavenged from Hitler's ruined chancellery. Views open up to an enormous sunken lawn lined by **sarcophagi** representing the then 16

of Berlin's most colourful districts are told in this converted red-brick factory. The permanent exhibit zeros in on such themes as Kreuzberg's radical legacy or how immigrants have shaped the area. The 1928 printing press on the mezzanine level can still be cranked into action on occasion.

AUFBAU HAUS CULTURAL BUILDING

Map p324 (www.aufbauhaus.de; Prinzenstrasse 85; [S]Moritzplatz) Injecting life into once drab and neglected Moritzplatz since 2011, the Aufbau Haus harbours a bright bouquet of art and cultural ventures, led by the venerable namesake publishing house Aufbau Verlag, which also operates a nonmainstream theatre. The eclectic offerings also include a gallery representing Roma and Sinti art, Coledampf's & Companies high-end cooking supply store and the nightclub Prince Charles.

MUSEUM DER DINGE MUSEUM

Map p324 (Museum of Things; ☎9210 6311; www.museumderdinge.de; Oranienstrasse 25; adult/concession €5/3; ⏰noon-7pm Fri-Mon; [S]Kottbusser Tor) With its extensive assemblage of everyday items and objects, the Museum of Things ostensibly traces German design history from the early 20th century to today but actually feels more like a cross between a cabinet of curiosities and a flea market. Alongside detergent boxes and cigarette cases are plenty of bizarre items, like a spherical washing machine, inflation money from 1923 and a swastika-adorned mug.

The collection is based on the archive of the Deutscher Werkbund (German Work Federation), an association of artists, architects, designers and industrialists formed in 1907 to integrate traditional crafts and industrial mass-production techniques. It was an important precursor of the 1920s Bauhaus movement.

Northern Neukölln

PUPPENTHEATER-MUSEUM BERLIN

Map p324 (☎687 8132; www.puppentheater-museum.de; Karl-Marx-Strasse 135, rear bldg; adult/child €3/2.50, shows €5; ⏰9am-3.30pm Mon-Fri, 11am-4pm Sun; [S]Karl-Marx-Strasse) At the little Puppet Theatre Museum, you'll enter a fantasy world inhabited by adorable hand puppets, marionettes, shadow puppets, stick figures and all manner of dolls, dragons and devils from around the world. Many of them hit the stage singing and dancing during shows that enthral both the young and the young at heart.

RIXDORF NEIGHBOURHOOD

Map p324 (Richardplatz; [S]Karl-Marx-Strasse, Neukölln) The contrast between the cacophonous

Soviet republics, each decorated with war scenes and Stalin quotes. This all culminates in a **mausoleum**, topped by a 13m statue of a Russian soldier clutching a child, his sword resting melodramatically on a shattered swastika. The socialist-realism mosaic within the plinth shows grateful Soviets honouring the fallen.

South of here, near the *Karpfenteich* (carp pond), is the **Archenhold Sternwarte** (☑536 063 719; www.sdtb.de; Alt-Treptow 1; exhibit adult/concession €2.50/2, tours €4/3; ⊙exhibit 2-4.30pm Wed-Sun, tours 8pm Thu, 3pm Sat & Sun; ⓢPlänterwald), Germany's oldest astronomical observatory. It was here in 1915 that Albert Einstein gave his first public speech in Berlin about the theory of relativity. The observatory's pride and joy is its 21m-long refracting telescope, the longest in the world, built in 1896 by astronomer Friedrich Simon Archenhold. Demonstrations of this giant of the optical arts usually take place at 3pm on Sunday. Exhibits in the foyer are a bit ho-hum but still impart fascinating nuggets about the planetary system, astronomy in general and the history of the observatory. Kids love having their picture taken next to a huge meteorite chunk.

Speaking of kids – generations of East Germans still have fond memories of the Kulturpark Plänterwald, a small state-run amusement park created in 1969 and privatised and renamed **Spreepark Berlin** in 1990. Dwindling visitor numbers forced it into bankruptcy in 2001; the owner fled to Peru. The Ferris wheel and other carousels have stood still ever since and the park's future remains uncertain, though its moody allure endures. It's illegal to enter the grounds except on guided tours offered by **Berliner Spreepark** (www.berliner-spreepark.de; Plänterwald; 2hr tour €15; ⓢPlänterwald).

Karl-Marx-Strasse and quiet Rixdorf, a tiny historic village centred on Richardplatz, seems almost surreal given that they're only steps apart. Weavers from Bohemia first settled here in the early 18th century and some of the original buildings still survive, including a **blacksmith** (Richardplatz 24), a **farmhouse** (Richardplatz 3a) and the 15th-century **Bethlehemskirche** (Richardplatz 22) church. From U-Bahn station Karl-Marx-Strasse, go south on Karl-Marx-Strasse for about 300m, then turn left into Karl-Marx-Platz and continue for another 300m to Richardplatz.

KÖRNERPARK   GARDENS
(Schierker Strasse; admission free; ⊙park 24hr, gallery noon-8pm Tue-Sun; ⓢNeukölln, Hermannstrasse) This elegant sunken baroque garden comes with a secret: strolling past the flower beds and the cascading fountain, you are actually standing in a reclaimed gravel pit! Ponder this as you grab a coffee in the elegant orangery, then check out the latest exhibit in the adjacent gallery. In summer you can join locals for free classical, jazz and world-music concerts. From Karl-Marx-Strasse U-Bahn station, head south on Karl-Marx-Strasse for 400m, turn right into Jonasstrasse and continue another 150m to the park.

🍴 EATING

Kreuzberg has become one of Berlin's most exciting foodie districts, with some of the best eating done in comfy neighbourhood restos, ethnic eateries and canal-side cafes. Northern Neukölln is still more of a drinking and partying zone but with new eateries opening all the time that's likely to change.

🍴 Bergmannkiez

TOMASA   INTERNATIONAL €€
Map p322 (☑8100 9885; www.tomasa.de; Kreuzbergstrasse 62; lunch specials €5.50, mains €6-19; ⊙9am-1am Sun-Thu, to 2am Fri & Sat; ⓢMehringdamm) Not only breakfast is a joy at this enchanting late-19th-century villa at the foot of the leafy Viktoriapark. The multitalented cooks also prepare creative salads, inspired vegetarian mains, *Flammekuche* (Alsatian pizza) and grilled meats. There's a kids' menu, plus a playroom and crayons to keep them entertained.

AUSTRIA   AUSTRIAN €€
Map p322 (☑694 4440; www.austria-berlin.de; Bergmannstrasse 30; mains €13-18; ⊙dinner; ⓢGneisenaustrasse) Deer antlers and Romy Schneider posters preside over this

LOCAL KNOWLEDGE

ALL ABOARD THE BADESCHIFF

Take an old river barge, fill with water, moor in the Spree and voila: **Badeschiff** (Map p324; ☎01578-591 4301; www.arena-berlin.de; Eichenstrasse 4; €4/3 summer adult/concession, €12 for 3hr winter; 🕒8am-midnight end May-Sep/Oct; [S]Schlesische Strasse, [R]Treptower Park) – an artist-designed urban lifestyle pool that is the preferred swim-and-tan spot for Berlin cool kids. With music blaring, a sandy beach, wooden decks, lots of hot bods and a bar to fuel the fun, the vibe is distinctly 'Ibiza on the Spree'. Come early on scorching days as it's often filled to capacity by noon. Or show up for sunset and night-time parties or concerts. In winter, an eerily glowing plastic membrane covers up the pool and a toasty chill zone is set up, including a sauna and bar. In winter (November to March) opening times range from 10am to 2pm and closing is from 10pm to 3am depending on the day of the week. The sauna is men-only from 10pm to 3am Mondays and women-only 10am to 2pm Wednesdays and Saturdays.

hunting-lodge-style restaurant perfect for camping out with a cold Kapsreiter beer. The baseball-glove-sized veal schnitzel are among the best in town and preferably enjoyed balancing atop the tasty potato salad. Thursday's suckling-pig special brings out local devotees in droves.

HARTMANNS INTERNATIONAL €€€

Map p324 (☎6120 1003; www.hartmanns-restaurant.de; Fichtestrasse 31; 3-/4-course dinner €58/66, mains €38; 🕒dinner Mon-Sat; [S]Südstern) Stefan Hartmann studied with star chefs in Hollywood and Berlin and now regales demanding diners with boundary-pushing Franco-German cuisine amid the vaulted ceilings, original art and lustily roaring fireplace of his romantic basement restaurant. *Loup de mer* with tarragon risotto or dove with duck liver confit are typical menu items on set menus featuring up to seven courses.

CURRY 36 GERMAN €

Map p322 (www.curry36.de; Mehringdamm 36; snacks €2-6; 🕒9am-4pm Mon-Sat, to 3pm Sun; [S]Mehringdamm) Day after day, night after night, a motley crowd of tattooed scenesters, office jockeys, noisy school kids and savvy tourists wait their turn at this top-ranked Currywurst purveyor that's been frying 'em up since 1981.

SEEROSE VEGETARIAN €

Map p322 (☎6981 5927; www.seerose-berlin.de; Mehringdamm 47; meals under €10; 🕒9am-midnight Mon-Sat, noon-11pm Sun; 🥕; [S]Mehringdamm) This been-here-forever cafe tempts taste buds with fresh, creative and completely animal-free pastas, casseroles, soups, salads and other healthy nosh. Order at the buffet-style counter, then start salivating at a pavement table or inside amid antique furniture and plenty of plants.

🍴 Kottbusser Tor & the Landwehrkanal

[TOP CHOICE] **CAFE JACQUES** INTERNATIONAL €€

Map p324 (☎694 1048; Maybachufer 8; mains €12-20; 🕒dinner; [S]Schönleinstrasse) A fave with off-duty chefs and local foodies, Jacques infallibly charms with flattering candlelight, warm decor and fantastic wine. It's the perfect date spot but, quite frankly, you only have to be in love with good food to appreciate the French- and North African–inspired blackboard menu. Charismatic owner Ahmad or his staff will happily recommend the perfect matching wine. Reservations essential.

DEFNE TURKISH €€

Map p324 (☎8179 7111; www.defne-restaurant.de; Planufer 92c; mains €7.50-16; 🕒dinner; [S]Kottbusser Tor, Schönleinstrasse) If you thought Turkish cuisine stopped at the doner kebab, canal-side Defne will teach you otherwise. The appetiser platter alone elicits intense food cravings (fabulous walnut-chilli paste!), but inventive mains such as *ali nacik* (sliced lamb with puréed eggplant and yoghurt) also warrant repeat visits.

BAR RAVAL SPANISH €€

Map p324 (☎8179 7111; www.barraval.de; Lübbener Strasse 1; tapas from €4; 🕒dinner; 📶; [S]Görlitzer Bahnhof) Forget folklore kitsch. Owned by actor Daniel Brühl (who played the male lead in *Good Bye Lenin!*), this tapas bar is fit for the 21st century. The delish

START BETHANIEN
END LEVIATHAN MURAL
DISTANCE 3KM
DURATION 1½ HOURS

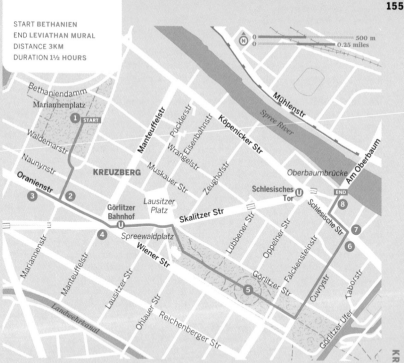

500 m
0.25 miles

Neighbourhood Walk
Radical Kreuzberg

Start the tour at the twin-turreted 1847
1 Bethanien, designed by three
students of Karl Friedrich Schinkel and
originally a hospital where writer and poet
Theodor Fontane worked as a pharmacist in
1848–49. Closed in 1970, it was saved from
demolition by squatters and preservation-
ists and was home to an artist community
from 1984 to 2010. Stroll over to Heinrich-
platz, where, in the '70s, the same antidevel-
opment protesters met at **2 Rote Harfe
& Zum Elefanten** to discuss how to prevent
the West Berlin Senate from tearing down
and gentrifying large swathes of eastern
Kreuzberg. A few steps away, the legendary
3 SO36 club began as an artist squat
in the early 1970s and soon evolved into
Berlin's seminal punk venue, known for wild
concerts by the Dead Kennedys, Die Ärzte
and Einstürzende Neubauten. Heading
down Oranienstrasse takes you to the site
of the **4 May Day Riot Supermarket**. On
May Day 1987 an initially peaceful protest
escalated into a full-fledged riot involving

looting and burning stores, including a supermarket on the corner now occupied by a
mosque. Follow Skalitzer Strasse to
5 Görlitzer Park, a patch of unkempt
grass and wacky ruins forged from a former
railway station and really more of an 'an-
tipark', though much beloved by locals.
Follow Cuvrystrasse to Schlesische Strasse
where **6 Barbie Deinhoff's** is pretty
much the last word in gender-fluid trash
kitsch art. The name was inspired by the
owner's fascination with both Barbie dolls
and the Baader-Meinhof terrorist gang.
Kreuzberg is street-art central and among
the finest pieces are the house-sized
7 Brothers Upside Down & Chains by
Italian artist Blu and his French colleague
JR, created in 2007 as part of a 21-day street
art festival called Planet Prozess. Another
Blu signature piece is the **8 Leviathan
mural**, an entire fire wall covered with a
huge pink body consisting of hundreds of
smaller bodies writhing like worms.

KREUZBERG & NORTHERN NEUKÖLLN NEIGHBOURHOOD WALK

homemade Iberian morsels pack comfort and complexity, as do the seasonal specials and hand-picked wines. Great *patatas bravas* (spicy potatoes) and *sobrasada* (a pâté-style sausage from Mallorca). Clued-in locals invade for paella night on Mondays.

MAX UND MORITZ — GERMAN €€

Map p324 (☎6951 5911; www.maxundmoritzberlin.de; Oranienstrasse 162; mains €9-15; 🕐dinner; [S]Moritzplatz) The patina of yesteryear hangs over this ode-to-old-school brewpub named for the cheeky Wilhelm Busch cartoon characters. Since 1902 it has packed hungry diners and drinkers into its rustic tile-and-stucco ornamented rooms for sudsy home brews and granny-style Berlin fare. A menu favourite is the *Kutschergulasch* (goulash cooked with beer).

HORVÁTH — AUSTRIAN €€€

Map p324 (☎6128 9992; www.restaurant-horvath.de; Paul-Lincke-Ufer 44a; 3-/7-course menu €40-76; 🕐dinner Tue-Sun; [S]Kottbusser Tor) At his canal-side bistro, newly minted Michelin chef Sebastian Frank performs culinary alchemy with Austrian classics, fearlessly combining textures, flavours and ingredients. To truly test his talents, order the 10-course small-plate dinner (€73). Despite the fanciful cuisine, the ambience in the elegantly rustic dining room remains relaxed; service is top-notch. Nice summer terrace.

HENNE — GERMAN €€

Map p324 (☎614 7730; www.henne-berlin.de; Leuschnerdamm 25; half chicken €7.90; 🕐dinner Tue-Sun; [S]Moritzplatz) This Old Berlin institution operates on the KISS (keep it simple, stupid!) principle: milk-fed chicken spun on the rotisserie for moist yet crispy perfection. That's all it's been serving for over a century, alongside tangy potato and white cabbage salads. Eat in the garden or in the cosy 1907 dining room that's resisted the tides of time. Reservations essential.

VOLT — MODERN GERMAN €€€

Map p324 (☎6107 4033; www.restaurant-volt.de; Paul-Lincke-Ufer 21; mains €24-32, 4-course meal €54; 🕐dinner Mon-Sat; [S]Görlitzer Bahnhof) The theatrical setting in a 1928 transformer station would alone be enough to seek out the culinary outpost of Matthias Geiss, crowned Berlin's most promising new chef in 2011. More drama awaits on the plates where smartly combined regional meats, fish and vegetables put on an artful show in innovative yet honest-to-goodness ways.

HASIR KREUZBERG — TURKISH €€

Map p324 (www.hasir.de; Adalbertstrasse 10; mains €8-13; 🕐24hr; [S]Kottbusser Tor) Tables at Hasir, the mother branch of a local Turkish mini-chain, are packed at all hours with patrons lusting after grilled meats, velvety hummus, stuffed grape leaves and other tasty morsels. Owner Mehmed Aygün invented the Berlin-style doner kebab back in 1971.

CICCIOLINA — ITALIAN €€

Map p324 (☎6165 7160; www.cicciolina-berlin.de; Spreewaldplatz 5; pizza €5-9.50, mains €7-18; 🕐noon-midnight; [S]Görlitzer Bahnhof) Conversation flows as freely as the wine at this convivial eatery whose eclectic clientele shares a passion for top-quality antipasti, soulful pastas and crispy-crust pizzas the size of wagon wheels. Weekly specials reflecting whatever's in season complement the menu. The name, by the way, honours a 1980s Italian porn-star-turned-politician.

LA RACLETTE — FRENCH €€€

Map p324 (☎6128 7121; www.la-raclette.de; Lausitzer Strasse 34; mains €14-20; 🕐dinner; [S]Görlitzer Bahnhof) With red-brick walls, a fireplace, good wine and delicious gooey raclette, this cosy hole-in-the-wall owned by German soap actor Peer Kusmagk is so fantastically French you half expect to see the Eiffel Tower through the window. There are plenty of noncheese dishes, too, from frogs' legs to steak and fish.

KIMCHI PRINCESS — KOREAN €€

Map p324 (☎0163 458 0203; www.kimchiprincess.com; Skalitzer Strasse 36; mains €9-24; 🕐dinner; [S]Görlitzer Bahnhof) New to Korean food? This hip hang-out is a fine place to lose your innocence. The kitchen delivers legit classics like *bibimbap* (hot pot rice dish) but it's the barbecue, grilled at your table and paired with tasty *panchan* (side dishes), that gets our vote for top menu pick. Elevated tolerance for spiciness required. Douse the fire with a cold Hite beer.

IL CASOLARE — ITALIAN €

Map p324 (☎6950 6610; Grimmstrasse 30; pizza €6-9; [S]Kottbusser Tor, Schönleinstrasse) The pizzas are truly dynamite – thin, crispy, cheap and gigantic – and the canal-side beer garden an idyllic spot to gobble them up. Staff can be frantic during busy times, so pack patience.

MAROUSH LEBANESE €

Map p324 (www.maroush-berlin.de; Adalbertstrasse 93; sandwiches €3; ⏰11am-2am; [S]Kottbusser Tor) This warm and woodsy hole-in-the-wall is tailor-made for restoring balance to the brain with terrific felafel or shawarma sandwiches paired with a glass of date juice or fresh mint tea.

🍴 Northern Neukölln

[TOP CHOICE] **LAVANDERIA VECCHIA** ITALIAN €€€

Map p324 (☎6272 2152; www.lavanderiavecchia.de; Flughafenstrasse 46; lunch from €4.50, 13-course dinner menu €45; ⏰lunch Tue-Fri, dinner Tue-Sat; [S]Boddinstrasse) From the crusty bread to the digestif, the country-style dinners at the 'Old Laundry' are truly a culinary first-class journey in a delightfully rustic-industrial space. You'll be spoiled with 10 cooked-to-order antipasti courses (the octopus carpaccio is tops!), followed by pasta or risotto and a fishy or meaty main, and dessert. Dinner starts at 7.30pm and includes half a bottle of wine per person, plus water and coffee. Reservations essential.

MARIAMULATA SPANISH €

Map p324 (www.mariamulata.de; Wildenbruchstrasse 88; tapas €2.50-5.50; ⏰dinner Tue-Sun; 🚌M41, [S]Rathaus Neukölln) The owner is Columbian, the chef is Basque and the tapas are divine at this convivial yet calming neighbourhood fave. Work your way through classic and creatively interpreted morsels, like *albondigas* (meatballs) in tangy tomato sauce, fried maniok or garlic shrimp. Service is sweet, the wines by the glass above par and the *crème catalán* swoon-worthy.

SAUVAGE PALEOLITHIC €€

Map p324 (☎5131 67547; www.sauvageberlin.com; Pflügerstrasse 25; mains €10-20; ⏰dinner Tue-Sun; [S]Hermannplatz) Sign up for a wild time at Berlin's first paleo restaurant, stylishly set up in a former brothel. Yup, at Sauvage you'll be eating like it was 10,000 BC: no grains, cheese or sugar but dishes featuring fish, meat, eggs, herbs, seeds, oils, fruit and wild vegetables, all organic, unprocessed and, usually, quite delicious.

HAMY VIETNAMESE €

Map p324 (☎6162 5959; www.hamycafe.com; Hasenheide 10; mains €4.90; ⏰from 5pm Wed-Sun; [S]Hermannplatz) If you're in the mood for a quick *pho* (soup), glass noodle salad or fragrant curry, follow the locals to this low-key landmark. Clever spicing and mountains of fresh herbs give dishes a special kick, and even during busy times you can be in and out in half an hour or less.

CITY CHICKEN MIDDLE EASTERN €

Map p324 (☎624 8600; Sonnenallee 59; chicken plate €5; ⏰11am-2am; [S]Rathaus Neukölln) There's chicken and then there's City Chicken, an absolute cult destination when it comes to juicy birds sent through the rotisserie for the perfect tan. Well worth ordering with the full complement of sides – especially the wicked garlic sauce and the creamy hummus.

BERLIN BURGER INTERNATIONAL AMERICAN €

Map p324 (www.berlinburgerinternational.com; Pannierstrasse 5; burger from €3.90; ⏰noon-midnight Mon-Thu, to 1am Fri, 5-11pm Sun; ✎; [S]Hermannplatz) The guys at BBI know that size matters. At least when it comes to burgers: handmade, two-fisted, bulging and sloppy contenders. Get 'em with a side of chilli cheese fries and you'll be in fast-food heaven. Paper towel is free. You'll need it.

🍴 Schlesisches Tor & the Spree

SPINDLER & KLATT FUSION €€€

Map p324 (☎319 881 860; www.spindlerklatt.com; Köpenicker Strasse 16-17; mains €18.50-26; ⏰8pm-1am; [S]Schlesisches Tor) It's not the hot spot it once was, but summer nights on the riverside terrace are magical in this Prussian bread factory turned stylish nosh and party spot. Sit at a long table or lounge on a platform bed while tucking into fearless fusion fare. The equally dazzling interior morphs into a dance club after 11pm on Friday and Saturday.

KATERSCHMAUS INTERNATIONAL €€€

Map p324 (☎5105 2134; www.katerholzig.de/restaurant; Michaelkirchstrasse 23; mains €16-26; ⏰dinner Tue-Sat; [S]Heinrich-Heine-Strasse) Trashy, irreverent, fabulous – the restaurant of the Kater Holzig club is as Berlin as you can get. Brave the dank, graffiti-festooned stairwell to arrive in an always slammed dining room filled with ephemera scavenged from flea markets, grandma's attic and chi-chi designer dens. Party people to politicians partake in the weekly menu that's often adventurous in its flavour pairings.

BURGERMEISTER AMERICAN €

Map p324 (www.burger-meister.de; Oberbaumstrasse 8; burger €3-4; ⏲11am-2am or later; [S]Schlesisches Tor) It's green, ornate, a century old and…it used to be a toilet. Now it's a burger joint on a traffic island beneath the elevated U-Bahn tracks. Don't fret, don't shudder: the plump all-beef patties are top-notch and best paired with fries and homemade dips such as peanut and mango curry.

FREISCHWIMMER FUSION €€

Map p324 (☎6107 4309; www.freischwimmer-berlin.de; Vor dem Schlesischen Tor 2a; mains €7-15; ⏲from 4pm Tue-Fri, 10am Sat & Sun; [S]Schlesisches Tor) In summertime, few places are more idyllic than this rustic 1930s boathouse turned canal-side chill zone. The menu draws inspiration from all corners of the world. Also a great spot for Sunday brunch and late-night warm-up drinks before hitting the area's clubs.

DRINKING & NIGHTLIFE

Bergmannkiez

HORST KRZBRG CLUB

Map p322 (www.myspace.com/horstkrzbrg; Tempelhofer Ufer 1; ⏲Fri & Sat; [S]Hallesches Tor) A former post office has taken on a new lease on life as a small electro club with a big sound system, cool lighting and a crowd that keeps it casual and attitude-free. The bar is great for socialising and the free mints and deodorant in the bathrooms come in handy in case of hook-ups.

GOLGATHA PUB

Map p322 (☎785 2453; www.golgatha-berlin.de; Dudenstrasse 48-64; ⏲from 10am Apr-Sep; [S]Platz der Luftbrücke, [R]Yorckstrasse) This classic beer garden right in Viktoriapark gets a changing cast of characters depending on where the hand of the clock points. Families invade in the daytime, lured by the adjacent adventure playground. Laid-back locals catch the day's final rays on the rooftop terrace, and wrinkle-free party folk arrive after 10pm when a DJ hits the decks.

GRETCHEN CLUB

Map p322 (www.gretchen-club.de; Obentrautstrasse 19-21; ⏲varies, always Fri & Sat; [S]Mehringdamm, Hallesches Tor) Berlin's newish drum 'n' bass temple has set up in the cross-vaulted stables of a former Prussian regiment, but Gretchen is no one-trick pony as other musical styles – electro to indie and jazz – get plenty of play as well. Pleasant door, unpretentious crowd.

SCHWUZ CLUB

Map p322 (☎693 7025; www.schwuz.de; Mehringdamm 61; ⏲from 11pm Fri & Sat; [S]Mehringdamm) Fortify yourself upstairs at the Melitta Sundström cafe, then drop down to this queer cellar institution for some high-energy flirting and dancing. Different nightly parties (eg Madonna Mania, Partysane, Popkicker) draw different punters, so check what's on before heading out. Good for easing into the gay party scene.

Kottbusser Tor & the Landwehrkanal

[TOP CHOICE] **MÖBEL OLFE** PUB

Map p324 (www.moebel-olfe.de; Reichenberger Strasse 177; ⏲Tue-Sun; [S]Kottbusser Tor) An old furniture store has been recast as an always-busy drinking den with cheap libations and a friendly crowd that's usually mixed but goes predominantly gay on Thursdays. Watch out: the skeletons above the bar get downright trippy after a few Polish beers or vodkas. Enter via Dresdner Strasse.

WÜRGEENGEL BAR

Map p324 (www.wuergeengel.de; Dresdner Strasse 122; ⏲from 7pm; [S]Kottbusser Tor) For a swish night out, point the compass to this '50s-style cocktail cave complete with glass ceiling, chandeliers and shiny black tables. It's especially busy after the final credits roll at the adjacent arthouse cinema. The name, by the way, pays homage to the surreal 1962

Buñuel movie *Exterminating Angel*. Smoking allowed.

LUZIA BAR

Map p324 (☎8179 9958; Oranienstrasse 34; ⏲noon-late; [S]Kottbusser Tor) Tarted up nicely with vintage furniture, baroque wallpaper and whimsical wall art by Berlin-based street artist Chin Chin, Luzia draws its crowd from eastern Kreuzberg's more sophisticated urban dwellers. Some punters have derided it as Mitte-goes-Kreuzberg, but it's still a comfy spot with lighting that gives even pasty-faced hipsters a glow. Smoker's lounge.

MONARCH BAR BAR

Map p324 (www.kottimonarch.de; Skalitzer Strasse 134; ⏲from 9pm Tue-Sat; [S]Kottbusser Tor) Behind a long steamed-up window front, eye level with the elevated U-Bahn tracks, Monarch is an ingenious blend of trashy sophistication, an international crowd and danceable tunes beyond the mainstream. Enter via the signless steel door adjacent to the doner kebab shop east of the Kaiser's supermarket. Smoking OK.

ANKERKLAUSE PUB

Map p324 (☎693 5649; www.ankerklause.de; Kottbusser Damm 104; ⏲from 4pm Mon, from 10am Tue-Sun; [S]Kottbusser Tor) Ahoy there! This nautical kitsch tavern with an ass-kicking jukebox sets sail in an old harbour-master's shack and is great for quaffing and waving to the boats puttering along the canal. Breakfast and snacks provide sustenance.

ROSES BAR

Map p324 (Oranienstrasse 187; ⏲from 9pm; [S]Kottbusser Tor) A palace of camp and kitsch with pink furry walls Barbie would love, Roses is a glittery fixture on the lesbigay Kreuzberg booze circuit. Drinks are cheap and the bartenders pour with a generous elbow, making this a packed – and polysexual – pit stop during hard-party nights. Smoking OK.

RITTER BUTZKE CLUB

Map p324 (www.ritterbutzke.de; Ritterstrasse 24; ⏲Fri & Sat; [S]Moritzplatz) After years in business, Ritter Butzke has thoroughly shed its underground patina and become a fixture on the Berlin house and electro party circuit. There's lots of dark nooks and crannies in this labyrinthine bi-level space inside a former lamp factory where mostly wrinkle-free hotties invade for extended weekend dance-floor jams.

SOJU BAR BAR, CLUB

Map p324 (www.soju-bar-com; Skalitzer Strasse 36; [S]Görlitzer Bahnhof) After a super-spicy meal at the adjacent – and affiliated – Kimchi Princess (p156), continue sweating to electro on the dance floor of this Asian-style bar complete with Korean neon signs and potent cocktails based on the namesake sweet-potato schnapps. Try the signature drink, a Seoul Mule, made with lime, cucumber and ginger beer.

BIERHIMMEL BAR

Map p324 (☎615 3122; www.bierhimmel-kreuzberg.de; Oranienstrasse 183; ⏲9am-1am Sun-Thu, to 3am Fri & Sat; [R]Kottbusser Tor) A hetero-friendly gay hang-out, this institution draws a coffee-and-cake-crowd in the afternoon but is also a relaxed place to get the evening in gear before moving on to naughtier places.

PRINCE CHARLES CLUB

Map p324 (☎200 950 933; www.princecharlesberlin.com; Prinzenstrasse 85f; ⏲from 7pm Wed-Sat ; [S]Moritzplatz) Prince Charles is a stylish mix of club and bar, with the latter cleverly set up within a former swimming pool backed by a kitschy-cute fish mural. There's electro on the turntable and inventive cocktails. The signature Prince Charles is a potent mix of vodka and Cointreau pimped up with lemon, cardamom, Earl Grey and espuma.

🍷 Northern Neukölln

Ä PUB

Map p324 (www.ae-neukoelln.de; Weserstrasse 40; ⏲from 5pm; [S]Rathaus Neukölln) Always wall-to-wall with globalists, this *Kiez* (neighbourhood) pioneer is a fine dressed-down watering hole to feed your party animal an appetiser, camp out for the night or turn in for that final drink. Expect to be eclectically entertained by pinball machines, DJs, live bands or (get this!) a monthly live soap opera starring cast-off stuffed animals.

CIRCUS LEMKE BAR

Map p324 (Selchower Strasse 31; ⏲from 3pm Mon, noon Tue-Fri, 10am Sat & Sun; 📶; [S]Boddinstrasse) Despite oozing the cosiness of an Alpine mountain cabin (complete with tile oven),

Circus Lemke is still very Berlin, tucked away in the increasingly hip Schillerkiez area of northern Neukölln. Yummy cakes, nice wines and fabulous cocktails make it a great stopover before or after visiting Tempelhofer Park.

KINDL STUBEN   PUB
Map p324 (✆5448 9722; Sonnenallee 92; ⊗from 10am; ☎; ⬡Rathaus Neukölln) Flanked by Turkish grocers, this laid-back lair gets kudos for fair drinks prices, swift and sweet service, and vintage furniture a couple of notches above the usual flea-market grunge. Bands invade on some nights and there's also movie screenings, swing night and other eclectic programming. Separate smoking lounge.

LOFTUS HALL   CLUB
Map p324 (www.loftushall.de; Maybachufer 48; ⊗Fri & Sat; ⬡Schönleinstrasse) Taking its name from a haunted mansion in Ireland, you half expect a resident ghost lurking behind the wood-panelled walls or heavy curtains in Loftus Hall's retro paradise. The music, however, is very today – that is very electro, mostly from smaller, hand-picked labels. Which is just how the global cast of tousled hipsters likes it.

KUSCHLOWSKI   BAR
Map p324 (✆0176 2438 9701; www.kuschlowski .de; Weserstrasse 202; ⊗from 8pm; ⬡Herman-

nplatz) When fierce winter winds blow in from the east, it's the perfect time to hole up by the crackling fireplace in this ex-bordello amid retro furniture and homemade lamps. The polyethnic crowd is united by a penchant for stiff drinks, especially the many Russian vodka varieties.

YUMA BAR   BAR
Map p324 (www.yuma-bar-de; Reuterstrasse 63; ⬡Hermannplatz) If you're in the mood for potent Belgian beer, hit this laid-back lounge bathed in an orange Kool Aid glow. Grown-up feeling by Kreuzkölln standards, it's also good for cocktails and civilised conversation. Local art on the walls, DJ nights and even an origami workshop mix things up.

SILVERFUTURE   BAR
Map p324 (✆7563 4987; www.silverfuture.net; Weserstrasse 206; ⬡Hermannplatz) Dressed in rich purple, burgundy and silver, this kitschy-campy queer pub collective is as charmingly over-the-top as a playful grope from your favourite drag queen. There's disco on the jukebox, Polish and Czech beer in the fridge and enough smiling faces for a dependably good time.

ROLLBERG BRAUEREI   BREWERY
Map p324 (www.rollberger.de; Werbellinstrasse 50; ⊗from 5pm Thu-Sun; ⬡Rathaus Neukölln, Boddinstrasse) Occupying a tiny section of the massive defunct Kindl brewery, the private Roll-

---

LOCAL KNOWLEDGE

BERLIN MUSIC SCENE: AN INSIDER'S VIEW

Thilo Schmied is a former sound engineer, music promoter, talent scout and owner of Fritz Music Tours (p289). He's been part of the Berlin music scene since the early '80s when Depeche Mode came into his life.

Best Live Music Venue
I really like Astra Kulturhaus (p176) for its sound and feeling. It's not so big and has a nice old East Berlin interior.

Best Clubs
Gretchen (p158) is really nice. It has a wonderful location and great booking policy. Also check out Prince Charles (p159) and **Chalet** (Map p324; Vor dem Schlesischen Tor 3; ⬡Schlesisches Tor) in Kreuzberg.

Good Place to Party on a Monday
You can still find a good crowd at Kater Holzig (p161). The legendary SO36 (p161) has good electronic nights. Also check out the concert line-up at Magnet Club (p161).

Good Sources for Plugging into the Music Scene
Check out the blog **Sugar High** (www.sugarhigh.de) and, of course, the good old-fashioned radio stations Radio Fritz (102.6FM), Radio Eins (95.8FM) and Flux FM (100.6FM).

berg Brauerei gets boutique brewery lovers salivating over delicious *helles* (light), *rotes* (ale) and *hefe* (wheat) beer. It's only sold in a few places around town for now, but it is really best sampled in the no-nonsense on-site pub anyway. Veer to the right as you enter the complex from Werbellinstrasse.

Schlesisches Tor & the Spree

CLUB DER VISIONÄRE   BAR, CLUB
Map p324 (✆6951 8942; www.clubdervisionaere.com; Am Flutgraben 1; ⊗from 2pm Mon-Fri, from noon Sat & Sun; ⓈSchlesisches Tor, ⓇTreptower Park) It's cold beer, crispy pizza and fine electro at this summertime chill and party playground in an old canal-side boatshed where entry rarely exceeds €3. Park yourself beneath the weeping willows or stake out some turf on the upstairs deck. At weekends party people invade 24/7. Toilets suck.

WATERGATE   CLUB
Map p324 (✆6128 0394; www.water-gate.de; Falckensteinstrasse 49a; ⊗from 11pm Fri & Sat; ⓈSchlesisches Tor) For a short night's journey into day, check into this high-octane riverside club with two floors, panoramic windows and a floating terrace overlooking the Oberbaumbrücke and Universal Music. Top DJs keep electro-hungry hipsters hot and sweaty till way past sunrise. Long queues, tight door on weekends.

KATER HOLZIG   CLUB
Map p324 (www.katerholzig.de; Michaelkirchstrasse 23; ⊗usually Thu-Sat; ⓈHeinrich-Heine-Strasse) This wicked kitty sits pretty in its surreal riverside playground set around a graffiti-slathered old soap factory. Parties often run for 72 hours, although there's also less excessive programming like readings, plays, concerts or film screenings, albeit usually with a wicked edge. Chill alfresco in the upstairs bar, on the wooden deck or by the beach bonfire. Tough door.

MADAME CLAUDE   PUB
Map p324 (Lübbener Strasse 19; ⊗from 7pm; ⓈSchlesisches Tor) Gravity is literally upended at this David Lynch-ian booze burrow where the furniture dangles from the ceiling and the moulding's on the floor. Don't worry, there are still comfy sofas for entertaining your crowd, plus live shows most nights at 9pm, including eXperimondays,

Wednesday's music quiz night and open-mike Sundays. The name honours a famous French prostitute – très apropos given the place's bordello pedigree.

SAN REMO UPFLAMÖR   PUB
Map p324 (✆7407 3088; Falckensteinstrasse 46; ⊗from 10am; ⓈSchlesisches Tor) Gather your posse at this laid-back hang-out before heading a few doors down to the area's celebrated clubs and concert venues. If chilled clientele, nice waiters, DJ sessions and cold beers won't get you in the party mood, what will? The odd name, by the way, ironically combines the two 'glamour towns' of San Remo, Italy, and tiny Upflamör in southern Germany. Coffee and cake in the daytime.

☆ ENTERTAINMENT

MAGNET CLUB   LIVE MUSIC
Map p324 (www.magnet-club.de; Falckensteinstrasse 48; ⓈSchlesisches Tor) This indie and alt-sound bastion is known for bookers with an astronomer's ability to detect stars in the making. After the last riff, the mostly student-age crowd hits the dance floor to – depending on the night – Britpop, indietronics, neodisco, rock and punk.

LIDO   LIVE MUSIC
Map p324 (✆6956 6840; www.lido-berlin.de; Cuvrystrasse 7; ⓈSchlesisches Tor) A 1950s cinema has been recycled into a rock-indie-electro-pop mecca with mosh-pit electricity and a crowd that cares more about the music than about looking good. Global DJs and talented upwardly mobile live noise-makers pull in the punters. Legendary Balkanbeats parties every few weeks.

SO36   CLUB
Map p324 (www.so36.de; Oranienstrasse 190; ⊗most nights; ⓈKottbusser Tor) The Dead Kennedys and Die Toten Hosen played gigs at this club collective when many of today's patrons were still in nappies. The actual crowd depends on what's on the program that night: an electro party, a punk concert, a lesbigay tea dance, a night flea market – anything goes at this long-time epicentre of Kreuzberg's scruffy alt-scene.

WILD AT HEART   CLUB
Map p324 (✆611 9231; www.wildatheartberlin.de; Wiener Strasse 20; ⓈGörlitzer Bahnhof)

SEX & THE CITY

The decadence of the Weimar years is alive and kicking in this city long known for its libertine leanings. While full-on sex clubs are most common in the gay scene (eg Lab. Oratory (p176), places such as Insomnia and the KitKatClub allow straights, gays, lesbians, the bi-curious and polysexuals to live out their fantasies in a safe if public setting. Surprisingly, there's nothing seedy about this, but you do need to check your inhibitions - and much of your clothing - at the door. If fetish gear doesn't do it for you, wear something sexy or glamorous; men can usually get away with tight pants and an open (or no) shirt. No normal street clothes, no tighty-whities. As elsewhere, couples and girl groups get in more easily than all-guy crews. And don't forget Mum's 'safe sex only' speech.

Insomnia (www.insomnia-berlin.de; Alt-Tempelhof 17-19; [S]Alt-Tempelhof) A late-19th-century ballroom has been reincarnated as a classy playground of passion. Besides the dance floor and big-screen Andrew Blake porn, there are performances and various pleasure pits, including a whirlpool, a gynaecological chair and a bondage room. Saturday's Circus Bizarre is good for first-timers; the special-themed sex parties during the week are for more advanced players and usually require preregistration. Check the website for full details. The club is right outside U-Bahn station Alt-Tempelhof.

KitKatClub (Map p324; www.kitkatclub.de; Köpenicker Strasse 76, enter via Brückenstrasse; 🕒Fri-Sun; [S]Heinrich-Heine-Strasse) This 'kitty' is naughty and sexy, raucous and decadent, listens to techno and house, and fancies leather and lace, vinyl and whips. It hides out at Sage with its four dance floors, shimmering pools and fire-breathing dragon. On weekends, the party never stops, starting with the classic Carneball Bizarre on Saturday and continuing through to midmorning Monday. The dress code varies; usually a combination of fetish, leather, uniforms, latex, costumes, Goth, evening dresses, glamour, or an extravagant outfit of any type. No dress code on Sunday.

Club Culture Houze (Map p324; ☎6170 9669; www.club-culture-houze.de; Görlitzer Strasse 71; 🕒Wed-Mon; [S]Görlitzer Bahnhof) Though predominantly gay, fetishistas of all sexual persuasions are welcome to get in on the action at this playground for advanced sexual experimentation on Wednesdays, Thursdays and Sundays. High kink factor.

Named after a David Lynch road movie, this kitsch-cool dive with its blood-red walls, tiki gods and Elvis paraphernalia hammers home punk, ska, surf-rock and rockabilly. Touring bands, including top acts such as Girlschool and Dick Dale, bring in the tattooed set nightly. It's really, REALLY loud, so if your ears need a break, head to the tiki-themed restaurant-bar next door.

ENGLISH THEATRE BERLIN — THEATRE

Map p322 (☎691 1211; www.etberlin.de; Fidicinstrasse 40; [S]Platz der Luftbrücke) Berlin's English-language theatre has brought Pinter, Williams and Beckett to the stage for over two decades. Every year, it puts on five new shows, mostly classical modern works with the occasional new play by emerging playwrights thrown into the mix. Visiting troupes provide additional impetus. All actors are native English speakers.

YORCKSCHLÖSSCHEN — LIVE MUSIC

Map p322 (☎215 8070; www.yorckschloesschen.de; Yorckstrasse 15; 🕒5pm-3am Mon-Sat, from 10am Sun; [S]Mehringdamm) Cosy and knick-knack-laden, Olaf Dähmlows's institution has been open since 1885 and plied an all-ages, all-comers crowd of jazz and blues lovers with tunes and booze for over 30 years. Toe-tapping bands invade several times weekly, but there's also a pool table, a garden for chilling, cold beer on tap and German comfort food served till 1am.

HEBBEL AM UFER — THEATRE

Map p322 (HAU; ☎2590 0427; www.hebbel-am-ufer.de) A pack of pit bulls mills about the seats while the audience gathers on the stage. An upside-down world? No, just another performance at Hebbel am Ufer, one of Germany's most avant-garde, groundbreaking and adventurous off-theatres. Performances can be, shall we say, challenging... Performances are held in three venues: **Hau 1** (Stresemannstr 29; [S]Möckernbrücke, Hallesches Tor), **Hau 2** (Map p322; Hallesches Ufer 32; [S]Möckernbrücke, [S]Hallesches Tor) and **Hau 3** (Map p322; Tempelhofer Ufer 10; [S]Möckernbrücke, [S]Hallesches Tor).

NEUKÖLLNER OPER — OPERA, MUSICAL

Map p324 (☎688 9070; www.neukoellneroper.de; Karl-Marx-Strasse 131-133, Northern Neukölln; [S]Karl-Marx-Strasse) Definitely not your upper-crust opera house, Neukölln's refurbished prewar ballroom has an actively anti-elitist repertoire presenting everything from intelligent musical theatre to original productions to experimental interpretations of classics. Many pick up on contemporary themes or topics relevant to Berlin.

FESTSAAL KREUZBERG — LIVE MUSIC

Map p324 (☎6165 6003; www.festsaal-kreuzberg.de; Skalitzer Strasse 130, SO36; 🕒from 8pm most nights; [S]Kottbusser Tor) This former Turkish wedding ballroom has become an essential space for globe-spanning music with at least one not-to-be-missed concert a week. The sound's good and prices moderate – only the ventilation could use a tune-up. Try scoring a spot on the balcony for bird's-eye views of the action. Parties, readings and performances pad the music schedule.

🛍 SHOPPING

Kreuzberg has a predictably eclectic shopping scene. Bergmannstrasse in the western district and Oranienstrasse both offer a fun cocktail of vintage frocks, and hot-label streetwear and clubwear alongside music and accessories. Nearby Kottbusser Damm is almost completely in Turkish hands, with vendors selling everything from billowing bridal gowns to water pipes and exotic teas and spices. On Tuesday and Friday the Türkenmarkt (Turkish market) lures crowds from outside the district with inexpensive fresh produce and other goods.

MARHEINEKE MARKTHALLE — FOOD

Map p322 (www.meine-markthalle.de; Marheinekeplatz; 🕒8am-8pm Mon-Fri, to 6pm Sat; [S]Gneisenaustrasse) After substantial renovations, this historic market hall has traded its grungy 19th-century charm for bright and modern digs. Its aisles are crammed with vendors plying everything from organic sausage to handmade cheeses, artisanal honey and other delicious bounty, both local and international. Snack stands feed tummy pangs.

MARKTHALLE IX — MARKET

Map p324 (☎577 094 661; www.markthalle9.de; Eisenbahnstrasse 42/43; 🕒noon-7pm Fri, 9am-4pm Sat; [S]Schlesisches Tor) A group of dedicated locals banded together to fight off a mega-supermarket wishing to take over this 1891 market hall with its iron-beam-supported ceiling. Instead, they turned it into an international food temple for local and regional producers. Stock up on apples from Brandenburg, baked goods from Neukölln or vegetables from an urban garden collective.

ANOTHER COUNTRY — BOOKS

Map p322 (☎6940 1160; www.anothercountry.de; Riemannstrasse 7; 🕒11am-8pm Mon-Fri, noon-4pm Sat; [S]Gneisenaustrasse) Presided over by eccentric owner Alan Raphaeline, this comfortably worn-round-the-edges 'culture club' overflows with around 20,000 used English-language books, from classic lit to a vast science fiction collection. Best of all, you can sell back any book you've purchased, minus a €1.50 borrowing fee. Also hosts an English Filmclub (8pm Tuesday), TV Night (8pm Thursday) and dinners (9pm Friday).

SPACE HALL — MUSIC

Map p322 (☎694 7664; www.space-hall.de; Zossener Strasse 33; 🕒11am-8pm Mon-Wed, to 10pm Thu & Fri, to 8pm Sat; [S]Gneisenaustrasse) This galaxy for electronic music gurus has four floors filled with everything from acid to techno by way of drum and bass, neotrance, dubstep and whatever other genres take your fancy. Alas, it's not terribly well organised and staff – while extremely knowledgeable – can be a tad snooty, so pack patience and you'll be fine.

HERRLICH — GIFTS, SOUVENIRS

Map p322 (☎6784 5395; www.herrlich-online.de; Bergmannstrasse 2; 🕒10am-8pm Mon-Sat; [S]Gneisenaustrasse) Next time you're looking for a gift for 'Him', peruse the racks of this fun store stocked with carefully culled men's delights. From retro alarm clocks to futuristic espresso machines – even a walking stick with hidden whisky flask – it's all here without a single sock or tie in sight.

TÜRKENMARKT MARKET

Map p324 (Turkish Market; www.tuerkenmarkt.de; Maybachufer; ⏲11am-6.30pm Tue & Fri; [S]Schönleinstrasse, Kottbusser Tor) Berlin goes Bosphorus at this lively canal-side farmers market where Turkish locals mix it up with impecunious students and hobby cooks. Stock up on fragrant olives, creamy cheese spreads, crusty flatbreads and mountains of fruit and vegetables, all at bargain prices. Grab your loot and head west along the canal to find a nice picnic spot.

VOO STORE FASHION, ACCESSORIES

Map p324 (☎6165 1119; www.vooberlin.com; Oranienstrasse 24; ⏲11am-8pm; [S]Kottbusser Tor) It takes chutzpah to open a concept store in an old backyard locksmith shop off gritty Oranienstrasse. But even Kreuzberg is changing, which is why party empresaria Ingrid Junker thought the time was ripe to open her industrial-flavoured emporium. Expect plenty of style-forward designer threads and accessories by Acne, Henrik Vibskov, Wood Wood and a couple dozen more.

HARD WAX MUSIC

Map p324 (☎6113 0111; www.hardwax.com; 3rd fl, door A, 2nd courtyard, Paul-Lincke-Ufer 44a; ⏲noon-8pm Mon-Sat; [S]Kottbusser Tor) This well-hidden outpost has been on the cutting edge of electronic music for about two decades and is a must-stop for fans of techno, house, minimal, dubstep and whatever sound permutation comes along next.

UVR CONNECTED FASHION

Map p324 (☎6981 4350; www.uvr-connected.de; Oranienstrasse 36; ⏲11am-8pm Mon-Sat; [S]Kottbusser Tor, Moritzplatz) This huge space is the flagship store of this Berlin label but also stocks the gamut of other coveted brands like Bench, Selected, Ben Sherman, Blutsgeschwister or local label Keregan. Plenty of accessories too. There are two more branches in **Schöneberg** (☎2196 2284; Goltzstrasse 40a; [S]Eisenacher Strasse) and **Friedrichshain** (Map p328; ☎2757 1498; Gärtnerstrasse 5; [S]Samariterstrasse).

UKO FASHION FASHION

Map p324 (☎693 8116; www.uko-fashion.de; Oranienstrasse 201; ⏲11am-8pm Mon-Fri, to 4pm Sat; [S]Görlitzer Bahnhof) High quality at low prices is the magic formula that has garnered this uncluttered clothing store a loyal clientele. It's a veritable gold mine for the latest girl threads by Pussy Deluxe and Muchacha, second-hand items from Esprit to Zappa and hot-label samples by Vero Moda, only and boyco.

KILLERBEAST FASHION

Map p324 (☎9926 0319; www.killerbeast.de; Schlesische Strasse 31; ⏲3-8pm Mon, 1-8pm Tue-Fri, 1-5pm Sat; [S]Schlesisches Tor) 'Kill uniformity' is the motto of this boutique where Claudia and her colleagues make new clothes from old ones right in the back of the store. No two pieces are alike and prices are very reasonable, and there's even a line for kids.

OVERKILL CLOTHING

Map p324 (☎6107 6633; www.overkill.de; Köpenicker Strasse 195a; ⏲11am-8pm; [S]Schlesisches Tor) What started as a graffiti magazine back in 1992 has evolved into one of Germany's top spots for sneakers and streetwear. Browse an entire wall of limited editions by such cult purveyors as Onitsuka Tiger, Converse and Asics (including vegan versions) alongside import threads by Stüssy, KidRobot, Cake, MHI and plenty of other hip labels.

MOTTO BOOKS

Map p324 (☎7544 2119; www.mottodistribution.com; Skalitzer Strasse 68; ⏲noon-8pm Mon-Sat; [S]Schlesisches Tor) Embark on a journey of discovery in this charmingly messy temple to the printed word. Motto stocks hundreds of international magazines you won't find at any kiosk and books by indie publishers from Afterall to Zoetrope that will never hit the shelves of high-street bookshops. Great for browsing for hours. Entrance is in the backyard.

SING BLACKBIRD VINTAGE

Map p324 (☎5484 5051; www.singblackbird.com; Sanderstrasse 11, Northern Neukölln; 📶; [S]Schönleinstrasse) Is it a store? Or a cafe? In fact, this blackbird sings its song for lovers of vintage clothing *and* fabulous homemade cakes and locally roasted java. Browse racks of neatly colour-sorted clothing (including designer labels) from the '70s to the '90s, then revel in your purchases over a steamy cuppa. On weekends, it serves Bloody Mary's, bagels and vegan pancakes.

NOWKOELLN FLOWMARKT MARKET

Map p324 (www.nowkoelln.de; Maybachufer; ⏲10am-6pm 1st & 3rd Sun of the month; [S]Kottbusser Tor, Schönleinstrasse) Setting up twice monthly along the Landwehrkanal, this flea market delivers secondhand bargains galore along with handmade threads and jewellery.

SAMEHEADS FASHION

Map p324 (www.sameheads.com; Richardstrasse 10; ⏲11am-late; [S]Karl-Marx-Strasse) Sameheads – that's Nathan, Leo and Harry, three Brit brothers whose shop-cafe-bar-club-party-space is a soapbox for budding talent of all stripes. Aside from stocking rare boho fashion labels, the subculture synergy extends to weird-cinema nights, a hilarious pub quiz, all-you-can-eat-buffet dinners and funky parties.

Friedrichshain

BOXHAGENER PLATZ AREA | WESTERN FRIEDRICHSHAIN

Neighbourhood Top Five

1 Confronting the ghosts of the Cold War at the world's longest outdoor artwork, the **East Side Gallery** (p168).

2 Partying through the night in rough-around-the-edges bars and clubs like **Suicide Circus** (p173) along Revaler Strasse.

3 Marvelling at the bombastic socialist architecture of **Karl-Marx-Allee** (p169), then learning the story behind it at **Café Sybille** (p170).

4 Shopping at the Sunday **flea market** (p177) on Boxhagener Platz, followed by brunch in a nearby cafe.

5 Pondering the day's events over sunset cocktails in a riverside beach bar like **Oststrand** (p175).

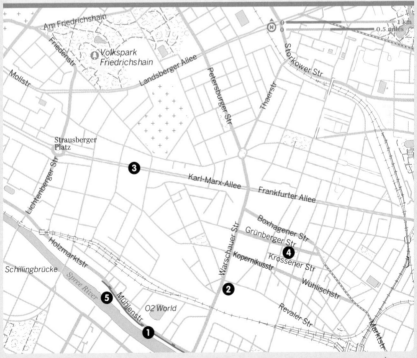

For more detail of this area, see Map p328 ➡

Explore: Friedrichshain

Rents may be rising and gentrification unstoppable but for now Friedrichshain is still largely the domain of the young and free-spirited, students, artists and eccentrics. There are few standout sights, but the web of boutique- and cafe-lined streets, especially around Boxhagener Platz, will repay those happy to simply wander and soak up the district's multilayered character. Daytime diversions include revelling in postreunification euphoria at the East Side Gallery or blowing your budget in sassy urban boutiques. Relax in sprawling Volkspark Friedrichshain, slurp a caipirinha in a riverside beach bar or enjoy a lazy lunch at a comfy cafe.

It's at night when Friedrichshain truly comes into its own. The district still celebrates its underground-punk-squatter roots in the derelict industrial bars and clubs along Revaler Strasse and around the Ostkreuz S-Bahn station. Steps away, Simon-Dach-Strasse is a bar-stumbling zone where the young and the restless drink, dance and flirt with mad exuberance. In the small hours, many will move on to a high-energy techno temple.

Local Life

➡ **Marketeering** Forage for vintage finds at flea markets on Boxhagener Platz (p177), at the RAW Flohmarkt (p177) and at Ostbahnhof (p177).

➡ **Picnic in the Park** Berlin's long summer evenings are perfect for chilling in rambling Volkspark Friedrichshain (p169), whether it's over a barbecue with friends or sunset with a six-pack.

➡ **Technotown** Become the master of the lost weekend partying at Berghain/Panorama Bar (p175) or less hyped – though no less fun – clubs like Suicide Circus (p173) or Salon zur Wilden Renate (p174).

Getting There & Away

➡ **Bus** Take bus 200 for Volkspark Friedrichshain from Mitte (eg Alexanderplatz); bus 240 from Ostbahnhof to Boxhagener Platz.

➡ **S-Bahn** Ostbahnhof is handy for the East Side Gallery; Warschauer Strasse and Ostkreuz for Boxhagener Platz and Revaler Strasse. Ringbahn trains (S41 and S42) stop at Frankfurter Allee and Ostkreuz.

➡ **Tram** M10 links Prenzlauer Berg and Warschauer Strasse; M13 runs from Warschauer Strasse to Boxhagener Platz.

➡ **U-Bahn** The U1 links Warschauer Strasse with Kreuzberg, Schöneberg and Charlottenburg; the U5 runs from Alexanderplatz down Karl-Marx-Allee and beyond.

Lonely Planet's Top Tip

Peel away the layers of Friedrichshain on a self-guided audio tour by **Stadt im Ohr** (www.stadt-im-ohr.de). The 2.5km tour costs €9 and starts at Café Sybille (p170).

FRIEDRICHSHAIN

Best Places to Eat
➡ Schneeweiss (p172)
➡ Spätzle & Knödel (p172)
➡ Schwarzer Hahn (p172)
➡ Lemon Leaf (p172)

For reviews, see p172 ➡

Best Places to Drink
➡ Astro Bar (p174)
➡ Hops & Barley (p174)
➡ Süss War Gestern (p174)
➡ Oststrand (p175)
➡ Aunt Benny (p176)

For reviews, see p173 ➡

Best Places to Dance
➡ Suicide Circus (p173)
➡ Berghain/Panorama Bar (p175)
➡ Salon zur Wilden Renate (p174)
➡ ://about blank (p174)

For reviews, see p173 ➡

TOP SIGHTS
EAST SIDE GALLERY

The year was 1989. After 28 years, the Berlin Wall, that grim divider of humanity, finally met its maker. Most of it was quickly dismantled, but along Mühlenstrasse, paralleling the Spree, a 1.3km stretch between Oberbaumbrücke and Ostbahnhof became the East Side Gallery, the world's largest open-air mural collection. In more than 100 paintings, dozens of artists from 21 countries translated the era's global euphoria and optimism into a mix of political statements, drug-induced musings and truly artistic visions.

Alas, time, taggers and tourists getting a kick out of signing their favourite picture took their toll over the years. In 2009, though, the entire thing got a makeover, a process accompanied by controversy since some artists considered the €3000 honorarium too low. In the end, though, all but six agreed to redo their work, leaving only half a dozen white patches. The relocation of a 45m section of the Gallery to create a plaza and boat landing docks for the O2 World arena also had its critics.

For graffiti-style street art, check out the river-facing side of the Wall, which is also where you'll find beach bars like Strandgut Berlin (p175). Here's a rundown of five of the more famous paintings, in the order you'll come across them if starting from the Ostbahnhof end:

➡ **It Happened in November (Kani Alavi)** A wave of people being squeezed through a breached Wall in a metaphorical rebirth reflects Kani Alavi's recollection of the events of 9 November 1989. Note the different expressions in the faces, ranging from hope, joy and euphoria to disbelief and fear.

➡ **Test the Rest (Birgit Kinder)** Another shutterbug favourite is Birgit Kinder's painting of a GDR-era Trabant car (known as a Trabi) bursting through the Wall with the licence plate reading 'November 9, 1989', the day the barrier was shattered. Originally called 'Test the Best', the artist renamed her work after the image's 2009 restoration.

➡ **Hommage to the Young Generation (Thierry Noir)** This Berlin-based French artist has done work for Wim Wenders and U2, but he's most famous for his cartoon-like heads gracing the Gallery. Naive, simple and boldly coloured, they symbolise the new-found freedom following the Wall's collapse.

➡ **Detour to the Japanese Sector (Thomas Klingenstein)** Born in East Berlin, Thomas Klingenstein spent time in a Stasi prison for dissent before being extradited to West Germany in 1980. This mural was inspired by his childhood love for Japan, where he ended up living from 1984 to the mid-'90s.

➡ **My God, Help Me Survive Amid this Deadly Love (Dimitry Vrubel)** The Gallery's best-known painting – showing Soviet and GDR leaders Leonid Breshnev and Erich Honecker locking lips with eyes closed – is based on an actual photograph taken by French journalist Remy Bossu during Breshnev's 1979 Berlin visit. This kind of kiss was an expression of great respect in socialist countries.

DON'T MISS...

➡ The five paintings described here

➡ Sunset drinks at a beach bar

PRACTICALITIES

➡ Map p328

➡ www.eastsidegallery-berlin.de

➡ Mühlenstrasse btwn Oberbaumbrücke & Ostbahnhof

➡ 🕒24hr

➡ [S]Warschauer Strasse, [U]Ostbahnhof, Warschauer Strasse

SIGHTS

Boxhagener Platz Area

BOXHAGENER PLATZ SQUARE

Map p328 (Boxhagener Platz; 🚌240, [S]Samariterstrasse, Warschauer Strasse, 🚇Warschauer Strasse) The heart of Friedrichshain, Boxhagener Platz is a lovely, leafy square with benches and a playground. It's framed by restored 19th-century buildings harbouring boho cafes and shabby-chic boutiques. The area is busiest during the Saturday farmers market and on Sundays when a flea market (p177) brings in folks from all over town.

RAW TEMPEL ARTS CENTRE

Map p328 (www.raw-tempel.de; Revaler Strasse; [S]Warschauer Strasse, 🚇Warschauer Strasse, Ostkreuz) The jumble of dilapidated buildings along Revaler Strasse was once a train repair station, founded in 1867 as the 'Reichsbahn-Ausbesserungs-Werk' (RAW for short), which remained in operation until 1994. Since 1999, the sprawling grounds have been a thriving alternative socio-cultural centre offering workspace for creatives of all stripes along with party venues, a skate hall and – in summer – a climbing cone, an outdoor cinema, a beer garden and a Sunday flea market (p177).

Western Friedrichshain

EAST SIDE GALLERY HISTORIC SITE

See p168.

KARL-MARX-ALLEE STREET

Map p328 ([S]Strausberger Platz, Weberwiese, Frankfurter Tor) It's easy to feel like Gulliver in the Land of Brobdingnag when walking down monumental Karl-Marx-Allee, one of Berlin's most impressive GDR-era relics.

TOP SIGHTS
VOLKSPARK FRIEDRICHSHAIN

Berlin's oldest public park has provided relief from urbanity since 1840, but has been hilly only since the late 1940s when wartime debris was piled up here to create two 'mountains', the taller one (**Mont Klamott,** Map p328) rising 78m high. Diversions include expansive lawns for lazing, tennis courts, a half-pipe for skaters, a couple of handily placed beer gardens and an outdoor cinema.

Kids in tow? There are imaginatively themed playgrounds and the enchanting 1913 **Märchenbrunnen** (Fairy-tale Fountain, Map p328) where turtles and frogs frolic in terraced water basins flanked by Cinderella, Snow White and other Brothers Grimm stars.

If you have a soft spot for revolutionaries, visit the park's communist-era memorial sites. Along Friedenstrasse, the **Denkmal der Spanienkämpfer** (Memorial to the Fighters in Spain, Map p328) pays respect to the German members of the International Brigades who died in the Spanish Civil War (1936–39). Off Landsberger Allee is the **Friedhof der Märzgefallenen** (Map p328; www.friedhof-der-maerzgefallenen.de; cnr Ernst-Zinna-Weg & Landsberger Allee; 🕐exhibit 10am-6pm), a cemetery for the victims of the revolutionary riots in March 1848, with a new exhibit set up inside a shipping container. Finally, in the northeastern corner, the **Deutsch-Polnisches Ehrenmal** (German-Polish Memorial, Map p328) honours the joint fight of Polish soldiers and the German resistance against the Nazis.

DON'T MISS...

- Märchenbrunnen
- Picnic on Mont Klamott
- Refreshments at Cafe Schönbrunn (p173)

PRACTICALITIES

- Map p328
- Bounded by Am Friedrichshain, Friedenstrasse, Danziger Strasse & Landsberger Allee
- 🚌200, [S]Schillingstrasse, 🚋M5, M6, M8 & M10

WORTH A DETOUR

STASI SIGHTS IN EAST BERLIN

In East Germany, the walls had ears. Modelled after the Soviet KGB, the GDR's Ministerium für Staatssicherheit (MfS, or Ministry of State Security, 'Stasi' for short) was founded in 1950. It was secret police, central intelligence agency and bureau of criminal investigation all rolled into one. Called the 'shield and sword' of the SED, the Socialist Unity Party of Germany, it put millions of GDR citizens under surveillance in order to suppress internal opposition. The Stasi grew steadily in power and size and, by the end, had 91,000 official full-time employees and 189,000 IMs (*inoffizielle Mitarbeiter*, unofficial informants). The latter were recruited among regular folks to spy on their coworkers, friends, family and neighbours. There were also 3000 IMs based in West Germany.

When the Wall fell, the Stasi fell with it. Thousands of citizens stormed the organisation's headquarters in January 1990, thus preventing the shredding of documents that reveal the full extent of institutionalised surveillance and repression through wire-tapping, videotape observation, opening private mail and other methods. The often cunningly low-tech surveillance devices (hidden in watering cans, rocks, even neckties) are among the more intriguing exhibits in the **Stasimuseum** (☎553 6854; www.stasimuseum.de; Haus 1, Ruschestrasse 103; adult/concession €5/4; 🕒11am-6pm Mon-Fri, noon-6pm Sat & Sun; [S]Magdalenenstrasse), which now occupies several floors of the former fortress-like ministry. At its peak, more than 8000 people worked in this compound alone; the scale model in the entrance foyer will help you grasp its vast dimensions.

Another museum highlight is the very 'lion's den' itself, the stuffy offices, private quarters and conference rooms of Erich Mielke, head of the Stasi for an incredible 32 years, from 1957 until the bitter end in 1989. Other rooms introduce the ideology, rituals and institutions of East German society. There's also background on the SED party and on the role of the youth organisation *Junge Pioneere* (Young Pioneers). Panelling is partly in English.

Built between 1952 and 1960, the 90m-wide boulevard runs for 2.3km between Alexanderplatz and Frankfurter Tor and is a fabulous showcase of East German architecture. A considerable source of national pride back then, it provided modern flats for thousands of people and served as a backdrop for military parades.

Until the early 1970s, this was also the 'Ku'damm of the East', lined with shops, cafes, restaurants and the glamorous Kino Kosmos. Living here was a privilege and, in fact, for a long time there was no better standard of living in East Germany. Flats featured such luxuries as central heating, lifts (elevators), tiled baths and built-in kitchens; facades were swathed in Meissen tiles.

Some of the finest East German architects of the day (Hartmann, Henselmann, Hopp, Leucht, Paulick and Souradny) collaborated on KMA's construction, looking to Moscow for inspiration. That's where Stalin favoured a style that was essentially a socialist reinterpretation of good old-fashioned neoclassicism. In East Berlin, Prussian building master Karl Friedrich Schinkel would be the stylistic godfather, not Walter Gropius and the boxy modernist aesthetic embraced in the West.

Now protected as a historic monument, KMA is undergoing a moderate renaissance with bars and businesses infusing some life into this huge concrete canyon. For visitors, though, its greater importance lies in being a unique architectural showcase.

[FREE] **CAFÉ SYBILLE** HISTORIC SITE

Map p328 (☎2935 2203; www.karlmarxallee.eu; Karl-Marx-Allee 72; exhibit free, viewing platform 1-5 people €15, extra person €3; 🕒10am-8pm Mon-Fri, noon-8pm Sat & Sun; [S]Weberwiese, Strausberger Platz) Today's Café Sybille is as old as Karl-Marx-Allee and was one of East Berlin's most popular cafes. Still oozing original 1960s GDR charm, it makes for a dapper coffee break and also features a small exhibit charting the milestones of KMA from inception to today. Call ahead to arrange for access to the rooftop terrace for bird's-eye views of the boulevard.

The exhibit features portraits and biographies of the architects of KMA, alongside posters, toys and other items from socialist times. There's even a piece of Stalin's mous-

No words are needed to understand the purpose of the van in the foyer. Outfitted with five teensy, lightless cells, it was used to transport suspects to the **Stasi prison** (☑9860 8230; www.stiftung-hsh.de; Genslerstrasse 66; tour adult/concession €5/2.50; ☉tours hourly 11am-3pm Mon-Fri, 10am-4pm Sat & Sun, English tour 2.30pm daily; ☒M5 to Freienwalder Strasse, then 1km walk via Freienwalder Strasse), which was only a few kilometres from the ministry. It too is a memorial site today – called Gedenkstätte Hohenschönhausen – and is, if anything, even more creepy than the Stasi Museum.

Tours, sometimes led by former prisoners, reveal the full extent of the terror and cruelty perpetrated upon thousands of suspected political opponents, many utterly innocent. If you've seen the Academy Award–winning film *The Lives of Others*, you may recognise many of the original settings.

Old maps of East Berlin show only a blank spot where the prison was: officially, it did not exist. In reality, though, the compound actually had three incarnations. Right after WWII, the Soviets used it to process prisoners (mostly Nazis, or those suspected to be) destined for the gulag. Over 3000 detainees died here because of atrocious conditions – usually by freezing to death in their unheated cells – until the Western Allies intervened in October 1946.

The Soviets then made it a regular prison, dreaded especially for its 'U-Boat', an underground tract of damp, windowless cells outfitted only with a wooden bench and a bucket. Prisoners were subjected to endless interrogations, beatings, sleep deprivation and water torture. Everybody signed a confession sooner or later.

In 1951 the Soviets handed over the prison to the Stasi, who ended up adopting its mentors' methods. Prisoners were locked up in the U-Boat until a new, much bigger cell block was built, with prison labour, in the late'50s. Psycho-terror now replaced physical torture: inmates had no idea of their whereabouts and suffered total isolation and sensory deprivation. Only the collapse of the GDR in 1989 put an end to the horror.

tache scavenged from the nearby statue that was torn down in 1961. The cafe is also the place to book guided tours of KMA or to pick up a booklet (€5) for more background.

COMPUTERSPIELEMUSEUM
MUSEUM

Map p328 (☑6098 8577; www.computerspiele museum.de; Karl-Marx-Allee 93a; adult/concession €8/5; ☉10am-8pm Wed-Mon; ☒Weberwiese) No matter if you grew up with PacMan or World of Warcraft or no games at all, this well-curated museum takes you on a fascinating trip down computer-game memory lane while putting the industry's evolution into a historical and cultural context. Colourful and engaging, it features lots of interactive stations alongside hundreds of original exhibits, including an ultra-rare 1972 Pong arcade machine and its twisted modern cousin, the 'PainStation' (must be 18 to play).

Other features include the **Wall of Hardware**, a gallerylike presentation of 50 consoles and computers from 1971 to 2001. **Games Milestones**, meanwhile, provides high-tech background on dozens of seminal games such as SimCity and Tomb Raider. Other parts of the exhibit explain how games are designed or how they transport players into virtual worlds through sound, music and 3D effects. But lest you thought it was all fun and games, one section also examines the medium's more sinister aspects, such as violence and addiction.

FREE SAMMLUNG HAUBROK
GALLERY

Map p328 (☑0172-210 9525; www.sammlung -haubrok.de; Strausberger Platz 19; ☉noon-6pm Sat & by appointment; ☒Strausberger Platz) His first purchase was a painting by Raoul de Keyser in 1988. Since then, investment consultant Axel Haubrok has amassed hundreds of contemporary works, many by such leading conceptual artists as Jonathan Monk, Christopher Williams and Martin Boyce. Selections from the collection are showcased in four shows per year on the 2nd floor of the GDR-era Henselmann-Tower on Karl-Marx-Allee.

OBERBAUMBRÜCKE
BRIDGE

Map p328 (Oberbaumstrasse; ☒Schlesisches Tor, Warschauer Strasse, ☒Warschauer Strasse) The Oberbaumbrücke (1896), which links Kreuzberg and Friedrichshain across the Spree, gets our nod for being Berlin's prettiest bridge. With its jaunty towers and turrets, crenellated walls and arched walkways, it has a fairy-tale quality and played a key scene in the movie *Run Lola Run*. There are great views of the Mitte skyline from here.

Looking south you'll spot the Universal Music HQ, MTV Europe and the extravagantly designed nHow hotel. On the Kreuzberg side is the Watergate club, the Badeschiff and, in the distance, a giant aluminium sculpture called **Molecule Man** (Map p324) by American artist Jonathan Borofsky. Right in the river, it shows three bodies embracing and is meant as a symbol of the joining together of the three districts of Kreuzberg, Friedrichshain and Treptow across the former watery border.

EATING

⊀ Boxhagener Platz Area

SPÄTZLE & KNÖDEL GERMAN €€
Map p328 (☑2757 1151; Wühlischstrasse 20; mains €8-15; ⊘dinner; Ⓢ Samariterstrasse) This elbows-on-the-table gastropub is a great place to get your southern German comfort food fix with waist-expanding portions of roast pork, goulash and of course the eponymous *Spätzle* (German mac 'n cheese) and *Knödel* (dumplings). Check the blackboard for seasonal specials like venison goulash or wild boar stew. Bonus: Augustiner, Riegele and Unertl on tap.

SCHWARZER HAHN GERMAN €€€
Map p328 (☑2197 0371; www.schwarzerhahn -heimatkueche.de; Seumestrasse 23; mains €14-21; ⊘lunch Mon-Fri, dinner Mon-Sat; Ⓢ Samariterstrasse, ⓜM13, Ⓡ Ostkreuz, Warschauer Strasse) The select menu at this delightful slow-food bistro shines the spotlight on regionally sourced German soul food, elegantly updated for the 21st century. Service is impeccable and so are the wines. The two-course lunches are superb value at just €6.50. At dinnertime, it's best to reserve ahead for seats at the long communal wooden table or the handful of private ones.

SCHNEEWEISS GERMAN €€
Map p328 (☑2904 9704; www.schneeweiss -berlin.de; Simplonstrasse 16; mains €10-20;

⊘dinner daily, brunch 10am-4pm Sat & Sun; Ⓢ Warschauer Strasse, Ⓡ Warschauer Strasse) The chilly-chic all-white decor with the eye-catching 'ice' chandelier is only the first thing to tip you off that Snow White is no student nosh spot. The menu here is inspired by the Alps, from classics like schnitzel or *Spätzle* to more innovative territory like braised ox cheeks or duck breast with bramble berries. The weekend brunch is a perennial bestseller.

TRANSIT ASIAN €
Map p328 (☑2694 8415; www.transit-restaurants .com; Sonntagstrasse 28; dishes €3; ⊘noon-midnight; ⋈; Ⓡ Ostkreuz) Sit beneath the colourful birdcages at this beloved Thai and Indonesian joint and order by ticking cheekily named dishes on a tear-off menu pad. There's great variety – papaya salad to spicy salmon soup – but quality can be hit or miss. Expect to order three or four dishes to get fed. There's another branch (p138) in Mitte.

SCHALANDER GERMAN €€
Map p328 (☑8961 7073; www.schalander-berlin .de; Bänschstrasse 91; snacks €3.50-10, mains €8-14; ⊘4pm-1am Mon-Fri, noon-1am Sat & Sun; ⋒; Ⓢ Samariterstrasse, Ⓡ Frankfurter Allee) See the pub action reflected in the very shiny steel vats that churn out the full-bodied Pilsner, Dunkel and Weizen at this old-school gastropub far off the tourist track. The menu is big on southern German comfort food along with *Flammkuche* (Alsatian pizza). Finish up by spooning homemade chocolate cream from an old-timey preserving jar.

LEMON LEAF ASIAN €
Map p328 (☑2900 9471; Grünberger Strasse 69; mains €5-9; ⊘noon-midnight; ⋈; Ⓢ Frankfurter Tor) Cheap and cheerful, this place is always swarmed by loyal local hipsters and for good reason: light, inventive and fresh, the Indochina menu here has few false notes. The modest menu is supplemented by daily specials, and the homemade mango lassi is rave-worthy.

KATER MIKESCH BOHEMIAN €€
Map p328 (☑0151 1579 7733; www.kater -mikesch.com; Proskauer Strasse 13; mains €8-14; ⊘4pm-late Mon-Fri, 11am-late Sat & Sun; Ⓢ Samariterstrasse) Although the Czech Republic is pretty close, there's a dearth of decent Bohemian food in Berlin, so Kater Mikesch fills a big void. And well. And generously. In fact, the plates of feisty goulash or chicken

paprikash are so huge, you may find it hard to leave room for the delicious sweet dumplings with vanilla sauce. Bonus points for the folklore-free, gallery-like setting.

VÖNER VEGAN €

Map p328 (☎9926 5423; www.voener.de; Boxhagener Strasse 56; dishes €2.50-4; 🕐noon-11pm; 🌿; [R]Ostkreuz) Holger, the owner of this funky vegan joint, used to live in a so-called *Wagenburg,* a countercultural commune made up of old vans, buses and caravans. A number of these 'wagon forts' are still around, but he now sells his juicy vegan 'Wagenburger' in this hole-in-the-wall where wall posters advertise the next antifascist demonstration.

The eponymous *'vöner'*, an anti-doner made from seitan and vegetables, is also a perennial bestseller. It's all paired with delicious homemade sauces (the garlic tahini rocks) and organic fries.

FISCHSCHUPPEN FISH €

Map p328 (☎0177 327 8847; Boxhagener Strasse 68; mains €7-14; 🕐10am-10.30pm; [R]Ostkreuz) It's mostly a shop, but this ship-cabin-sized purveyor of fresh fish also grills up seabass, pike perch, cod or whatever else lakes and the sea have yielded that day right on the spot. To fill up on a budget, get your hands greasy with a serving of fish 'n chips (€4).

VINERIA DEL ESTE SPANISH €€

Map p328 (☎4202 4943; www.vineriaytapas.de; Bänschstrasse 41; tapas €2.60-7.90, mains €12-17; 🕐3pm-midnight; [S]Samariterstrasse) Off the tourist track, this low-key Iberian jumps with local foodies hungry for a piñata of flavours. The tapas menu covers all the classics (bacon-wrapped dates, fried shrimp, garlic mushrooms etc), while the weekly changing mains can bring grilled roast beef or blood-sausage-stuffed squid. Savour it all with a glass of tasty Spanish or Uruguayan wine.

🍴 Western Friedrichshain

MICHELBERGER MEDITERRANEAN €

Map p328 (Warschauer Strasse 39-40; mains €5-10; 🕐lunch Mon-Fri; 📶; [S]Warschauer Strasse, [R]Warschauer Strasse) One of Berlin's hippest hotels, Michelberger does weekday lunches to feed hungry desk-jockeys and East Side Gallery visitors in an airy, tiled dining room. Dishes change daily but always have a Mediterranean streak as exemplified by ratatouille, polenta and creative pastas.

LOCAL KNOWLEDGE

HERE'S THE SCOOP!

There's ice cream and then there's **Caramello** (Map p328; Wühlischstrasse 31; 🕐from 11am; [R]Warschauer Strasse, Frankfurter Tor, Warschauer Strasse). Join the inevitable queue for over 40 var ieties of taste-bud-teasers from pistachio to bitter-orange, all of them organic and homemade. There are even soy-based concoctions for vegans and the lactose-intolerant, plus strong coffees and other tempting sweets.

CAFE SCHÖNBRUNN AUSTRIAN-MEDITERRANEAN €€

Map p328 (☎453 056 525; www.schoenbrunn.net; Am Schwanenteich im Volkspark; mains €10-18; 🕐10am-midnight Mar-Sep; 🚌200) Austrian fare meets magical setting with views of snow-white swans drifting around their pond in the middle of Volkspark Friedrichshain. If you're not in the mood for the formal restaurant, report to the beer garden for a cold one paired with pizza or sausage. Breakfast is served until 2pm.

PAVILLON IM VOLKSPARK FRIEDRICHSHAIN INTERNATIONAL €€

Map p328 (☎0172 750 4724; www.pavillon-berlin.de; Friedenstrasse 101; mains €6-12; 🕐11am-midnight; 📶; 🚌200) An institution since 1973, Pavillon is best on sunny days when you can dig into schnitzel, pasta or pancakes in the sprawling beer garden. Otherwise, tables beckon inside the cosy restaurant lidded by a huge thatched roof. Breakfast until 4pm and occasional parties.

🍷 DRINKING & NIGHTLIFE

🍷 Boxhagener Platz Area

SUICIDE CIRCUS CLUB

Map p328 (www.suicide-berlin.com; Revaler Strasse 99; 🕐usually Wed-Sun; [R]Warschauer Strasse) Tousled hipsters hungry for an eclectic electro shower invade this gritty dancing den that at times can feel like a mini-Berghain – sweaty, edgy, industrial and with a top-notch sound system. In summer, watch the stars fade on the outdoor floor with chillier sounds and grilled bratwurst.

SALON ZUR WILDEN RENATE   CLUB
Map p329 (www.renate.cc; Alt Stralau 70; ⊘Fri & Sat; ⓡOstkreuz) Yes, things can indeed get pretty wild at Renate where stellar local spinners feed self-ironic freethinkers with sweat-inducing electro in the rambling rooms of an abandoned residential building. Sofas, a fireplace room and several bars provide suitable chill zones. Crowd skews young.

:// ABOUT BLANK   CLUB
Map p328 (www.aboutparty.net; Markgrafendamm 24c; ⊘Fri & Sat; ⓡOstkreuz) This club collective also organises cultural and political events that often segue into long, intense club nights when talented DJs feed a diverse bunch of revellers with dance-worthy electronic gruel. Drinks are fairly priced, and if you get the spirit of openness and tolerance, you'll have a grand old time here.

CASSIOPEIA   CLUB
Map p328 (www.cassiopeia-berlin.de; Revaler Strasse 99, Gate 2; ⊘Tue-Sun; ⓢWarschauer Strasse, ⓡWarschauer Strasse) The college-age crowd at this grungy, chill party den defines the word eclectic and so does the music. Dive deep into a sound spectrum ranging from vintage hip hop to hard funk, reggae and punk to electronic beats.

HOPS & BARLEY   PUB
Map p328 (⌨2936 7534; Wühlischstrasse 40; ⓢWarschauer Strasse, ⓡWarschauer Strasse) Conversation flows as freely as the unfiltered pilsner, malty dunkel (dark) fruity *weizen* (wheat) and potent cider produced right at this congenial microbrewery inside a former butcher's shop. Fellow beer lovers range from skinny-jean hipsters to suits swilling postwork pints among ceramic-tiled walls and shiny copper vats.

SÜSS WAR GESTERN   BAR
Map p328 (Wühlischstrasse 43; ⓢWarschauer Strasse, Samariterstrasse, ⓡWarschauer Strasse, Ostkreuz) Chilled electro and well-mixed cocktails fuel the party spirit and the low light makes everyone look good. Beware of the ubercomfy retro sofas – it may be hard to get up to order that next drink,

for instance the eponymous house cocktail made with real root ginger, ginger ale and whisky. Smoking OK.

PLACE CLICHY   BAR
Map p328 (⌨2313 8703; Simon-Dach-Strasse 22; ⊘Tue-Sat; ⓢWarschauer Strasse, ⓡWarschauer Strasse) *Chapeau!* Clichy brings a whiff of Paris to the lower end of Simon-Dach-Strasse. Candle-lit, artist-designed and cosy, the postage-stamp-sized boîte exudes an almost existentialist vibe, so don your black turtleneck and join the chatty crowd for Bordeaux and sweaty cheeses.

ASTRO BAR   BAR
Map p328 (www.astro-bar.de; Simon-Dach-Strasse 40; ⓢWarschauer Strasse, Frankfurter Tor, ⓡWarschauer Strasse) Get 'beamed' into this cosmic lounge where sci-fi fiends from the hood and beyond drown in cheap drinks and long conversations, often until the stars begin to fade. DJs kick into action after 10pm. One of the few respectable spots on this well-trodden party drag.

TUSSY LOUNGE   BAR
Map p328 (⌨8411 1795; www.tussylounge.de; Sonntagstrasse 22; ⊘from 3pm; ⓡOstkreuz) This pint-sized, living-room-style bar cum hair salon is nicely dressed in genuine *Mad Men*–era vintage. It's a most beautilicious place to get those highlights while catching up on gossip and getting liquefied on coffee, wine or cocktails, pinkie raised and all.

KPTN A MÜLLER   PUB
Map p328 (www.kptn.de; Simon-Dach-Strasse 32; ☏; ⓢWarschauer Strasse, ⓡWarschauer Strasse) Arrgh, matey, the captain's in town, bringing much-needed relief from the strip's cookie-cutter cocktail lounge circuit. Pretensions are checked at the door of this self-service joint where drinks are cheap and table football and wi-fi free. The Matterhorn photo wallpaper in the DJ room out back makes for an easy conversation starter.

ZUM SCHMUTZIGEN HOBBY   GAY
Map p328 (www.ninaqueer.com; Revaler Strasse 99, RAW Tempel, gate 2; ⓢWarschauer Strasse, ⓡWarschauer Strasse) Berlin's trash-drag deity Nina Queer has flown her long-time Prenzlauer Berg coop and reopened her louche den of kitsch and glam in less hostile environs amid the Friedrichshain kool kids. Wednesday's 'Glamour Trivia Quiz' is legendary.

HIMMELREICH   GAY

Map p328 (www.himmelreich-berlin.de; Simon-Dach-Strasse 36; **S**Warschauer Strasse, **R**Warschauer Strasse) Confirming all those stereotypes about gays having good taste, this smart red-hued cocktail bar cum retro-style lounge makes most of the competition look like a straight guy's bedsit. Tuesdays are women-only and on Wednesdays drinks are 2-4-1.

SANATORIUM 23   BAR

Map p328 (✆4202 1193; www.sanatorium23.de; Frankfurter Allee 23; ⊘from 5pm; 🔊; **S**Frankfurter Tor) This Zen-meets-pop-art-in-hospital lounge is likely to cure whatever ails you. At first, though, risk chemistry class flashbacks when facing the drinks menu set up like a periodic table: ordering an *He* gets a Hemingway sour, *Ps* a prosecco and *Mi* a mojito. From Thursday to Saturday DJs turn the place into an electro party zone after 9pm.

GROSSE FREIHEIT   GAY

Map p328 (www.gay-friedrichshain.de/grosse-freiheit; Boxhagener Strasse 114; ⊘Tue-Sun; **S**Frankfurter Tor) Named for a lane in Hamburg's red-light district where the Beatles cut their teeth, Grosse Freiheit is a key cruising joint but also a harbour for just a drink and meet-up. The fabulous nautical decor looks just like most '80s films portrayed gay bars. Best day: 2-4-1 Wednesdays. DJs get toes tapping on weekends.

🍸 Western Friedrichshain

BERGHAIN/PANORAMA BAR   CLUB

Map p328 (www.berghain.de; Wriezener Bahnhof; ⊘midnight Fri-Mon morning; **R**Ostbahnhof) Still the holy grail of techno-electro clubs. Only world-class spinmasters heat up this hedonistic bass junkie hellhole inside a labyrinthine ex-power plant. The big factory floor (Berghain) is gay-leaning and pounds with minimal techno beats. One floor up, Panorama Bar is smaller, more mixed and pulsating with house and electro.

Provocative art more than hints at the club's sexually libertine nature with its busy darkrooms, alcoves and toilets. Awesome sound system that feels as though the gods are barking orders. Best time: after 4am. Strict door, no cameras. The adjacent **Kantine @ Berghain** is more relaxed and also open on some weeknights. In summer, the beer garden invites daytime chilling.

BERLIN'S BOAT OF BABBLE

Meet friendly Berliners, expats and visitors over beer and bratwurst at the 'Boat Party & Barbecue' held Wednesday from 7pm in the cool retro-lounge on the Eastern Comfort Hostelboat (p222). It brings together an easy-going, all-ages, international crowd, including lots of regulars, but don't be shy – people are friendly and eager to welcome newcomers. Admission, which is added to your first drink, is €1 until 8.30pm, €2 after that, which pays for the band that kicks into gear at 10pm. Check MC Charles' website, www.english-events-in-berlin.de, for updates and additional meet-ups.

OSTSTRAND   BEACH BAR

Map p328 (www.oststrand.de; Mühlenstrasse, Rummelsburger Platz; ⊘from 10am; **R**Ostbahnhof) Drag your flip-flops to this funky beach paradise along the East Side Gallery and enjoy cocktails while wiggling your toes in the sand or relaxing beneath colourful party lights on an old barge. Tanning and chilling in the daytime, party at night.

STRANDGUT BERLIN   BEACH BAR

Map p328 (www.strandgut-berlin.com; Mühlenstrasse 61-63; ⊘from 10am; **R**Ostbahnhof) Drink a toast to Berlin at this chic riverside beach bar where the beer is cold, the cocktails strong, the crowd grown-up and the DJs tops.

MONSTER RONSON'S ICHIBAN KARAOKE   KARAOKE

Map p328 (✆8975 1327; www.karaokemonster.com; Warschauer Strasse 34; **S**Warschauer Strasse, **R**Warschauer Strasse) Knock back a couple of brewskis if you need to loosen your nerves before belting out your best Britney or Lady Gaga at this mad, great karaoke joint. *Pop Idol* wannabes can pick from thousands of songs and hit the stage; shy types may prefer music and mischief in a private party room. Some nights are GLBT-geared, like Mondays Multisexual Box Hopping.

CSA   BAR

Map p328 (✆2904 4741; www.csa-bar.de; Karl-Marx-Allee 96; ⊘from 7pm; **S**Weberwiese) This sophisticated bar right on Karl-Marx-Allee has been carved out of the eponymous Czech national airline offices and sports a wonderful 1960s vintage vibe. Dim lights and classic cocktails mean that a more grown-up set balances on the white leather bar stools.

AUNT BENNY CAFE

Map p328 (☎6640 5300; www.auntbenny.com; Oderstrasse 7, enter on Jessnerstrasse; 🕐9am-7pm Tue-Fri, from 10am Sat & Sun; 📶; [S]Frankfurter Allee, 🚇Frankfurter Allee) Owned by two Canadians, this urban daytime cafe in an unhurried yet central section of Friedrichshain combines urban sophistication with downhomey treats. Catch up on your reading over potent coffee and homemade carrot cake or banana bread. No wi-fi on weekends.

LAB.ORATORY CLUB

Map p328 (www.lab-oratory.de; Am Wriezener Bahnhof; 🕐Thu-Mon; 🚇Ostbahnhof) Part of the Berghain complex, this well-equipped 'lab' has plenty of toys and rooms for advanced sexual experimentation in what looks like the engine room of an aircraft carrier. Party names like Yellow Facts, Naked Sex Party and Fausthouse leave little to the imagination. Hedonism pure. Come before midnight and skip the aftershave.

NAHERHOLUNG STERNCHEN CLUB

Map p328 (www.naherholung-sternchen.de; Berolinastrasse 7; [S]Schillingstrasse) Hipsters tired of Mitte's see-and-be-seen scene pack into this funkytown collective in a classic socialist-era building. The booking policy hop-scotches from concerts to readings, movies to parties, usually with a non-mainstream bent, which goes well with the fair drinks prices and fabulous GDR-era vibe.

> **LOCAL KNOWLEDGE**
>
> **AMAZING MAZE**
>
> For a spooky mind-bender kind of experience, plunge into the **Peristal Singum** (www.karmanoia.com; Alt-Stralau 70; €10; 🕐6pm-midnight, last entry 10pm; 🚇Ostkreuz), an art installation and trippy labyrinth set up in the dark and dank bowels of Salon zur Wilden Renate. Prepare to be launched on a metaphysical self-exploration in this 'landscape of wafting thoughts' that has all the warped intensity of a Dalí painting gone 3D. Definitely not for the claustrophobic!

☆ ENTERTAINMENT

ASTRA KULTURHAUS LIVE MUSIC

Map p328 (☎2005 6767; www.astra-berlin.de; Revaler Strasse 99; [S]Warschauer Strasse, 🚇Warschauer Strasse) With space for 1500, Astra is one of the bigger indie venues in town, yet often fills up easily, and not just for such headliners as Melissa Etheridge, Kasabian or Paul van Dyk's Vandit Records label parties. Bonus: the sweet '50s GDR decor. Beer garden in summer.

RADIALSYSTEM V PERFORMING ARTS

Map p328 (☎2887 8850; www.radialsystem.de; Holzmarktstrasse 33; 📶; 🚇Ostbahnhof) Contemporary dance meets medieval music, poetry meets pop tunes, painting meets digital. This progressive performance space in an old riverside pump station blurs the boundaries between the arts to nurture new forms of creative expression. Nice riverside cafe-bar from 10am.

KINO INTERNATIONAL CINEMA

Map p328 (☎2475 6011; www.yorck.de; Karl-Marx-Allee 33; [S]Schillingstrasse) The East German film elite once held movie premieres in this 1960s cinema, whose cavalcade of glass chandeliers, glitter curtains and parquet floors is a show in itself. Some movies are screened in the original language, usually English. Monday is 'MonGay' with gay-themed classics, imports and previews. The space is also used for glamtastic monthly lesbigay parties such as Klub International and Girls Town.

K17 LIVE MUSIC, CLUB

Map p328 (☎4208 9300; www.k17-berlin.de; Pettenkoferstrasse 17a; 🕐Thu-Sat; [S]Frankfurter Allee, 🚇Frankfurter Allee) K17 used to be the go-to club for all things Goth, industrial, metal and other dark music. Although bands like Icon of Coil, Debauchery and Deadlock still hit the stage here, softer sounds have made inroads as well, especially on party nights when there's four floors feeding different musical appetites, from electropop and Nu-Wave to hip hop.

MARKETS GALORE

If you're into marketeering, Sundays are a great time to swing by Friedrichshain. If it's genuine antiques you're after, head straight to the **Antikmarkt am Ostbahnhof** (Map p328; www.oldthings.de; Erich-Steinfurth-Strasse; ⊘9am-5pm Sun; ⌗Ostbahnhof), which starts right outside the Ostbahnhof station's north exit. The 'Grosser Antik-markt' (large antiques market) is more professional and brims with genuine collecti-bles – old coins, Iron Curtain–era relics, gramophone records, books, stamps, jewel-lery etc. It segues neatly into the 'Kleiner Antikmarkt' (small antiques market) which has more bric-a-brac and lower prices.

The smallest, and newest, of the bunch is the **RAW Flohmarkt** (Map p328; http://raw-flohmarkt.de; Revaler Strasse 99; ⊘sunrise-8pm Sun; ⌗Warschauer Strasse, Warschau-er Strasse) on the grounds of the RAW Tempel creative colony. It's wonderfully free of professional sellers, meaning you'll find everything from the proverbial kitchen sink to preloved Carhartt hoodies. Bargains are plentiful.

The most popular market is the **Flohmarkt am Boxhagener Platz** (Map p328; Boxhagener Platz; ⊘10am-6pm Sun; ⓢWarschauer Strasse, Frankfurter Tor, ⌗Warschauer Strasse), which gets some pros along with regular folks here to unload their spring-cleaning detritus for cheap. Best of all, stalls are just a java whiff away from Sunday brunch cafes.

🛍 SHOPPING

Friedrichshain has come quite along in the shopping department, with increasingly chic indie clothing boutiques and speciality stores sprinkled around Boxhagener Platz, Sonntagsstrasse and its side streets near Ostkreuz. On Sundays, a flea market sets up on Boxhagener Platz and an antique market at Ostbahnhof.

PRACHTMÄDCHEN   FASHION

Map p328 (☑9700 2780; www.prachtmaedchen.de; Wühlischstrasse 28; ⊘11am-8pm Mon-Fri, to 4pm Sat; ⓢFrankfurter Tor, Warschauer Strasse, ⌗Warschauer Strasse) In business since 2004, this sweet store was a pioneer on Wühlischstrasse, aka Friedrichshain's 'fashion mile'. Low-key and friendly, it's great for kitting yourself out head to toe in grown-up streetwear by such labels as Blutsgeschwister, skunkfunk and Who's That Girl. Also: chic undies by Pussy Deluxe and Vive Maria.

MONDOS ARTS   GIFTS, SOUVENIRS

Map p328 (☑4201 0778; www.mondosarts.de; Schreinerstrasse 6; ⊘10am-7pm Mon-Fri, 11am-4pm Sat; ⓢSamariterstrasse) Cult and kitsch seem to be the GDR's strongest survivors at this funky little shop, named after Mondos, a GDR-era brand of condoms. It's fun to have a look even if you didn't grow up drinking Red October beer, falling asleep to the *Sandmän-nchen* (Little Sandman) TV show or listening to rock by the Puhdys.

PERLEREI   JEWELLERY

Map p328 (☑9788 2028; www.perlerei.de; Len-bachstrasse 7; ⊘noon-8pm Tue-Fri, to 6pm Sat; ⌗Ostkreuz) Looking for a unique souvenir to bring back from Berlin? Simply make it yourself. Piece of jewellery, that is. Don't worry if you don't know how. At Meike Köster's bead boutique, you select your bau-bles and then turn them into beautiful neck-laces, earrings, brooches or bracelets, with her help if you want it, at no extra charge, right there in the in-store workshop.

ZIGARREN HERZOG AM HAFEN   CIGARS

(☑2904 7015; www.herzog-am-hafen.de; Stral-auer Allee 9; ⊘11am-9pm Mon-Sat; ⓢWarschauer Strasse, ⌗Warschauer Strasse) If you're a friend of Belinda, Cohiba or Trinidad, you can indulge your passion in this upmarket cigar boutique in a 1909 riverside ware-house with a waterfront terrace for puff-ing up a smooth one at sunset. All cigars come straight from Havana and can be pur-chased by the date they were boxed or even by wrapping colour.

Prenzlauer Berg

Neighbourhood Top Five

1 Spending a sunny Sunday afternoon foraging for flea-market treasures and cheering on karaoke crooners in the **Mauerpark** (p180).

2 Taking a leisurely ramble around the leafy **Kollwit-** **zplatz** (p181) neighbourhood with its beautiful townhouses, convivial cafes and upmarket indie boutiques.

3 Treating yourself and a friend to the tiered breakfast tray for two at the charming **Anna Blume** (p186) cafe.

4 Coming face to face with Berlin's subterranean mysteries on a WWII bunker tour with **Berliner Unterwelten** (p182).

5 Catching a concert or other cultural event at the **Kulturbrauerei** (p181).

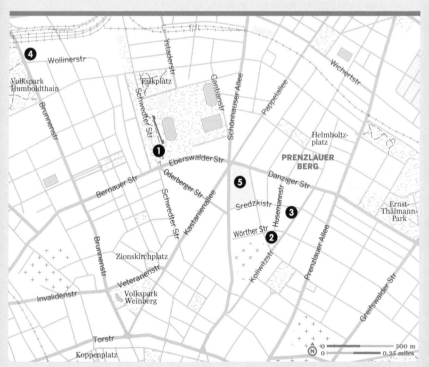

For more detail of this area, see Map p330 ➡

Explore: Prenzlauer Berg

Once a neglected backwater, Prenzlauer Berg went from rags to riches after reunification to emerge as one of Berlin's most desirable and expensive neighbourhoods. There are no major sights, but the ample charms reveal themselves in subtler, often unexpected ways and are best experienced on a leisurely meander. Look up at restored townhouses that recently bore the scars of war. Push open an ornamented wooden door to stumble upon quiet courtyards. Source Berlin-made fashions on boho-trendy Kastanienallee or comb quiet side streets for indie boutiques selling handmade jewellery or organic baby clothes.

Prenzlauer Berg also has one of the city's best cafe scenes. Carve out a spot in a cafe on Kollwitzplatz or Helmholtzplatz, or bask in the sun with views of a handsome historic water tower. On Sundays, the Mauerpark draws tens of thousands to the city's best flea market, outdoor karaoke, pick-up basketball and other fun and games.

This is one of the most family-friendly districts in town: safe, quiet and with plenty of playgrounds, toy stores and children's cafes.

Local Life

➜ **Outdoor Quaffing** Days get long, temperatures climb and spirits soar. Time to celebrate summer beneath the chestnut trees of the Prater (p185) beer garden, on the rooftop terrace of Deck 5 (p187) or at a sunny sidewalk table at Bar Gagarin (p187). Alternatively, pick up a bottle of beer at a local market and stake out some turf in the Mauerpark.

➜ **Shopping** Prenzlauer Berg's side streets are nirvana for indie shoppers. Browse for chic bags at Ta(u)sche (p188), Berlin designers at Flagshipstore (p188) or retro threads at the Flohmarkt am Mauerpark (p180).

➜ **Eating Out** Foodies have plenty to like about this neighbourhood, where perennial favourites include Frau Mittenmang (p182) for modern German, A Magica (p185) for pizza and Konnopke's Imbiss (p185) for Currywurst. The organic farmers market on Kollwitzplatz is a fabulous place to stock up on quality fruit, veg and meat along with locally made pestos, honey and pasta.

Getting There & Away

➜ **U-Bahn** The U2 stops at Senefelderplatz, Eberswalder Strasse and Schönhauser Allee.

➜ **Tram** The M1 links Museumsinsel and Prenzlauer Berg via the Scheunenviertel, Kastanienallee and Schönhauser Allee.

➜ *** S-Bahn** Ringbahn (Circle Line) trains S41 and S42 stop at Schönhauser Allee.

Lonely Planet's Top Tip

This family-dominated district is no longer known for its late-night partying, but if you find yourself in need of a drink at 3am, your best bets are the bars along Lychener Strasse like August Fengler (p186) or Zu mir oder zu dir. If you're in dancing mood, try Alte Kantine on Wednesdays (free admission if you're over 27) or Frannz Club on weekends; both are located in the Kulturbrauerei (p181). Gays should head to Chantals at Bassy on Thursdays.

✖ Best Places to Eat

➜ Frau Mittenmang (p182)
➜ Der Fischladen (p184)
➜ Lucky Leek (p184)
➜ Der Hahn ist tot! (p182)
➜ Oderquelle (p182)

For reviews, see p182 ➜

♟ Best Places to Drink

➜ Prater (p185)
➜ Becketts Kopf (p186)
➜ August Fengler (p186)
➜ Mauersegler (p187)
➜ Deck 5 (p187)

For reviews, see p185 ➜

🔒 Best Places to Shop

➜ Flagshipstore (p188)
➜ Flohmarkt am Mauerpark (p180)
➜ Luxus International (p188)
➜ Ta(u)sche (p188)

For reviews, see p188 ➜

TOP SIGHTS MAUERPARK

Long-time locals, neo-Berliners and the international tourist brigade – everyone flocks to the Mauerpark, especially on Sundays. It's a wild and wacky urban tapestry where a flea market, outdoor karaoke, artists and bands provide entertainment, and people gather for barbecues, basketball and boules.

Pretty it ain't, with its scraggly bushes and anaemic lawn, but then it was forged from the former death strip. Yup, the Berlin Wall once cut right through what has become an urban playground. In fact, a 300m-long section of the Wall still looms above it all, having taken on new life as legal practice ground for budding graffiti artists. Views across the park are terrific from up here and downright romantic at sunset, especially in summer.

The floodlights behind the wall belong to the **Friedrich-Ludwig-Jahn-Sportpark** (Map p330; ☎4430 3730; Cantianstrasse 24; [S]Eberswalder Strasse), the stadium where Erich Mielke, head of the feared East German secret police (the Stasi), used to cheer on his beloved Dynamo Berlin soccer team. Just north of here is the **Max-Schmeling-Halle** (Map p330; ☎tickets 4430 4430; www.max-schmeling-halle.de; Falkplatz 1; Eberswalder Strasse), a venue for concerts, competitions and sports events.

But the magic of Mauerpark isn't about its facilities. It's about the relaxed, almost neo-hippie vibe that attracts folks from all walks of life, many still unencumbered by the traps and trappings of adulthood. Even tots are happy here romping around playgrounds, testing their mettle on the climbing wall or meeting barnyard animals at a children's farm.

DON'T MISS...

- Sunday flea market
- Bearpit Karaoke
- Sunset watching
- Street art on the Berlin Wall remnant

PRACTICALITIES

- Map p330
- www.mauerpark.info
- btwn Bernauer Strasse, Schwedter Strasse & Gleimstrasse
- [S]Eberswalder Strasse, 🚋M1

Flea Market

Join the throngs of thrifty trinket hunters, bleary-eyed clubbers and excited visitors sifting for treasure at the vibrant **Flohmarkt am Mauerpark** (Map p330; www.mauerparkmarkt.de; Bernauer Strasse 63-64; ⏲10am-5pm Sun; [S]Eberwalder Strasse). Search among the retro threads, local-designer T-shirts, communist memorabilia, vintage vinyl and all manner of offbeat stuff. Despite an inevitable smattering of pros, many vendors are locals cleaning out their closets, which means real bargains are still a possibility. Plenty of ethnic food stands provide sustenance, too.

Bearpit Karaoke

Berlin's greatest free entertainment, **Bearpit Karaoke** (Map p330; www.bearpitkaraoke.de) kicks off on Sundays around 3pm (roughly from late April to September) when Irish import Joe Hatchiban sets up his custom-made mobile karaoke unit in the Mauerpark's amphitheatre. As many as 2000 people cram onto the stone bleachers to cheer and clap for eager crooners ranging from giggling 11-year-olds to Broadway-calibre belters.

Northern Mauerpark

To escape the usual Mauerpark frenzy and see where the locals relax, head to the park's extension north of Gleimstrasse. This is also where you'll find the **Jugendhof Moritzdorf** (Map p330; ☎4402 4220; www.jugendfarm-moritzhof.de; Schwedter Strasse 90; ⏲11.30am-6pm Mon-Fri, 1-6pm Sat; [S]Schönhauser Allee, [R]Schönhauser Allee), an educational farm playground complete with horses, goats and other barnyard animals. Further along you can watch vertigo-free daredevils scale the **Schwedter Northface** (Schwedter Nordwand; Map p330; www.alpinclub-berlin.de; [S]Schönhauser Allee, [R]Schönhauser Allee), a climbing wall operated by the German Alpine Club.

SIGHTS

MAUERPARK PARK

See p180.

KOLLWITZPLATZ SQUARE

Map p330 ([S]Senefelderplatz) Triangular Kollwitzplatz is the epicentre of Prenzlauer Berg poshification. To pick up on the local vibe, linger with macchiato mamas and media daddies in a street cafe or join them at the organic farmers market (p189). The park in the square's middle is tot heaven with three playgrounds plus a bronze sculpture of the artist Käthe Kollwitz for clambering on.

JÜDISCHER FRIEDHOF SCHÖNHAUSER ALLEE CEMETERY

Map p330 (☎441 9824; Schönhauser Allee 23-25; 🕘8am-4pm Mon-Thu, 7.30am-2.30pm Fri; [S]Senefelderplatz) Berlin's second Jewish cemetery opened in 1827 and hosts many well-known dearly departed, such as the artist Max Liebermann and the composer Giacomo Meyerbeer. It's a pretty place with dappled light filtering through big old trees and a sense of melancholy emanating from overgrown graves and toppled tombstones. The nicest and oldest have been moved to the Lapidarium by the main entrance.

Liebermann's tomb is next to his family's crypt roughly in the centre along the back wall. Men must cover their heads; pick up a free skullcap by the entrance.

KULTURBRAUEREI HISTORIC BUILDING

Map p330 (☎4431 5152; www.kulturbrauerei.de; Schönhauser Allee 36; tours adult/concession €7.50/6; [S]Eberswalder Strasse, 🚋M1) The fanciful red-and-yellow brick buildings of this 19th-century brewery have been recycled into a cultural powerhouse with a small village's worth of venues, from concert and theatre halls to restaurants, nightclubs, galleries and a multiscreen cinema. The bike touring company Berlin on Bike (p288) also has its home here. In December, the old buildings make a lovely backdrop for a Swedish-style Lucia Christmas market.

GETHSEMANEKIRCHE CHURCH

Map p330 (☎445 7745; www.gethsemanekirche.de; Stargarder Strasse 77; [S]Schönhauser Allee) This 1893 neo-Gothic church was a hotbed of dissent in the final days of the GDR, attracting the attention of Stasi which brutally quashed a peaceful gathering here in 1989. Ernst Barlach's *Geistkämpfer* (Ghost Fighter, 1928) sculpture stands outside the church, which is usually closed except for concerts and Sunday services.

Designed by August Orth, the Gethsemane Church was among the dozens commissioned by Emperor Wilhelm II to 'create a bulwark against socialism, communism and atheism' which, he feared, were fomenting in Berlin's working-class districts. Ironically, rather than stifling such movements, the church seemed to encourage them and

WORTH A DETOUR

SCHLOSS SCHÖNHAUSEN

In Pankow, just north of Prenzlauer Berg, **Schloss Schönhausen** (☎3949 2622; www.spsg.de; Tschaikowskistrasse 1; adult/concession €6/5; 🕘10am-6pm Tue-Sun Apr-Sep, to 5pm Oct-Mar) is surrounded by a lovely park and packs a lot of German history into its pint-size frame. Originally a country estate of Prussian nobles, in 1740 it became the summer residence of Frederick II's estranged wife Elisabeth Christine, who had it enlarged and rendered in playful rococo. Taking a page from *Sleeping Beauty*, the palace fell into a long slumber after her death in 1797 until the Nazis used the dilapidated structure as a storeroom for 'degenerate' modern art. In 1949, the building was restored once more and became the seat of East Germany's first head of state, Wilhelm Pieck, before later becoming the country's state guesthouse.

Open again after a final mega-makeover, the palace now sparkles in renewed splendour. The downstairs rooms, where the queen had her private quarters, reflect the 18th-century style with partly original furniture and wallpaper. More interesting – largely for their uniqueness – are the upstairs rooms where GDR fustiness is alive in the heavy furniture of Pieck's 1950s office and in the baby-blue bedspread in the Gentlemen's Bedroom where Castro, Ceaucesçu, Ghaddafi and other 'bad boys' slept. To get to the palace, catch tram M1 to the Tschaikowskistrasse stop, then walk about 300m east on Tschaikowskistrasse.

WWII BUNKER TOURS

After you've checked off the Brandenburg Gate and the TV Tower, why not explore Berlin's dark and dank underbelly? Join **Berliner Unterwelten** (4991 0517; www .berliner-unterwelten.de; Brunnenstrasse 105; adult/concession €10/8; English tours 11am Wed-Mon, 1pm Mon, no tours Wed Dec-Feb; Gesundbrunnen, Gesundbrunnen) on a gripping tour of a WWII underground bunker and pick your way through a warren of low-ceilinged rooms, past heavy steel doors, hospital beds, helmets, guns, boots and glowing arrows pointing towards exit doors. Listen on in horror and fascination as guides bring alive the stories of the thousands of ordinary Berliners cooped up here, crammed and scared, as the bombs rained down on Berlin. Five other tours, including one of a wartime anti-aircraft tower, are also offered. Buy tickets at the kiosk outside the south exit of Gesundbrunnen U-Bahn station (in front of Kaufland).

its congregation can look back on a proud tradition as a haven for nonconformists and freethinkers, even long before GDR times.

ZEISS GROSSPLANETARIUM   PLANETARIUM
Map p330 (421 8450; www.sdtb.de; Prenzlauer Allee 80; adult/concession €5/4; Wed-Sun, show times vary; Prenzlauer Allee) The people of East Berlin were not allowed to see what was across the Wall, but at least they could gaze at the entire universe at this fine planetarium. It opened in 1987 as one of the largest star theatres in Europe, boasting a 'Cosmorama', back then the finest star projector ever built. Today, programming ranges from traditional narrated shows (in German) to 'music under the stars' and children's events.

EATING

Being largely residential, Prenzlauer Berg has an exceptionally high density of neighbourhood restaurants to cater for on-the-go locals with more money than time. Most are convivial, elbows-on-the-table kind of places where nobody bats an eye if you're still in your sightseeing outfit or are toting the kids along. There are no Michelin shrines here, but there's still lots of good chowing down to be done.

FRAU MITTENMANG   MODERN GERMAN €€
(444 5654; www.fraumittenmang.de; Rodenbergstrasse 37; mains €9-17; dinner; Schönhauser Allee, M1, Schönhauser Allee) This unhurried neighbourhood-adored restaurant with sidewalk seating delivers a daily changing menu that folds international influences into classic German dishes. Hunker down at a polished wooden table and join locals for a meal, the house brew or a glass of excellent

wine. Walk 200m north on Schönhauser Allee from the eponymous U/S-Bahn station, then turn right on Rodenbergstrasse and continue for another 300m.

ZIA MARIA   ITALIAN €
Map p330 (www.zia-maria.de/website; Pappelallee 32a; slices €1.50-3.50; noon-midnight; Schönhauser Allee, Schönhauser Allee) This shoebox-sized pizza kitchen fills up with patrons lusting after habit-forming crispy-crust pies decorated with such non-run-of-the-mill toppings as wafer-thin prosciutto, nutmeglaced artichokes or pungent Italian sausage. Sit outside at red beer tables or in the grottolike dining room that doubles as a gallery. The eggless tiramisu is a perfect finish.

ODERQUELLE   GERMAN €€
Map p330 (4400 8080; Oderberger Strasse 27; mains €8-16; dinner; Eberswalder Strasse) It's always fun to pop by this woodsy resto and see what's inspired the chef today. Most likely, it'll be a delicious well-crafted German meal, perhaps with a slight Mediterranean nuance. The generously topped and crispy *Flammkuche* (Alsatian pizza) are a reliable standby. In summer, try scoring an outside table for keeping an eye on the buzzy action along this pretty street.

DER HAHN IST TOT!   FRENCH €€
Map p330 (6570 6756; www.der-hahn-ist-tot .de; Zionskirchstrasse 40; 4-course dinner €18; dinner Tue-Sun; Eberswalder Strasse, M1) The name translates as 'The rooster is dead!' and the fowl in question would be coq au vin, the classic French country stew that's the signature dish of this warm and pretension-free restaurant. Every night, staff dish up two different four-course dinners costing a mere €18. Either main course can always be substituted for coq au vin or a meat-free dish.

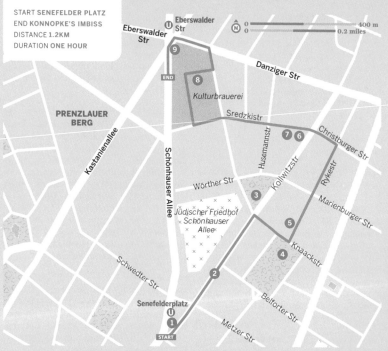

START SENEFELDER PLATZ
END KONNOPKE'S IMBISS
DISTANCE 1.2KM
DURATION ONE HOUR

Neighbourhood Walk
Poking Around Prenzlauer Berg

This easy walk takes you through the pretty Kollwitzkiez. Start out at **1 Senefelder Platz**, a triangular patch of green named for Alois Senefelder, an Austro-German actor who invented lithography. Note the marble statue with his name chiselled into the pedestal in mirror-writing, just as it would be using his printing technique. Head north on **2 Kollwitzstrasse**, where the huge LPG organic supermarket, the brand-new ultra-deluxe Palais Kolle-Belle apartment complex and a sprawling adventure playground are solid indicators of the *Kiez's* (neighbhourhood's) upmarket demographics.

You'll soon arrive at **3 Kollwitzplatz**, a square named for the artist Käthe Kollwitz, who lived here with her husband for over 40 years while tending to the destitute. A bronze statue in the square's centre park and a plaque on the blue building at Kollwitzstrasse 58 honour her legacy.

Follow Knaackstrasse to Rykestrasse, past a row of popular cafes, and note the round **4 Wasserturm** (water tower)

which went through a sinister stint as a Nazi-era prison and is now honeycombed with flats shaped like pie slices. Follow Rykestrasse, noting the handsome facades of its restored townhouses. At No 53 is the **5 Synagoge Rykestrasse**, which survived WWII and again hosts Shabbat services. It's not open to the general public.

Continue on Rykestrasse to Sredzki strasse, perhaps stopping for a cuppa at darling cafe **6 Anna Blume**. There's plenty to look at along Sredzkistrasse, including the kooky **7 Bücher Tauschbaum**, a free book exchange made from tree trunks. Soon the turrets and towers of the yellow-and-red brick **8 Kulturbrauerei** come into view. Enter this sprawling brewery-turned-cultural-complex from Sredzskistrasse. It's usually pretty quiet in the daytime, but the beautiful architecture is still worth seeing. There's also a district tourist office here. Leave the Kulturbrauerei via the north exit and turn left on Danziger Strasse to wrap up your walk with a Currywurst from cult purveyor **9 Konnopke's Imbiss**.

LUCKY LEEK
VEGAN €€

Map p330 (☑6640 8710; www.lucky-leek.de; Kollwitzstrasse 46; mains around €12; ☺dinner Tue & Thu-Sun; ☑; ⑤Senefelderplatz) It didn't take long for Lucky Leek to become one of Berlin's top vegan restaurants. Quality ingredients, fearless flavour combinations, creative and colourful presentation and enthusiastic staff should make believers of even the most dedicated carnivores. Creamy sweet-potato risotto, stuffed chilli tofu with orange-cinnamon glaze and white chocolate mousse are typical menu entries.

DER FISCHLADEN
SEAFOOD €€

Map p330 (☑4000 5612; www.derfischladen. com; Schönhauser Allee 128; mains €3.50-15; ☺10am-9pm Mon-Sat, 2-9pm Sun; ⑤Schönhauser Allee, ⑱Schönhauser Allee) Great fish at fabulous prices. Berlin may be landlocked but Der Fischladen shows that this does not have to be a detriment to sourcing superfresh fish and seafood. It's a shop and takeaway place as well as a simple but nice spot to stick around for crunchy fish and chips, Sicilian shrimp or the grilled fish platter.

TAPITAS
SPANISH €€

Map p330 (☑4673 6837; Gleimstrasse 23; tapas €2.50-6; ☺4-11pm; ⑤Eberswalder Strasse, ⑱M1) This darling teensy tapas bar is a top pick on Gleimstrasse restaurant row. All the classics are there – *jamón serrano*, bacon-wrapped dates, tortillas etc – along with a changing roster of hot tapas like chicken in lime sauce. Fabulous aioli and robust Spanish wines to boot.

BIRD
AMERICAN €€

Map p330 (☑030-5105 3283; www.thebirdinberlin.com; Am Falkplatz 5; mains €6.50-13, steaks from €15; ☺6pm-midnight Mon-Sat, from noon Sun; ⑤Schönhauser Allee, ⑱Schönhauser Allee) New York meets Berlin at this buzzy, boozy gastropub whose steaks, burgers and fries justify the hype. Sink your teeth into a dripping half-pounder made from freshly ground dry-aged Angus beef trapped between a toasted English muffin (yes, it's messy – that's what the kitchen roll is for!). Sauces, dressings and even the cheesecake are all made from scratch.

GUGELHOF
FRENCH €€

Map p330 (☑442 9229; www.gugelhof.de; Knaackstrasse 37; mains €7.50-23; ☺4pm-midnight Mon-Fri, from 10am Sat & Sun; ⑤Senefelderplatz) This country-French jewel made

headlines when feeding Bill Clinton back in 2000 but thankfully it hasn't coasted on its fame since. Chefs still keep things real with robust *choucroute* (a sauerkraut-based stew), cheese fondue, *Flammkuche* and other Alsatian soul food, plus inventive daily specials. Fabulous hand-picked French and German wines.

NEUGRÜNS KÖCHE
GERMAN €€€

Map p330 (☑4401 2092; www.neugruenskoeche .de; Schönhauser Allee 135a; mains €21, 4-course dinner €43; ☺dinner Tue-Sat; ⑤Eberswalder Strasse) Fresh ingredients play off each other beautifully at this homely-stylish restaurant whose chefs whip up two four-course menus with a passion every night. One orchestrates flavours with a regional focus, while the other travels to the Mediterranean for inspiration. No flights of fancy, just dependably good food. Only downside: squished together tables allow for little privacy.

I DUE FORNI
ITALIAN €€

Map p330 (☑4401 7373; Schönhauser Allee 12; pizzas €6-12; ☺noon-midnight; ⑤Senefelderplatz) In this hectic hall run by a crew of Italian punks, the pizza is king, not you. Service can be slow and rude, but tattooed scenesters, fresh-faced students and boho families are not deterred: the pizzas are just that good. With its scribbled walls and pseudo-revolutionary decor, this place is quintessential Berlin. Make reservations if you hope to get fed between 8pm and 10pm.

AZNAVOURIAN
FRENCH €€

Map p330 (☑4862 3131; www.aznavourian.de; Rykestrasse 2; mains €10-19; ☺11am-2am; ⑤Senefelderplatz) Aznavourian is as fantastically French as its namesake, *chanson* crooner Charles Aznavour. Black-and-white pictures of the man are mixed with giant mirrors to create a cosy ambience enhanced by dark wooden tables and candlelight. Go easy on the baguette and vampire-repellent aioli to save your appetite for bouillabaisse, salad nicoise, coq au vin, bourguignon-style snails and other Gallic classics. Good-value lunches.

SI AN
VIETNAMESE €€

Map p330 (☑4050 5775; www.sian-berlin.de; Rykestrasse 36; mains €7-11; ☺noon-midnight; ⑤Eberswalder Strasse) Sian Truong used to manage Monsieur Vuong in Mitte, the place that started the Vietnamese food craze in Berlin. His own stylish nosh spot is considerably less hectic and welcomes a steady stream of tousled hipsters, yoga mamas and even the occasional celeb. Everything's prepared freshly, seasonally, healthily and using traditional recipes from the ancient monasteries of Vietnam. Afterwards wind down in the adjacent teahouse.

SCHUSTERJUNGE GERMAN €€
Map p330 (🖉442 7654; Danziger Strasse 9; mains €5-12; ⏰11am-midnight; ⓢEberswalder Strasse) At this rustic corner pub, authentic Berlin charm is doled out with as much abandon as the delish home cooking. Big platters of goulash, roast pork and *Sauerbraten* feed both tummy and soul as do the regionally brewed Bürgerbräu and Bernauer Schwarzbier.

LA MUSE GUEULE FRENCH €€
Map p330 (🖉4320 6596; Sredzkistrasse 14; mains €8-16; ⏰dinner; ⓢEberswalder Strasse) It's the living room of Prenzlauer Berg's sizeable French community, but also popular for kicking back before or after attending an event at the Kulturbrauerei (p181). The country-style cuisine is as unpretentious as the chatty patrons, with blackboard specials showing especially imaginative flourishes. Even just sticking to a glass of luscious red wine and the earthy cheese-and-sausage appetiser has its rewards.

A MAGICA ITALIAN €
Map p330 (🖉2280 8290; Greifenhagener Strasse 54; pizzas €5-10; ⏰4pm-midnight; ⓢSchönhauser Allee, 🚇M1, 🚋Schönhauser Allee) This always-packed joint consistently delivers Neapolitan pizzas with pizazz straight out of the wood-burning oven in full view of tables in the cosy, candlelit dining room. They go down well with luscious red house wine served in water glasses. Come by 8pm before local groupies have snapped up all the tables.

KONNOPKE'S IMBISS SAUSAGES €
Map p330 (Schönhauser Allee 44a; sausages €1.30-1.70; ⏰10am-8pm Mon-Fri, noon-8pm Sat; ⓢEberswalder Strasse) Brave the inevitable queue for great Currywurst from one of the city's cult sausage kitchens, now in shiny new glass digs but in the same historic spot since 1930.

DAIRY INTERNATIONAL €
Map p330 (www.thedairy.de; Raumerstrasse 12; mains €3-8; 📶; ⓢEberswalder Strasse, 🚇M1) There's certainly no shortage of bohemian

daytime cafes in Prenzlauer Berg, but this New Zealander-owned hole-in-the-wall on Helmholtzplatz got our attention for its kick-ass coffee, granny-style baked goods, bulging sandwiches and homemade blackboard specials: steak-and-Guinness stew or wild-boar sandwich anyone?

W- DER IMBISS FUSION €
Map p330 (www.w-derimbiss.de; Kastanienallee 49; dishes €2-8; ⏰noon-midnight; 📶; ⓢRosenthaler Platz, 🚇M1) The love child of Italian and Indian cooking, W's signature naan pizza is freshly baked in the tandoor oven and mouth-wateringly topped with everything from goat cheese to smoked salmon to guacamole. The wok curries and tortilla wraps are tasty too, while the spirulina-laced apple juice keeps hangovers at bay.

NAKED LUNCH INTERNATIONAL €€
Map p330 (🖉3034 6461; www.naked-lunch.net; Anklamer Strasse 38, 2nd courtyard; mains €8-18; ⏰11.30am-5pm Mon, to 10.30pm Tue-Fri, 10am-5pm Sat & Sun; ⓢBernauer Strasse) Nothing to do with the famous novel by William S Burroughs, this purist oasis tucked into a back courtyard of an all-women start-up complex has simple cafeteria flair by day but turns into a more grown-up restaurant at night. 'Naked' refers to the complete absence of artificial flavour enhancers.

ULA BERLIN JAPANESE €€€
Map p330 (www.ula-berlin.com; Anklamer Strasse 8; mains €16-29; ⏰dinner Tue-Sun; 🚋Bernauer Strasse) Ula means 'unexpected' and indeed, this avant-garde parlour goes way beyond sushi with such tempting modern Japanese morsels as sesame-flavoured roasted tuna or grilled sea bream with citrus sauce. The owner and the chef hail from Tokyo, sending the authenticity-scale sky-high. The stylish interior gives it instant hipster cred. It's 360m north of the intersection of Invalidenstrasse and Ackerstrasse.

🍷 DRINKING & NIGHTLIFE

⎍ᴛᴏᴘ⎎ PRATER BEER GARDEN
Map p330 (🖉448 5688; www.pratergarten.de; Kastanienallee 7-9; ⏰from noon Apr-Sep in good weather; ⓢEberswalder Strasse) Berlin's oldest beer garden (since 1837) has kept much

A CASE STUDY OF GENTRIFICATION

Badly pummelled but not destroyed during WWII, Prenzlauer Berg languished for decades, its grand but crumbling 19th-century townhouses becoming the domain of artists, creatives, intellectuals, gays and political dissidents. It was this community that stood up when the East German government came within a whisker of tearing down the old buildings in the late '80s. And it was they who fanned the flames of opposition that led to the Peaceful Revolution of 1989.

After the Wall collapsed, the district became party central but was also among the first to show up in the crosshairs of developers. They snapped up the decrepit buildings for virtual pennies and scrubbed away decades of grime to reveal gorgeous facades and stucco-ornamented interiors. Nowadays, the sleekly renovated lofts are the haunts of worldly boho-bourgeois professionals, including many expats from France, Italy, the US and Britain.

These relatively recent arrivals have displaced nearly 80% of pre-unification residents who could simply no longer afford the ever-rising rents or felt no cultural affinity for fancy coffee drinks. The demographic changes also account for the death of many long-standing party venues that have had to cede to developers (eg Klub der Republic and Icon) or have come under fire from noise-sensitive neighbours (eg Knaack and Magnet).

of its traditional charm and is a fantastic place to hang and guzzle a cold one beneath the ancient chestnut trees (self-service). Kids can romp around the small play area. In foul weather or winter, the adjacent woodsy restaurant is a fine place to sample classic Berlin dishes (mains €8 to €19).

BECKETTS KOPF — BAR

Map p330 (www.becketts-kopf.de; Pappel allee 64; ⏲Tue-Sun; [S]Schönhauser Allee, 🚋12, [R]Schönhauser Allee) Beyond Samuel Beckett's head in the window, the art of cocktail-making is taken very seriously. Settle into a heavy, wine-coloured armchair in the warmly lit room and look on as the barkeeps whip high-calibre spirits, fresh juices and secret ingredients into classic and creative concoctions intended to appeal to all the senses.

MARIETTA — CAFE, BAR

Map p330 (☎4372 0646; www.marietta-bar.de; Stargarder Strasse 13; ⏲from 10am; [S]Schönhauser Allee, 🚋M1, [R]Schönhauser Allee) Retro is now at this neighbourly self-service retreat where you can check out passing eye candy through the big window or lug your beverage to the dimly lit back room for quiet bantering. On Wednesday nights it's a launch pad for the local gay party circuit.

AUGUST FENGLER — BAR

Map p330 (www.augustfengler.de; Lychener Strasse 11; [S]Eberswalder Strasse, 🚋M1) With its flirty vibe, blazing dance floor and foosball in the cellar, this local institution scores a trifecta on key ingredients for a good night out. Wallet-friendly drinks prices, charming bar staff and a pretence-free crowd don't hurt either. Best in the wee hours for that last drink.

ST GAUDY CAFE — CAFE

Map p330 (☎4435 0732; www.gaudycafe.com; Gaudystrasse 1; ⏲8am-8pm, later on event nights; [S]Schönhauser Allee, 🚋M1, [R]Schönhauser Allee) In a former East German pub, this unpretentious hang-out is as warm and welcoming as a hug from an old friend. It's run by expats for expats and offers plenty of fun programming, from concerts to quiz nights to the biweekly German-English Language Exchange. Fabulous cakes and meat-free dishes along with one of the best cappuccinos in town.

ANNA BLUME — CAFE

Map p330 (☎4404 8749; www.cafe-anna-blume.de; Kollwitzstrasse 83; ⏲8am-2am; [S]Eberswalder Strasse) Potent java, homemade cakes and flowers from the attached shop perfume the art nouveau interior of this corner cafe named for a Kurt Schwitters poem. In fine weather the sidewalk terrace is the best people-watching perch. Great for breakfast, especially the tiered tray for two.

MORNING GLORY — CAFE

Map p330 (Kastanienallee 35; ⏲8.30am-6pm Nov-Mar, to 8pm Apr-Oct; [S]Eberswalder Strasse, 🚋M1) This bright and low-key gem on the sunny side of Kastanienallee is the perfect place to banish hangovers with vitamin-packed smoothies, catch up on your reading over a top-shelf cappuccino or dig into an energy-restoring *panino* (sandwich). Charming staff adds to the feel-good vibe.

MAUERSEGLER
BEER GARDEN

Map p330 (🖉9788 0904; www.mauersegler -berlin.de; Bernauer Strasse 63; ⊙11am-2am May-Oct, 9am-7pm Sun year-round; 🛜; Ⓢ Eberswalder Strasse) Pram-pushing mummies, iPad toters and laid-back students all congregate at this funky-romantic beer garden for cold beers, cakes and barbecues. Part of the Mauerpark (p180), it's busiest during the Sunday flea market. Check the website for parties, live concerts and sports screenings.

DECK 5
BAR

Map p330 (www.freilufttrebellen.de/deck-5; Schönhauser Allee 80; ⊙10am-midnight, in good summer weather only; Ⓢ Schönhauser Allee, 🚇M1, 🚊Schönhauser Allee) Soak up the sunset at this beach bar in the sky while sinking your toes into tonnes of sand lugged to the top parking deck of the Schönhauser Arkaden mall. Take the lift from within the mall or enter via a never-ending flight of stairs from Greifenhagener Strasse.

BONANZA COFFEE HEROES
CAFE

Map p330 (🖉0171 563 0795; Oderberger Strasse 35; ⊙8.30am-7pm Mon-Fri, 10am-7pm Sat & Sun; Ⓢ Eberswalder Strasse) If Synesso Cyncra and 'third-wave coffee' are not mere gobbledygook to you, you speak the language of Kiduk and Yumi, owners of this pocket-sized shrine for javaholics. It's daytime only and often packed to the rafters.

BAR GAGARIN
CAFE, BAR

Map p330 (🖉442 8807; www.bar-gagarin.com; Knaackstrasse 22-24; ⊙10am-2am; Ⓢ Senefelderplatz) Prepare for lift-off with vodka, Moskwa beer and borscht at this retro homage to Soviet cosmonaut Yuri Gagarin, the first man in space. It's one of several cafes along Knaackstrasse. Good breakfast and Sunday brunch. Free toiletries in the loos.

KAFFEE PAKOLAT
CAFE

Map p330 (Raumerstrasse 40; ⊙10am-7pm Mon-Fri, to 6pm Sat & Sun; Ⓢ Eberswalder Strasse, 🚇M1) Flash back to the 19th century in this olde-worlde cafe-cum-store where the coffee is roasted on-site, the bread and cakes are made in the backroom bakery and

the money is deposited in a ring-a-ding till from 1913. Antique furniture, enamel signs and sweet, unhurried service complete the illusion. Breakfast and snacks are available.

WOHNZIMMER BAR
BAR

Map p330 (🖉445 5458; Lettestrasse 6; ⊙10am-4am; Ⓢ Eberswalder Strasse) Bask in the vintage vibe of this cult 'living room' (the translation of *Wohnzimmer*), where talkative types hang out for vegetarian brekkie, cakes and beer on mismatched flea-market sofas and armchairs. It's buzzy at night, but daytime can be slow.

BASSY
CLUB

Map p330 (🖉281 8323; www.bassy-club.de; Schönhauser Allee 176a; ⊙Mon-Sat; Ⓢ Senefelderplatz) Most punters here have a post-Woodstock birth date but happily ride the retro wave at this trashy-charming den of darkness, which plays only pre-1969 sounds – surf music, rockabilly, swing, R&B and whatever else gets people tapping their toes. Concerts, burlesque and cabaret nights and the weekly infamous Chantals House of Shame gay party beef up the program.

ROADRUNNER'S CLUB
CLUB

Map p330 (www.roadrunners-paradise.de; 3rd courtyard, Saarbrücker Strasse 24; Ⓢ Senefelderplatz) Rock and roll temple for rebels without a cause. Girls in petticoats and guys with slicked-back pompadours invade for kick-ass rockabilly parties amid a fantasy world of '50s and '60s Americana tucked into the back of a labyrinthine red-brick ex-brewery. No need to sport the look to shake your own hips at concerts and parties (see website for upcoming events).

ⓘ

KIEZ INFO

Stop by the local **tourist info centre** (🖉4435 2170; Maschinenhaus, Kulturbrauerei, Schönhauser Allee 36; ⊙11am-7pm; Ⓢ Eberswalder Strasse) in the Kulturbrauerei, which has maps, flyers and booklets to help you plug into the Prenzlauer Berg neighbourhood. It also sells tickets to events around town.

PRENZLAUER BERG DRINKING & NIGHTLIFE

GREIFBAR BAR

Map p330 (☎444 0828; www.greifbar.com; Wichertstrasse 10; ⏰10pm-6am; [S]Schönhauser Allee, 🚆Schönhauser Allee) Men-Film-Cruising: Greifbar's motto says it all. This Prenzlauer Berg staple draws a mixed crowd of jeans, sneakers, leather and skin sniffing each other out below the big-screen video in the comfortable bar before retiring to the sweaty play zone in the back. Beers are half-price on Mondays.

☆ ENTERTAINMENT

DOCK 11 DANCE

Map p330 (☎448 1222; www.dock11-berlin.de; Kastanienallee 79; [S]Eberswalder Strasse, 🚋M1) For cutting-edge, experimental dance, there are few better places in town than this unpretentious space tucked into an old factory. Many productions are original works developed in-house as a result of courses and workshops offered throughout the week.

LICHTBLICK KINO CINEMA

Map p330 (☎4405 8179; www.lichtblick-kino.org; Kastanienallee 77; [S]Eberswalder Strasse, 🚋M1) With space for 32 cineastes, there's not a bad seat in Berlin's smallest cinema, run by a collective and known for its eclectic programming of fine retrospectives, political documentaries, shorts, Berlin-made movies and global avant-garde fare. Luis Buñuel is honoured with a special filmic line-up every year on his birthday on 22 February.

KOOKABURRA COMEDY CLUB

Map p330 (☎4862 3186; www.comedyclub.de; Schönhauser Allee 184; [S]Rosa-Luxemburg-Platz) Living-room-style comedy club delivers an assembly line of laughs in cosy digs at a former bank building. On Tuesday nights and late on Saturdays (from 11.45pm), funny folk from English-speaking countries spin everyday material into comedy gold. Other treats: improv nights, open mike nights and the inimitable Fish & Whips burlesque shows.

🛍 SHOPPING

Kastanienallee and Oderberger Strasse are popular for Berlin-made fashions and streetwear. More indie stores hold forth along Stargarder Strasse and in the streets around Helmholtzplatz, especially lower Dunckerstrasse. Cool-hunters should also steer to the Mauerpark and Arkonaplatz to forage for flea-market treasure. For everyday needs stop by the Schönhauser Allee Arcaden mall right by the eponymous U-/S-Bahn station.

[TOP CHOICE] **FLAGSHIPSTORE** FASHION

Map p330 (☎4373 5327; www.flagshipstore-berlin.de; Oderberger Strasse 53; ⏰noon-8pm Mon-Sat; [S]Eberswalder Strasse, 🚋M1) Beata and Johanna are geniuses when it comes to ferreting out the finest, limited-edition streetwear, mostly from young Berlin labels (Hazelnut, Betty Bund, Stoffbruch etc), as well as a few imports. There's unconventional but wearable fashion for him and her, plus plenty of accessories. Definitely one of the coolest shops along Kastanienallee.

LUXUS INTERNATIONAL GIFTS, SOUVENIRS

Map p330 (☎4432 4877; www.luxus-international.de; Kastanienallee 101; ⏰11am-8pm Mon-Fri, 1.30-7.30pm Sat; [S]Eberswalder Strasse, 🚋M1) There's no shortage of creative spirits in Berlin, but not many of them can afford their own store. In comes Luxus International, a unique concept store that rents them a shelf or two to display their original designs: T-shirts, tote bags, ashtrays, lamps, candles, mugs etc. You never know what you'll find, but you can bet it's a Berlin original.

TA(U)SCHE ACCESSORIES

Map p330 (☎4030 1770; www.tausche.de; Raumerstrasse 8; ⏰11am-8pm Mon-Fri, to 6pm Sat; [S]Eberswalder Strasse) Heike Braun and Antje Strubels, both landscape architects by training, are the masterminds behind these ingenious messenger-style bags kitted out with exchangeable flaps that zip off and on in seconds. Bags come in 11 sizes with two flaps included. Additional ones can be purchased individually along with various inserts, depending on whether you need to lug a laptop, a camera or nappies.

FLOHMARKT AM ARKONAPLATZ FLEA MARKET

Map p330 (www.mauerparkmarkt.de; Arkonaplatz; ⏰10am-4pm Sun; [S]Bernauer Strasse) Surrounded by cafes perfect for carbo-loading, this smallish flea market lets you ride the retro frenzy with plenty of groovy furniture, accessories, clothing, vinyl and books, including some GDR-era stuff. It's easily combined with a visit to the nearby Flohmarkt am Mauerpark (p180).

KOLLWITZPLATZMARKT MARKET

Map p330 (Kollwitzstrasse; ⏲noon-7pm Thu, 9am-4pm Sat; [S]Senefelderplatz) Berlin's poshest farmers market has everything you need to put together a gourmet picnic or meal. Velvety gorgonzolas, juniper-berry smoked ham, crusty sourdough bread and homemade pesto are among the exquisite morsels scooped up by well-heeled locals. The Saturday edition also features handicrafts.

ERFINDERLADEN GIFTS, SOUVENIRS

Map p330 (www.erfinderladen-berlin.de; Lychener Strasse 8; [S]Eberswalder Strasse, 🚋M1) Notepads for the shower, a toilet paper holder made from vinyl records, an antimonster spray for your kids – the Inventor Store is chockfull of items ranging from whimsical and bizarre to stylish and practical. Also check out the prototypes in the small museum in back.

SAINT GEORGES BOOKS

Map p330 (☎8179 8333; www.saintgeorgesbookshop.com; Wörther Strasse 27; ⏲11am-8pm Mon-Fri, to 7pm Sat; 📶; [S]Senefelderplatz) Laid-back and low-key, Saint Georges bookshop is a sterling spot to track down new and used Berlin-themed fiction and nonfiction. The history section alone makes for some great time wasting (as do the Chesterfield sofas).

GOLDHAHN & SAMPSON FOOD

Map p330 (☎4119 8366; www.goldhahnundsampson.de; Dunckerstrasse 9; ⏲8am-8pm Mon-Fri, 10am-8pm Sat; [S]Eberswalder Strasse) Pink Himalaya salt, Moroccan argan oil and crusty German bread are among the temptingly displayed delicacies at this posh food gallery. Owners Sasha and Andreas hand-source all items, most of them rare, organic and from small suppliers. For inspiration, nose around the cookbook library or book a class at the on-site cooking school.

RATZEKATZ TOYS

Map p330 (☎681 9564; www.ratzekatz.de; Raumerstrasse 7; ⏲10am-7pm Mon-Sat; [S]Eberswalder Strasse) Packed with quality playthings, this adorable store made headlines a few years ago when Angelina Jolie and son Maddox picked out a Jurassic Park's worth of dinosaurs. Even without the celeb glow, it's a fine place to source everything from Siku cars and trucks to Ravensburger jigsaws, Lego and piles of plush toys.

VEB ORANGE GIFTS, SOUVENIRS

Map p330 (☎9788 6886; www.veborange.de; Oderberger Strasse 29; ⏲10am-8pm Mon-Sat; [S]Eberswalder Strasse) Viva retro! With its selection of the most beautiful things from the '60s and '70s, this place will remind you of how colourful, plastic and fun home decor once used to be. VEB Orange sells all kinds of orange furnishings, accessories, lamps and fashions, much of it reflecting that often irresistibly campy GDR design.

AWEAR FASHION

Map p330 (www.above-berlin.de; Kastanienallee 75; ⏲noon-8pm Mon-Fri, to 7pm Sat; [S]Eberswalder Strasse, 🚋M1) This trendy streetwear concept store feeds the urban-fashion craze with hats, hoodies, sneakers, tees and more by Dr Denim, Sixpack France, Wood Wood, Just Female, dico Copenhagen and plenty of other cool-hunter faves.

COLEDAMPF'S CULTURCENTRUM HOMEWARES

Map p330 (☎4373 5225; www.coledampfs.de; Wörther Strasse 39; ⏲10am-8pm Mon-Fri, to 6pm Sat; [S]Senefelderplatz) The ultimate chef's playground, this store is stuffed with everything from the functional to the frivolous. From shiny copper pans to ravioli cutters, iced-tea glasses to espresso pots – you're sure to find something you can't live without among the 8000 or so items stocked here.

THATCHERS FASHION

Map p330 (☎2462 7751; www.thatchers.de; Kastanienallee 21; ⏲11am-7pm; [S]Eberswalder Strasse, 🚋M1) Berlin fashion veterans Ralf Hensellek and Thomas Mrozek specialise in well-tailored clothing that's feminine and versatile. Their smart dresses, skirts and shirts look almost plain on the rack but are transformed when worn as the sort of stylish garments that go from office to dinner to nightclub – but not hurriedly out of fashion. Also located at Court IV of the **Hackesche Höfe** (Map p320; ☎2758 2210; Rosenthaler Strasse 40-41; ⏲11am-8pm Mon-Fri, to 6pm Sat; 🚆Hackescher Markt).

City West & Charlottenburg

SCHLOSS CHARLOTTENBURG | KURFÜRSTENDAMM

Neighbourhood Top Five

1 Marvelling at the Prussian royal lifestyle at **Schloss Charlottenburg** (p192), then relaxing with a picnic by the carp pond in the palace park.

2 Tempting your taste buds in the fabulous food hall of the **KaDeWe** (p202) department store.

3 Meditating upon the futility of war at the still hauntingly majestic **Kaiser-Wilhelm-Gedächtniskirche** (p197).

4 Travelling back to the 1920s while enjoying merriment in the retro-styled cabaret of **Bar Jeder Vernunft** (p202).

5 Getting under the skin of Berlin's tumultuous history at the **Story of Berlin** (p197).

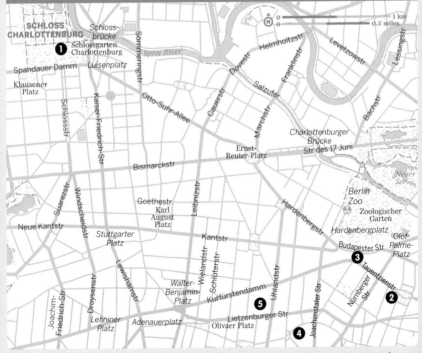

For more detail of this area see Map p333 and p334 ➡

Explore: City West & Charlottenburg

The glittering heart of West Berlin during the Cold War, Charlottenburg is nirvana for shopaholics, royal groupies and culture lovers. On its main artery – Kurfürsten damm – fashionable boutiques mix it up with high-street chains and department stores. The holy grail among the latter is the KaDeWe on nearby Tauentzienstrasse. There's more shopping in leafy side streets that are also home to relaxed cafes, neighbourhood-adored restaurants and old-timey pubs.

Eclipsed by historic Mitte and other eastern districts after reunification, Charlottenburg is now working hard to reclaim the limelight with new construction and redevelopment, especially in the City West, the area centred near the Zoologischer Garten train station.

Since 2012, the 32-storey Waldorf Astoria Hotel has dramatically changed the skyline. Nearby, the historic Zoopalast cinema, which once hosted glamorous Berlin ale events, is getting a major makeover, as is the adjacent so-called Bikinihaus, until recently the haunt of souvenir shops.

About 3.5km northwest of here, Schloss Charlottenburg is not only the best preserved royal palace in Berlin but also surrounded by a lovely park and a trio of top museums. Budget at least one full day to do this area justice.

Local Life

⇒ **Shopping** Shop till you drop at high-street chains and high-fashion boutiques along Ku'damm and its side streets and be bowled over by the KaDeWe (p202) consumer temple.

⇒ **The Asian Mile** Find your favourite among the authentic Chinese eateries in Berlin's Little Asia (p200) along Kantstrasse.

⇒ **Culture** Applaud top-rated opera productions alongside Berliners at the vast Deutsche Oper (p202) and the Staatsoper Unter den Linden (p202), exiled to Charlottenburg while its Mitte pad is under long-term renovation.

Getting There & Away

⇒ **Bus** Zoologischer Garten is the western terminal for buses 100 and 200. M19, M29 and X10 travel along Kurfürstendamm. The M45 goes to Schloss Charlottenburg.

⇒ **S-Bahn** Zoologischer Garten is the most central station.

⇒ **U-Bahn** Uhlandstrasse, Kurfürstendamm and Wittenbergplatz stations put you right into shopping central.

Lonely Planet's Top Tip

Grab a lounge chair and enjoy a movie under the stars against the backdrop of gorgeous Schloss Charlottenburg in July and August. See www.openaircharlotten burg.de for details.

Best Places to Eat

⇒ Osteria Centrale (p199)
⇒ Ottenthal (p201)
⇒ Good Friends (p200)
⇒ Mr Hai Kabuki (p200)

For reviews, see p198 ⇒

Best Places to Drink

⇒ Gainsbourg (p201)
⇒ Puro Skylounge (p201)
⇒ Universum Lounge (p201)

For reviews, see p201 ⇒

Best Museums

⇒ Museum Berggruen (p194)
⇒ Käthe-Kollwitz-Museum (p196)
⇒ Sammlung Scharf-Gerstenberg (p194)
⇒ Story of Berlin (p197)

For reviews, see p196 ⇒

CITY WEST & CHARLOTTENBURG

TOP SIGHTS
SCHLOSS CHARLOTTENBURG

Schloss Charlottenburg is an exquisite baroque palace and one of the few sites in Berlin that still reflects the one-time grandeur of the royal Hohenzollern clan. A visit is especially pleasant in summer when you can fold a stroll, sunbathing session or picnic by the carp pond into a day of peeking at royal treasures. These treasures include lavishly furnished period rooms reflecting royal tastes and lifestyles from the baroque to the 20th century, as well as the largest collection of 18th-century French paintings outside of France.

The grandest Prussian palace to survive in Berlin consists of the main building and three smaller structures scattered about the sprawling Schlossgarten Charlottenburg (palace park), which is part formal French, part unruly English and all idyllic playground. Hidden among the shady paths, flower beds, lawns, mature trees and carp pond are two smaller buildings, the sombre Mausoleum and the playful Belvedere.

DON'T MISS...

- Frederick the Great's apartments in the Neuer Flügel
- A stroll around the Schlossgarten
- Paintings by French masters in the Altes Schloss
- Sarcophagi in the Mausoleum

PRACTICALITIES

- Map p333
- ☎320 911
- www.spsg.de
- Spandauer Damm 20-24
- day pass adult/concession €15/11
- 🚌145, 309, [S]Richard-Wagner-Platz, Sophie-Charlotte-Platz

Altes Schloss

Also known as the Nering-Eosander Building after its two architects, the **Altes Schloss** (Map p333; ☎320 911; www.spsg.de; Spandauer Damm; adult/concession €12/8; 🕒10am-6pm Tue-Sun Apr-Oct, to 5pm Tue-Sun Nov-Mar; 🚌145, 309, [S]Richard-Wagner-Platz, Sophie-Charlotte-Platz) is the central, and oldest, section of the palace and fronted by Andreas Schlüter's grand **equestrian statue of the Great Elector** (1699). Inside, the baroque living quarters of Friedrich I and Sophie-Charlotte are an extravaganza in stucco, brocade and overall opulence. Highlights include the **Oak Gallery**, a wood-panelled festival hall; the charming **Oval Hall** overlooking the park; Friedrich I's bedchamber, with the first-ever bathroom in a baroque palace; and the **Eosander Chapel**, with its trompe l'oeil arches. The king's passion for Chinese and Japanese blueware is reflected in the dazzling **Porcelain Chamber**.

Upstairs are paintings, vases, tapestries, weapons, porcelain, a 2600-piece silver table setting and other items essential to a royal lifestyle.

Neuer Flügel

The palace's most beautiful rooms are the flamboyant private chambers of Frederick the Great in the **Neuer Flügel** (New Wing; Map p333; ☎320 911; www.spsg.de; Spandauer Damm 20-24; adult/concession incl audioguide €6/5; ⏰10am-6pm Wed-Mon Apr-Oct, to 5pm Wed-Mon Nov-Mar; 🚌M45, 309, [S]Richard-Wagner-Platz, Sophie-Charlotte-Platz), designed in 1746 by royal buddy and 'starchitect du jour' Georg Wenzeslaus von Knobelsdorff. The confection-like White Hall banquet room and the Golden Gallery, a rococo fantasy of mirrors and gilding, are both standouts. Other rooms display superb paintings by such 18th-century French masters as Watteau and Pesne. Another highlight is the recently recreated apartment of Luise (1776–1810), a popular queen and wife of King Friedrich Wilhelm III. Note the lavish chandeliers, period furniture and hand-painted silk wall coverings.

Neuer Pavillon

Returning from a trip to Italy, Friedrich Wilhelm III (r 1797–1848) commissioned Karl Friedrich Schinkel to design the **Neuer Pavillon** (New Pavilion; Map p333; ☎320 910; www.spsg.de; Spandauer Damm 20-24; adult/concession incl audioguide €4/3; ⏰10am-6pm Tue-Sun Apr-Oct, to 5pm Nov-Mar; 🚌309, [S]Richard-Wagner-Platz, Sophie-Charlotte-Platz) as a summer refuge modelled on a villa in Naples. After a five-year renovation, the minipalace is again a sparkling backdrop for masterpieces by such Schinkel-era artists as Caspar David Friedrich, Eduard Gaertner and Carl Blechen. Rooms on the ground floor are furnished in Biedermeier style and feature many original pieces.

Belvedere

The pint-size **Belvedere** (Map p333; ☎3209 1445; www.spsg.de; Spandauer Damm 20-24; adult/concession €3/2.50; ⏰10am-6pm Tue-Sun Apr-Oct, noon-4pm Tue-Sun Nov-Mar; [S]Sophie-Charlotte-Platz, then bus 309, [S]Richard-Wagner-Platz, then bus 145) palace with the distinctive cupola got its start in 1788 as a teahouse for Friedrich Wilhelm II. Here he listened to chamber music and held spiritual sessions with fellow members of the mystical Order of the Rosicrucians. These days it makes an elegant backdrop for porcelain masterpieces by the royal manufacturer KPM.

TOP TIPS

Each Schloss building charges separately so invest in the *Tageskarte* (adult/concession €15/11) for one-day admission to every open building. Come between Wednesday and Sunday when all are open and arrive early, especially on weekends and in summer when queues can be long.

The Schloss is at its most photogenic from the front and when seen from the carp pond in the Schlosspark. If you want to take noncommercial photographs inside the palaces, you need to buy a photo permit for €3.

BAROQUE CONCERTS

Feel like a member of the Prussian court during the **Berliner Residenz Konzerte** (Map p333; ☎258 1035; www.concerts-berlin.com; Spandauer Damm 22-24; ⏰usually 8pm Wed, Fri & Sat; 🚌145, 309, [S]Richard-Wagner-Platz, Sophie-Charlotte-Platz), a series of classical concerts held by candlelight with musicians dressed in powdered wigs and historical costumes and playing Bach, Mozart, Händel or Haydn. Various packages are available, including one featuring a preconcert dinner.

Mausoleum

In the Schlosspark, west of the carp pond, the 1810 neoclassical **Mausoleum** (Map p333; ☎3209 1446; www.spsg.de; Spandauer Damm 20-24; 🕙10am-6pm Tue-Sun Apr-Oct; 🚌145, 309, [S]Richard-Wagner-Platz, Sophie-Charlotte-Platz) was conceived as the final resting place of Queen Luise but twice expanded to make room for other royals, including Luise's husband Friedrich Wilhelm III, and Emperor William I and his wife Augusta. Their ornate marble sarcophagi are great works of art. More royals are in the crypt (closed to the public).

Sammlung Scharf-Gerstenberg

The stellar **Scharf-Gerstenberg Collection** (Map p333; ☎266 424 242; www.smb.museum/ssg; Schlossstrasse 70; adult/concession €6/3; 🕙10am-6pm Tue-Sun; [S]Sophie-Charlotte-Platz, then bus 309, [S]Richard-Wagner-Platz, then bus 145) in the former palace stables showcases a complete survey of surrealist art, with large bodies of work by René Magritte and Max Ernst alongside dreamscapes by Dalí and Dubuffet. Standouts among their 18th-century forerunners include Goya's spooky etchings and the creepy dungeon scenes by Italian engraver Giovanni Battista Piranesi.

Regularly screened films by Buñuel, Dalí and contemporary directors show how the surrealist aesthetic was interpreted on screen.

Tickets to this museum are also valid for same-day admission to the Museum für Fotografie (p197) near Zoologischer Garten U-/S-Bahn station.

Museum Berggruen

Fans of classical modern art will be in their element at the delightful **Museum Berggruen** (Map p333; ☎266 424 242; www.smb.museum/mb; Schlossstrasse 1; 🕙closed for renovation; 🚌145, 309, [S]Richard-Wagner-Platz, Sophie-Charlotte-Platz), which just started a major extension. Picasso is especially well represented with paintings, drawings and sculptures from all major creative phases. Elsewhere it's off to Paul Klee's emotional world, Matisse's paper cut-outs, Giacometti's famous sculptures and a sprinkling of African art that inspired both Klee and Picasso. Standouts by the latter include the *Seated Harlequin* from the early blue and rose periods, bold

THE PALACE THROUGH THE AGES

Schloss Charlottenburg wasn't always so large and lavish. It started out rather modestly as a petite summer retreat – called Lietzenburg – built for Sophie-Charlotte, wife of Elector Friedrich III. Arnold Nering drew up the initial plans, which were expanded in the mode of Versailles by Johann Friedrich Eosander after the elector became *King* Friedrich I in 1701. After Sophie-Charlotte died in 1705, he renamed the palace in her honour.

Subsequent royals dabbled with the compound, most notably Frederick the Great, who built the spectacular Neuer Flügel (p193). Eventually, the facade extended for an impressive 505m, only 65m less than its French model. In 1812, the three-wing palace got its landmark central dome. It's topped by a gilded statue of the goddess Fortuna that moves with the wind, making it sort of a glamorous weather vane.

Bombed in 1943, the rebuilding of the Schloss became a priority in West Berlin after the East German leadership detonated the only other surviving Hohenzollern palace, the Berliner Stadtschloss on Unter den Linden, in 1951. When reconstruction was completed in 1966, the equestrian statue of the Great Elector (1699) by Andreas Schlüter was returned to the front courtyard. At press time, restoration of the main palace exterior was expected to have begun, but there won't be any interruptions to the visiting schedule.

Museum interior, Schloss Charlottenburg

cubist canvases like his portrait of George Braque and the more mellow paintings of his later years, including *The Yellow Pullover* from 1939.

Bröhan Museum

The fine **Bröhan Museum** (Map p333; ⌨3269 0600; www.broehan-museum.de; Schlossstrasse 1a; adult/concession €6/4; ☺10am-6pm Tue-Sun; §Sophie-Charlotte-Platz, Richard-Wagner-Platz) trains the spotlight on art nouveau, art deco and functionalism, all decorative styles in vogue between 1889 and 1939 and considered the midwives of modern design. Highlights include fully furnished and decorated period rooms by Hector Guimard and Peter Behrens, a Berlin Secession picture gallery and a section dedicated to Henry van de Velde.

Abguss-Sammlung Antiker Plastik Berlin

If you are a fan of classical sculpture or simply enjoy studying naked guys with missing noses or other body protrusions, see the **Abguss-Sammlung Antiker Plastik Berlin** (Antique Plaster-Cast Collection; Map p333; ⌨342 4054; www.abguss-sammlung-berlin.de; Schlossstrasse 69b; ☺2-5pm Thu-Sun; §Sophie-Charlotte-Platz, then bus 309, §Richard-Wagner-Platz, then bus 145). With works spanning 3500 years, created by cultures as diverse as the Minoan, Roman or Byzantine, you will be able to trace the evolution of this ancient art form. The shop sells plaster-cast copies.

Schloss Charlottenburg is about 3km northwest of Bahnhof Zoologischer Garten. The most scenic approach is from the south via Schlossstrasse (get off at U-Bahn stop Sophie-Charlotte-Platz), a leafy avenue flanked by dignified townhouses built for senior court officials.

THE SCHLOSS BY BOAT

From April to early October, a lovely way to travel to or from Schloss Charlottenburg is by boat cruise operated by **Stern und Kreisschiffahrt** (⌨536 3600; www.sternundkreis.de; one way €15, round-trip €20). Both the 1¼-hour tour along the Spree River and the three-hour tour via the Landwehrkanal leave from landing docks at Jannowitzbrücke in Mitte, near Alexanderplatz. The Schloss Charlottenburg boat landing is just outside the northeast corner of the park.

There's a pretty cafe with tree-shaded outdoor seating in the Kleine Orangerie building near the entrance to the palace gardens. Or for a hearty meal and cold beer, try Brauhaus Lemke (p198), a short walk from the palace.

CITY WEST & CHARLOTTENBURG SCHLOSS CHARLOTTENBURG

TOP SIGHTS
SCHLOSS CHARLOTTENBURG

SIGHTS

Schloss Charlottenburg

SCHLOSS CHARLOTTENBURG PALACE

See p192.

Kurfürstendamm

The 3.5km-long Kurfürstendamm is a ribbon of commerce that began as a bridle path to the royal hunting lodge in the Grunewald forest. In the early 1870s, Otto von Bismarck, the Iron Chancellor, decided that the capital of the newly founded German Reich needed its own representative boulevard, bigger and better even than the Champs-Élysées.

EUROPA-CENTER LANDMARK

Map p334 (www.europa-center-berlin.de; Breitscheidplatz; ⌚building 24hr; [S]Kurfürstendamm, Zoologischer Garte, 🚆Zoologischer Garten) With its giant Mercedes star spinning on its rooftop, the 103m-high Europa-Center was Berlin's first 'skyscraper' at its 1965 opening. These days, the 20-storey shopping centre exudes charming retro flair and is packed with such quirky sights as the Lotus Fountain on the ground floor and the psychedelic *Flow of Time Clock* by Bernard Gitton in the basement.

You can also catch the lift to the 20th floor to enjoy the panorama or get an eyeful of pretty people and Berlin at the swish Puro Skylounge (p201). It was built on the site of the Romanisches Cafe, a key hangout of 1920s glitterati and intellectuals.

KÄTHE-KOLLWITZ-MUSEUM MUSEUM

Map p334 (☎882 5210; www.kaethe-kollwitz.de; Fasanenstrasse 24; adult/concession €6/3, audio guide €3; ⌚11am-6pm; [S]Uhlandstrasse) This exquisite museum is devoted to Käthe Kollwitz (1867–1945), one of Germany's greatest women artists, whose social and political awareness lent a tortured power to her lithographs, graphics, woodcuts, sculptures and drawings. Recurring themes include motherhood and death; sometimes the two are strangely intertwined as in works that show death as a nurturing figure, cradling its victims.

TOP SIGHTS
BERLIN ZOO & AQUARIUM

Germany's oldest animal park was established in 1844 under King Friedrich Wilhelm IV, who not only donated the land but also pheasants and other animals from the royal family's private reserve on the Pfaueninsel. The zoo made worldwide headlines a few years ago with the birth of a polar bear named Knut, who died suddenly in 2011. Still, an astonishing 18,000 critters representing 1570 species make their home here, many of them in open – but moated – enclosures. The menagerie includes orangutans, koalas, rhinos, penguins and Bao Bao, the only giant panda on view in Germany. There are feeding sessions scheduled in the afternoon; ask for the day's schedule when buying your ticket.

The zoo can be entered via Hardenbergplatz or through the exotic **Elephant Gate** on Budapester Strasse. Just east of the latter, the **aquarium** (Map p334; ☎254 010; www.aquarium-berlin.de; Budapester Strasse 32; adult/child €13/6.50, with zoo €20/10; ⌚9am-6pm; [S]Zoologischer Garten, 🚆Zoologischer Garten) presents three floors of exotic fish, amphibians and reptiles in endearingly old-fashioned darkened halls and glowing tanks. Some of the specimens in the famous **Crocodile Hall** could be the stuff of nightmares, but jellyfish, iridescent poison frogs and a real-life 'Nemo' should bring smiles to most youngsters.

DON'T MISS...

- Bao Bao
- Jellyfish tanks
- Penguin hall

PRACTICALITIES

- Map p334
- ☎254 010
- www.zoo-berlin.de
- Hardenbergplatz 8
- adult/child €13/6.50, with aquarium €20/10
- ⌚9am-7pm Apr–mid-Oct, 9am-5pm mid-Oct–Mar
- [S]Zoologischer Garten, 🚆Zoologischer Garten

⊙ TOP SIGHTS
KAISER-WILHELM-GEDÄCHTNISKIRCHE

One of Berlin's most photographed landmarks is the bombed-out tower of the Kaiser Wilhelm Memorial Church. It now serves as an antiwar memorial, standing quiet and dignified among the roaring traffic. The original church was a magnificent neo-Romanesque pile built in 1895 to honour Kaiser Wilhelm I. The few surviving mosaics, marble reliefs and liturgical objects in the memorial hall at the foot of the tower only hint at its one-time splendour. Before and after photographs will help you visualise its former grandeur.

In 1961, a modern bell tower and octagonal hall of worship designed by Egon Eiermann were built next to the church ruin. Stepping inside the latter feels a bit like entering a giant crystal because of the intensely midnight-blue glass walls. The nave's single most striking element is the giant golden Jesus figure 'floating' above the altar. Also note the *Stalingrad Madonna* (a charcoal drawing made by a German soldier trapped in Russia during the winter of 1942).

Restoration of the tower, under way at the time of writing, may be completed by the time you're reading this.

DON'T MISS...

➡ Historic exhibit in the tower

➡ Memorial hall

PRACTICALITIES

➡ Kaiser Wilhelm Memorial Church

➡ Map p334

➡ ☑218 5023

➡ www.gedaechtni skirche.com

➡ Breitscheidplatz

➡ ⊙9am-7pm

➡ Ⓢ Zoologischer Garten, Kurfürstendamm, ⓇZoologischer Garten

CITY WEST & CHARLOTTENBURG SIGHTS

Highlights include the antihunger lithography *Brot!* (Bread!, 1924) and the woodcut series *Krieg* (War, 1922–23). There's also a copy of Gustav Seitz' Kollwitz sculpture on Kollwitzplatz in Prenzlauer Berg. Special exhibits supplement the permanent exhibit twice annually.

MUSEUM FÜR FOTOGRAFIE   MUSEUM

Map p334 (☑3186 4825; www.smb.museum/mf; Jebensstrasse 2; adult/concession €8/4; ⊙10am-6pm Tue, Wed & Fri-Sun, to 10pm Thu; ⓈZoologischer Garten, ⓇZoologischer Garten) Berlin's Museum of Photography is still a work in progress. For now, its biggest tenant is the Helmut Newton Collection, which chronicles the artistic legacy of this Berlin-born enfant terrible of fashion and lifestyle photography on two floors of this former Prussian officers' casino behind Bahnhof Zoologischer Garten. On the top floor, the gloriously restored barrel-vaulted **Kaisersaal** (Emperor's Hall) forms a grand backdrop for high-calibre changing exhibits of photography drawn from the archive of the State Art Library.

Shortly before his fatal car crash in 2004, Newton donated 1500 images along with personal effects to the city in which he was born in 1920. He had studied photography here with famed fashion photographer Yva before fleeing Nazi Germany in 1938. His work reflects a lifelong obsession with the female body, which he often portrayed in controversial, quasi-pornographic poses. One famous image shows a crouched model wearing a horse's saddle, while his best-known work – the 'Big Nudes' series – stars a flock of stark-naked Amazons. Even his landscapes and still lifes are often charged with cold eroticism. The galleries on the 1st floor showcase his vision, while the ground floor is essentially a shrine to the man. Highlights include his partially recreated office in Monte Carlo, his first camera (an Agfa Box he bought aged 12) and his blue Jeep (dubbed the Newton-Mobile).

Tickets to this museum are also valid for same-day admission to the surrealist art collection of the Sammlung Scharf-Gerstenberg (p194).

STORY OF BERLIN   MUSEUM

Map p334 (☑8872 0100; www.story-of-berlin.de; Kurfürstendamm 207-208, enter via Ku'damm Karree mall; adult/concession €10/8; ⊙10am-8pm, last admission 6pm; ⓈUhlandstrasse) This multimedia museum breaks down 800 years of Berlin history into bite-sized chunks that are easy to swallow but substantial enough

WORTH A DETOUR

OLYMPIASTADION & AROUND

The main attraction in far western Berlin is the Olympiastadion. Even though it was put through a total modernisation for the 2006 FIFA World Cup, it's hard to ignore the fact that this massive coliseum-like stadium was built by the Nazis for the 1936 Olympic Games. The bombastic bulk of the structure undoubtedly remains but has been softened by the addition of a spidery oval roof, snazzy VIP boxes and top-notch sound, lighting and projection systems. It seats up to 74,400 people for games played by the local Hertha BSC soccer team, concerts, the Pope or Madonna. On nonevent days, you can explore the stadium on your own, although renting an audioguide is recommended (€3). Several times daily, guided tours take you into the locker rooms, warm-up areas and VIP areas that are otherwise off-limits. Access the stadium from the Osttor (eastern gate).

Admission also includes access to the 77m-high **Glockenturm** (Bell Tower; ☎305 8123; www.glockenturm.de; Am Glockenturm; adult/concession incl Olympiastadion €7/5; ⏲9am-8pm Jun–mid-Sep, 9am-7pm late Mar-May & mid-Sep–Oct, 10am-4pm Nov–mid-Mar weather permitting; [R]Pichelsberg) just west of the stadium. It's well worth riding the lift to the viewing platform to truly appreciate the structure's massive dimensions. On good days, you can see all the way into town and as far as Potsdam. An exhibit on the ground floor chronicles the infamous 1936 games; the documentary featuring rare original footage from the event is also well worth watching.

to be satisfying. Each of the 23 rooms encapsulates a different theme or epoch in the city's history, from its founding in 1237 to the fall of the Berlin Wall. A highlight is a tour of a still functional atomic bunker beneath the building.

DAS VERBORGENE MUSEUM MUSEUM

Map p334 (Hidden Museum; ☎313 3656; www.dasverborgenemuseum.de; Schlüterstrasse 70; adult/concession €2/1; ⏲3-7pm Thu & Fri, noon-4pm Sat & Sun; [S]Ernst-Reuter-Platz, [R]Savignyplatz) Founded by a pair of feminist artists and art historians, the nonprofit Hidden Museum has a unique focus: the largely forgotten works by early-20th-century women artists, mostly from Germany. Past exhibits have highlighted the works of expressionist artist Ilse Heller-Lazard and photographs by Henriette Grindat. Curators mount about two exhibits annually, which run for three or four months each. At other times, the museum is closed.

LOCAL KNOWLEDGE

WATER MEATBALL FOUNTAIN

Flanked by the Kaiser-Wilhelm-Gedächtniskirche and the Europa-Center, bustling Breitscheidplatz is where everyone from foot-sore tourists to buskers, punks and souvenir hawkers gathers around the quirky **Weltbrunnen** (World Fountain; Map p334; Breitscheidplatz; 🚌100, [S]Kurfürstendamm, Zoologischer Garten, [R]Zoologischer Garten), a 1983 creation of local artist Joachim Schmettau. Nicknamed *Wasserklops* (water meatball), it's made from red granite and bronze, and festooned with sculptures of humans and animals.

🍴 EATING

The dining quality in Charlottenburg is dependably high. Savignyplatz exudes the relaxed and bustling vibe of an Italian piazza on balmy summer nights, while Kantstrasse is lined with many excellent Asian and Spanish eateries.

🍴 Schloss Charlottenburg

BRAUHAUS LEMKE GERMAN €€

Map p333 (☎3087 8979; www.brauhaus-lemke.com; Luisenplatz 1; mains €7-20; ⏲11am-midnight; 🚌M45, [S]Richard-Wagner-Platz) There are not too many worthy eating options right by Schloss Charlottenburg, but this congenial brewpub is the go-to place for solid – if a bit pricey – German home-

About 1.5km south of the stadium, the **Georg Kolbe Museum** (☎304 2144; www.georg-kolbe-museum.de; Sensburger Allee 25; adult/concession €5/3; ⏰10am-6pm Tue-Sun; [R]Heerstrasse) is dedicated to one of Germany's most influential sculptors in the first half of the 20th century. A member of the Berlin Secession, Kolbe became a chief exponent of the idealised male nude, an approach that found favour with the Nazis. The museum shows works from all phases of his life alongside temporary exhibits often drawn from his rich private collection of 20th-century sculpture and paintings. The sculpture garden is an oasis of tranquillity and the cafe one of the nicest in a Berlin museum.

About 2km northwest of the stadium, right next to the trade-fair grounds, looms another Berlin landmark, the 129m-high **Funkturm** (Radio Tower; ☎3038 1905; Messedamm 22; adult/concession €4.50/2.50; ⏰platform 10am-8pm Mon, to 11pm Tue-Sun, weather permitting; [S]Kaiserdamm, [R]Messe Nord/ICC). Its filigree outline bears an uncanny resemblance to Paris' Eiffel Tower and looks especially attractive when lit up at night. It started transmitting signals in 1925; 10 years later the world's first regular TV program was broadcast from here. From the viewing platform at 126m or the restaurant at 55m you can enjoy sweeping views of the Grunewald forest and the western city, as well as the **AVUS**, Germany's first car-racing track, which opened in 1921; AVUS stands for Automobil-, Verkehrs- und Übungsstrasse (auto, traffic and practice track). The Nazis made it part of the autobahn system, which it still is today.

cooking. Although it's only been in business since 1987, the decor seeks to evoke old-timey Berlin. In summer the terrace tables with palace view are the most desirable.

ROGACKI GERMAN €€

Map p334 (☎343 8250; www.rogacki.de; Wilmersdorfer Strasse 145; meals €4.50-13; ⏰9am-6pm Mon-Wed, to 7pm Thu, 8am-7pm Fri, 8am-4pm Sat; [S]Bismarckstrasse) Family-run since 1928, Rogacki is chiefly a deli that's a foodie's daydream, where glass display cases are piled high with cheeses, cold cuts, bread, game, salads, smoked fish (done in-house) and whatever else demanding palates desire. Put together a picnic-to-go, or stay put and join locals crowded around the stand-up tables for oysters and wine, a feisty stew or a plate of pasta.

NATURAL'MENTE VEGETARIAN €€

Map p333 (☎341 4166; www.naturalmente.de; Schustehrusstrasse 26; mains €9-12; ⏰noon-3.30pm Mon-Fri; 🌱; [S]Richard-Wagner-Platz) This Macrobiotic Society–run resto has been supplying herbivores with reliable, healthy and organic lunches long before vegetarianism became sexy. It's got a bit of an institutional feel but is a nicely untouristed spot to break up a day of sightseeing in nearby Schloss Charlottenburg. From the Schloss, walk 250m south on Schlosstrasse, then turn left and follow Schustehrusstrasse for another 200m.

🍴 Kurfürstendamm

ALI BABA ITALIAN €

Map p334 (☎881 1350; www.alibaba-berlin.de; Bleibtreustrasse 45; dishes €3-9; ⏰11am-2am Sun-Thu, to 3am Fri & Sat; [R]Savignyplatz) Every body feels like family at this been-here-forever port of call where the thin-crust pizza is delicious, the pasta piping hot and nothing costs more than €9. Popular with party people and posh Charlottenburgers in slumming mood.

SCHLEUSENKRUG GERMAN €

Map p334 (☎313 9909; www.schleusenkrug.de; Müller-Breslau-Strasse; mains €3.50-13; ⏰10am-11pm May-Sep, to 7pm Oct-Apr; [S]Zoologischer Garten, [R]Zoologischer Garten) Sitting pretty on the edge of the Tiergarten, next to a Landwehrkanal lock, Schleusenkrug truly comes into its own in summer when the beer garden kicks into full swing. People from all walks of life hunker over mugs of foamy beer and satisfying comfort food, from grilled sausages to *Flammkuche* (Alsatian pizza) and weekly changing specials. Breakfast is served until 3pm.

OSTERIA CENTRALE ITALIAN €€

Map p334 (☎3101 3263; Bleibtreustrasse 51; mains €10-20; ⏰dinner Mon-Sat; [R]Savignyplatz) This neighbourhood Italian fits like a well-worn shoe and lets you dip into a pool of pleasurable classics from around the Boot. Staples like octopus carpaccio, grilled calamari, truffle pasta or rosemary-scented beef stew are creatively perfected and keep regulars coming back for more.

GOOD FRIENDS
CHINESE €€

Map p334 (☑313 2659; www.goodfriends-berlin .de; Kantstrasse 30; mains €10-20; ☺noon-2am; ᕼSavignyplatz) Sinophiles tired of the Kung Pao school of Chinese cooking will appreciate the real thing at this top-flight Cantonese restaurant. The ducks dangling in the window are the overture to a menu long enough to confuse Confucius. If jellyfish with eggs or fried pork belly prove too challenging, you can always fall back on, well, Kung Pao chicken.

MR HAI KABUKI
JAPANESE €€

(☑8862 8136; www.mrhai.de; Olivaer Platz 10; platters €12-22; ᕲM19, 109, ᔆAdenauerplatz, Uhlandstrasse) The menu here features classic nigiri and maki but most regulars flock to Mr Hai for more unconventional sushi morsels, composed like little works of art. Some creations feature kimchi, pumpkin and cream cheese or are flambéed and deep-fried. Sounds bizarre, but it works. From U-Bahn station Uhlandstrasse, take bus 109 or M19 two stops to Olivaer Platz.

JULES VERNE
INTERNATIONAL €€

Map p334 (☑3180 9410; www.jules-verne-berlin .de; Schlüterstrasse 61; breakfast €4-9, 2-course lunch €5.50-7.50, dinner mains €7-17.50; ☺9am-1am; ☑; ᕼSavignyplatz) Jules Verne was a well-travelled man, so it's only fitting that a cafe bearing his name would feature a globetrotting menu. French oysters, Austrian schnitzel and Moroccan couscous are all perennial bestsellers. It also has great breakfasts named after Verne's books served until 3pm and a buffet at weekends.

FRANKE
INTERNATIONAL €€

Map p334 (www.frankrestaurant.de; Excelsior Hotel, Hardenbergstrasse 14; 2-course lunch €12, dinner mains €12-20; ᔆZoologischer Garten, ᕼZoologischer Garten) Yes, it's in a hotel but this is not your usual hotel restaurant. Say goodbye to dry chicken Kiev and hello to fresh, healthy international fare infused with Israeli touches: duck breast marinaded in date honey and chilli, or tiger shrimp paired with mint and black pasta are

typical menu entries. Sit close to the open kitchen if you want to watch the cooks in action.

CAFÉ-RESTAURANT WINTERGARTEN IM LITERATURHAUS
INTERNATIONAL €€

Map p334 (☑882 5414; www.literaturhaus-berlin .de; Fasanenstrasse 23; mains €8-16; ☺9.30am-1am; ᔆUhlandstrasse) The hustle and bustle of Ku'damm is only a block away from this genteel art nouveau villa with attached bookstore. Tuck into seasonal bistro cuisine amid elegant Old Berlin flair in the gracefully stucco-ornamented rooms or, if weather permits, in the idyllic garden. Breakfast is served 2pm.

DICKE WIRTIN
GERMAN €€

Map p334 (☑312 4952; www.dicke-wirtin.de; Carmerstrasse 9; mains €6-15; ☺from noon; ᕼSavignyplatz) Old Berlin charm oozes from every nook and cranny of this been-here-forever pub which pours eight draught beers (including the superb Kloster Andechs) and nearly three dozen homemade schnapps varieties. Hearty local fare like roast pork, fried liver or breaded schnitzel keeps brains balanced.

BREL
FRENCH, BELGIAN €€

Map p334 (☑3180 0020; www.cafebrel.de; Savignyplatz 1; 3-course lunch €9, mains €11-21; ☺9am-1am; ᕼSavignyplatz) Belgian cult crooner Jacques Brel is the namesake of this corner bistro in a former bordello that now draws bleary-eyed bohos for coffee and croissants, suits and tourists for €9 lunches, and artsy types and stylish couples for

BERLIN'S LITTLE ASIA

It's not quite Chinatown, but if you're in the mood for Asian food, simply head to Kantstrasse between Savignyplatz and Wilmersdorfer Strasse to find the city's densest concentration of authentic Chinese restaurants, including the perennial popular Good Friends (p200). At lunchtime, most offer value-priced specials perfect for filling up on the cheap. In between are Chinese furniture stores, massage parlours and Asian supermarkets as well as various Vietnamese and Thai eateries.

frog legs, steaks and snails at dinnertime. Also one of the best places for *moules frites* during mussel season (September to February). Breakfast until 6pm.

MOON THAI
THAI €€

Map p334 (**2**3180 9743; www.moonthai-restaurant.com; Kantstrasse 32; mains €8.50-14.50; ⊙noon-midnight Mon-Fri, 1pm-midnight Sat & Sun; **2**; **R**Savignyplatz) Orange walls accented with exotic art create a feel-good ambience at this family affair serving classic Thai dishes with more than a modicum of authenticity. Anything revolving around duck or squid is excellent and even the seitan dishes strut their stuff when paired with fresh vegetables and bold spices.

ENOTECA IL CALICE
ITALIAN €€€

Map p334 (**2**324 2308; www.ilcalice.de; Walter-Benjamin-Platz 4; mains €13-34; ⊙dinner, lunch Mon-Sat; **S**Adenauerplatz) Superb wines from all regions of 'the Boot' flow as freely as the conversation at this elegant Italian outpost. Resist the temptation to make a meal of the antipasto alone so you can test the chef's considerable talents over such out-there concoctions as coffee-oil-poached sturgeon or air-dried mullet-roe pasta.

OTTENTHAL
AUSTRIAN €€€

Map p334 (**2**313 3162; www.ottenthal.com; Kantstrasse 153; mains €14-32; ⊙dinner; **S**Zoologischer Garten, Uhlandstrasse, **R**Zoologischer Garten) This neighbourhood-adored restaurant features a little shrine to Mozart and the old church clockwork from the owner's Austrian hometown of Ottenthal, and has classic alpine cuisine with a modern workout. The Wiener schnitzel is a dependable staple but more innovative creations like roast pike perch with red pepper cream are at least as pleasurable.

DUKE
FRENCH €€€

Map p334 (**2**683 154 000; www.duke-restaurant.com; Ellington Hotel, Nürnberger Strasse 50-55; 2-/3-course lunch €15/19.50, 5-course dinner €60, dinner mains €12.50-29; ⊙11.30am-midnight; **S**Augsburger Strasse) Head chef Florian Gauert has a knack for pairing punctilious craftsmanship with complementary combinations of flavours, textures and aromas. Spring vegetables, for instance, are matched with preserved blueberries, capers and shaved mushrooms, and sea bass meets saffron gnocchi and glazed cucum-

ber. Whenever possible, local or regional organic ingredients are used.

🍷 DRINKING & NIGHTLIFE

GAINSBOURG
BAR

Map p334 (**2**313 7464; www.gainsbourg.de; Jeanne-Mammen-Bogen 576/577; ⊙from 4pm; **R**Savignyplatz) The spirit of namesake crooner Serge Gainsbourg seems to waft through this West Berlin institution, now in larger digs beneath the S-Bahn arches. Round tables, candlelight and *chansons* all exude a cosy Paris vibe that speaks to a crowd probably old enough to have made out to *'Je t'aime'*, Serge's steamy 1969 duet with Jane Birkin. Classic cocktails. Gauloises cigarettes optional.

PURO SKYLOUNGE
BAR, CLUB

Map p334 (**2**2636 7875; www.puro-berlin.de; Tauentzienstrasse 11; ⊙Tue-Sat; **S**Kurfürstendamm) Puro has quite literally raised the bar in Charlottenburg – by moving it to the 20th floor of the Europa Center, that is. Trade Berlin funky-trash for sleek decor, fabulous views and high-heeled hotties. The crowd skews young but moneyed. Dress up or forget about it.

ZWIEBELFISCH
PUB

Map p334 (**2**312 7363; www.zwiebelfisch-berlin.de; Savignyplatz 5; ⊙noon-6am; **R**Savignyplatz) With its clientele of grizzled and aspiring artists, actors and writers, this cosy pub has been Charlottenburg at its boho best since the patchouli-perfumed 1960s. Arrested in time, it's a fabulous sliver of pre-reunification West Berlin and ideal for guzzling that final drink while the suits are gearing up for the office grind.

UNIVERSUM LOUNGE
BAR

(**2**8906 4995; www.universumlounge.com; Kurfürstendamm 153; ⊙6pm-3am; **S**Adenauerplatz) The curvaceous teak bar and white leather banquettes of this spacey, retroglam libation station fill up quickly after the curtain falls at the Schaubühne theatre, a 1920s gem by the esteemed Erich Mendelsohn in the same building. The bar is about 300m west of U-Bahn station Adenauerplatz.

★ ENTERTAINMENT

[TOP CHOICE] **BAR JEDER VERNUNFT** CABARET
(☎883 1582; www.bar-jeder-vernunft.de; Schaperstrasse 24; [S]Spichernstrasse) Life's still a cabaret at this intimate 1912 art nouveau mirrored tent, which puts on song-and-dance shows, comedy and *chanson* evenings plus, intermittently, the famous *Cabaret* cult musical itself. From the U-Bahn station, follow Meierottostrasse northwest for 200m, then turn right and continue on Schaperstrasse for another 100m. The entrance is on your right behind a parking lot.

STAATSOPER UNTER DEN LINDEN @ SCHILLERTHEATER OPERA
Map p334 (☎information 203 540, tickets 2035 4555; www.staatsoper-berlin.de; Bismarckstrasse 110; [S]Ernst-Reuter-Platz) Point your highbrow compass towards the Daniel Barenboim-led Staatsoper, Berlin's top opera company. While its historic digs on Unter den Linden are getting a facelift (probably until 2014), the high-calibre productions are staged at the Schiller Theater in Charlottenburg. All operas are sung in their original language.

QUASIMODO LIVE MUSIC
Map p334 (☎312 8086; www.quasimodo.de; Kantstrasse 12a; ⏲Tue-Sat Sep-Jul; [S]Zoologischer Garten, 🚆Zoologischer Garten) One of Berlin's oldest jazz clubs has diversified its programming and now also pulls in fans of blues, rock, soul, funk and Motown acts to its intimate cellar space with a low ceiling and black walls. If that gets too claustrophobic, escape to the upstairs cafe, in summer with outside terrace. Wednesday's jam sessions are free.

ASTOR FILM LOUNGE CINEMA
Map p334 (☎883 8551; www.astor-filmlounge.de; Kurfürstendamm 225; [S]Kurfürstendamm, Uhlandstrasse) Demanding celluloid lovers flock to this ultradeluxe movie temple that has hosted star-studded premieres since the 1950s. Plop down into a generously spaced and adjustable leather seat, order cocktails or snacks and lean back to enjoy the superb projection and ear-popping surround-sound. It's also a venue to catch live opera broadcasts from around the world.

DEUTSCHE OPER OPERA
Map p334 (☎3438 4343; www.deutscheoperberlin.de; Bismarckstrasse 35; [S]Deutsche Oper) The German Opera was founded by local citizens in 1912 as a counterpoint to the royal opera (today's Staatsoper) on Unter den Linden. The original building was destroyed in WWII and rebuilt by 1961 as a huge, modernist venue with seating for nearly 1900 people. It boasts a repertory of around 70 operas, which are all sung in their original language.

A-TRANE JAZZ
Map p334 (☎313 2550; www.a-trane.de; Bleibtreustrasse 1; ⏲Mon-Sat; 🚆Savignyplatz) Herbie Hancock and Diana Krall have anointed the stage of this intimate jazz club, but mostly it's emerging talent bringing their A-game to the A-Trane. Entry is free on Monday when local boy Andreas Schmidt shows off his skills, and after 12.30am on Saturday for the late-night jam session.

SHOPPING

Kurfürstendamm and Tauentzienstrasse are chock-a-block with multiple outlets of international chains flogging fashion and accessories. Further west on Ku'damm are the more high-end boutiques such as Hermès, Cartier and Bulgari. Kantstrasse is the go-to zone for home designs. Connecting side streets, such as Bleibtreustrasse and Schlüterstrasse, house upscale indie and designer boutiques, bookstores and galleries.

[TOP CHOICE] **KADEWE** DEPARTMENT STORE
(www.kadewe.de; Tauentzienstrasse 21-24; ⏲10am-8pm Mon-Thu, to 9pm Fri, 9.30am-8pm Sat; [S]Wittenbergplatz) Just past the centennial mark, this venerable department store has an assortment so vast that a pirate-style campaign is the best way to plunder its bounty. If pushed for time, at least hurry up to the legendary 6th-floor gourmet food hall. The name, by the way, stands for *Kaufhaus des Westens* (department store of the West). It's right outside U-Bahn station Wittenbergplatz.

SCHROPP BOOKS
Map p334 (☎2355 7320; www.landkartenschropp.de; Hardenbergstrasse 9a; ⏲10am-8pm Mon-Fri, to 6pm Sat; [S]Ernst-Reuter-Platz) No other shop in Berlin is better placed than Schropp to tell you where to go. It's been in business for more than 250 years, and you'll find the entire world beneath its roof

with every conceivable map, travel guide, dictionary and globe. Come here for some quality armchair travelling or to plan your next trip.

HAUTNAH   FASHION

Map p334 (✆882 3434; www.hautnahberlin.de; Uhlandstrasse 170; ⊙noon-8pm Mon-Fri, 11am-4pm Sat; Ⓢ Uhlandstrasse) Being the sort of city Berlin is, sooner or later you may just need to update your fetish wardrobe, and Hautnah's three floors of erotic costuming should do the job naughtily. Expect a vast range of latex bodices, leather goods, themed get-ups, sex toys and vertiginous footwear, plus an interesting wine selection (Marquis de Sade champagne anyone?).

KÄTHE WOHLFAHRT   HANDICRAFTS

Map p334 (✆www.wohlfahrt.com; Kurfürstendamm 225-226; ⊙10am-8pm Mon-Sat, 1-6pm Sun May-Dec; Ⓢ Kurfürstendamm) With its mind-boggling assortment of Yuletide decorations and ornaments, this huge shop lets you celebrate Christmas every day of the year. Many of the items are handcrafted with amazing skill and imagination.

STILWERK   HOMEWARES

Map p334 (✆315 150; www.stilwerk.de; Kantstrasse 17; Ⓡ Savignyplatz) This four-storey temple of good taste will have devotees of the finer things itching to redecorate. Everything you could possibly want for home and hearth – from tactile key rings to glossy grand pianos and quality vintage design –

is here, plus all the top names (eg Bang & Olufsen, Ligne Roset, Niessing).

STEIFF GALERIE IN BERLIN   TOYS

Map p334 (✆8862 5006; www.steiff.de; Kurfürstendamm 38/39; Ⓢ Uhlandstrasse) The cuddly creations of this famous stuffed-animal company, founded in 1880 by Margarete Steiff (who in 1902 invented the teddy bear – named for US president Teddy Roosevelt, whom she admired), are tailor-made for snuggles. The fluffy menagerie at this central store will have all ages feeling warm and fuzzy.

BERLINER TRÖDELMARKT   MARKET

Map p334 (www.berliner-troedelmarkt.de; Strasse des 17 Juni; ⊙10am-5pm Sat & Sun; Ⓡ Tiergarten) Vendors vie for your euros with yesteryear's fur coats, silverware, jewellery, lamps, dolls, hats and plenty of other stuff one might find in Granny's attic at Berlin's oldest flea market set up west of Tiergarten S-Bahn station. The attached arts and crafts market sells mostly new stuff.

TITUS ZOOPREME   FASHION

Map p334 (✆3259 3239; www.titus.de; Meinekestrasse 2; Ⓢ Kurfürstendamm) Perhaps not what you were expecting in this quiet street off Ku'damm, but definitely the place to come for streetwear and skate-wear (for both men and women) plus an impressive selection of skate decks. It's part of a Germany-wide chain and the clued-up staff can also provide information about the local skating scene.

Day Trips from Berlin

Potsdam p205
It's practically impossible not to be enchanted by this rambling park and palace ensemble, including Schloss Sanssouci.

Sachsenhausen Concentration Camp p209
The horrors of the Third Reich become all too real at what's left of one of Germany's oldest Nazi-built concentration camps.

Spandau p211
Anchored by a delightful Altstadt (old town), this northwestern Berlin district flaunts its historical pedigree.

Grunewald & Dahlem p212
Tree-lined streets with mansions and manicured lawns lace Berlin's poshest area, which also boasts plenty of culture cred.

Wannsee p214
Hemmed in by the Havel River, Berlin's southwesternmost district counts palaces, forests and historical sights among its assets.

Köpenick p216
Home to Berlin's largest lake, sprawling forest, a handsome baroque castle and medieval centre.

Potsdam

9.30am-6pm Mon-Fri, to 4pm Sat & Sun Apr-Oct, 10am-6pm Mon-Fri, 9.30am-2pm Sat & Sun Nov-Mar; ⓡHauptbahnhof)

Explore

Potsdam, on the Havel River just southwest of Berlin, is the capital and crown jewel of the state of Brandenburg. Scores of visitors are drawn to the stunning architecture of this former Prussian royal seat to soak up the air of history that hangs over its elegant parks. Large parts of the city garnered Unesco World Heritage status in 1990.

Headlining the roll call of palaces is Schloss Sanssouci, the private retreat of King Friedrich II (Frederick the Great) who was also the visionary behind many of Potsdam's other fabulous palaces and parks, which miraculously survived WWII with nary a shrapnel wound. When the shooting stopped, the Allies chose Schloss Cecilienhof for the Potsdam Conference of August 1945 to decide Germany's postwar fate.

The Best...

➡ **Sight** Schloss Sanssouci (p205)
➡ **Place to Eat** Maison Charlotte (p209)
➡ **Place to Drink** Hafthorn (p209)

Top Tip

Cold War history buffs should visit the memorial exhibit in the grim former **KGB Prison** (www.gedenkstaette-leistikowstrasse.de; Leistikowstrasse 1; ⊙2-6pm Tue-Sun) that was part of Military Station 7, where Soviet military lived and worked.

Getting There & Away

Car Take the A100 to the A115.
Train Regional trains leaving from Berlin-Hauptbahnhof and Zoologischer Garten take only 25 minutes to reach Potsdam Hauptbahnhof; some continue on to Potsdam-Charlottenhof and Potsdam-Sanssouci, which are actually closer to Park Sanssouci. The S7 from central Berlin makes the trip in about 40 minutes. You need a ticket covering zones A, B and C (€3.10) for either service.

Need to Know

➡ **Area Code** ☎0331
➡ **Location** 24km southwest of Berlin
➡ **Tourist Office** (☎2755 8899; www .potsdam-tourism.com; Brandenburger Strasse 3;

⦿ SIGHTS

⦿ Schloss & Park Sanssouci

This glorious park and palace ensemble is what happens when a king has good taste, plenty of cash and access to the finest architects and artists of the day. Sanssouci was dreamed up by Frederick the Great (1712–86) and was his favourite summer retreat, a place where he could be 'sans souci' (without cares). His grave is nearby. Frederick's great-great nephew, King Friedrich Wilhelm IV (1795–1861), added a few more buildings to this vast landscaped expanse of mature trees, undulating paths and rare plants. Unesco gave the entire complex World Heritage status in 1990.

SCHLOSS SANSSOUCI   PALACE
(www.spsg.de; adult/concession incl audioguide Apr-Oct €12/8, Nov-Mar €8/5; ⊙10am-6pm Tue-Sun Apr-Oct, to 5pm Nov-Mar; ⓠ695, 606) The biggest stunner, and what everyone comes to see at Schloss and Park Sanssouci, is Schloss Sanssouci, the celebrated rococo palace designed by Georg Wenzeslaus von Knobelsdorff in 1747. The timed tickets sometimes sell out by noon – arrive early, preferably at opening, and avoid weekends and holidays. You can only enter the palace at the time printed on your ticket. Only city tours booked through the tourist office guarantee entry to the Schloss.

This rococo jewel of a palace sits daintily above vine-draped terraces with Frederick

SIGHTSEEING FLOATS

Boats operated by **Schiffahrt in Potsdam** (Map p206; ☎275 9210; www .schiffahrt-in-potsdam.de; Lange Brücke 6; ⊙departures 10am-7pm Apr-Oct) depart throughout the day from the docks near Lange Brücke, by the towering Hotel Mercure. Choose from a 90-minute palaces cruise (€13), a three-hour trip around several Havel lakes (€16), or the two-hour 'seven lake cruise' to Wannsee (€14).

Potsdam

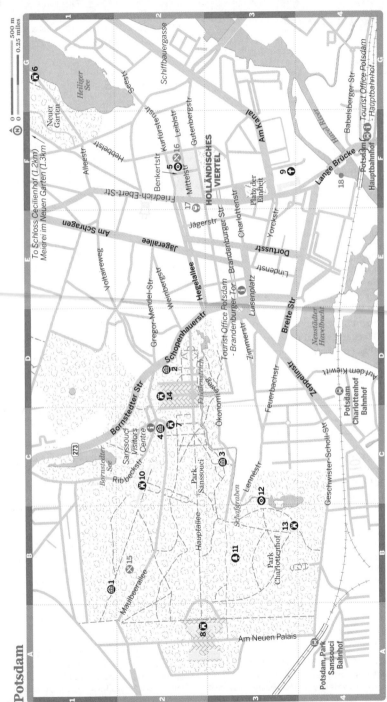

500 m
0.25 miles

Heiliger See

Neuer Garten

Seestr

Schiffbauergasse

G

To Schloss Cecilienhof (1.2km)
Meierei im Neuen Garten (1.3km)

Alleestr

Hebbelstr

Kurfürstenstr

Benkertstr

Leiblstr

Gutenbergstr

5

16

Mittelstr

Friedrich-Ebert-Str

HOLLÄNDISCHES
VIERTEL

Am Kanal

17

Jägerstr

Brandenburger Str

Charlottenstr

Platz der
Einheit

Yorckstr

9

Lange Brücke

18

Babelsberger Str

Potsdam
Hauptbahnhof

Tourist Office Potsdam
– Hauptbahnhof

Am Schragen

Jägerallee

Hegelallee

Voltaireweg

Weinbergstr

Gregor-Mendel-Str

Schopenhauerstr

2

Friedrich

Tourist Office Potsdam
– Brandenburger Tor

Zimmerstr

Luisenplatz

Lindenstr

Breite Str

Neustädter
Havelbucht

Bornstedter See

273

Bornstedter Str

Sanssouci
Visitors
Centre

4

7

14

Ribbeckstr

10

Ökonomieweg

3

Park
Sanssouci

Feuerbachstr

Zeppelinstr

Auf dem Kiewitt

Potsdam
Charlottenhof
Bahnhof

Hauptallee

Schafgraben

Lennéstr

12

13

11

Park
Charlottenhof

Maulbeerallee

15

1

8

Am Neuen Palais

Potsdam, Park
Sanssouci
Bahnhof

Geschwister-Scholl-Str

Potsdam

the Great's grave nearby. Standouts on the audioguided tours include the **Konzertsaal** (Concert Hall), whimsically decorated with vines, grapes and even a cobweb where sculpted spiders frolic. The king himself gave flute recitals here. Also note the intimate **Bibliothek** (library), lidded by a gilded sunburst ceiling, where the king would seek solace amid 2000 leather-bound tomes ranging from Greek poetry to the latest releases by his friend Voltaire. Another highlight is the **Marmorsaal** (Marble Room), an elegant white Carrara marble symphony modelled after the Pantheon in Rome.

As you exit the palace, don't be fooled by the **Ruinenberg**, a pile of classical 'ruins' looming in the distance: they're merely a folly conceived by Frederick the Great.

BILDERGALERIE
GALLERY

Map p206 (Im Park Sanssouci 4; adult/concession €3/2.50; ☉10am-6pm Tue-Sun May-Oct; ◻695, 606) The Picture Gallery is the oldest royal museum in Germany, rather plain on the outside but resplendent in yellow and white marble and elaborate stuccowork on the inside. It shelters Frederick the Great's collection of Old Masters, including such pearls as Caravaggio's *Doubting Thomas*, Anthony van Dyk's *Pentecost* and several works by Peter Paul Rubens.

NEUE KAMMERN
PALACE

Map p206 (Park Sanssouci; adult/concession incl tour or audioguide €4/3; ☉10am-6pm Tue-Sun Apr-Oct, to 5pm Nov-Mar; ◻695, 606) The New Chambers were originally an orangery and later converted into a guesthouse. The interior drips with opulence, most notably in the **Ovidsaal**, a grand ballroom with gilded reliefs depicting scenes from *Meta-morphosis*, and in the **Jasper Hall**, which is drenched in precious stones and topped by a ceiling fresco starring Venus.

CHINESISCHES HAUS
HISTORIC BUILDING

Map p206 (Am Grünen Gitter; admission €2; ☉10am-6pm Tue-Sun May-Oct; ◻605 to Schloss Charlottenhof, 606 or 695 to Schloss Sanssouci, ◻91 to Schloss Charlottenhof) The Far East was all the rage in the 18th century, as reflected in the adorable Chinese House. The clover leaf–shaped pavilion is among the park's most photographed buildings, thanks to its enchanting exterior of exotically dressed gilded figures shown sipping tea, dancing and playing musical instruments. Inside is a precious collection of Chinese and Meissen porcelain.

ORANGERIESCHLOSS
PALACE

Map p206 (An der Orangerie 3-5; tour adult/concession €4/3; ☉10am-6pm Tue-Sun May-Oct, 10am-6pm Sat & Sun Apr) The 300m-long Orangery Palace was Friedrich Wilhelm IV's favourite building project and reflects his love for all things Italian. Tours take in the **Raphaelsaal**, which brims with 19th-century copies of the famous painter's masterpieces, while the **tower** (€2) delivers sweeping park views. The greenhouses are still used for storing potted plants in winter.

BELVEDERE AUF DEM KLAUSBERG
HISTORIC BUILDING

Map p206 (☑ 969 4206; An der Orangerie 1; admission €2; ☉10am-6pm Sat & Sun May-Oct) From the Orangerieschloss, a tree-lined path forms a visual axis to the templelike Belvedere, modelled on Nero's palace in Rome. From here you can enjoy a panorama taking in the park, lakes and Potsdam itself. The upstairs hall has an impressive frescoed dome, oak parquet and fanciful stucco marble. En route you'll pass the **Drachenhaus** (Dragon House; 1770), a fantastical Chinese minipalace inspired by the Ta-Ho pagoda in Canton and guarded by a small army of dragons. It now houses a cafe-restaurant (p209).

HISTORISCHE MÜHLE HISTORIC BUILDING

Map p206 (Historical Mill; adult/child incl tour €3/2, without tour €2.50/1.50; ⊘10am-6pm daily Apr-Oct, 10am-4pm Sat & Sun Nov & Jan-Mar) This is a functioning replica of the palace's original Dutch-style 18th-century windmill. Admission buys access to three floors of exhibits on mill technology, a close-up of the grinding mechanism and a top-floor viewing platform.

NEUES PALAIS PALACE

Map p206 (New Palace; ☑969 4200; Am Neuen Palais; adult/concession €6/5; ⊘10am-6pm Wed-Mon Apr-Oct, to 5pm Nov-Mar; ☐695 or 605 to Neues Palais, ☐to Potsdam, Park Sanssouci Bahnhof) At the far western end of the park, the Neues Palais has made-to-impress dimensions, a central dome and a lavish exterior capped with a parade of sandstone figures. It was the final and largest palace commissioned by Frederick the Great, built in only six years, largely to demonstrate the undiminished power of the Prussian state following the bloody Seven Years War (1756-63). The king himself rarely camped out here, preferring the intimacy of Schloss Sanssouci and using it for representational purposes only. Only the last German Kaiser, Wilhelm II, used it as a residence until 1918.

The interior attests to the high level of artistry and craftsmanship of the time. It's an opulent symphony of ceiling frescoes, gilded stucco ornamentation, ornately carved wainscoting and fanciful wall coverings alongside paintings (eg by Antoine Pesne) and richly crafted furniture.

Memorable rooms include the **Grottensaal** (Grotto Hall), a rococo delight with shells, fossils and baubles set into the walls and ceilings; the **Marmorsaal**, a large banquet hall of Carrara marble with a wonderful ceiling fresco; and the **Jagdkammer** (Hunting Chamber), with lots of dead furry things and fine gold tracery on the walls. Frederick the Great's **private apartments** (Königswohnung; Map p206; adult/concession €5/4; ⊘ tours 10am, noon, 2pm & 4pm Wed-Mon Apr-Oct) can only be seen on guided tours.

On weekends, admission also includes a peek inside the **Pesne-Galerie** (Map p206; adult/concession €2/1.50; ⊘10am-6pm Sat &

Sun Apr-Oct) with a fine selection of works by this French painter.

The **Schlosstheater** in the south wing is only open during concerts. The pair of lavish buildings behind the Schloss is called the **Communs**. It originally housed the palace servants and kitchens and is now part of Potsdam University.

PARK CHARLOTTENHOF PARK

Map p206 Laid out by Peter Lenné for Friedrich Wilhelm IV, this park segues imperceptibly from Park Sanssouci but gets far fewer visitors. Buildings in this quiet corner bear the stamp of Karl Friedrich Schinkel, most notably the small neoclassical **Schloss Charlottenhof** (Map p206; tour adult/concession €4/3; ⊘10am-6pm Tue-Sun May-Oct), which was modelled after a Roman villa and features a Doric portico and bronze fountain. Schinkel, aided by his student Ludwig Persius, also dreamed up the nearby **Römische Bäder** (Roman Baths; Map p206; adult/concession €3/2.50; ⊘10am-6pm Tue-Sun May-Oct), a picturesque ensemble of an Italian country villa. A same-day combination ticket is €5 (concession €4).

⊙ Other Potsdam Sights

East of the park, you'll quickly reach Potsdam's Altstadt (old town), whose sightseeing highlights are the picturesque **Holländisches Viertel** (Dutch Quarter; Map p206), a cluster of 18th-century gabled red-brick houses built for Dutch workers and now home to cafes and galleries. Mittelstrasse is especially scenic. Landmarks include the Brandenburger Tor and the 1850 Schinkel-designed **Nikolaikirche** (Map p206; ☑270 8602; www.nikolai-potsdam.de; Am Alten Markt 1; tower €5; ⊘9am-7pm Mon-Sat, 11.30am-7pm Sun), easily recognised by its mighty dome. Next door, the old royal city palace is being reconstructed as the new home of the Brandenburg state parliament.

North of here is another lovely park, the **Neuer Garten** (New Garden), laid out in natural English style on the western shore of the Heiliger See. Its key sight is **Schloss Cecilienhof** (☑969 4244; www.spsg.de; Im Neuen Garten 11; tours adult/concession €6/5; ⊘10am-6pm Tue-Sun Apr-Oct, to 5pm Nov-Mar; ☐603), famous as the site of the 1945 Potsdam Conference where Stalin, Truman and Churchill hammered out Germany's postwar fate. The conference room looks as though the delegates had just left. The park's other palace,

➡ Park Sanssouci is open from dawn till dusk year-round. Admission is free, but there are machines by the entrance where you can make a voluntary donation of €2.

➡ The palaces all have different hours and admission prices. Most are closed on Monday; in the off-season, some of the lesser sights open only at weekends and on holidays. Some are closed from November to April.

➡ A one-day pass valid at all Potsdam palaces is €19 (concession €14) and is sold only at Schloss Sanssouci. A day pass to all palaces *except* Schloss Sanssouci is €15 (concession €11) and sold at any of them as well as at the **Sanssouci Visitors Centre** (📞969 4200; www.spsg.de; An der Orangerie 1; ⊙8.30am-6pm Apr-Oct, to 5pm Nov-Mar) at the Historische Mühle (Historical Mill). There's also a €3 day fee for taking pictures inside the palaces.

➡ The palaces are fairly well spaced – it's almost 2km between the Neues Palais (New Palace) and Schloss Sanssouci. Take your sweet time wandering along the park's meandering paths to discover your personal favourite spot.

➡ Cycling is officially permitted along Ökonomieweg and Maulbeerallee, which is also the route followed by bus 695, the main line to the park from the Hauptbahnhof.

the late 18th-century **Marmorpalais** (Map p206; 📞969 4550; www.spsg.de; Im Neuen Garten 10; tour adult/concession €5/4; ⊙10am-6pm Tue-Sun May-Oct, 10am-4pm Sat & Sun Nov-Mar, 10am-6pm Sat & Sun Apr; 🚌603), is especially notable for its fanciful Oriental Cabinet, an upstairs room that resembles a Turkish tent.

🍴 EATING & DRINKING

HAFTHORN   PUB
Map p206 (📞280 0820; www.hafthorn.de; Friedrich-Ebert-Strasse 90; mains €4-8; ⊙from 6pm) Check your pretence at the door of this cheerily charming pub, the home of quirky metal lamps, big burgers and cheap, delicious Bohemian beer. An all-ages crowd shares laughter inside this former bakery and, in summer, along candlelit benches in the courtyard.

⎡TOP⎤ MAISON CHARLOTTE   FRENCH $$$
Map p206 (📞280 5450; www.maison-charlotte.de; Mittelstrasse 20; mains around €20, Flammkuche €8-13; ⊙noon-11pm) There's a rustic lyricism to the French country cuisine in this darling Dutch Quarter bistro, no matter whether your appetite runs more towards a simple *Flammkuche* (Alsatian pizza), Breton fish soup or a full four-course menu (€47). Budget bon vivants come for the daily lunch special: €7.50, including a glass of wine.

MEIEREI IM NEUEN GARTEN   GERMAN $$
(📞704 3211; www.meierei-potsdam.de; Im Neuen Garten 10; snacks €3-7, mains €10-13;

⊙11am-11pm Mon-Sat, to 8.30pm Sun; 🚌603 to Höhenstrasse) The Berlin Wall once ran right past this brewpub that's especially lovely in summer when you can count the boats sailing on the Jungfernsee from your beer-garden table. The hearty dishes are a perfect match for the delicious Helles and seasonal suds brewed on the premises. Service can be challenged on busy days. It's at the northern end of the Neuer Garten.

DRACHENHAUS   GERMAN $$
Map p206 (📞505 3808; www.drachenhaus.de; Maulbeerallee 4a; mains €7.50-25; ⊙11am-7pm or later Apr-Oct, to 6pm Tue-Sun Nov-Feb) Right in Park Sanssouci, the exotic Dragon House is now a pleasant cafe-restaurant serving coffee, homemade cakes and regional cuisine – in summer beneath a tree canopy.

Sachsenhausen Concentration Camp

Explore
Built by prisoners brought here from another concentration camp, Sachsenhausen opened in 1936 as a model for other camps. By 1945 about 200,000 people had passed through its gates, initially mostly political

GUIDED TOURS

Nonprofit **Mosaic Tours** (☑0176 8754 5620; www.mosaic.de; adult/student €15/12; ☑10am Tue, Thu & Sun year-round, also Fri & Sat Apr-Oct) specialises in Sachsenhausen lasting about six hours. Meet at 10am at the foot of the TV Tower, next to the Alexanderplatz S-Bahn station. No reservations are necessary.

The English-language walking tour companies Berlin Walks (p288), Insider Tour Berlin (p288) and New Berlin Tours (p288) also operate guided tours of Sachsenhausen several times weekly.

opponents but later also gypsies, gays, Jews and, after 1939, POWs from Eastern Europe, especially the Soviet Union. Tens of thousands died here from hunger, exhaustion, illness, exposure, medical experiments and executions. Thousands more succumbed during the death march of April 1945, when the Nazis evacuated the camp in advance of the Red Army. There's a memorial plaque to these victims as you approach the camp, at the corner of Strasse der Einheit and Strasse der Nationen.

After the war, the Soviets imprisoned some 60,000 German POWs in what was now Speziallager No 7 (Special Camp No 7); about 12,000 died of malnutrition and disease before it was dissolved in 1950. Soviet and GDR military continued using the grounds for another decade until the camp became a memorial site in 1961. Updated many times since, today's memorial delivers a predictably sobering experience.

Top Tip

Although the memorial site is open daily, we recommend that you don't visit on a Monday when all of the indoor exhibits are closed.

Getting There & Away

Train The S1 makes the trip thrice hourly from central Berlin (eg Friedrichstrasse) to Oranienburg (€3.10, 45 minutes). Hourly regional RE5 and RB12 trains leaving from Hauptbahnhof are faster (€3.10, 25 minutes). The camp is about 2km from the Oranienburg train station. Turn right onto Stralsunder Strasse, right on Bernauer Strasse, left on Strasse der Einheit and right on Strasse

der Nationen. Alternatively, bus 804 makes hourly trips.

Need to Know

→ **Area Code** ☑03301

→ **Location** About 35km north of central Berlin

→ **Tourist Office** (☑2000; www.stiftung-bg.de; Strasse der Nationen 22; ☑8.30am-6pm mid-Mar-mid-Oct, to 4.30pm mid-Oct-mid-Mar)

⊙ SIGHTS

FREE GEDENKSTÄTTE UND MUSEUM
SACHSENHAUSEN   MEMORIAL

(☑2000; www.stiftung-bg.de; Strasse der Nationen 22; ☑8.30am-6pm mid-Mar–mid-Oct, to 4.30pm mid-Oct–mid-Mar, most exhibits closed Mon) Unless you're on a guided tour, pick up a leaflet (€0.50) or, better yet, an audio guide (€3, including leaflet) at the visitor centre to get a better grasp of this huge site. The approach to the camp takes you past photographs taken during the death march and the camp's liberation. Just beyond the perimeter is the **Neues Museum** (New Museum), which has only moderately interesting exhibits on the history of the memorial site since GDR days as well as on the Oranienburg concentration camp, the precursor to Sachsenhausen set up in 1933 in a nearby disused brewery.

Proceed to **Tower A**, the entrance gate, cynically labelled, as at Auschwitz, *Arbeit Macht Frei* (Work Sets You Free). Beyond here is the roll-call area, with barracks and other buildings fanning out beyond. Off to the right, two restored barracks illustrate the abysmal living conditions prisoners were subjected to. **Barrack 38** has an exhibit on Jewish inmates, while **Barrack 39** graphically portrays daily life at the camp. The **prison**, where famous inmates included Hitler would-be assassin Georg Elser and the minister Martin Niemöller, is next door. The two original **infirmary barracks** on the other side of the roll-call area have exhibits about the camp's poor medical care and on the horrid medical experiments performed on prisoners.

Moving towards the centre, the **Prisoners' Kitchen** zeroes in on key moments in the camp's history during its various phases. Exhibits include instruments of torture (such as a 'beating bench'), the original gallows that stood in the roll-call area and, in the cellar, heart-wrenching artwork scratched into the wall by prisoners.

The most sickening displays, though, deal with the extermination area called **Station Z**, which consisted of an execution trench, a crematorium and a gas chamber. Nearby, there's a more in-depth exhibit right at the actual entrance to this horrific section of the camp, which was separated by a wall from the rest of the grounds. In autumn 1941, more than 10,000 Soviet POWs were executed here in four weeks by being shot in the back of the neck through a hidden hole in the wall while ostensibly being measured for a uniform. Bullets were then retrieved and reused.

In the far right corner, a new building and two original barracks house the **Soviet Special Camp** exhibit, which documents how Sachsenhausen was used by the Soviets between 1945 and 1950.

🍴 EATING & DRINKING

No food is available at the memorial site, although a vending machine in the Neues Museum dispenses hot drinks. There are cafes, bakeries and stores outside Oranienburg train station.

Spandau

Explore

Spandau is a congenial mix of green expanses, rivers, industry and almost rural residential areas wrapped around a medieval core famous for its 16th-century fortress, the Zitadelle Spandau (Spandau Citadel). Older than Berlin by a few years, Spandau thrived as an independent city for nearly eight centuries and only became part of Berlin in 1920. Its people, though, continue to feel as Spandauers first, Berliners second. To this day, they talk about 'going to Berlin' when heading to any other city district. Nearly all sights handily cluster in and around the Altstadt.

The Best...

- **Sight** Zitadelle Spandau (p211)
- **Place to Eat** Restaurant Kolk (p212)
- **Place to Drink** satt und selig (p212)

Top Tip

Every summer, the Zitadelle Spandau is an atmospheric backdrop for the rock, pop and classical music concerts of the **Citadel Music Festival** (www.citadel-musicfestival.de). There are also year-round concerts in the Gothic Hall.

Getting There & Away

U-Bahn The recommended route is via the U7 which travels to Spandau in 30 to 40 minutes and stops at the Zitadelle, the Altstadt and the Rathaus.

S-Bahn The S5 makes the trip to central Spandau in about 30 to 40 minutes.

Need to Know

- **Area Code** ☎030
- **Location** About 13km northwest of central Berlin
- **Tourist Office** (☎333 9388; www.partner-fuer-spandau.de; Breite Strasse 32; 🕒10am-6pm Mon-Sat; [S]Altstadt Spandau, [R]Spandau)

👁 SIGHTS

ZITADELLE SPANDAU CASTLE

(☎354 9440; www.zitadelle-spandau.de; Am Juliusturm 64; adult/concession €4.50/2.50, audioguide €2; 🕒10am-5pm; [S]Zitadelle) The 16th-century Spandau Citadel, on a little island in the Havel River, is one of the world's best-preserved Renaissance fortresses. With its moat, drawbridge and arrowhead-shaped bastions, it is also a veritable textbook in military architecture. These days, the impressive complex multitasks as museum, cultural venue and wintering ground for thousands of bats. Climb the 30m-high Julius Tower for sweeping views.

NIKOLAIKIRCHE CHURCH

(☎333 5639; www.nikolai-spandau.de; Reformationsplatz 6; tower €1; 🕒noon-4pm Mon-Fri, 11am-3pm Sat, 2-4pm Sun, tower tours 12.30pm Sat, 2.30pm Sun Apr-Oct; [S]Altstadt Spandau) The Gothic Church of St Nicholas is

WORTH A DETOUR

LUFTWAFFENMUSEUM

Military and airplane buffs may want to make the detour about 9km south of Altstadt Spandau to the **Luftwaffenmuseum** (German Air Force Museum; ☑811 0769; www.luftwaffenmuseum.de; Kladower Damm 182; ☺10am-6pm Tue-Sun Apr-Oct, 9am-4pm Nov-Mar, last entry 1hr before closing; Zoologischer Garten, then bus X34), which spreads its wings over a military air field used both by the Nazis and the Royal Air Force. Exhibits in the hangar and control tower cover German military aviation since 1884. Over 100 fighter jets, bombers, helicopters and weapons systems litter the runway, including such gems as WWI biplanes, a Russian MiG-21, a Messerschmidt ME-163 Komet and a GDR-era Antonov An-14.

famous for hosting Brandenburg's first public Lutheran-style worship service back in 1539, under Elector Joachim II, whose bronze statue stands outside the church. Inside, important treasures include a 14th-century baptismal font, a baroque pulpit and a late-Renaissance altar. Tours up the 77m-high tower are available at weekends.

FREE GOTISCHES HAUS HISTORIC BUILDING

(☑333 9388; Breite Strasse 32; ☺10am-6pm Mon-Sat; Ⓢ Altstadt Spandau) Whoever built this late-medieval Gothic House must not have been hurting for money, for it's made of stone, not wood, as was customary in those times. This well-preserved Altstadt gem sports ornate net-ribbed vaulting on the ground floor, which houses the local tourist office. Check out the Biedermeier-era living room and late-19th-century kitchen upstairs.

✖ EATING & DRINKING

RESTAURANT KOLK GERMAN $$

(☑333 8879; www.kolk.im-netz.de; Hoher Steinweg 7; mains €10-16; ☺11am-11pm; Ⓢ Altstadt Spandau) Even with 20 years of business, this old-timey restaurant in a 19th-century firehouse hasn't lost its grip on the crowd.

The rustic ambience matches a menu headlined by Huguenot and Eastern European dishes, including hearty goulash, meatballs in caper sauce and boiled eel in dill sauce. Snag a garden table in fine weather.

SATT UND SELIG INTERNATIONAL $$

(☑3675 3877; www.sattundselig.de; Carl-Schurz-Strasse 47; mains €8-16; ☺9am-11pm; Ⓢ Altstadt Spandau) In a baroque half-timbered house near the Nikolaikirche, this snug neighbourhood favourite gets things right from morning to night. The breakfast selection is legendary, the cakes homemade and the main dishes creative, fresh and ample. In summer, terrace tables spill out onto the pedestrian zone.

Grunewald & Dahlem

Explore

Berlin's most upper-crust suburbs, Dahlem and Grunewald are packed with cultural and natural appeal. Set between their leafy streets and lavish villa colonies are gardens, parks, palaces and a sprinkling of museums, most notably the Museen Dahlem with its stunning ethnological collections from around the world. After WWII, the area was part of the American sector, a legacy reflected in such institutions as the AlliiertenMuseum (Allied Museum). A respite not only for local residents is the Grunewald forest, a vast fresh-air refuge crisscrossed by paths and dotted with lakes extending all the way west to the Havel River.

The Best...

➡ **Sight** Museen Dahlem (p213)
➡ **Place to Eat** Galileo (p214)
➡ **Place to Drink** Luise (p214)

Top Tip

The fragrant Botanischer Garten (Botanical Garden) is the glorious backdrop for al fresco summer concerts – jazz to flamenco to classical – held every Friday from 6pm. Tickets cost €15 and include garden access.

Getting There & Away

U-Bahn The U3 meanders through this area, with key stops being Dahlem-Dorf for the museums and Krumme Lanke for easy access to the Grunewald forest.

S-Bahn The S1 skirts southern Dahlem, while the S7 runs straight through the Grunewald forest.

Need to Know

- **Area Code** ☎030
- **Location** 11km southwest of central Berlin

SIGHTS

MUSEEN DAHLEM MUSEUM

(☎266 424 242; www.smb.museum; Lansstrasse 8; adult/concession/child €6/3/free; ⏲10am-6pm Tue-Fri, 11am-6pm Sat & Sun, Junior Museum 1-6pm Tue-Fri, 11am-6pm Sat & Sun; [S]Dahlem-Dorf) Unless some mad scientist invents a magic time-travel-teleporter machine, the three collections within the Museen Dahlem are your best bet for exploring the world in a single afternoon. Highlights of the **Museum of Ethnology** include masks and musical instruments in the Africa exhibit and the outriggers and traditional huts in the South Seas hall. In another wing, the **Museum of Asian Art** displays six millennia of art. Don't miss the Japanese tearoom and a 16th-century Chinese imperial throne made of lacquered rosewood with mother-of-pearl inlay. There's also the **Museum of European Cultures** whose exhibits range from Swedish armoires to a black Venetian gondola and a giant mechanical nativity scene from Germany. Small kids can have their horizons expanded at the touchy-feely Junior Museum.

BRÜCKE MUSEUM GALLERY

(☎831 2029; www.bruecke-museum.de; Bussardsteig 9; adult/concession €5/3; ⏲11am-5pm Wed-Mon; [S]Oskar-Helene-Heim, then bus 115 to Pücklerstrasse) In 1905 Karl Schmidt-Rottluff, Erich Heckel and Ernst Ludwig Kirchner founded Germany's first modern-artist group, called *Die Brücke* (The Bridge), thereby paving the way for German expressionism and modern art in general. Schmitt-Rottluff's personal collection forms the core of this superb presentation of expressionist art. The gallery is about 2.5km north of U-Bahn station Oskar-Helene-Heim via Clayallee. Bus 115 makes the trip from the station several times hourly.

To get there, take bus 115 to Pücklerstrasse from the U-Bahn station.

[FREE] **ALLIIERTENMUSEUM** MUSEUM

(☎818 1990; www.alliiertenmuseum.de; Clayallee 135; ⏲10am-6pm Thu-Tue; [S]Oskar-Helene-Heim) The original Checkpoint Charlie guard cabin, a Berlin Airlift plane and a reconstructed spy tunnel are among the poignant exhibits at the Allied Museum, which documents the history and challenges faced by the Western Allies during the Cold War. The museum is about 800m north of U-Bahn station Oskar-Helene-Heim.

BOTANISCHER GARTEN GARDENS

(☎8385 0100; www.bgbm.org; Königin-Luise-Strasse 6-8; adult/concession €6/3, museum only €2.50/1.50; ⏲garden 9am-dusk, museum 10am-6pm; [S]Dahlem-Dorf, [R]Botanischer Garten) Berlin's vast botanical garden boasts 22,000 plant species and is an inspirational spot to reconnect with nature. Especially enchanting is the Grosse Tropenhaus greenhouse, the muggy home of an entire bamboo forest. Exhibits in the museum are rather academic. Enter from Unter den Eichen or Königin-Luise-Platz.

TRACKS OF DEATH

The Holocaust Memorial in central Berlin may be more prominent and artistic, but there is another commemorative site that is at least as poignant: **Gleis 17** (track 17), next to S-Bahn station Grunewald (S7). It was from these tracks that 186 trains left for Theresienstadt, Riga, Lodz and Auschwitz, carrying their Jewish cargo like cattle to the slaughter. More than 50,000 Berliners were deported between 1941 and 1945. Weathered iron plaques recording the number of people and destination by date along the platform edge honour their memory. It's quiet here, with only the trees rustling in the breeze, but the silence speaks loudly.

✕ EATING & DRINKING

The Botanischer Garten and the Museen Dahlem both have nice cafes for a post-sightseeing pick-me-up.

LUISE   INTERNATIONAL $$

(☑841 8880; www.luise-dahlem.de; Königin-Luise-Strasse 40-42; mains €5-22; ⊙10am-1am; ⓢDahlem-Dorf) This cafe-restaurant-beer-garden combo is a Dahlem institution with a long menu likely to please everyone from salad heads to schnitzel fiends to pizza punters. Scrumptious breakfasts are served until 2pm and there are seven beers on tap to enjoy beneath the chestnut trees.

GALILEO   ITALIAN $$

(☑831 2377; www.ristorantegalileo.de; Otto-von-Simson-Strasse 26; mains €4-16; ⊙10am-10pm Mon-Fri; ⓢDahlem-Dorf) On the edge of the Free University campus, Galileo has plied students, faculty and clued-in locals with cheap, authentic Italian fare for nearly 25 years. If homemade pasta and pizza don't do it for you, go for the more elaborate daily specials – grilled tuna, perhaps, or rosemary-scented lamb filet.

Wannsee

Explore

Leafy Wannsee, Berlin's southwesternmost suburb, is named for the enormous Wannsee lake, which is really just a bulge in the Havel River. In fine weather, it's a fantastic place to leave the city bustle behind. You can cruise around the lake, walk in the forest, visit an enchanting island, tour a royal pal-

ace or work on your tan in the Strandbad Wannsee, a lakeside lido with a 1200m long sandy beach. Famous Nazi and Cold War sites are among its more sinister attractions.

The Best...

➡ **Sight** Pfaueninsel (p215)
➡ **Place to Eat** Restaurant Seehaase (p215)
➡ **Place to Drink** Loretta am Wannsee (p216)

Top Tip

For cruising on the cheap, catch the ferry from Wannsee to Kladow using just a normal public transport ticket.

Getting There & Away

S-Bahn S1 or S7 from central Berlin to Wannsee, then walk or bus depending on where you're headed.

Need to Know

➡ **Area Code** ☑030
➡ **Location** 25km southwest of central Berlin

⊙ SIGHTS

FREE HAUS DER WANNSEE-
KONFERENZ   MEMORIAL SITE

(☑805 0010; www.ghwk.de; Am Grossen Wannsee 56-58; ⊙10am-6pm; ⓡWannsee, then bus 114) In January 1942 a group of 15 high-ranking Nazi officials met in a stately villa near Lake Wannsee to hammer out the details of the 'Final Solution': the system-

---

IN & ON THE WANNSEE

Stern und Kreisschiffahrt (☑536 3600; www.sternundkreis.de) From April to mid-October, Stern und Kreisschiffahrt operates two-hour cruises around seven lakes from landing docks near Wannsee S-Bahn station. Boats depart hourly from 10.30am to 5.30pm and the trip costs €11.

Strandbad Wannsee (www.strandbadwannsee.de; Wannseebadweg 25; adult/concession €4/2.50; ⊙Apr-Sep; ⓡNikolassee) A lakeside public pool that has delighted water rats for over a century. On hot days, its 1200m long sandy beach can get very busy. Besides swimming, you can rent boats, play volleyball, basketball or table tennis or grab a snack or drink. In August, operas are performed on a floating stage. The Strandbad is about 1.3km northwest of the S-Bahn station Nikolassee. Walk north on Borussen-strasse, then turn left onto Wannseebadweg.

BRIDGE OF SPIES

There's been a bridge linking Berlin with Potsdam across the Havel for over 300 years, but the 125m-long **Glienicker Brücke** only gained fame during the Cold War when the first spy exchange between the Soviets and the US took place in 1962. At 8.52am, Gary Powers, the U2 pilot who'd been shot down over Russia, and exposed KGB intelligence officer Rudolf Abel, crossed the white line that had been painted in the middle of the bridge to mark the border of the Iron Curtain. Over the course of the Cold War there were more than two dozen prisoner exchanges but only two more took place on Glienicker Brücke, in 1975 and 1986. However, that didn't stop writers like John Le Carré from elevating it to near mythical status in print and on celluloid. For more background, visit www.glienicker-bruecke.de.

atic deportation and murder of European Jews in Eastern Europe. Today, the same building houses a memorial exhibit and an education centre about this sinister meeting and its ramifications. The site is about 2.5km northwest of Wannsee S-Bahn station and served from there by bus 114 several times hourly.

PFAUENINSEL   OUTDOORS

(☑8058 6831; www.spsg.de; Nikolskoer Weg; adult/concession ferry €3/2.50, palace €3/2.50, Meierei €2/1.50; ⊙ferry 8am-9pm May-Aug, shorter hours Sep-Apr; ⊠Wannsee, then bus 218) Back to nature was the dictum in the 18th century, so Friedrich Wilhelm II had this little island turned into an idyllic playground, perfect for retreating from state affairs and for frolicking with his mistress in a snowy-white fairy-tale palace. To heighten the romance factor, he brought in a flock of peacocks that gave the island its name and that are strutting their stuff to this day.

A stand-out among the smattering of other buildings is the **Meierei**, a dairy farm in the shape of a Gothic monastery at the island's eastern end. The island is a nature preserve, so no smoking, cycling or swimming. Picnicking, though, remains legal and this is a nice place to do it. There are no cafes or restaurants. The island is about 4km northwest of S-Bahn station Wannsee, from where it's served several times hourly by bus 218.

SCHLOSS GLIENICKE   PALACE

(☑8058 6750; www.spsg.de; Königstrasse 36; palace tours adult/concession €5/4, Casino €1; ⊙10am-6pm Tue-Sun Apr-Oct, 10am-5pm Sat & Sun Nov-Mar; ⊠Wannsee, then bus 316) Glienicke Palace is the result of a rich royal kid travelling to Italy and falling in love with the country. Prince Carl of Prussia (1801–83) was only 21 when he returned to

Berlin giddy with dreams of building his own Italian villa, so he hired starchitect du jour Karl Friedrich Schinkel to turn an existing garden estate into an elegant, antique-looking compound. Schinkel not only expanded the mansion but added a smaller guesthouse (the 'Casino') and two charming pavilions, the 'Small Curiosity' and 'Great Curiosity'. The palace itself is richly decorated with marble fireplaces, sparkling crystal chandeliers, gold-framed paintings and fine furniture. The palace is about 6km west of S-Bahn station Wannsee and served several times hourly by bus 316.

LIEBERMANN-VILLA AM WANNSEE   MUSEUM

(☑8058 5900; www.max-liebermann.de; Colomierstrasse 3; adult/concession €6/4, audioguide €3; ⊙10am-6pm Wed & Fri-Mon, to 8pm Thu Apr-Sep, 11am-5pm Wed-Mon Oct-Mar; ⊠Wannsee, then bus 114) This lovely villa was the summer home of Berlin Secession founder Max Liebermann from 1909 until his death in 1935. Liebermann loved the lyricism of nature and gardens in particular and often painted the scenery right outside his window. Some can be seen in the upstairs rooms and in his barrel-vaulted studio. In summer, there are few more languid spots than the garden and Wannsee-facing cafe terrace. The villa is about 2km northwest of S-Bahn station Wannsee and served several times hourly by bus 114.

🍴 EATING & DRINKING

RESTAURANT SEEHAASE   INTERNATIONAL $$

(☑8049 6474; www.restaurant-seehaase.de; Am Grossen Wannsee 58-60; mains €7-17; ⊙11am-10pm; ⊠114, ⊠Wannsee) Most of the waterfront lots are in private hands, so the

DAY TRIPS FROM BERLIN WANNSEE

Seehaase with its lake views is justifiably popular. The menu is mostly classic German but also features pasta, *Flammkuche* (Alsatian pizza) and an interesting array of Turkish appetisers. It's close to the Haus der Wannsee-Konferenz. Take bus 114 from Wannsee station.

LORETTA AM WANNSEE   GERMAN $$
(☑8010 5333; www.loretta-berlin.de; Kronprinzessinnenweg 260; mains €7-15; ⊙11am-11pm; ⊠Wannsee) The view of Wannsee lake is fabulous at this traditional beer garden that's an enchanting place for a hearty Bavarian meal and big mug of amber liquid. Have a simple *Brotzeit* (dark bread and cold meats) or go the whole hog with pork leg braised in black beer. Augustiner and Erdinger on tap. It's about 350m south of Wannsee station via Kronprinzessinnenweg.

Köpenick

Explore

A 20-minute S-Bahn ride away from central Berlin, Köpenick is famous for its handsome baroque castle, a picturesque Altstadt (old town) and a trio of superlative natural assets: largest lake (Müggelsee), largest forest (Köpenicker Stadtforst) and highest natural elevation (Müggelberge, 115m) in Berlin. A leisurely ramble, relaxed boat ride or cooling dip in the water will quickly restore balance to an overstimulated brain.

The Best...

➡ **Sight** Schloss Köpenick (p216)
➡ **Place to Eat** Ratskeller Köpenick (p217)
➡ **Place to Drink** Krokodil (p217)

Top Tip

For a more in-depth understanding of Köpenick's history, take a self-guided tour with the help of an audioguide (€5) dispensed by the tourist office.

Getting There & Away

S-Bahn For the Altstadt, take the S3 to S-Bahn station Köpenick, then walk 1.5km south along Bahnhofstrasse or take tram 62

to the Schloss Köpenick. For the Müggelsee get off at S-Bahn station Friedrichshagen.

Need to Know

➡ **Area Code** ☑030
➡ **Location** 16km southeast of central Berlin
➡ **Tourist Office** (☑655 7550; www.berlin-tourismus-online.de; Alt-Köpenick 31-33; ⊙9am-6.30pm Mon-Fri year-round, 10am-4pm Sat May-Sep, 10am-1pm Sat Oct-Apr; ⊠62, ⊠Köpenick) Near Schloss Köpenick. Tram 62 will take you there from S-Bahn station Köpenick.

◉ SIGHTS

SCHLOSS KÖPENICK   PALACE, MUSEUM
(☑266 424 242; www.smb.museum/kgm; Schlossinsel 1; adult/concession €4/2, under 18 yr free; ⊙10am-6pm Tue-Sun; ⊠62, ⊠Köpenick) Berlin's only surviving baroque palace, on a little island just south of the Altstadt, houses a branch of the **Kunstgewerbemuseum** (Museum of Decorative Arts). It's a rich and eclectic collection of furniture, tapestries, porcelain, silverware, glass and other frilly objects from the Renaissance, baroque and rococo periods. Highlights include four lavishly panelled rooms and the stunning **Wappensaal** (Coat of Arms Hall).

It was in this very hall where, in 1730, a military court sentenced Crown Prince Friedrich (the later Frederick the Great) and his friend Hans Katte to death for attempted desertion. The future king was eventually spared, but forced by his father to watch his friend's beheading. Tram 62 will take you there from S-Bahn station Köpenick.

FREE RATHAUS KÖPENICK   HISTORIC BUILDING
(Alt-Köpenick 21; ⊙10am-5.30pm; ⊠62 or 68 to Rathaus Köpenick) With its frilly turrets, soaring tower and stepped gable, Köpenick's town hall exudes a fairy tale quality but is actually more famous for an incident back in 1906. It involved an unemployed cobbler named Wilhelm Voigt, who managed to make a laughing stock of the Prussian authorities. Costumed as an army captain, he marched upon the town hall, arrested the mayor, confiscated the city coffers and disappeared with the loot. And no one questioned his authority! At least not initially. Although

DEUTSCH-RUSSISCHES MUSEUM BERLIN-KARLSHORST

On 8 May 1945, six years of madness ended with the unconditional surrender of the Wehrmacht in the headquarters of the Soviet army in what is today the **Deutsch-Russisches Museum Berlin-Karlshorst** (German-Russian Museum Berlin-Karlshorst; ☑5015 0810; www.museum-karlshorst.de; Zwieseler Strasse 4; ☺10am-6pm Tue-Sun; ⓡKarlshorst). Stand in the hall where the signing took place, then browse the info commemorating this fateful day as well as the history of WWII from the Russian perspective. The museum was being reorganised at press time but should reopen in April 2013. Outside is a battery of Soviet weapons, including a Howitzer canon and the 'Stalin's organ' rocket launcher. The museum is a 10- to 15-minute walk from the S-Bahn station; take the Treskowallee exit, then turn right onto Rheinsteinstrasse.

quickly caught and convicted, Voigt became quite a celebrity for his chutzpah. Today, his bronze statue guards the town hall, which also harbours a small exhibit about this infamous 'Hauptmann von Köpenick' (Captain of Köpenick). The story is also re-enacted every summer during a raucous festival.

GROSSER MÜGGELSEE   LAKE

(ⓐ60, ⓡFriedrichshagen) Berlin's largest lake, the Müggelsee is hemmed in by forest on two sides and hugely popular for swimming and boating on hot summer days. The easiest access is by taking the S-Bahn to the Friedrichshagen station, followed by a tram ride (tram 60) or 1.5km walk down historic and cafe-lined Bölschestrasse. This culminates at the Müggelpark, near where the lake and the Spree River meet. Besides restaurants and beer gardens, there's also the landing docks of Stern und Kreisschiffahrt (p214), which runs one-hour lake tours several times daily from April to mid-October (€7). For a walk in the woods, head to the other side of the Spree via the nearby **Spreetunnel**. The closest public lake beach, with boat rental, **Seebad Friedrichshagen** (☑645 5756; www.seebad-friedrichshagen.de; Müggelseedamm 216; adult/concession €0.50/2.50; ☺from 9am) is about 300m east of the Müggelpark. On Sundays, there's a flea market around S-Bahn station Friedrichshagen. Tram 60 will take you there from S-Bahn station Friedrichshagen.

✖ EATING & DRINKING

RATSKELLER KÖPENICK   GERMAN **$$**

(☑655 5178; www.ratskellerkoepenick.de; Alt-Köpenick 21; mains €7-19; ☺11am-11pm; ⓐ62 or 68, ⓡKöpenick) 'Ratskeller' restaurants in many city town hall cellars are often overpriced tourist traps, but this one is a happy exception. The olde-worlde ambience is fun and the menu full of classic rib-stickers (smoked roast pork, blood sausage) alongside smaller dishes, meatless selections and fish. Many ingredients are locally sourced. Reservations advised for the Friday and Saturday live jazz nights. Tram 62 or 68 will take you there from S-Bahn station Köpenick.

KROKODIL   MEDITERRANEAN **$$**

(☑6588 0094; www.der-coepenicker.de; Gartenstrasse 46-48; mains €7-15; ☺dinner daily, brunch Sun; ⓐ62 or 68, ⓡKöpenick) The food is great but what you're more likely to remember about Krokodil is its idyllic setting on the eastern shore of the Dahme River, about 700m south of the Altstadt. With its own beach and boat rental, it's perfect for afternoon lounging, followed by sunset dinner on seasonal fare with Mediterranean inflections. There's even a hostel attached, in case you want to stay (dorm/double €17/66). To get there from S-Bahn station Köpenick, take tram 62 or 68 to Schlossplatz, then follow Müggelheimer Strasse east for 300m and turn south on Kietz for another 400m.

Sleeping

Berlin offers the gamut of places to unpack your suitcase. Just about every international chain now has a flagship in the German capital, but more interesting options that better reflect the city's verve and spirit abound. You can sleep in a former bank, boat or factory, in the home of a silent-movie diva, in a 'flying bed' or even a coffin.

Hotels

You'll find an entire range of hotels in Berlin, from frill-free cookie-cutter chains to all-out boutique hotels with top-notch amenities and fall-over-backwards service. For style-minded wallet-watchers, there's now an increasing number of budget designer hotels with chic interiors but small rooms and minimal amenities. Design-lovers with deeper pockets can choose from lifestyle and boutique hotels as well as *Kunsthotels* (art hotels), which are designed by artists and/or liberally sprinkled with original art.

Hostels

Berlin's hostel scene is as vibrant as ever and consists of both classic backpacker hostels and trendy 'lifestyle' versions with hotel-like amenities. You'll find them in all districts but especially in Kreuzberg and Friedrichshain, putting you within stumbling distance of bars and clubs. Dorm beds can be had for as little as €9 but spending a little more gets you a smaller dorm or even a private room.

B&Bs

Nostalgic types seeking Old Berlin flavour should check into a charismatic B&B, called *Hotel-Pension* or simply *Pension*. They're a dying breed, but for now there's still plenty of them, mostly in the western district of Charlottenburg, around Kurfürstendamm.

Furnished Apartments

Furnished flats are a popular – and economical – alternative to hotels in Berlin. The benefit of space, privacy and independence makes them especially attractive to families and small groups (see p230).

Rates

Standards are high but fierce competition has kept prices low compared to other capital cities in Europe. Prices spike during major trade shows, festivals and public holidays, when early reservations are essential. Business-geared hotels often have good deals on weekends. In winter, prices often plummet outside holidays, with five-star rooms costing as little as €100.

Amenities

When it comes to mid-range options, expect clean, comfortable and decent-sized rooms with at least a modicum of style, a private bathroom and cable TV. Budget places are generally hostels and other basic properties where facilities may be shared. Top-end hotels have an international standard of amenities, designer decor and perhaps a scenic location or historical ambience.

Overall, rooms tend to be on the small side. You'll usually find that BBC and CNN are the only English-language channels on TV (nearly all foreign shows and films are dubbed into German) and that air-con is a rare commodity. Most hotels now have wi-fi, although the additional cost can be as high as €20 per day.

Lonely Planet's Top Choices

Circus Hotel (p225) The perfect synthesis of style, comfort, location and value.

Michelberger Hotel (p228) Fun base with eccentric design and party pedigree.

Honigmond Garden Hotel (p225) A charmer with plenty of historic touches.

Hotel Askanischer Hof (p229) The class and romance of the 1920s in one smart package.

EastSeven Berlin Hostel (p229) Small, friendly and spotless crash pad.

Hostel One80° (p222) Central hipster design hostel with progressive amenities.

Best by Budget

€
Grand Hostel (p227)
Plus Hostel (p228)
Motel One Berlin-Alexanderplatz (p222)

€€
Hotel Amano (p225)
Miniloft Berlin (p230)
Hotel Honigmond (p227)

€€€
Hotel de Rome (p221)
Mandala Hotel (p224)
Ritz-Carlton Berlin (p224)

Best Hostels

Circus Hostel (p226)
Plus Hostel (p228)
Grand Hostel (p227)
Raise a Smile Hostel (p228)
Wombat's City Hostel Berlin (p225)

Best Historic Charmers

Hotel-Pension Funk (p231)
Hotel Bogota (p231)
Hotel Adlon Kempinski (p221)
Grand Hostel (p227)

Best Cool Factor

Soho House Berlin (p225)
Weinmeister (p226)
Casa Camper (p225)
Hostel One80° (p222)

Best for Families

Abion Spreebogen Waterside Hotel (p224)
Adina Apartment Hotel Berlin Checkpoint Charlie (p221)
Ritz-Carlton Berlin (p224)
Radisson Blu Hotel (p223)

Best for Romance

Ackselhaus & Blue Home (p229)
Soho House Berlin (p225)
Hotel Riehmers Hofgarten (p227)
Honigmond Garden Hotel (p225)

Best Artsy Abodes

Arte Luise Kunsthotel (p221)
art'otel berlin mitte (p224)
Propeller Island City Lodge (p222)
mitArt Hotel & Café (p227)

Best Room with a View

Hotel Adlon Kempinski (p221)
Park Inn Berlin-Alexanderplatz (p222)
Ritz-Carlton Berlin (p224)
nhow (p228)

NEED TO KNOW

Price Ranges
The following room rates are only a guideline. Rates are for a standard double room with private bathroom during high season but outside of major events, holidays or trade-show periods. Many properties have pricier rooms in higher categories. Rates include 7% VAT and breakfast (usually a generous buffet), unless noted.

➡ €   under €80
➡ €€   €80 to €160
➡ €€€   over €160

Reservations
Berlin has lots of beds, but the best ones often sell out early, so make reservations, especially around major holidays, cultural events and trade shows.

Websites
For online bookings for hostels try www.hostelworld.com and www.hostelbookers.com, for hotels www.booking.com and www.hrs.com, and for furnished apartments www.airbnb.com and www.homeaway.com.

Visit Berlin (www.visitberlin.de) Official tourist office books rooms at partner hotels with a best-price guarantee.

Lonely Planet (hotels.lonelyplanet.com) Bookings.

Which Floor?
In Germany, 'ground floor' refers to the floor at street level. The 1st floor is the floor above that. The book follows local usage of the terms.

SLEEPING

Where to Stay

Neighbourhood	For	Against
Historic Mitte	Close to major sights; great transport links; mostly high-end hotels; great restaurants	Touristy, expensive, pretty dead at night
Museumsinsel & Alexanderplatz	Supercentral; easy transport access; close to shopping; large and new hotels	Noisy, busy, ugly
Potsdamer Platz & Tiergarten	Urban flair; high-end international hotels; top museums and Philharmonie; next to huge city park	Limited eating and nightlife options; pricey
Scheunenviertel	Trendy, historic, central; brims with boutique/designer hotels; superb shopping, eating, cafe scene	Pricey, busy, noisy
Kreuzberg & Northern Neukölln	Best for bar-hopping, clubbing; cheap; lots of hostels; multicultural feel	Gritty, noisy; away from main sights
Friedrichshain	Vibrant nightlife; inexpensive; superb Cold War–era sights	Limited sleeping options; not so central for sightseeing
Prenzlauer Berg	Clean, charming residential area; lively cafe and restaurant scene; indie boutiques and flea market	Limited late-night dark action, no major sights
Charlottenburg	Great shopping, 'Old Berlin' bars and B&Bs, top restaurants, good value	Sedate; far from key sights and happening nightlife

🛏 Historic Mitte

HOTEL DE ROME LUXURY HOTEL **$$$**

Map p314 (☎460 6090; www.hotelderome.com; Behrenstrasse 37; d from €395; [P]🚭❄[@]📶🏊; 🚌100, 200, [S]Hausvogteiplatz) To feed your luxury cravings, set up shop in this 19th-century bank on historic Bebelplatz for a delightful alchemy of historic and contemporary flair. The opulently beautiful rooms come with all the latest tech accoutrements, marble baths with heated mosaic floors, and extra-high ceilings. Wind down in the former vault that is now the pool/spa area or over cocktails at the exquisite Bebel Bar (p90). In summer, drinks are also served on the rooftop terrace. Optional breakfast is €30.

HOTEL ADLON KEMPINSKI LUXURY HOTEL **$$$**

Map p314 (☎226 10; www.kempinski.com; Pariser Platz, Unter den Linden 77; r from €250; ❄[@]📶🏊; [S]Brandenburger Tor, 🚇Brandenburger Tor) Opposite Brandenburger Tor, the Adlon has been Berlin's most high-profile defender of the grand tradition since 1907. The striking lobby is a mere overture to the full symphony of luxury awaiting in spacious, amenity-laden rooms and suites where the decor is old fashioned in a regal sort of way. A ritzy day spa, gourmet restaurants and the swank Felix nightclub add 21st-century spice.

ARTE LUISE KUNSTHOTEL BOUTIQUE HOTEL **$$**

Map p319 (☎284 480; www.luise-berlin.com; Luisenstrasse 19; d €100-210, with shared bathroom €80-110; ❄[@]📶; [S]Friedrichstrasse, 🚇Friedrichstrasse) At this 'gallery with rooms', each unit is designed by different artists who receive royalties whenever it's rented. They're all wonderfully imaginative but we especially like No 107 with its giant bed and the boudoir-red 'Cabaret' (No 206). Cash-strapped art fans should enquire about the smaller, bathless rooms. Avoid those facing the train tracks. Optional breakfast is €11.

ADINA APARTMENT HOTEL BERLIN CHECKPOINT CHARLIE APARTMENT **$$**

Map p314 (☎200 7670; www.adina.eu; Krausenstrasse 35-36; d €110-160, 1-bedroom apt from €140; [P]❄[@]📶🏊; [S]Stadtmitte, Spittelmarkt) Adina's contemporary and roomy one- and two-bedroom apartments with full kitchens are tailor-made for cost-conscious families, anyone in need of elbow room, and self-caterers (a supermarket is a minute away). Hotel rooms without kitchens are also available. Staff are accommodating and the pool and sauna make soothing sore muscles at day's end a snap. See the website for details about other Adina properties in town. Optional breakfast is €15.

ARCOTEL JOHN F HOTEL **$$**

Map p314 (☎405 0460; www.arcotelhotels.com; Werderscher Market 11; r €90-190; [P]❄[@]📶; [S]Hausvogteiplatz) This urbane lifestyle hotel pays homage to President John F Kennedy with plenty of whimsical detail, including hand-carved rocking chairs (because the President had a back problem that rockers helped him with) and curvaceous lamps inspired by Jackie's ball gowns. Rooms are smartly dressed in dark zebrano wood and a silver-white colour scheme; some overlook the Friedrichswerdersche Kirche, others the German Foreign Office. Optional breakfast is €18.

COSMO HOTEL BERLIN HOTEL **$$**

Map p314 (☎5858 2222; www.cosmo-hotel.de; Spittelmarkt 13; d €100-210; [P]❄[@]📶; [S]Spittelmarkt) Despite its ho-hum location on a busy street, this hotel scores high for comfort and design. The lobby with its extravagant lamps and armchairs sets the tone for rooms decked out in cinnamon and silver hues. The cheaper ones don't fit a ton of luggage, but all have 'dream machine' beds and blackout blinds that are great jet-lag antidotes. Wi-fi in public areas only. Continental breakfast is €5, the full buffet €14.

SOFITEL BERLIN GENDARMENMARKT HOTEL **$$$**

Map p314 (☎203 750; www.sofitel.com; Charlottenstrasse 50-52; d €180-270; [P]❄[@]📶; [S]Französische Strasse) This cocoon of quiet sophistication has a killer location facing elegant Gendarmenmarkt and 92 rooms and suites that are a flawless interplay of marble, glass and light. The nicest have a private balcony facing the Französischer Dom (French Cathedral), although light sleepers might prefer those facing the inner courtyard. There's a top-floor sauna and gym, and an upmarket restaurant serving German and Austrian food, including breakfast for €28.

🛏 Museumsinsel & Alexanderplatz

[TOP CHOICE] HOSTEL ONE80° HOSTEL $

Map p318 (☎2804 4620; www.one80hostels.com; Otto-Braun-Strasse 65; dm €12-32; 🚭@📶; [S]Alexanderplatz, 🚇Alexanderplatz) As soon you enter, stylish designer sofas, cool music and an industrial-chic dining area signal that One80° has redefined the hostel concept – let's call it a next-generation lifestyle hostel. Dorms sleep four to eight in ultra-comfy bunk beds and have reading lamps, two electrical outlets and two lockers – per person. It's a big place but the lobby bar and basement club are conducive to making friends. Optional breakfast is €4.90.

MOTEL ONE BERLIN-ALEXANDERPLATZ HOTEL $

Map p318 (☎2005 4080; www.motel-one.de; Dircksenstrasse 36; d from €69; [P]❄@📶; [S]Alexanderplatz, 🚇Alexanderplatz) If you value location over luxury, this fast-growing budget designer chain makes for an excellent crash pad. Smallish rooms come with up-to-the-minute touches (flat-screen TVs, granite counters, massage showerheads, air-con) that are normally the staples of posher players. Arne Jacobsen's turquoise egg chairs accent the hip lobby. This is the most central of eight Motel One properties, including one at Zoo station and another at Hauptbahnhof. Check the website for details. Optional breakfast is €7.50.

PARK INN BERLIN-ALEXANDERPLATZ HOTEL $$

Map p318 (☎238 90; www.parkinn-berlin.de; Alexanderplatz 7; d €110-200; ❄@📶; [S]Alexanderplatz, 🚇Alexanderplatz) Views, views, views! Berlin's tallest and second-largest hotel has got them. Right in the belly of Alexanderplatz, this sleek tower is honeycombed with 1012 rooms (some rather snug) sporting panoramic windows, soothing earth

QUIRKY SLEEPS

Propeller Island City Lodge (☎891 9016; www.propeller-island.de; Albrecht-Achilles-Strasse 58; d €94-130; 📶; [S]Adenauerplatz) This hotel's name was inspired by a novel by the master of imagination, Jules Verne, and indeed each of the 32 rooms is a journey to a unique, surreal and slightly wicked world. To be stranded on Propeller Island may have you waking up on the ceiling, in a prison cell or inside a kaleidoscope... Artist-composer-owner Lars Stroschen designed and crafted all the furniture and fixtures, creating sinks from metal beer barrels, faucets made from heater valves and table bases from tree trunks. Don't expect TV, room service or pillow treats. Check-in is by prior arrangement and optional breakfast is €7.50. Located in City West & Charlottenburg. From U-Bahn station Alexanderplatz, walk 200m west on Kurfürstendamm, then 250m south on Albrecht-Achilles-Strasse.

Eastern Comfort Hostelboat (Map p328; ☎6676 3806; www.eastern-comfort.com; Mühlenstrasse 73-77; dm €16-19, d €50-78; @📶; [S]Warschauer Strasse, 🚇Warschauer Strasse) Let the Spree River murmur you to sleep while you're snugly ensconced in this two-boat floating hostel right by the East Side Gallery. Cabins are carpeted and trimmed in wood, but pretty snug (except for 'first-class'); all but the dorms have their own shower and toilet. The party zones of Kreuzberg and Friedrichshain are handily within staggering distance. On Wednesdays, the hostel hosts the convivial Boat Party & Barbecue (p**175**). Located in Friedrichshain.

Hüttenpalast (Map p324; ☎3730 5806; www.huettenpalast.de; Hobrechtstrasse 66; d campervans & cabins/hotel with shared bathrooms €65/85; 📶; [S]Hermannplatz) Sure, it has rooms with private bath, but who wants those when you can sleep in a romantic wooden hut with rooftop terrace or in a quirky vintage caravan fitted with a homemade light sculpture? Welcome to Hüttenpalast, an indoor campground in an old vacuum-cleaner factory that's an unusual place to hang your hat even by Berlin standards. Wacky and welcoming, the compound also includes an idyllic garden and a cafe for socialising that's open to everyone. Check-in from 3pm to 6pm or by arrangement and optional breakfast is €5. Located in Northern Neukölln.

tones, flat-screen TVs and noiseless air-con. For superb sunsets, snag a room facing the Fernsehturm. In fine weather, the 39th-floor panorama terrace with bar and lounge chairs is tailor-made for starring in your very own king of the world scene. Optional breakfast is €19.

HOTEL INDIGO BERLIN-ALEXANDERPLATZ
HOTEL $$

Map p318 (☑505 0860; www.hotelindigoberlin.com; Bernhard-Weiss-Strasse 5; d €120-170; ➡✳🛜; 🚇Alexanderplatz, 🚈Alexanderplatz) Sophisticated, efficient and supercentral, this mod designer hotel spoils you with amenities normally reserved for pricier abodes (fluffy bathrobes, iPod docking station, Tassimo coffeemaker). Rooms, though rather small, are decorated in a minimal modern style and get a sense of place from imagery of the nearby Neptune fountain on the glass wall separating bedroom from bathroom. Free landline calls to 19 countries.

ALEXANDER PLAZA
HOTEL $$

Map p318 (☑240 010; www.hotel-alexander-plaza.de; Rosenstrasse 1; d from €135; ℗✳@🛜; 🚈Hackescher Markt) This 92-room boutique hotel in a sensitively restored 19-century fur-trading house retains such period details as a mosaic floor and a stucco-adorned floating stairway. Rooms are good-sized, have panoramic windows and a pleasing cherry-and-charcoal colour scheme. Kick back in the sauna. One hour of free wi-fi per day.

RADISSON BLU HOTEL
HOTEL $$$

Map p318 (☑238 280; www.radissonblu.com/hotel-berlin; Karl-Liebknecht-Strasse 3; d €155-340; ℗✳@🛜🛟; 🚍100, 200, 🚈Hackescher Markt) At this swish and super-central contender, right next to Museumsinsel (Museum Island), you will quite literally 'sleep with the fishes', thanks to the Aquadom, a 25m-high tropical aquarium in the lobby. Streamlined design radiates urban poshness in the 427 rooms and throughout the two restaurants and various social nooks.

Alte Bäckerei Pankow (☑486 4669; www.alte-baeckerei-pankow.de; Wollankstrasse 130; d €70; ➡; 🚈Wollankstrasse) Yesteryear is now in this small rooftop apartment in a 19th-century bakery. Bedrooms and sitting rooms are furnished country-style and the bathroom has a deep wooden tub. The building also houses a childhood museum, and fresh bread is still baked between 3pm and 6pm Tuesday and Friday. Located in Prenzlauer Berg.

Das Andere Haus VIII (☑5544 0331; www.dasanderehaus8.de; Erich-Müller-Strasse 12; d €60-65; ℗➡🛜; 🚈Rummelsburg) GDR leader Erich Honecker was one of the last prisoners of this 19th-century GDR-era jailhouse overlooking scenic Rummelburger Bucht. These days, anyone can stay in the five 'cells' that are snug and sparsely though comfortably furnished; all have private baths, some come with bay views. The waterfront walkway invites strolling or exploring by bike. Located in Friedrichshain. From S-Bahn station Rummelsburg, take tram 21 from Hauptstrasse to Kosanke-Siedlung and then walk 350m via Georg-Löwenstein-Strasse.

Yes Residenz (Map p330; ☑0176 4010 8772; www.yes-berlin.de; Fehrbelliner Strasse 84; d €66; ➡; 🚇Rosenthaler Platz, Senefelderplatz) Fancy sleeping on camping beds in a tent and taking showers from a watering can, all without roughing it in the woods? In this teensy yet undeniably unique mini-apartment, you can do just that. Architect Julian Marhold has created a charmingly unique space, complete with forest wallpaper, right in a regular Berlin building, so you can have your own Hansel and Gretel moment without leaving town. Rates include a welcome drink. Located in Prenzlauer Berg.

Ostel Hostel (Map p328; ☑2576 8660; www.ostel.eu; Wriezener Karree 5; dm/d/apt from €15/64/80; ℗@🛜; 🚇Ostbahnhof) This unusual hostel resuscitates socialist-era East German charm with original furnishings sourced from flea markets, grannies' attics and eBay. With portraits of Honecker and other party apparatchiks peering down on you, you can stay in a 'pioneer'-room dorm, colourfully furnished private rooms or a '70s holiday apartment. Optional breakfast is €7.50. Located in Friedrichshain.

Flat-screen TVs and coffee- and tea-makers are among standard amenities, as are free wi-fi and access to the 24/7 spa area with pool, steam room, sauna and fitness equipment. Optional breakfast is €25.

DUDE
BOUTIQUE HOTEL $$$

Map p318 (☑411 988 177; www.thedudeberlin .com; Köpenicker Strasse 92; d €170-190; ⓅⓈ; ⓈMärkisches Museum, Heinrich-Heine-Platz) With only 30 rooms, the Dude is living proof that good things can indeed come in small packages. Hand-picked furniture, lamps and colour schemes inspired by the proprietors' decades of travel exude an aura of timeless elegance. The most stunning element in this hushed 1822 hideaway is a Schinkel-designed spiral staircase. Breakfast (from €6) is served in the on-site deli, while the Brooklyn Beef Club (p109) gets top marks for its Angus steaks at dinnertime. The hotel is about 200m from the Märkisches Ufer U-Bahn station. Walk east on Wallstrasse, then south on Inselstrasse.

ART'OTEL BERLIN MITTE
HOTEL $$

Map p318 (☑240 620; www.artotels.de; Wallstrasse 70-73; d €90-150; ⓅⓈ; ⓈMärkisches Museum) This boutique hotel wears its 'art' moniker with a justified swagger: more than 400 works by renowned contemporary German artist Georg Baselitz decorate its 109 rooms and the public areas. Fans of cutting-edge Italian design will also be happy here, especially in the suites with their extra-cool bathrooms; those on the 6th floor even have small balconies for rewinding the day's events against a panorama of the historic harbour and the 368m-high Fernsehturm (TV Tower). Optional breakfast is €16.

PANGEA PEOPLE HOSTEL
HOSTEL $

Map p318 (☑886 695 810; www.pangeapeoples .com; Karl-Liebknecht-Strasse 34; dm €13-22, d from €58; @⌂; ⓈAlexanderplatz, ⓇAlexanderplatz) Before there were continents, there was Pangea, a single supercontinent that united the earth's landmass. At this central hostel, the name is the game for the goal is to reunite people from all cultures, be it in dorms equipped with customised beds and lockers or in the bar over beer, snacks or karaoke. Other assets: good security, spicand-span bathrooms and an international crew. Optional breakfast is €5.50. The hostel is about 200m northwest of Alexanderplatz via Karl-Liebknecht-Strasse.

🛏 Potsdamer Platz & Tiergarten

MANDALA HOTEL
LUXURY HOTEL $$$

Map p316 (☑590 050 000; www.themandala.de; Potsdamer Strasse 3; ste €145-360; ⓅⓈ@⌂; ⓈPotsdamer Platz, ⓇPotsdamer Platz) How 'suite' it is to be staying at this swank cocoon of sophistication and unfussy ambience. Suites come in six sizes (40 to 101 sq metres) and are equipped with a kitchenette, walk-in closets and spacious desks in case you're here to ink that deal. Wind down at the on-site spa before drinks at Qiu (p125), perhaps followed by a Michelin-starred dinner at Facil (p125).

RITZ-CARLTON BERLIN
LUXURY HOTEL $$$

Map p316 (☑337 777; www.ritzcarlton.com; Potsdamer Platz 3; d €176-455; ⓅⓈ@⌂⛴; ⓈPotsdamer Platz, ⓇPotsdamer Platz) At one of Berlin's most popular full-on luxury addresses, rooms and suites are done up in natural hues and classical dark-wood furniture enhanced by watercolours by German contemporary artist Markus Lüpertz. Expect all the trappings of a big-league player, including a high-end restaurant, bar, spa and extensive Ritz Kids program. Optional breakfast is €38.

ABION SPREEBOGEN WATERSIDE HOTEL
HOTEL $$

(☑3992 0990; www.abion-hotel.de; Alt-Moabit 99; d €85-225; ⓅⓈ; ⓈTurmstrasse) In a converted dairy farm right on the Spree River, the Abion goes mostly for the suit brigade but also comes with easy access to the major sights, though not to happening nightlife. Spend a bit extra on the newly renovated river-facing rooms. The bilevel family rooms include a baby or child amenity kit. Boat cruises stop in front and a waterfront walkway invites strolling. Optional breakfast €7.50. The hotel is located about 1.6km west of the Hauptbahnhof via Invalidenstrasse and Alt-Moabit. From Turmstrasse U-Bahn station, walk 250m east on Alt-Moabit.

SCANDIC BERLIN POTSDAMER PLATZ
HOTEL $$

Map p316 (☑700 7790; www.scandichotels .com; Gabriele-Tegit-Promenade 19; d €90-200; ⓅⓈ@⌂; ⓈMendelssohn-Bartholdy-Park) This Scandinavian import gets kudos for central location and spacious blond-wood rooms with big bathrooms, as well as for going the extra mile when it comes to being green. Water conservation, for instance, is taken so seriously that you may see staff watering plants with a carafe of leftover water from the restaurant. It's a big city hotel, with all the commensurate comforts, including a restaurant (breakfast €20), bar and gym. You can even borrow bikes or walking sticks for spins around Tiergarten. Free minibar drinks.

MÖVENPICK HOTEL BERLIN — HOTEL $$
Map p316 (☑230 060; www.moevenpick-berlin.com; Schöneberger Strasse 3; d €120-300; P✻@🖥; ⓇAnhalter Bahnhof) This snazzy hotel cleverly marries bold contemporary design with the industrial aesthetic of the historic Siemenshöfe, a protected building where Werner von Siemens founded the world-renowned Siemens electronics and electrical engineering company in 1847. This makes it a chic base of operations for both the suit brigade and city-breakers. Rooms vamp it up with glass cube walls, sensuous olive wood furniture and zany bath-tubs designed by Philippe Starck. The hotel centres on its Mediterranean courtyard restaurant with a glass roof that can be opened for al fresco dining. Optional breakfast is €22. The hotel entrance is just 50m west of Anhalter Bahnhof station.

🛏 Scheunenviertel

TOP CHOICE CIRCUS HOTEL — HOTEL $$
Map p320 (☑2000 3939; www.circus-berlin.de; Rosenthaler Strasse 1; d €80-110; @🖥; ⓈRosenthaler Platz) At our favourite budget boutique hotel, none of the mod rooms are alike but all feature upbeat colours, thoughtful design details, sleek oak floors and quality beds. Baths have walk-in rainforest showers. Unexpected perks include a well-stocked library and free iPod, netbook and DVD player rentals. Fabulous breakfast buffet to boot. Simply good value all-round.

WOMBAT'S CITY HOSTEL BERLIN — HOSTEL $
Map p320 (☑8471 0820; www.wombats-hostels.com; Alte Schönhauser Strasse 2; dm/d €25/70; @🖥; ⓈRosa-Luxemburg-Platz) Wombat's has a long track record at getting hostelling right. From backpack-sized in-room lockers to individual reading lamps and a guest kitchen with dishwasher, the attention to detail here is impressive. Spacious en suite rooms are as de rigueur as freebie linen and a welcome drink, best enjoyed with fellow party pilgrims at the 7th-floor Wombar. Optional breakfast is €3.80.

HOTEL AMANO — HOTEL $$
Map p320 (☑809 4150; www.amanogroup.de; Auguststrasse 43; d €80-160; P✻@🖥; ⓈRosenthaler Platz) Easy on the budget, this instant hit with designer-hotel devotees has inviting public areas dressed in brushed-copper walls and cocoa-hued banquettes. In rooms, white furniture teams up with oak floors and natural-toned fabrics to create crisp cosiness. The standard rooms are a case study in efficiency, so get an apartment (with kitchen) for more elbow room. Great bar and fabulous summer rooftop terrace.

CASA CAMPER — HOTEL $$$
Map p320 (☑2000 3410; www.casacamper.com; Weinmeisterstrasse 1; r/ste from €185/325; P🖥; ⓈWeinmeisterstrasse) Catalan shoemaker Camper has translated its concept of chic yet sensible footwear into this style pit for trend-conscious travellers. Rooms are mod if minimalist and come with day-lit bathrooms and beds that invite hitting the snooze button. Minibars are eschewed for a top-floor lounge with stellar views, free breakfast and 24/7 snacks and drinks.

HONIGMOND GARDEN HOTEL — BOUTIQUE HOTEL $$
Map p319 (☑284 4550; www.honigmond-berlin.de; Invalidenstrasse 122; d €125-230; P@🖥; ⓈNaturkundemuseum) Never mind the busy thoroughfare, this well-managed 20-room guesthouse managed by the same folks as the Hotel Honigmond is an utterly sweet retreat. Reach your comfortable, classically styled room via an enchanting garden with koi pond, fountain and old trees. The communal lounge comes with an honour bar and magazines. Avoid rooms facing the road (tram noise).

SOHO HOUSE BERLIN — BOUTIQUE HOTEL $$$
Map p320 (☑405 0440; www.sohohouseberlin.com; Torstrasse 1; d €270-380; P✻🖥🏊; ⓈRosa-Luxemburg-Platz) This in-crowd darling packs plenty of design cachet into its eclectic-mod rooms equipped with such lifestyle essentials as Bose iPod docking stations, huge plasma flat-screen TVs and

rainforest showers. Staying here also buys access to members-only areas such as the restaurant, the rooftop pool/bar and a small movie theatre. It's all in a Bauhaus building that's seen stints as a department store, Hitler Youth HQ and East German party elite offices.

WEINMEISTER — HOTEL $$$

Map p320 (☎755 6670; www.the-weinmeister.com; Weinmeisterstrasse 2; d €140-300; [P][✻] [@][☎]; [S]Weinmeisterstrasse) Behind its shiny facade, this sassy glamour bastion unapologetically curries favour with creatives from fashion, music and film. Heck, British band Hurts and DJ Mousse T have designed their own rooms (numbers 501 and 401, respectively). You don't need to run with this crowd to appreciate the sleek rooms dressed in charcoal and chocolate, although a certain tech-savvy comes in handy when figuring out how to watch TV on the iMac.

MANI HOTEL — BOUTIQUE HOTEL $$

Map p320 (☎5302 8080; www.hotel-mani.com; Torstrasse 136; d €73-174; [P][☎]; [S]Rosenthaler Platz) Located behind an elegant black facade on trendy Torstrasse, Mani flaunts an uncluttered urban feel and rooms that pack plenty of design cachet and creature comforts into a compact package. It's great val-

ue for the money, even if facilities are limited to the recommended restaurant that wows local cool-hunters with its French-Israeli fare. Optional breakfast is €15.

CIRCUS HOSTEL — HOSTEL $

Map p320 (☎2000 3939; www.circus-hostel.de; Weinbergsweg 1a; dm €23-29, d from €80, with shared bathroom from €64, 2-/4-person apt €95/150; [@][☎]; [S]Rosenthaler Platz) Clean, cheerfully painted rooms, abundant showers and helpful staff are among the factors that have kept Circus at the top of the hostel heap since 1997. Stay in dorms, private rooms (some with en suite baths) or one of 10 penthouse apartments with kitchen and terrace. The downstairs cafe serves inexpensive breakfasts, drinks and snacks, while the basement bar has bands, karaoke, bingo and parties every night (free beer on Mondays!). Welcome tech touches include laptop and Skype phone rentals and laptop-sized in-room lockers with integrated electrical plug.

FLOWER'S BOARDINGHOUSE MITTE — APARTMENT $$

Map p320 (☎2804 5306; www.flowersberlin.de; Mulackstrasse 1; apt €89-133; ⊘reception 9am-6pm; [☎]; [S]Weinmeisterstrasse, Rosa-Luxemburg-Platz) Self-caterers won't miss many of the comforts of home in these breezy

GAY SLEEPS

All Berlin hotels are, of course, open to gays but these places are especially geared to (male) scene crawlers.

Axel Hotel (☎2100 2893; www.axelhotels.com/berlin; Lietzenburger Strasse 13/15; d €130-210; [P][✻][☎]; [S]Wittenbergplatz) Next to Schöneberg's 'gay village', Axel cheekily bills itself as hetero-friendly but is squarely aimed at the gay community. The soundproof rooms are stylish if on the twee side but come with king-sized beds, bathrobes and above-average amenities. Follow a workout in the rooftop gym with a massage or a soak in the outdoor jacuzzi. In summer, the Sky Bar is the perfect launch pad for a night out. Optional breakfast is €11.50. The hotel is about 200m south of U-Bahn station Wittenbergplatz via Bayreuther Strasse.

Gay Hostel (☎2100 5709; www.gay-hostel.de; Motzstrasse 28; dm €22-25, s/d €48/56; ⊝☎; [S]Nollendorfplatz) It's a hostel, so you know the drill. Except that this one is in the heart of Queertown and open to gay men only. Rooms (all with shared bathrooms) are bright and contempo and come with lockers; private rooms also have flat-screen TVs. The communal kitchen and lounge provide plenty of mingling opportunities. Check-in at **Tom's Hotel** (☎030 2196 6604; www.toms-hotel.de; Motzstrasse 19).

Enjoy B&B (☎2362 3610; www.ebab.de; Nollendorfplatz 5; s/d from €20/40; [S]Nollendorfplatz) This private-room referral service caters specifically for gays and lesbians. It has an office inside the Mann-O-Meter (p59) gay information centre, open noon to 9.30pm Monday to Friday, 4.30pm to 9.30pm Saturday and Sunday, but it's easiest to make your reservations online. The website has all the details.

apartments whose heart-of-Scheunenviertel location makes them quite a steal. Choose from three sizes – L, XL and XXL – the latter being a split-level unit sleeping up to six and letting you peer out over the Scheunenviertel rooftops. Units come with full kitchens; rates include free wi-fi and a small breakfast (rolls, coffee, tea) you pick up at reception.

HOTEL HONIGMOND   HOTEL $$

Map p319 (✆284 4550; www.honigmond -berlin.de; Tieckstrasse 12; d €145-235; [P][@][🛜]; [S]Oranienburger Tor) This delightful hotel scores a perfect 10 on our 'charm-o-meter', not for being particularly lavish but for its familiar yet elegant ambience. Rabbits frolic in the garden, the restaurant is a local favourite and rooms sparkle in restored glory. The nicest are in the new wing and flaunt their historic features – ornate stucco ceilings, frescoes, parquet floors – to maximum effect.

MITART HOTEL & CAFÉ   BOUTIQUE HOTEL $$

Map p319 (✆2839 0430; www.mitart.de; Linienstrasse 139-140; d €110-180; [🛜]; [S]Oranienburger Tor) If you'd like to 'sleep with an original', book into this 'hotel gallery' whose 33 rooms are decorated with changing canvases by emerging local artists. The owners go the extra mile when it comes to being green by using only natural materials, organic food and ecominded cleaning products. Rooms are pretty basic given the price (eg no TV), but the central location and dedication to the arts and the environment score bonus points with us.

🛏 Kreuzberg & Northern Neukölln

GRAND HOSTEL   HOSTEL $

Map p322 (✆209 5450; www.grandhostel-berlin .de; Tempelhofer Ufer 14; dm €12-15, d €58; [@][🛜]; [S]Möckernbrücke) Afternoon tea in the library? Check. Rooms with stucco-ornamented ceilings? Got 'em. Canal views? Yup. OK, the Grand Hostel may be no five-star hotel, but it is one of Berlin's most supremely comfortable and atmospheric hostels. Ensconced in a wonderful 1870s building are private rooms and dorms with quality single beds (linen costs €3) and large lockers. The on-site Grandwich Bar serves sandwiches and weekend brunch.

HOTEL SAROTTI-HÖFE   HOTEL $$

Map p322 (✆6003 1680; www.sarotti-hoefe.de; Mehringdamm 55; d €100-180; [P][@][🛜]; [S]Mehringdamm) You'll have sweet dreams in this 19th-century ex-chocolate factory whose courtyard-cloistered rooms are quiet despite being smack dab in the bustling quarter around Bergmannstrasse. Rooms exude elegant yesteryear flair with rich earth-toned fabrics and dark-wood furniture. The nicest (deluxe category) even have a small private terrace. Check-in is at the on-site Cafe Sarotti-Höfe where you'll be spoiled for choice at breakfast time. Optional breakfast is €10.

HOTEL RIEHMERS HOFGARTEN   HOTEL $$

Map p322 (✆7809 8800; www.riehmers-hofga rten.de; Yorckstrasse 83; d €126-143; [🛜]; [S]Mehringdamm) Take a romantic 19th-century building, add contemporary art, stir in a few zeitgeist touches such as iPod docking stations and you'll get one winning cocktail of a hotel. Riehmers' high-ceilinged rooms are modern but not stark; if you're noise-sensitive, get a courtyard-facing room. Assets include in-room tea and coffee, free laptop rentals and a popular gourmet restaurant.

HOTEL JOHANN   HOTEL $$

Map p322 (✆225 0740; www.hotel-johann-berlin .de; Johanniterstrasse 8; d €95-120; [P][@][🛜]; [S]Prinzenstrasse, Hallesches Tor) This 33-room hotel consistently tops the popularity charts, thanks to its eager-to-please service and light-flooded rooms where minimalist designer style contrasts with such historic flourishes as scalloped ceilings and brick walls. The small garden is perfect for summery breakfasts, while happening Bergmannstrasse and the Jüdisches Museum are within strolling distance.

RIVERSIDE LODGE HOSTEL   HOSTEL $

Map p324 (✆6951 5510; www.riverside-lodge .de; Hobrechtstrasse 43; dm €21-22, d €52; [@][🛜]; [S]Schönleinstrasse) This sweet little 12-bed hostel is as warm and welcoming as an old friend's hug thanks to its wonderful owners, Jutta and Liane. Both avid travellers, they have created a cosy, communicative hang-out near the Landwehrkanal in booming northern Neukölln. In the six-bed dorm, beds can be curtained off for extra privacy. Check-in is from 11am to 2pm and 7pm to 9.30pm. There's an extra fee of €3 for linen. Optional breakfast is €4.

Friedrichshain

[TOP CHOICE] **MICHELBERGER HOTEL** HOTEL $$
Map p328 (☎2977 8590; www.michelbergerhotel.com; Warschauer Strasse 39; d €80-180; 📶; [S]Warschauer Strasse, [R]Warschauer Strasse) The ultimate in creative crash pads, Michelsberger perfectly encapsulates Berlin's offbeat DIY spirit. Rooms don't hide their factory pedigree but are comfortable and come in sizes suitable for lovebirds, families or rock bands. Staff is friendly and clued-in. On weekends, there's often some sort of party or concert going on in the bar-reception-lobby. Great for the young and forever young. Optional breakfast is €8.

NHOW HOTEL $$
Map p328 (☎290 2990; www.nhow-hotels.com; Stralauer Allee 3; d €115-275; [P]📶; [S]Warschauer Strasse, [R]Warschauer Strasse) nhow bills itself as a music and lifestyle hotel, and underscores the point by having its own on-site recording studios. The look of the place is certainly dynamic, what with a sideways tower jutting out over the Spree and Karim Rashid's vibrant digi-pop design that would make Barbie proud. Rooms are more subdued, despite the pink, blue and black colour scheme.

PLUS HOSTEL HOSTEL $
Map p328 (☎2123 8501; www.plushostels.com/plusberlin; Warschauer Platz 6; dm/d from €13/25; 🚭❄[@]📶🏊; [S]Warschauer Strasse, [R]Warschauer Strasse) A hostel with a pool and sauna? Yup. Within stumbling distance of Berlin's best nightlife, Plus has definitely upped the hostelling ante. There's a bar for easing into the night and a courtyard with pet rabbits and a tranquil atmosphere to get rid of that hangover. Spacious dorms have bunks, desks and lockers, while private rooms have beds, TV and air-con. All have en suites. Optional breakfast is €6.

RAISE A SMILE HOSTEL HOSTEL $
Map p328 (☎0172 855 6064; www.raise-a-smile-hostel-berlin.com; Weidenweg 51; dm/d from €10/40; [@]📶; [S]Frankfurter Tor, 🚊M10 to Bersarinplatz) Elephants, zebras, giraffes and big cats watch over guests in smallish dorms and private rooms with shared facilities at this African-themed hostel. With only 18 beds, it's definitely not a party hostel, but great for banding up with fellow travellers in the lounge or the communal kitchen. The hostel donates 100% of all profits to children's projects in Zambia. Two-night minimum. Breakfast by donation.

ODYSSEE GLOBETROTTER HOSTEL HOSTEL $
Map p328 (☎2900 0081; www.globetrotterhostel.de; Grünberger Strasse 23; dm €16.50-24, d €73; [@]📶; [S]Warschauer Strasse, 🚊M10 to Grünberger Strasse, [R]Warschauer Strasse) Young, social types give high marks to this eastside hostel that puts the 'fun' in funky and is a great launching pad for in-depth nightlife explorations. Clean rooms sport pine beds, lockers and artsy styling: here a vertigo-inducing ceiling swirl, there a bright orange flower-power homage or a giant puzzle. Guest kitchen, backyard and on-site pub are all great socialising zones. Beer for €1 during happy hour (4pm to 6pm). Optional breakfast is €3.

🍃 **HOTEL 26** HOTEL $$
Map p328 (☎297 7780; www.hotel26-berlin.de; Grünberger Strasse 26; d from €90; [P][@]📶; [S]Warschauer Strasse, 🚊M10 to Grünberger Strasse, [R]Warschauer Strasse) Set back from the street and with a lovely garden out back, this architect-owned hotel in a revamped factory sparkles in cheery citrus colours that instantly put you in a good mood. Clear lines and blond-wood furniture dominate both public areas and the rooms. Hotel 26 also has a lot going on in the eco-department with such things as natural soaps, filtered water and a cafe serving mostly sustainable and organic products.

EAST-SIDE HOTEL HOTEL $$
Map p328 (☎293 833; www.eastsidehotel.de; Mühlenstrasse 6; d €80-120; [P]📶; [S]Warschauer Strasse, [R]Warschauer Strasse) One of the older properties in these parts, but still good value-for-money. Behind the white-and-butter-yellow classical facade hide 36 rooms that are a meditation on minimalism. Hard to beat, though, is the location across from the East Side Gallery (Berlin Wall remnant) and the Spree River with its beach bars and steps from the O2 World arena and the Kreuzberg and Friedrichshain fun zones.

UPSTALSBOOM HOTEL FRIEDRICHSHAIN HOTEL $$
Map p328 (☎293 750; www.upstalsboom.de; Gubener Strasse 42, enter via Kopernikusstrasse; [P]📶; [S]Frankfurter Tor, [R]Warschauer Strasse,

[S]Warschauer Strasse) If this modern and well-kept hotel feels like a breath of fresh air, it may be because it's the Berlin branch of a small chain of German seaside resorts. Subtle maritime flair pervades the public areas, including the fish restaurant, while rooms have a clean, uncluttered look, pleasing colours and come in four sizes. Small spa and great views from the rooftop terrace.

Prenzlauer Berg

[TOP CHOICE] EASTSEVEN BERLIN HOSTEL HOSTEL $

Map p330 (☎9362 2240; www.eastseven.de; Schwedter Strasse 7; dm €17-19, d €50; @📶; [S]Senefelderplatz) Perfect for solo travellers, this small, friendly and fun hostel is within strolling distance of hip hang-outs and public transport. Cultural and language barriers melt away quickly over a barbecue in the idyllic back garden, spaghetti dinner in the modern kitchen (with dishwasher!) or chilling in the retro lounge. Come bedtime, retreat to comfy pine beds in brightly painted dorms with lockers or a private room. Each floor has several gender-separated bathrooms.

🍃 HOTEL KASTANIENHOF HOTEL $$

Map p330 (☎443 050; www.kastanienhof.biz; Kastanienallee 65; d €105-140; [P]@📶; [S]Rosenthaler Platz, 🚊M1 to Zionskirchstrasse, [S]Senefelderplatz) In contrast to its location on trendy Kastanienallee with its cafes, restaurants and boutiques, this charmer itself has more of a lovable traditional bent. Family-owned and with fall-over-backwards staff, its 35 good-sized rooms pair historical touches with flat-screen TVs, modern bathrooms and free wi-fi. Bikes rent for €12.50 per day.

MEININGER HOTEL BERLIN PRENZLAUER BERG HOSTEL, HOTEL $

Map p330 (☎6663 6100; www.meininger-hotels.com; Schönhauser Allee 19; dm €15-28, d €44-100; @📶; [S]Senefelderplatz) This popular hotel-hostel combo appeals to everyone from school groups to flashpackers, which makes for an interesting mix at breakfast time (optional breakfast is €5.90). A lift whisks you to mod and spacious en suite rooms and dorms with quality furnishings, flat-screen TVs and handy blackout blinds to combat jetlag (or hangovers). Other assets: the all-day cafe-bar, guest kitchen and proximity of sights, eats and parties. Check the website for the five other Berlin locations, including recommended ones near the Hauptbahnhof and on Oranienburger Strasse.

ACKSELHAUS & BLUE HOME BOUTIQUE HOTEL $$

Map p330 (☎4433 7633; www.ackselhaus.de; Belforter Strasse 21; ste from €105, apt from €150; @📶; [S]Senefelderplatz) At this charismatic retreat in a 19th-century building you'll sleep in large, classily decorated themed rooms (eg Africa, Rome, Maritime), each with thoughtfully picked special features; a freestanding tub, perhaps, a four-poster bed or Chinese antiques. Many face the idyllic courtyard garden. Breakfast is served – beneath crystal chandeliers – until 11am (until 12.30pm at weekends).

PRECISE HOTEL MYER'S BERLIN BOUTIQUE HOTEL $$

Map p330 (☎440 140; www.myershotel.de; Metzer Strasse 26; d €135-255; 🚭❄📶; [S]Senefelder Platz) This 56-room boutique hotel combines the elegance of your rich uncle's mansion, the cheerful warmth of your parents' home and the casual comforts of your best friend's pad. You'll sleep well in classically furnished rooms with stucco-ornamented ceilings and wooden floors, and find pleasing unwinding spots in the 24-hour lobby bar, the sauna and steam room, or the bucolic garden. Rave-worthy breakfast.

HOTEL GREIFSWALD HOTEL $

Map p330 (☎4442 7888; www.hotel-greifswald.de; Greifswalder Strasse 211; d €65-75; [P]@📶; 🚊M4 to Hufelandstrasse) This 30-room hotel, tucked into a back building away from tram and traffic noise, has a serious rock pedigree. The tiny lobby doubles as a veritable hall of fame for former guests, including Mitch Ryder and Steppenwolf. Rooms are handsome, if rather generic, but it's the awesome breakfast spread – served until noon and an optional €7.50 – that gets our thumbs up. Great value, overall.

City West & Charlottenburg

[TOP CHOICE] HOTEL ASKANISCHER HOF HOTEL $$

Map p334 (☎881 8033; www.askanischer-hof.de; Kurfürstendamm 53; d €120-180; 📶;

S Adenauerplatz) If you're after character and vintage flair, you'll find heaps of both at this 17-room jewel with a Roaring Twenties pedigree. An ornate oak door leads to a quiet oasis where no two rooms are alike but all are filled with antiques, lace curtains, frilly chandeliers and time-worn oriental rugs. The quaint Old Berlin charms make a popular setting for fashion shoots.

BLEIBTREU BERLIN BOUTIQUE HOTEL $$

Map p334 (☎884 740; www.bleibtreu.com; Bleibtreustrasse 31; d €120-200; @ ; S Uhlandstrasse) On a leafy avenue, the stylish Bleibtreu pioneered sustainable hospitality long before everyone else jumped on the bandwagon. Furniture made from untreated oak, virgin wool carpets and walls daubed with organic paint are among the thoughtful features. Rooms don't fit a ton of luggage but, heck, the minibar is free and breakfast (€17) is available all day at the on-site deli.

HOTEL CONCORDE BERLIN HOTEL $$$

Map p334 (☎800 9990; www.concorde-hotels.com/concordeberlin; Augsburger Strasse 41; d €150-300; P @ ; S Kurfürstendamm) If you like edgy design combined with the amenities of a big-city property, the Concorde should fit the bill. Designed by German architect Jan Kleihues, from the curved limestone facade to the door knobs, it channels New York efficiency, French lightness of being and Berlin-style unpretentiousness. The 311 rooms and suites are supersized, warmly furnished and accented with quality prints by contemporary German artists. Free wi-fi. Optional breakfast is €28.

LOUISA'S PLACE BOUTIQUE HOTEL $$$

(☎631 030; www.louisas-place.de; Kurfürstendamm 160; ste €135-595; P @ ; S Adenauerplatz) Louisa's is the kind of place that dazzles with class not glitz; it's a discreet deluxe hideaway that puts great emphasis on customised guest services. Suites here

FURNISHED APARTMENTS

For self-caterers, independent types, families and anyone wanting extra privacy, a short-term furnished-apartment rental may well be the cat's pyjamas. Also check **airbnb** (www.airbnb.com), **Be My Guest** (www.be-my-guest.com) or **HomeAway** (www.homeaway.com).

Miniloft Berlin (Map p319; ☎847 1090; www.miniloft.com; Hessische Strasse 5, Scheunenviertel; apt from €138; ; S Naturkundemuseum) Eight stunning lofts in an architect-converted building, some with south-facing panorama windows, others with cosy alcoves, all outfitted with modern designer furniture and kitchenettes. Near the Natural History Museum.

Brilliant Apartments (Map p330; ☎8061 4796; www.brilliant-apartments.de; Prenzlauer Berg; apt from €84; ; S Eberswalder Strasse) Tthese 11 stylish and modern units with full kitchens sleep from one to six people. They're located on Oderberger Strasse and Rykestrasse, both hip drags in Prenzlauer Berg that put you close to good eats, bars and shops.

ÏMA Loft Apartments (Map p324; ☎6162 8913; www.imalofts.com; Ritterstrasse 12-14; apt €55-200; ; S Moritzplatz) These uncluttered, contemporary apartments are part of the ÏMA Design Village, an old factory shared by design studios and a dance and theatre academy. They sleep from one to four.

T&C Apartments (Map p330; ☎030 405 046 612; www.tc-apartments-berlin.de; Kopenhagener Strasse 72; studio apt from €75; S Schönhauser Allee) Huge selection of stylish, hand-picked, one- to four-room apartments in Mitte, Prenzlauer Berg, Tiergarten and Schöneberg; main office is in Prenzlauer Berg.

Berlin Lofts (☎0151 2121 9126; www.berlinlofts.com; Stephanstrasse 60; apt from €127; @ ; S Westhafen, Birkenstrasse, R Westhafen) Rents huge lofts in handsomely converted historic buildings, including an old smithy and a bilevel horse barn. The area, alas, is not nearly as hip, although public transport connections are decent. Trivia bonus: Kommune 1, Germany's first politically motivated student commune, formed in 1967, once hung out in one of the apartments.

are luxe and huge and have kitchens, the pool is small but refreshing and the library palatial. A high-end restaurant shares the premises. Optional breakfast is €20. The hotel is 150m west on Kurfürstendamm from U-Bahn station Adenauerplatz.

ELLINGTON HOTEL   HOTEL $$
Map p334 (☑683 150; www.ellington-hotel.com; Nürnberger Strasse 50-55; d €130-270; P✿@; SAugsburger Strasse) Duke and Ella gave concerts in the jazz cellar and Bowie and Prince partied in the Dschungel nightclub, then the lights went out in the '90s. Now the handsome 1920s building has been resuscitated as a high-concept jewel that wraps all that's great about Berlin – history, innovation, *joie de vivre* – into one attractive package. Rooms are stylishly minimalist. Optional breakfast is €20.

HOTEL ART NOUVEAU   B&B $$
Map p334 (☑327 7440; www.hotelartnouveau.de; Leibnizstrasse 59; d €96-176; P@☎; SAdenauerplatz) A rickety birdcage lift drops you off with belle époque flourish at this arty B&B. Rooms skimp neither on space nor charisma and offer a blend of youthful flair and tradition. The affable owners are fluent English-speakers with a knack for colour and sourcing fantastic pieces of art and furniture. No two rooms are alike. Bonus points for the superb beds, the organic breakfast and the honour bar.

HOTEL BOGOTA   HOTEL $$
Map p334 (☑881 5001; www.bogota.de; Schlüterstrasse 45; d €90-150, with shared bathroom €64-77; ☎; SUhlandstrasse) Bogota has charmed travellers with charisma and vintage flair since 1964. Helmut Newton studied with fashion photographer Yva here in the 1930s and to this day the rambling retro landmark hosts glam-mag photo shoots. Room sizes and amenities vary greatly, so ask to see a few before settling in. Love those Gregorian chants in the courtyard!

HOTEL-PENSION FUNK   B&B $$
Map p334 (☑882 7193; www.hotel-pensionfunk.de; Fasanenstrasse 69; d €82-129; ➔☎; SUhlandstrasse, Kurfürstendamm) Time-travel back to the Golden Twenties at this charismatic little pension in the home of silent-movie siren Asta Nielsen. With its antique furniture and period decor, it's a great choice if you value old-fashioned charm over mod-cons. Rooms vary quite significantly, so if size

matters bring up the subject when booking. Cheaper ones have partial or shared facilities.

SAVOY HOTEL   HOTEL $$$
Map p334 (☑311 030, reservations 0800 7286 9468; www.hotel-savoy.com; Fasanenstrasse 9-10; d €150-280; ✿@☎; SZoologischer Garten, ℝZoologischer Garten) History streams through this intimate grand hotel as strongly as the Thames does through London. In business since 1929, there's something comfortably old-school about the place that writer Thomas Mann called 'charming and cosy' and Talking Heads' David Byrne considered 'friendly and helpful'. The handsome rooms are classically furnished; some in the superior category have canopy beds and air-con. Free wi-fi. Parking across the street. Optional breakfast is €19.

MITTENDRIN   B&B $$
Map p334 (☑2362 8861; www.boutique-hotel-berlin.de; Nürnberger Strasse 16; d €100-200; ☎; SAugsburger Strasse, Wittenbergplatz) This actress-run sweet retreat close to primo shopping is a fantastic find for those who value individual service over fancy lobbies or rooftop bars. All four rooms bulge with character, handpicked furnishings and homey extras like fresh flowers and candles. Breakfasts are gourmet affairs and, if desired, served in bed at no extra charge.

HOTEL-PENSION DITTBERNER   B&B $$
Map p334 (☑881 6485; www.hotel-dittberner.de; Wielandstrasse 26; d €115; P@☎; SAdenauerplatz) Travel back in time aboard a century-old lift that deposits you at this charming pension with a hospitality pedigree going back to the 1930s. With its old furniture, plush rugs and armloads of artwork, it's a quiet place that appeals to more mature and solo travellers. Rooms are rather large and sport such old-school touches as crisp white linen and floor-length curtains.

HOTEL Q!   BOUTIQUE HOTEL $$
Map p334 (☑810 0660; www.loock-hotels.com; Knesebeckstrasse 67; d €95-215; P✿☎; Uhlandstrasse) No fancy marquee, only a plain facade conceals this snazzy boutique hotel with its retro-futuristic sculptural design. Corners are eschewed, from the red-hot lobby to the sexy rooms, some with pod chairs, others with tubs right next to the bed. Note that the cheapest ones are tiny. Nice touch: the spa with indoor beach

for relaxing. Members-only bar. Optional breakfast is €20.

HOTEL OTTO   HOTEL $$

Map p334 (☎5471 0080; www.hotelotto.com; Knesebeckstrasse 10; d €100-140; P 🛜; S Ernst-Reuter-Platz) Otto would be just another business hotel were it not for the helpful staff and thoughtful extras such as free DVDs and a rooftop lounge with sun terrace and free afternoon cake and refreshments. Rooms are fairly functional but get character from bright colour accents and warm textures, even if those in the 'standard' category are pretty small. Optional breakfast is €15.

KU' DAMM 101   HOTEL $$

(☎520 0550; www.kudamm101.com; Kurfürstendamm 101; d €120-250; P ❄ @ 🛜; 🚌M19 to Joachim-Friedrich-Strasse, 🚇Halensee) If it were in Mitte, this sassy lifestyle hotel would be hipster central. But, alas, it's kinda out there in the far west, albeit close to the trade-fair grounds and with easy access to public transport. The mod rooms are dressed in a colour scheme inspired by Modernist architect Le Corbusier and are replete with stylish furniture by young German designers. Breakfast (€15) is served in an airy 7th-floor lounge with a feast of views. It's a 500m walk or one stop on the M19 from S-Bahn station Halensee. The M19 bus stops 50m from the hotel.

EXCELSIOR HOTEL   HOTEL $$

Map p334 (☎303 1550; www.hotel-excelsior.de; Hardenbergstrasse 14; d €80-130; ❄ 🛜; S Zoologischer Garten, 🚇Zoologischer Garten) It must have taken a considerable amount of cash to turn the stuffy old Excelsior into this progressively designed outpost that should suit buttoned-up business types as much as couples on a getaway. Get at least a superior room if you want a large flat-screen, cloud-soft bedding and a tub for postsightseeing unwinding. The Franke (p200) restaurant gets high marks.

Understand Berlin

Berlin Today

Berlin is a city that is truly 24/7, where creativity, sensory overload and hedonism roar with unapologetic abandon. Where New York might be the 'Big Apple', the German capital is the 'Big Appetite', and the hunger for experimentation and challenge is rarely sated. It's a city where you can fairly hear and feel the collision between past and future, what is possible and what is realistic and the cultural hopes and the culture clashes between people who've joined together from around the globe in one big experiment.

Best on Film

The Lives of Others (2006) This Academy Award winner reveals the stranglehold the East German secret police had on innocent people.

Downfall (2004) Chilling account of Hitler's last 12 days holed up in his Berlin bunker.

Good Bye, Lenin! (2003) Cult comedy tells the story of a young East Berliner's quest to keep the fall of the Wall from his ailing mother.

Russendisko (2012) Berlin as experienced by three young Russians who move here after the fall of the Berlin Wall.

Best in Print

Goodbye to Berlin (Christopher Isherwood; 1939) Brilliant semi-autobiographical account of early 1930s Berlin through the eyes of a gay Anglo-American journalist.

Berlin Alexanderplatz (Alfred Döblin; 1929) This stylised meander through the seamy 1920s is still an essential Berlin text.

Russian Disco (Wladimir Kaminer; 2000) Entertaining vignettes portraying postreunification Berlin.

Stasiland (Anna Funder; 2004) The Stasi's vast spying apparatus from the perspectives of both victims and perpetrators.

Economic Upswing

Long mired in the economic doldrums, Berlin is finally seeing slivers of sunlight on the horizon. In 2010 its economy grew by 2.7%, nearly 1% more than Germany as a whole. Exports are up, and so are investments, especially in such high-tech fields as biotechnology, communication and environmental technologies and transportation. Tourism is another driving force, with the number of annual visitors soaring to 22 million, more than double what it was in 2002. Since 2006 Berlin has also been the start-up capital of Germany with venture capitalists, many of them foreign, increasingly willing to finance budding visionaries.

It's not all good news, though. Although unemployment has dropped, at 13% it's still more than double the national average. No other German city has more welfare recipients than Berlin. And keeping the books balanced is tough with a city debt hovering around €62 billion that demands €2 billion in annual interest payments.

Gentrification

Try to put your finger on the pulse of Berlin and you'll find that, much like the mysterious movements on a Ouija board, the pulse is already moving on to another location. Today's downtrodden neighbourhood becomes tomorrow's dream of students and artists, young entrepreneurs and, eventually, developers. The city's famously low rents have become a thing of the past, office buildings have displaced beloved riverside party venues, and 'loft-living' is the new buzzword.

In other words, Berlin is fully in the grip of gentrification. And although it results in cleaner streets, nicer flats and chic bars and restaurants, many locals don't like it one bit.

Kreuzberg, with its punk and squatter roots, is especially worried about losing its edge and going the way Prenzlauer Berg and Mitte have already gone – from free-wheeling alt-flavoured districts to high-income, well-educated monocultures. And indeed, in recent years rents have surged citywide; nowhere faster than in Kreuzberg. In 2011 alone, the district saw rents increase by 11.1% and it replaced Charlottenburg as Berlin's most expensive area. Adjacent northern Neukölln, which has gone from quasi-ghetto to hipster haven within a few years, shares a similar fate (8.2% increase in 2011).

Many long-term residents, a good number of them low-income earners or unemployed, are forced to move away. In their frustration, some have pointed the finger at affluent foreigners and newcomers from western Germany who can afford and are willing to pay the higher rents. Even tourists have come in for their share of blame, be it for being noisy, for staying in unlicensed holiday flats or for swarming locals' bars and pubs in large groups. Controlling growth and keeping rents in check will be among the major challenges the government will have to face in years to come.

The Airport Quagmire

And unchecked gentrification may not be the worst of it. The delayed opening of the new central Berlin Brandenburg Airport, which has been taking shape on the city's southeastern edge since 2006, is putting a major stain on the city's image. Originally expected to open in November 2011, the date was pushed back to June 2012. However, only weeks before the first flights were to hit the tarmac, the supervisory board announced a nine-month delay because of flaws in the fire safety system. At the time of writing, safety concerns had further delayed the opening to October 2013.

All this back and forth has been a major embarrassment for local politicians and placed a heavy burden on the public purse. So far, the delays have entailed a projected 30% cost overrun and pushed the overall budget to €3.1 billion. In fact, each month of delay in opening adds €100 million to the final tally. Naturally, there's been quite a bit of public scapegoating. Berlin mayor Klaus Wowereit and Brandenburg governor Matthias Platzeck, who both serve on the airport supervisory board, have blamed airport officials who in turn, along with the airlines and retailers, have pointed the finger right back at the politicians. Who will pay for the airport's inflated cost, and when it will actually open, remains anybody's guess.

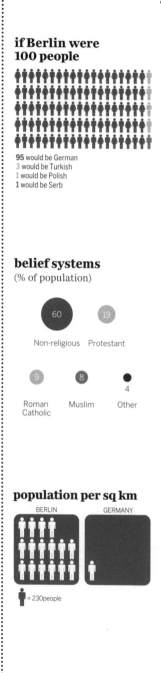

BERLIN TODAY

if Berlin were 100 people

95 would be German
3 would be Turkish
1 would be Polish
1 would be Serb

belief systems
(% of population)

60 Non-religious
19 Protestant
9 Roman Catholic
8 Muslim
4 Other

population per sq km

BERLIN   GERMANY

≈ 230people

History

Berlin has long been in the cross-hairs of history: it staged a revolution, was headquartered by fascists, bombed to bits, ripped in half and finally reunited – and that was just in the 20th century! Yet, Berlin is very much an accidental capital whose medieval birth was a mere blip on the map of history. It continued to exist in relative obscurity until becoming the royal capital of Prussia some 400 years later, but it wasn't until the 20th century that it significantly impacted on European – and indeed world – history.

MEDIEVAL BERLIN

The recent discovery of an oak beam suggests that Berlin may have roots going back to 1183 but, for now, the city was officially founded in the 13th century by itinerant merchants as twin trading posts. Called Berlin and Cölln, the settlements flanked the Spree River in an area just southwest of today's Alexanderplatz. It was a profitable spot along a natural east–west trade route, about halfway between the fortified towns of Köpenick to the southeast and Spandau to the northwest whose origins can be traced to the 8th century. The tiny settlements grew in leaps and bounds and, in 1307, merged into a single town for reasons of power and protection. As the centre of the March (duchy) of Brandenburg, it continued to assert its political and economic independence and even became a player in the Hanseatic League in 1360.

Such confidence did not sit well with Sigismund, king of the Germans, who, in 1411, put one of his cronies, Friedrich von Hohenzollern, in charge of Brandenburg, thereby ushering in five centuries of uninterrupted rule by the House of Hohenzollern.

Berlin's medieval birthplace around the Nikolaikirche was devastated during the WWII bombing raids. Today's 'Nikolaiviertel' is actually a replica of the quarter, dreamed up by the East German government in celebration of the city's 750th anniversary in 1987.

REFORMATION & THE THIRTY YEARS' WAR

The Reformation, kick-started in 1517 by Martin Luther in nearby Wittenberg, was slow to arrive in Berlin. Eventually, though, the wave of reform reached Brandenburg, leaving Elector Joachim II (r 1535–71) no choice

TIMELINE	1244	1307	1360
	Berlin is referenced in a document for the first time in recorded history, but the city's birthday is pegged to the first mention of its sister settlement Cölln seven years earlier in 1237.	Berlin and Cölln join forces by merging into a single town to assert their independence from local rulers.	The twin town of Berlin-Cölln joins the Hanseatic League but never plays a major role in the alliance and quits its membership in 1518.

but to subscribe to Protestantism. On 1 November 1539 the court celebrated the first Lutheran-style service in the Nikolaikirche in Spandau. The event is still celebrated as an official holiday (Reformationstag) in Brandenburg, the German federal state that surrounds Berlin, although not in the city state of Berlin itself.

Berlin prospered for the ensuing decades until drawn into the Thirty Years' War (1618–48), a conflict between Catholics and Protestants that left Europe's soil drenched with the blood of millions. Elector Georg Wilhelm (r 1620–40) tried to maintain a policy of neutrality, only to see his territory repeatedly pillaged and plundered by both sides. By the time the war ended, Berlin lay largely in shambles – broke, ruined and decimated by starvation, murder and disease.

ROAD TO A KINGDOM

Stability finally returned during the long reign of Georg Wilhelm's son, Friedrich Wilhelm (r 1640–88). Also known as the Great Elector, he took several steps that helped chart Brandenburg's rise to the status of a European powerhouse. His first order of business was to increase Berlin's safety by turning it into a garrison town encircled by fortifications with 13 bastions. He also levied a new sales tax, using the money to build three new neighbourhoods (Friedrichswerder, Dorotheenstadt and Friedrichstadt), a canal linking the Spree and the Oder rivers (thereby cementing Berlin's position as a trading hub), as well as the Lustgarten and Unter den Linden.

But the Great Elector's most lasting legacy was replenishing Berlin's population by encouraging the settlement of refugees. In 1671, 50 Jewish families arrived from Vienna, followed by thousands of Protestant Huguenots – many of them highly skilled – who had been expelled from France by Louis XIV in 1685. The Französischer Dom (French Cathedral) on Gendarmenmarkt serves as a tangible reminder of Huguenot influence. Between 1680 and 1710, Berlin saw its population nearly triple to 56,000, making it one of the largest cities in the Holy Roman Empire.

The Great Elector's son, Friedrich III, was a man of great ambition with a penchant for the arts and sciences. Together with his beloved wife, Sophie-Charlotte, he presided over a lively and intellectual court, founding the Academy of Arts in 1696 and the Academy of Sciences in 1700. One year later, he advanced his career by promoting himself to King Friedrich I (elector 1688–1701, king 1701–13) of Prussia, making Berlin a royal residence and the capital of the new state of Brandenburg-Prussia.

An 8m-long section is all that survives of Berlin's original city wall, built around 1250 from crude boulders and bricks and standing up to 2m tall. Go to see it on Littenstrasse, near Alexanderplatz.

FIRST BERLIN WALL

1411	1415	1443	1539
German King Sigismund puts Friedrich von Hohenzollern in charge as administrator of Brandenburg, marking the beginning of 500 years of Hohenzollern rule.	Friedrich von Hohenzollern's grip on power solidifies when Sigismund promotes him to elector and margrave of Brandenburg at the Council of Constance.	Construction of the Berlin Stadtschloss (City Palace) on the Spree island begins and becomes the electors' permanent residence in 1486.	Elector Joachim II celebrates the first Lutheran service and a year later passes a church ordinance making the new religion binding throughout Brandenburg.

THE AGE OF PRUSSIA

All cultural and intellectual life screeched to a halt under Friedrich's son, Friedrich Wilhelm I (r 1713–40), who laid the groundwork for Prussian military might. Soldiers were this king's main obsession and he dedicated much of his life to building up an army of 80,000, partly by instituting the draft (highly unpopular even then, and eventually repealed) and by persuading his fellow rulers to trade him men for treasure. History quite appropriately knows him as the *Soldatenkönig* (soldier king).

Ironically, these soldiers didn't see action until his son and successor Friedrich II (aka Frederick the Great; r 1740–86) came to power. Friedrich fought tooth and nail for two decades to wrest Silesia (in today's Poland) from Austria and Saxony. When not busy on the battlefield 'Old Fritz', as he was also called, sought greatness through building. His Forum Fridericianum, a grand architectural master plan for Unter den Linden, although never completed, gave Berlin the Staatsoper Unter den Linden (State Opera House), Sankt-Hedwigs-Kathedrale, a former palace now housing the Humboldt Universität (Humboldt University) and other major attractions.

Frederick also embraced the ideas of the Enlightenment, abolishing torture, guaranteeing religious freedom and introducing legal reforms. With some of the leading thinkers in town (Moses Mendelssohn, Voltaire and Gotthold Ephraim Lessing among them), Berlin blossomed into a great cultural capital, known as 'Athens on the Spree'.

NAPOLEON & REFORMS

One of the definitive histories on Prussia, Christopher Clark's *Iron Kingdom: The Rise and Downfall of Prussia* covers the period from 1600 to 1947 and shows the central role this powerhouse played in shaping modern Europe.

Old Fritz's death sent Prussia into a downward spiral, culminating in a serious trouncing of its army by Napoleon at Jena-Auerstedt in 1806. The French marched triumphantly into Berlin on 27 October and left two years later, their coffers bursting with loot. Among the pint-sized conqueror's favourite souvenirs was the *Quadriga* sculpture from atop the Brandenburg Gate.

The post-Napoleonic period saw Berlin caught up in the reform movement sweeping through Europe. Public servants, academics and merchants now questioned the right of the nobility to rule. Friedrich Wilhelm III (r 1797–1840) instituted a few token reforms (easing guild regulations, abolishing bonded labour and granting Jews civic equality), but meaningful constitutional reform was not forthcoming. Power continued to be centred in the Prussian state.

The ensuing period of political stability was paired with an intellectual flourishing in Berlin's cafes and salons. The newly founded Universität zu Berlin (Humboldt Universität) was helmed by the philosopher Johann Gottlieb Fichte and, as it grew in status, attracted other leading think-

1618	1640
Religious conflict and territorial power struggles escalate into the bloody Thirty Years' War, devastating Berlin financially and decimating its population by half, to a mere 6000 people.	Friedrich Wilhelm, who will go down in history as the Great Elector, comes to power and restores a semblance of normality by building major fortifications and rebuilding infrastructure.

CAROLA KOSEROWSKY / GETTY IMAGES ©

Friedrich Wilhelm statue, Museumsinsel (p95)

ers of the day, including Hegel and Ranke. This was also the age of Karl Friedrich Schinkel, whose many projects – from the Neue Wache (New Guardhouse) to the Altes Museum (Old Museum) – still beautify Berlin.

REVOLUTION(S)

The Industrial Revolution snuck up on Berliners in the second quarter of the 19th century, with companies like Siemens and Borsig vastly spurring the city's growth. In 1838 trains began chuffing between Berlin and Potsdam, giving birth to the Prussian railway system and spurring the founding of more than 1000 factories, including electrical giants AEG and Siemens. In 1841 August Borsig built the world's fastest locomotive, besting even the British in a race.

Tens of thousands of people now streamed into Berlin to work in the factories, swelling the population to over 400,000 by 1847 and bringing the city's infrastructure close to collapse. A year later, due to social volatility and restricted freedoms, Berlin joined with other German cities in a bourgeois democratic revolution. On 18 March two shots rang out during a demonstration, which then escalated into a full-fledged revolution. Barricades went up and a bloody fight ensued, leaving 183 revolutionaries and 18 soldiers dead by the time Friedrich Wilhelm IV ordered his troops back. The dead revolutionaries are commemorated on Platz des 18 März immediately west of the Brandenburg Gate. In a complete turnabout, the king now put himself at the head of the movement and ostensibly professed support for liberalism and nationalism. On 21 March, while riding to the funeral of the revolutionaries in the Volkspark Friedrichshain, he donned the red, black and gold tricolour of German unity. An elected Prussian national assembly met on 5 May.

However, disagreements between delegates from the different factions kept parliament weak and ineffective, making restoration of the monarchy child's play for General von Wrangel, who led 13,000 Prussian soldiers who had remained faithful to the king into the city in November 1848. Ever the opportunist, the king quickly switched sides again, dissolved the parliament and proposed his own constitution while insisting on maintaining supreme power. The revolution was dead. Many of its participants fled into exile.

BISMARCK & THE BIRTH OF AN EMPIRE

When Friedrich Wilhelm IV suffered a stroke in 1857, his brother Wilhelm became first regent and then, in 1861, King Wilhelm I (r 1861–88). Unlike his brother, Wilhelm had his finger on the pulse of the times and

Historical Reads

Berlin Rising: Biography of a City (Anthony Read, David Fisher)

Berlin (David Clay Large)

Berlin Diary: Journal of a Foreign Correspondent 1934-41 (William Shirer)

The Candy Bombers (Andrei Cherny)

The Berlin Wall (Frederick Taylor)

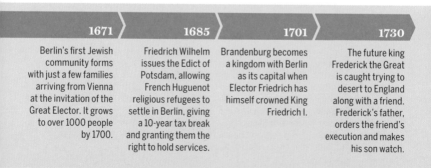

1671	1685	1701	1730
Berlin's first Jewish community forms with just a few families arriving from Vienna at the invitation of the Great Elector. It grows to over 1000 people by 1700.	Friedrich Wilhelm issues the Edict of Potsdam, allowing French Huguenot religious refugees to settle in Berlin, giving a 10-year tax break and granting them the right to hold services.	Brandenburg becomes a kingdom with Berlin as its capital when Elector Friedrich has himself crowned King Friedrich I.	The future king Frederick the Great is caught trying to desert to England along with a friend. Frederick's father orders the friend's execution and makes his son watch.

PISSOIRS

was less averse to progress. One of his key moves was to appoint Otto von Bismarck as Prussian prime minister in 1862.

Bismarck's glorious ambition was the creation of a unified Germany with Prussia at the helm. An old-guard militarist, he used intricate diplomacy and a series of wars with neighbouring Denmark and Austria to achieve his aims. By 1871 Berlin stood as the proud capital of the German Reich (empire), a bicameral, constitutional monarchy. On 18 January the Prussian king was crowned Kaiser at Versailles, with Bismarck as his 'Iron Chancellor'.

The early years of the German empire – a period called *Gründerzeit* (foundation years) – were marked by major economic growth, fuelled in part by a steady flow of French reparation payments. Hundreds of thousands of people poured into Berlin in search of work in the factories. Housing shortages were solved by building labyrinthine tenements (*Mietskasernen*, literally 'rental barracks'), where entire families subsisted in tiny and poorly ventilated flats without indoor plumbing.

New political parties gave a voice to the proletariat, foremost the Socialist Workers' Party (SAP), the forerunner of the Sozialdemokratische Partei Deutschlands (SPD; Social Democratic Party of Germany). Founded in 1875, the SAP captured 40% of the Berlin vote only two years later. Bismarck tried to make the party illegal but eventually, under pressure from the growing and increasingly antagonistic socialist movement, he enacted Germany's first modern social reforms, though this was not his true nature. When Wilhelm II (r 1888–1918) came to power, he wanted to extend social reform while Bismarck wanted stricter antisocialist laws. Finally, in March 1890, the Kaiser's scalpel excised his renegade chancellor from the political scene. After that, the legacy of Bismarck's diplomacy unravelled and a wealthy, unified and industrially powerful Germany paddled into the new century.

The green octagonal public pissoirs scattered around Berlin are a legacy of the late 19th century when the municipal sanitation system could not keep up with the exploding population. About two dozen survive, including one on Chamissoplatz in Kreuzberg and another on Senefelderplatz in Prenzlauer Berg.

WWI & REVOLUTION (AGAIN)

The assassination of Archduke Franz Ferdinand, the heir to the Austrian throne, on 28 June 1914 triggered a series of diplomatic decisions that led to WWI, the bloodiest European conflict since the Thirty Years' War. In Berlin and elsewhere, initial euphoria and faith in a quick victory soon gave way to despair as casualties piled up in the battlefield trenches and stomachs grumbled on the home front. When peace came with defeat in 1918, it ushered in a period of turmoil and violence.

On 9 November 1918, Kaiser Wilhelm II abdicated, bringing an inglorious end to the monarchy and 500 years of Hohenzollern rule. Power was transferred to the SPD, the largest party in the Reichstag, and its

1740	1806	1810	1830
Frederick the Great, the philosopher king, turns Berlin into 'Athens on the Spree', a centre of the Enlightenment and an architectural showcase; French is the main language of the ruling elite.	After defeating Prussia, Napoleon leads his troops on a triumphant march through the Brandenburg Gate, marking the start of a two-year occupation of Berlin.	After the Napoleonic occupation ends in 1808, Berlin embarks on a period of reconstruction and reform that includes the creation of its first university by Wilhelm von Humboldt.	The Altes Museum opens as the first of five repositories on Museumsinsel (Museum Island). The last (the Pergamonmuseum) opens exactly 100 years later.

leader, Friedrich Ebert. This would not go unchallenged. Shortly after the Kaiser's exit, prominent SPD member Philipp Scheidemann stepped to a window of the Reichstag to announce the birth of the German Republic. Two hours later, Karl Liebknecht of the Spartakusbund (Spartacist League) proclaimed a socialist republic from a balcony of the royal palace on Unter den Linden. The struggle for power was on.

Founded by Liebknecht and Rosa Luxemburg, the Spartacist League sought to establish a left-wing, Marxist-style government; by year's end it had merged with other radical groups into the German Communist Party. The SPD's goal, meanwhile, was to establish a parliamentary democracy.

Supporters of the SPD and Spartacist League took their rivalry to the streets, culminating in the Spartacist Revolt in early January 1919. On the orders of Ebert, government forces quickly quashed the uprising. Liebknecht and Luxemburg were arrested and murdered en route to prison by Freikorps soldiers (right-leaning war volunteers); their bodies were dumped in the Landwehrkanal.

Discover stat after stat on Berlin at the website of the Office of Statistics in Berlin (www.statistik-berlin-brandenburg.de).

THE WEIMAR REPUBLIC

In July 1919 the federalist constitution of the fledgling republic – Germany's first serious experiment with democracy – was adopted in the town of Weimar, where the constituent assembly had sought refuge from the chaos of Berlin. It gave women the vote and established basic human rights, but it also gave the chancellor the right to rule by decree – a concession that would later prove critical in Hitler's rise to power.

The so-called Weimar Republic (1920–33) was governed by a coalition of left and centre parties, headed by Friedrich Ebert and later Paul von Hindenburg – both of the SPD, which remained Germany's largest party until 1932. The republic, however, pleased neither communists nor monarchists. Trouble erupted as early as March 1920 when right-wing militants led by Wolfgang Kapp forcibly occupied the government quarter in Berlin. The government fled to Dresden, but in Berlin a general strike soon brought the 'Kapp Putsch' to a collapse.

THE GOLDEN TWENTIES

The giant metropolis of Berlin as we know it today was forged in 1920 from the region's many independent towns and villages (Charlottenburg, Schöneberg, Spandau etc), making Berlin one of the world's largest cities, with around 3.8 million inhabitants.

Otherwise, the 1920s began as anything but golden, marked by the humiliation of a lost war, social and political instability, hyperinflation,

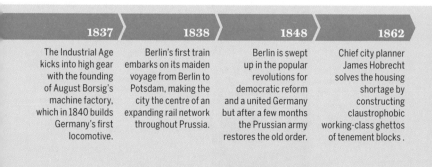

1837	1838	1848	1862
The Industrial Age kicks into high gear with the founding of August Borsig's machine factory, which in 1840 builds Germany's first locomotive.	Berlin's first train embarks on its maiden voyage from Berlin to Potsdam, making the city the centre of an expanding rail network throughout Prussia.	Berlin is swept up in the popular revolutions for democratic reform and a united Germany but after a few months the Prussian army restores the old order.	Chief city planner James Hobrecht solves the housing shortage by constructing claustrophobic working-class ghettos of tenement blocks .

hunger and disease. Around 235,000 Berliners were unemployed, and strikes, demonstrations and riots became nearly everyday occurrences. Economic stability gradually returned after a new currency, the *Rentenmark*, was introduced in 1923 and the Dawes Plan in 1924, which limited the crippling reparation payments imposed on Germany after WWI.

Berliners responded like there was no tomorrow and made their city as much a den of decadence as a cauldron of creativity (not unlike today...). Cabaret, Dada and jazz flourished. Pleasure pits popped up everywhere, turning the city into a 'sextropolis' of Dionysian dimensions. Bursting with energy, it became a laboratory for anything new and modern, drawing giants of architecture (Bruno Taut, Martin Wagner, Hans Scharoun and Walter Gropius), fine arts (George Grosz, Max Beckmann and Lovis Corinth) and literature (Bertolt Brecht, Kurt Tucholsky, WH Auden and Christopher Isherwood).

The fun came to an instant end when the US stock market crashed in 1929, plunging the world into economic depression. Within weeks, half a million Berliners were jobless, and riots and demonstrations again ruled the streets. The volatile, increasingly polarised political climate led to clashes between communists and members of a party that had been patiently waiting in the wings – the Nationalsozialistische Deutsche Arbeiterpartei (NSDAP, National Socialist German Workers' Party, or Nazi Party), led by a failed Austrian artist and WWI corporal named Adolf Hitler. Soon jack boots, brown shirts, oppression and fear would dominate daily life in Germany.

The Siegessäule (Victory Column) in Tiergarten park has had starring roles in Wim Wenders movie *Wings of Desire* and U2's 'Stay' music video. It also inspired Paul van Dyk's 1998 trance hit 'For an Angel' and the name of Berlin's leading gay magazine. In 1998 it served as a backdrop for Barack Obama's speech.

HITLER'S RISE TO POWER

The Weimar government's inability to improve conditions during the Depression spurred the popularity of Hitler's NSDAP, which gained 18% of the national vote in the 1930 elections. In the 1932 presidential election, Hitler challenged Hindenburg and won 37% of the second-round vote. A year later, on 30 January 1933, faced with failed economic reforms and persuasive right-wing advisors, Hindenburg appointed Hitler chancellor. That evening, NSDAP celebrated its rise to power with a torchlit procession through the Brandenburg Gate. Not everyone cheered. Observing the scene from his Pariser Platz home, artist Max Liebermann famously commented: 'I couldn't possibly eat as much as I would like to puke'.

As chancellor, Hitler moved quickly to consolidate absolute power and to turn the nation's democracy into a one-party dictatorship. The Reichstag fire in March 1933 gave him the opportunity to request temporary emergency powers to arrest communists and liberal opponents

1871	1877	1891
Employing an effective strategy of war and diplomacy, Prussian chancellor Otto von Bismarck forges a unified Germany with Prussia at its helm and Berlin as its capital.	Berlin's population reaches the one million mark, which almost doubles again by 1900.	Aviation pioneer and Berlin engineer Otto Lilienthal, known as the 'Glider King', makes the world's first successful flight aboard a glider, staying in the air for 25m. Five years later he dies in an air accident.

FINE ART IMAGES / GETTY IMAGES ©

Portrait of Otto von Bismarck

and push through his proposed Enabling Law, allowing him to decree laws and change the constitution without consulting parliament. When Hindenburg died a year later, Hitler fused the offices of president and chancellor to become Führer of the Third Reich.

NAZI BERLIN

The rise of the Nazis had instant, far-reaching consequences for the entire population. Within three months of Hitler's power grab, all non-Nazi parties, organisations and labour unions ceased to exist. Political opponents, intellectuals and artists were rounded up and detained without trial; many went underground or into exile. There was a

OLYMPICS UNDER THE SWASTIKA

When the International Olympics Committee awarded the 1936 Games to Germany in 1931, the gesture was supposed to welcome the country back into the world community after its defeat in WWI and the tumultuous 1920s. No one could have known that only two years later, the fledgling democracy would be helmed by a dictator with an agenda to take over the world.

As Hitler opened the Games on 1 August in Berlin's Olympic Stadium, prisoners were putting the finishing touches on the first large-scale Nazi concentration camp at Sachsenhausen just north of town. As famous composer Richard Strauss conducted the Olympic hymn during the opening ceremony, fighter squadrons were headed to Spain in support of Franco's dictatorship. Only while the Olympic flame was flickering were political and racial persecution suspended and anti-Semitic signs taken down.

The Olympics were truly a perfect opportunity for the Nazi propaganda machine, which excelled at staging grand public spectacles and rallies, as was so powerfully captured by Leni Riefenstahl in her epic movie *Olympia*. Participants and spectators were impressed by the choreographed pageantry and warm German hospitality. The fact that these were the first Games to be broadcast internationally on radio did not fail to impress either.

From an athletic point of view, the Games were also a big success, with around 4000 participants from 49 countries competing in 129 events and setting numerous records. The biggest star was African-American track-and-fieldster Jesse Owens, who was awarded four gold medals in the 100m, 200m, 4 x 100m relay and the long jump, winning the hearts of the German public and putting paid to Nazi beliefs in the physical superiority of the Aryan race. German Jews, meanwhile, were excluded from participating, with the one token exception being half-Jewish fencer Helene Mayer. She took home a silver medal.

1902	1918	1919	1920
After two decades of debate and eight years of construction, the first segment of the Berlin U-Bahn network is inaugurated, ferrying passengers between Warschauer Strasse and Ernst-Reuter-Platz.	WWI ends on 11 November with Germany's capitulation, following the resignation of Kaiser Wilhelm II and his escape to Holland. The Prussian monarchy is dead.	The Spartacist Revolt led by Liebknecht, Luxemburg and Pieck is violently suppressed and ends with the murder of Liebknecht and Luxemburg by right-wing Freikorps troops.	On 1 October Berlin becomes Germany's largest city after seven independent towns, 59 villages and 27 estates are amalgamated into a single administrative unit. The population reaches 3.8 million.

THE NIGHT OF THE LONG KNIVES

The brown-shirted Sturmabteilung (SA, or Storm Troopers) was a Nazi organisation charged mainly with policing Nazi party meetings and disrupting those convened by political opponents. Although it played an important role in Hitler's ascent to power, by 1934 it had become quite powerful in its own right thanks, in large part, to its leader Ernst Röhm. On 30 June of that year, feeling threatened, Hitler ordered the black-shirted Schutzstaffel (SS) to round up and kill the SA leadership (including Röhm and at least 75 others) to bring the organisation to heel.

Hitler hushed up what came to be known as the 'Night of the Long Knives' until 13 July, when he announced to the Reichstag that, from now on, the SA (which numbered two million, thus easily outnumbering the army) would serve under the command of the army which, in turn, would swear an oath of allegiance to Hitler. Justice would be executed by the SS under the leadership of former chicken farmer Heinrich Himmler, effectively giving the SS unchallenged power and making it Nazi Germany's most powerful – and feared – force.

burgeoning culture of terror and denunciation, and the terrorisation of Jews started to escalate.

Hitler's brown-shirted Nazi state police, the Sturmabteilung (SA), pursued opponents, arresting, torturing and murdering people in improvised concentration camps, such as the one in the Wasserturm in Prenzlauer Berg. North of Berlin, construction began on Sachsenhausen concentration camp. During the so-called Köpenicker Blut woche (Bloody Week) in June 1933, around 90 people were murdered. On 10 May, right-wing students burned 'un-German' books on Bebelplatz, prompting countless intellectuals and artists to rush into exile.

JEWISH PERSECUTION

Jews were a Nazi target from the start. In April 1933 Joseph Goebbels, *Gauleiter* (district leader) of Berlin and head of the well-oiled Ministry of Propaganda, announced a boycott of Jewish businesses. Soon after, Jews were expelled from public service and banned from many professions, trades and industries. The Nuremberg Laws of 1935 deprived 'non-Aryans' of German citizenship and forbade them to marry or have sexual relations with Aryans.

The international community, meanwhile, turned a blind eye to the situation in Germany, perhaps because many leaders were keen to see some order restored to the country after decades of political upheaval. Hitler's

1920s	1921	1923	1929
Berlin evolves into a cultural metropolis, exerting a pull on leading artists, scientists and philosophers of the day, including Einstein, Brecht and Otto Dix.	The world's first highway – called AVUS – opens in the Grunewald after eight years of construction.	The Golden Twenties show their dark side when inflation reaches its peak and a loaf of bread costs 3.5 million marks – an entire wheelbarrow's worth.	The Great Depression hits Berlin, leaving half a million people unemployed. The city parliament elects 13 members of the National Socialist German Workers' Party

success at stabilising the shaky economy – largely by pumping public money into employment programmes, many involving re-armament and heavy industry – was widely admired. The 1936 Olympic summer games in Berlin were a PR triumph, as Hitler launched a charm offensive, but terror and persecution resumed soon after the closing ceremony.

For Jews, the horror escalated on 9 November 1938, with the Reichspogromnacht (often called Kristallnacht, or Night of Broken Glass). Using the assassination of a German consular official by a Polish Jew in Paris as a pretext, Nazi thugs desecrated, burned and demolished synagogues, Jewish cemeteries, property and businesses across the country. Jews had begun to emigrate after 1933, but this event set off a stampede.

The fate of those Jews who stayed behind deteriorated after the outbreak of WWII in 1939. At Hitler's request, a conference in January 1942 in Berlin's Wannsee came up with the Endlösung (Final Solution): the systematic, bureaucratic and meticulously documented annihilation of European Jews, carried out by around 100,000 Germans. Sinti and Roma (gypsies), political opponents, priests, gays and habitual criminals were targeted as well. Of the roughly seven million people who were sent to concentration camps, only 500,000 survived. In Berlin, the Holocaust Memorial is one of many commemorating this grim period in history.

RESISTANCE

Resistance to Hitler was quashed early by the powerful Nazi machinery of terror, but it never vanished entirely, as is thoroughly documented in the excellent exhibit called Topographie des Terrors (Topography of Terror; p86). One of the best known acts of defiance was the 20 July 1944 assassination attempt on the Führer that was led by senior army officer Claus Graf Schenk von Stauffenberg. On that fateful day, Stauffenberg brought a briefcase packed with explosives to a meeting of the high command at the Wolfschanze (Wolf's Lair), Hitler's eastern-front military headquarters. He placed the briefcase under the conference table near Hitler's seat, then excused himself and heard the bomb detonate from a distance. What he didn't know was that Hitler had escaped with minor injuries thanks to the solid oak table which shielded him from the blast.

Stauffenberg and his co-conspirators were quickly identified and shot by firing squad at the army headquarters in the Bendlerblock in Berlin. The rooms where they hatched their plot now house the Gedenkstätte Deutscher Widerstand (p121), an exhibit about the efforts of the German Nazi resistance.

Top Five WWII Sites

Topographie des Terrors

Haus der Wannsee Konferenz

Holocaust Memorial

Sachsenhausen concentration camp

Gedenkstätte Deutscher Widerstand

1933
Hitler is appointed chancellor; the Reichstag burns; construction starts on Sachsenhausen concentration camp; the National Socialist German Workers' Party rules Germany.

1935
Germany's first public TV broadcast is made from Berlin. It is shown three times weekly but most people can only watch it in so-called *Fernsehstuben* (TV parlours).

1936
The 11th modern Olympic Games held in Berlin in August are a PR triumph for Hitler and a showcase of Nazi power; anti-Jewish propaganda is suspended during the period.

Sachsenhausen (p209)

BERNHARD CLASSEN / ALAMY ©

HISTORY RESISTANCE

WWII & THE BATTLE OF BERLIN

World War II began on 1 September 1939 with the Nazi attack on Poland. Although France and Britain declared war on Germany two days later, this could not prevent the quick defeat of Poland, Belgium, the Netherlands and France. Other countries, including Denmark and Norway, were also soon brought into the Nazi fold.

In June 1941 Germany broke its nonaggression pact with Stalin by attacking the USSR. Though successful at first, Operation Barbarossa quickly ran into problems, culminating in the defeat at Stalingrad (today Volgograd) the following winter, forcing the Germans to retreat.

With the Normandy invasion of June 1944, Allied troops arrived in formidable force on the European mainland, supported by unrelenting air raids on Berlin and most other German cities. The final Battle of Berlin began in mid-April 1945. More than 1.5 million Soviet soldiers barrelled towards the capital from the east, reaching Berlin on 21 April and encircling it on 25 April. Two days later they were in the city centre, fighting running street battles with the remaining troops, many of them boys and elderly men. On 30 April the fighting reached the government quarter where Hitler was ensconced in his bunker behind the chancellery, with his long-time mistress Eva Braun, whom he'd married just a day earlier. Finally accepting the inevitability of defeat, Hitler shot himself that afternoon; his wife swallowed a cyanide pill. As their bodies were burned in the chancellery courtyard, Red Army soldiers raised the Soviet flag above the Reichstag.

> Did you know that 9 November is Germany's 'destiny date'? It was the end of the monarchy in 1918, the day of the 1923 Hitler *putsch* in Munich, the Night of Broken Glass in 1938 and the day the Wall fell in 1989.

DEFEAT & AFTERMATH

The Battle of Berlin ended on 2 May with the unconditional surrender by Helmuth Weidling, the commander of the Berlin Defence Area, to General Vasily Chuikov of the Soviet army. Peace was signed at the US military headquarters in Reims (France) and at the Soviet military headquarters in Berlin-Karlshorst, now a German-Soviet history museum (Deutsch-Russisches Museum Berlin-Karlshorst). On 8 May 1945, WWII in Europe officially came to an end.

The fighting had taken an enormous toll on Berlin and its people. Entire neighbourhoods lay in smouldering rubble and at least 125,000 Berliners had lost their lives. With around one million women and children evacuated, only 2.8 million people were left in the city in May 1945 (compared to 4.3 million in 1939), two-thirds of them women. It fell to them to start clearing up the 25 million tonnes of rubble, earning them the name *Trümmerfrauen* (rubble women). In fact, many of Ber-

> One of many fabulous films by Germany's best-known female director, Margarethe von Trotta, *Rosenstrasse* (2003) is a moving portrayal of a 1943 protest by a group of non-Jewish women trying to save their Jewish husbands from deportation.

1938	1942	1944	1945
On 9 November Nazis set fire to nine of Berlin's 12 synagogues, vandalise Jewish businesses and terrorise Jewish citizens during a night of pogroms called 'Kristallnacht'.	At the so-called Wannsee Conference, leading members of the SS decide on the systematic murder of European Jews, cynically called the 'Final Solution.'	On 20 July, senior army officers led by Claus Graf Schenk von Stauffenberg stage an assassination attempt on Hitler. Their failure costs their own and countless other lives.	Soviet troops advance on Berlin in the final days of the war, devastating the city; Hitler commits suicide on 30 April, fighting stops on 2 May and the armistice is signed on 8 May.

lin's modest hills are actually *Trümmerberge* (rubble mountains), piled up from wartime debris and then reborn as parks and recreational areas. The best known are the Teufelsberg in the Grunewald and Mont Klamott in the Volkspark Friedrichshain.

Some small triumphs came quickly: U-Bahn service resumed on 14 May 1945, newspaper printing presses began rolling again on 15 May, and the Berliner Philharmonie gave its first postwar concert on 26 May.

OCCUPATION

At the Yalta Conference in February 1945, Winston Churchill, Franklin D Roosevelt and Joseph Stalin had agreed to carve up Germany and Berlin into four zones of occupation controlled by Britain, the USA, the USSR and France. By July 1945, Stalin, Clement Attlee (who replaced Churchill after a surprise election win) and Roosevelt's successor, Harry S Truman, were at the table in Schloss Cecilienhof in Potsdam to hammer out the details.

Berlin was sliced up into 20 administrative areas. The British sector encompassed Charlottenburg, Tiergarten and Spandau; the French got Wedding and Reinickendorf; and the US was in charge of Zehlendorf, Steglitz, Wilmersdorf, Tempelhof, Kreuzberg and Neukölln. All these districts later formed West Berlin. The Soviets, meanwhile, held on to eight districts in the east, including Mitte, Prenzlauer Berg, Friedrichshain, Treptow and Köpenick, which would later become East Berlin. The Soviets also occupied the land surrounding Berlin, leaving West Berlin completely encircled by territories under Soviet control.

> **Top Five Cold War Sites**
>
> Gedenkstätte Berliner Mauer
> ....
> East Side Gallery
> ....
> Allierten Museum
> ....
> Stasi Prison
> ....
> DDR Museum

THE BIG CHILL

Friction between the Western Allies and the Soviets quickly emerged. For the Western Allies, a main priority was to help Germany get back on its feet by kick-starting the devastated economy. The Soviets, though, insisted on massive reparations and began brutalising and exploiting their own zone of occupation. Tens of thousands of able-bodied men and POWs ended up in labour camps deep in the Soviet Union. In the Allied zones, meanwhile, democracy was beginning to take root as Germany elected state parliaments in 1946–47.

The showdown came in June 1948 when the Allies introduced the Deutschmark in their zones. The USSR regarded this as a breach of the Potsdam Agreement, whereby the powers had agreed to treat Germany as one economic zone. The Soviets issued their own currency,

1948
After the Western Allies introduce the Deutschmark, the Soviets blockade West Berlin; in response the US and Britain launch the Berlin Airlift, ferrying necessities to the isolated city.

1949
Two countries are born – West Germany and East Germany (known as the German Democratic Republic or GDR); Berlin remains under Allied supervision.

AFP/GETTY IMAGES ©

Exhibits, Gedenkstätte Deutscher Widerstand (p121)

the Ostmark, and promptly announced a full-scale economic blockade of West Berlin. The Allies responded with the remarkable Berlin Airlift.

THE TWO GERMAN STATES

In 1949 the division of Germany – and Berlin – was formalised. The western zones evolved into the Bundesrepublik Deutschland (BRD, Federal Republic of Germany or FRG) with Konrad Adenauer as its first chancellor and Bonn, on the Rhine River, as its capital. An economic aid package dubbed the Marshall Plan created the basis for West Germany's *Wirtschaftswunder* (economic miracle), which saw the economy grow at an average 8% per year between 1951 and 1961. The recovery was largely engineered by economics minister Ludwig Erhard, who dealt with an acute labour shortage by inviting about 2.3 million foreign workers, mainly from Turkey, Yugoslavia and Italy, to Germany, thereby laying the foundation for today's multicultural society.

The Soviet zone, meanwhile, grew into the Deutsche Demokratische Republik (German Democratic Republic or GDR), making East Berlin

THE BERLIN AIRLIFT

The Berlin Airlift was a triumph of determination and a glorious chapter in Berlin's post-WWII history. On 24 June 1948, the Soviets cut off all rail and road traffic into the city to force the Western Allies to give up their sectors and bring the entire city under their control.

Faced with such provocation, many in the Allied camp urged responses that would have been the opening barrages of WWIII. In the end wiser heads prevailed, and a mere day after the blockade began the US Air Force launched 'Operation Vittles'. The British followed suit on 28 June with 'Operation Plane Fare'.

For the next 11 months Allied planes flew in food, coal, machinery and other supplies to now-closed Tempelhof airport in the western city, 24/7. By the time the Soviets backed down, they had made 278,000 flights, logged a distance equivalent to 250 round trips to the moon and delivered 2.5 million tonnes of cargo. The Luftbrückendenkmal (Berlin Airlift Memorial; p151) outside the airport honours the effort and those who died carrying it out.

It was a monumental achievement that profoundly changed the relationship between Germany and the Western Allies, who were no longer regarded merely as occupational forces but as *Schutzmächte* (protective powers).

1950	1950s	1953	1961
GDR leaders raze the remains of the Prussian city palace for ideological reasons, despite worldwide protest.	Hundreds of thousand of East Germans move to West Berlin and western Germany, depleting the GDR's brain and brawn power.	The uprising of construction workers on the Stalinallee (today's Karl-Marx-Allee) spreads across the entire GDR before being crushed by Soviet tanks, leaving several hundred dead and over 1000 injured.	Tragedy strikes just 11 days after the first stone of the Berlin Wall is laid. On 24 August Günter Litfin is gunned down by border guards while attempting to swim across Humboldt Harbour.

its capital and Wilhelm Pieck its president. From the outset, though, the Sozialistische Einheitspartei Deutschlands (SED, Socialist Unity Party of Germany), led by party boss Walter Ulbricht, dominated economic, judicial and security policy. In order to counter any opposition, the Ministry for State Security, or Stasi, was established in 1950 and based its headquarters in Lichtenberg. Regime opponents were incarcerated at the supersecret Gedenkstätte Hohenschönhausen (Stasi Prison) nearby.

Economically, East Germany stagnated, in large part because of the Soviets' continued policy of asset stripping and reparation payments. Stalin's death in 1953 raised hopes for reform but only spurred the GDR government to raise production goals even higher. Smouldering discontent erupted in violence on 17 June 1953 when 10% of GDR workers took to the streets. Soviet troops quashed the uprising, with scores of deaths and the arrest of about 1200 people.

THE WALL: WHAT GOES UP...

Through the 1950s the economic gulf between the two Germanys widened, prompting hundreds of thousands of East Berliners to seek a future in the west. Eventually, the exodus of mostly young and well-educated East Germans strained the troubled GDR economy so much that – with Soviet consent – its government built a wall to keep them in. Construction of the Berlin Wall, the Cold War's most potent symbol, began on the night of 13 August 1961.

This stealthy act left Berliners stunned. Formal protests from the Western Allies, as well as massive demonstrations in West Berlin, were ignored. Tense times followed. In October 1961 US and Soviet tanks faced off at Checkpoint Charlie, pushing the world to the brink of WWIII. In 1963 US president John F Kennedy made a visit to West Berlin, praising locals for their pro-freedom stance in his famous 'Ich bin ein Berliner' speech at the Rathaus Schöneberg.

The appointment of Erich Honecker (1912–94) in 1971 opened the way for rapprochement with the West and enhanced international acceptance of the GDR. In September that year the Western Allies and the Soviet Union signed a new Four Power Accord in the *Kammergericht* (courthouse) in Schöneberg. It guaranteed access to West Berlin from West Germany and eased travel restrictions between East and West Berlin. The accord paved the way for the Basic Treaty, signed a year later, in which the two countries recognised each other's sovereignty and borders and committed to setting up 'permanent missions' in Bonn and East Berlin, respectively.

To alleviate acute housing shortages, three new satellite cities – Marzahn, Hohenschönhausen and Hellersdorf – consisting of massive prefab housing blocks for 300,000 were built in the 1970s and '80s on East Berlin's outskirts. Equipped with mod cons like central heating and indoor plumbing, these apartments were much coveted.

More Great Quotes...

'Berlin is poor but sexy' – Wowereit, 2004

'We want Berlin to become rich and stay sexy' – Wowereit, 2011

1963	1964	1967	1971
US president John F Kennedy professes his solidarity with the people of Berlin when giving his famous 'Ich bin ein Berliner' speech at the town hall in West Berlin's Schöneberg on 26 June.	A master plan begins to turn Alexanderplatz, East Berlin's central square, into a socialist architectural showcase. Its crowning glory, the TV Tower, opens in 1969.	The death of Benno Ohnesorg, an unarmed student who is shot by a policeman while demonstrating against the visit to West Berlin of the Shah of Persia, draws attention to the student movement.	The four Allies sign the Four Power Accord, which confirms Berlin's independent status. East and West Germany recognise each other's sovereignty in the Basic Treaty.

JEWISH BERLIN: MENDELSSOHN TO LIBESKIND

Since reunification, Berlin has had the fastest-growing Jewish community in the world. Their background is diverse; most are Russian Jewish immigrants but there are also Jews of German heritage, Israelis wishing to escape their war-torn homeland and American expats lured by Berlin's low-cost living and limitless creativity. Today there are about 13,000 active members of the Jewish community, including 1000 belonging to the Orthodox congregation Adass Yisroel. However, since not all Jews choose to be affiliated with a synagogue, the actual population is estimated to be at least twice as high.

The community supports 10 synagogues, two *mikve* ritual baths, several schools, numerous cultural institutions and a handful of kosher restaurants and shops. The golden-domed Neue Synagoge (New Synagogue) on Oranienburger Strasse is the most visible beacon of Jewish revival, even though today it's not primarily a house of worship but a community and exhibition space. In Kreuzberg, the Jüdisches Museum (Jewish Museum; p148), a spectacular structure by Daniel Libeskind, tracks the ups and downs of Jewish life in Germany for almost 2000 years. Other key Jewish sites include the Alter Jüdischer Friedhof, Berlin's

...MUST COME DOWN

Hearts and minds in Eastern Europe had long been restless for change, but German reunification came as a surprise to the world and ushered in a new and exciting era. The so-called *Wende* (turning point, ie the fall of communism) came about as a gradual development that ended in a big bang – the collapse of the Berlin Wall on 9 November 1989 (see p40).

The Germany of today, with 16 unified states, was hammered out after a volatile political debate and a series of treaties to end post-WWII occupation zones. The newly united city of Berlin became a separate city-state. Economic union took force in mid-1990, and in August 1990 the Unification Treaty was signed in the Kronprinzenpalais on Unter den Linden. A common currency came into being in July 1990. Also in July, Pink Floyd replayed the original music of their 1980s album *The Wall* to a crowd of 200,000 (and a TV audience of millions worldwide) on Potsdamer Platz.

In September 1990, representatives of East and West Germany, the USSR, France, the UK and the US met in Moscow to sign the Two-Plus-Four Treaty, ending postwar occupation zones and paving the way for formal German reunification. One month later, the East German state was dissolved; in December Germany held its first unified post-WWII elections.

1976 〉	1987 〉		1989 〉
The Palace of the Republic, which houses the GDR parliament and an entertainment centre, opens on 23 April on the site where the royal Hohenzollern palace had been demolished in 1950.	East and West Berlin celebrate the city's 750th birthday separately. On 12 June Ronald Reagan stands before the Brandenburg Gate to say 'Mr Gorbachev, tear down this Wall!'.		On 9 October, East Germany celebrates the 40th anniversary of its founding as demonstrations in favour of reforms reverberate through East Berlin.

MARK DAFFEY / GETTY IMAGES ©

Flag, near Reichstag (p76)

oldest Jewish cemetery and final resting home of Enlightenment philosopher Moses Mendelssohn, who arrived in Berlin in 1743. His progressive thinking and lobbying paved the way for the Emancipation Edict of 1812, which made Jews full citizens of Prussia, with equal rights and duties.

By the end of the 19th century, many of Berlin's Jews, numbering about 5% of the population, had become thoroughly German in speech and identity. When a wave of Hasidic Jews escaping the pogroms of Eastern Europe arrived around the same time, they found their way to today's Scheunenviertel, which at that time was an immigrant slum with cheap housing. By 1933 Berlin's Jewish population had grown to around 160,000 and constituted one third of all Jews living in Germany. The well-known horrors of the Nazi years sent most into exile and left 55,000 dead. Only about 1000 to 2000 Jews are believed to have survived the war years in Berlin, often with the help of their non-Jewish neighbours. Many memorials throughout the city commemorate the Nazi victims. The most prominent is, of course, the Holocaust Memorial (p79) near the Brandenburg Gate.

In 1991 a small majority (338 to 320) of members in the Bundestag (German parliament) voted in favour of moving the government to Berlin and of making Berlin the German capital once again. On 8 September 1994 the last Allied troops stationed in Berlin left the city after a festive ceremony.

THE POSTUNIFICATION YEARS

With reunification, Berlin once again became the German capital in 1991 and the seat of government in 1999. Mega-sized construction projects such as Potsdamer Platz and the government quarter eradicated the physical scars of division but did little to improve the city's balance sheet or unemployment statistics. It didn't help that Berlin lost the hefty federal subsidies it had received during the years of division. More than 250,000 manufacturing jobs were lost between 1991 and 2006, most of them through closures of unprofitable factories in East Berlin. Add to that the mismanagement, corruption and excessive spending under the city government led by governing mayor Eberhard Diepgen and it's no surprise that the city ran up a whopping debt of €60 million.

Australian journalist Anna Funder documents the Stasi, East Germany's vast domestic spy apparatus, by letting both victims and perpetrators tell their stories in her 2004 book *Stasiland*.

1989	1991	1994	1999
On 4 November, half a million Berliners demand freedom of speech, press and assembly. The Berlin Wall opens on 9 November without a single bullet being fired.	Members of the Bundestag (German parliament) vote to reinstate Berlin as Germany's capital and to move the federal government here. Berliners elect the first joint city government.	The last British, French, Russian and American troops withdraw from Berlin, thereby ending nearly half a century of occupation and protection.	The German parliament holds its first session in the historic Reichstag building, after the building's complete restoration by Lord Norman Foster.

Elected in 2001, the new government mayor Klaus Wowereit responded by making across-the-board spending cuts, but with a tax base eroded by high unemployment and ever-growing welfare payments, they did little initially to get Berlin out of the poorhouse. Eventually, though, the economic restructure away from a manufacturing base and towards the service sector began to bear fruit. Job creation here has outpaced that of Germany in general for almost 10 years. No German city has a greater number of business start-ups. Its export quota has risen steadily, as has its population. The health, transport and green technology industries are growing in leaps and bounds.

On the cultural front, Berlin exploded into a hive of cultural cool with unbridled nightlife, a dynamic art scene and booming fashion and design industries. In 2006 it became part of Unesco's Creative Cities Network. Some 170,000 people are employed in the cultural sector, which generates an annual turnover of some €13 billion. An especially important subsector is music, with nearly 10% of all related companies, including Universal and MTV, moving to Berlin over the past 20 years.

2001	2006	2007	2011
Openly gay politician Klaus Wowereit is elected governing mayor of Berlin.	Berlin's first central train station, the Hauptbahnhof, opens. Germany kicks off the 2006 FIFA World Cup. In the final match on 9 July, Italy defeats France in a penalty shoot-out.	Polar bear Knut is raised by a zookeeper at the Berlin Zoo after being rejected by his mum and becomes an international media star. He dies suddenly in 2011 by drowning.	Berlin's population passes the 3.5 million mark, growing 1.2%, the most within a single year since reunification in 1990. Most of the growth comes from people moving to Berlin.

Arts

The arts are fundamental to everything Berlin holds dear, and the sheer scope of creative activity in the city is astounding. Half the reason Berliners are always so busy is because of the efforts required to keep up with the ever-changing cultural kaleidoscope of trends and events. And with a history of international excellence in most fields, expectations and standards are always set high. The city itself provides an iconic setting for any number of books, films, paintings and songs, its unmistakable presence influencing artists and residents just as it does those canny visitors who take the time to dive in.

PAINTING & SCULPTURE

Early Beginnings

Fine art only began to flourish in Berlin in the late 17th century, when self-crowned King Friedrich I founded the Akademie der Künste (Academy of Arts) in 1696, egged on by court sculptor Andreas Schlüter. Schlüter repaid the favour with outstanding sculptures, including the *Great Elector on Horseback*, now in front of Schloss Charlottenburg, and the haunting masks of dying warriors in the courtyard of today's Deutsches Historiches Museum (German Historical Museum). Artistic accents in painting were set by Frenchman Antoine Pesne, who became Friedrich I's court painter in 1710. His main legacy is his elaborate portraits of the royal family members.

The arts also reached a heyday under Friedrich I's grandson, Friedrich II (Frederick the Great), who became king in 1740. Friedrich drew heavily on the artistic expertise of his friend Georg Wenzeslaus von Knobelsdorff, a student of Pesne, and also amassed a sizeable collection of works by such French artists as Jean Antoine Watteau.

The 19th Century

Neoclassicism emerged as a dominant sculptural style in the 19th century. Johann Gottfried Schadow's *Quadriga* – the horse-drawn chariot atop the Brandenburg Gate – epitomises the period. Schadow's student Christian Daniel Rauch had a special knack for representing idealised, classical beauty in a realistic fashion. His most famous work is the 1851 monument of Frederick the Great on horseback on Unter den Linden. For a thorough survey of 19th-century sculpture, visit the Friedrichswerdersche Kirche (p83).

In painting, heart-on-your-sleeve Romanticism that drew heavily on emotion and a dreamy idealism dominated the 19th century. Top dog of the era was Caspar David Friedrich, best known for his moody, allegorical landscapes. Although more famous as an architect, Karl Friedrich Schinkel also created some fanciful canvases. Eduard Gärtner's paintings documenting Berlin's evolving cityscape found special appeal among the middle classes. The Alte Nationalgalerie (Old National Gallery; p102) on Museumsinsel (Museum Island) and the Neuer Pavillon (New Pavilion; p193) of Schloss Charlottenburg are both showcases of 19th-century art.

GALLERY WEEKEND

Art-world honchos descend upon Berlin in late April for the annual Gallery Weekend when you can hop-scotch around 40 galleries, and the Berlin Biennale, a curated forum for contemporary art held over two months in spring every other year.

Berliner Secession

The Berliner Secession was formed in 1898 by a group of progressive-minded artists who rejected the traditional teachings of the arts academies that stifled any new forms of expression. The schism was triggered in 1891, when the established Verein Berliner Künstler refused to show paintings by Edvard Munch at its annual salon, and reached its apex in 1898 when the salon jury rejected a landscape painting by Walter Leistikow. Consequently, 65 artists banded together under leadership of Leistikow and Max Liebermann and seceded from the Verein. Other famous Berlin Secession members included Lovis Corinth, Max Slevogt, Ernst Ludwig Kirchner, Max Beckmann and Käthe Kollwitz.

Expressionism

In 1905 Kirchner, along with Erich Heckel and Karl Schmidt-Rottluff, founded the artist group Die Brücke (The Bridge) in Dresden that turned the art world on its head with ground-breaking visions that paved the way for German expressionism. Shapes and figures that teeter on the abstract – without ever quite getting there – drenched with bright colours, characterise the aesthetic of Die Brücke. It moved to Berlin in 1911 and disbanded in 1913. The small Brücke Museum (p213) in the Grunewald has a fantastic collection of these influential canvases.

Ironically, it was the expressionists that splintered off from the Berlin Secession in 1910 after their work had been rejected by the Secession jury. With Max Pechstein at the helm, they formed the Neue Secession. The original group continued but saw its influence waning, especially after the Nazi power grab in 1933.

The Bauhaus

The year 1919 saw the founding of the Bauhaus movement and school in Weimar. It was was based on practical anti-elitist principles bringing form and function together, and had a profound effect on all modern design – visit the Bauhaus Archiv (p122) for ample examples. Although the school moved to Dessau in 1925 and only to Berlin in 1932, many of its most influential figures worked in Berlin. It was forced by the Nazis to close down in 1933.

After the Nazi takeover many artists left the country and others ended up in prison or concentration camps, their works confiscated or destroyed. The art promoted instead was often terrible, favouring

ZILLE SEASON

Born in Dresden in 1858, Heinrich Zille moved to Berlin with his family when he was a child. A lithographer by trade, he became the first prominent artist to evoke the social development of the city as the tendrils of modernity reached Berlin. His instantly recognisable style depicted everyday life and real people, often featuring the bleak *Hinterhöfe* (back courtyards) around which so much of their lives revolved. Even during his lifetime Zille was acknowledged as one of the definitive documenters of his time, and since his death in 1929 his prolific photographic work has also come to be seen as a valuable historical record.

In 1903 Zille was accepted into the Berlin Secession, although he didn't really regard himself as an 'artist' as such, but more as a hard-working illustrator. When he died, thousands of Berliners turned out to pay their respects to the man whose pictures chronicled their daily lives with sharp humour and unsentimental honesty. There's a Zille Museum (p105) in the Nikolaiviertel dedicated to his life and work.

straightforward 'Aryan' forms and epic styles. Propaganda artist Mjöl-nir defined the typical look of the time with block Gothic scripts and idealised figures.

Berlin Dada

Dada was an avant-garde art movement formed in Zurich in 1916 in reaction to the horrors of WWI. It spread to Berlin in 1918 with the help of Richard Huelsenbeck, who held the first Dada event in a gallery in February that year and later produced the First German Dada Manifesto. Founding members included George Grosz, photomontage inventor John Heartfield and Hannah Höch, but Marcel Duchamp, Kurt Schwitters and Hans Arp were also among the many others who dabbled in Dada.

Uncompromisingly turning away from convention, Dada took an irrational, satirical and often absurdist approach that found expression not only in the visual arts but also in theatre, dance and literature. Dadaists embraced collage and montage and considered chance and spontaneity integral parts of the artistic process. In Berlin especially, there was often a political undercurrent and a tendency to shock and provoke. The First International Dada Fair in 1920, for instance, took place beneath a suspended German officer dummy with a pig's head.

Post WWII

After WWII, Berlin's art scene was as fragmented as the city itself. In the east, artists were forced to toe the 'socialist-realist' line, at least until the late 1960s when artists of the so-called Berliner Schule, including Manfred Böttcher and Harald Metzkes, sought to embrace a more interpretative and emotional form of expression inspired by the colours and aesthetic of Beckmann, Matisse, Picasso and other classical modernists. In the '70s, when conflicts of the individual in society became a prominent theme, underground galleries flourished in Prenzlauer Berg and art became a collective endeavour.

In postwar West Berlin, artists eagerly embraced abstract art. Pioneers included Zone 5, which revolved around Hans Thiemann, and surrealists Heinz Trökes and Mac Zimmermann. In the 1960s politics was a primary concern and a new style called 'critical realism' emerged, propagated by artists like Ulrich Baehr, Hans-Jürgen Diehl and Wolfgang Petrick. The 1973 movement Schule der Neuen Prächtigkeit (School of New Magnificence) had a similar approach. In the late 1970s and early 1980s, expressionism found its way back onto the canvasses of Salomé, Helmut Middendorf and Rainer Fetting, a group known as the Junge Wilde (Young Wild Ones). One of the best-known German neo-expressionist painters is Georg Baselitz, who lives in Berlin and who became internationally famous in the 1970s with his 'upside-down' works.

The Present

Art aficionados will find their compass on perpetual spin in Berlin, which has developed one of the most exciting and dynamic arts scenes in Europe. With an active community of some 10,000, there have been some notable successes, most famously perhaps Danish-Icelandic artist Olafur Eliasson. Other major leaguers like Thomas Demand, Jonathan Meese, Via Lewandowsky, Isa Genzken, Tino Seghal, Esra Ersen, John Bock and the artist duo Ingar Dragset and Michael Elmgreen all live and work in Berlin, or at least have a second residence here. To keep a tab on the scene, check out the latest shows at the city's many high-calibre galleries like **Galerie Eigen+Art** (Map p320; 280 6605; www.eigen-art.com; Auguststrasse 26; 11am-6pm Tue-Sat; Oranienburger Strasse)

ARTS PAINTING & SCULPTURE

Some of Gerhart Hauptmann's plays were so provocative that several of his premieres ended in riots. An 1892 production of his *Die Weber* (The Weavers), depicting the misery of Silesian weavers, even prompted the Kaiser to cancel his subscription at the Deutsches Theater.

If you want to plug into the city's jazz scene, check out www.jazzinitiative berlin.de and www.jazz-guide -berlin.de.

or **Contemporary Fine Arts** (Map p314; ☑288 7870; www.cfa-berlin.com; Am Kupfergraben 10; ⊙10am-1pm & 2-6pm Tue-Fri, 11am-4pm Sat; ⊠Friedrichstrasse) and visit the collections at Hamburger Bahnhof (p129) and the Sammlung Boros (p134).

LITERATURE

For an insightful introduction to Berlin, get a hold of *City-Lit Berlin* (2009), an anthology of excerpts from writings about the city from a diverse bunch of authors, Fontane to Bowie to blogger Simon Cole.

Since its beginnings, Berlin's literary scene has reflected a peculiar blend of provincialism and worldliness. As with the other arts, Berlin didn't emerge as a centre of literature until relatively late, reaching its zenith during the dynamic 1920s. Overall, the city was less a place that generated influential writers than one where they came to meet each other, exchange ideas and be intellectually stimulated.

First Words

Berlin's literary history began during the Enlightenment in the late 18th century, an epoch dominated by humanistic ideals. A major author was Gotthold Ephraim Lessing, noted for his critical works, fables and tragedies, who wrote the play *Minna von Barnhelm* (1763) in Berlin.

Literary greats working in Berlin during the Romantic period, an outgrowth of the Enlightenment, included Friedrich and August Wilhelm von Schlegel, and the Romantic poets Achim von Arnim, Clemens Brentano and Heinrich von Kleist.

In the mid-19th century, realist novels and novellas captured the imagination of the newly emerging middle class. It was Theodor Fontane who raised the Berlin society novel to an art form by showing both the aristocracy and the middle class mired in their societal confinements. His 1894 novel *Effi Briest* is perhaps his best-known work.

Naturalism, a spin-off of realism, took things even further by painstakingly recreating the milieu of entire social classes. In Berlin, the genre's most high-profile exponent was Gerhard Hauptmann, whose plays and novels focused on social injustice and the harsh life of the working class. In 1912 he won the Nobel Prize for Literature.

THRILL CITY: CRIME & SPY NOVELS SET IN BERLIN

Berlin has often served as inspiration in the setting of crime and spy novels written by outsiders. The city's bullet-scarred history, divided loyalties and political intrigues make for some clever twists and turns. Here are some of the best:

➡ **Berlin Game, Mexico Set, London Match** (Len Deighton; 1983, 1984, 1985) There are more unexpected twists and turns than on a roller-coaster ride in this classic spy trilogy set in '80s Berlin.

➡ **Berlin Noir Trilogy** (Phillip Kerr; 1994) Kerr's compelling depictions of Berlin in the murky days before, during and after WWII follow private investigator Bernie Gunther through the city's seamy side.

➡ **Pavel & I** (Dan Vyleta; 2008) Beautifully written, this novel explores the friendship between a US soldier and a German orphan in the aftermath of WWII, during the bitterly cold winter of 1946–47.

➡ **Rift Zone** (Raelynn Hillhouse; 2004) A female smuggler operating between the East and the West in 1989 becomes a pawn in a KGB agent's game.

➡ **The Spy Who Came in from the Cold** (John le Carré; 1963) Graham Greene called the tale of British spook Alex Leamas in early Cold War Berlin the finest spy story ever written.

ARTS MUSIC

Modernism & Modernity

In the 1920s Berlin became a literary hotbed, drawing writers such as Alfred Döblin, whose definitive *Berlin Alexanderplatz* is a stylised meander through the seamy 1920s, and Anglo-American import Christopher Isherwood whose brilliant semi-autobiographical *Berlin Stories* formed the basis of the musical and film *Cabaret*. Other notables include the political satirists Kurt Tucholsky and Erich Kästner. Many artists left Germany after the Nazis came to power, and those who stayed often went into 'inner emigration', keeping their mouths shut and working underground, if at all.

In West Berlin, the postwar literary revival was led by Günter Grass's *Die Blechtrommel* (The Tin Drum; 1958), which traces recent German history through the eyes of a child who refuses to grow and quickly made Grass a household name. In 1999 he became the ninth German to win the Nobel Prize for Literature.

In the mid-1970s a segment of the East Berlin literary scene began to detach itself slowly from the socialist party grip. Authors such as Christa Wolf and Heiner Müller belonged to loose literary circles that regularly met in private houses. Wolf is one of the best and most controversial East German writers, while Müller had the distinction of being unpalatable in both Germanys. His dense, difficult works include *Der Lohndrücker* (The Man Who Kept Down Wages) and the *Germania* trilogy of plays.

Post-1990

After reunification, literary achievement stagnated at first as writers from the East and West began a process of self-examination, but picked up steam in the late 1990s. Thomas Brussig's tongue-in-cheek *Helden wie Wir* (Heroes Like Us; 1998) was one of the first postreunification novels and offers a look look at East German society. In *Zonenkinder* (2002), Jana Hensel, who was 13 when the Wall fell, reflects upon the loss of identity and the challenge of adapting to a new society.

Sven Regener, the frontman of the Berlin band Element of Crime, penned the hugely successful *Herr Lehmann* (2001; *Berlin Blues*), a boozy trawl through Kreuzberg nights at the time of the fall of the Wall. The runaway success story, however, has been Russian-born author Wladimir Kaminer, whose amusing, stranger-than-fiction vignettes *Russendisko* (Russian Disco; 2000) established both the author and his Russian disco parties firmly on the Berlin scenescape. Both were made into feature films.

> Aside from the headline-grabbing Berlinale, there are dozens of other film festivals held throughout the year, including Achtung Berlin and the Porn Film Festival. See http://berliner-filmfestivals.de for the schedule.

MUSIC

For centuries, Berlin was largely eclipsed by Vienna, Leipzig and other European cities when it came to music. In 1882, however, the Berliner Philharmoniker was established, gaining international stature under Hans von Bülow and Arthur Nikisch. In 1923 Wilhelm Furtwängler became artistic director, a post he held (with interruptions during and shortly after the Nazi years) until 1954.

The pulsating 1920s also drew numerous musicians to Berlin, including Arnold Schönberg and Paul Hindemith, who taught at the Akademie der Künste and the Berliner Hochschule, respectively. Schönberg's atonal compositions found a following here, as did his experimentation with noise and sound effects. Hindemith explored the new medium of radio and taught a seminar on film music.

After WWII, it was the legendary Herbert von Karajan who helped gain the Philharmoniker world fame. In East Germany, a key figure was Hanns Eisler, who composed the national anthem of the German Democratic Republic (GDR) and taught at the state conservatory in East Berlin.

For an overview of popular music in the 1920s, see p274. Details about the last 50 years of music in Berlin are in the Music: Punk to Techno chapter on p280.

FILM

Before 1945

Berlin's pioneering role in movie history is undeniable. America had Edison, France the Lumière brothers, and Berlin had Max Skladanowsky, a former fairground showman whose 1895 'bioscope' – a prototype film projector – paved the way for the first era of film-making in Germany. By 1910, Berlin had 139 Kinematographentheater (which gives us the German word for cinema, Kino) showing mostly slapstick, melodramas and short documentaries. One of the world's oldest film studios, the legendary UFA (Universum Film AG), was founded in nearby Potsdam in 1912.

The 1920s and early '30s were a boom time for Berlin cinema, with Marlene Dietrich's bone structure and distinctive voice seducing the world, and the mighty UFA Studios producing virtually all of Germany's celluloid output. Dominant directors were Georg Wilhelm Pabst, whose use of montage and characterisation defined the Neue Sachlichkeit (New Objectivity) movement, and Fritz Lang, whose seminal works *Metropolis* (1926) and *M* (1931) brought him international fame. After 1933, however, film-makers found their artistic freedom, not to mention funding, increasingly curtailed; by 1939 practically the entire industry had fled abroad.

DOCUMENTING EVIL

'I filmed the truth as it was then. Nothing more.'
Leni Riefenstahl

Films made during the Nazi period bring their own historical dilemma, none more so than the works of brilliant if controversial Berlin-born director Leni Riefenstahl (1902–2003). Her most famous film, *Triumph of the Will*, documents the 1934 Nuremberg Nazi party rally. *Olympia*, which chronicles the 1936 Berlin Olympic Games, was another seminal work.

While breakthroughs in aesthetics and filming techniques brought her lasting fame, it was her close association with Adolf Hitler that would forever haunt her after the war. Riefenstahl maintained that she had held no fascist sympathies, protesting both her right as a film-maker to record such events and her lack of choice in the matter under the Nazis.

After WWII, Riefenstahl focused on photography, producing several books about the Sudanese people, which went some way towards refuting accusations of racism. In 1992 she published her autobiography and subsequently found herself the subject of a number of documentaries, including *The Wonderful Horrible Life of Leni Riefenstahl* (2003). She made only one more film, the nature documentary *Impressionen unter Wasser* (Impressions under Water; 2002).

When she died in 2003, aged 101, she left no real answers in the debate over art and complicity.

After 1945

Like most of the arts, film-making has generally been well funded in Berlin since 1945. During the 1970s in particular, large subsidies lured directors back to the city, including such Neuer Deutscher Film (New German Film) luminaries as Rainer Werner Fassbinder, Volker Schlöndorf, Wim Wenders and Werner Herzog. It was Wenders who made one of the seminal Berlin films, the highly acclaimed *Der Himmel über Berlin* (Wings of Desire; 1987).

As befits a city with such a chequered past, history has always been a popular topic with Berlin film-makers. Some of the best films about the Nazi era include Wolfgang Staudte's *Die Mörder sind unter uns* (Murderers Among Us; 1946); Fassbinder's *Die Ehe der Maria Braun* (The Marriage of Maria Braun; 1979); Margarethe von Trotta's *Rosenstrasse* (2003), and Oliver Hierschbiegel's extraordinary *Der Untergang* (The Downfall; 2004) about Hitler's final days.

The first round of postreunification feature films about life in East Germany were light-hearted comedy dramas, including the smash hit *Good Bye, Lenin!* (2003), Wolfgang Becker's witty and heart-warming tale of a son trying to re-create the minutiae of GDR life to reassure his sick mother. It was Florian von Donnersmarck who trained the spotlight on the darker side of the GDR with his Academy Award–winning film *Das Leben der Anderen* (The Lives of Others; 2006).

GoArt (p35) demystifies Berlin's complex art scene on customised tours that visit private collections, artist studios, edgy galleries and street-art locations.

ARTS FILM

Architecture

From the majestic dome atop the Reichstag to the cloud-piercing Fernsehturm (TV Tower), the jagged angles of the Jüdisches Museum (Jewish Museum) to the baroque splendour of Schloss Charlottenburg and the warped dynamism of the Berliner Philharmonie – Berlin boasts some of the world's finest architecture. It's an eclectic mix, to be sure, shaped by the city's unique history, especially the destruction of WWII and the contrasting urban-planning visions during the years of division. Since reunification, though, Berlin has become a virtual laboratory for the world's elite architects, David Chipperfield, Lord Norman Foster and Daniel Libeskind among them.

MODEST BEGINNINGS

Very few buildings from the Middle Ages until the 1700s have survived time, war and modernist town planning. Only two Gothic churches – the red-brick Nikolaikirche (1230) and Marienkirche (1294) – bear silent witness to the days when today's metropolis was just a small trading town. The former anchors the Nikolaiviertel, a mock-medieval quarter built on the site of the city's original settlement as East Germany's contribution to Berlin's 750th anniversary celebrations in 1987. It's a hodgepodge of

Interior of Nikolaikirche (p104)

SYLVAIN SONNET / CORBIS ©

Berliner Dom (p106)

genuine historic buildings like the Knoblochhaus and replicas of historic buildings such as the Gaststätte Zum Nussbaum.

A hint of residential medieval architecture also survives in the outer district of Spandau, both in the Gotisches Haus and the half-timbered houses of the Kolk quarter.

Traces of the Renaissance, which reached Berlin in the early 16th century, are rarer still, but notable survivors include the Jagdschloss Grunewald and the Zitadelle Spandau.

GOING FOR BAROQUE

As Berlin grew, so did the representational needs of its rulers, especially in the 17th and 18th centuries. In Berlin, this role fell to Great Elector Friedrich Wilhelm, who systematically expanded the city by adding three residential quarters, a fortified town wall and a tree-lined boulevard known as Unter den Linden.

This was the age of baroque, a style merging architecture, sculpture, ornamentation and painting into a single *Gesamtkunstwerk* (complete work of art). In Berlin and northern Germany it retained a formal and precise bent, never quite reaching the exuberance favoured in regions further south.

The Great Elector may have laid the groundwork, but it was only under his son, Elector Friedrich III, that Berlin acquired the stature of an exalted residence, especially after he was promoted to *King* Friedrich I in 1701. Two major baroque buildings survive from his reign, both blueprinted by Johann Arnold Nering: Schloss Charlottenburg, which Johann Friedrich Eosander later expanded into a Versailles-inspired three-wing palace topped by a domed central tower; and the Zeughaus (armoury, today's Deutsches Historisches Museum) on Unter den Linden. The museum's courtyard, graced

Top Five Prussian Palaces

Schloss Sanssouci, Potsdam

Schloss Charlottenburg

Neues Palais, Potsdam

Schlösschen auf der Pfaueninsel

Jagdschloss Grunewald

with Andreas Schlüter's celebrated masks of dying warriors, was lidded by a glass roof during renovations that started in the late 1990s. The modern annex, named the IM Pei Bau (IM Pei Building) after its architect, was also added during this time. Fronted by a transparent, spiral staircase shaped like a snail shell, it's a harmonious interplay of glass, natural stone and light and an excellent example of Pei's muted postmodernist approach.

Meanwhile, back in the early 18th century, two formidable churches were taking shape on Gendarmenmarkt in the heart of the immigrant Huguenot community. These were the Deutscher Dom (German Cathedral) by Martin Grünberg, and the Französischer Dom (French Cathedral) by Louis Cayart; the latter was modelled on the Huguenots' destroyed mother church in Charenton, France.

Built as a summer palace for King Friedrich I's wife Sophie-Charlotte, Schloss Charlottenburg was originally called Schloss Lietzenburg but renamed after the popular queen's sudden death in 1705.

No king had a greater impact on Berlin's physical layout than Frederick the Great. Together with his childhood friend, architect Georg Wenzeslaus von Knobelsdorff, he masterminded the Forum Fridericianum, a cultural quarter centred on today's Bebelplatz. It was built in a style called 'Frederician Rococo' that blended baroque and neoclassical elements. Since the king's war exploits had emptied his coffers, he could only afford to partially realise his vision by building the neoclassical Staatsoper (State Opera House); the Sankt-Hedwigs-Kathedrale (St Hedwig Cathedral), inspired by Rome's Pantheon; the playful Alte Königliche Bibliothek (Old Royal Library); and the Humboldt Universität (Humboldt University), originally a palace for the king's brother Heinrich. Knobelsdorff also added the Neuer Flügel (New Wing) to Schloss Charlottenburg. His crowning achievement, though, was Schloss Sanssouci (Sanssouci Palace) in Potsdam.

After Knobelsdorff's death in 1753, two architects continued in his tradition: Philipp Daniel Boumann – who designed Schloss Bellevue (Bellevue Palace) for Frederick's youngest brother, August Ferdinand – and Carl von Gontard, who added the domed towers to the Deutscher Dom and Französischer Dom on Gendarmenmarkt.

THE SCHINKEL TOUCH

The architectural style that most shaped Berlin was neoclassicism, thanks in large part to one man: Karl Friedrich Schinkel, arguably Prussia's finest architect. Turning away from baroque flourishes, neoclassicism drew upon columns, pediments, domes and other design elements that had been popular throughout antiquity.

Berlin's architectural growth was significantly shaped by advancements in transportation. The first train chugged from Berlin to Potsdam in 1838, the first S-Bahn rumbled along in 1882 and the U-Bahn kicked into service in 1902.

Schinkel's first Berlin commission was the Mausoleum, built for Queen Luise in Schloss Charlottenburg's park, although he didn't really make his mark until 1818 with the Neue Wache (New Guardhouse) on Unter den Linden. Originally an army guardhouse, it is now an antiwar memorial accented with a haunting sculpture by Käthe Kollwitz.

The nearby Altes Museum (Old Museum), on Museumsinsel (Museum Island), with its colonnaded front, is considered Schinkel's most mature work. Other neoclassical masterpieces include the magnificent Schauspielhaus (now the Konzerthaus Berlin) on Gendarmenmarkt, and the small Neuer Pavillon (New Pavilion) in Schlossgarten Charlottenburg. Schinkel's most significant departure from neoclassicism, the turreted Friedrichswerdersche Kirche, was inspired by a Gothic Revival in early-19th-century England.

After Schinkel's death in 1841, several of his disciples kept his legacy alive, notably Friedrich August Stüler, who built the original Neues Museum (New Museum) and the Alte Nationalgalerie (Old National Gallery), both on Museumsinsel, as well as the Matthäuskirche (Church of St Matthew) in today's Kulturforum.

HOUSING FOR THE MASSES

In his 1930 book *Das Steinerne Berlin* (Stony Berlin), Werner Hege mann fittingly refers to Berlin as 'the largest tenement city in the world.' The onset of industrialisation in the middle of the 19th century lured hundreds of thousands to the capital who dreamed of improving their lot in the factories. Something had to be done to beef up the city's infrastructure and provide cheap housing for the masses, and quick. A plan drawn up in 1862 under chief city planner James Hobrecht called for a city expansion along two circular ring roads bisected by diagonal roads radiating in all directions from the centre – much like the spokes of a wheel. The land in between was divided into large lots and sold to speculators and developers. Building codes were limited to a maximum building height of 22m (equivalent to five stories) and a minimum courtyard size of 5.34m by 5.34m, just large enough for fire-fighting equipment to operate in.

Such lax regulations led to the uncontrolled spread of sprawling working-class tenements called *Mietskasernen* (literally 'rental barracks') in newly created peripheral districts such as Prenzlauer Berg, Kreuzberg, Wedding and Friedrichshain. Covering one huge 'Berlin Block', the buildings had front, rear and side wings enclosing multiple courtyards. Each was designed to squeeze the maximum number of people into the smallest possible space. Living conditions were sub human, with entire families crammed into tiny, lightless flats reached via internal staircases that also provided access to shared toilets. Many flats doubled as workshops or sewing studios. Only those in the street-facing front offered light, space and balconies – and they were reserved for the bourgeoisie.

Walking around Berlin, it's hard to visualise what the city looked like before WWII. In comes Nick Gay's book *Berlin Then and Now*, which handily juxtaposes historical and recent images of major landmarks, streets and squares.

THE EMPIRE YEARS

The architecture in vogue after the creation of the German Empire in 1871 reflects the representational needs of the united Germany and tends towards the pompous. No new style as such emerged as architects essentially recycled earlier ones (eg Romanesque, Renaissance, baroque, sometimes weaving them all together) in an approach called Historismus (Historicism) or Wilhelmismus, after Emperor Wilhelm I.

PRUSSIA'S BUILDING MASTER: KARL FRIEDRICH SCHINKEL

The most prominent and mature architect of German neoclassicism, Karl Friedrich Schinkel (1781–1841), studied architecture under Friedrich Gilly and his father David at the Building Academy in Berlin. He continued his education during a two-year trip to Italy (1803–1805) to study classical architecture up close only to return to a Prussia hamstrung by Napoleonic occupation. While unable to practise his craft, he scraped by as a romantic painter and furniture and set designer.

Schinkel's career took off as soon as the French left Berlin. He steadily rose through the ranks of the Prussian civil service, starting as surveyor to the Prussian Building Commission and ending as chief building director for the entire kingdom. He travelled tirelessly throughout the land, designing buildings, supervising construction and even developing principles for the protection of historic monuments.

His travels in Italy notwithstanding, Schinkel actually drew greater inspiration from classical Greek architecture. From 1810 to 1840 his vision very much defined Prussian architecture and Berlin even came to be known as 'Athens on the Spree'. In his buildings he strove for the perfect balance between functionality and beauty, achieved through clear lines, symmetry and an impeccable sense for aesthetics. Schinkel fell into a coma in 1840 and died one year later in Berlin.

STEFANO AMANTINI / 4CORNERS ©

Staatsbibliothek zu Berlin (State Library) on Bebelplatz (p83)

As a result, many buildings in Berlin look much older than they actually are. Prominent examples include the Reichstag by Paul Wallot and the Berliner Dom (Berlin Cathedral) by Julius Raschdorff, both in neo-Renaissance style. Franz Schwechten's Anhalter Bahnhof and the Kaiser-Wilhelm-Gedächtniskirche (Memorial Church), both in ruins, reflect the neo-Romanesque, while the Staatsbibliothek zu Berlin (State Library) and the Bodemuseum by Ernst von Ihne are neo-baroque in style.

While squalid working-class neighbourhoods hemmed in the north, east and south of the city centre, western Berlin (Charlottenburg, Wilmersdorf) was being developed for the middle and upper classes under none other than the 'Iron Chancellor' Otto von Bismarck himself. He widened the Kurfürstendamm, lining it and its side streets with attractive town houses. Like the *Mietskasernen*, they were four or five storeys high and wrapped around a central courtyard, but that's where the similarities ended. Courtyards were large, allowing light to enter the roomy flats, some of which had as many as 10 rooms. These days, some harbour charming old-Berlin-style B&Bs, such as the Hotel-Pension Funk and Hotel Askanischer Hof.

Those with serious money and status moved even further west, away from the claustrophobic centre. The villa colonies in leafy Grunewald and Dahlem are another Bismarck legacy and still among the ritziest residential areas today.

> The Industrial Age saw Berlin's population explode. It more than doubled to 969,050 between 1858 and 1875, doubling again by 1905 and fuelling the need for cheap and plentiful housing.

THE BIRTH OF MODERNISM

While most late-19th-century architects were looking to the past, a few progressive minds managed to make their mark, mostly in industrial and commercial design. The main trailblazer was Peter Behrens (1868–1940), who is sometimes called the 'father of modern architecture' and taught later modernist luminaries such as Le Corbusier, Walter Gropius and Ludwig Mies van der Rohe. One of his earliest works, the 1909 AEG Turbinenhalle at Huttenstrasse 12-14 in Moabit, is an airy, functional and light-flooded 'industrial cathedral' and considered an icon of early industrial architecture.

After WWI, the 1920s spirit of innovation lured some of the finest avant-garde architects to Berlin, including Bruno and Max Taut, Le Corbusier, Mies van der Rohe, Erich Mendelsohn, Hans Poelzig and Hans Scharoun. In 1924 they formed an architectural collective called Der Ring (The Ring) whose members were united by the desire to break with traditional aesthetics (especially the derivative Historicism) and to promote a modern, affordable and socially responsible approach to building.

Their theories were put into practice as Berlin entered another housing shortage. Led by chief city planner Martin Wagner, Ring members devised a new form of social housing called *Siedlungen* (housing estates). It opened up living space and incorporated gardens, schools, shops and other communal areas that facilitated social interaction. Together with

UNCOMMON ENVIRONS FOR THE COMMON MAN

Architecturally speaking, Museumsinsel, Schloss Sanssouci and the Hufeisensiedlung in Neukölln could not be more different. Yet all have one thing in common: they are Unesco World Heritage Sites. Along with five other working-class housing estates throughout Berlin, the Hufeisensiedlung was inducted onto this illustrious list in July 2008.

Created between 1910 and 1933 by such leading architects of the day as Bruno Taut and Martin Wagner, these icons of modernism are the earliest examples of innovative, streamlined and functional – yet human-scale – mass housing and stand in stark contrast to the slumlike, crowded tenements of the late 19th century. The flats, though modest, were functionally laid out and had kitchens, private baths and balconies that let in light and fresh air. For further details, see http://whc.unesco.org.

Hufeisensiedlung (Lowise-Reuter-Ring; dParchimer Allee) Taut and Wagner dreamed up the three-storey-high horseshoe-shaped colony (1933–35) with 1000 balconied flats wrapping around a central park. Head north on Fritz-Reuter-Allee from the U-Bahn station.

Gartenstadt Falkenberg (Akazienhof, Am Falkenberg & Gartenstadtweg, Köpenick; dGrünau) Built by Taut between 1910 and 1913, the oldest of the six Unesco-honoured estates is a cheerful jumble of colourfully painted cottages. From the S-Bahn, approach from Am Falkenberg.

Grossiedlung Siemensstadt (Geisslerpfad, Goebelstrasse, Heckerdamm, Jungfernheideweg, Mäckeritzstrasse, Charlottenburg; dSiemensdamm) This huge development (1929–31) combines Walter Gropius' minimalism, Hugo Häring's organic approach and Hans Scharoun's ship-inspired designs. Best approach is via Jungfernheideweg.

Schillerpark Siedlung (Barfussstrasse, Bristolstrasse, Corker Strasse, Dubliner Strasse, Oxforder Strasse, Windsorer Strasse, Wedding; dRehberge) Inspired by Dutch architecture, this large colony by Taut (1924–30) sports a dynamic red-and-white-brick facade. Best approach is via Barfussstrasse.

Weisse Stadt (Aroser Allee, Baseler Strasse, Bieler Strasse, Emmentaler Strasse, Genfer Strasse, Gotthardstrasse, Romanshorner Weg, Schillerring, Sankt-Galler-Strasse; dParacelusbad, Residenzstrasse) Martin Wagner's 'White City' (1929–31) includes shops, a kindergarten, cafe, central laundry and other communal facilities. Best approach is via Aroser Allee.

Wohnstadt Carl Legien (Map p330; Erich-Weinert-Strasse, Georg-Blank-Strasse, Gubitzstrasse, Küselstrasse, Lindenhoekweg, Sodtkestrasse, Sültstrasse, Trachtenbrodtstrasse; ⓇPrenzlauer Allee) For this development (1928–30), the one closest to the city centre, Taut arranged rows of four-to-five-storey-high houses and garden areas in a semi-open space. Approach via Erich-Weinert-Strasse.

Bruno Taut, Wagner himself designed the Hufeisensiedlung (Horseshoe Colony) in Neukölln which, in 2008, became one of six Berlin housing estates recognised as a Unesco World Heritage Site.

In nonresidential architecture, expressionism flourished with Erich Mendelsohn as its leading exponent. This organic, sculptural approach is nicely exemplified by the Universum Kino (Universum Cinema; 1926), which is today's Schaubühne am Lehniner Platz; it greatly influenced the Streamline Moderne movie palaces of the 1930s. Emil Fahrenkamp's 1931 Shell-Haus at Reichspietschufer 60 follows similar design principles. Reminiscent of a giant upright staircase, it was one of Berlin's earliest steel-frame structures concealed beneath a skin of travertine. Its extravagant silhouette is best appreciated from the southern bank of the Landwehrkanal.

NAZI MONUMENTALISM

Modernist architecture had its legs cut out from under it as soon as Hitler came to power in 1933. The new regime immediately shut down the Bauhaus School, one of the most influential forces in 20th-century building and design. Founded by Walter Gropius in 1919, it had moved to Berlin from Dessau only in 1932. Many of its visionary teachers, including Gropius, Mies van der Rohe, Wagner and Mendelsohn, went into exile in the USA.

Back in Berlin, Hitler, who was a big fan of architectural monumentalism, put Albert Speer in charge of turning Berlin into the 'Welthauptstadt Germania', the future capital of the Reich. Today, only a few buildings offer a hint of what Berlin might have looked like had history taken a different turn. These include the coliseum-like Olympiastadion by Walter and Werner March, and Ernst Sagebiel's Tempelhof Airport. Heinrich Wolff designed the Reichsbank on Kurstrasse which, along with a modern

Bauhaus Archiv (p122), designed by Walter Gropius

Football (p30), Olympic Stadium

annex by Thomas Müller and Ivan Reimann on Werderscher Markt, now houses the Federal Foreign Office. In the Diplomatenviertel (Diplomatic Quarter) south of Tiergarten – another Speer idea – the embassies of Nazi allies Italy and Japan reflect a similarly pompous grandeur.

A TALE OF TWO CITIES

Even before the Wall was built in 1961, the clash of ideologies and economic systems between East and West also found expression in the architectural arena.

East Berlin

East Germans looked to Moscow, where Stalin favoured a style that was essentially a socialist reinterpretation of good old-fashioned neoclassicism. The most prominent German Democratic Republic (GDR) architect was Hermann Henselmann, the brains behind the Karl-Marx-Allee (called Stalinallee until 1961) in Friedrichshain. Built between 1952 and 1965, it was East Berlin's showcase 'socialist boulevard' and, with its Moscow-style 'wedding-cake buildings', the epitome of Stalin-era pomposity. It culminates at Alexanderplatz, the central square that also got a socialist makeover in the 1960s. The only remaining prewar buildings are Peter Behrens' Berolinahaus (1930) and Alexanderhaus (1932).

While Alexanderplatz and the Karl-Marx-Allee were prestige projects, they did not solve the need for inexpensive, modern housing to accommodate growing populations. The government responded by building three massive satellite cities on the periphery – Marzahn, Hohenschönhausen and Hellersdorf – that leapt off the drawing board in the 1970s and '80s. Like a virtual Legoland for giants, these huge housing developments largely consist of row upon row of rectangular high-rise *Plattenbauten*, ie buildings made from large, precast concrete slabs. Marzahn

GERMANIA MANIA

Part of Hitler's Third Reich vision was to transform Berlin into Germania, the utopian world capital of a Nazi empire. Masterminded by Albert Speer (1905–81) and Hitler himself, there would be two major intersecting roads at its heart: the north–south axis running from the Reichstag to Tempelhof, and the east–west axis (today's Strasse des 17 Juni) linking the Brandenburg Gate with Theodor-Heuss-Platz (then Adolf-Hitler-Platz) in Charlottenburg. At the top of the north–south axis, near today's Reichstag, would rise the Grosse Halle des Volkes (Great Hall of the People), big enough to hold 180,000 people and topped by a 250m-wide dome.

Entire neighbourhoods north and east of Tiergarten were bulldozed to make room for these ambitious architectural projects. In the end, though, Speer only got as far as the Reichskanzlei (Hitler's office, now destroyed) on Vosstrasse before the realities of WWII put paid to his vision.

Speer was sentenced to 20 years at the Nuremberg Trials. He spent most of them at a prison in Spandau where he penned a couple of autobiographical books, including *Inside the Third Reich* (1970), a detailed account of the day-to-day operations of Hitler's inner circle. Read it alongside Gitta Sereny's biography *Albert Speer: His Battle with Truth* (1996) for full insight into this controversial Nazi figure.

alone could accommodate 165,000 people in 62,000 flats. Since they offered such mod cons as private baths and lifts, this type of housing was very popular among East Germans, despite the monotony of the design.

West Berlin

In West Berlin, urban planners sought to eradicate any hint of monumentalism and determined to rebuild the city in a modernist fashion. Their equivalent of the Karl-Marx-Allee became the Hansaviertel, a loosely structured leafy neighbourhood of midrise apartment buildings and single-family homes, northwest of Tiergarten. Built from 1954 to 1957, it drew the world's top architects, including Gropius, Luciano Baldessari, Alvar Aalto and Le Corbusier and was intended to be a model for other residential quarters. Although looking dated today, it represented the pinnacle of architectural vision in the 1950s, and is still a popular and pricey neighbourhood.

The 1960s saw the birth of a large-scale public building project, the Kulturforum, a museum and concert-hall complex conceived by Hans Scharoun. His Berliner Philharmonie, the first building to be completed in 1963, is considered a masterpiece of sculptural modernism. Among the museums, Mies van der Rohe's templelike Neue Nationalgalerie (New National Gallery) is a standout. A massive glass-and-steel cube, it perches on a raised granite podium and is lidded by a coffered, steel-ribbed roof that seems to defy gravity.

The West also struggled with a housing shortage and, in one of the few parallel developments, also combated it by building mass-scale housing projects. The Walter Gropius–planned 'Grosssiedlung Berlin-Buckow' in southern Neukölln (renamed Gropiusstadt after his death) and the Märkisches Viertel in Reinickendorf, in northwest Berlin, are two such megasuburbs that provided quick and cheap housing for tens of thousands.

INTERBAU 1987

While mass housing mushroomed on the peripheries, the inner city suffered from decay and neglect on both sides of the Wall. In West Berlin, an international architectural exposition called IBA 1987 was to set new initiatives in urban renewal by blending two architectural principles: Careful Urban Renewal would focus on rehabilitating existing buildings; and Critical Reconstruction, which would require any new buildings to fit in with the existing urban fabric.

Planning director Josef Paul Kleihues invited the royalty of international architecture to take up the challenges of Interbau, among them Rob Krier, Peter Eisenman, James Stirling, Aldo Rossi, Arata Isozaki and OM Ungers. *Time* magazine called it 'the most ambitious showcase of world architecture in this generation'. Eastern Kreuzberg and the area south of Tiergarten park received the most attention. Good places to study the legacy of Interbau 1987 are on a stroll along the Fraenkelufer in Kreuzberg and along the streets surrounding the Jüdisches Museum such as Lindenstrasse, Ritterstrasse and Alte Jakobstrasse.

In the 1920s Adolf Hitler's stepbrother Alois was a waiter at Weinhaus Huth, the only complete building on Potsdamer Platz to survive WWII intact. During the Cold War, it stood forlorn in the middle of the death strip for decades.

THE NEW BERLIN

Reunification presented Berlin with both the challenge and the opportunity to redefine itself architecturally. With the Wall gone, the two city halves had to be physically rejoined across huge gashes of empty space. Critical reconstruction continued to be the guiding vision under city planning director Hans Stimmann. Architects had to follow a long catalogue of parameters with regard to building heights, facade materials and other criteria with the goal of rebuilding Berlin within its historic forms rather than creating a modern, vertical city.

Potsdamer Platz

The biggest and grandest of the post-1990 Berlin developments, Potsdamer Platz is a modern reinterpretation of the historic square that was Berlin's bustling heart until WWII. From the Cold War–era death strip has sprung an urban quarter laid out along a dense, irregular street

PETER LANGER / DESIGN PICS / CORBIS ©

Jüdisches Museum (p148)

grid reminiscent of a 'European city'. Led by Renzo Piano, it's a collaboration of an international roster of renowned architects, including Helmut Jahn, Richard Rogers and Rafael Moneo. Structures are of medium height, except for three gateway high-rises overlooking the intersection of Potsdamer Strasse and Ebertstrasse.

Pariser Platz

Top Five Buildings since 1990

Jüdisches Museum (Daniel Libeskind)
....
Reichstag Dome (Lord Norman Foster)
....
Sony Center (Helmut Jahn)
....
Neues Museum (David Chipperfield)
....
Hauptbahnhof (central train station; Gerkan, Marg und Partner)

Pariser Platz was also reconstructed from the ground up. It's a formal, introspective square framed by banks, embassies and the Hotel Adlon that, in keeping with Critical Reconstruction, had to have natural stone facades. The one exception is the glass-fronted Akademie der Künste (Academy of Arts). Its architect, Günter Behnisch, had to fight tooth and nail for this facade, arguing that the square's only public building should feel open, inviting and transparent. The Adlon, meanwhile, is an almost exact replica of the 1907 original.

Diplomatenviertel

Some of Berlin's most exciting new architecture is clustered in the revitalised Diplomatenviertel (Diplomatic Quarter) on the southern edge of Tiergarten, where many countries rebuilt their embassies on their historic pre-WWII sites.

Government Quarter

The 1991 decision to move the federal government back to Berlin resulted in a flurry of building activity in the empty space between the Reichstag and the Spree River. Designed by Axel Schultes and Charlotte Frank and arranged in linear east–west fashion are the Federal Chancellery, the Paul-Löbe-Haus and the Marie-Elisabeth-Lüders-Haus. Together they form the Band des Bundes (Band of Federal Buildings) in a symbolic linking of the formerly divided city halves across the Spree River.

Overlooking all these shiny new structures is the Reichstag, home of the Bundestag (German parliament), the glass cupola of which is the most visible element of the building's total makeover masterminded by Lord Norman Foster.

The glass-and-steel 'spaceship' on the northern river bank is Berlin's first-ever central train station, the sparkling Hauptbahnhof designed by the Hamburg firm of Gerkan, Marg und Partner and completed in 2006.

More Architectural Trophies

If you want to learn more about Berlin's contemporary architecture, sign up for a tour (also in English) with Ticket B (www. ticket-b.de), an architect-run guide company.

In Kreuzberg, Daniel Libeskind's deconstructivist Jüdisches Museum (1999) is among the most daring and provocative structures in the new Berlin. With its irregular, zigzagging floor plan and shiny zinc skin pierced by gashlike windows, it is not merely a museum but a powerful metaphor for the troubled history of the Jewish people. An extension under construction in a nearby former flower market is expected to be completed by the time you read this.

Near Gendarmenmarkt, along Friedrichstrasse, the Friedrichstadtpassagen (1996) is a trio of luxurious shopping complexes, including the glamorous Galeries Lafayette, that hide their jewel-like interiors behind postmodern facades.

Another remarkable building is the Dutch Embassy (2004), at Klosterstrasse 50, a starkly geometric glass cube by Rem Koolhaas, intended to embody 'Dutch openness'. It has a large terrace offering good views of the Spree River.

Hauptbahnhof (p285)

Kudos for ground-breaking energy-efficiency go to the headquarters of the real-estate company GSW (1999) at Charlottenstrasse 4, which was designed by Louisa Hutton and Matthias Sauerbruch. Among other features, it sports a double-layer convection facade with blinds that automatically change colour depending on the temperature.

Across town, in the City West, several new structures have added some spice to the rather drab postwar architecture around Kurfürstendamm. The Ludwig-Erhard-Haus (1997), home of the Berlin stock market, is a great example of the organic architecture of the UK's Nicholas Grimshaw. Nearby, Kleihues' Kantdreieck (1995) establishes a visual accent on Kantstrasse by virtue of its rooftop metal 'sail'. Noteworthy buildings along Ku'damm itself are Helmut Jahn's Neues Kranzler Eck (2000) and the 2001 Neue Ku-Damm-Eck (2001), a corner building with a gradated and rounded facade, designed by Gerkan, Marg und Partner and festooned with sculptures by Markus Lüpertz.

More recently, the building that captured worldwide headlines was David Chipperfield's reconstruction of the Neues Museum (2009) on Museumsinsel. Like a giant jigsaw puzzle, it beautifully blends fragments from the original structure, which was destroyed in WWII, with modern elements. The result is so harmonious and impressive, it immediately racked up the accolades, including the prestigious award from the Royal Institute of British Architects (RIBA) in 2010.

With its cool and calm facade, the DZ Bank on Pariser Platz seems untypical for its exuberant architect, Frank Gehry. The surprise, though, lurks beyond the foyer leading to a light-flooded atrium anchored by an enormous sci-fi-esque stainless-steel sculpture used as a conference room.

THE FUTURE

You'd think that the ballet of cranes would finally stand still almost 25 years after reunification, but there are still plenty of large-scale projects on the drawing board or, as in the case of the new headquarters of the Bundesnachrichtendienst (Germany's foreign intelligence agency), under construction. Designed by Kleihues + Kleihues, the enormous complex on Chausseestrasse is taking shape on a lot formerly occupied by the GDR-era Stadium of the World Youth. After several delays, it is expected to open in 2015.

Across town, new life is being injected into the City West. The most visible project, the high-rise Waldorf Astoria Hotel, should have opened by the time you're reading this. Nearby, the Zoopalast cinema is getting a serious facelift and may once again roll out the red carpet for the Berlinale film festival in 2014. The Bikinihaus next door, which is being rehabilitated to house shops, offices and a hotel, should have already reopened by then.

The opening of Berlin's central airport, the Berlin Brandenburg Airport in Schönefeld, has been delayed several times and may now open in late 2013. Plans on what to do with Tempelhof Airport, which closed in 2008 and for the moment is a giant park, keep shifting, much to the delight of Berliners who cherish the open space.

Also delayed is the beginning of the reconstruction of the Berliner Stadtschloss (Berlin City Palace) in its historic site on Schlossplatz, currently envisioned for 2014.

The Golden Twenties

In the 1920s the great cities of the world – Paris, London, New York – went through times of peril, uncertainty and creative abandonment. But nowhere did this Zeitgeist express itself more frenetically than in Berlin. Humiliated and penniless after WWI, Berliners compensated for their despair by throwing themselves headlong into hedonism in exuberant cabarets, theatres and music halls. In the city's cafes, artists and intellectuals sipped absinthe and forged groundbreaking forms of expression. Was it all daring? Certainly. Was it all fun? Undoubtedly. Was it all 'golden'? Decidedly not.

PARTY TOWN

The centre of nightlife was in the western city centre, where Kurfürstendamm had become a glittering ribbon of commerce. Cabarets, theatres and snazzy movie palaces like the Marmorpalast lined the boulevard and its side streets. The Romanisches Cafe, which stood on the site of today's Europa-Center, was practically the second living room for artists, actors, writers, photographers, film producers and other creative types. Some were

Marlene Dietrich

The 1997 movie *The Harmonists*, directed by Joseph Vilsmaier, charts the course of the Comedian Harmonists' career from the day they first met in 1927 until 1934.

famous, like Bertolt Brecht, Otto Dix and Billy Wilder. Most were not. German satirical writer Erich Kästner even called it the 'waiting room of the talented'. In fact, the cafe was split into two areas: the 'small room' for the success stories and the 'large room' for the wanna-bes. The Cafe des Westens on Kurfürstendamm was another popular gathering spot for artists and intellectuals.

Not far from here, the area around Nollendorfplatz had emerged as Berlin's gay mecca. This is where men met boys at the Eldorado, a famous transvestite bar also favored by local gals Marlene Dietrich, Claire Waldorff and the beau monde of the day. Another Schöneberg resident was Anglo-American writer Christopher Isherwood, whose collected novellas in *Berlin Stories* form the basis of the film and musical *Cabaret*. Pay homage to him at his former residence at Nollendorfstrasse 17.

CABARET

Cabaret may have been born in 1880s Paris, but it became a wild and libidinous grown-up in 1920s Berlin. In those giddy Weimar years, when creativity and decadence blossomed, cabarets provided a titillating fantasy of play and display, where transvestites, singers, magicians, dancers and other entertainers made audiences forget about the harsh realities of daily life. It was a smoke-filled world vividly portrayed in the 1930 movie *Der Blaue Engel* (The Blue Angel), starring femme fatale Marlene Dietrich as Lola, and of course in Bob Fosse's acclaimed film musical *Cabaret* (1972) with Liza Minnelli.

Jazz became the dominant cabaret sound, especially after American performer Josephine Baker's headline-grabbing performances at the Theater des Westens dressed in nothing but a banana skirt. Across town, in the Admiralspalast, The Chocolate Kiddies, also from the US, delighted their audiences with Duke Ellington music.

A more traditional, home-grown 1920s musical style entertaining the crowds in cabarets, dance halls and variety theatres was the Berlin Schlager – light-hearted songs with titles like 'Mein Papagei frisst keine harten Eier' ('My parakeet doesn't eat hard-boiled eggs') and 'Ich hab das Fräulein Helen baden sehen' ('I've seen Miss Helen in the bathtub') that teetered on the silly and surreal.

The most successful singing group performing this type of music was the Comedian Harmonists, a 'boy band' founded in Berlin in 1927 by Harry Frommermann in the vein of the American group The Revelers. With a baritone, a bass, three tenors and a piano player, they performed perfect harmonies with their voices sounding like musical instruments. The group disbanded in 1934 because three of its members were Jewish; they subsequently fled Germany.

Another runaway hit was *The Threepenny Opera*, written by Bertolt Brecht with music by Kurt Weill. It premiered in 1928 with such famous songs as 'Mack the Knife' and combined classical music with cabaret and pop songs. It was a fine example of Brecht's 'epic theatre', a style he developed after moving to Berlin in 1924. Unlike 'dramatic theatre', it forces its audience to detach themselves emotionally from the play and its characters and to reason critically and intellectually.

For a vivid and insightful chronicle of the rise and fall of cabaret in Berlin, read Peter Jelavich's *Berlin Cabaret* (2005).

Friedrich Hollaender was also a key composer in the cabaret scene, noted for his wit, improvisational talent and clever lyrics. Among his most famous songs is 'Falling in Love Again', sung by Marlene Dietrich in *Der Blaue Engel*, where he cameoed as a pianist. Like so many other talents (including Weill and Brecht), Hollaender left Germany when the Nazis brought down the curtain and continued his career in Hollywood.

MARLENE DIETRICH

Marlene Dietrich (1901–92) was born Marie Magdalena von Losch into a good middle-class Berlin family. After acting school, she first captivated her audience as a hard-living, libertine flapper in 1920s silent movies, but quickly carved a niche as the dangerously seductive femme fatale, best typified by the 1930 talkie *Der Blaue Engel* (The Blue Angel), which turned her into a Hollywood star.

This film was the start of a five-year collaboration with director Josef von Sternberg, during which time Dietrich built on her image of erotic opulence – dominant and severe, but always with a touch of self-irony. Dressed in men's suits for *Morocco* in 1930, she weighed in with her 'sexuality is power' attitude and bisexual mystique, winning a new audience overnight.

Dietrich stayed in Hollywood after the Nazi rise to power, though Hitler, not immune to her charms, reportedly promised perks and the red-carpet treatment if she moved back to Germany. She responded with an empty offer to return if she could bring along Sternberg – a Jew and no Nazi favourite. She took US citizenship in 1937 and entertained Allied soldiers on the front.

After the war, Dietrich retreated slowly from the public eye, making occasional appearances in films, but mostly cutting records and performing live. Her final years were spent in Paris, bedridden and accepting few visitors, immortal in spirit as mortality caught up with her.

THE GOLDEN TWENTIES FILM

FILM

The willingness to experiment with bold ideas and new artistic styles that characterised the Weimar years also translated to the big screen. Based in Babelsberg, just outside Berlin, the mighty UFA (Universum Film AG) emerged as Germany's flagship dream factory. As early as 1919, Ernst Lubitsch produced historical films and comedies like *Madame Dubarry*, starring Pola Negri and Emil Jannings; the latter went on to win the Best Actor Award at the very first Academy Award ceremony in 1927. Later movies were heavily expressionistic, using stark contrast, sharp angles, heavy shadows and other distorting elements. Well-known flicks employing these techniques include *Nosferatu*, a 1922 Dracula adaptation by FW Murnau, and the ground-breaking *Metropolis* (1927) by Fritz Lang. One of the earliest seminal talkies was Josef von Sternberg's *Der Blaue Engel*, which starred the ubiquitous Emil Jannings.

Marlene Dietrich makes her final home in a surprisingly unglamourous plot on Friedhof Schöneberg. Her tombstone simply says 'Marlene' along with the inscription: 'Here I stand on the marker of my days'.

DANCE

In dance, Berlin gave birth to a new form of physical expression, the so-called grotesque dance. Influenced by Dadaism, it was characterised by excessive, often comical expressiveness. One of its prime practitioners was Valeska Gert, the film star and founder of the Kohlkopp cabaret. Even more influential was Mary Wigman, who regarded body and movement as tools to express the universal experience of life. Her style inspired the late Pina Bausch as well as Reinhild Hoffmann and other leading German choreographers. Another famous Berlin hoofer from the 1920s was the notorious 'erotic dancer' Anita Berber, immortalised in a famous portrait by Otto Dix in 1925.

Life in the Divided City

For 45 years, Berlin was a political exclave in the cross-hairs of the Cold War, carved up by the victorious Allies into West Berlin, which comprised the American, French and British sectors, and East Berlin, which was controlled by the Soviets. In 1949 East Berlin became the capital of East Germany, while West Berlin was part of West Germany but formally administered by the Western Allies until 1990.

After the Berlin Wall was built in 1961, the two city halves developed as completely separate entities. What was life like on either side? This chapter takes a look at some unique aspects of both societies.

CONSUMERISM & SHOPPING

West Berlin could not have survived economically without heavy subsidies from the West German government in the form of corporate tax incentives and a so-called *Berlinzulage*, a monthly tax-free bonus of 8% on pretax income, for every working Berliner.

Buying a Trabant or Wartburg car in East Germany easily entailed wait times of 15 years or more.

West Berliners enjoyed the same fruits of capitalism as all other West Germans with full access to a wide range of quality consumer goods, the latest technology and imported foods. Then as now, the main shopping spine was Kurfürstendamm and its extension, Tauentzienstrasse, the crown jewel of which, the KaDeWe department store, left no shopping desires unfulfilled.

In East Berlin, the standard of living was higher than in the rest of the German Democratic Republic (GDR), with the Centrum Warenhaus on Alexanderplatz (today's Galeria Kaufhof) being a flagship store. Still, while basic foods (bread, milk, butter, some produce) were cheap and plentiful, fancier foods and high-quality goods were in short supply and could often only be obtained with connections and patience. Queues outside shops were a common sight and many items were only available as so-called *Bückware*, meaning that they were hidden from plain view and required the sales clerk to bend down (*bücken*) to retrieve them from beneath the counter. Bartering for goods was also common practice.

Western products could only be purchased in government-run retail stores called *Intershops*, and then only by the privileged few who had access to hard currency. The East German mark was not accepted payment.

ARTS & CULTURE

During the Cold War, ritzy Charlottenburg was the glittering heart of West Berlin. This is where the jet set gorged on steak and lobster in chic restaurants, debated politics in smoke-filled cafes and disco-foxed at cocaine-addled parties in glamorous Kurfürstendamm haunts. For high-brow entertainment, people flocked to the Deutsche Oper (German Operahouse) and the Ku'damm theatres that had delighted audiences since the 1920s.

BUYING A CAR

West Berlin spearheaded many of Germany's popular music revolutions. The late 1960s brought Tangerine Dream's psychedelic sound, while a decade later Kreuzberg's subculture launched the punk movement at SO36 and other seminal clubs. SO36 regulars included David Bowie and Iggy Pop, who were flat buddies in Schöneberg in the late 1970s. Trying to kick a drug addition and greatly inspired by Berlin's brooding quality, Bowie partly wrote and recorded his Berlin Trilogy (*Low, Heroes, Lodger*) at the famous Hansa Studios, which he dubbed the 'Hall by the Wall'. See p282 for more on the West Berlin music scene.

Airwaves know no walls, so East Berliners had access to western radio and television, even though they were not officially permitted to listen to or watch it; few western stars were invited to perform live in East Berlin.

Overall, though, the arts, especially theatre, enjoyed great popularity. Prestige stages included the Bertolt Brecht-founded Berliner Ensemble, the Volksbühne, the Deutsches Theater and the Staatsoper Unter den Linden. People also flocked to the fancy Kino Kosmos and Kino International, both on Karl-Marx-Allee, to catch the latest movies produced by the state-owned DEFA film studios in Potsdam.

East Berlin–based artists, however, faced severe restrictions of their artistic freedom. Lyrics and productions had to be approved and performances were monitored. Some popular pop and rock bands like The Puhdys, Karat, Silly and City managed to get around the censors by disguising criticism in seemingly innocuous metaphors or by deliberately inserting provocative lyrics they fully expected to be deleted.

Many nonconformists were placed under an occupational ban and prohibited from performing. Singer-songwriter Wolf Biermann became a cause célèbre when, in 1976, he was not allowed to return to the GDR from a concert series in the West despite being an avid – albeit regime-critical – socialist. When other artists rallied to his support, they too were expatriated, including Biermann's stepdaughter Nina Hagen, an East Berlin pop singer who later became a West Berlin punk pioneer. The East Berlin punk scene, meanwhile, produced Sandow and Feeling B, members of whom went on to found Rammstein.

TRAVEL & HOLIDAYS

After the Wall went up in 1961, East Berliners, along with other East Germans, were only allowed to travel within the GDR and to other Eastern Bloc countries. Most holiday trips were state-subsidised and

OSTALGIE

Postreunification movies like the smash hit *Good Bye, Lenin!* (2003) looked at the German Democratic Republic (GDR) with humour and bathos. They also fuelled Ostalgie (a hybrid of 'east' and 'nostalgia') – a longing for aspects of East German life that swept through Berlin and eastern Germany in the early 2000s. All of a sudden, it became fashionable to drink Vita Cola or wear T-Shirts emblazoned with the Interflug (East German airline) logo. The tinny Trabant car rose to cult status and in Friedrichshain, the Ostel hostel began offering 'GDR designer style'. Ostalgie was also largely responsible for saving the Ampelmännchen, the jaunty little East Berlin traffic-light man.

These days, Ostalgie has lost its hip factor, and not just since another movie, *The Lives of Others* (2006), peeled back the layer on the sinister side of life in the GDR with its legions of powerful secret police.

SPOTLIGHT ON 9 NOVEMBER 1989

Matthias Rau (www.matthiasrau-berlin.de) grew up in a Brandenburg village and moved to East Berlin in 1971 where he has led thematic city tours since 1984. Here is his eyewitness report of the events of 9 November 1989:

'I was at a pub with friends when suddenly the rumour spread that the Wall had opened. We didn't want to miss that and took the S-Bahn to the Warschauer Strasse station and headed down to the Oberbaumbrücke. When we got there shortly before midnight, it was utter chaos. Masses of people had piled up outside a steel door next to the border-control shack. Then suddenly, just when I stood in front of it, the door opened and I was the first one through. Others pushed on behind me and the West Berliners came from the other side. It's hard to imagine the euphoria on the bridge. Everyone was in each others arms, crying and laughing, drinking *Sekt* (sparkling wine) from the bottle – it was pure, almost hysterical, joy. Right then I knew that this was the end of the GDR.'

organised by the Freier Deutscher Gewerkschaftsbund (FDGB, Free German Trade Union Federation) that nearly every employee and worker belonged to. Who went where, when and for how long might have depended on such factors as an individual's productivity and level of social and political engagement. Those who could afford it, could book a package holiday abroad through the Reisebüro der DDR (GDR Travel Agency). A two-week trip to Bulgaria cost roughly an average monthly net income (1500 East German marks).

West Berlin, meanwhile, was completely surrounded by East Berlin and East Germany, prompting its residents to joke that no matter in which direction you went, you were always going east. Still, West Berliners suffered no restrictions on travel and were free to leave and return as they pleased, as well as to choose their holiday destinations.

The city was linked to West Germany by air, train and four transit roads, which were normal autobahns or highways also used by East Germans. Transit travellers were not allowed to leave the main road. Border checks were common and often involved harassment and time-consuming searches.

Until 1975, East Berlin had 12 holidays per year, which was increased to 21 days in 1980. West Berliners were guaranteed 18 days starting in 1963 and up to 28 days since the late '70s.

WOMEN & SOCIETY

In keeping with socialist tradition, women ostensibly enjoyed equality in East Germany. An extensive government-run child care system made it easier to combine motherhood and employment, and nearly 90% of all women were gainfully employed, many in such 'nontraditional' fields as engineering and construction. Gender equality, however, did not necessarily translate into the private sphere, where women remained largely responsible for child-raising and domestic chores. Rising through the ranks at work or in organisations was also rare. In fact, the only female member of the Ministerrat (Council of Ministers) was Erich Honecker's wife, Margot Honecker.

In West Germany, it took the women's movement of the 1970s to bring about legal changes and increase women's rights. Until then, for instance, women had to take their husband's name at marriage, were obligated by law to take care of the household, and were not granted divorces without their husband's consent. Despite progress made in the '70s, West German women continued to earn at least a third less than men for the same position and saw their careers held back by the proverbial 'glass ceiling'.

POLITICAL SOCIALISATION

From the outset, East Germany's economic, judicial and security policy was dominated by a single party, the Sozialistische Einheitspartei Deutschlands (SED, Socialist Unity Party of Germany). Among its prime objectives was the moulding of its citizens into loyal members of a new socialist society. Children as young as six years old were folded into a tight network of state-run mass organisations such as the Ernst Thälmann Pioniere and the Freie Deutsche Jugend (FDJ, Free German Youth). In the workplace, the FDGB was in charge of ideological control and conformity. Officially, membership in any of these groups was voluntary, but in reality refusing to join usually led to repercussions with regard to access to higher education and career choices. It could also incite the suspicion of the much-feared Ministerium für Staatssicherheit (Ministry for State Security, Stasi for short), which was headquartered in East Berlin. For more on the Stasi, see p171.

Music: From Punk to Techno

Just like the city itself, Berlin's music scene is a shape-shifter, a dynamic and restlessly inventive creature fed by the city's appetite for diversity and change. With at least 2000 active bands and dozens of indie labels, including Bpitch Control, Get Physical and Shitkatapult, the city is Germany's undisputed music capital. About 60% of the country's music revenue is generated here, up from a paltry 8% in 1998. It's where Universal Music and MTV have their European headquarters, to a large extent accounting for this boom. And every September, the Berlin Music Week brings together labels, agents, performers, DJs, club owners and fans for seven days of musical immersion.

POP, PUNK & ROCK BEFORE 1990

Since the end of WWII, Berlin has spearheaded most of Germany's popular music innovations. In the late '60s Tangerine Dream helped to propagate the psychedelic sound. Meanwhile, across the Iron Curtain, Nina Hagen got an early taste of fame in East Germany as a pop singer with the band Automobil only to become the diva of punk after following her parents to West Germany. Founded in 1977, her Nina Hagen Band delighted teens (and shocked their parents) with provocative lyrics, shrieking voices and theatrical performances. Hagen also helped pave the way for the major musical movement of the early '80s, Neue Deutsche Welle (NDW; German new wave), which gave the stage to Berlin bands like D.A.F, Trio, the Neonbabies, Ideal and UKW and, in East Berlin, Rockhaus.

The '80s saw the birth of Die Ärzte, who released their 26th album, *auch*, in 2012. Another seminal band from that era is Einstürzende Neubauten, who pioneered an experimental, proto-industrial sound that transformed oil drums, electric drills and chainsaws into musical instruments. The indie rock band Element of Crime, with singer-cum-novelist Sven Regener at the helm, also came onto the scene in the mid '80s.

In East Germany, access to Western rock and other popular music was restricted, but a slew of home-grown *Ostrock* (eastern rock) bands emerged. Major ones, like Die Puhdys, Karat, City and Silly, were allowed to perform in the West and built up huge followings on both sides of the Wall. The small but vital East Berlin underground scene was led by the punk band Feeling B; two of its permanent members went on to form the industrial metal band Rammstein in 1994. Although its dark and provocative songs are almost entirely performed in German, the band is the country's top musical export.

An excellent movie about Germany's early techno scene and culture is *We Call it Techno!*, released in 2008 by Sense Music & Media.

EARLY TECHNO

POP, ROCK & RAP AFTER 1990

Since reunification, hundreds of indie, punk, alternative and gothic bands have gigged to appreciative Berlin audiences. The still (or once again) active Die Ärzte, Element of Crime and Einstürzende Neubauten were joined by other successful exports, such as alternative punk rockers Beatsteaks, which had its breakthrough in 2004 as Best German Act at the MTV Europe Music Awards.

Other fine Berlin exports come from a jazz/breaks angle (electrojazz and breakbeats, favouring lush grooves, obscure samples and chilled rhythms). Remix masters Jazzanova are top dogs of the downtempo scene. They're represented by the Sonar Kollektiv label that also champions a number of successful similar artists, including Micatone.

Few other European cities offer such a thriving reggae-dancehall scene as Berlin. Founded in 1998, Seeed ruled the genre for years and finally released its much anticipated new album in 2012. Its frontman Peter Fox's solo album *Stadtaffe* (2008) was one of the best-selling albums in Germany and also won the 2010 Album of the Year Echo Award (the 'German Grammy'). Also commercially successful is Culcha Candela, who have essentially pop-ified the Seeed sound and released their fifth studio album – *Flätrate* – in 2011.

Home-grown rap and hip hop has a huge following, thanks to such early key players as 'gangsta-rappers' Sido, Fler, Bushido and Kool Savas, who cofounded Masters of Rap (MOR) in 1996. Also hugely successful are Berlin-based hip hoppers Casper and Marteria. K.I.Z., meanwhile, see themselves as a parody of gangsta rappers and released their most successful album thus far, *Urlaub fürs Gehirn* (Vacation for the Brain), in 2011. For a historical survey of the early scene, check out the DVDs *Rap City Berlin* (2005) and *Rap City Berlin II* (2006).

TECHNO TOWN

Call it techno, electro, house, minimal – electronic music is the sound of Berlin and its near-mythical club culture has, to no small degree, defined the capital's cool factor and put it on the map of global hedonists. The sound may have its roots in Detroit-based house music, but it came of age in the German capital.

What today is a huge industry germinated in a dark and dank cellar club called UFO on Köpenicker Strasse back in 1988. The 'godfathers' of the Berlin sound, Dr Motte, Westbam and Kid Paul, played their first gigs here, mostly sweat-driven acid house all-night raves. It was Motte who, a few months later, came up with the bright idea to take the party to the street with a truck, loud beats and a bunch of friends dancing behind it – the Love Parade was born (it peaked in 1999 with dozens of trucks and 1.5 million people swarming Berlin's streets).

It was the fall of the Wall in 1989, and the vacuum of artistic freedom it created, that catapulted techno out of the subcultural corner. The associated euphoria, the sudden access to derelict and abandoned spaces in eastern Berlin and the lack of control by the authorities were all defining factors in the explosive growth of the techno scene and in making Berlin into its mecca.

MUSIC: FROM PUNK TO TECHNO · TECHNO TOWN

BERLIN TRACKS THROUGH THE YEARS

1977
Heroes (David Bowie) Two lovers in the shadow of the 'Wall of Shame'.

1991
Zoo Station (U2) Bono embarks on a surreal journey inspired by a Berlin train station.

1995
Born to Die in Berlin (The Ramones) Drug-addled musings reveal Berlin's dark side.

2000
Dickes B (Seeed) Reggae Ode to the 'Big B' (ie Berlin).

2007
Kreuzberg (Bloc Party) Looking for true love...

2008
Schwarz zu Blau (Peter Fox) Perfect portrait of Kottbusser Tor grit and grunge.

2011
Brandenburg Gate (Lou Reed & Metallica) Expressionistic, dark ode to the sordid side of the 1920s.

HALL BY THE WALL

Complete this analogy: London is to Abbey Road what Berlin is to...

Well? Hansa Studios, of course, that seminal recording studio that has exerted a gravitational pull on top international artists since the Cold War. The 'Big Hall by the Wall' was how David Bowie fittingly dubbed its glorious Studio 2, better known as the Meistersaal (Masters' Hall). Through its arched windows one could look across the concrete barrier and wave at the gun-toting guards in their watchtowers. In the late '70s the 'White Duke' recorded his tortured visions in the seminal album *Heroes* after completing *Low*, both part of his Berlin Trilogy. Bowie also coproduced *The Idiot* and *Lust for Life* with his buddy Iggy Pop.

There's a long list of other music legends who have taken advantage of Studio 2's special sound quality, including Nina Hagen, Nick Cave, David Byrne, Einstürzende Neubauten, Die Ärzte, Snow Patrol, Green Day, REM and The Hives. Depeche Mode produced three albums here – *Construction Time Again*, *Some Great Reward* and *Black Celebration* – between 1983 and 1986.

The only way to get inside this hallowed hall (and find out why Depeche Mode's Martin Gore stripped down naked for the recording of a love song) is with the highly recommended Fritz Music Tours (p289).

In 1991, after the second UFO club closed, the techno-sonic brotherhood followed UFO founder Dimitri Hegemann to Tresor, which launched camouflage-sporting DJ Tanith along with trance pioneer Paul van Dyk. Other key venues in the early 1990s were Walfisch (in the space of today's KitKatClub) and, after 1993, the vast E-Werk. Tresor closed in 2005, only to reopen in its current location two years later. Today, its Tresor record label is an international brand representing Jeff Mills, Blake Baxter and Cristian Vogel, among many others.

Another seminal Berlin techno label is BPitch Control. Founded by Ellen Allien in 1999, it launched the careers of Modeselektor, Apparat and Sascha Funke and has also signed talent from around the world, including Thomas Muller from France and We Love from Italy. Another BPitch artist is Paul Kalkbrenner, whose 2008 semi-autobiographical *Berlin Calling* was the first mature film about Berlin and techno. Bpitch's varied roster points up the diversification of Berlin's techno-electro music scene that is now influenced by all sorts of sounds, from IDM (intelligent dance music) to pop and indie.

Another heavyweight label is Get Physical, a collective of almost 20 artists, including the dynamic duo M.A.N.D.Y., who are known for infusing house and electro with minimal and funk and thus creating a highly danceable – physical – sound. More of an underground label is the charmingly named Shitkatapult, founded in 1997 by Marco Haas (aka T.Raumschmiere), which gives techno a hard electro tinge and counts Oval and Rechenzentrum among its artists.

Foreign artists too have influenced the Berlin scene, including the provocative Canadian songstress and performance artist Peaches, UK–Canadian techno innovator Richie Hawtin and Chilean minimalist master Ricardo Villalobos.

These days, techno is big business in Berlin, but clubs and labels are still run by the same people who started it all. Venues have become more professional, equipped with state-of-the-art sound systems, while preserving an artistic integrity that continues to lure the world's finest DJs. The scene too has become more international as weekends bring in a flood of visitors that now account for up to 80% of people partying at such megaclubs as Berghain, Watergate and Tresor.

Check out Thomas Jerome Seabrook's *Bowie in Berlin: A New Career in a New Town* (2008) for a cool insight into those heady days.

Survival Guide

Transport

GETTING TO BERLIN

Most visitors arrive in Berlin by air. Until the opening of the new Berlin Brandenburg Airport (October 2013 at the time of research), which has been taking shape about 24km southeast of the city centre since 2006, flights will continue to land at Tegel and Schönefeld airports.

Lufthansa and nearly all other major European airlines and low-cost carriers (including Air Berlin, easyJet, Ryanair and Germanwings) operate direct flights to Berlin from throughout Europe. There are a few direct flights from US gateway cities such as Los Angeles and New York, but normally travel from outside Europe involves a change of planes in another European city such as Frankfurt or Amsterdam.

Travel to Berlin by train or bus may be a viable alternative. Berlin is linked by overnight train to many European cities, including Amsterdam and Vienna. Coming from London, you could be in Berlin in as little as nine hours by taking a combination of the Eurostar and German highspeed trains.

Flights, cars and tours can be booked online at lonelyplanet.com.

Tegel Airport

Tegel Airport (TXL; 01805 000 186; www.berlin-airport.de) is located in the northwestern suburb of Tegel, about 8km from the city centre.

Bus

➡ The TXL express bus connects Tegel to Alexanderplatz (€2.40, Tariff AB; 40 minutes) via Hauptbahnhof (central train station) every 10 minutes.The TXL goes via Saatwinkler Damm, Beusselstrasse, Turmstrasse, Alt-Moabit, Invalidenstrasse (passing by Hauptbahnhof) and Unter den Linden.

➡ For the City West around Zoologischer Garten take bus X9 (€2.40, Tariff AB; 20 minutes), which also runs at 10-minute intervals. The X9 runs along Otto-Suhr-Allee and Hardenbergstrasse, via Ernst-Reuter-Platz.

➡ Bus 109 heads to U-/S-Bahn station Zoologischer Garten and is slower and useful only if you're headed somewhere along Kurfürstendamm (€2.40, Tariff AB; 20 to 30 minutes).

U-Bahn

➡ Tegel is not served directly by the U-Bahn, but both bus 109 and X9 stop at Jakob-Kaiser-Platz, the station closest to the airport. From this station the U7 takes you directly to Schöneberg and Kreuzberg.

➡ Trips costs €2.40 (Tariff AB).

S-Bahn

The closest S-Bahn station is Jungfernheide, which is a stop on the S41/S42 (the Ringbahn, or circle line). It is linked to the airport by bus X9.

Taxi

Taxi rides cost about €20 to Zoologischer Garten and €23 to Alexanderplatz and take 30 to 45 minutes. There's a €0.50 surcharge for trips originating at the airport.

Schönefeld Airport

Schönefeld Airport (SXF; 0180 5000 186; www.berlin-airport.de) is located about 22km southeast of the city centre.

S-Bahn & Regional Trains

The airport train station is 400m from the terminals. Free shuttle buses run every 10 minutes; walking takes five to 10 minutes. You need a transport ticket covering zones ABC (€3.10) for any of the following trips.

➡ Airport-Express trains make the trip to central Berlin twice hourly. Note: these are regular Deutsche Bahn regional trains denoted as RE7 and RB14 in timetables. The journey takes 20 minutes to Alexanderplatz and 30 minutes to Zoologischer Garten.

➡ The S-Bahn S9 runs every 20 minutes and is slower but useful if you're headed to Friedrichshain (eg Ostkreuz, 30 minutes)

or Prenzlauer Berg
(eg Schönhauser Allee,
45 minutes).

➡ For the Messe (trade fair grounds), take the S45 to Süd-kreuz and change to the S41 to Messe Nord/ICC. Trains run every 20 minutes and the journey takes 55 minutes.

U-Bahn

Schönefeld is not served by the U-Bahn. The nearest station, Rudow, is linked to the airport by bus X7 every 20 minutes (€3.10, Tariff ABC; eight minutes) and by bus 171 (€3.10, Tariff ABC; 11 minutes). From Rudow, the U7 will take you into town. This connection is useful if you're headed for Neukölln or Kreuzberg.

Taxi

A cab ride to central Berlin averages €40 and takes 40 minutes to an hour.

Berlin Brandenburg Airport

Berlin's new central airport is located about 24km southeast of the city centre, next to Schönefeld airport.

Regional Train

Airport-Express trains are expected to depart every 15 minutes from the airport's own station and travel to central Berlin (€3.40, Tariff ABC; 20 to 30 minutes).

Taxi

Taxis make the trip into town in about 45 minutes to an hour and cost €42 to €50, including a €1.50 airport surcharge.

Train

Berlin is well connected by train to other German cities and destinations such as Prague, Czech Republic, War-saw, Poland and Amsterdam. For the full low-down, check out **Rail Europe** (www.rail europe.com).

Hauptbahnhof

➡ Berlin's central train station shelters five floors of tracks and services. North- and southbound trains depart from the lowest floor; east- and westbound trains, as well as the S-Bahn, run from the top level.

➡ Buy tickets in the *Reisezentrum* (travel centre) located between tracks 14 and 15 on the first upper level (OG1). A second travel centre on the first lower level (UG1) also has a **EurAide** (www.euraide.de; Hauptbahnhof, DB Reisezentrum, 1st lower level (UG1); 11am-7pm Mar, Apr & Oct, 10am-8pm May-Jul, 10am-7pm Aug-Oct, 11am-6.30pm Nov, 10am-7.30pm Dec; Hauptbahnhof, Hauptbahnhof) desk. Tickets are also sold online at www.bahn.de and, for

TICKETS & PASSES

➡ The network is divided into fare zones A, B and C with tickets available for zones AB, BC or ABC. One ticket is valid for travel on all forms of public transportation.

➡ Most trips within Berlin require an AB ticket, which is valid for two hours (interruptions and transfers allowed, but not round-trips). Notable exceptions include trips to Potsdam, Schönefeld Airport and, once in operation, Berlin Brandenburg Airport, where the ABC tariff applies.

➡ Children aged six to 14 qualify for reduced (*ermässigt*) rates, kids under six travel free.

➡ Buy tickets from bus drivers, at vending machines at U- or S-Bahn stations (English instructions available) and aboard trams, and at station offices and news kiosks sporting the yellow BVG logo. Some vending machines accept debit cards. Tram vending machines only take cash.

➡ Single tickets, except those bought from bus drivers and in trams, must be validated (stamped) at station platform entrances. Anyone caught without a valid ticket must pay a €40 fine payable on the spot.

➡ If you're taking more than two trips in a day, a day pass (*Tageskarte*) will save you money. It's valid for unlimited rides on all forms of public transport until 3am the following day. The group day pass (*Kleingruppenkarte*) is valid for up to five people travelling together.

➡ For short trips, buy the *Kurzstreckenticket*, which is good for three stops on the U-Bahn and S-Bahn or six on any bus or tram; no changes allowed.

➡ For longer stays, consider the seven-day pass (*Wochenkarte*), which is transferable and lets you take along another adult and up to three children aged six to 14 for free after 8pm Monday to Friday and all day on Saturday, Sunday and holidays.

TRAVEL FARES

TICKET TYPE	AB (€)	BC (€)	ABC (€)
Einzelfahrschein (single)	2.40	2.80	3.10
Ermässigt (reduced, single)	1.50	1.90	2.20
Tageskarte (day pass)	6.50	6.80	7
Kleingruppenkarte (group day pass)	15.50	15.80	16
Wochenkarte (7-day pass)	28	28.90	34.60

shorter distances, at station vending machines.

➡ The left-luggage office (€5 per piece, per 24 hours) is behind the Reisebank currency exchange on level OG1, opposite the Reisezentrum.

➡ Other services include a 24-hour pharmacy, tourist office, supermarket and other stores open daily from 8am to 10pm.

Bus

Berlin's 'central' bus station is in far western Berlin, about 4km west of Zoologischer Garten station.

Eurolines is the umbrella organisation of 32 long-haul operators connecting 500 destinations across Europe. Midweek fares to Berlin can be as low as £39 from London, €75 from Milan and €55 from Vienna.

GETTING AROUND BERLIN

Berlin's extensive and efficient public transport system is operated by BVG (☎194 49; www.bvg.de) and consists of U-Bahn (underground, subway), S-Bahn (light rail), buses and trams. For trip planning and general information, call the 24-hour hotline or check the website.

The U-Bahn is the most efficient way of getting around town, while the S-Bahn comes in handy for covering longer distances. Buses, trams and bicycles are useful for shorter journeys.

U-Bahn

➡ The U-Bahn is the quickest way of getting around Berlin. Lines (referred to as U1, U2 etc in this book) operate from 4am until about 12.30am and throughout the night on Friday, Saturday and public holidays (all lines except the U4 and U55). From Sunday to Thursday, night buses take over in the interim.

➡ Our listings indicate the closest station, preceded by the ⓈL icon.

S-Bahn & Regional Trains

➡ S-Bahn trains (S1, S2 etc) don't run as frequently as the U-Bahn but make fewer stops and thus are useful for covering longer distances. Trains operate from 4am to 12.30am and all night on Friday, Saturday and public holidays. Individual reviews indicate the closest stations.

➡ Destinations further afield are served by RB and RE trains. You'll need an ABC or Deutsche Bahn ticket to use these trains.

➡ Our listings indicate the closest station, preceded by the Ⓢ icon.

Bus

➡ Buses are slow but useful for sightseeing on the cheap (especially routes 100 and 200).

They run frequently between 4.30am and 12.30am. Night buses (N19, N23 etc) take over in the interim.

➡ MetroBuses, designated M19, M41 etc, operate 24/7.

➡ In our listings, buses are preceded by the 🚌 icon.

Tram

Trams (Strassenbahn) operate almost exclusively in the eastern districts. Those designated M1, M2 etc, run 24/7. A useful line is the M1, which links Prenzlauer Berg with Museum Island via Hackescher Markt. Individual reviews mention the nearest stop. Listings mention the nearest stop, preceded by the 🚊 icon.

Bicycle

Bicycles are handy both for in-depth explorations of local neighbourhoods and for getting across town. More than 650km of dedicated bike paths make getting around easy even for less confident riders. Do watch out for tram tracks, though.

Bicycles may be taken aboard designated U-Bahn and S-Bahn carriages (usually the last ones; look for the bicycle logo) as well as on night buses (Sunday to Thursday only) and trams. You need a separate ticket called a Fahrradkarte (bicycle ticket; €1.60). Taking a bike on regional trains (RE, RB) costs €5 per trip.

The websites www.bbbike.de and www.vmz-info.de are handy.

Hire

Many hostels and hotels have guest bicycles, often for free or a nominal fee. If not, rental stations are practically at every corner. These include not only the expected (bike shops, gas stations) but also convenience stores, cafes and even clothing boutiques.

Prices start at €6 per day, although the definition of 'day' can mean anything from eight hours to 24 hours. A cash or credit-card deposit and/or photo ID is usually required.

The following outfits are recommended. Call or check the website for branches and be sure to book ahead, especially in summer.

Fahrradstation (☎0180-510 8000; www.fahrradstation.com) Large fleet of quality bikes (including e-bikes), English-speaking staff and six branches in Mitte, Kreuzberg, Charlottenburg and Prenzlauer Berg. Bike rentals start at €15 per day or €50 per week.

Little John Bikes (www.little-john-bikes.de; Warschauer Strasse 31; [S]Warschauer Strasse, [U]Warschauer Strasse) A full store with branches in Schöneberg, Friedrichshain, Kreuzberg and Wilmersdorf that rents bicycles for €15 per 24 hours or €80 per week (€10/50 at the Friedrichshain branch).

Prenzlberger Orangebikes (Map p330; ☎4435 6852; Kollwitzstrasse 37, Prenzlauer Berg; per 24hr €6; 🕐noon-6pm Apr-Nov; [S]Senefelderplatz) The cheapest bike rentals in town (€6 for 24 hours) with proceeds going to a social-project adventure playground.

Lila Bike (Map p330; ☎0176 6112 5909, 4209 3446; www.berlin-citytours-by-bike.de; Schönhauser Allee 41; 🕐10am-8pm Mon-Sat, 11am-8pm Sun; [S]Eberswalder Strasse) Small outfit with just one branch in Prenzlauer Berg and great prices. The first 24-hour rental is charged at €8, subsequent ones at €5.

Taxi

You can order a **taxi** (☎44 33 11, 20 20 20) by phone, flag one down or pick one up at a rank. At night, cars often line up outside theatres, clubs and other venues. Up to four passengers travel for the price of one.

Flag fall is €3.20, then it's €1.65 per kilometre up to 7km and €1.28 for each additional kilometre. There's a surcharge of €1.50 if paying by credit or debit card, but none for night trips. Bulky luggage that does not fit into the trunk is charged at €1.

Tip about 10%.

TAXI SAMPLE FARES

DEPARTURE POINT	DESTINATION	COST
Alexanderplatz	Zoologischer Garten	€13
Kollwitzplatz	Gendarmenmarkt	€9
East Side Gallery	Brandenburger Tor	€15
Jewish Museum	Hackescher Markt	€10

Car & Motorcycle

Driving in Berlin is more hassle than it's worth, especially since parking is expensive and hard to find. If you're bringing in your own car, be aware that central Berlin (defined as the area bounded by the S-Bahn circle line) is a restricted low-emission zone, meaning that all cars entering must display a special sticker called *Umwelt-plakette*. Drivers caught without one will be fined €40. In order to buy one, go to www.umwelt-plakette.de.

Hire

All the big internationals maintain branches at the airports, major train stations and throughout town. Book in advance for the best rates.

Avis (www.avis.com)

Budget (www.budget.com)

Europcar (www.europcar.com)

Hertz (www.hertz.com)

If you get 'Harley hunger', head to **Classic Bike** (☎616 7930; www.classic-bike.de; Salzufer 6; 🕐9am-7pm Mon-Fri, 10am-3pm Sat Apr-Sep, 10am-6pm Mon-Fri, 10am-3pm Sat Oct-Mar; [U]Tiergarten). Daily (24-hour) rates range from €80 to €135.

Taking your rental vehicle into an Eastern European country, such as the Czech Republic or Poland, is often a no-no; check in advance if you're planning a side trip from Berlin.

TRAVELLING AT NIGHT

No matter what time it is, there's always a way to get around Berlin.

- U-Bahn lines run every 15 minutes throughout the night on Friday, Saturday and public holidays (all but the U4 and U55).
- From Sunday to Thursday, night buses (N1, N2 etc) serve the U-Bahn routes between 12.30am and 4am at 30-minute intervals.
- MetroBuses (M11, M19 etc) and MetroTrams (M1, M2 etc) run nightly every 30 minutes between 12.30am and 4.30am.

TOURS

Walking Tours

Several English-language walking-tour companies run introductory spins that take in both blockbuster and offbeat sights, plus themed tours (eg Third Reich, Cold War, Sachsenhausen, Potsdam). Tours don't require reservations – just show up at one of the meeting points. Since these change quite frequently, keep an eye out for flyers in hotel or hostel lobbies or at tourist offices; alternatively, contact the companies directly.

Alternative Berlin Tours (☎0162 819 8264; www.alternativeberlin.com) Free twice-daily subculture tours plus a street art workshop, the 666 Anti-Pubcrawl and a seriously wacky Twilight Tour.

Berlin Walks (☎301 9194; www.berlinwalks.de; tours €12-15, concession €9-12) Local expert guides of Berlin's longest-running English-language walking tour company.

Brewer's Berlin Tours (☎0177 388 1537; www.brewersberlintours.com; adult/concession €15/12) Purveyors of the epic all-day Best of Berlin tour and a donation-based Berlin Express tour.

Insider Tour Berlin (☎692 3149; www.insidertour.com; tours €12-15, concession €9-12) Insightful tours of Berlin, plus day trips to Dresden and a pub crawl.

New Berlin Tours (www.newberlintours.com; adult €12-15, concession €10-15) Energetic and entertaining city spins by the pioneers of the donation-based 'free tour' and the pub crawl.

Bicycle Tours

Companies listed below both get top marks for their various English-language tours. Reservations are recommended.

Berlin on Bike (Map p330; ☎4373 9999; www.berlinonbike.de; Knaackstrasse 97; tours incl bike €19, concession €17; 🕒Mar-Oct; [S]Eberswalder Strasse) Well-established company with an intriguing repertory, including excursions deep behind the 'Iron Curtain', along the Berlin Wall, into alt-flavoured Kreuzberg or Berlin's hidden oases. Tours leave from Court 4 in the Kulturbrauerei.

Fat Tire Bike Tours (Map p318; ☎2404 7991; www.fattirebiketours.com/berlin; Panoramastrasse 1a; tours €24, concession €22; [S]Alexanderplatz, [U]Alexanderplatz) Has classic Berlin, Nazi and Cold War tours as well as the fascinating Raw Tour, which addresses such hot-button issues as gentrification, urban renewal and multicultural living. Tours leave from the Fernsehturm (TV Tower) main entrance.

Boat Tours

Tours range from one-hour spins around Museumsinsel (from €11) to longer trips to Schloss Charlottenburg and

CALL A BIKE

Call a Bike (☎07000 522 5522; www.callabike-interaktiv.de) is an automated cycle-hire scheme offered by Deutsche Bahn (German Rail). The idea is simple: pick up a bike from one of dozens of docking stations around town (the website has a map). Cycle. Drop it off at another docking station.

Using the scheme requires that you preregister online for free with a credit card. The website is currently only in German. Signing up by phone is an alternative, although there's a €5 service charge.

The fee for renting a bike is €0.08 per minute up to a maximum of €15 per 24 hours.

Hiring a Bike

Once you've signed up, picking up a bike is actually pretty straightforward.

➡ **Unlocking a Bike at a Terminal** Touch the screen and identify yourself with your credit, debit or customer card. Select the number of bicycles (maximum of two per customer). Go to the assigned bicycle and tap on the lock display to open the lock.

➡ **Unlocking a Bike by Phone** Select a bike and call the red-rimmed phone number on the lock. Confirm your request. Tap on the lock display to open the lock.

➡ **Interrupting Your Trip** Lock the bike. To unlock it, you need your personal ID code, which you'll be given after registering. It also displays briefly on your lock when locking the bike.

➡ **Returning the Bike** Return the bike at any rental station. Lock the rear wheel and push the button on the right side of the lock. Wait for confirmation.

CLIMATE CHANGE & TRAVEL

Every form of transport that relies on carbon-based fuel generates CO_2, the main cause of human-induced climate change. Modern travel is dependent on aeroplanes, which might use less fuel per person than most cars but travel much greater distances. The altitude at which aircraft emit gases (including CO_2) and particles also contributes to their climate change impact. Many websites offer 'carbon calculators' that allow people to estimate the carbon emissions generated by their journey and, for those who wish to do so, to offset the impact of the greenhouse gases emitted with contributions to portfolios of climate-friendly initiatives throughout the world. Lonely Planet offsets the carbon footprint of all staff and author travel.

beyond (from €15). Young children usually travel for free; those under 14 and seniors get 50% off. Most tours offer live commentary in English and German and sell refreshments on board. **Stern und Kreisschiffahrt** (536 3600; www.sternund kreis.de) is one of the major operators. The main season runs from April to mid-October with a limited schedule in the winter months.

Bus Tours

Colourful buses tick off the key sights on two-hour loops with basic taped commentary in eight languages. You're free to get off and back on at any of the stops, paying only once. Buses depart roughly every 15 or 30 minutes between 10am and 5pm or 6pm daily; tickets cost from €10 to €20 (half-price for teens, free for children). Traditional tours where you don't get off the bus, combination boat and bus tours as well as trips to Potsdam and the Spreewald are also available. Look for flyers in hotel lobbies or at the tourist offices.

Speciality Tours

Berlinagenten (4372 0701; www.berlinagenten.com; 3hr tour for groups up to 10 from €350) Opens doors to hot and/

or hidden bars, boutiques, restaurants, clubs, private homes and sights. The Gastro-Rallye delivers an insider's primer on the city's culinary scene.

Berliner Unterwelten (4991 0517; www.berliner -unterwelten.de; Brunnenstrasse 105; adult/concession €10/8; English tours 11am Wed-Mon, 1pm Mon, no tours Wed Dec-Feb; SGesundbrunnen, RGesundbrunnen) Pick your way past heavy steel doors, hospital beds and filter systems on a tour of a WWII underground bunker. Buy tickets at the kiosk next to the south exit of the Gesundbrunnen U-Bahn station.

Fritz Music Tours (Map p314; 3087 5633; www.musictours-berlin.com; Unter den Linden 77; bus/walking tours €19/12, minibus tours per person €45, Hansa Studios €10-20; English bus tour 12.30pm Sun, walking tour 4pm Fri; SBrandenburger Tor, RBrandenburger Tor) Get the low-down on Berlin's legendary music history on a dynamic 2½-hour bus tour. Tours meet in front of the Hotel Adlon Kempinski. Fritz also offers: two-hour walking tours leaving from the tourist office in the **Kulturbrauerei** (Map p330; 4431 5152; www. kulturbrauerei.de; Schönhauser

Allee 36; tours adult/concession €7.50/6; SEberswalder Strasse, M1); private minibus tours (two-person minimum); and monthly tours of the Hansa Studios. Prices of the latter two vary by group size. Reservations are required for all tours.

Sta Tours Berlin (3010 5151; www.sta-tours.de; for groups of up to 6, per person €35; by appointment) If you're a German-film buff, first visit the Museum für Film & Fernsehen, then let celluloid expert Birgit Wetzig-Zalkind take you on two-hour van tours of the places where Billy Wilder, Leni Riefenstahl, Nastassja Kinski, Horst Buchholz, Marlene Dietrich and other legends lived and played.

Trabi Safari (Map p314; 2759 2273; www.trabi-safari. de; Zimmerstrasse 97, Historic Mitte; per person €30-90, Wall Ride €79-89, prices depending on group size; SKochstrasse) Catch the *Good Bye, Lenin!* vibe on tours of Berlin's classic sights or the 'Wild East' with you driving or riding in convoy of GDR-made Trabant cars (Trabi) with live commentary (in English by prior arrangement) piped into your vehicle. The two-hour Wall Ride has you steering towards Berlin Wall–related stops. Drivers need to bring their licence.

Directory
A–Z

Business Hours

The following list summarises standard opening hours. See p45 for late night and Sunday shopping.

Banks 9.30am to 6pm Monday to Friday, some to 1pm Saturday

Bars 6pm to 1am or later

Boutiques 11am to 7pm Monday to Friday, to 4pm Saturday

Cafes 8am to 8pm

Clubs 11pm to 5am or later

Post Offices 9am to 6pm Monday to Friday, to 1pm Saturday

Shops 10am to 8pm Monday to Saturday

Restaurants 11am to 10.30pm

Supermarkets 8am to 8pm, some until midnight, some 24hr

Customs Regulations

Goods brought in and out of countries within the EU incur no additional taxes provided duty has been paid somewhere within the EU and the goods are only for personal use. Duty-free shopping is only available if you're leaving the EU.

Discount Cards

Berlin Welcome Card

(www.visitberlin.de; 48/72hr €17.90/23.90, 48hr incl Potsdam & up to 3 children under 15yr €19.90, 72hr incl Museum Island €34) Entitles you to unlimited public transport and up to 50% discount to 200 sights, attractions and tours for periods of two, three or five days. Sold at U-Bahn and S-Bahn station ticket vending machines, tourist offices, BVG offices and many hotels.

CityTourCard (www.city tourcard.com; 48hr/72hr/5 days €16.90/22.90/29.90) Operates on a similar scheme as the Berlin Welcome Card; it's a bit cheaper, but offers fewer discounts. Available online, at some hotels and from U-Bahn and S-Bahn vending machines.

Berlin Museum Pass (www.visitberlin.de; adult/concession €19/9.50) Buys admission to the permanent exhibits of about 60 museums for three consecutive days, including big draws like the Pergamonmuseum. Sold at tourist offices and participating museums.

IMPORT RESTRICTIONS

ITEM	DUTY-FREE	TAX & DUTY PAID
Tobacco	200 cigarettes or 100 cigarillos or 50 cigars or 250g tobacco	3200 cigarettes, 200 cigars, 400 cigarillos or 3kg tobacco
Spirits & liqueurs	1L spirit or 2L of fortified wine	10L spirit or 20L fortified wine
Beer & wine	16L beer, 4L wine	110L beer, 90L wine
Other goods	Up to a value of €300 if arriving by land or €430 if arriving by sea or air (€175 for under 15yr)	n/a

Electricity

230V/50Hz

220V/50Hz

Emergency

Ambulance (☏112)
Fire Department (☏112)
Police (☏110)

Internet Access

➡ Many hotels, hostels and *Pensions* (B&Bs) have wireless internet access (called W-Lan;

pronounced vee-lan), DSL or an internet corner for their guests, often at no charge. If they don't, staff should be able to direct you to the nearest internet cafe. They're identified in this book with the internet icon **@**.

➡ Note that at some hotels or hostels wi-fi may be limited to some rooms and/or public areas. Some hotels (usually top-end and business hotels) charge as much as €20 per day for wi-fi access. The wi-fi icon 🛜 is used if a cafe, bar or lodging property has…you guessed it… wi-fi access.

➡ Numerous cafes and bars tout free wi-fi hotspots. If necessary, you'll be given a password when placing your order.

➡ Internet cafes tend to have the lifespan of a fruit fly, so we have not listed any. If you need one, ask at your hotel.

➡ To pin down wi-fi hotspots use www.hotspot-locations.com or www.free-hotspot.com.

Legal Matters

➡ By law you must carry some form of photographic identification, such as your passport, national identity card or driving licence.

➡ The permissible blood-alcohol limit is 0.05% for drivers and 0.16% for bicyclists. Anyone caught exceeding this amount is subject to stiff fines, a confiscated licence or even jail time. Drinking in public is not illegal, but be discreet about it.

➡ Cannabis possession is a criminal offence and punishment ranges from a warning to a court appearance; stiffer penalties apply to people caught with any 'harder' recreational drugs like heroin or cocaine. Searches upon entering clubs are common.

➡ If arrested, you have the right to make a phone call and are presumed innocent until proven guilty, although you may be held in custody until

trial. If you don't know a lawyer, contact your embassy.

Medical Services

➡ The standard of healthcare is high and there are many English-speaking doctors (*Ärzte*) in Berlin. Try **Call-a-Doc** (☎01805 321 303; www.calladoc.com; ⊙24hr), a free nonemergency physician referral in whatever your mother tongue is.

➡ The most central hospital with a 24-hour emergency room is the renowned **Charité Mitte** (☏450 50; www.charite.de; Charitéplatz 1; ⊙24hr; 🚌147, Ⓢ Oranienburger Tor).

➡ If you are a citizen of the EU, the European Health Insurance Card (EHIC) entitles you to reduced-cost or free medical treatment for illness or injury, but not emergency repatriation home. Check with your local health authorities for information on how to obtain an EHIC. Non-EU citizens should check if a similar reciprocal agreement exists between their country and Germany, or if their policy at home provides worldwide healthcare coverage.

➡ If you need to buy travel health insurance, be sure to get a policy that also covers emergency flights back home. While some plans pay doctors or hospitals directly, note that many healthcare providers may still demand immediate payment from nonlocals. Most do not accept credit cards.

➡ There are no vaccinations required to visit Germany.

Pharmacies

➡ German chemists (drugstores, *Drogerien*) do not sell any kind of medication, not even aspirin. Even over-the-counter (*rezeptfrei*) medications for minor health concerns, such as a cold or upset stomach, are only available at a pharmacy (*Apotheke*). For more serious conditions, you will need to produce a prescription (*Rezept*) from a licensed physician. If you take regular medication, be sure to bring a full supply for your entire trip, as the same brand may not be available in Germany.

➡ The names and addresses of pharmacies open after hours (these rotate) are posted in every pharmacy window; or call ☎011 41 for a recorded message outlining which pharmacies are open after hours.

Money

ATMs & Debit Cards

➡ The easiest and quickest way to obtain cash is by using your debit (bank) card at an ATM (*Geldautomat*) linked to international networks such as Cirrus, Plus, Star and Maestro. ATMs are ubiquitous and accessible 24/7.

➡ Many ATM cards double as debit cards and many shops hotels, restaurants and other businesses accept them as payment. Cards use the 'chip and pin' system: instead of signing, you enter your PIN. If you're from overseas and your card isn't chip-and-pin enabled, you may be able to sign the receipt – ask first.

Cash

Cash is king in Germany, so always carry some with you and plan to pay in cash almost everywhere.

Changing Money

Currency exchange offices (Wechselstuben) can be found at airports and major train stations.

Reisebank (www.reisebank.de) Branches at Zoologischer Garten, Hauptbahnhof, Ostbahnhof and Bahnhof Friedrichstrasse.

Euro-Change (www. euro-change.de) Branches at Zoologischer Garten and Alexanderplatz stations; Friedrichstrasse 80.

Reisebank keeps slightly longer hours (at least until 8pm); on Sundays, the airports are your only option.

Credit Cards

➡ Credit cards are becoming more widely accepted (especially in hotels and upmarket shops and restaurants), but it's best not to assume that you'll be able to use one – enquire first.

➡ Visa and MasterCard are more commonly accepted than American Express.

Tipping

➡ Restaurant bills always include a *Bedienung* (service charge) but most people add 5% or 10% unless the service was truly abhorrent.

➡ It's considered rude to leave the tip on the table. Instead, tell the server the total amount you want to pay (for instance, if the bill is €28, say €30). If you don't want change back, say 'Stimmt so' (that's fine).

The following tips are recommended.

Bar 5%

Room cleaners Per day €1 to €2

Hotel porter Per bag €1 to €1.50

Restaurant 5 to 10%

Taxi drivers 10%

Toilet attendants €0.20 to €0.50

Tour guide Per person €1 to €2

Post

You can buy stamps at post offices and at convenience stores offering postal services. The rate for standard-sized letters up to 20g is €0.55 to destinations within Germany and €0.75 elsewhere in the world. For other rates, see www.deutschepost.de.

Mail takes a day or two within Germany, three to five days to the USA and European destinations, and five to seven days to Australasia.

Central post office branches with late hours:

Charlottenburg (Europa Presse Center, Tauentzienstrasse 9; ◷8am-10.30pm Mon-Fri, to 10pm Sat, 11am-8pm Sun; Ⓢ Zoologischer Garten, Ⓡ Zoologischer Garten)

Mitte (Grunerstrasse 20; ◷8am-9pm Mon-Sat; Ⓢ Alexanderplatz, Ⓡ Alexanderplatz)

Public Holidays

Shops, banks and public and private offices are closed on the following *gesetzliche Feiertage* (public holidays):

Neujahrstag (New Year's Day) 1 January

Ostern (Easter) March/April; Good Friday, Easter Sunday and Easter Monday

Christi Himmelfahrt (Ascension Day) Forty days after Easter, always on a Thursday

Maifeiertag (Labour Day) 1 May

SMOKING REGULATIONS

After years of foot-dragging, a total smoking ban in all gastro establishments was to take effect in Berlin on 1 July 2008. But less than a month later, Germany's highest court ruled the sweeping ban unconstitutional. Now smoking is again allowed, but only in single-room bars and clubs that are smaller than 75 sq metres, don't serve anything to eat and keep out customers under 18. Huh?

Some places allow smoking, others don't; at some you can puff away after 10pm, at others only in certain areas. In short, Berlin-style laissez-faire at its finest!

Pfingsten (Whitsun/ Pentecost Sunday and Monday) May/June

Tag der Deutschen Einheit (Day of German Unity) 3 October

Reformationstag (Reformation Day; Brandenburg state only) 31 October

Weihnachtstag (Christmas Day) 25 December

Zweiter Weihnachtstag (Boxing Day) 26 December

Safe Travel

➨ Travellers will rarely get tricked, cheated or conned simply because they're tourists. In fact, Berlin is one of the safest and most tolerant of European cities. Walking about at night, even for a woman alone, is not usually dangerous. Of course, you should keep your wits about you just as you would at home. Always carry enough cash for a cab ride back to the hotel.

➨ The most headline-grabbing crimes are racial or homophobic attacks, but these are very rare. Ask hotel staff about particulars.

➨ If people on the street approach you for cash, they are generally not dangerous – just ignore them. The same goes for people standing near U-Bahn entrances trying to sell you used tickets for a few cents. Don't fall for it – it's illegal and most likely the ticket is no longer valid.

Taxes & Refunds

Prices for goods and services include a value-added tax (VAT; *Mehrwertsteuer*), which is 19% for regular goods and 7% for food and books. If your permanent residence is outside the EU, a large portion of the VAT can be refunded, if you shop at a store displaying the 'Tax-free for tourists' sign and obtain a tax-free form for your purchase. At the

airport, show this form, your unused goods and the receipt to a customs official before checking your luggage. The customs official will stamp the form, which you can then take straight to the cash refund office at the airport.

Telephone

Mobile Phones

➨ Mobile phones (*Handys*) work on GSM900/1800. If your home country uses a different standard, you'll need a multiband GSM phone in Germany.

➨ To avoid high roaming costs, consider buying a prepaid, rechargeable local SIM card, provided you have an unlocked phone that works in Germany. The cheapest and least complicated of these are sold at discount supermarkets such as Aldi, Netto and Lidl, which are ubiquitous in Berlin.

➨ Calls made to German mobile phone numbers are charged at higher rates than those to landlines, but incoming calls are free.

Phone Codes

German phone numbers consist of an area code, which starts with 0, and the local number.

PRACTICALITIES

➨ **Currency** The German currency is the euro (€), divided into 100 cents.

➨ **Clothing Sizes** For women's clothing sizes, a German size 36 equals a size 6 in the US and a size 10 in the UK, then increases in increments of two, making size 38 a US 8 and UK 12, and so on.

➨ **DVD** Germany is in region code 2.

➨ **Laundry** There are dry cleaners (*Reinigung*) and self-service laundrettes (*Waschsalon*) scattered all over Berlin. Most hostels often have washing machines for guest use, while hotels offer a cleaning service as well, although this is quite pricey.

➨ **Newspapers & Magazines** Widely read dailies are *Tagesspiegel*, *Berliner Zeitung*, *Berliner Morgenpost* and *taz*.

➨ **Weights & Measures** The metric system is used.

The area code for Berlin is ☑030. If dialling from a landline within the same city, you don't need to dial the area code. If using a mobile, you must dial it.

Calling Berlin from abroad Dial your country's international access code, then 49 (Germany's country code), then the area code (dropping the initial 0, so just 30) and the local number.

Calling internationally from Berlin Dial 00 (the international access code), then the country code, the area code (without the zero if there is one) and the local number.

Phonecards

➨ Most public payphones only work with Deutsche Telecom (DT) phonecards, available in denominations of €5, €10 and €20 from DT stores, post offices, newsagents and tourist offices.

➨ For long-distance and international calls, prepaid calling cards issued by other providers tend to offer better rates. Those sold at Reisebank branches are reliable and offer fairly competitive rates. Landline calls within Germany and to the UK, for instance, are charged at €0.05 per minute, to the US at €0.06. Calls made from mobile phones cost an extra €0.23 per minute.

Time

Clocks in Germany are set to central European time (GMT/UTC plus one hour). Daylight-savings time kicks in on the last Sunday in March and ends on the last Sunday in October. The use of the 24-hour clock is common.

CITY	NOON IN BERLIN
Auckland	11pm
Cape Town	noon
London	11am
New York	6am
San Francisco	3am
Sydney	9am
Tokyo	8pm

Toilets

- German toilets are sit-down affairs. Men are expected to sit down when peeing.
- Free-standing, 24-hour self-cleaning toilet pods have become quite commonplace. The cost is €0.50 and you have 15 minutes to finish your business. Most are wheelchair-accessible.
- Toilets in malls, clubs, beer gardens etc often have an attendant who expects a tip of between €0.20 and €0.50.

Tourist Information

Visit Berlin (www.visitberlin.de), the Berlin tourist board, operates three walk-in offices and a **call centre** (☎250 025; 🕒8am-7pm Mon-Fri, 9am-6pm Sat & Sun) whose multilingual staff field general questions and make hotel and ticket bookings.

Brandenburger Tor (Pariser Platz; 🕒9.30am-7pm daily; [S]Brandenburger Tor, 🚆Brandenburger Tor) Extended hours April to October.

Hauptbahnhof (inside train station, ground fl, Europaplatz (north) entrance; 🕒8am-10pm; [S]Hauptbahnhof, 🚆Hauptbahnhof)

Neues Kranzler Eck (Kurfürstendamm 22; 🕒9.30am-8pm Mon-Sat, to 6pm Sun; [S]Kurfürstendamm) Extended hours April to October.

Travellers with Disabilities

- Access ramps and/or lifts are available in many public buildings, including train stations, museums, concert halls and cinemas. Newer hotels have lifts and rooms with extra-wide doors and spacious bathrooms. For a data bank assessing the accessibility of cafes, restaurants, hotels, theatres and other public spaces, check with **Mobidat** (☎7477 7115; www.mobidat.de).
- Most buses and trams are wheelchair-accessible and many U-Bahn and S-Bahn stations are equipped with ramps or lifts. For trip-planning assistance, contact the **BVG** (☎194 49; www.bvg.de). Many stations also have grooved platforms to assist blind and vision-impaired passengers. Seeing-eye dogs are allowed everywhere. Hearing-impaired passengers can check upcoming station names on displays installed in all forms of public transport.
- **Rollstuhlpannendienst** (☎0177 833 5773) provides 24-hour wheelchair repairs. The same company also offers wheelchair rentals.

Visas

- EU nationals only need their national identity card or passport to enter, stay and work in Germany. If you intend to stay for an extended period, you must register with the authorities (*Bürgeramt*, or Citizens' Office) within two weeks of arrival.
- Citizens of Australia, Canada, Israel, Japan, New Zealand, Switzerland and the US are among those who only need a valid passport (no visa) if entering as tourists for a stay of up to three months within a six-month period. Passports must be valid for at least another four months beyond the planned departure date.
- Nationals from other countries need a Schengen Visa. Applications for a Schengen Visa must be filed with the embassy or consulate of the country that is your primary destination. It is valid for stays of up to 90 days. Legal residency in any Schengen country makes a visa unnecessary, regardless of your nationality.
- For full details and current regulations, see www.auswaertiges-amt.de or check with a German consulate in your country.

Women Travellers

- Berlin is remarkably safe for women to explore, even solo. Simply use the same common sense you would at home.
- Going alone to cafes and restaurants is perfectly acceptable, even at night.
- It's quite normal to split dinner bills, even on dates.
- In bars and nightclubs, solo women are likely to attract some attention, but if you don't want company, most men will respect a firm 'no, thank you'. Drinks spiked with rohypnol or other drugs are a potential problem in some places – don't leave your drink unattended!
- If assaulted, call the police ☎(110) or contact the **Women's Crisis Hotline** (☎251 2828, 615 4243, 216 8888) whose staff members are trained to help deal with the emotional and physical trauma associated with an attack. The hotlines are not staffed around the clock, but don't get discouraged and try again later.

Language

German belongs to the West Germanic language family and has around 100 million speakers. It is commonly divided into Low German (*Plattdeutsch*) and High German (*Hochdeutsch*). Low German is an umbrella term used for the dialects spoken in Northern Germany. High German is the standard form; it's also used in this chapter.

German is easy for English speakers to pronounce because almost all of its sounds are also found in English. If you read our coloured pronunciation guides as if they were English, you should be understood just fine. Note that kh sounds like the 'ch' in 'Bach' or in the Scottish 'loch' (pronounced at the back of the throat), r is also pronounced at the back of the throat, zh is pronounced as the 's' in 'measure', and ü as the 'ee' in 'see' but with rounded lips. The stressed syllables are indicated with italics in our pronunciation guides. The markers (pol) and (inf) indicate polite and informal forms.

BASICS

Hello.	Guten Tag.	goo·ten tahk
Goodbye.	Auf Wiedersehen.	owf vee·der·zay·en
Yes./No.	Ja./Nein.	yah/nain
Please.	Bitte.	bi·te
Thank you.	Danke.	dang·ke
You're welcome.	Bitte.	bi·te
Excuse me.	Entschuldigung.	ent·shul·di·gung
Sorry.	Entschuldigung.	ent·shul·di·gung

WANT MORE?

For in-depth language information and handy phrases, check out Lonely Planet's *German Phrasebook*. You'll find it at **shop.lonelyplanet.com**, or you can buy Lonely Planet's iPhone phrasebooks at the Apple App Store.

How are you?
Wie geht es Ihnen/dir? (pol/inf) — vee gayt es ee·nen/deer

Fine. And you?
Danke, gut. Und Ihnen/dir? (pol/inf) — dang·ke goot unt ee·nen/deer

What's your name?
Wie ist Ihr Name? (pol) — vee ist eer nah·me
Wie heißt du? (inf) — vee haist doo

My name is ...
Mein Name ist ... (pol) — main nah·me ist ...
Ich heiße ... (inf) — ikh hai·se ...

Do you speak English?
Sprechen Sie Englisch? (pol) — shpre·khen zee eng·lish
Sprichst du Englisch? (inf) — shprikhst doo eng·lish

I don't understand.
Ich verstehe nicht. — ikh fer·shtay·e nikht

ACCOMMODATION

guesthouse	Pension	pahng·zyawn
hotel	Hotel	ho·tel
inn	Gasthof	gast·hawf
youth hostel	Jugend-herberge	yoo·gent·her·ber·ge

Do you have a ... room?	Haben Sie ein ...?	hah·ben zee ain ...
double	Doppelzimmer	do·pel·tsi·mer
single	Einzelzimmer	ain·tsel·tsi·mer

How much is it per ...?	Wie viel kostet es pro ...?	vee feel kos·tet es praw ...
night	Nacht	nakht
person	Person	per·zawn

Is breakfast included?
Ist das Frühstück inklusive? — ist das frü·shtük in·kloo·zee·ve

DIRECTIONS

Where's ...?
Wo ist ...? — vaw ist ...

What's the address?
Wie ist die Adresse? — vee ist dee a·dre·se

How far is it?
Wie weit ist es? — vee vait ist es

Can you show me (on the map)?
Können Sie es mir — ker·nen zee es meer
(auf der Karte) zeigen? — (owf dair kar·te) tsai·gen

How can I get there?
Wie kann ich da — vee kan ikh dah
hinkommen? — hin·ko·men

Turn ...	Biegen Sie ... ab.	bee·gen zee ... ab
at the corner	an der Ecke	an dair e·ke
at the traffic lights	bei der Ampel	bai dair am·pel
left	links	lingks
right	rechts	rekhts

EATING & DRINKING

I'd like to reserve a table for ...	Ich möchte einen Tisch für ... reservieren.	ikh merkh·te ai·nen tish für ... re·zer·vee·ren
(eight) o'clock	(acht) Uhr	(akht) oor
(two) people	(zwei) Personen	(tsvai) per·zaw·nen

I'd like the menu, please.
Ich hätte gern die — ikh he·te gern dee
Speisekarte, bitte. — shpai·ze·kar·te bi·te

What would you recommend?
Was empfehlen Sie? — vas emp·fay·len zee

What's in that dish?
Was ist in diesem — vas ist in dee·zem
Gericht? — ge·rikht

I'm a vegetarian.
Ich bin Vegetarier/ — ikh bin ve·ge·tah·ri·er/
Vegetarierin. (m/f) — ve·ge·tah·ri·e·rin

That was delicious.
Das hat hervorragend — das hat her·fawr·rah·gent
geschmeckt. — ge·shmekt

Cheers!
Prost! — prawst

Please bring the bill.
Bitte bringen Sie — bi·te bring·en zee
die Rechnung. — dee rekh·nung

Key Words

bar (pub)	Kneipe	knai·pe
bottle	Flasche	fla·she

KEY PATTERNS

To get by in German, mix and match these simple patterns with words of your choice:

When's (the next flight)?
Wann ist (der — van ist (dair
nächste Flug)? — naykhs·te flook)

Where's (the station)?
Wo ist (der Bahnhof)? — vaw ist (dair bahn·hawf)

Where can I (buy a ticket)?
Wo kann ich (eine — vaw kan ikh (ai·ne
Fahrkarte kaufen)? — fahr·kar·te kow·fen)

Do you have (a map)?
Haben Sie — hah·ben zee
(eine Karte)? — (ai·ne kar·te)

Is there (a toilet)?
Gibt es (eine Toilette)? — gipt es (ai·ne to·a·le·te)

I'd like (a coffee).
Ich möchte — ikh merkh·te
(einen Kaffee). — (ai·nen ka·fay)

I'd like (to hire a car).
Ich möchte — ikh merkh·te
(ein Auto mieten). — (ain ow·to mee·ten)

Can I (enter)?
Darf ich — darf ikh
(hereinkommen)? — (her·ein·ko·men)

Could you please (help me)?
Könnten Sie — kern·ten zee
(mir helfen)? — (meer hel·fen)

Do I have to (book a seat)?
Muss ich (einen Platz — mus ikh (ai·nen plats
reservieren lassen)? — re·zer·vee·ren la·sen)

bowl	Schüssel	shü·sel
breakfast	Frühstück	frü·shtük
cold	kalt	kalt
cup	Tasse	ta·se
daily special	Gericht des Tages	ge·rikht des tah·ges
delicatessen	Feinkostgeschäft	fain·kost·ge·sheft
desserts	Nachspeisen	nahkh·shpai·zen
dinner	Abendessen	ah·bent·e·sen
drink list	Getränkekarte	ge·treng·ke·kar·te
fork	Gabel	gah·bel
glass	Glas	glahs
grocery store	Lebensmittelladen	lay·bens·mi·tel·lah·den
hot (warm)	warm	warm
knife	Messer	me·ser
lunch	Mittagessen	mi·tahk·e·sen

market	Markt	markt
plate	Teller	te·ler
restaurant	Restaurant	res·to·rahng
set menu	Menü	may·nü
spicy	würzig	vür·tsikh
spoon	Löffel	ler·fel
with/without	mit/ohne	mit/aw·ne

Meat & Fish

beef	Rindfleisch	rint·flaish
carp	Karpfen	karp·fen
fish	Fisch	fish
herring	Hering	hay·ring
lamb	Lammfleisch	lam·flaish
meat	Fleisch	flaish
pork	Schweinefleisch	shvai·ne·flaish
poultry	Geflügelfleisch	ge·flü·gel·flaish
salmon	Lachs	laks
sausage	Wurst	vurst
seafood	Meeresfrüchte	mair·res·frükh·te
shellfish	Schaltiere	shahl·tee·re
trout	Forelle	fo·re·le
veal	Kalbfleisch	kalp·flaish

Fruit & Vegetables

apple	Apfel	ap·fel
banana	Banane	ba·nah·ne
bean	Bohne	baw·ne
cabbage	Kraut	krowt
capsicum	Paprika	pap·ri·kah
carrot	Mohrrübe	mawr·rü·be
cucumber	Gurke	gur·ke
fruit	Frucht/Obst	frukht/awpst
grapes	Weintrauben	vain·trow·ben
lemon	Zitrone	tsi·traw·ne
lentil	Linse	lin·ze
lettuce	Kopfsalat	kopf·za·laht
mushroom	Pilz	pilts
nuts	Nüsse	nü·se
onion	Zwiebel	tsvee·bel
orange	Orange	o·rahng·zhe
pea	Erbse	erp·se
plum	Pflaume	pflow·me
potato	Kartoffel	kar·to·fel
spinach	Spinat	shpi·naht
strawberry	Erdbeere	ert·bair·re

tomato	Tomate	to·mah·te
vegetable	Gemüse	ge·mü·ze
watermelon	Wassermelone	va·ser·me·law·ne

Other

bread	Brot	brawt
butter	Butter	bu·ter
cheese	Käse	kay·ze
egg/eggs	Ei/Eier	ai/ai·er
honey	Honig	haw·nikh
jam	Marmelade	mar·me·lah·de
pasta	Nudeln	noo·deln
pepper	Pfeffer	pfe·fer
rice	Reis	rais
salt	Salz	zalts
soup	Suppe	zu·pe
sugar	Zucker	tsu·ker

Drinks

beer	Bier	beer
coffee	Kaffee	ka·fay
juice	Saft	zaft
milk	Milch	milkh
orange juice	Orangensaft	o·rang·zhen·zaft
red wine	Rotwein	rawt·vain
sparkling wine	Sekt	zekt
tea	Tee	tay
water	Wasser	va·ser
white wine	Weißwein	vais·vain

EMERGENCIES

Help!	Hilfe!	hil·fe
Go away!	Gehen Sie weg!	gay·en zee vek

Signs

Ausgang	Exit
Damen	Women
Eingang	Entrance
Geschlossen	Closed
Herren	Men
Toiletten (WC)	Toilets
Offen	Open
Verboten	Prohibited

Call the police!
Rufen Sie die Polizei!   roo·fen zee dee po·li·*tsai*

Call a doctor!
Rufen Sie einen Arzt!   roo·fen zee *ai*·nen artst

Where are the toilets?
Wo ist die Toilette?   vo ist dee to·a·*le*·te

I'm lost.
Ich habe mich verirrt.   ikh *hah*·be mikh fer·*irt*

I'm sick.
Ich bin krank.   ikh bin krangk

It hurts here.
Es tut hier weh.   es toot heer vay

I'm allergic to ...
Ich bin allergisch   ikh bin a·*lair*·gish
gegen ...   *gay*·gen ...

SHOPPING & SERVICES

I'd like to buy ...
Ich möchte ... kaufen.   ikh *merkh*·te ... *kow*·fen

I'm just looking.
Ich schaue mich nur um.   ikh *show*·e mikh noor um

Can I look at it?
Können Sie es mir   *ker*·nen zee es meer
zeigen?   *tsai*·gen

How much is this?
Wie viel kostet das?   vee feel *kos*·tet das

That's too expensive.
Das ist zu teuer.   das ist tsoo *toy*·er

Can you lower the price?
Können Sie mit dem   *ker*·nen zee mit dem
Preis heruntergehen?   prais he·*run*·ter·gay·en

There's a mistake in the bill.
Da ist ein Fehler   dah ist ain *fay*·ler
in der Rechnung.   in dair *rekh*·nung

ATM	*Geldautomat*	*gelt*·ow·to·maht
post office	*Postamt*	*post*·amt
tourist office	*Fremden-*	*frem*·den-
	verkehrsbüro	fer·kairs·bü·raw

TIME & DATES

What time is it?
Wie spät ist es?   vee shpayt ist es

It's (10) o'clock.
Es ist (zehn) Uhr.   es ist (tsayn) oor

Question Words		
What?	*Was?*	vas
When?	*Wann?*	van
Where?	*Wo?*	vaw
Who?	*Wer?*	vair
Why?	*Warum?*	va·*rum*

At what time?
Um wie viel Uhr?   um vee feel oor

At ...
Um ...   um ...

morning	*Morgen*	*mor*·gen
afternoon	*Nachmittag*	*nahkh*·mi·tahk
evening	*Abend*	*ah*·bent
yesterday	*gestern*	*ges*·tern
today	*heute*	*hoy*·te
tomorrow	*morgen*	*mor*·gen
Monday	*Montag*	*mawn*·tahk
Tuesday	*Dienstag*	*deens*·tahk
Wednesday	*Mittwoch*	*mit*·vokh
Thursday	*Donnerstag*	*do*·ners·tahk
Friday	*Freitag*	*frai*·tahk
Saturday	*Samstag*	*zams*·tahk
Sunday	*Sonntag*	*zon*·tahk
January	*Januar*	*yan*·u·ahr
February	*Februar*	*fay*·bru·ahr
March	*März*	merts
April	*April*	a·*pril*
May	*Mai*	mai
June	*Juni*	*yoo*·ni
July	*Juli*	*yoo*·li
August	*August*	ow·*gust*
September	*September*	zep·*tem*·ber
October	*Oktober*	ok·*taw*·ber
November	*November*	no·*vem*·ber
December	*Dezember*	de·*tsem*·ber

TRANSPORT

Public Transport

boat	*Boot*	bawt
bus	*Bus*	bus
metro	*U-Bahn*	*oo*·bahn
plane	*Flugzeug*	*flook*·tsoyk
train	*Zug*	tsook
At what time's the ... bus?	*Wann fährt der ... Bus?*	van fairt dair... bus
first	*erste*	*ers*·te
last	*letzte*	*lets*·te
next	*nächste*	*naykhs*·te

Numbers

1	eins	ains
2	zwei	tsvai
3	drei	drai
4	vier	feer
5	fünf	fünf
6	sechs	zeks
7	sieben	zee·ben
8	acht	akht
9	neun	noyn
10	zehn	tsayn
20	zwanzig	tsvan·tsikh
30	dreißig	drai·tsikh
40	vierzig	feer·tsikh
50	fünfzig	fünf·tsikh
60	sechzig	zekh·tsikh
70	siebzig	zeep·tsikh
80	achtzig	akht·tsikh
90	neunzig	noyn·tsikh
100	hundert	hun·dert
1000	tausend	tow·sent

A ... to (Cologne).	Eine ... nach (Köln).	ai·ne ... nahkh (kerln)
1st-/2nd-class ticket	Fahrkarte erster/zweiter Klasse	fahr·kar·te ers·ter/tsvai·ter kla·se
one-way ticket	einfache Fahrkarte	ain·fa·khe fahr·kar·te
return ticket	Rückfahrkarte	rük·fahr·kar·te

At what time does it arrive?
Wann kommt es an? van komt es an

Is it a direct route?
Ist es eine direkte ist es ai·ne di·rek·te
Verbindung? fer·bin·dung

Does it stop at ...?
Hält es in ...? helt es in ...

What station is this?
Welcher Bahnhof vel·kher bahn·hawf
ist das? ist das

What's the next stop?
Welches ist der vel·khes ist dair
nächste Halt? naykh·ste halt

I want to get off here.
Ich möchte hier ikh merkh·te heer
aussteigen. ows·shtai·gen

Please tell me when we get to ....
Könnten Sie mir bitte kern·ten zee meer bi·te
sagen, wann wir in zah·gen van veer in
... ankommen? ... an·ko·men

Please take me to (this address).
Bitte bringen Sie mich bi·te bring·en zee mikh
zu (dieser Adresse). tsoo (dee·zer a·dre·se)

platform	Bahnsteig	bahn·shtaik
ticket office	Fahrkarten-verkauf	fahr·kar·ten-fer·kowf
timetable	Fahrplan	fahr·plan

Driving & Cycling

I'd like to hire a ...	Ich möchte ein ... mieten.	ikh merkh·te ain ... mee·ten
4WD	Allrad-fahrzeug	al·raht-fahr·tsoyk
bicycle	Fahrrad	fahr·raht
car	Auto	ow·to
motorbike	Motorrad	maw·tor·raht

How much is it per ...?	Wie viel kostet es pro ...?	vee feel kos·tet es praw ...
day	Tag	tahk
week	Woche	vo·khe

bicycle pump	Fahrradpumpe	fahr·raht·pum·pe
child seat	Kindersitz	kin·der·zits
helmet	Helm	helm
petrol	Benzin	ben·tseen

Does this road go to ...?
Führt diese Straße fürt dee·ze shtrah·se
nach ...? nahkh ...

(How long) Can I park here?
(Wie lange) Kann ich (vee lang·e) kan ikh
hier parken? heer par·ken

Where's a petrol station?
Wo ist eine Tankstelle? vaw ist ai·ne tangk·shte·le

I need a mechanic.
Ich brauche einen ikh brow·khe ai·nen
Mechaniker. me·khah·ni·ker

My car/motorbike has broken down (at ...).
Ich habe (in ...) eine ikh hah·be (in ...) ai·ne
Panne mit meinem pa·ne mit mai·nem
Auto/Motorrad. ow·to/maw·tor·raht

I've run out of petrol.
Ich habe kein ikh hah·be kain
Benzin mehr. ben·tseen mair

I have a flat tyre.
Ich habe eine ikh hah·be ai·ne
Reifenpanne. rai·fen·pa·ne

Are there cycling paths?
Gibt es Fahrradwege? geept es fahr·raht·vay·ge

Is there bicycle parking?
Gibt es Fahrrad- geept es fahr·raht·
Parkplätze? park·ple·tse

GLOSSARY

You may encounter the following terms and abbreviations while in Berlin.

Bahnhof (Bf) – train station

Berg – mountain

Bibliothek – library

BRD – Bundesrepublik Deutschland (abbreviated in English as FRG – Federal Republic of Germany); see also DDR

Brücke – bridge

Brunnen – fountain or well

Bundestag – German parliament

CDU – Christliche Demokratische Union (Christian Democratic Union), centre-right party

DDR – Deutsche Demokratische Republik (abbreviated in English as GDR – German Democratic Republic); the name for the former East Germany; see also BRD

Denkmal – memorial, monument

Dom – cathedral

ermässigt – reduced (eg admission fee)

Fahrrad – bicycle

Flohmarkt – flea market

Flughafen – airport

FRG – Federal Republic of Germany; see also BRD

Gasse – lane or alley

Gästehaus, Gasthaus – guesthouse

GDR – German Democratic Republic (the former East Germany); see also DDR

Gedenkstätte – memorial site

Gestapo – Geheime Staatspolizei (Nazi secret police)

Gründerzeit – literally 'foundation time'; early years of German empire, roughly 1871–90

Hafen – harbour, port

Hauptbahnhof (Hbf) – main train station

Hof (Höfe) – courtyard(s)

Imbiss – snack bar, takeaway stand

Insel – island

Kaiser – emperor; derived from 'Caesar'

Kapelle – chapel

Karte – ticket

Kiez(e) – neighbourhood(s)

Kino – cinema

König – king

Konzentrationslager (KZ) – concentration camp

Kristallnacht – literally 'Night of Broken Glass'; Nazi pogrom against Jewish businesses and institutions on 9 November 1938

Kunst – art

Kunsthotels – hotels either designed by artists or liberally furnished with art

Mietskaserne(n) – tenement(s) built around successive courtyards

Ostalgie – fusion of the words Ost and Nostalgie, meaning nostalgia for East Germany

Palais – small palace

Palast – palace

Passage – shopping arcade

Platz – square

Rathaus – town hall

Reich – empire

Reisezentrum – travel centre in train or bus stations

Saal (Säle) – hall(s), large room(s)

Sammlung – collection

S-Bahn – metro/regional rail service with fewer stops than the U-Bahn

Schiff – ship

Schloss – palace

See – lake

SPD – Sozialdemokratische Partei Deutschlands (Social Democratic Party of Germany)

SS – Schutzstaffel; organisation within the Nazi Party that supplied Hitler's bodyguards, as well as concentration camp guards and the Waffen-SS troops in WWII

Stasi – GDR secret police (from Ministerium für Staatssicherheit, or Ministry of State Security)

Strasse (Str) – street

Tageskarte – daily menu; day ticket on public transport

Tor – gate

Trabant – GDR-era car boasting a two-stroke engine

Turm – tower

Trümmerberge – rubble mountains

U-Bahn – rapid transit railway, mostly underground; best choice for metro trips

Ufer – bank

Viertel – quarter, neighbourhood

Wald – forest

Weg – way, path

Weihnachtsmarkt – Christmas market

Wende – 'change' or 'turning point' of 1989, ie the collapse of the GDR and the resulting German reunification

Behind the Scenes

SEND US YOUR FEEDBACK

We love to hear from travellers – your comments keep us on our toes and help make our books better. Our well-travelled team reads every word on what you loved or loathed about this book. Although we cannot reply individually to postal submissions, we always guarantee that your feedback goes straight to the appropriate authors, in time for the next edition. Each person who sends us information is thanked in the next edition – and the most useful submissions are rewarded with a selection of digital PDF chapters.

Visit **lonelyplanet.com/contact** to submit your updates and suggestions or to ask for help. Our award-winning website also features inspirational travel stories, news and discussions.

Note: We may edit, reproduce and incorporate your comments in Lonely Planet products such as guidebooks, websites and digital products, so let us know if you don't want your comments reproduced or your name acknowledged. For a copy of our privacy policy visit lonelyplanet.com/privacy.

OUR READERS

Many thanks to the travellers who used the last edition and wrote to us with helpful hints, useful advice and interesting anecdotes:

Álvaro Márquez Barba, Arie van Oosterwijk, Brian & Cate Quinn, Chris Roloff, Christian Oelsner, Clemens Maria Schreiner, Cynthia Romero, Elmar Vieregge, Emanuele Ciola, Emma Hoiberg, James Browne, Jeannette Kreutzberger, Jeen van Beusekom, Jonny Vancutsem, Josianne Boucher, Lorenzo Scacchia, Martin D Rich, Michaela Grill, Noemi Cipollone, P Lystrup, Paolosbg Vattelapesca, Paul Martinez, Risma Utami, Tony Plunkett, Torsten Alisch, Uli Schuster, Vilppu Välimäki

AUTHOR THANKS
Andrea Schulte-Peevers

Big heartfelt thanks to all these wonderful people who plied me with tips, insights, information, ideas and encouragement (in no particular order): Henrik Tidefjärd, Miriam Bers, Petra Gümmer, Julia Schwarz, Frank Engster, Myriel Walter, Cookie, Heiner Schuster, Steffi Gretschel, Renate Freiling, Silke Neumann, Kirsten Schmidt, Michael Radder, Christoph Münch, Christoph Lehmann, Patrick Schwarzkopf, Danilo Hommel, Dr Jasper Freiherr von Richthofen, Uve Teschner, Elisabeth Herms-Lübbe, Julia Schröder, Jan Czyszke and, of course, David Peevers. Kudos to the entire LP team responsible for producing such a kick-ass book.

ACKNOWLEDGMENTS

Climate map data adapted from Peel MC, Finlayson BL & McMahon TA (2007) 'Updated World Map of the Köppen-Geiger Climate Classification', Hydrology and Earth System Sciences, 11, 163344.

Cover photograph: Brandenburg Gate; Mark Daffey/Getty Images.

THIS BOOK

This 8th edition of Lonely Planet's *Berlin* guidebook was researched and written by Andrea Schulte-Peevers. Andrea has worked on all eight editions of this book; the first alongside David Peevers, the 4th and 5th editions with the late Tom Parkinson, and the 6th edition with Anthony Haywood and Sally O'Brien. This guidebook was commissioned in Lonely Planet's London office, and produced by the following:

Commissioning Editors Katie O'Connell, Anna Tyler

Coordinating Editors Karyn Noble, Tracy Whitmey

Coordinating Cartographer Julie Dodkins

Coordinating Layout Designer Katherine Marsh

Managing Editors Sasha Baskett, Barbara Delissen, Brigitte Ellemor

Managing Cartographers Anita Bahn, Mark Griffiths, Adrian Persoglia

Managing Layout Designer Jane Hart

Assisting Editors Janet Austin, Elin Berglund, Samantha Forge, Carly Hall, Gabrielle Innes, Charlotte Orr

Assisting Cartographers Jeff Cameron, Rachel Imeson

Assisting Layout Designer Joseph Spanti

Cover Research Naomi Parker

Internal Image Research Kylie McLaughlin

Language Content Branislava Vladisavljevic

Thanks to Dan Austin, Ryan Evans, Justin Flynn, Larissa Frost, Tobias Gattineau, Chris Girdler, Lorna Goodyer, Briohny Hooper, Asha Ioculari, Jouve India, Anna Metcalfe, Trent Paton, Raphael Richards, Averil Robertson, Fiona Siseman, Luna Soo, Angela Tinson, Gerard Walker, Clifton Wilkinson

See also separate subindexes for:

🍴 **EATING P307**

🍷 **DRINKING & NIGHTLIFE P308**

☆ **ENTERTAINMENT P309**

🛍 **SHOPPING P309**

🛏 **SLEEPING P310**

Index

Berlin Maps

Map Legend

Sights
- Beach
- Buddhist
- Castle
- Christian
- Hindu
- Islamic
- Jewish
- Monument
- Museum/Gallery
- Ruin
- Winery/Vineyard
- Zoo
- Other Sight

Eating
- Eating

Drinking & Nightlife
- Drinking & Nightlife
- Cafe

Entertainment
- Entertainment

Shopping
- Shopping

Sleeping
- Sleeping
- Camping

Sports & Activities
- Diving/Snorkelling
- Canoeing/Kayaking
- Skiing
- Surfing
- Swimming/Pool
- Walking
- Windsurfing
- Other Sports & Activities

Information
- Post Office
- Tourist Information

Transport
- Airport
- Border Crossing
- Bus
- Cable Car/Funicular
- Cycling
- Ferry
- Monorail
- Parking
- S-Bahn
- Taxi
- Train/Railway
- Tram
- Tube Station
- U-Bahn
- Underground Train Station
- Other Transport

Routes
- Tollway
- Freeway
- Primary
- Secondary
- Tertiary
- Lane
- Unsealed Road
- Plaza/Mall
- Steps
- Tunnel
- Pedestrian Overpass
- Walking Tour
- Walking Tour Detour
- Path

Boundaries
- International
- State/Province
- Disputed
- Regional/Suburb
- Marine Park
- Cliff
- Wall

Geographic
- Hut/Shelter
- Lighthouse
- Lookout
- Mountain/Volcano
- Oasis
- Park
- Pass
- Picnic Area
- Waterfall

Hydrography
- River/Creek
- Intermittent River
- Swamp/Mangrove
- Reef
- Canal
- Water
- Dry/Salt/Intermittent Lake
- Glacier

Areas
- Beach/Desert
- Cemetery (Christian)
- Cemetery (Other)
- Park/Forest
- Sportsground
- Sight (Building)
- Top Sight (Building)

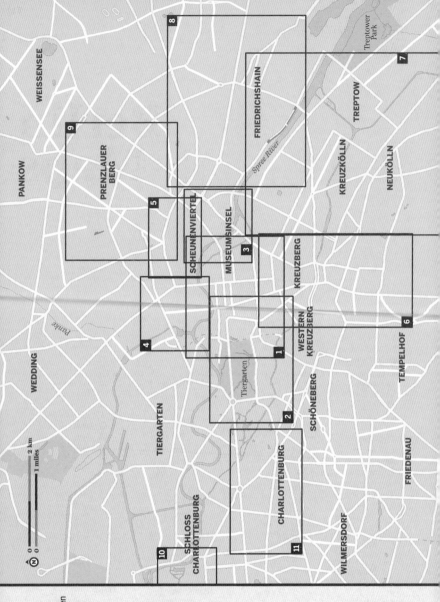

MAP INDEX

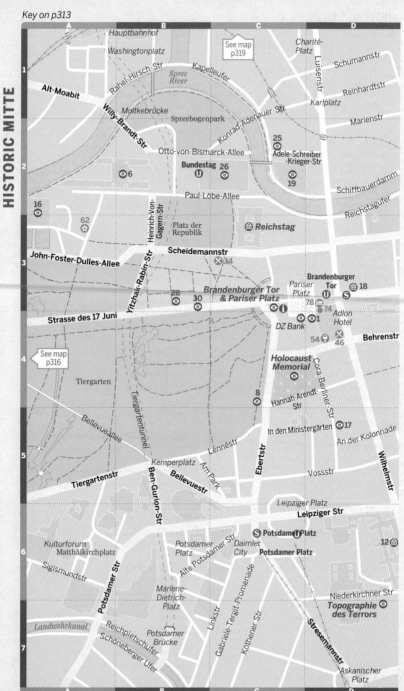

HISTORIC MITTE

Hauptbahnhof

Washingtonplatz

Alt-Moabit

Rahel-Hirsch-Str

Willy-Brandt-Str

Spree River

Kapelleufer

See map p319

Charité-Platz

Luisenstr

Schumannstr

Reinhardtstr

Moltkebrücke

Spreebogenpark

Karlplatz

Marienstr

Otto-von-Bismarck-Allee

Konrad-Adenauer-Str

⊙ 6

Bundestag Ⓤ

26

Adele-Schreiber-Krieger-Str

25

19

Schiffbauerdamm

16

Paul-Löbe-Allee

Reichstagufer

62 ☆

Heinrich-Von-Gagern-Str

Platz der Republik

🏛 Reichstag

John-Foster-Dulles-Allee

Yitzhak-Rabin-Str

Scheidemannstr

× 34

Brandenburger Tor & Pariser Platz

Pariser Platz

Brandenburger Tor

🏛 18

28

30

Ⓤ

Ⓢ

Strasse des 17 Juni

⊙ i

78

74

Adlon Hotel

⊙ 1

See map p316

DZ Bank

54

× 46

Behrenstr

Tiergarten

Tiergartentunnel

Holocaust Memorial

⊙

Cora-Berliner-Str

Bellevueallee

8

Hannah-Arendt-Str

Lennéstr

In den Ministergärten

⊙ 17

An der Kolonnade

Kemperplatz

Am Park

Ebertstr

Vossstr

Wilhelmstr

Tiergartenstr

Ben-Gurion-Str

Bellevuestr

Leipziger Platz

Leipziger Str

Kulturforum Matthäikirchplatz

Potsdamer Str

Potsdamer Platz

Alte Potsdamer Str

Daimler City

Ⓢ Potsdamer Ⓤ Platz

Potsdamer Platz

12 🏛

Sigismundstr

Marlene-Dietrich-Platz

Linkstr

Gabriele-Tergit-Promenade

Köthener Str

Niederkirchner Str

Topographie des Terrors ⊙

Landwehrkanal

Reichpietschufer

Schöneberger Ufer

Potsdamer Brücke

Stresemannstr

Askanischer Platz

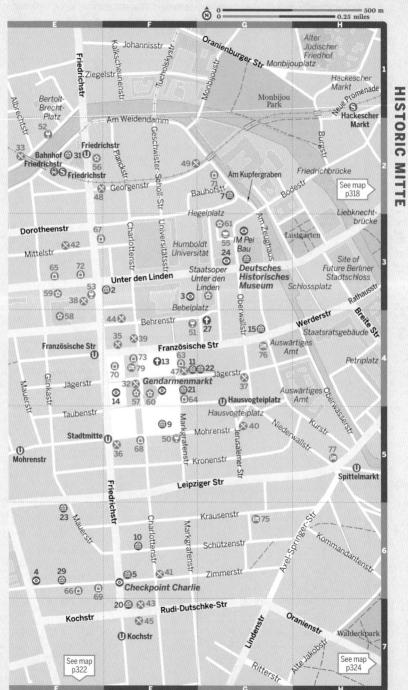

0
0
500 m
0.25 miles

Johannisstr

Kalkscheunenstr

Oranienburger Str

Monbijoustr

Alter Jüdischer Friedhof

Monbijouplatz

Monbijou Park

Hackescher Markt

Neue Promenade

Hackescher Markt

Friedrichstr

Ziegelstr

Tucholskystr

Geschwister-Scholl-Str

Bertolt-Brecht-Platz

Albrechtstr

Am Weidendamm

52

33

Bahnhof 31

Friedrichstr

Friedrichstr 56

48

Planckstr

Georgenstr

49

71

Bauhofstr

7

Am Kupfergraben

Friedrichbrücke

Bodestr

Burgstr

See map
p318

Hegelplatz

Dorotheenstr

67

42

Mittelstr

65

72

Charlottenstr

Universitätsstr

Humboldt Universität

61

55

51

IM Pei Bau

24

Liebknecht-brücke

Lustgarten

Site of Future Berliner Stadtschloss

Unter den Linden

59

38

53

2

58

Staatsoper Unter den Linden

3

Bebelplatz

44

35

39

Behrenstr

Französische Str

Französische Str

Deutsches Historisches Museum

Oberwallstr

Schlossplatz

Rathausstr

Breite Str

27

51

15

Werderstr

Staatsratsgebäude

Auswärtiges Amt

76

Petriplatz

Glinkastr

Mauerstr

Jägerstr

70

73

79

13

63

11

47

22

Gendarmenmarkt

Jägerstr

32

14

57

60

21

64

37

Auswärtiges Amt

Niederwallstr

Kurstr

Oberwasserstr

Taubenstr

Stadtmitte

Mohrenstr

36

68

9

50

Hausvogteiplatz

Hausvogteiplatz

40

Mohrenstr

Markgrafenstr

Kronenstr

Jerusalemer Str

77

Spittelmarkt

Leipziger Str

23

Mauerstr

Friedrichstr

10

Charlottenstr

Krausenstr

Schützenstr

Markgrafenstr

75

Axel-Springer-Str

Kommandantenstr

4

29

66

69

5

41

Checkpoint Charlie

Zimmerstr

20

43

45

Kochstr

Kochstr

Rudi-Dutschke-Str

Lindenstr

Oranienstr

Waldeckpark

See map
p322

Alte Jakobstr

Rittstr

See map
p324

POTSDAMER PLATZ & TIERGARTEN

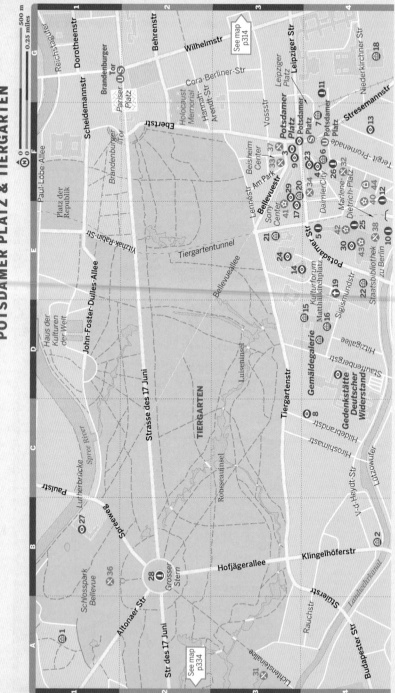

500 m
0.25 miles

See map p314

See map p334

TIERGARTEN

POTSDAMER PLATZ & TIERGARTEN

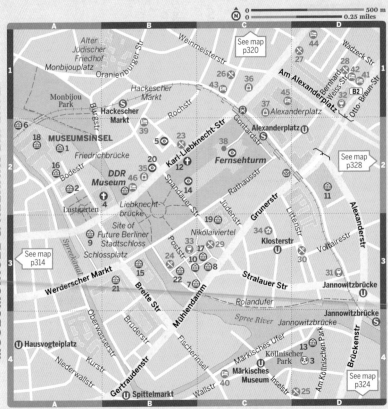

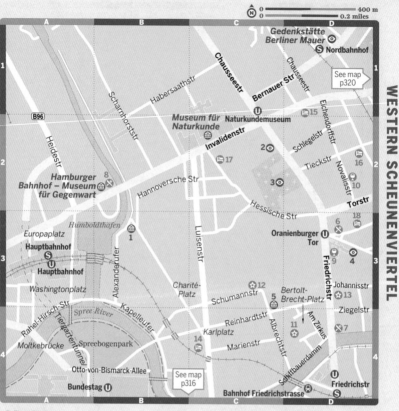

SCHEUNENVIERTEL

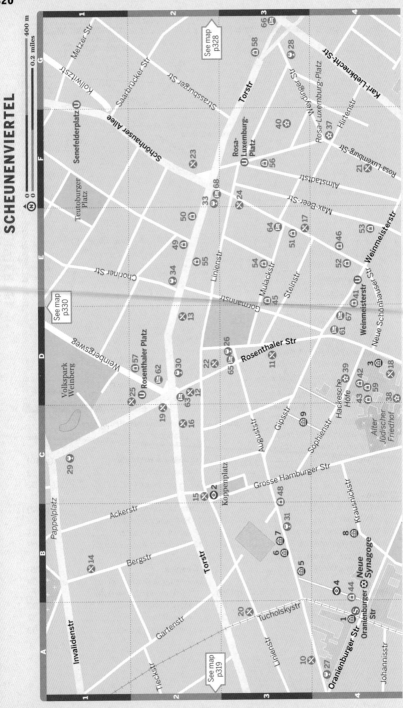

N

0   400 m
0   0.2 miles

See map p328

See map p330

See map p319

Metzer Str

Kollwitzstr

Saarbrücker Str

Strassburger Str

Schönhauser Allee

Senefelderplatz

Teutburger Platz

Torstr

Rosa-Luxemburg-Platz

Rosa-Luxemburg-Str

Karl-Liebknecht-Str

Hirtenstr

Weydinger Str

Almstadtstr

Max-Beer-Str

Gormannstr

Mulackstr

Steinstr

Linienstr

Choriner Str

Weinbergsweg

Volkspark Weinberg

Pappelplatz

Invalidenstr

Tieckstr

Gartenstr

Ackerstr

Bergstr

Torstr

Linienstr

Koppenplatz

Grosse Hamburger Str

Augustrstr

Gipsstr

Sophienstr

Rosenthaler Platz

Rosenthaler Str

Weinmeisterstr

Neue Schönhauser Str

Weinmeisterstr

Hackesche Höfe

Alter Jüdischer Friedhof

Krausnickstr

Neue Synagoge

Oranienburger Str

Oranienburger Str

Tucholskystr

Johannisstr

66
58
28
37
40
56
23
68
33
24
50
17
64
51
46
53
52
49
34
55
54
45
41
67
61
13
26
57
62
30
22
11
65
63
12
16
19
25
29
39
42
3
18
59
43
38
9
48
15
2
31
7
6
5
44
4
8
1
20
10
27
14
21

Ziegelstr
Monbijoustr
Monbijouplatz
Monbijou Park
Spree River
Am Kupfergraben
Burgstr
Hackesche Höfe
Neue Promenade
Hackescher Markt
See map p318
Dircksenstr
Rochstr
Münzstr
Am Alexanderplatz
36
35
60
32
47
A
B
C
D
E
F
G
5

Top Sights (p129)
Hackesche Höfe D5
Neue Synagoge B4

Sights (p132)
Anne Frank Zentrum (see 3)
1 C/O Berlin A4
2 Der Verlassene Raum C2
Gedenkstätte Stille Helden .... (see 3)
3 Haus Schwarzenberg...... D4
4 Heckmannhöfe................ B4
5 Jüdische Mädchenschule B3
6 KW Institute for Contemporary Art........ B3
7 Me Collectors Room B3
Museum Blindenwerkstatt Otto Weidt .... (see 3)
Museum The Kennedys..(see 5)
8 Ramones Museum.......... B4
9 Sammlung Hoffmann C3

Eating (p136)
Barcomi's Deli ....(see 9)
10 Café Nord-Sud................A3
11 Chèn Chè D3
12 Côcô...............................D2
Fleischerei Imbiss.. (see 30)
13 Hartweizen D2
14 Katz Orange.................... B1
15 Kopps..............................C2
16 Mani C2
Mogg & Melzer ....(see 5)
17 Monsieur Vuong E3
18 Pan Asia..........................D4
Pauly Saal ....(see 5)
19 Rosenburger...................C2
Rosenthaler Grill- und Schlemmerbuffet (see 19)
20 Schwarzwaldstuben........A3
21 Susuru F4
22 Transit D2
23 White Trash Fast Food.... F2
24 Yam Yam F3
25 Zagreus Projekt D2

Drinking & Nightlife (p140)
26 Amano Bar D3
27 August II A4
28 Bar 3...............................G3
29 Buck and Breck.............. C1
30 Butcher's........................ D2
Café Bravo................(see 6)
31 Clärchens Ballhaus B3
32 Flamingo.........................C5
33 Kaffee Burger..................F2
Mein Haus am See . (see 19)
34 Neue Odessa Bar E2
35 Strandbar Mitte.............. B5

Entertainment (p142)
36 Amphitheater.................. B5
37 Babylon F4
B-Flat......................(see 11)
38 Chamäleon Varieté D4
Freiluftkino Mitte...... (see 3)
Sonntagskonzerte ..(see 31)
39 Sophiensaele.................. D4
40 Volksbühne am Rosa-Luxemburg-Platz.F3

Shopping (p143)
41 1. Absinth Depot Berlin....E4
42 Ampelmann Galerie.........D4
43 Berlin Fashion Network D4
44 Bonbonmacherei.............B4
45 C'est Tout E3
46 Claudia Skoda E4
East Berlin .... (see 46)
47 Fun Factory D5
48 Galerie Eigen+Art C3
49 Grober Unfug..................E2
50 Happy Shop....................E2
51 Herr Von Eden E3
52 Hundt Hammer Stein......E4
53 IC! Berlin.........................E4
54 Lala Berlin.......................E3
55 No 74 Berlin....................E2
56 Pro QM...........................F3
57 Rotation Records............ D2
58 Schwarzer Reiter G3
59 Thatchers........................ D4

Sports & Activities (p27)
60 Kinderbad Monbijou B5

Sleeping (p225)
61 Casa Camper D4
62 Circus Hostel D2
63 Circus Hotel D2
64 Flower's Boardinghouse Mitte.............................E3
65 Hotel Amano D3
Mani Hotel..............(see 16)
66 Soho House Berlin G3
67 The Weinmeister............ D4
68 Wombat's City Hostel Berlin F2

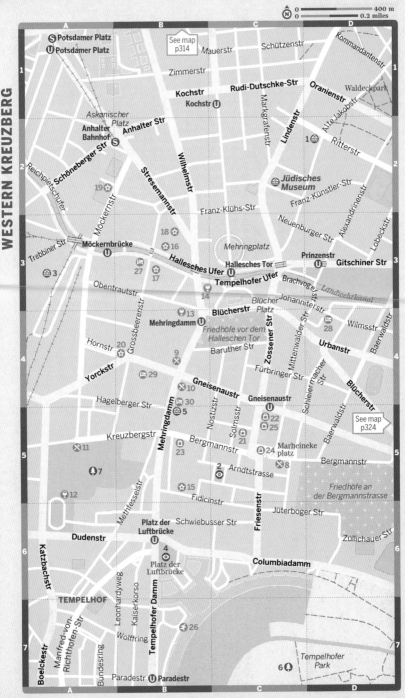

WESTERN KREUZBERG

0 — 400 m
0 — 0.2 miles

Potsdamer Platz
Potsdamer Platz

See map p314

Mauerstr
Schützenstr
Kommandantenstr
Zimmerstr
Waldeckpark
Kochstr
Rudi-Dutschke-Str
Oranienstr
Kochstr
Markgrafenstr
Alte Jakobstr
Ritterstr
Askanischer Platz
Anhalter Str
Lindenstr
1
Anhalter Bahnhof
Schöneberger Str
Wilhelmstr
Jüdisches Museum
Franz-Künstler-Str
19
Möckernstr
Stresemannstr
Franz-Klühs-Str
Neuenburger Str
Reichpietschufer
Alexandrinenstr
Lobeckstr
Trebbiner Str
18
16
Mehringplatz
Möckernbrücke
27
17
Hallesches Ufer
Hallesches Tor
Prinzenstr
Gitschiner Str
Obentrautstr
Tempelhofer Ufer
14
Brachvogelstr
Johanniterstr
Landwehrkanal
Blücher Platz
28
Wilmsstr
13
Blücherstr
Mehringdamm
Friedhöfe vor dem Halleschen Tor
Zossener Str
Urbanstr
Baerwaldstr
Hornstr
20
Grossbeerenstr
Baruther Str
Mittenwalder Str
Blücherstr
9
Fürbringer Str
Schleiermacher Str
See map p324
Yorckstr
29
Gneisenaustr
10
30
Hagelberger Str
5
Gneisenaustr
22
25
Baerwaldstr
Nostizstr
Solmsstr
21
Kreuzbergstr
11
23
Bergmannstr
24
Marheineke platz
8
7
2
Arndtstrasse
Bergmannstr
Friesenstr
Friedhöfe an der Bergmannstrasse
12
15
Fidicinstr
Juterboger Str
Platz der Luftbrücke
Schwiebusser Str
Dudenstr
4
Zullichauer Str
Platz der Luftbrücke
Columbiadamm
Katzbachstr
TEMPELHOF
Mathieustr
Leonhardyweg
Kaiserkorso
Tempelhofer Damm
26
Tempelhofer Park
6
Manfred-von-Richthofen-Str
Bundesring
Wolffring
Boelckestr
Paradestr
Paradestr

WESTERN KREUZBERG

WESTERN KREUZBERG

EASTERN KREUZBERG & NORTHERN NEUKÖLLN

See map p328

See map p318

Key on p326

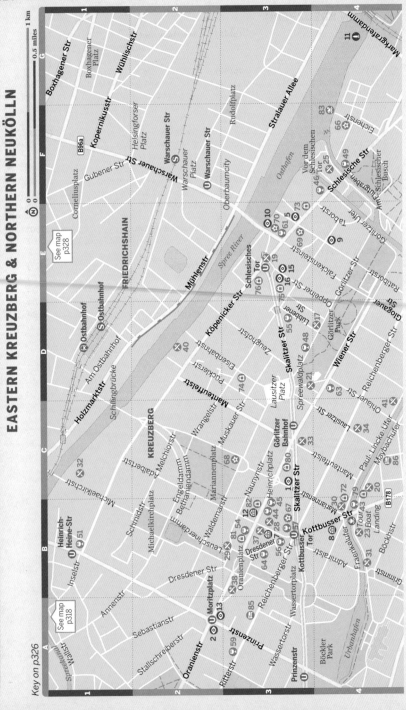

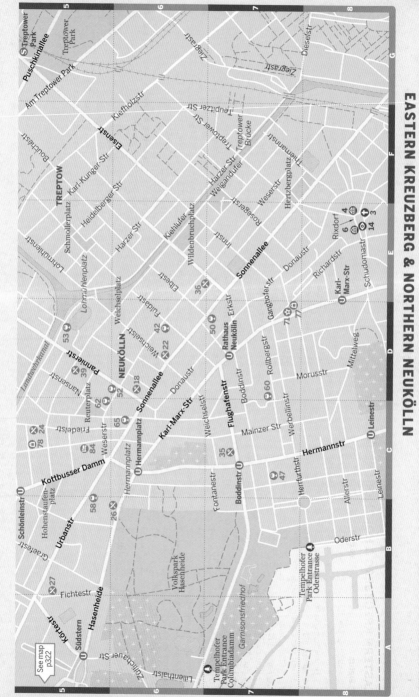

TREPTOW

NEUKÖLLN

See map
p322

Treptower Park

Puschkinallee
Am Treptower Park
Bouchéstr
Eisenstr
Kieholzstr
Lohmühlenstr
Lohmühlenstr
Landwehrkanal
Nansenstr
Pannierstr
Reuterplatz
Weichselplatz
Weichselstr
Weichselstr
Friedelstr
Weserstr
Hermannplatz
Hermannstr
Sonnenallee
Karl-Marx-Str
Karl-Kunger-Str
Heidelberger Str
Harzer Str
Schollerplatz
Kiefholzstr
Harzer Str
Weigandufer
Kiehlufer
Wildenbruchplatz
Elbestr
Fuldastr
Donaustr
Donaustr
Fontanestr
Zeughofstr
Ziegrastr
Ziegrastr
Dieselstr
Teupitzer Str
Teupitzer Str
Treptower Brücke
Thielenstr
Hertzbergplatz
Weserstr
Roseggerstr
Innstr
Sonnenallee
Donaustr
Ganghofer str
Rollbergstr
Boddinstr
Mainzer Str
Werbellinstr
Morusstr
Richardstr
Karl-Marx-Str
Schudomastr
Mittelweg
Rixdorf
Leinestr
Herrfurthstr
Allerstr
Leinestr
Oderstr
Oderstrasse
Kottbusser Damm
Schönleinstr
Hohenstaufen-platz
Urbanstr
Gräfestr
Fichtestr
Hasenheide
Körtestr
Südstern
Zülpichtstr
Lilienthalstr
Lilienthalstr
Volkspark
Hasenheide
Garnisonsfriedhof
Tempelhofer
Park Entrance
Columbiadamm
Tempelhofer
Park Entrance
Oderstrasse

Rathaus
Neukölln
Flughafenstr
Boddinstr

53
42
22
36
50
60
71
77
6 / 4
14 3
18
39
52
62
65
78 24
84
35
47
58
26
27

EASTERN KREUZBERG & NORTHERN NEUKÖLLN

EASTERN KREUZBERG & NORTHERN NEUKÖLLN Map on p324

FRIEDRICHSHAIN *Map on p328*

FRIEDRICHSHAIN

FRIEDRICHSHAIN

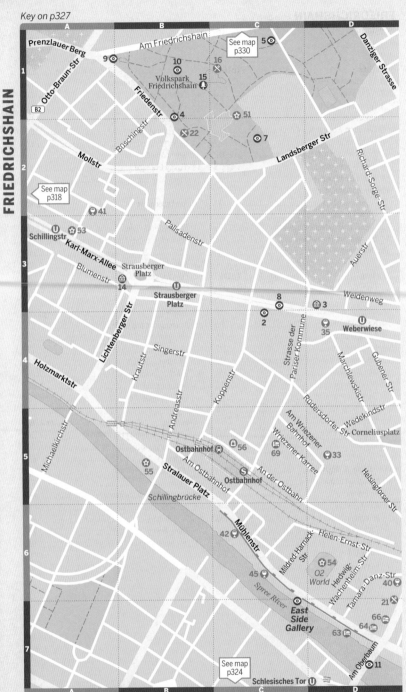

Prenzlauer Berg

Am Friedrichshain

See map p330

Otto-Braun-Str

B2

9

10

16

Volkspark
Friedrichshain

15

5

Danziger Strasse

Friedenstr

4

51

Büschingstr

22

7

Landsberger Str

Mollstr

Richard-Sorge-Str

See map p318

41

Schillingstr

53

Karl-Marx-Allee

Pallasadenstr

Auerstr

Blumenstr

Strausberger
Platz

14

Strausberger
Platz

Weidenweg

Lichtenberger Str

8

3

2

35

Weberwiese

Singerstr

Krautstr

Koppenstr

Andreasstr

Strasse der
Pariser Kommune

Rüdersdorfer Str

Marchlewskistr

Wedekindstr

Corneliusplatz

Gubener Str

Holzmarkstr

Michaelkirchstr

Ostbahnhof

56

Am Wriezener
Bahnhof

Wriezener Karree

69

33

Helsingforser Str

Stralauer Platz

55

Am Ostbahnhof

Ostbahnhof

An der Ostbahn

Schillingbrücke

Mühlenstr

42

Helen-Ernst-Str

Mildred-Harnack-Str

54

O2
World

Hedwig-Wachenheim-Str

Tamara-Danz-Str

40

45

21

Spree River

East
Side
Gallery

66

64

63

11

See map p324

Schlesisches Tor

Am Oberbaum

FRIEDRICHSHAIN

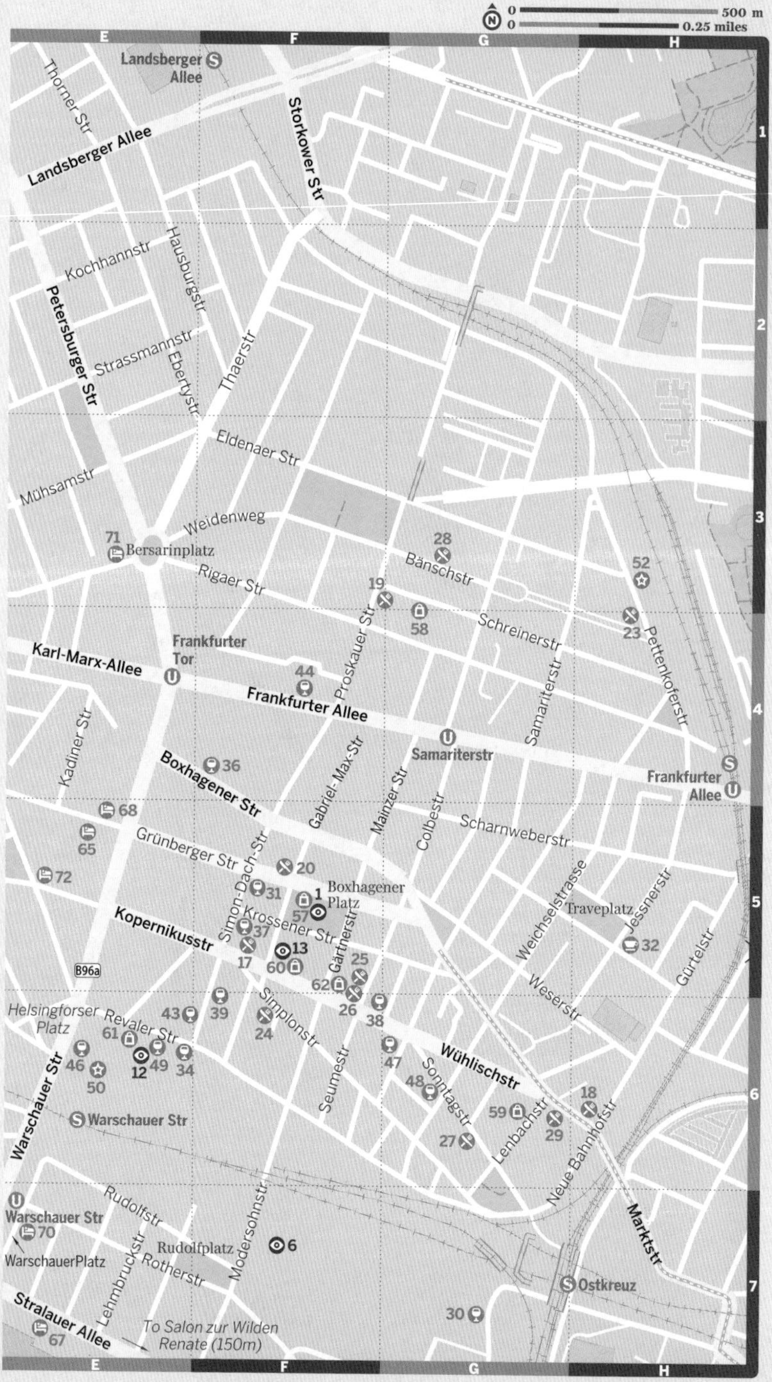
0
500 m
0
0.25 miles
E
F
G
H
1
2
3
4
5
6
7
Landsberger Allee
Landsberger Allee
Thorner Str
Storkower Str
Kochhannstr
Hausburgstr
Petersburger Str
Strassmannstr
Ebertystr
Thaerstr
Eldenaer Str
Mühsamstr
Weidenweg
71
Bersarinplatz
Rigaer Str
28
Bänschstr
52
19
58
Schreinerstr
23
Pettenkoferstr
Frankfurter Tor
Karl-Marx-Allee
44
Proskauer Str
Frankfurter Allee
Samariterstr
Samariterstr
Frankfurter Allee
Kadiner Str
Boxhagener Str
36
Gabriel-Max-Str
Mainzer Str
Colbestr
Scharnweberstr
68
65
Grünberger Str
72
Simon-Dach-Str
20
31
1
Boxhagener Platz
57
Krossener Str
37
Kopernikusstr
Gärtnerstr
17
13
60
25
62
26
B96a
Simplonstr
Traveplatz
Weichselstrasse
Jessnerstr
32
Weserstr
Gürtelstr
Helsingforser Platz
Revaler Str
43
39
24
38
61
46
12
49
34
47
Wühlischstr
50
Warschauer Str
Seumestr
Sonntagstr
48
59
Lenbachstr
29
18
Warschauer Str
27
Neue Bahnhofstr
Marktstr
Warschauer Str
70
Rudolfstr
Warschauer Platz
Rudolfplatz
Rotherstr
Lehmbruckstr
Modersohnstr
6
Ostkreuz
Stralauer Allee
67
To Salon zur Wilden Renate (150m)
30

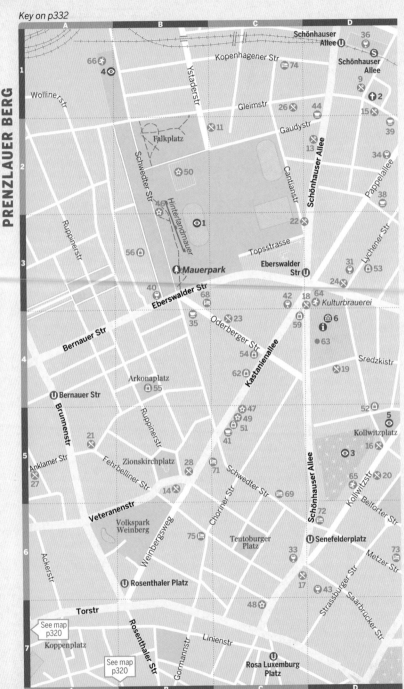

Key on p332

PRENZLAUER BERG

Schönhauser Allee

36

Schönhauser Allee

66

4

Kopenhagener Str

74

Wolliner Str

9

2

Gleimstr

26

44

15

Ystaderstr

39

Falkplatz

11

Gaudystr

13

34

50

Schwedter Str

Cantianstr

Schönhauser Allee

Pappelallee

38

1

Hinterlandmauer

22

Lychener Str

56

Topsstrasse

31

53

Mauerpark

Eberswalder Str

24

40

Eberswalder Str

68

42

18

64

Kulturbrauerei

35

23

Oderberger Str

59

6

Kastanienallee

54

63

Sredzkistr

62

19

Arkonaplatz

55

47

52

5

49

Kollwitzplatz

51

16

41

3

Ruppinerstr

21

28

65

20

Anklamer Str

71

Schwedter Str

Kollwitzstr

Belforter Str

27

Zionskirchplatz

Fehrbelliner Str

14

Choriner Str

69

72

Veteranenstr

Weinbergsweg

Volkspark Weinberg

75

Teutoburger Platz

Senefelderplatz

Ackerstr

Rosenthaler Platz

33

73

Metzer Str

17

43

Torstr

48

Strassburger Str

Saarbrucker Str

See map p320

Koppenplatz

Rosenthaler Str

Gormannstr

Linienstr

Rosa Luxemburg Platz

See map p320

Brunnenstr

Bernauer Str

Bernauer Str

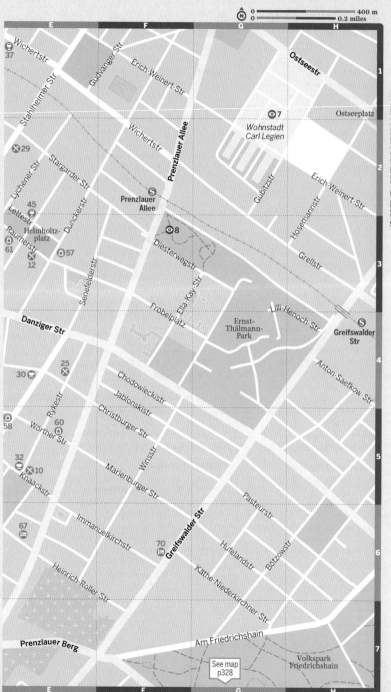

0   400 m
0   0.2 miles

Wichertstr
37

Ostseestr

Stahlheimer Str

Gudvanger Str

Erich-Weinert-Str

7
Ostseeplatz

Wohnstadt
Carl Legien

Wichertstr

Prenzlauer Allee

Gubitzstr

29

Stargarder Str

Lychener Str

Erich-Weinert-Str

Prenzlauer
Allee

Hosemannstr

45

Lettestr

Dunckerstr

Grellstr

Raumerstr
61

Helmholtz-
platz

8
Diesterwegstr

12

57

Senefelderstr

Ella-Kay-Str

Lilli-Henoch-Str

Danziger Str

Fröbelplatz

Ernst-
Thälmann-
Park

Greifswalder
Str

30

25

Anton-Saefkow-Str

Rykestr

Chodowieckistr

Jablonskistr

58

Wörther Str

60

Christburger Str

Winsstr

Pasteurstr

32

10

Marienburger Str

Knaackstr

Immanuelkirchstr

67

70
Greifswalder Str

Hufelandstr

Bötzowstr

Heinrich-Roller-Str

Käthe-Niederkirchner-Str

Prenzlauer Berg

Am Friedrichshain

See map
p328

Volkspark
Friedrichshain

PRENZLAUER BERG *Map on p330*

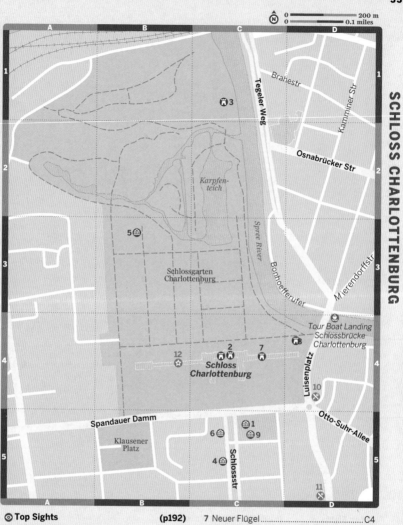

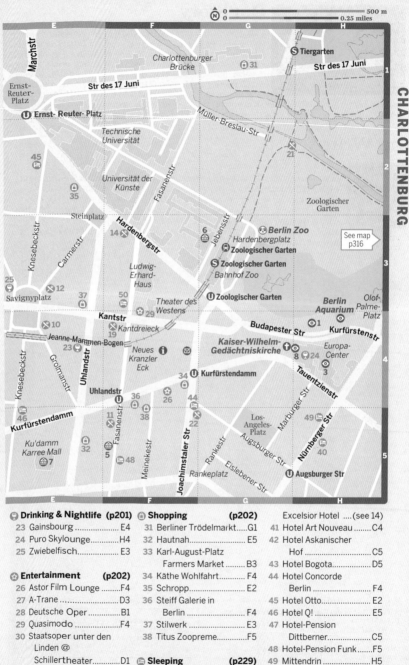

Our Story

A beat-up old car, a few dollars in the pocket and a sense of adventure. In 1972 that's all Tony and Maureen Wheeler needed for the trip of a lifetime – across Europe and Asia overland to Australia. It took several months, and at the end – broke but inspired – they sat at their kitchen table writing and stapling together their first travel guide, *Across Asia on the Cheap*. Within a week they'd sold 1500 copies. Lonely Planet was born.

Today, Lonely Planet has offices in Melbourne, London and Oakland, with more than 600 staff and writers. We share Tony's belief that 'a great guidebook should do three things: inform, educate and amuse'.

Our Writer

Andrea Schulte-Peevers

Born and raised in Germany and educated in London and at UCLA, Andrea has travelled the distance to the moon and back in her visits to some 65 countries. She's written about her native country for two decades and authored or contributed to some 60 Lonely Planet titles, including all editions of this guide, the *Germany* country guide, the *Discover Germany* guide and the Berlin *Pocket* guide. After years of living in LA, Andrea couldn't be happier to finally make her home in a lovely Berlin flat.

Published by Lonely Planet Publications Pty Ltd
ABN 36 005 607 983
8th edition – Mar 2013
ISBN 978 1 74220 053 8
© Lonely Planet 2013   Photographs © as indicated 2013
10 9 8 7 6 5 4 3 2 1
Printed in China